fashion

fashion

THE DEFINITIVE VISUAL GUIDE

NEW EDITION

SECOND EDITION
Senior Editor Kathryn Hennessy
Project Art Editor Katie Cavanagh
Managing Editor Gareth Jones
Senior Managing Art Editor Lee Griffith
Producer, Pre-Production Gillian Reid
Senior Producer Rachel Ng
Lead Jacket Designer Surabhi-Wadhwa Ghandhi
Jacket Editor Emma Dawson
Jacket Design Development Manager Sophia MTT

DK INDIA
Senior Jacket Designer Suhita Dharamjit
Senior DTP Designer Harish Aggarwal
Jackets Editorial Coordinator Priyanka Sharma
Managing Jackets Editor Saloni Singh

FIRST EDITION
Senior Editor Kathryn Hennessy
Senior Art Editor Gadi Farfour
Project Art Editor Amy Orsborne
Editors Anna Fischel, Ann Baggaley,
Scarlett O'Hara, Alison Sturgeon,
Camilla Gersh, Ashwin Khurana
Designers Paul Drislane, Kirsty Tizzard
Art Worker Philip Fitzgerald
Glossary Illustrator Katie John
Editorial Assistants Alexandra Beeden,
Damilare Olugbode
Photographers Gary Ombler, Paul Self
Picture Researchers Liz Moore, Sarah Smithies
DK Picture Library Claire Bowers,
Emma Shepherd, Claire Cordier
Database Rob Laidler, David Roberts
Jacket Designer Mark Cavanagh
US Senior Editor Shannon Beatty
US Editor Jane Perlmutter
US Consultant Carol Pelletier
Production Editor Ben Marcus
Repro Opus Multimedia Services, Delhi
Producer Sophie Argyris

Managing Editor Esther Ripley
Managing Art Editor Karen Self
Publisher Laura Buller
Art Director Phil Ormerod
Associate Publishing Director Liz Wheeler
Publishing Director Jonathan Metcalf

DK INDIA
Senior Art Editors Anjana Nair, Chhaya Sajwan
Art Editors Neha Sharma, Nidhi Mehra,
Supriya Mahajan, and Shipra Jain
Assistant Art Editors Vidit Vashisht, Namita,
Niyati Gosain, and Payal Rosalind Malik
Design Managers Arunesh Talapatra
and Sudakshina Basu
Senior Editors Garima Sharma, Sreshtha Bhattacharya
Editor Roma Malik
Assistant Editors Archana Ramachandran
Editorial Manager Pakshalika Jayaprakash
DTP Designers Nand Kishor Acharya,
Mohammad Usman, Dheeraj Arora, and Anita Yadav
DTP Manager Balwant Singh
Production Manager Pankaj Sharma
Picture Research Nivisha Sinha and Sakshi Saluja

Smithsonian

Smithsonian Project Coordinator Ellen Nanney

This American Edition, 2019
First American Edition, 2012
Published in the United States by
DK Publishing
1450 Broadway, Suite 801
New York, New York 10018

Copyright © 2012, 2019 Dorling Kindersley Limited
DK, a Division of Penguin Random House LLC
19 20 21 22 23 10 9 8 7 6 5 4 3 2 1
001–314816–Sep/2019

All rights reserved.
Without limiting the rights under copyright reserved above, no part of this publication may be reproduced,
stored in or introduced into a retrieval system, or transmitted, in any form, or by any means (electronic, mechanical,
photocoping, recording, or otherwise), without the prior written permission of both the copyright owner and the above
publisher of this book.
Published in Great Britain by Dorling Kindersley Limited.

A catalog record for this book is available from the Library of Congress.

ISBN: 978-1-4654-8640-0

DK books are available at special discounts when purchased in bulk for sales promotions, premiums, fund-raising,
or educational use. For details, contact:
DK Publishing Special Markets, 1450 Broadway, Suite 801, New York, New York 10018
or SpecialSales@dk.com

Printed and bound in China by Hung Hing Printing Co., Ltd

A WORLD OF IDEAS:
SEE ALL THERE IS TO KNOW
www.dk.com

CHAPTER 1

PREHISTORY–600 CE

THE ANCIENT WORLD

CHAPTER 2
600–1449

MEDIEVAL ROMANCE AND TRADE

CHAPTER 3
1450–1624

RENAISSANCE SPLENDOR

CHAPTER 4
1625–1789

BAROQUE AND ROCOCO

CONTENTS

CHAPTER 5

1790–1900

FROM REVOLUTION TO FRIVOLITY

CHAPTER 6

1901–1928

LA BELLE EPOQUE AND THE JAZZ AGE

CHAPTER 7

1929–1946

FROM GLAMOUR TO UTILITY

CHAPTER 8

1947–1963

OPTIMISM AND YOUTH

CHAPTER 9

1964–1979

SWINGING SIXTIES TO GLAM ROCK

CHAPTER 10

1980 ONWARD

THE DESIGNER DECADES

REFERENCE

FOREWORD

Like art, music, and literature, fashion has its own rich history. While we associate fashion with an almost relentless newness, it is also in a constant dialogue with its own past: just as Picasso reverently dissected Goya, Balenciaga examined the form of medieval religious vestments, and Mick Jagger channeled Beau Brummel in much the way that Prokofiev reframed Haydn.

While fashion historians may assert that fashion began with the development of fitted garments, and critics may argue that only a small number of wealthy individuals truly participate in the fashion system, for most of us fashion conjures an essential, perhaps innate, will to adorn and beautify our bodies, faces, and hair. Even our early human representations, the prehistoric, so-called Venus figurines, wear nonfunctional garments, string skirts that offered little protection or coverage. We see and are seen: we voraciously consume images of the human figure, inhabit or reject those images in our own self-presentation, and become ourselves the subject of further image making. The sources of representation are punctuated by personalities—men and women of style, from royalty to rock stars, designers, movie stars, and models, who epitomized "the look" of any given moment in time. Photographer Bill Cunningham's weekly "On the Street" column in *The New York Times* celebrates the complexity and exuberance of this complex visual reverberation.

"The main thing I love about street photography," he says, "is that you find the answers you don't see at the fashion shows. You find information for readers so they can visualize themselves." ("Bill on Bill," October 27, 2002). Whether an individual act of style takes place in the design studio, behind the camera lens, or at home in front of the mirror, it forms part of one of our culture's oldest and most participatory expressions, one which utterly shapes everyday human experience.

Susan Brown
Smithsonian consultant
Susan Brown is Associate Curator, Cooper-Hewitt, National Design Museum, Smithsonian and most recently collaborated on the exhibition and catalog *Color Moves: Art and Fashion* by Sonia Delaunay with Matilda McQuaid. She teaches in the Masters Program in the History of Decorative Arts and Design offered by the Museum with Parsons The New School for Design, as well as lecturing regularly for the Institute of Fine Arts at NYU. Prior to joining the Smithsonian, she designed costumes for theater, opera, and television.

CONSULTANT AUTHORS

Beatrice Behlen
La Belle Epoque and the Jazz Age/From Glamour to Utility
Beatrice Behlen studied fashion design in Germany and the history of dress at the Courtauld Institute of Art. Having lectured at art colleges and curated at Historical Royal Palaces, she is now Senior Curator of Fashion and Decorative Arts at the Museum of London.

Alison Carter
From Revolution to Frivolity
Senior Keeper of Art and Design at Hampshire Museums for 25 years (1986–2011), Alison Carter is the author of *Underwear: the Fashion History* and Chair of the Southern Counties Costume Society.

Hilary Davidson
Medieval Romance and Trade/Renaissance Splendor
Hilary Davidson is Curator of Fashion and Decorative Arts at the Museum of London. She teaches, publishes, and lectures on topics ranging from medieval dress to cultural theory.

Rosemary Harden
Baroque and Rococo/Optimism and Youth/Swinging Sixties to Glam Rock/The Designer Decades
Rosemary Harden is the curator at the Fashion Museum in Bath, where she has organized many exhibitions, including *The Diana Dresses* and *Sport and Fashion*.

Jackie Herald
The Ancient World
Jackie Herald studied at The Courtauld Institute of Art and is a former lecturer in fashion history at art colleges.

Jemima Klenk
In-house Consultant
Jemima Klenk has an MA in the history of dress from the Courtauld Institute of Art, London.

Judith Watt
General Consultant
Judith Watt is course director of the MA in fashion journalism at Kingston University, and teaches fashion history at Central St. Martin's College of Art, London.

WRITERS

Alexandra Black
A contributor to *Elle*, *Marie Claire*, and *Vogue Living*, Alexandra Black is the author of *Ski Style*, *Dusk Till Dawn: a history of the evening dress*, and *The Party Dress: a history of fashionable occasions*.

Oriole Cullen
Oriole Cullen is curator for Fashion and Textiles at the Victoria and Albert Museum, London, specializing in 20th- and 21st-century fashion.

Ann Kay
Designer and fashion icon profiles
Ann Kay has authored or contributed to around 25 books. She has an MA in art history and specializes in art, design, and cultural history.

Sally Regan
Designer and fashion icon profiles
Sally Regan has contributed to a number of Dorling Kindersley titles and is an award-winning documentary filmmaker on a range of history subjects for the BBC, Granada, and Channel Four.

Shelley Tobin
Shelley Tobin is Curator at Killerton House, Devon, and assistant curator (Costume and Textiles) at Royal Albert Memorial Museum and Art Gallery, Exeter.

Heather Vaughan
Heather Vaughan is an author and editor of fashion history publications. She writes the blog *Fashion Historia* and holds an MA in Visual Culture: Costume Studies from New York University.

Additional writing: Andrea Mills, Lorrie Mack, Marcus Weeks, Katie John (glossary)

THE ANCIENT WORLD

PREHISTORY–600 CE

THE ANCIENT WORLD

The ancient world is a jigsaw of images and objects that historians are trying to piece together. Paintings, sculpture, artifacts, and scraps of clothing and jewelry all provide clues as to how people lived and dressed. Many of the early civilizations reached impressive levels of development. Sophisticated technologies and craft skills coexisted in different corners of the world, as they still do today, and influenced each other as cultures met through war, exploration, and commercial exchange. Clothing and accessories—including protective armor and talismanic jewelry—were often produced to extremely high standards. Fine linen was woven on the banks of the Nile in Egypt; sericulture from China supplied the wider world with exquisite silks; the Greeks and Romans created fantastic wool tapestries; and the Etruscans crafted ornate, tooled metalwork.

Starting points
Many shapes and styles in dress date back thousands of years, having necessity, function, and the materials available as their starting points. For example, connecting two pieces of material to form a garment may once have meant no more than using a simple fastening such as a pin or a few basic stitches, but from such crude beginnings wonderful pieces of embroidery evolved, providing decoration and reinforcement at the same time. Embroidery on traditional dress from, say, eastern Europe or southwest China is often concentrated around the neck, hem, shoulders, and wrist—the areas that are most visible and most subject to wear and tear.

Cycle of fashion
If the clothes people wore in the distant past often look remarkably modern and familiar, this is because of the way styles are continually revived and reinterpreted through cycles of history and waves of fashion. Modern designers have borrowed again and again from the styles—and style icons—of the past. Numerous examples can be listed of fashions that have had their day and gone, only to reappear with a new spin: the elegant draperies of classical Greek and Roman goddesses; Ancient Egypt's massive jewelry and the kohl-eyed, black-bobbed "Cleopatra look"; Chinese and Japanese silks and sashes; exotic Middle Eastern asymmetry and A-line cut garments; colorful, patterned textiles from India and southern Asia; and dynamic geometric, anthropomorphic patterns from pre-Columbian civilizations. From couture house to main-street store, the modern fashion world owes much to the past.

TO 10,000 BCE	10,000–4000 BCE	4000–3500 BCE
c. 500,000–100,000 BCE The first clothing, the hides of animals, are worn, sometimes tied on with beltlike strips of hide. ▼ Stripped buffalo hide	**c. 10,000 BCE** The earliest surviving shoes are sandals discovered in a cave in Oregon, woven from tree bark, fashioned at least 10,000 years ago.	▼ Egyptian sandals c. 4000 BCE
	c. 10,000 BCE Wool cloth starts with the domesticated sheep, bred for soft wool as opposed to fur.	
	7500–5700 BCE Dyed textiles are in use in Çatal Höyük, southern Anatolia (present-day Turkey), as evidenced by traces of red dye, possibly ocher, found at the site.	**c. 4000 BCE** These thonged leather sandals, c. 6,000 years old, are part of daily wear in Ancient Egypt.
c. 40,000 BCE People punch holes in skins and furs, lacing them together. The earliest bone needle dates to c. 30,000 BCE.	**7500–5700 BCE** Seals such as this one from the settlement of Çatal Höyük, Turkey, are used during the Neolithic period to stamp decorative designs in dye onto skin or cloth. ▶ Neolithic baked clay seal	
c. 30,000 BCE Cave painters use pigments such as ocher, hematite, and charcoal to color their art, and probably to decorate their own bodies, too. ▶ Prehistoric rock art, Acacus National Park, Libya		**c. 3600 BCE** Flax is the predominant fiber used to create clothing in Egypt.

> We live not according to reason, but according to fashion.

SENECA, ROMAN PHILOSOPHER, 1ST CENTURY CE

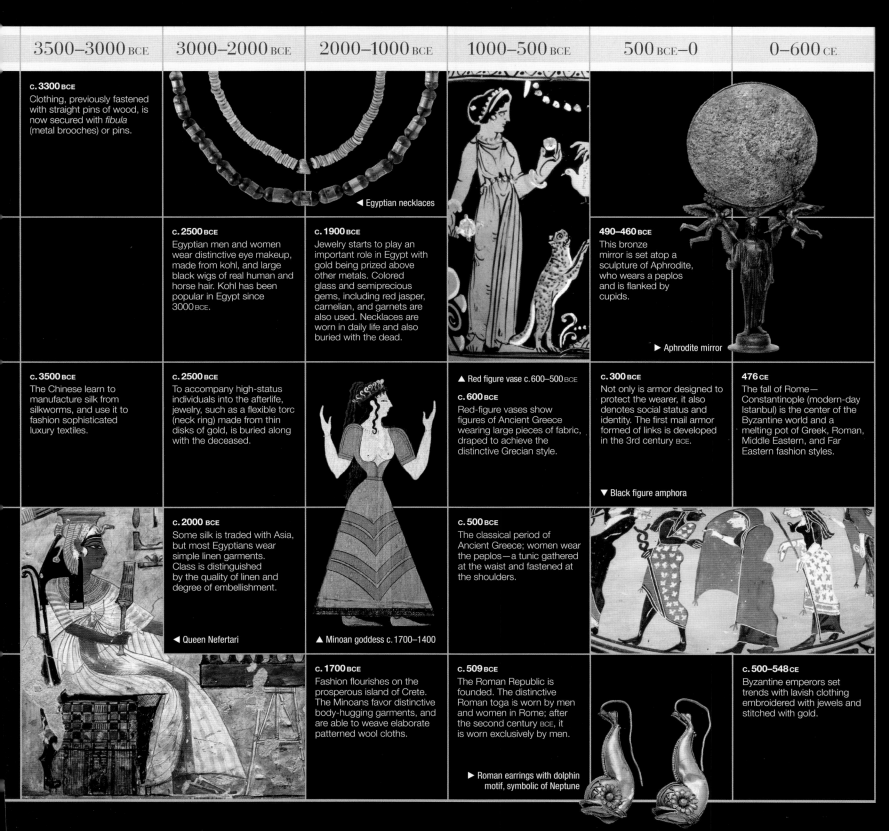

3500–3000 BCE	3000–2000 BCE	2000–1000 BCE	1000–500 BCE	500 BCE–0	0–600 CE

c. 3300 BCE
Clothing, previously fastened with straight pins of wood, is now secured with *fibula* (metal brooches) or pins.

◄ Egyptian necklaces

c. 2500 BCE
Egyptian men and women wear distinctive eye makeup, made from kohl, and large black wigs of real human and horse hair. Kohl has been popular in Egypt since 3000 BCE.

c. 1900 BCE
Jewelry starts to play an important role in Egypt with gold being prized above other metals. Colored glass and semiprecious gems, including red jasper, carnelian, and garnets are also used. Necklaces are worn in daily life and also buried with the dead.

490–460 BCE
This bronze mirror is set atop a sculpture of Aphrodite, who wears a peplos and is flanked by cupids.

► Aphrodite mirror

c. 3500 BCE
The Chinese learn to manufacture silk from silkworms, and use it to fashion sophisticated luxury textiles.

c. 2500 BCE
To accompany high-status individuals into the afterlife, jewelry, such as a flexible torc (neck ring) made from thin disks of gold, is buried along with the deceased.

▲ Red figure vase c. 600–500 BCE

c. 600 BCE
Red-figure vases show figures of Ancient Greece wearing large pieces of fabric, draped to achieve the distinctive Grecian style.

c. 300 BCE
Not only is armor designed to protect the wearer, it also denotes social status and identity. The first mail armor formed of links is developed in the 3rd century BCE.

476 CE
The fall of Rome—Constantinople (modern-day Istanbul) is the center of the Byzantine world and a melting pot of Greek, Roman, Middle Eastern, and Far Eastern fashion styles.

▼ Black figure amphora

c. 2000 BCE
Some silk is traded with Asia, but most Egyptians wear simple linen garments. Class is distinguished by the quality of linen and degree of embellishment.

◄ Queen Nefertari

c. 500 BCE
The classical period of Ancient Greece; women wear the peplos—a tunic gathered at the waist and fastened at the shoulders.

▲ Minoan goddess c. 1700–1400

c. 1700 BCE
Fashion flourishes on the prosperous island of Crete. The Minoans favor distinctive body-hugging garments, and are able to weave elaborate patterned wool cloths.

c. 509 BCE
The Roman Republic is founded. The distinctive Roman toga is worn by men and women in Rome; after the second century BCE, it is worn exclusively by men.

► Roman earrings with dolphin motif, symbolic of Neptune

c. 500–548 CE
Byzantine emperors set trends with lavish clothing embroidered with jewels and stitched with gold.

PREHISTORY– 600 CE
FROM FUNCTION TO IDENTITY

For Scythian nomads in Asia, Sumerians in Mesopotamia (now Iraq), Nubians in Africa, and the earliest Chinese dynasty, the picture of early clothing continues to emerge from archaeological sites. Although little cloth survives, there are impressions of prehistoric textiles in pottery, and bone sewing needles, reindeer horn buttons, amber necklaces, and wooden weaving sticks are found. Where animal and vegetal fibers exist, they suggest that rudimentary clothes, skins, and furs were largely uncut and often unsewn, held by a pin or a tie-cord. When warp-weighted looms came into use, possibly as early as the Neolithic period, a semicircle or T-shaped tunic could be woven. Textile technology determined the shape and degree of stretch, durability, and warmth of garments. Stitching was used to strengthen garments, for decoration, and to express identity. Climate and lifestyle also dictated attire—for example, nomadic Steppe men and women wore trousers for riding.

Helmet

Leaf-shaped sword

Frame-hilted dagger on leather or textile belt

Short tunic

Thick wool cape

Sardinian chieftain A tribal chieftain is shown wearing a cloak in this 7th century BCE bronze statuette from Sardinia. He is armed with a dagger across his chest and a sword, and holds a staff. The cloak gave the body some protection while leaving the arms free for fighting.

HELMETS

The earliest helmets were leather, followed by metal helmets, fashioned first from bronze and then iron. Ancient helmets could be simple conical or hemispherical shapes, or more elaborate, with additional guards for the nose, cheeks, and neck. Helmets provided protection, but also an opportunity for decoration and display, with detailing on the metalwork, such as animal motifs, or topped with crests. Celtic crests could be extremely tall, and warriors were known to add figural metal pieces, feathers, or horsehair plumes to their helmets. Some intricately patterned and adorned helmets were created solely for ceremonial purposes.

Coiffed hair

Handlebar mustache

Tunic sleeves and shoulders have decorated seams

Patterned cape could be made of spotted fur

Close-fitting tunic and trousers

Ankle boots

Scythian rider A Scythian on horseback is shown in a detail from a 5th–4th-century BCE carpet discovered in the frozen tombs of Pazyryk, Siberia. Made of colored felt, the shapes are stylized, but show the saddle, patterned cape, close-fitting garments, and distinctive mustache and hairstyle.

A Celtic Iron Age horned helmet 150–50 BCE, made from riveted sheet bronze pieces. It may originally have been adorned with red glass.

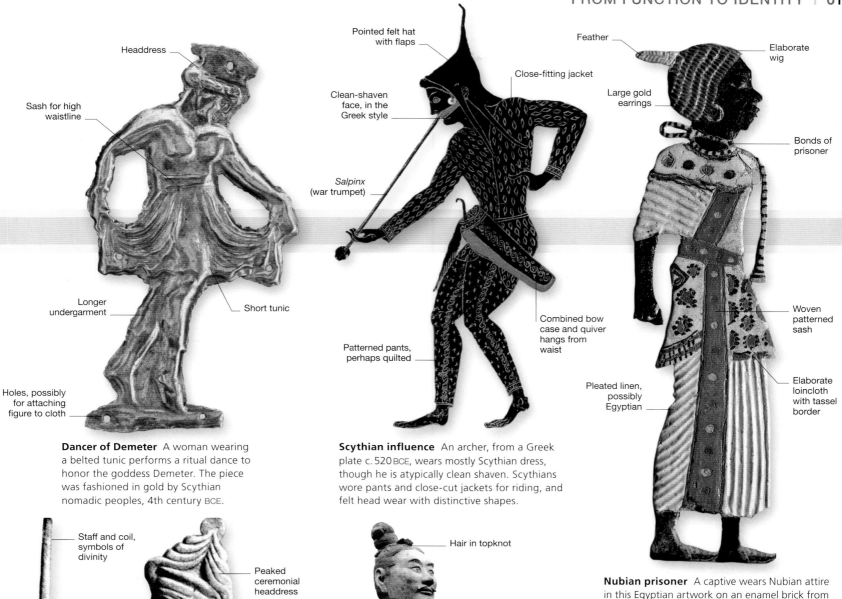

Dancer of Demeter A woman wearing a belted tunic performs a ritual dance to honor the goddess Demeter. The piece was fashioned in gold by Scythian nomadic peoples, 4th century BCE.

- Headdress
- Sash for high waistline
- Longer undergarment
- Short tunic
- Holes, possibly for attaching figure to cloth

Scythian influence An archer, from a Greek plate c. 520 BCE, wears mostly Scythian dress, though he is atypically clean shaven. Scythians wore pants and close-cut jackets for riding, and felt head wear with distinctive shapes.

- Pointed felt hat with flaps
- Close-fitting jacket
- Clean-shaven face, in the Greek style
- *Salpinx* (war trumpet)
- Combined bow case and quiver hangs from waist
- Patterned pants, perhaps quilted

Nubian prisoner A captive wears Nubian attire in this Egyptian artwork on an enamel brick from the Royal Palace of Medinet Habu, c. 16th–13th century BCE. Egyptians typically portrayed Nubians with gold earrings and elaborate wigs.

- Feather
- Elaborate wig
- Large gold earrings
- Bonds of prisoner
- Woven patterned sash
- Pleated linen, possibly Egyptian
- Elaborate loincloth with tassel border

Sumerian dress The moon god Nannar reigns in a detail from the Sumerian Stele of Ur-Nammu, c. 2060 BCE. *Kaunakes* cloth started out as goat or sheep skin with long hair turned outward. Gradually cloth was woven with added tufts to imitate this effect.

- Staff and coil, symbols of divinity
- Peaked ceremonial headdress
- Long curled beard with square end
- Hair knot at back of head
- *Kaunakes* (tufted cloth) with long fringing wrapped asymmetrically around body
- Sumerians went barefoot

Chinese warrior A terra-cotta warrior from Emperor Qin Shihuangdi's tomb, China, c. 210 BCE kneels. His armor is of laced plates made of either bronze or hardened leather. The scarf is one of the earliest examples of men's neckwear.

- Hair in topknot
- Plates laced together
- Silk scarf
- Padded coat
- Leggings
- Square-toed footwear
- Padded tunic

JEWELRY

Bone, stone, and shell jewelry survive from prehistoric times, and were probably worn as marks of status or symbolic protection. As metalworking evolved, greater sophistication in design emerged. Gold was prized and items were often buried with the dead, such as the *lunulae*, collars of beaten gold, c. 2000 BCE found in Ireland.

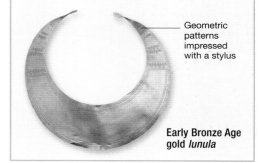

- Geometric patterns impressed with a stylus

Early Bronze Age gold *lunula*

3150 BCE – 30 CE
ANCIENT EGYPT

For three thousand years almost all clothing worn by the Ancient Egyptians was of linen, made from flax grown in the Nile Valley. The fabric suited the hot climate because it was cool and airy. Clothes were very simple in shape, with minimal cutting of cloth. Men wore a *schenti* cloth wrapped around the hips which hung in folds in front. Women wore a *kalasiris* (sheathlike dress), often with detachable sleeves. The *mss* (bag-shirt) was worn in the Middle Kingdom and later became general wear for men, women, and children. The silhouette was influenced by two key factors: the fineness and finish of the linen—either left with a natural crimp after laundering, or (in the New Kingdom) arranged in crisp pleats—and by the wearing of decorative collars and belts. These accessories were rich in color and texture.

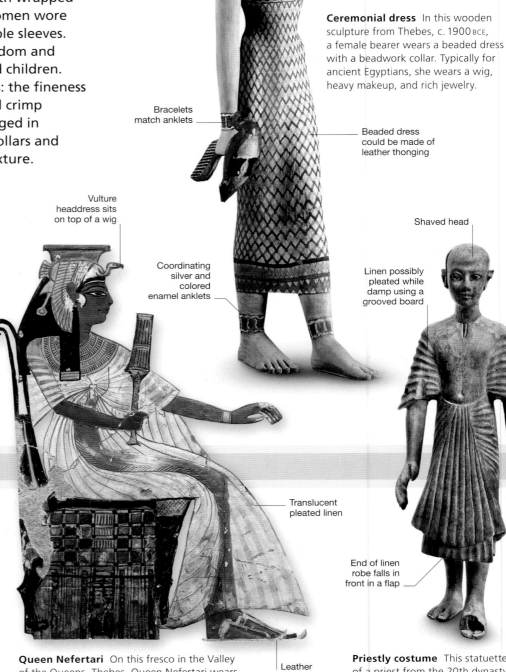

Box of offerings for the gods

Kohl accentuates eyes

Indigo-dyed wig

Bracelets match anklets

Ceremonial dress In this wooden sculpture from Thebes, c. 1900 BCE, a female bearer wears a beaded dress with a beadwork collar. Typically for ancient Egyptians, she wears a wig, heavy makeup, and rich jewelry.

Beaded dress could be made of leather thonging

Coordinating silver and colored enamel anklets

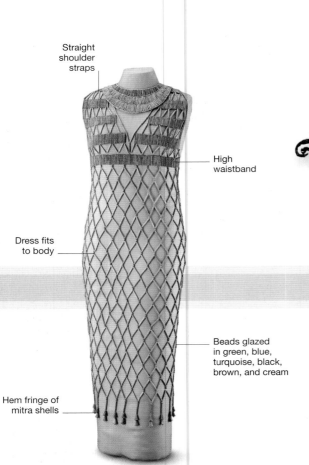

Straight shoulder straps

High waistband

Dress fits to body

Beads glazed in green, blue, turquoise, black, brown, and cream

Hem fringe of mitra shells

Beaded dress This bead-net dress from about 2400 BCE is made of 3,000 cylindrical and disk-shaped colored beads. It is decorated with shells and breast caps. A dancing girl may have worn it for entertaining at banquets.

Vulture headdress sits on top of a wig

Translucent pleated linen

Leather sandals

Queen Nefertari On this fresco in the Valley of the Queens, Thebes, Queen Nefertari wears the finest linen, which is almost transparent. She has an elaborate headdress featuring a gilded figure of a vulture, as well as a gold collar.

Shaved head

Linen possibly pleated while damp using a grooved board

End of linen robe falls in front in a flap

Priestly costume This statuette of a priest from the 20th dynasty (c. 1187–1064 BCE) shows his pleated robe, which may have had fringed ends. There are traces of kohl around his eyes.

Gold jewelry on indigo-dyed wig

Both wear gold disks and plumes over gold headdress and blue wigs, tied in place by richly decorated bands

Women used colored cosmetics

Inlaid gold bracelet

Heavily jeweled pectoral (wide collar)

Finely pleated linen *kalasiris*

Hoop earrings made from Nubian gold

Beaded wig ends

Collar of precious stones

Fine transparent linen reveals *schenti* cloth around hips

Lotus flower in her hand and on her headdress

Royal robes Tutankhamun and his wife, Ankhesenamun, are wearing elaborate headdresses and wigs dyed with indigo in this image (c. 1330 BCE). The pharaoh's robe is tied at the waist with ornate bands. Ankhesenamun's robe has pleats falling in different directions, showing how a long piece of cloth wraps around the body.

Princely robes A mural of a prince and his wife from the Tomb of Senneferi, Thebes, shows the couple wearing wigs. Elaborate wigs were made of human hair attached to a net. Their straight, plain linen robes contrast with the decorative collars, armlets, and earrings they are wearing.

Cone of scented wax

Offerings of flowers to the deity

Wig of human hair

Gold armlets

The gauzy appearance indicates a fine linen

Complete leopard skin

Dress stitched up its length

Finest linen was pure white

Excess fabric gathers on ground

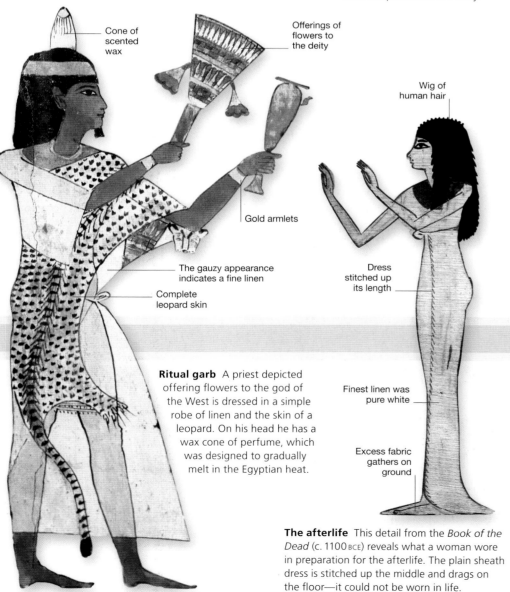

Ritual garb A priest depicted offering flowers to the god of the West is dressed in a simple robe of linen and the skin of a leopard. On his head he has a wax cone of perfume, which was designed to gradually melt in the Egyptian heat.

The afterlife This detail from the *Book of the Dead* (c. 1100 BCE) reveals what a woman wore in preparation for the afterlife. The plain sheath dress is stitched up the middle and drags on the floor—it could not be worn in life.

JEWELRY

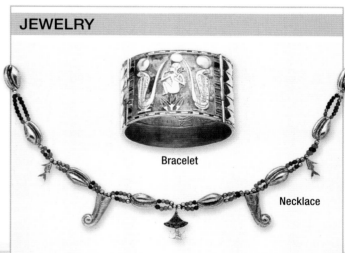

Bracelet

Necklace

Jewelry was worn from top to bottom by wealthy Egyptian men and women—and even by their sacred animals. Always colorful, the pieces featured motifs from the natural world, including green palm leaves, white lotus flowers, and yellow mandrake fruits. Gold came from Nubia (present-day Ethiopia), and silver was rarer and more expensive than gold. Semiprecious stones included lapis lazuli (imported from Afghanistan), green and red jasper, amethyst, cornelian, turquoise, and quartz. Glass and glazed composite were used to imitate precious stones. Steatite, a soft stone, was carved into small objects, including pendants and scarabs.

Gold and silver rings

FASHION ICON
QUEEN NEFERTITI

△ **PAINTED LIMESTONE BUST**
One of the world's most famous images (c. 1350 BCE, Egyptian Museum, Berlin), Nefertiti wears a flat-topped crown with a decorative ribbon and the remains of a *uraeus*—a protective cobra and royal symbol—on the front. Reddened lips and kohl-rimmed eyes typify the Egyptian love of makeup, while a decorative collar circles her neck and shoulders.

SENSUAL DRAPERY ▷
This red sandstone sculpture from the 14th century BCE is thought to be of Nefertiti. The contemporary garment style—finely pleated linen gathered at a point under the bust and extended over one shoulder—showcases a voluptuously hipped body symbolic of fertility.

The Egyptian Queen Nefertiti—whose name translates as "a beautiful woman has come"—is famed for possessing both political influence and great beauty. She was the wife of Akhenaten (named after his worship of the sun disk, Aten), who reigned over 18th-dynasty Ancient Egypt in the 14th century BCE, during the New Kingdom era, and created a glittering city at Amarna. Nefertiti's allure is heightened by mystery—she seems to have disappeared without trace and theories abound about her fate.

Dressing a goddess
Contemporary statues and reliefs depict a woman with a striking face, and some show a curvaceous form highlighted by clinging garments. Such images would have been idealized according to the era's spiritual values. Nefertiti (along with her six daughters) would have constituted a living fertility goddess, emphasized by those images that portray her as wide hipped or in tight clothes; surviving evidence suggests that contemporary garments were in fact looser than depicted.

Nefertiti's clothing trademarks include a distinctive tall, straight-sided and flat-topped crown worn exclusively by her (left). Her garments were in the fine, pleated linen worn by New Kingdom royals and often depicted as being so fine that it became transparent—an aid to showing off the divine body. The linen was probably thicker in reality. Images of Nefertiti show how Egyptian linen lent itself to draping, folding, and well-defined pleating. Ancient Egyptian styles remained similar for centuries, but during the 18th dynasty in which Nefertiti lived, a more complex draping of larger pieces of fabric developed (alongside the basic *kalasiris* sheath).

Nefertiti is depicted wearing long, fine tunics draped in ways typical of New Kingdom times. Frequently the material's gathering appears to center on one point, often close to the bust, creating a distinctive high-waisted shape; she appears with and without sleeves. A famous painted limestone statue of the royal couple, hand in hand, from around 1340 BCE, shows Nefertiti in a long, pleated linen tunic (often called a *haik*), caught between the waist and bust, gathered to produce undefined sleeves, and clinging especially closely to the lower body. Since dyeing linen is difficult and it was the staple fiber, Egyptian clothing tends to be white. Rich color was added with accessories by most levels of society.

An icon for the modern age
More than 3,500 years have elapsed, yet Nefertiti and all things Egyptian continue to inspire today's designers. The seminal blue-crowned bust (far left) was unearthed in 1912 and made its way to Berlin's Egyptian Museum, where it remains. Upon its Berlin unveiling, in 1923, this arresting image had an immediate impact on the public, cementing a fascination for all things Egyptian that had been fired the year before by the discovery of the tomb of boy-pharaoh Tutankhamun. "Egyptomania" gripped fashion design of the Art Deco era, from scarab jewelry to flowing, draped dresses, exotic embroidery, pyramid and lotus-flower motifs, dramatic deep headbands, and a love of Nile-green and bright blues. There was even a mummy wrap dress in the 1920s, an idea interpreted afresh in the skintight bandage dresses of the 2000s. Flappers' love of dark hair, red lips, and darkly outlined eyes was part of Egyptomania, and would most likely have been encouraged by Nefertiti's famed bust.

TIMELINE

1550 BCE Start of 18th dynasty, which brings in more complex, pleated garments

c. 1353 BCE King Akhenaten's reign begins, with Nefertiti as his wife

c. 1350 BCE Nefertiti appears on Theban reliefs

1340s BCE ▷ Akhenaten's court moves to Amarna. Nefertiti's image shows her in colorful jewelry similar to this brooch with sacred motifs such as falcons and scarabs

c. 1340 BCE Nefertiti seems to vanish

1295 BCE End of 18th dynasty

c. 1335 BCE Akhenaten's reign ends

1912 CE Nefertiti bust unearthed by Ludwig Borchardt

1923 ▷ Unveiling of Nefertiti bust in Berlin bolsters Art Deco–era Egyptomania. Egyptian motifs appear on 1920s dresses, jewelry, and ornaments

○ 1550 BCE   ○ 1350 BCE   ○ 1340 BCE   ○ 1335 BCE   ○ 1295 BCE   ○ 1920 CE

ROYAL FASHIONS Thought to be Akhenaten and Nefertiti, both are wearing white pleated linen, decorative collars and aprons, and cobra-adorned headgear. ▷

c. 3000–1500 BCE
MINOAN CULTURE

Centered on the island of Crete, the Minoan civilization was at its height around 1600 BCE; it was advanced and prosperous with widespread trade contacts. Minoan dress from this isolated island society stands out among other ancient European Bronze Age cultures for its cut and stitched body-hugging garments. The small, cinched waist, a key feature of both male and female attire, was emphasized in women by the hats, hairstyles, and embellished sleeves worn above, and the wide, flounced skirts below. Men wore peaked caps, wrapped loincloths around their hips, and showed off their bare torsos—although tunics appeared in the later years of Minoan civilization. The art of weaving complicated, patterned wool cloths flourished on the peaceful, wealthy island and clothing was more elaborate than that of later mainland Greek people. Minoan ideas influenced fashion in Egypt, Mycenae (Ancient Greece), and farther afield.

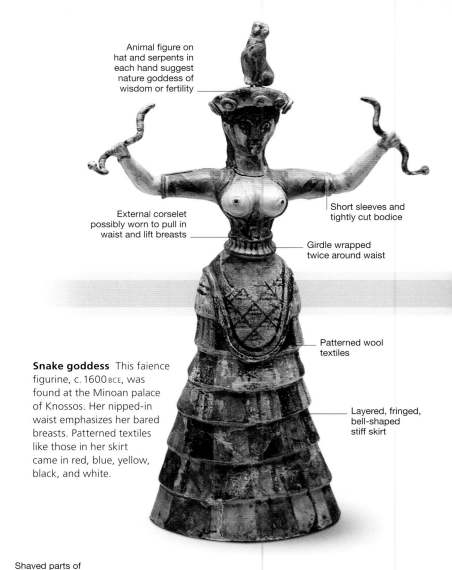

Animal figure on hat and serpents in each hand suggest nature goddess of wisdom or fertility

Short sleeves and tightly cut bodice

External corselet possibly worn to pull in waist and lift breasts

Girdle wrapped twice around waist

Patterned wool textiles

Layered, fringed, bell-shaped stiff skirt

Snake goddess This faience figurine, c. 1600 BCE, was found at the Minoan palace of Knossos. Her nipped-in waist emphasizes her bared breasts. Patterned textiles like those in her skirt came in red, blue, yellow, black, and white.

JEWELRY COLLECTION

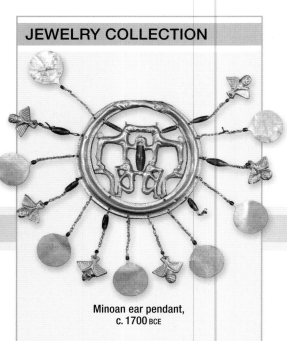

Minoan ear pendant, c. 1700 BCE

Many pieces of jewelry have survived from Minoan culture. The gold pendant shown above is part of a collection known as the Aegina Treasure, thought to be from the island of Aegina. An outer ring in the shape of a two-headed serpent, representing longevity, encircles paired leopards and monkeys. Radiating strings of beads are decorated with sun disks and birds.

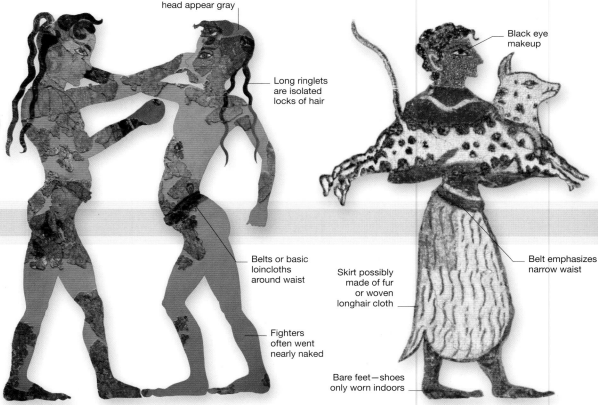

Shaved parts of head appear gray

Long ringlets are isolated locks of hair

Belts or basic loincloths around waist

Fighters often went nearly naked

Fresco from Thira In a detail from a 16th-century BCE fresco from the island of Thira (also known as Thera or Santorini), two boys fight in the nude, wearing just boxing gloves and a belt. Similarly to women, they use eye makeup and wear their hair in ringlets.

Black eye makeup

Belt emphasizes narrow waist

Skirt possibly made of fur or woven longhair cloth

Bare feet—shoes only worn indoors

Priest, Hagia Triada sarcophagus Part of a funerary scene painted on a stone coffin found on Crete, c. 1400 BCE, this priest offers an animal as a gift to the dead. His clothes are probably made of animal hair and skin.

Diadem and ribbons decorate hair

Sleeves embroidered with gold and colored threads

Gold earplugs

Matching bracelets and armlets

Flaring skirt with stylized representation of flounces

Double-layered linen loincloths

Fresco of goddess and worshippers
Men of apparently African origin worship a bare-breasted goddess, 1700–1400 BCE. They wear striped loincloths, probably woven with gold thread, and tight belts at the waist.

Serpent coiled around hat

Snake goddess in tall hat Various faience figurines of the Minoan snake goddess have survived. This one from 1600 BCE wears a towering hat and has two or three snakes entwined around her body. Her apron, which has a deep embroidered border, repeats the curves of the snakes.

Short sleeves

Snakes entwined around arms

Curved apron suggests cutting to shape

Only women wore yellow clothes

Network of fringing around hemline

Peacock feathers

Lily motif on crown

Long, oiled and curled hair

Gold neck chain with lily motif

Elaborate, beribboned headdress

Eyes painted with liner

Band of embroidery or woven bands emphasize close fit of dress

Linen bodice with contrasting bands

Skirt resembles a *kaunakes*—ancient garment made of woven long animal hair

Close-fitted loincloth

Outer loincloth of folded linen layers

Hagia Triada sarcophagus, offering libations
The woman on the right wears a dress with decorative bands at the neck, along the side seams, and around the hem. Her companion wears a skirt that may be made of skins.

Prince Found in fragments at Knossos on Crete, this fresco of a young priest-king, c. 1550 BCE, has been heavily restored. A feathered headdress was a symbol of power in many cultures.

LADIES IN BLUE

The Minoan civilization was named after the legendary King Minos, whose supposed palace of Knossos on the island of Crete was excavated by British archaeologist Arthur Evans at the turn of the 20th century. Among the discoveries at Knossos were the fragments of dynamic frescoes depicting sports events and also various scenes portraying both men and women taking part in everyday life.

With their oiled, ringleted hair and open-fronted, tight-waisted bodices, the three Minoan ladies display the styles peculiar to their culture. Their hairdressed locks are draped with beads and clipped in with thin metal headbands (fillets). They wear delicate bracelets and hold the bodice tops together with more accessories. The modern restoration highlights the complex woven textiles Crete was famous for.

Little of the original paintings has survived. In the 1920s Evans employed Dutch architect and artist Piet de Jong to assemble the fragments, and reconstitute the rest. At that time illustrators of chic fashion journals were setting models against backdrops of Mediterranean resorts, and stylized folk embroidery was influencing textile patterns. The restoration of the frescoes was criticized—perhaps with some justification—for being overly influenced by current fashion tastes.

> 66
>
> It is impossible to disregard the suspicion that their painters have tempered their zeal for accurate reconstruction with a somewhat inappropriate predilection for covers of *Vogue*.
>
> **EVELYN WAUGH,** 1920s
>
> 99

◁ **WALL PAINTING, KNOSSOS, C.1600 BCE**
These ladies of the Minoan court display their wealth with elaborate necklaces, bracelets, and hair ornaments.

C. 500–323 BCE

CLASSICAL GREECE

Clothing worn during the classical period of ancient Greece was made of simple elements draped to sophisticated effect. Loose-fitting and free-flowing, it was adaptable to different seasons. The key garment for both men and women was the *chiton*, a tunic comprising two rectangles of cloth attached at the shoulders and sides. It could be arranged in many ways, and cut to different lengths. Worn over the *chiton* was a cloaklike garment, the *himation*; this was made of heavy material for outdoors, or of lighter cloth for a more fashionable effect indoors or in warmer weather. Women also wore an alternative version of the tunic, called a *peplos*, which was gathered in at the waist and partially fastened at the top of the shoulders, allowing the free corners to drape. The *chlamys*, a cape shaped like the clamshell it was named after, was originally worn by soldiers but, like many functional garments, became a fashion item.

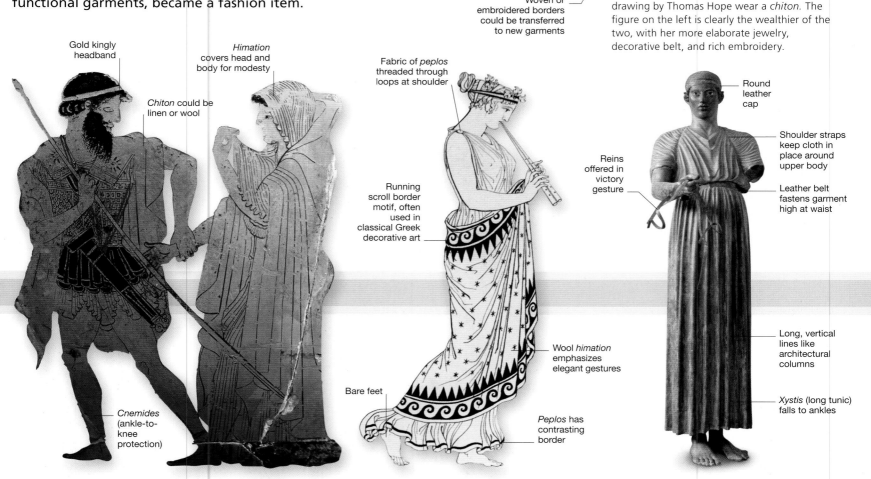

Gold diadem and decorative hairstyle

Short *chiton* worn over chemise

Sunburst and flower motifs resemble Minoan patterns

Leather shoes

Woven or embroidered borders could be transferred to new garments

Chiton Both these women from a 19th-century drawing by Thomas Hope wear a *chiton*. The figure on the left is clearly the wealthier of the two, with her more elaborate jewelry, decorative belt, and rich embroidery.

Gold kingly headband

Himation covers head and body for modesty

Chiton could be linen or wool

Cnemides (ankle-to-knee protection)

Fabric of *peplos* threaded through loops at shoulder

Running scroll border motif, often used in classical Greek decorative art

Wool *himation* emphasizes elegant gestures

Bare feet

Peplos has contrasting border

Round leather cap

Shoulder straps keep cloth in place around upper body

Leather belt fastens garment high at waist

Reins offered in victory gesture

Long, vertical lines like architectural columns

Xystis (long tunic) falls to ankles

Royal dress In a scene drawn from Greek legend, King Agamemnon abducts Princess Briseis during the Trojan War. The king wears a short *chiton*, which is covered by protective, armored battle dress, c. 480 BCE.

Decorative border Wealthy citizens hired musicians to entertain guests at banquets and festivities. A woman plays a flute in this 19th-century drawing. This classical profile is a prototype for figures in later European fashion.

Charioteer's tunic This young driver has just won a race and makes a victory gesture, c. 470 BCE. He wears a type of long *chiton* known as a *xystis*, which was the usual dress for a charioteer at that time.

Water jar

Unadorned hair of working woman

Himation

Draped clothing needed constant rearrangement to keep lines

Working dress This detail was painted on a 6th-century BCE amphora from Vulci, Italy, a center for Greek crafts. The plainly dressed figure is a working woman, perhaps a slave. Slaves did much of the weaving for clothing.

Hair bound in knot and held in stretchy net band

Women's wear These female figures are from an *epinetron*, a pottery item women wore over their knees to protect clothes while weaving, 450–323 BCE. The seated figure wears a *chiton*, while her companion is dressed in a peplos.

Peplos drapes loosely over shoulders

Girdle gathers in waist

Pleated linen

Himation draped over *chiton*

Bare feet

Wool *himation* worn over *chiton* for warmth in winter

Hair parted in middle and waved

Classical dress often more colorful than contemporary representations show

Himation could be draped in many ways to suit taste and fashion

Himation and chiton Like many of the numerous small figures found at Tanagra in Boeotia, Greece, this one is a naturalistic image of a fashionably dressed woman, c. 470 BCE. Few traces remain of the statuette's original bright colors.

HAIRSTYLES

The Greeks paid as much attention to their hair as to their clothing. In the classical period it was the fashion for young men to crop their hair short. Women teased, frizzed, and curled their hair, using combs made of ivory, tortoiseshell, bone, olive wood, or bronze, depending on personal wealth.

Women never cut their hair (except in mourning, or if they were slaves), letting it hang in long locks, or wearing it twisted with ribbons and piled up in a chignon. Both men and women perfumed their hair with scents or fragrant oils. Children had long hair—little girls tied their hair in ponytails.

Short crop: Charioteer of Delphi c. 470 BCE

Waves and braids: statue, 480 BCE

FLUID
DRAPERY

The elegant language of drapery, and the way in which it both reveals and conceals the human form, was well understood by the stone carvers of ancient Greece. They observed acutely the silhouettes achieved by tucking, folding, and draping combinations or sections of fabric that had been cut in triangles, squares, or circles.

Classical Greek drapery was a widespread and long-lasting style, in both fashion and art. It passed from Greece to Rome when Augustus (63 BCE–14 CE), the first Roman emperor, aspired to surpassing the achievements of the golden age of Greece. Retrospective styles in drapery flourished accordingly. Romans, of the upper classes at least, wore graceful, draped garments, but the influence of Greece was not confined to clothing. Fountains, sculpture, and monumental vases in the gardens and villas of wealthy Romans were invariably decorated with drapery styles borrowed from Greek sculpture of 500 years before.

In the modern world, from the 18th century onward, a number of neoclassical movements in fashion have drawn on the soft, draped styles of the classical past. Often these have had a particular purpose—for example, helping to liberate women from the constraints of tight clothing and cumbersome layers of petticoats and shaped padding.

66

The rectangle of fabric, when it is well chosen, is better for making the human form emerge. The angles form exterior parts which, in falling, rise up upon themselves in tiers and sinuous falls …

MADELEINE VIONNET, *GAZETTE DU BON TON,* 1924–1925

99

GREEK VOTIVE RELIEF, 410 BCE ▷
Draped in flowing folds of stone, Artemis and her nymphs stand before a river god.

PREHISTORY TO 600 CE

PROWESS AND PROTECTION

In some parts of the ancient world, men spent much of their lives away from home on active military service. What they wore depended to a large extent on money and rank. Men who dressed in armor were likely to have paid for it themselves—like the hoplites (Greek foot soldiers) in the 5th century BCE, who were drawn from the middle classes and could afford to provide their own body protection. Early armor included metal plates, scales, hardened leather, and padded linen. The invention of mail shirts, made from individually forged interlocking rings, is attributed to the Celts in about 300 BCE. Chain was expensive to produce, and was probably restricted to the highest ranking warriors. A mail shirt allowed more limb movement than some other forms of protection, but at 30 lb (15 kg) it weighed the wearer down. Battle-dress styles sometimes depended on attitude—the fearless Spartans marched to war in red capes to disguise bloodstains.

PROTECTIVE FEATHERS

Getting closer to the gods and gaining protection from evil by wearing plumes, or representations of birds, is common in many cultures, from Egypt to Peru. Feathers are inherently powerful, being light, yet flexible and tough. In the pre-Columbian Amazonian and Andean cultures, headdresses and ceremonial garments were adorned with feathers— especially the contour plumes of wing and tail that aided flight. In Ancient Egypt, after death, the spirit's "heart" was weighed on a golden scale against Ma'at, the feather of truth. If the heart was the lighter, the spirit went directly to the heavenly afterlife.

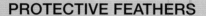

Peruvian feathered headdress

Horned helmet designed to intimidate

Jacketlike garment with lapels shows Persian influence

Molded leather leg protectors

Bronze warrior This 5th-century BCE votive figure from the Etruscan civilization may represent Mars, god of war. Soldiers held their shields on the left side, overlapping them when in line to create a wall of defense.

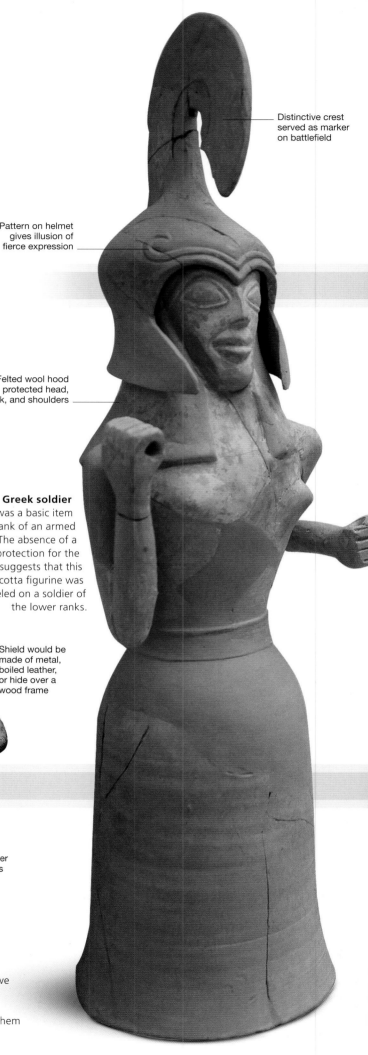

Distinctive crest served as marker on battlefield

Pattern on helmet gives illusion of fierce expression

Felted wool hood protected head, neck, and shoulders

Ancient Greek soldier A helmet was a basic item for any rank of an armed force. The absence of a cuirass (protection for the torso) suggests that this terra-cotta figurine was modeled on a soldier of the lower ranks.

Shield would be made of metal, boiled leather, or hide over a wood frame

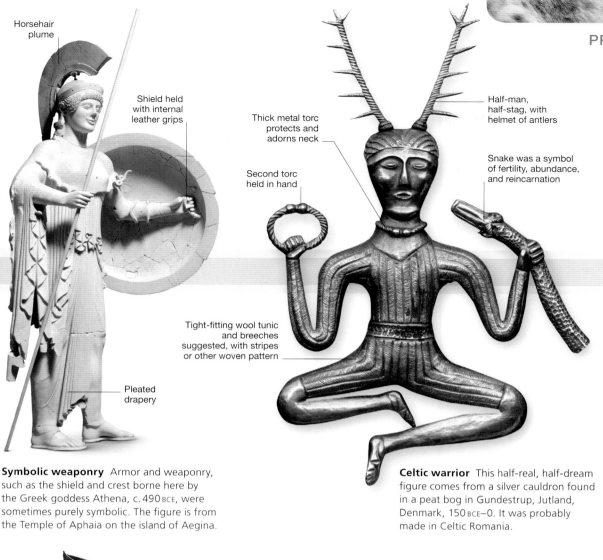

Horsehair
plume

Shield held
with internal
leather grips

Pleated
drapery

Thick metal torc
protects and
adorns neck

Second torc
held in hand

Tight-fitting wool tunic
and breeches
suggested, with stripes
or other woven pattern

Half-man,
half-stag, with
helmet of antlers

Snake was a symbol
of fertility, abundance,
and reincarnation

Symbolic weaponry Armor and weaponry, such as the shield and crest borne here by the Greek goddess Athena, c. 490 BCE, were sometimes purely symbolic. The figure is from the Temple of Aphaia on the island of Aegina.

Celtic warrior This half-real, half-dream figure comes from a silver cauldron found in a peat bog in Gundestrup, Jutland, Denmark, 150 BCE–0. It was probably made in Celtic Romania.

ARMOR

Greek helmet

Heroic cuirass

Other than the helmet, the cuirass was one of the most protective elements of a suit of armor. It covered the front of the torso, and was usually connected to a back piece for all-around protection. The so-called muscle or heroic cuirass of the classical world was cast to the wearer's body, and was designed to mimic an idealized human physique. Greek and Roman art often depicts generals and emperors wearing the heroic cuirass, but real soldiers would have used much simpler armor in battle.

Warrior wears a
mask, probably
to protect face

Shield may show
identifying colors
of soldier's army

Shin shields
end at knee

Etruscan-Corinthian warrior Painted on an alabastron (perfume bottle) probably made in Etruria (now Tuscany) in the 6th century BCE, the soldier has some protective wear but mainly relies on his shield.

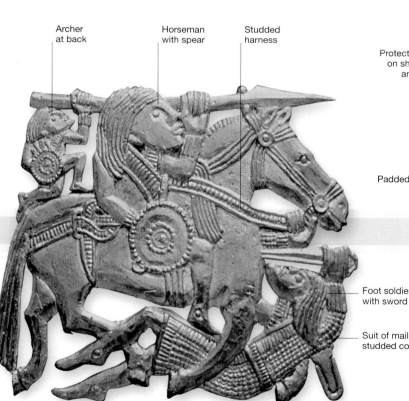

Archer
at back

Horseman
with spear

Studded
harness

Foot soldier
with sword

Suit of mail or
studded coat

Anglo-Saxon ranks This helmet fragment from the 7th-century CE Sutton Hoo burial site in Suffolk, east England, shows different ranks of soldiers. The men wear protective clothing but no helmets over their long, flowing hair.

Felted
wool hood

Protective mail
on shoulders
and torso

Padded leather
cotun

Scottish soldier This early medieval carving from a grave slab in the West Highlands of Scotland shows a man dressed in a long, padded leather garment known as a *cotun*, which gave reasonable protection in battle.

200 BCE – 600 CE
STYLE IN THE EAST

C hina was known as Ceres (from the word for silk) in the ancient world after its legendary and luxurious silks that were traded to the West along the Silk Road. The rich stashes of garments and accessories found in ancient tombs show how sophisticated the textiles and clothing were. They included highly patterned, light-reflective fabrics, and translucent gauze weaves. By layering garments of different lengths, and adding contrasting linings, waist sashes, and bands around the neck, strikingly colorful combinations were achieved. Elaborate cloth turbans and wide sleeves were to influence fashion in the West. The T-shaped kimono-style garments from China and Japan had wide sleeves that hung from the elbow over the wrist and different proportions than Western-style tunics. In central Asian and Persian areas (modern Iran and Iraq) clothing was more fitted, tight to the wrists and with shaped skirts, influenced by the nomadic, horse-riding peoples.

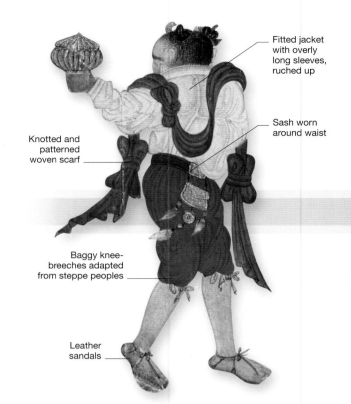

Fitted jacket with overly long sleeves, ruched up

Knotted and patterned woven scarf

Sash worn around waist

Baggy knee-breeches adapted from steppe peoples

Leather sandals

Chinese merchant On a piece of painted silk, this trader is portrayed as part of a group of merchants transporting their wares. His clothes are brightly colored but practical: knee-breeches and a fitted jacket.

Bronze oil lamp

Hair covering

Peacock-feather neck adornment

Standing collar made by straight edge on robe

Large hoop earrings

Carrying framework with silk panels

Wide sleeves

Sleeves folded back to form deep cuffs

Robe wraps across body

Embroidered panels around hem

Leather sandals

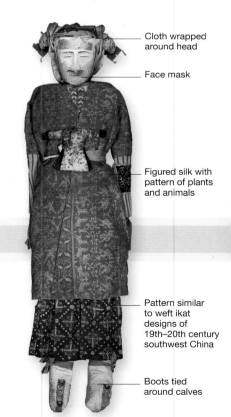

Cloth wrapped around head

Face mask

Figured silk with pattern of plants and animals

Pattern similar to weft ikat designs of 19th–20th century southwest China

Boots tied around calves

Servant girl The kneeling girl holding a functional oil lamp wears a simple robe that wraps around the body and is tied at the side. It has a distinct collar and cuffs. The lamp is from the Western Han dynasty (c. 206 BCE to 9th century CE).

Chinese scholar Xuanzang was a renowned Chinese Buddhist and scholar, depicted here returning from his pilgrimage to India. He is shown wearing a Chinese-style, wide-sleeved robe over loose breeches.

Yingpan Man This 4th–5th-century BCE masked Caucasoid mummy from the Tarim Basin, China, is dressed in a patterned silk coat and wraparound skirt. Discoveries like this along the Silk Road reveal the sophistication of silk weaving at the time.

Hair tied back smoothly

Noblewoman A figurine of a woman from an excavated tomb in Hunan province, China, wears a white silk wrap-front robe covered in the fine silk floral embroidery practiced in China for centuries.

Wide sleeves can cover the hands

Sash in contrasting color, knotted at the front

Red silk lining shows in turned-back collar

Long, tubular skirt

Upturned toes on shoes a northern fashion

Kimono's origins The distinctive, loose T-shape of the garment later called a kimono is apparent in this Chinese man's outfit. Men's and women's clothing were similar. Japan adopted clothing from the Chinese Han Dynasty early in the Common Era.

Tall, decorated turban implies wealth and status

Pointed full beard

Buttons fasten at front

Shorter sleeves of outer *caftan*

Decorative sash hanging down

Caftan with A-line skirt

Ancient Persian This Sassanid-era (200–600 CE) nobleman wears a tall hat and wide-skirted *caftan* (robe). The tailoring is sophisticated—it is fitted and has tight sleeves. Persians wore silk two centuries before the Byzantines.

Mandarin-style hat

Robe wrapped around body

Richly embroidered decoration

Hands tucked into sleeves

Diagonal front of robe unknown in Europe

Contrasting silk border

SILK ROAD

The Silk Road was not one but several trading routes through the mountains and deserts between Asia, the Arabian peninsula, and the Mediterranean. Silk was a prime commodity, along with precious stones and spices. Excavations along the Silk Road offer glimpses into the cloths being traded. For example, at Palmyra in Syria—a major trading center that handled goods from China, India, and Iran in the Roman period—Chinese silks have been found in tombs.

After Western cultures fell for silk's allure, their goal was to learn the secrets of sericulture (obtaining silk from silkworms) for themselves. The Persians succeeded by the 3rd century CE.

Western Han Dynasty silk banner, c. 180 BCE, found in a tomb in Hunan province, China

Wound turban cloth

Decorative work on sleeves

Skirt width created by adding triangles of fabric to rectangles

Long pants tucked into boots underneath

Sassanid noble Horse-riding tribes originally cut curved fitted clothes from skins, rather than straight woven lengths. Clothes convenient for riding—long sleeves, split skirts, and shaped waists—became the norm.

c. 900–200 BCE
ETRUSCANS

Before the rise of Roman civilization, a people known as the Etruscans flourished in Etruria, an area of Italy corresponding broadly to modern Tuscany. The origin of the Etruscans is uncertain but they are thought to have come from Asia Minor. By the 7th century BCE these people had established a wide-reaching commercial network and were trading all over Europe. As a result, Etruscans enjoyed a comfortable lifestyle and the means to dress up—as paintings, sculpture, and pottery, mostly recovered from the burial sites of the wealthy, testify. Their clothes combined influences from both Greece and Asia and included garments that later became classic items of Roman wear. For example, the colorful *tebenna*, a wide, embroidered cape that was worn throughout Etruria, evolved into the Roman toga. The purple robes of later Roman emperors were also worn in Etruria.

Striped cloak A young musician, depicted on the wall of a tomb in the city of Tarquinia (c. 500 BCE), wears a dramatically striped *tebenna*, the classic Etruscan cloak, flung casually over his tunic.

Colorful *tebenna* worn over tunic

Sandals were one of the most common types of footwear

Minoan-influenced hairstyle

Colored border

Long *chiton* (gown)

Pointed boots

Tunic of fine linen, probably pleated

Trio of circles motif on cloak

Plated leather cuirass

Perizoma (very short breeches) under cuirass

ACCESSORIES

Gold pendant (portraying Achelous, the river god) c. 6th century BCE

Leech-shaped gold brooch, c. 7th century BCE

The highly skilled Etruscan jewelers created marvellous accessories in bronze, silver, and gold. These included pendants, bracelets, necklaces, earrings, bracelets, clasps, and brooches. A gold-working technique known as granulation was developed, whereby tiny grains of gold were soldered on to a smooth background to create a glittering effect. Some of the showiest pieces date from the 7th century BCE. Between the 6th and 4th centuries BCE the work was fine but less extravagant. Around 550 BCE engraved gemstones were imported from Greece.

Dancing clothes Paintings in the Tomb of the Jugglers at Tarquinia (c. 500 BCE) depict various entertainers. This dancer wears pointed boots and a *chiton* with a contrasting border. Bracelets and large, disk-shaped earrings complete her costume.

Age and youth This Thomas Hope line illustration shows an older man wearing a cloak with the trio of circles motif often seen in Etruscan art. However, the younger man's leather armor is more imaginative than authentic.

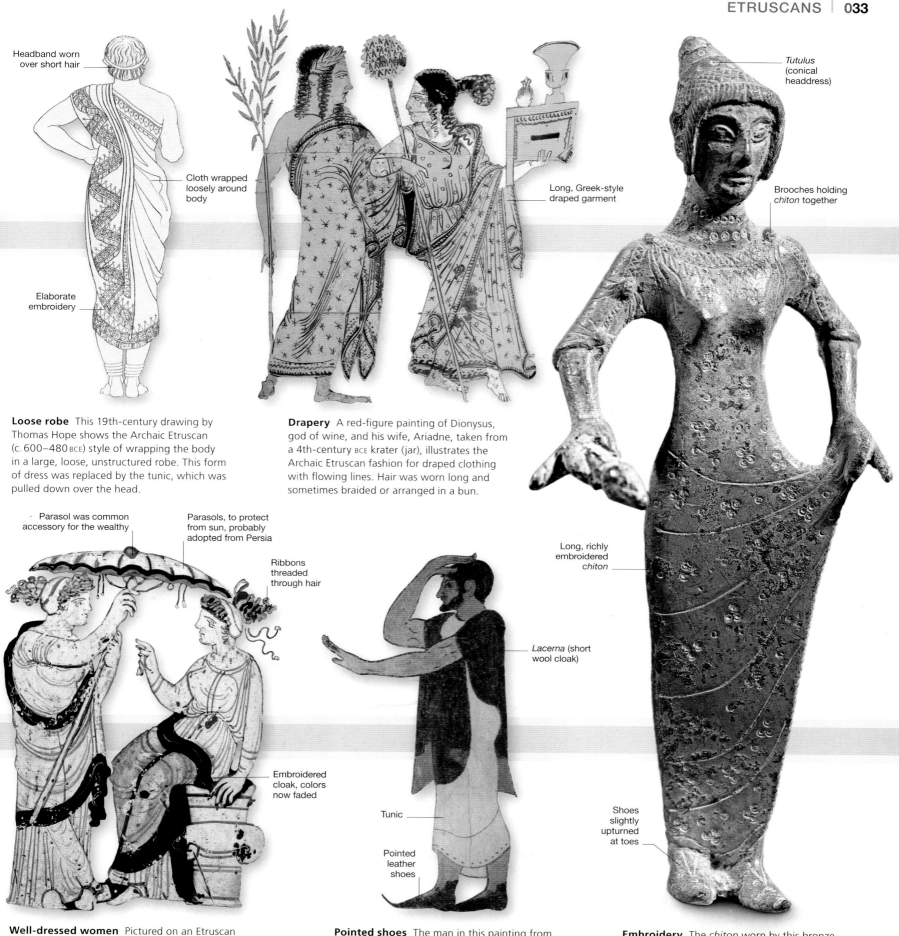

Headband worn over short hair

Cloth wrapped loosely around body

Elaborate embroidery

Loose robe This 19th-century drawing by Thomas Hope shows the Archaic Etruscan (c. 600–480 BCE) style of wrapping the body in a large, loose, unstructured robe. This form of dress was replaced by the tunic, which was pulled down over the head.

Long, Greek-style draped garment

Drapery A red-figure painting of Dionysus, god of wine, and his wife, Ariadne, taken from a 4th-century BCE krater (jar), illustrates the Archaic Etruscan fashion for draped clothing with flowing lines. Hair was worn long and sometimes braided or arranged in a bun.

Tutulus (conical headdress)

Brooches holding *chiton* together

Long, richly embroidered *chiton*

Parasol was common accessory for the wealthy

Parasols, to protect from sun, probably adopted from Persia

Ribbons threaded through hair

Embroidered cloak, colors now faded

Well-dressed women Pictured on an Etruscan vase, the woman on the right wears a Greek-style peplos, a type of sleeveless dress; her companion, left, wears a gown called a *chiton*. In typical Etruscan style, both flaunt richly colored cloaks.

Lacerna (short wool cloak)

Tunic

Pointed leather shoes

Pointed shoes The man in this painting from the Tomb of the Augurs at Tarquinia (c. 500 BCE) may be a priest or a relative of the deceased. His shoes, with pointed and curved toes, show Greek, Persian, or Middle Eastern influences.

Shoes slightly upturned at toes

Embroidery The *chiton* worn by this bronze votive figure (c. 520–470 BCE) is embroidered with the popular Etruscan trio of circles motif. A close-fitting conical headdress, known as a *tutulus*, covers the figure's hair.

509 BCE – 476 CE
ROMAN EMPIRE

Dress was carefully prescribed in Roman society, especially for men; rank and status determined whether the toga could be worn (only by Roman citizens) and whether it might be colored. Only the emperor could wear purple, but priests, senators, and equestrians (serving in the army or the administration) might wear a stripe of purple on their robes. A women's basic garment was the *stola*, a robe which hung in pleats from the shoulders, where it fastened with brooches or clasps called *fibulae* and was often held in under the bust and around the waist with a belt. Over this, ladies wore a *palla* (shawl), which might cover the head. Madder (red), saffron (yellow), and indigo (blue) dyes were available, and clothes were sometimes embroidered. Most garments were wool or linen, but silk was imported for the wealthy. Foreign captives and slaves wore a *tunica* (tunic). Leather sandals or boots protected the feet.

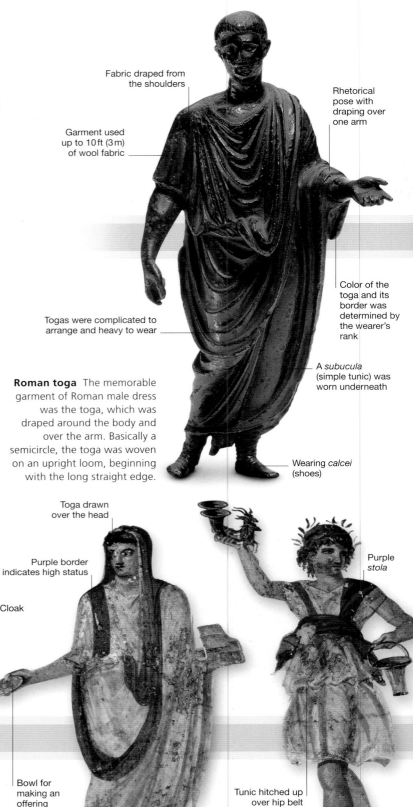

Fabric draped from the shoulders

Garment used up to 10 ft (3 m) of wool fabric

Rhetorical pose with draping over one arm

Togas were complicated to arrange and heavy to wear

Color of the toga and its border was determined by the wearer's rank

A *subucula* (simple tunic) was worn underneath

Wearing *calcei* (shoes)

Roman toga The memorable garment of Roman male dress was the toga, which was draped around the body and over the arm. Basically a semicircle, the toga was woven on an upright loom, beginning with the long straight edge.

HAIRSTYLES

Curls were made using heated metal curling tongs

Women's hairstyle

Hair pomades and creams were made from animal fats

Men's hairstyle

Hairstyling was important for both men and women, and hair fashions changed often. During the Imperial period (27 BCE–3 CE) styles became increasingly elaborate, particularly for the nobility. Men generally kept their hair short and neat, and were clean shaven. Wealthy women had slaves to help them curl and dress their hair using ointments and *calamistrum* (curling irons). To create styles such as the raised curls above, hair pieces or wigs were used, sometimes made with blonde hair from Germanic peoples.

Horsehair plume

Helmet with cheek guards

Cloak

Apron skirt of studded leather strips

Bowl for making an offering

Shin guards

Caliga (leather sandals)

Toga drawn over the head

Purple border indicates high status

Purple *stola*

Tunic hitched up over hip belt

Boots are called *solea*

Roman soldier Wearing a leather cuirass, this reconstructed legionnaire has a metal helmet and shin guards to protect him in battle. His wool cloak was also a blanket.

Draped figure In this fresco from a household shrine in Pompeii, the master of the house is offering a sacrifice. His priestly function is marked by draping the purple-bordered praetexta over his head.

Dancing spirit This *lar* is a mythological figure who protects the household. His tunic is tucked up in a simple rustic style. It is bound at the waist with a girdle.

Hair is curled and pinned up

Strophium—band of fabric worn over breasts

Pagne (loincloth) made of linen

Playful crown of leaves

Both men and women wore loincloths

Double-girdled *chiton*—folded over in two places

Female gymnasts A mosaic from the Villa Romana del Casale in Sicily of 200–300 CE shows women wearing bikinis. The upper garment is a simple scarf tied around the bust and the lower piece is a loincloth. Shaped leather Roman underwear from the same period has been found.

Crown of laurel leaves

Pallium (cloak) of saffron-dyed wool

Greek influence
A 1st-century CE fresco from Pompeii shows Greek hero Jason wearing a *chiton* (tunic) in the knee-length "Ionic" style, with long sleeves and held up at the waist. The Roman *tunica* was based on this garment.

No beard—Roman fashion was clean shaven

Applied ornament was called *segmenta*

Tunic embellished with tapestry-woven bands

Wool was the only fabric available to most people

Long country boots called *pero*

Hunting gear Wearing a tunic and practical boots, this man, in a mosaic from 4th-century CE Sicily, is returning from a hunting trip. Only Roman citizens could wear the toga—foreigners and slaves wore simple tunics.

Laurel wreath worn by people of rank

Colors are probably fanciful on this fresco

Purple dye was the most highly prized

Purple border called a *clavus*

Ceremonial toga A house fresco in Pompeii shows Greek king Agamemnon in a toga. By decree, togas were white, called *pura*. Only emperors, magistrates, and priests could wear the expensive purple edging.

Gallicae (knee-high boots)

Headdress of horns and jewels

Gauzy *stola* of precious silk

Leather sandals

Silky nymph Roman mythology included stories about gods and nymphs. The beautiful nymph Io, the lover of Argos, is shown dressed in a *stola* (diaphanous silk robe). She was turned into a heifer so her headdress has small horns.

476–600 CE
BYZANTINE STYLE

After the fall of Rome in 476 CE, Constantinople (present-day Istanbul) became the center of the Byzantine world. With the rise of the empire came opulence and a fusion of Greek, Roman, Middle Eastern, and Oriental styles. Clothes indicated social status. The richest and grandest figures, exemplified by the Emperor Justinian I and his consort Theodora, had their long, flowing gowns of richly patterned silks encrusted with jewels and gold thread. The veils and silks worn by women, and the T-shaped tunics and cloaks worn by men, were developed from Roman official dress. Some of the garments, notably the *pallium* (cloak), chasuble (outer garment), and *dalmatikon* (wide-sleeved tunic), were formalized into vestments of the Orthodox and Catholic churches. Poor working people wore plain wool tunics, knee-length for men, with leggings, boots, and a long cloak on top.

EMPRESS THEODORA

"May I never be without the purple I wear, nor live to see the day when men do not call me 'Your Majesty,'" proclaimed Theodora in 532 CE, in defiance of the revolt against her husband Justinian's rule. The empress's lavish dress emphasized her wealth and status. Gold thread decorated her garments, which were colored with expensive Tyrian purple dye and embroidered with jewels.

Her fashion influence has traveled down through the centuries—designer Karl Lagerfeld drew on Theodora's embellished style for his Paris–Byzance Spring 2011 collection for Chanel.

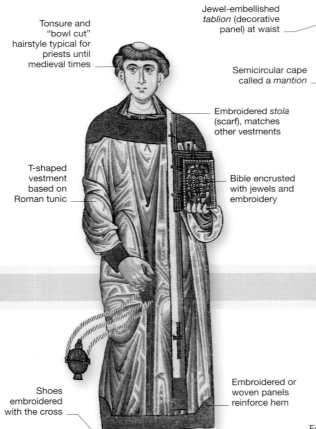

Tonsure and "bowl cut" hairstyle typical for priests until medieval times

T-shaped vestment based on Roman tunic

Embroidered *stola* (scarf), matches other vestments

Bible encrusted with jewels and embroidery

Shoes embroidered with the cross

Embroidered or woven panels reinforce hem

Holy man This mosaic of St. Stephen from Monreale Cathedral, Palermo, Sicily, shows him wearing bands of heavy embroidery, his vestments following the style of Roman tunics. He also wears a *stola* over his left shoulder.

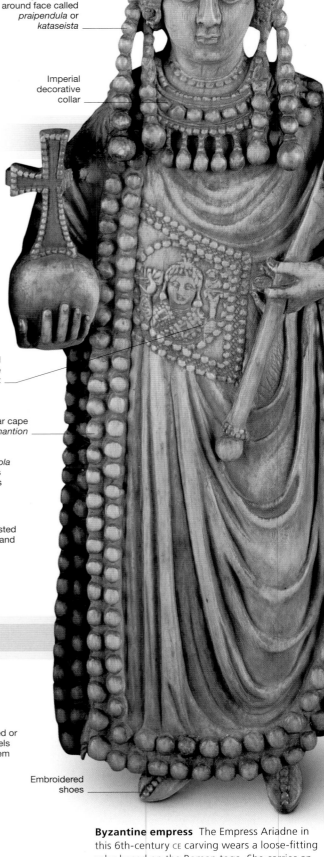

Padded headdress called *propoloma*

Strings of pearls around face called *praipendula* or *kataseista*

Imperial decorative collar

Jewel-embellished *tablion* (decorative panel) at waist

Semicircular cape called a *mantion*

Embroidered shoes

Byzantine empress The Empress Ariadne in this 6th-century CE carving wears a loose-fitting robe based on the Roman toga. She carries an orb and scepter as symbols of her imperial power over the state and the Orthodox Church.

Sleeves are separate pieces of cloth joined at shoulder

Head cloth called *vilarion*

Short-sleeved overtunic

Sleeves of tightly fitting linen undertunic may be stitched to fit at wrist

Rich colors of brown and red

Floor-length outer garment

Beard may imply foreign mercenary

Sash knotted in particular way

Crown inlaid with jewels

Praipendula—jewels hanging around face

Large fibula holds mantle in place

Gold and silk woven *tablion* (decorative panel)

Striped textile This woman's striped textile, depicted in a mosaic, probably came from a near-Eastern source. The direction of the stripes down the body and arm indicate that the sleeves were stitched into the shoulder.

Foreign soldier This figure of a soldier from a chapel in Palermo, Sicily, is shown dressed in clothes probably from a near-Eastern location such as Anatolia or Mesopotamia. The artist intended him to appear foreign.

Diadem inlaid with semiprecious stones

Band of pearl-encrusted embroidery

Diaphanous silk veil with fringed ends—symbol of the virgin bride

Stola worn around both shoulders

Ornate outer chasuble

Wide-sleeved *dalmatikon* (tunic)

Patterned silks probably woven in imperial state workshops

Embroidered end panel of a waist sash

Wide-sleeved vestment has black woven bands derived from Roman tunic

Open leather shoes with white wool socks

Shoes embroidered and encrusted with pearls

Silken virgin This detail from a mosaic in a church in Ravenna, Italy, shows one of the holy virgins. She wears a figured silk overgown. The secrets of silk production were smuggled into Constantinople.

Justinian's clergyman Emperor Justinian's retinue included clergymen in vestments that indicated the transition from formal imperial Roman dress to liturgical wear. The *stola* has evolved into a symbolic garment without practical function.

Imperial purple Emperor Justinian wears a long mantle colored from large quantities of enormously expensive Tyrian purple dye. His tunic sleeve is visible underneath.

PREHISTORY TO 600 CE
DYES AND PIGMENTS

There was much more color in the ancient world than many faded objects and buildings that remain would suggest. Mixing naturally occurring pigments with water or oil is evident in prehistoric cave paintings, and ancient people found colors to dye cloth, decorate their skin, and create jewelry. The most commonly used dyes and pigments were locally available. Many came from plants; insects were the source of a few rich colors; and rocks, minerals, or soil provided others. The best quality, rarest, and most expensive dyes, such as Tyrian purple from sea snails, were traded across cultures and continents. Color—sometimes in the form of pattern—differentiated class, customs, and geographic origin. It could also be symbolic.

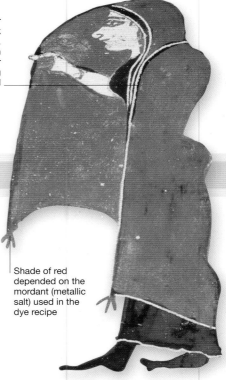

Sources of dye for black trim of cloak were tree bark, oak galls, green walnuts, and other plants containing tannic acid

Shade of red depended on the mordant (metallic salt) used in the dye recipe

Red Swathed in two tones of red, this female figure is depicted on an Etruscan jar from the 6th century BCE. The word "crimson" comes from kermes, an insect that feeds on holm oaks in the Mediterranean, and the source of the dye.

Bow painted to match

Embroidered wool felt cap

Sleeves and leggings probably made from sprang, a stretchy netted textile

Yellow dyes were easily obtained from a number of plants

Repeat patterns probably woven in on the loom, possibly using tapestry techniques

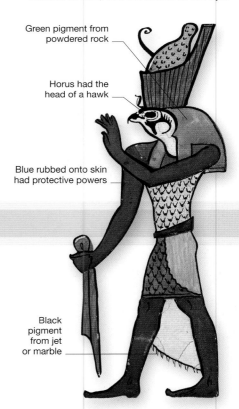

Green pigment from powdered rock

Horus had the head of a hawk

Blue rubbed onto skin had protective powers

Black pigment from jet or marble

Bright colors Ancient Greek statues and buildings were vividly painted with mineral pigments and indigo when they were first made. This reproduction of an archer from c. 490 BCE suggests how these statues appeared.

Ancient Egyptian blue This detail from the back of a mummy mask shows Horus, god of the sky and protector of the ruler of Egypt. Blue, the color of the sky and so of heaven, was used symbolically in honor of the dead.

Purple from overdyeing red and blue

Some rare examples of green dye in South America

Red dye from cochineal beetle

Green from overdyeing blue and yellow

Undyed, rich brown native wool or cotton

Tabards were often worn

THE POPULARITY OF INDIGO

While some cosmetics were ruinous to health and beauty in the long term, indigo had special healing properties. Indigo is a natural antiseptic and was traditionally used in tattooing the skin. A major international trading commodity, indigo is one of the most readily available natural dyes around the world, although the quality and intensity can vary. It is sourced from different plants, depending on the climate. In Europe *Isatis tinctoria* (woad) was the source. Different species for indigo exist far and wide, from sub-Saharan Africa to Japan and India.

Fermented, compacted leaves look like a rock

Compressed indigo

Orange and ocher The ocher on the woman's robe is an earth color used in paintings—like this 1st-century CE fresco from Pompeii—but not in textiles. The cloth could have been dyed with cheap weld or goldenrod, or rare, expensive saffron from crocus stems.

Green and contrasting color This stylized figure is woven into a llama wool cloth for wrapping a mummy in the 3rd-century BCE Paracas culture of Peru. The lively textile patterns of pre-Columbian cultures use contrasting colors and shapes.

Madder red from roots of the madder plant

Indigo dyed

Tyrian purple dyed cloth a rich red-violet and did not fade

White silk or cotton baggy pants

Saffron yellow sash

Blue from Indian indigo

White is the natural background color

Chinese blue Blue from indigo was the most easily available dye, since the plants grew freely. This detail from a painted panel of Chinese silk shows a man both wearing blue and carrying a blue-and-white teapot.

Patterned clothing The patterns distinguish these Semite women of c. 1900 BCE from Egyptians. Striped or patterned cloth may have been the biblical Joseph's "coat of many colors." The white cotton was block printed with wax to resist the dye, like batik.

Purple Tyrian, also called true, Imperial, or murex (from the sea snail that secreted it) purple was a precious dye farmed in the Mediterranean. It was reserved for imperial and high religious use or for rich diplomatic gifts. The Phoenician city of Tyre was a trade center.

RECONSTRUCTION
SHORT TUNIC

Typically worn in the Saxon era, this short ungored (without panel inserts) tunic has been re-created in gray lozenge-twill wool by reconstruction dressmaker Sarah Thursfield. Short tunics were worn by young men and workers from the 3rd or 4th century CE in northern Germany right through to late Saxon times. Tunics based on rectangles and triangles were the basic unit of clothing across Europe. They were usually worn with *braccas* (wool pants), often with leg windings, and leather shoes. The final appearance of a tunic was a matter of personal preference and style: the wearer arranged the spare width of the fabric over the tied fabric belt, gently pouched or sometimes in the stylish pleats seen in late Saxon illustrations. Later tunics often had fuller gored skirts.

◁ **RURAL WEAR**
A peasant tends his sheep in a rural idyll on a late Anglo-Saxon vellum. He wears a simple tunic draped over a fabric belt—a style and shape that endured for centuries.

Fullness at top of arms allows freedom of movement

No armhole shaping

Full-length sleeves

Short skirt pouched over belt

◁ **SIMPLE CONSTRUCTION**
The tunic back and front are made from two unshaped rectangles of cloth with added sleeves that taper at the wrist. A fabric belt defines the waist and gathers in the width.

Brooches at each
shoulder did not
always match

Natural opening
created for arms

Linen undershift
could be laundered

Garment falls
in heavy folds

RECONSTRUCTION
PEPLOS STYLE

Combinations of wrapped dresses and sleeved linen shifts were worn from the Bronze Age (more than 4,000 years ago) and formed the basis of Ancient Greek and Roman women's wardrobes. An example of this dress style survives from a Danish "bog body" of around 500 BCE, and the garments only appear to have gone out of fashion with the Northern European move to Christianity. The peplos-style dress is simply a large tube of cloth. The fold at the top controls the length in wear, and two brooches hold it in place at the shoulders.

IN DETAIL

◁ **IRON-AGE REPLICAS**
Bronze safety-pin brooches made from a single piece of coiled wire are used to hold the peplos together at the shoulder. The changing style of brooches is revealed through finds in early Saxon graves and often give an indication of the wealth of the individual.

◁ **WOVEN BORDERS**
The wool fabric would have been woven on an upright loom, either warp weighted or with upper and lower beams. On these looms it was possible to weave the cloth either as a continuous tube or as a single large piece. The border design is part of the weave.

◁ **WARMTH AND PROTECTION**
As with the tunic, this garment is managed by the wearer and may be worn with a belt and shortened for practical work. The dense wool provides good protection and an extra peplos-style outer garment could be added in cold weather.

◁ **DRESSING VENUS**
Two attendants dress Venus, drawing her peplos up over a filmy shift in this detail of the birth of Venus from a marble relief on the Ludovisi Throne, c. 470–60 BCE.

MEDIEVAL ROMANCE AND TRADE

AND TRADE

600–1449

MEDIEVAL ROMANCE AND TRADE

Throughout this period, clothes for most people were very simple, based on little more than two draped rectangles sewn into a tunic. Tunics and cloaks were made of wool and linen, though leather and furs were also worn, especially in the colder northern regions of Europe. Silk was an extremely expensive item throughout the medieval era. After the fall of the Roman Empire in 476 CE people began to travel across Europe, learning new customs, techniques, and fashions. The Church split into two branches: the Eastern (Byzantine) and the Western (Holy Roman Empire) with different styles of clothing for each. Ecclesiastical clothing was decided at this time by papal decree and religious vestments today still follow these templates.

New skills and tools

Most people in the Middle Ages wore a variation on a tunic, but, as cutting improved slowly from the 12th to the 14th centuries, clothing became more shaped to the body. Also at this time, vertical looms were replaced by horizontal ones, which allowed fabric to be woven more quickly and increased textile production; it became cheaper to buy clothing. Byzantium retained the most advanced and luxurious culture—its clothing styles were much imitated by Western courts and monarchs such as Charlemagne. Europeans traveling to and trading with Middle Eastern areas discovered new styles and fabrics, eventually finding out the secrets of sericulture (silk production). Fine lampas, cloth-of-gold, and brocaded silks were produced in Italy and Spain, no longer relying on expensive imports.

Birth of fashion

By the later Middle Ages fashion and clothing became more complicated. There was a wider choice of garments and accessories and a greater range of fabrics; colors were brighter and closures more varied. With a certain novelty and more choice, fashion can be said to have been born, styles changed more quickly, and the idea of change for change's sake arrived. Improved production of textiles meant wastage, and innovation was possible. Garment shapes began to be curved, and edges could be snipped or dagged.

Place in society

Despite these changes, some things remained rigid. Women were expected to keep their heads covered, and clothes dictated an individual's place in society—they revealed who you were and what you did. It was frowned upon, and there were even laws against, non-nobility attempting to dress as nobility. At the same time differences between social classes increased—the rich looked a lot richer than the poor.

600–800	801–1070	1071–1100

664
In England, the Synod of Whitby decides that the Roman tonsure (top of the head shaved) is to be adopted over the Celtic tonsure (front of the head shaved).

▼ Priest being tonsured

▶ Detail from the Bayeux Tapestry

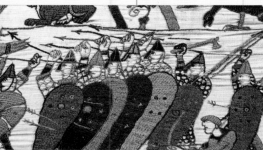

985
Eric the Red sails from Iceland to Greenland with Norse settlers and establishes a colony. Clothing from burials during the 14th and 15th centuries give an insight into dress at the edge of the European world.

1070s
The Bayeux Tapestry, made of linen and embroidered with colored wool yarns, is created. It reveals hallmarks of Anglo-Saxon embroidery techniques.

680
Anglo-Saxon England has silk by the late 600s, brought back from Rome by Benedict Biscop and others. It is an essential, and portable, purchase for well-off pilgrims to Rome or the Holy Land.

▲ Eric depicted in 1688

1095
The First Crusade begins, opening additional routes and bringing back Eastern fabrics and styles to influence Europe.

711
The conquest of Spain by the Moors brings an Islamic and Moorish influence to Iberia and the development of Hispano–Moresque style (silk textiles that have geometric patterns).

1066
Beginning of the Norman Conquest in England, when Norman styles from the continent began to have a major influence on English dress.

▶ Byzantine fabrics traveled to Europe

> A merchant was there with a forked beard, In mottelee and hye on horse he sat; Upon his head a Flaundrish bever hat …

GEOFFREY CHAUCER, *THE MERCHANT'S TALE*, C. 1380

1101–1200	1201–1210	1211–1300	1301–1359	1360–1380	1381–1449
1150 Horizontal looms, around since the 11th century in Europe and much earlier in the East, become mechanized in the 12th century.	**1200s** Buttons start to appear in European clothing.	**1215** The Fourth Council of the Lateran rules that Jews and Muslims must be distinguishable by their dress, beginning the process that transformed the conical Jewish hat from something worn as a voluntary mark of difference, to an enforced one. Clerical dress also becomes mandatory.	**1350** A fashion for mi-parti or parti-colored garments made of two contrasting fabrics, one on each side, emerges in the mid-14th century for men.		**c. 1390** Chaucer's *Prologues to The Canterbury Tales* includes details of the pilgrims' clothing, showing how medieval people can determine status and position from what someone is wearing.

▲ 13th-century metal button

| | **1204** The capture of Constantinople in the Fourth Crusade diminishes the power of the Byzantine empire, and its hold on dress style. | | | **1367** King Richard II of England (reigned 1367–1399) is credited with having invented the cloth handkerchief. The item, "little pieces [of cloth] for the lord King to wipe and clean his nose," appears in the Household Rolls (accounts)—the first documentation of their use. | |

▲ Map showing Marco Polo's route and the Silk Road

1150 Damask is first produced in the city of Damascus in the 12th century. Damask fabrics rely on contrasting weave textures rather than color to render patterns.

c. 1380 Women's shoulders are revealed for the first time in low-necked fitted dresses. Clerics and critics are predictably outraged. They also accuse women of padding their busts to give them a better appearance.

▲ Fitted tunic worn over footed hose

1271 Venetian Marco Polo sets off on his 24-year-long travels along the Silk Road. His voyage passes through all the centers of silk innovations, manufacture, and trading, and he returns to Venice with riches and treasures.

1350 The gown for men is abandoned and instead a tight top over the torso, with breeches or pants below, is worn. These become the distinctive feature of European men's fashion for centuries to come.

▲ Woman in conical headdress

c. 1430 The headdress in the shape of a cone or "steeple"— the stereotypical princess hat—makes an appearance.

▲ Damask patterned fabric

c. 1205 The word "breeches" first appears in the English language.

1278 Velvet is woven in Spain and Italy in the late 13th century. It is documented in 1278 that the English King Edward I has a velvet bed covering.

1351 Edward III of England establishes an embroidery workshop in the Tower of London.

1431 Joan of Arc, the Maid of Orleans claiming divine guidance, leads the French armies to victory against the English. She is burned as a heretic on May 30, 1431. One of the main charges against her was that she wore male clothing and cut her hair short—transvestitism was against church doctrine.

▲ The Maid of Orleans

600–1100
THE AGE OF MIGRATIONS

After the western Roman Empire collapsed, people started migrating to new areas, sometimes by invasion and conquest, sometimes through peaceful settlement. In Northern European areas, Germanic, Frankish, and Norse-speaking peoples needed warm, water-repelling clothes in the cold climate, so wool was the main cloth used. People in warmer Mediterranean regions had lighter clothing in linens, wools, and sometimes silk—if they could afford it. Both men and women wore loose tunics, based on rectangles sewn together in different styles, and caught with belts. Mantles (cloaks) were draped over tunics, sometimes with status-enhancing fur linings. Men wore trews (the forerunner of pants) below the waist, wrapped with wool bands or leather below the knee. Linen shirts were worn as undergarments beneath tunics, and sometimes worn on their own in summer. Surviving clothing from burials reveals a love of finery in embroidery, tablet-woven braids, and intricate jewelry.

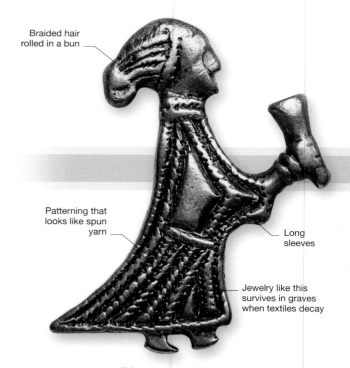

Braided hair rolled in a bun

Patterning that looks like spun yarn

Long sleeves

Jewelry like this survives in graves when textiles decay

Viking woman Women in some Scandinavian countries wore apron-dresses or apron-skirts. Round or oval brooches were used to hold up the dresses and further decoration came from pendants such as this silver example.

TEXTILE PRODUCTION

Before the horizontal loom's introduction, c.1000, all European weaving was done on vertical looms, held under tension with warp-weights at the bottom. Producing cloth was extremely labor intensive and women did most of it at home. Wool, the most common fiber, had to be shorn, cleaned, and carded (brushed), then spun with a drop-spindle. The loom was set up with vertical warp threads, and finally the weft threads were woven horizontally over and under the warp to make cloth. Clothing was based mostly on straight lines, connecting the selvedges (fabric edges) to minimize waste.

Coptic wool tunic, c.600

Mythological motifs

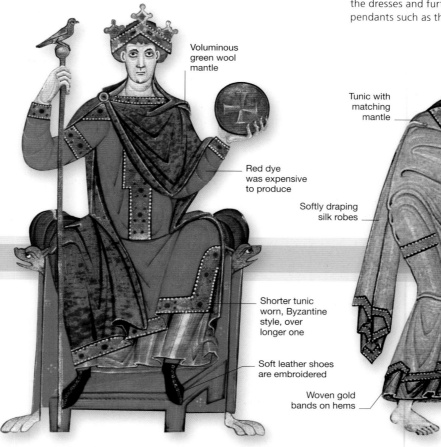

Voluminous green wool mantle

Red dye was expensive to produce

Shorter tunic worn, Byzantine style, over longer one

Soft leather shoes are embroidered

Imperial majesty This illumination, c.990, shows the Holy Roman Emperor Otto III in the finest attire possible. His silk tunic is dyed with costly red and embellished with gems and gold. The crown, orb, and scepter mark his authority.

Tunic with matching mantle

Softly draping silk robes

Long undertunic revealed by shorter outer garments

Woven gold bands on hems

Byzantine silk A 10th-century woman wears sumptuous textiles. Byzantine silk was light and clung to the shape of the body. The undertunic, painted to look blue, was probably made of white linen.

Beard and long hair

Men wore conical helmets, or caps of fur, leather, or wool

Loose wool tunic tapers at wrists

Vikings at work Two 12th-century Norwegian men fixing a sword wear wool tunics, belted at the waist. Summer Viking raids brought new fashions and rare accessories back to Norse regions.

Long hair

Undergarment shows at wrists

Close-fitting linen leg coverings

Drapery lines reveal rich quantity of fabric

Tunic based on rectangles

Applied bands show wealth

Catalan noble Men's and women's dress could be so similar that it was hard to tell the sexes apart. This Iberian noble from the 7th century could be a lord or a lady, since both wore long clothes, soft shoes, and long hair.

Mantle worn sideways in fashionable style

Length hitched up over belt

Fine, supple leather boots

Tunic could be made of luxurious silk

Royal splendor As befits a ruler, Frankish King Charles II wears fine-quality clothing, c. 870. His long mantle covers a tunic and leg coverings, although classical writers thought that pants were barbaric.

Pointed crown in Byzantine style

Underarm gusset gives sleeves fullness

Elegant draping, even with simple construction

Embroidered leg garment and leather leg wrappings

Carolingian style Emperor Charlemagne's son, Louis the Pious, d. 840, wears sumptuous silk and gem-encrusted clothing. The damask mantle is particularly extravagant in its color and pearl motifs.

JEWELRY

Thor's hammer

Replica Viking amulets

Jewelry was a means of adornment and also a form of portable wealth, easily carried and used as payment. People living around the Baltic Sea collected amber, the fossilized resin of prehistoric trees, and traded it across Europe and beyond. Precious metals, such as gold, and jewels had a nearly sacred attribution due to their rarity. Other metals used included bronze, iron, copper, and tin. Glass beads appear in many Norse graves. Men and women held clothing together with ornate round pins and brooches, and wore shapely belt buckles, rings, and earrings.

900–1100

THE EARLY MIDDLE AGES

As people began to settle into stable societies, different styles of dress evolved. Charlemagne's Holy Roman Empire and the monasteries of Anglo-Saxon England recorded clothing details in illuminated manuscripts. The modern words "kirtle" (undertunic) and "mantle" (cloak) originated from the Anglo-Saxon *cyrtel* and *mantel*. Women wore a kirtle over a linen undergarment, and often an outer gown as well. There was still little difference between clerical and secular dress, all continuing to be based on Ancient Roman principles of draped rectangles. Southern areas around modern Spain and Italy particularly wanted to show links with the former empire in Romanesque style. Women covered their heads with veils according to Christian ideas of pious modesty. As textile technology improved, people used more fabric in their clothing. Eastern silk from as far as China outstripped local products in complexity and beauty, making it highly prized.

Body completely covered

Mantel is a huge rectangle covering her top half

Cyrtel reaches the ankles

Vamp stripe on leather ankle shoes

Beards in style

Large gold shoulder brooch

Anglo-Saxon *cyrtel, mantel*, and veil In the 1060s Judith, Countess of Flanders, is shown draped with cloth. Her long, semicircular linen veil wraps over her head and shoulders. The *mantel* is draped sideways.

Fit for a king Biblical King David, in a manuscript of 1050, wears a long, dignified gown in quality fabric—the signs of a ruler—with a woven pattern and frilled hem. The gartering holding his *braccas* (pants) is carefully interlaced.

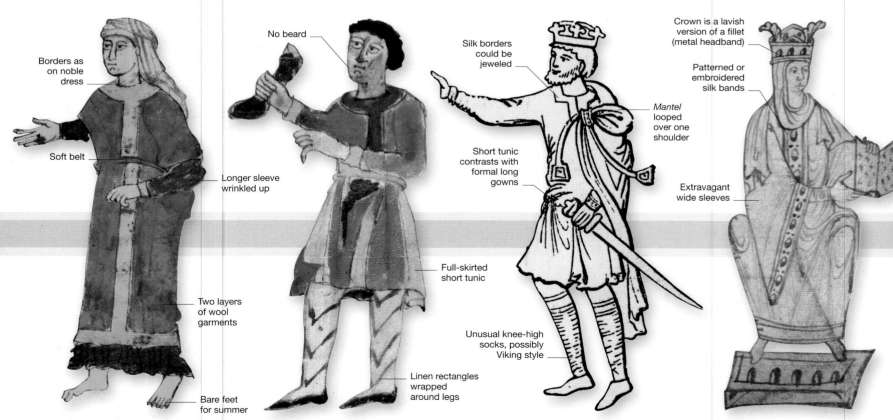

Borders as on noble dress

Soft belt

Two layers of wool garments

Bare feet for summer

No beard

Longer sleeve wrinkled up

Full-skirted short tunic

Linen rectangles wrapped around legs

Silk borders could be jeweled

Mantel looped over one shoulder

Short tunic contrasts with formal long gowns

Unusual knee-high socks, possibly Viking style

Crown is a lavish version of a fillet (metal headband)

Patterned or embroidered silk bands

Extravagant wide sleeves

Everyday wear A linen veil is wrapped around this 11th-century woman's head. Her outer gown has short sleeves, and it covers a much fuller, longer tunic.

Simple dress In the 1020s this man has the keyhole neckline seen in noble dress, but in a plain fabric. His tunic is short and easy to move in, with tight cuffs.

Anglo-Saxon king More modest than continental rulers, Cnut of Wessex wears a silk-bordered tunic. A later Anglo-Saxon king's clothing was "interwoven with gold and sumptuously embellished."

Anglo-Saxon queen Noblewomen like Aelfgyfu-Emma, King Cnut's wife, enjoyed wearing sumptuous dress. Her clothing, c. 1040, was probably dyed with costly colors.

Pinned veil

Long, straight sleeves

Fillet (metal headband) holds second veil

Circular mantle

Borders embroidered with gold

Slim fit reflects frugal fabric use

Blue silk tunic in fine folds

Feet could be bare

Longer white linen tunic under top tunic

French dancer This dancer's lively movement contrasts with formal poses. Her pinned, extremely long veil is coming loose and the tunic is cut with a minimum of material. The 11th-century painted colors are inaccurate but show people's love of bright dyes.

Luxury dress An 11th-century French manuscript honors St. Radegund by clothing her in an imported Byzantine mantle of the most expensive purple silk. Her two tunics are clearly defined.

Mustache with no beard, a Norman fashion

Classically inspired clothing

Tight sleeves

Leather sword belt

Tunic with divided skirt, like culottes

Braccas (pants) or *hosa* (hose) on legs

Norman warrior The embroidered wool stitches of the Bayeux Tapestry, made in the 1070s, show the natural vegetable dyes used to color textiles. Cropped hair was a practical choice beneath helmets.

MARKERS OF LUXURY

Jewelry shows the distinct medieval styles. Gold and enamel jewelry had symmetrical Celtic patterns or the stylized animals favored by Anglo-Saxons. Other markers of a settled, richer society were women's fine embroidery, applied to hangings, copes (capes), and clothing, imports such as silk, as well as furs, kermes (red dye), and fine wools.

TRENDS IN TUNICS

The Bayeux Tapestry (actually an embroidery) documenting the Norman invasion of England in 1066 illustrates the fashion of the time: the tunic, shaped like a "T" with insertions for fullness. It was the basic clothing for Saxons and Normans, but the trend for wearing short tunics was relatively new—one of many continental fashions that King Edward the Confessor introduced when he came to the English throne in 1042 after exile at the Court of Normandy.

Most men wore two tunics: a linen undergarment covered by an overtunic. The undertunic was sometimes longer, so that the bottom of it peeped out below the hem of the overtunic. Pulled on over the head, tunics had a slit at the front of the neck, bordered by a band or collar, often in a contrasting color. A belt was worn, sitting at the waist or low on the hips, and could be used to tuck up extra length.

Although tunics were ubiquitous, the quality of the cloth reflected the wealth of the wearer. The aristocracy, often shown in the tapestry as pointing and giving orders, wore sumptuous silk tunics with gold embroidery imported from the East. The bright colors showed off expensive dyes. Much simpler, coarse-cloth tunics with close-fitting leggings were worn by laborers. The colors available to the ordinary people were shades of natural gray and brown, and greens and blues from plants.

> 66
>
> The English did Frenchify themselves … and make themselves ridiculous by their fantastic fashions …
>
> **WILLIAM OF MALMESBURY,** 1095–1143
>
> 99

◁ **HISTORIC TUNICS**
The Bayeux Tapestry, probably embroidered during the 1070s, provides a picture of the clothes worn by both nobles and serfs in the 11th century. Here, tunic-clad laborers build a fortified Norman base.

1100–1200
COURTLY LOVE AND CRUSADES

Fashion became increasingly flamboyant in the 12th century—a time of Crusaders, romances, and chivalry. Vivacious, sophisticated fashions cultivated in the south spread north from Mediterranean shores. Clothing became more seductively fitted, showing the body's shape for the first time. Tales of courtly love celebrated this effect, conjuring visions of figure-hugging silk gowns revealing embroidered chemises beneath laced sides. Garments were still based mainly on rectangular and triangular fabric cuts, but with lacing to crush straight shapes against the curved figure. Even ordinary women wore their tunics more closely over waist, arms, and hips. Men's clothing also lengthened and tightened. Noble people of both sexes wore the bliaut or brial, a tunic made of fine, expensive silk with trailing hems and long sleeves. Accessories were long, pointed shoes, long hair, and elaborate cloaks and mantles. Religious and secular clothing styles began to differ.

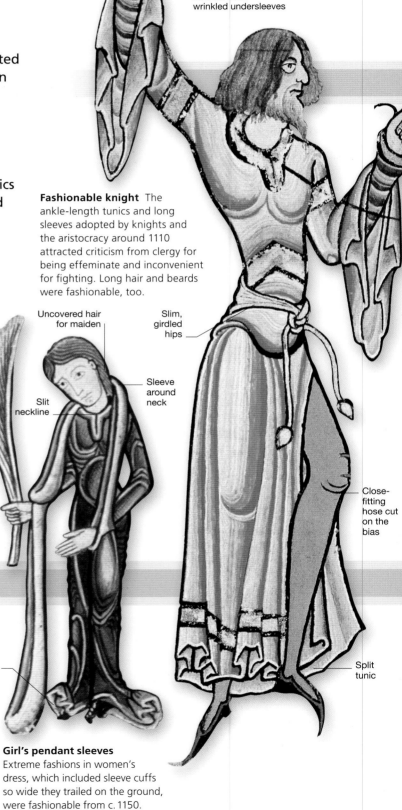

Fashionable knight The ankle-length tunics and long sleeves adopted by knights and the aristocracy around 1110 attracted criticism from clergy for being effeminate and inconvenient for fighting. Long hair and beards were fashionable, too.

Loose hanging sleeves show wrinkled undersleeves

Uncovered hair for maiden

Slim, girdled hips

Sleeve around neck

Slit neckline

Close-fitting hose cut on the bias

Split tunic

SILK

Silk lampas

This fragment of silk lampas with a pattern of lions and harpies shows the extraordinary skill of 12th-century weavers. Luxury silk textiles were highly prized and expensive, with alluring names like samite, Alexandria, ciclaton, taffeta, and lampas recorded in romance tales of the times.

Silks were either rich and stiff or valued for their delicacy, transparency, and light draping. Silks made ideal high-status gifts, since they were light and unbreakable during long-distance travel.

Round fillet holding fine veil

V-neckline

Wide, hanging sleeves

Pleated or finely gathered long skirt of bliaut

Long lines When women finally revealed their hair, they added false hair into their braids for dramatic length. French noblewomen wore bliauts of the finest Asian silks; fine pleating contributed to the vertical illusion.

Contrasting lining

Girl's pendant sleeves Extreme fashions in women's dress, which included sleeve cuffs so wide they trailed on the ground, were fashionable from c. 1150. Thinner fabrics clung to the body, outlining the shape.

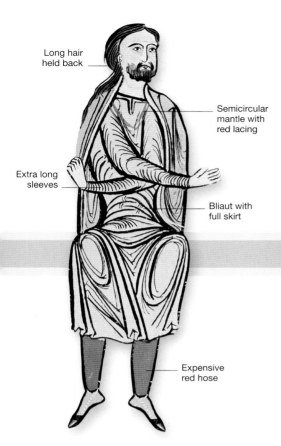

Long hair held back

Semicircular mantle with red lacing

Extra long sleeves

Bliaut with full skirt

Expensive red hose

Southern dress This Provençal viscount's tunic, c. 1110, follows the body, but is not fashionably skintight, though its tight sleeves had to be sewn shut at each wearing. Aquitanian fashion was more sensuous than that of northern France.

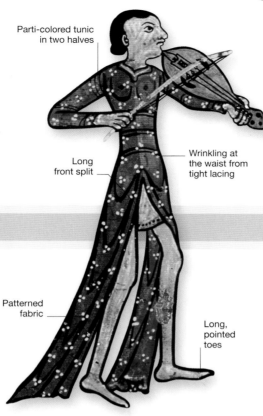

Parti-colored tunic in two halves

Long front split

Wrinkling at the waist from tight lacing

Patterned fabric

Long, pointed toes

Split tunic This is what French Abbot Bernard of Clairvaux meant when he complained that split clothing "revealed intimate parts." A young 12th-century Frenchman's shirt hangs over tight hose that look like naked legs.

Short, curled hair

Round neckline

Slim waist widening from hips

Ankle shoes with vamp stripe

Colored hose

Elegant draping This musician has used his hip belt to hitch up his tunic and create flowing lines. Sideways wrinkles show the closeness over the ribs. The wider sleeves of the outer tunic do not interfere with his playing.

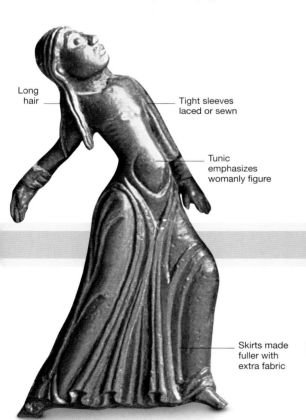

Long hair

Tight sleeves laced or sewn

Tunic emphasizes womanly figure

Skirts made fuller with extra fabric

Body-revealing dress This young Veronan girl's tunic is skintight—probably through lacing—and reveals all her feminine curves. The contrast with the full flaring skirt shows the new seductive fit appearing in clothing.

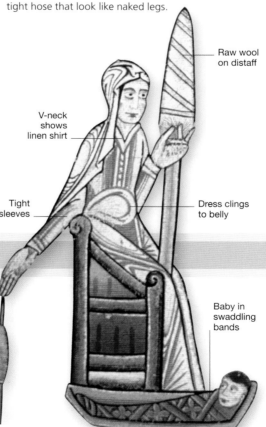

Raw wool on distaff

V-neck shows linen shirt

Tight sleeves

Dress clings to belly

Baby in swaddling bands

Noble Englishwoman This image from around 1170 shows a woman in the modest dress of married women, spinning yarn with a distaff and spindle. The veil is still long and covers all her hair. The tunic may have buttons at the front, and fits closely.

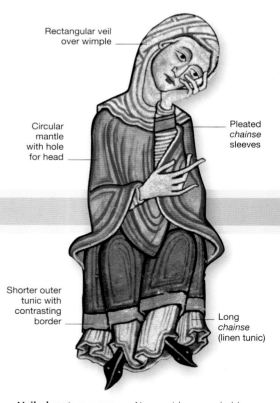

Rectangular veil over wimple

Circular mantle with hole for head

Pleated *chainse* sleeves

Shorter outer tunic with contrasting border

Long *chainse* (linen tunic)

Veiled mature woman Nuns, widows, and older women left fashion behind and veiled their heads throughout the Middle Ages and Renaissance period. Wimples, which concealed the neck and chin, were pinned at the top of the head and covered with a veil.

FASHION ICON

ELEANOR OF AQUITAINE

Eleanor of Aquitaine (c. 1124–1204) is one of the most important and well-known figures of the Middle Ages, due to her huge influence on the cultural life of the time. Born into the ruling family of the Duchy of Aquitaine, a large province that covered most of southwest France, this cultured, sophisticated, and most eligible heiress in Europe had an extraordinary zest for life. At 15 she married the future King Louis VII of France and moved to Paris. Used to luxury and splendor, Eleanor found the city bleak and gray. She immediately set about transforming Paris into a center of art and beauty. With her strong sense of style, she introduced new fashions, fabrics, and etiquette from the more sophisticated south. Nobles from Aquitaine had a reputation for being fashion conscious, and the new queen shocked Louis' courtiers with her jewels, kohl, and rouge. Chronicler Bernard of Clairvaux remarked that her gowns were "not so much adorned as loaded down with gold, silver, and precious stones." She was said to be tall and extremely beautiful and continued to enchant men across the known world into her old age.

Setting the trend

Under her influence, women's clothing became increasingly elaborate. The bliaut, a long overgown, was a new trend. In Eleanor's reign it grew tighter around the bodice, fitting snugly down to the hips, and was worn with a decorative belt or girdle. The bodice was split down either side from underarm to hip and attached with ribbons, which could be tied to tighten the fabric across the body.

The skirt was cut wide, falling in light folds and pleats down to the feet. This emphasized the conspicuous use of rich fabrics. Silk from the Middle East was readily available throughout Europe and used extensively by the royal court.

In a palette of blues, grays, burgundies, and earth tones, the silk was highly embellished and heavily embroidered in costly metallic threads. The garments' sumptuous flow outraged church fathers: Bernard of Clairvaux complained about the ladies at court who "drag after them trains of precious material that makes a cloud of dust."

Bliaut sleeves also drew attention; they were tight from shoulder to elbow, then flared out into enormous cuffs long enough to drag on the ground. Sleeves were knotted to shorten them and to make them more manageable.

Impact abroad

A formidable woman, Eleanor accompanied her husband in 1147 on the Second Crusade (1145–1149), traveling to Constantinople (modern Istanbul) and Jerusalem. She took chests of the finest clothing with her so she might appear as a sophisticated Provençal queen instead of a Frankish rustic. She cut a dashing figure. The Greek chronicler Niketas Choniates noted Eleanor's ride into Byzantium: "... even women traveled in the ranks of the crusaders, boldly sitting astride in their saddles as men do … At the head of these was one in particular, richly dressed, who because of the gold embroidery on the hem of her dress, was nicknamed *Chrysopous* [Golden Foot]."

Eleanor was granted an annulment of her marriage to Louis in 1152 and went on to marry Henry of Anjou as a love match. In 1154 he became King of England. As in Paris, Eleanor began to turn primitive England into an illustrious court, introducing art, makeup, romance, and poetry under the influence of her glamorous personality. Wherever she went, Eleanor challenged tradition, developing the style and sophistication, romance, and chivalry for which the medieval period became famous.

△ **INTERNATIONAL INFLUENCES**
In this effigy from Fontevraud Abbey, the queen's dress was originally covered with diagonal bars of gold, representing an expensive Eastern silk. She wears the barbette and is reading a book—a literate woman in illiterate times.

◁ **NOBLE COLORS**
Wealthy noblewomen wear the bliaut with extravagant sleeves in this 12th-century stained-glass window in the Abbey of Saint-Denis, France. Courtly romances describe how the gowns could be open at the side to reveal delicate underwear.

TIMELINE

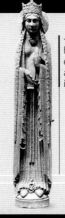

1137 Marries Louis and becomes Queen of France, bringing sophistication to the Paris court

1140s ▷ Popularizes the bliaut and other long overgowns with trailing sleeves and hems

1140s Patronizes the troubadour poets of her native court. In turn, they praise her "lovely eyes and noble countenance"

1147 Takes part in the Second Crusade. Her cloaks are sumptuous and heavily embroidered

1154 Becomes Queen of England, and introduces new style and standards of living to the English court—drinking wine instead of beer, and bringing in costly silks and love poets

◁ **1167** Popularizes long braided hair. Returns to France, after being estranged from Henry II, and cultivates a court in Poitiers unmatched by any in Europe for its cultural influence

1173 Is imprisoned for 16 years after taking part in a revolt against Henry II

O 1130   O 1140   O 1150   O 1160   O 1170   O 1180

◁ **ELEANOR RIDES INTO CAPTIVITY** A 12th–13th-century fresco shows Eleanor, cloaked upon a horse, bidding farewell to her sons as she is imprisoned by Henry II, after taking part in a revolt against him

1000–1450
PRIESTS AND THE PEOPLE

In the Middle Ages fashionable, luxurious dress was only possible for the wealthy minority, including nobility, merchants, and clergy. Ordinary people—peasants and freeholders, artisans and trade workers, or professionals—wore simpler versions that allowed them to do their work. Their clothes were shorter or plainer, in coarser, often home-produced, fabrics. Garments such as aprons could double as tools, to carry items or as protection. Laborers stripped to cool linen underclothes for heavy field work. Learned and professional men wore long robes that marked their education. Although religious clothing kept to older tunic styles, the Church used the best-quality fabrics with the finest embroidery and weaving to dress cardinals and bishops, as well as to adorn altars.

Milk jar

Rectangular linen veil covering head

Long hair and linen veil

Large decorative brooch

Belt from which items can be attached

Pleated leather purse

Close-fitting but not tight tunic

Red undertunic

Leather shoes fit foot's shape

Imitating fashion This 12th-century Italian working woman sowing grain uses her wide sleeves like a bag. Though simple and ankle length, her tunic has the large, pointed sleeves of noblewomen, with a brooch at the neck.

English dairywoman The Luttrell Psalter manuscript of the 1330s shows peasants going about their everyday tasks. This older woman wears a long wool tunic with close-fitting sleeves.

DYEING CLOTH

Ordinary people did wear colored clothes in the Middle Ages, but linen was hard to dye and was used in its natural pale gray or bleached white. Dark sheep gave dark wool, while paler fleeces could be dyed. Common plant dyes made browns, yellows (weld, goldenrod), and blues (woad, indigo). Dyestuffs were fixed with mordants, minerals that "bit" color into cloth. Reds and purples were difficult and costly to produce, left to professionals like the 15th-century dyers above.

Tippet (long sleeve end) reveals fur lining

Linen coif under skullcap

Liripipe (tail) on youth's hood

Doublet with open seams underneath

Tight hose covering the legs

Pointed shoes with ankle strap

Italian doctor A professional man such as this doctor from c. 1345 wore long garments, and a skullcap and coif to mark his position. This contrasts with his patient's shorter tunic. Both wear fashionable hoods and tippet sleeves.

Scholarly attire Roman author Pliny the Elder is imagined in the 1480s in the Italian clothing worn by medieval scholars. Academic dress today still derives from 15th-century robes, with open sleeves, pleated backs, and soft caps.

Hood with tail

Beard of older man

Long hanging split sleeves

Ankle-length robe

Hood with shoulder cape and short liripipe (tail)

Hat hanging down back

Sienese country man An Italian 1380s fresco shows warm-weather country clothing—cool, loose linen *braies* (trousers) over bare legs, a wool tunic open at the neck and tucked back to reveal a long linen shirt, and a wide-brimmed straw hat.

Braided straw hat keeps off sun

CHURCH TEXTILES

Syon Cope

Few pieces of medieval clothing are still in existence. Of those that survive, most are exceptionally high-quality miters (bishop's hats), chasubles (vestments), and copes (semicircular capes) made for the Church.

English church embroidery became famous as *opus anglicanum* (English work). It was the finest of its day and exported all over Europe. An exquisite example of this is the Syon Cope, made between 1300 and 1320. Precious metal threads mix with silk stitches to illustrate biblical stories, like a wearable illumination.

Large wool coat

Buttoned up the front

French woodcutter This 13th-century peasant is wrapped up against the cold in a large wool coat over a red tunic. Leather shoes help keep his feet warm and dry. The painted colors are not true to life.

Shaved tonsure

Expensive textiles—silk and gold

Bishop's crosier

Plain, humble dress

Chasuble

Pilgrim's *sclavein* (coarse tunic)

Sturdy leather boots

Frayed hem on edge of tunic

Robes from classical tradition

Cassock

Alb

Leather ankle shoes

Pallium reaches to hem

Pilgrim's clothing Pilgrims who set off to visit religious sites wore practical dress, including a hat to keep off the sun, robust wool clothes to keep out wind and rain, a staff, and a leather satchel.

Bishop's robes Many of these 12th-century liturgical vestments are still worn today. A patterned red chasuble is worn over a blue cassock and white linen alb. A pallium (stole) drapes around his shoulders to the hem.

800–1453

THE EAST
IN THE WEST

In medieval times, the Mediterranean basin was the most advanced center in the world for learning, technology, and trade. The importing of luxury goods into the Mediterranean regions and Northern Europe had a long history, both before and after the age of the Crusades (1095–1291). Expensive textiles came from China along the ancient Silk Road, the great trade route running through Central Asia. Eastern weaving techniques made their way to Byzantium and Persia, to Islamic areas in North Africa, and to Al-Andalus, the Moorish kingdom in southern Spain. Venice made its fortune through controlling the trade in luxuries with the Middle East. Throughout the Middle Ages, the cultures of East and West constantly exchanged and merged styles.

Pillbox cap, possibly beaded

Tight *aljuba* (tunic) with red side lacing

Low-slung belt or girdle

Decorated shoes

Assyrian-style hat

Gold buttons down front

Outer robe known as *kabbadion*

Woven gold borders

Turban of striped fabric

Extremely wide sleeves with *tiraz* (inscribed) bands

Tunic known as *aljuba*

Greek doctor This doctor wears the long robe popular in Orthodox countries, with the fashionable 14th-century fitted torso. The material's pattern of roundels containing animals is typical of high-quality Byzantine silk weaving.

Moorish musician A detail from a mid-13th-century illumination, this lutenist combines the Moorish tunic, turban, and beard of Islamic southern Spain with the *pellote* (sleeveless surcoat) then fashionable in northern Europe.

Crossover style In 13th-century Spain Christians, Muslims, and Jews lived together and influenced each other's clothing. Details, such as the side lacing on this musician's tunic, show how they blended into an "Iberian" style.

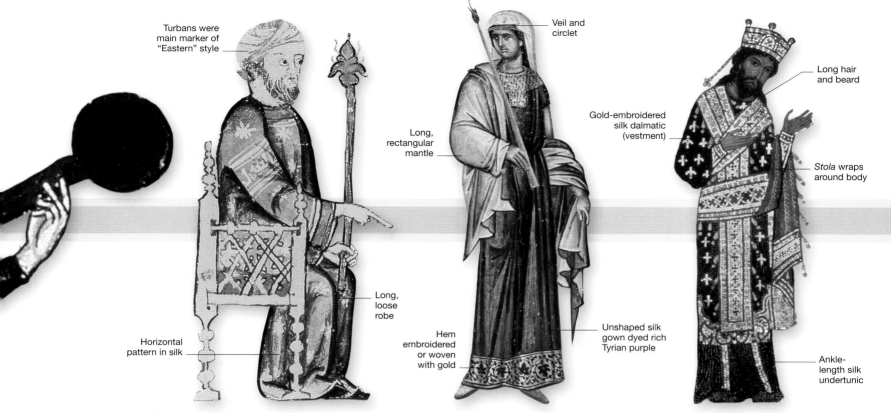

Turbans were main marker of "Eastern" style

Long, loose robe

Horizontal pattern in silk

Veil and circlet

Long, rectangular mantle

Hem embroidered or woven with gold

Unshaped silk gown dyed rich Tyrian purple

Long hair and beard

Gold-embroidered silk dalmatic (vestment)

Stola wraps around body

Ankle-length silk undertunic

Turbaned king Alfonso X, king of Castile and León 1252–1284, sits in a Moorish turban and robe to rule his northern Spanish Christian kingdoms. At that time, half of the Iberian peninsula was a Muslim kingdom.

Serbian matron The Eastern Orthodox women's dress of the 14th century shows a continuation of classical styles, not the fitted clothing of Western Europe. This reflects the kingdom's link with Byzantine traditions.

Byzantine splendor Norman King Roger II of Sicily wears Byzantine imperial clothing for his 1133 coronation. The magnificent wide gold band encrusted with pearls and precious stones is a long *stola* (scarf) wrapped around his body.

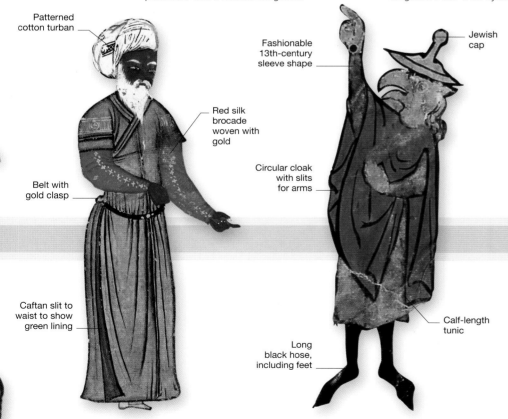

Patterned cotton turban

Red silk brocade woven with gold

Belt with gold clasp

Caftan slit to waist to show green lining

Fashionable 13th-century sleeve shape

Jewish cap

Circular cloak with slits for arms

Calf-length tunic

Long black hose, including feet

Persian caftan An older African man wears a caftan with a diagonal wrap front, a style never seen in European dress. This was worn all across Asia as far as China. Islamic men and women's clothing often had the same feature.

Jewish dress This figure from a Jewish text known as the *Bird's Head Haggadah* (c. 1300) shows the cap sometimes worn by Jewish men. Christian countries often made people of other faiths identify themselves with specific clothing.

SICILIAN SILK

Crusading travelers who visited the Middle Eastern Latin kingdoms were astonished at the quantities of silk worn there. One renowned center for silk weaving was Sicily. When King Roger II of Sicily was crowned, his clothing included a semicircular silk coronation mantle made in Palermo's royal workshops. This valuable treasure is embroidered in gold with symmetrical patterns of lions attacking camels—symbolizing Normans versus Saracens. Each animal is outlined with hundreds of seed pearls. The inscription around the edge is in Arabic calligraphy.

1200–1300
SOCIAL STATEMENTS

Clothing became more voluminous in the 13th century, and men's and women's garments followed the same changes in shape. Tunic sleeves had tight lower arms, but more fabric around the armhole, and the surcoat (sleeveless overtunic) became a wardrobe staple. Though cuts were still simple and elegantly draped, head wear became more complex. Women wore hairnets, or wimples (chin bands) and circlets around the head, and men wore small, round caps. Beards went out; curled hair came in. Romance poetry with its glamorous ideals of dress and behavior inspired women to walk gracefully with swaying hips or to hold a mantle so as to display a slim waist. Fabrics were more widely available so the leisured and merchant classes could imitate noble fashions. Such mimicry of their betters prompted litigation: laws were introduced to control what people at different social levels could wear. Called sumptuary laws, these regulations were rarely effective.

Wedding clothes A wedding scene from around 1300 shows the main trends for women's fashion. The bride's mother wears a dress with tight cuffs but loose upper sleeves. Holding laces keep her mantle forward.

Barbette fillet with wimple under chin

Holding laces

Mantle

Dress trails on ground

Hair getting longer and curled

Buttons still unusual, featured like jewelry

Leather belt

Hunting outfit This horseman, from around 1260, wears a linen coif (close-fitting cap) under another narrow, round cap, and his tunic closes with buttons. The heavy leather gauntlet, needed for protection from the falcon's sharp talons, is decorated on the cuff.

Elegant folds in skirt indicate fine-quality wool

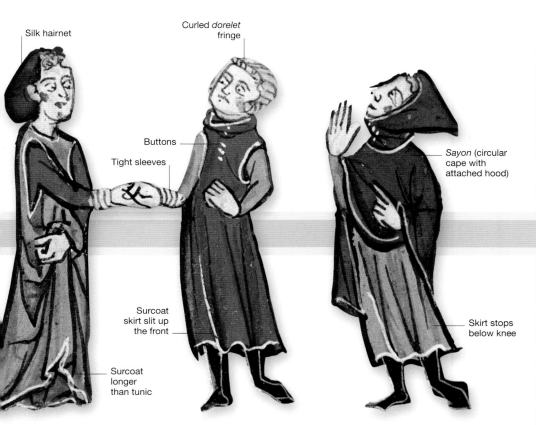

Silk hairnet

Curled *dorelet* fringe

Buttons

Tight sleeves

Sayon (circular cape with attached hood)

Surcoat skirt slit up the front

Surcoat longer than tunic

Skirt stops below knee

Bride and groom The bride's hair is gathered into a net, and she wears a sleeveless surcoat over her long dress. The groom's red wool surcoat has a hood and a fur lining.

Groom's friend The groom's companion has a larger cape, also lined with fur. Both men achieve a closer fit with buttons, which were beginning to emerge as popular closures.

SURVIVING MEDIEVAL CLOTHING

Very little complete medieval clothing has survived. Some of the best examples date from the 13th century; one such find was of members of the Castilian royal family buried in tombs in the Monasterio de las Huelgas in Burgos, Spain, dressed in royal garb. One young prince's grave from 1275 revealed a laced *aljuba* (tunic), sideless surcoat (right), and a mantle. The set of matching clothes, called a "robe," is of the finest Moorish silk and gold samite woven with the royal coats of arms of the kingdoms of Castile and León. The finds confirm the accuracy of contemporary illuminations and their usefulness as historical records. The images also bring written descriptions of noble finery to life.

Slit at the neck

Pellote (surcoat) belonging to Don Fernando de la Cerda

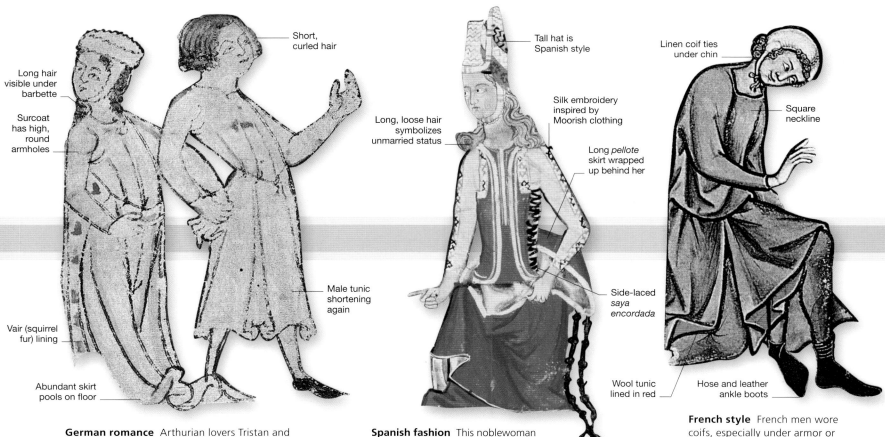

Short, curled hair

Long hair visible under barbette

Surcoat has high, round armholes

Vair (squirrel fur) lining

Abundant skirt pools on floor

Male tunic shortening again

German romance Arthurian lovers Tristan and Isolde sport the latest youthful fashions: shorter tunic for him; surcoat, fillet (headband), and an elegant hips-forward posture for her. Isolde's mantle is lined with vair (fur from a squirrel's winter coat).

Tall hat is Spanish style

Silk embroidery inspired by Moorish clothing

Long, loose hair symbolizes unmarried status

Long *pellote* skirt wrapped up behind her

Side-laced *saya encordada*

Wool tunic lined in red

Spanish fashion This noblewoman wears a red *saya encordada* (side-laced gown) under a *pellote* (surcoat). Since both are sleeveless, the embroidered sleeves of her *camisa* (linen undergarment) show. Spanish-style clothes were especially formfitting.

Linen coif ties under chin

Square neckline

Hose and leather ankle boots

French style French men wore coifs, especially under armor or mail. The split tunic made riding easier. It reveals the long hose, which could be footless or include feet with leather soles.

RECONSTRUCTION
COTE-HARDIE

This carefully constructed replica of a parti-colored medieval *cote-hardie* (outer dress), with its undergarments, is in blue and murrey (mulberry-red). It follows the styles found on memorial brasses from around 1375–1385, which show the wives of knights and barons in formal or courtly dress. The cut and construction—four A-line, floor-length panels of fulled (thickened) wool twill with short inset sleeves—have been conjectured by dressmaker Sarah Thursfield. Although the shape looks simple to modern eyes, the figure-hugging cut and low neck were considered shocking at the time, and the bright dyes and rows of tiny buttons were condemned as extravagant. Under the dress is a gray wool kirtle, lined with blue linen and laced at the center front.

Neckline is cut straight across the back

Shaped sleeve head set into a close-fitting armhole is a 14th-century innovation

Sleeves of the gray kirtle (undergarment) visible beneath the shorter sleeves of the *cote-hardie*, but the linen shift is entirely concealed

Narrow cut at the waist gives a smooth, flat outline

Simple A-line shape is created from four panels

Dress widens and becomes fuller toward the hem

SIDE VIEW

TWO FOR ONE △ ▷
The mi-parti (part-colored) effect of this dress was very fashionable. The dress is constructed in identical halves so it appears entirely red from one side and entirely blue from the other.

SIDE VIEW

BACK VIEW

INNOVATIONS ▷

Earlier dresses had long tippets cut as part of the sleeve and faced with fur. The white cloth streamers on this *cote-hardie* could be a successor to these. Buttons were fashionable for both men and women: the most expensive, with precious stones, were made by goldsmiths; cheaper ones were cast in pewter.

The curved neckline is cut to sit low on the shoulders

White streamers are made of worsted cloth

FRONT VIEW

IN DETAIL

◁ **BUTTONING TECHNIQUE**
The buttons shown here are those used in the 14th century. Rather than being sewn, they are secured onto the dress with a single length of cord, a technique that was employed on similar dresses at the time.

◁ **BUTTONHOLES**
Buttonholes are hand sewn using silk thread, and all unlined wool edgings of the dress are finished with silk facings. The dress buttons left-over-right, the same as men's clothes. The convention that women's clothing buttons right-over-left came much later.

◁ **SINGLE LACE**
The neckline is opened here to reveal the gray wool kirtle beneath, front-laced down the center to hip level with a single lace, as was the practice in medieval times.

◁ **EYELETS**
Hand-stitched eyelets are set close together and tight to the garment's edge so the lacing is discreet and functional.

◁ **SELF-COVERED BUTTONS**
The sleeves of the kirtle narrow to long cuffs fastened with up to 50 self-cloth buttons, each one made from a circle of fabric sewn tightly to form a firm ball. These long cuffs would have been impractical for anyone who had to do manual work.

◁ **OPENED CUFF**
An unbuttoned cuff reveals a simple linen shift worn next to the skin. Wealth was reflected in the quality and number of shifts the wearer owned and how frequently they were changed and laundered.

1300–1380
FITTING TO THE BODY

The biggest development of the 14th century was the move from flat, draped garments belted for shape to the cutting of curved pieces with more complex construction to fit the body—the beginning of tailoring. Closures, especially buttons, became more important, used on new front openings and along very tight long sleeves. Close fitting revealed men's and women's figures to great effect: sideless surcoats drew attention to slim waists and new waist seams, and low belts emphasized the hips. Chests looked larger—both sexes made use of padding. Colors began to contrast instead of match, and parti-coloring became popular. Many believe that changes in "fashion" began increasing in speed from this time. Clothing had tended to reflect one's place in society. However, a greater variety of fabrics and accessories, such as hoods, belts, veils, gloves, and shoes, made it possible to blur social distinctions.

Sheer silk or linen veil, shown lifted by the wind

Neckline becomes lower

Sleeves become tighter

Long, trailing hem

Higher hairstyle Women's braids were arranged over each ear in a variety of styles, pinned to metal circlets wrapped in colored silk threads. This sheer veil, fluttering in a breeze, barely covers the hair.

Long, loose hair for unmarried girls

Round neckline

Sleeves fit more tightly around the armhole

Fashionable swayback posture

Saya (gown) longer than feet

Side lacing Lacing was still a feature in Spain in 1320. In other areas, the laces that could help achieve the fashionable tightness are rarely seen in images. This red undertunic draws attention to a narrow waist and swelling hips.

Fillet (thin headband)

Silk veil

Crespinette (net) under veil confines hair

Central plastron section of *cote-hardie*

Fur trim on surcoat

Full skirt of surcoat hangs from narrow center

Youthful short hair

Outer robe with hood and loose, short sleeves

Stitching instead of buttons

Bone needle, linen thread

Horizontal decoration was fashionable, especially in Italian areas

Shoes with buttoned ankle strap

Short elbow sleeve with hanging tippet

Short, curled hair

Pourpoint (doublet) cut to fit body, not draped

Jeweled hip belt carries dagger

Hose and shoes

Shoulder hood with gold border

Wool coat with baggy upper sleeves

Gold sword belt

Tight red cloth hose have leather soles

Reproduction sideless surcoat The surcoat armholes are enlarged to display the sides of the body clad in a clinging *cote-hardie* beneath. The central plastron section could be richly jeweled or embroidered, or have elaborate buttons.

Sewing a sleeve For the fashionable man, getting dressed might involve sewing sleeve and other seams together for a smooth, perfect fit. This man's long robe prefigures the *houppelande*, a wide-sleeved, flared outer garment.

A southern French hunter A hunting companion in 1343 has slung his hood with a long *cornette* (tail) over one shoulder. Separate hoods ended in shoulder capes and offered another site for elegant arrangement.

French knight This 1378 image shows the classic 14th-century male shape: hair at ear-length; nipped-in waist; round chest; tight lower sleeves over the hand; slim, fitted hips with no fullness below, set off with a belt; and pointed toes.

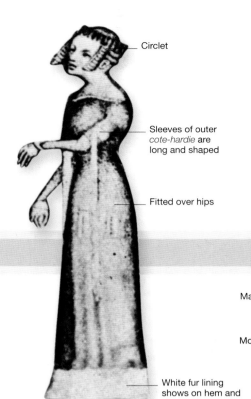

Circlet

Sleeves of outer *cote-hardie* are long and shaped

Fitted over hips

White fur lining shows on hem and sleeve streamers

Perfect fit This lady's 1370 *cote-hardie* (outer tunic) cleaves exactly to her upper body. The high, round chest was also favored in men's fashion. The wide, boat neckline shows off her shoulders, and her braided-back hair is brought forward in loops over her ears.

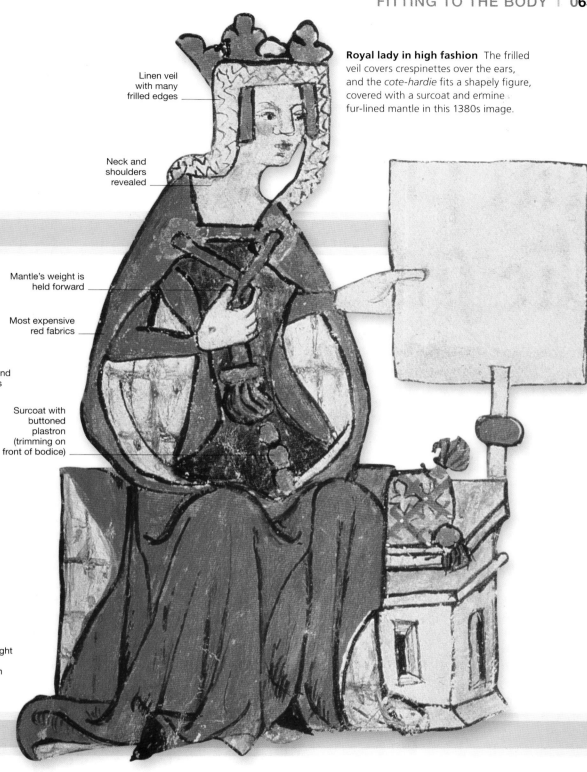

Linen veil with many frilled edges

Neck and shoulders revealed

Mantle's weight is held forward

Most expensive red fabrics

Surcoat with buttoned plastron (trimming on front of bodice)

Royal lady in high fashion The frilled veil covers crespinettes over the ears, and the *cote-hardie* fits a shapely figure, covered with a surcoat and ermine fur-lined mantle in this 1380s image.

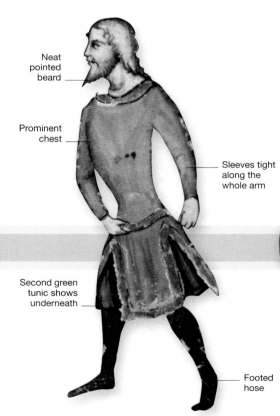

Neat pointed beard

Prominent chest

Sleeves tight along the whole arm

Second green tunic shows underneath

Footed hose

Getting slimmer A 1350s Neapolitan illumination shows how the amount of fabric used in tunics was reduced as fit improved. This man still has a fuller skirt, slit over each thigh. His hose are made of wool fabric cut on the bias (diagonally) to stretch around the leg.

LEATHER SHOES

Medieval leather shoes survive in much greater numbers than fragile textiles. These London examples show some of the styles. Piercing or incising with decorative patterns was popular and showed off colored hose underneath. The long "poulaine" toe was stuffed with whalebone, wool, or moss to keep the shape. Noblemen's shoes were embroidered with silks. It was hard to keep feet dry, so people wore pattens—overshoes with raised wooden soles that kept feet above the mud and filth as they walked.

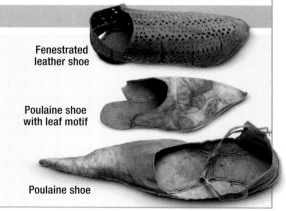

Fenestrated leather shoe

Poulaine shoe with leaf motif

Poulaine shoe

TRAILING ELEGANCE

At the turn of the 15th century, fashion for the nobility became more extravagant. Improved technology allowed weavers to run riot with patterns of twining symmetrical fruit and flowers, or geometric motifs. Italians invented velvet, with its sumptuous pile. Better looms meant the aristocracy could buy more of their favorite taffetas and damask, and indulge in more complex patterns. Long gowns trailed on the ground, implying that the wearer was rich enough to afford copious amounts of material. Both sexes wore a voluminous outer garment called a *houppelande*. It fit on the shoulders, was full and often belted, and draped in folds. The sleeves could be long and wide, sometimes adorned with tinkling bells.

For women, the silhouette was long, with a high waist and small bosom. It was the fashion to walk with the belly slightly protruding and the hips thrust forward. This helped to carry the weight of the fabric and balance the headgear, as well as to suggest fertility. In this painting, the young couple celebrate their betrothal. The red turban of the young man is decorated with dagged (snipped) material. His fur-lined *houppelande* trails on the ground. Fur and feathers decorate his fiancée's turban, and her dress, derived from the *houppelande*, has a bodice that fits tightly to the hips. The trailing finery and elaborate headgear of the nobility raised moral indignation among the clergy, who reminded the rich that such ostentation was not good for the soul.

> 66
>
> So much pouncing of chisel to make holes, so much dagging of shears, with the superfluity in length of the aforesaid gowns, trailing in the dung and mire, on horse and ... foot, as well of man as of woman ...
>
> GEOFFREY CHAUCER, *THE PARSON'S TALE*, 1386–1395
>
> 99

◁ **LES TRES RICHES HEURES DU DUC DE BERRY**
Known simply as *The Book of Hours*, this richly decorated prayer book was commissioned by John, Duke of Berry, between 1412 and 1416. The page here represents April, and shows a young couple exchanging engagement rings.

600–1449
KNIGHTS IN ARMOR

The arms and armor used by medieval warriors changed over time with new developments in weapons and improved technical skills in shaping metal. A knight needed to be proficient in handling many different kinds of weapon and had to be able to defend himself against similar weapons wielded by his opponents. In the early middle ages men fought with axes, spears, swords, and bows and arrows, either on foot or on horseback, and protected their bodies with short-sleeved shirts of chain mail made of interlocking metal rings. Plate armor began to be developed in the 13th century as a defense against more efficient crossbows, which fired bolts that could pierce soft mail. Armor was also sometimes made from leather hardened by boiling. By the mid-15th century, knights were completely encased in suits of shining armor, draped with their heraldic coats of arms.

Norman archer This 11th-century longbowman depicted on the Bayeux Tapestry wears mail: circular links of steel riveted together to form a flexible, armored mesh tunic.

Pointed helmet with nose piece

Mail tunic

Quiver to hold arrows

Leg bindings

Bascinet helmet with symbolic crown

Mail "aventail" protects neck

Rerebrace: protection for upper arms

Vambrace: protection for lower arms

Cylindrical great helm with decorations

Padded jupon underneath surcoat

Sabautons (articulated foot plates)

Heraldic trappings

METALWORKING

10th-century helmet

Single sheet of metal forged into a cone

Nose piece is sole face protection

Advances in the technology of metalworking played a large part in determining what knights wore. In the 10th and 11th centuries soldiers carried a shield as a first line of defense. They wore a coat of chain mail with a hood covered by a helmet that protected the head. Only a nasal guard covered the face. Sections of plate supplemented the chain mail over the centuries. By the 15th century, soldiers and horsemen wore full plate armor, made from multiple sheets of metal, and no longer needed a shield.

While armor provided practical protection, chivalrous and romantic ideals inspired the knight in battle. His lady would give him a piece of her clothing—a sleeve, veil, or belt—to tie to his armor as a token of her favor.

German knight In the 14th-century jousting field, a knight's appearance was as much a part of his display as the fighting. This nobleman bears his heraldic coat of arms. The "wings" on his helm were a Teutonic knightly fashion.

Edward III of England The 14th-century king wears a surcoat with the royal coat of arms over a padded gold jupon (seen at his elbows and knees). His low gold belt follows civilian style.

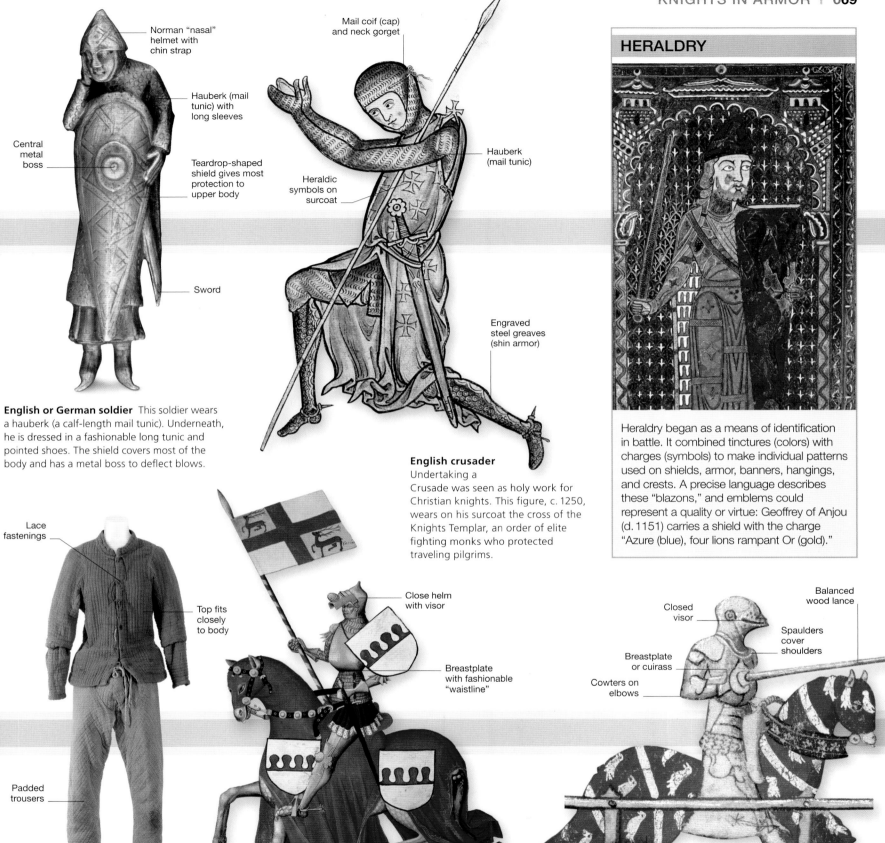

Norman "nasal" helmet with chin strap

Hauberk (mail tunic) with long sleeves

Central metal boss

Teardrop-shaped shield gives most protection to upper body

Sword

Mail coif (cap) and neck gorget

Hauberk (mail tunic)

Heraldic symbols on surcoat

Engraved steel greaves (shin armor)

English or German soldier This soldier wears a hauberk (a calf-length mail tunic). Underneath, he is dressed in a fashionable long tunic and pointed shoes. The shield covers most of the body and has a metal boss to deflect blows.

English crusader Undertaking a Crusade was seen as holy work for Christian knights. This figure, c. 1250, wears on his surcoat the cross of the Knights Templar, an order of elite fighting monks who protected traveling pilgrims.

HERALDRY

Heraldry began as a means of identification in battle. It combined tinctures (colors) with charges (symbols) to make individual patterns used on shields, armor, banners, hangings, and crests. A precise language describes these "blazons," and emblems could represent a quality or virtue: Geoffrey of Anjou (d. 1151) carries a shield with the charge "Azure (blue), four lions rampant Or (gold)."

Lace fastenings

Top fits closely to body

Padded trousers

Close helm with visor

Breastplate with fashionable "waistline"

Closed visor

Breastplate or cuirass

Cowters on elbows

Balanced wood lance

Spaulders cover shoulders

Horse trappings in gules (red) and argent (white or silver)

Quilted clothing In the 14th century thick, quilted or stuffed clothing, as in this reconstruction, was worn under chain mail and plate armor to buffer the body against the metal, distribute weight, and cushion blows.

Medieval tournament A man fighting on horseback needed different armor than a foot soldier. Full plate armor had to protect the whole body but be light and flexible enough to allow the rider to mount his horse unaided.

French chain mail and plate armor All the individual pieces of armor making up a suit of mid-15th-century plate were tied to a fitted and padded arming doublet, using laces attached to the doublet. Knights dressed from the legs upward.

RECONSTRUCTION
DOUBLET
AND HOSE

Closely based on the pourpoint (quilted doublet) of Charles de Blois, dated to 1364 and housed in the Musée des Tissus in Lyon, this sumptuous blue silk paltock (doublet) with brocaded gilt leaves is the work of reconstruction dressmaker Sarah Thursfield. A feature of the garment is the deep armhole shape evolved to allow a skintight but nonrestrictive fit on heavily muscled fighting men. Although both this version and the original are covered in expensive silk, plain linen doublets were usually made for the battlefield. The long hose are suspended from points laced inside the doublet, and the feet are soled with leather to create the shape of fashionable shoes. They would be worn with wood pattens if needed.

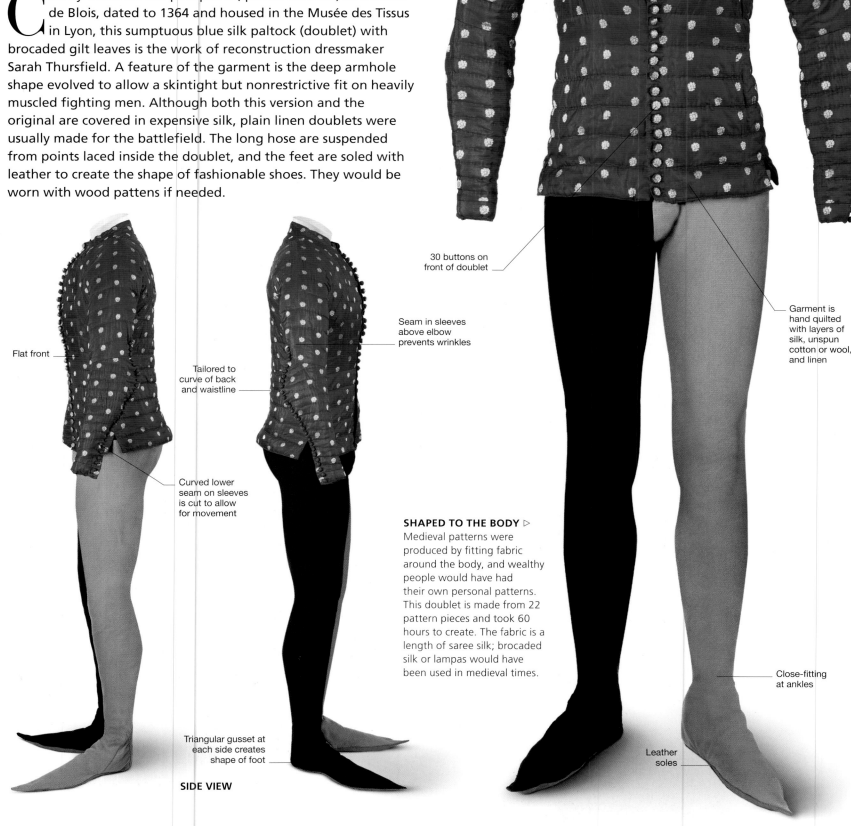

Close-fitting collar

30 buttons on front of doublet

Garment is hand quilted with layers of silk, unspun cotton or wool, and linen

Flat front

Seam in sleeves above elbow prevents wrinkles

Tailored to curve of back and waistline

Curved lower seam on sleeves is cut to allow for movement

SHAPED TO THE BODY ▷
Medieval patterns were produced by fitting fabric around the body, and wealthy people would have had their own personal patterns. This doublet is made from 22 pattern pieces and took 60 hours to create. The fabric is a length of saree silk; brocaded silk or lampas would have been used in medieval times.

Close-fitting at ankles

Triangular gusset at each side creates shape of foot

SIDE VIEW

Leather soles

Seam curves
around over the
shoulder blades

Additional layers of
padding protect the
back, shoulders, chest,
and upper arms

IN DETAIL

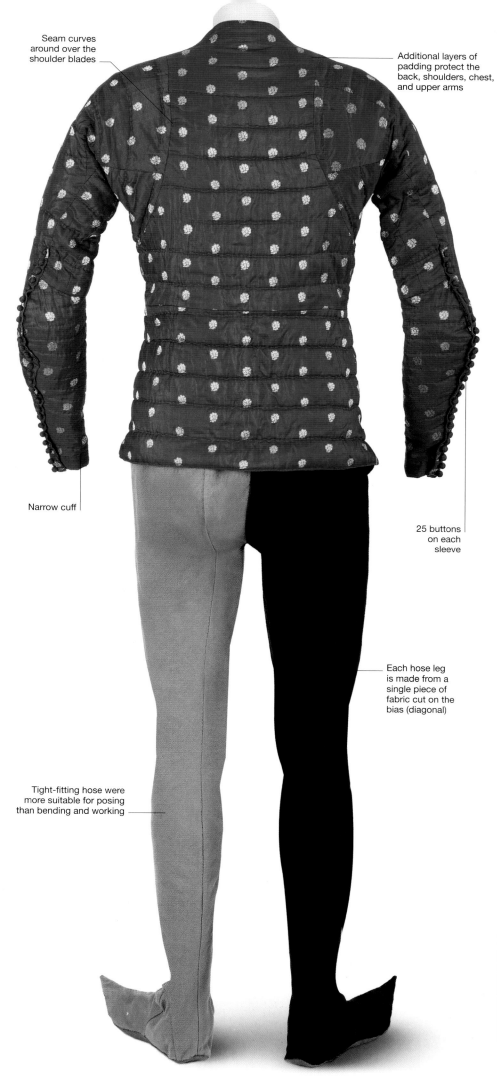

Narrow cuff

25 buttons
on each
sleeve

Each hose leg
is made from a
single piece of
fabric cut on the
bias (diagonal)

Tight-fitting hose were
more suitable for posing
than bending and working

◁ TAILORING

A close view of the back curve of
the armhole shows the gussets
that create the *grande assiette*—
the large plate shape that defines
the armhole. Each sleeve has nine
pattern pieces. The many pieces
economically use up every scrap
of the highly expensive fabric.

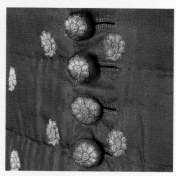

◁ FLATTENED BUTTONS

The doublet's 50 sleeve buttons
and 30 buttons at the front
opening are made from a circle
of silk stuffed with cotton fiber
and sewn into a tight, firm ball.
Toward the waist, flatter buttons
with a wooden or bone interior
allow a belt to be worn
comfortably.

◁ SLASHED VENTS

Slashes at each side seam at the
same level as the points (where
the hose are attached) help the
wearer to move freely.

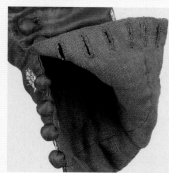

◁ LINING AND CUFFS

The lining of the doublet is fine
blue linen, which is overlaid with
a thin layer of cotton fiber and
then a layer of silk. The garment
is then quilted through all the
layers. Buttonholes are stitched
with silk thread.

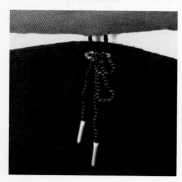

◁ SUSPENDED HOSE

The hose are suspended from the
doublet by five pairs of laces with
metal aglets or chapes. These
are sewn into the doublet and
threaded through eyelets on the
hose. Later garments had eyelets
on the doublet, too.

1380–1450
REGIONAL FLAIR

The 15th century saw an eclectic mix of regional styles and the beginnings of pants. For men, the fitted cote (tunic) became even shorter. It was worn on its own or underneath long outer garments called *houppelandes*, using vast amounts of fabric and bringing back wide sleeves. Clothing became more vivid as dyeing and weaving improved. At the same time black grew more fashionable, especially for the middle classes, who spent more and more on clothes. Better wools led to the craze for cutting raw edges as decoration, and fur use reached its peak. Individual hose legs were stitched together to create full-bottomed hose—a key development and the origin of today's pants. Headgear offered variety—high felt cones, draped cloth *chaperons* and hoods, wide-brimmed straw hats, and large silk and fur bonnets. Sleeve shapes also grew more inventive.

High collar

Open at wrists

Tight foundation for loose outer clothes

Braies could reach to the knee—these are short

Hood has heavily dagged tail

Waist neatly marked

Leather pouch hangs from belt

Linen underwear A man undressing shows 1420s underclothes. The loose shirt hangs over a pair of short *braies* (fitted underpants). Doublets had many front buttons and a waist seam for a close fit.

Doublet collar shows underneath robe neck

Center front closing

Paternoster (rosary) beads

Leather purse with metal-edged top flap

Fur lining shows at hem

Hose in open-backed slippers

Split tunic seams show off dagging

Lattice cutwork boots show hose underneath

High collar

Gathered sleeve heads

Clothes lined in contrasting colors

In France cut edges were considered a German style

Sleeves draped over wrist

Contrasting panels of dagged cloth

Parti-colored shoes and hose

Portable accessories Men and women hung all the items they needed during the day off their belts, a handy way of carrying before pockets. This English man's hat has a liripipe (long tail) draped over his shoulder.

Dagged edges This Italian man from around 1400 wears fashionable wool clothes in different bright colors, with decorative cuts, called dagging, around the edges. The cloth was so tightly woven that edges did not fray. The tight sleeves of a green doublet cover his hands.

Shorter French robe This *haincelin* (shorter robe) has dagged (decoratively cut) edges. The earlier hood became a hat by putting the face hole on top of the head and elegantly arranging the extra material.

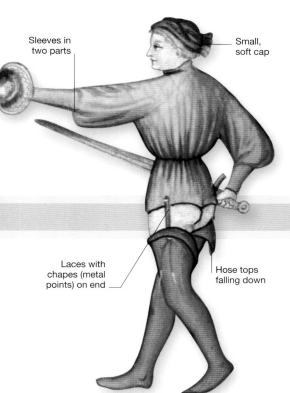

Sleeves in two parts

Small, soft cap

Laces with chapes (metal points) on end

Hose tops falling down

Hose laced to doublet Young men practicing sword fighting would strip to their basic garments. Laces tie the individual legs of the thigh-high hose to the bottom of the doublet to hold them up. Linen drawers show underneath.

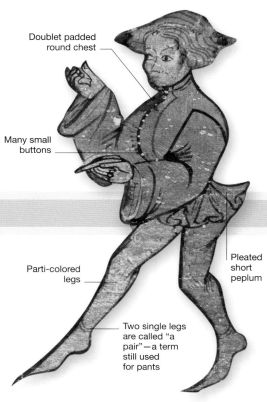

Doublet padded round chest

Many small buttons

Pleated short peplum

Parti-colored legs

Two single legs are called "a pair"—a term still used for pants

Spaniard in short doublet The dramatic shortening of men's top garments exposed the gaps in their hose. For modesty, hose were soon stitched together at the back, with a triangular piece of fabric over the crotch. Breeches were born.

FURS IN GREAT DEMAND

The Little Ice Age made temperatures in Europe dip in the 14th century. Demand for fur clothing was huge; sometimes up to 2,000 animals were used in one garment. Most luxury furs came from Russia: ermine, a stoat's winter coat; sable, a brown or black weasel fur; and brown marten skins. Cheaper local furs were budge (lambs' wool), coney (rabbit or hare), fox, and wolf.

The 14th-century Italian merchants above inspecting vair (winter squirrel fur) have the same fur lining their hoods. Furs had heraldic meanings, and painters, too, represented them with stylized patterns.

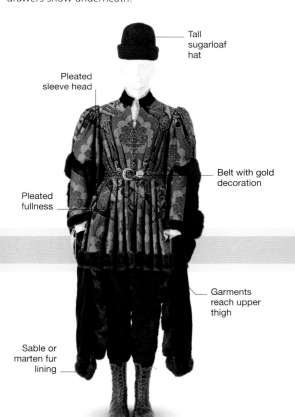

Tall sugarloaf hat

Pleated sleeve head

Pleated fullness

Belt with gold decoration

Garments reach upper thigh

Sable or marten fur lining

English style Shorter doublets with long sleeves were an English fashion. The cut of this reproduction exploits the silk's symmetrical formal pomegranate pattern. To economize, doublets could have plain bodies with silk used only for the sleeves.

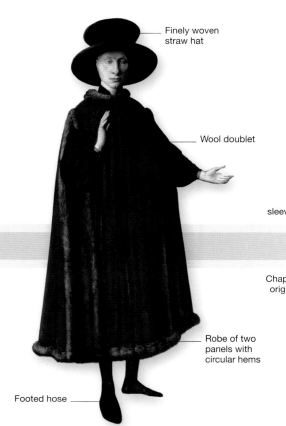

Finely woven straw hat

Wool doublet

Robe of two panels with circular hems

Footed hose

Italian merchant in Flemish dress In van Eyck's 1434 portrait, the sleeveless burgundy velvet *heuque* (cloak) is lined in marten fur. It has open sides, leaving the arms free. The ensemble is somber, respectable, and of high quality.

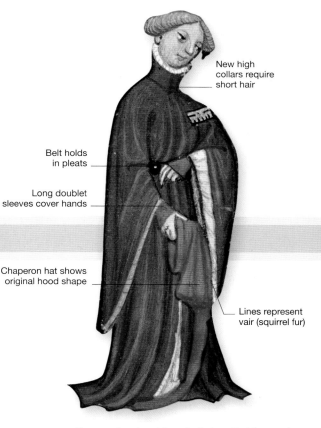

New high collars require short hair

Belt holds in pleats

Long doublet sleeves cover hands

Chaperon hat shows original hood shape

Lines represent vair (squirrel fur)

Houppelande **with vair lining** Fashion took advantage of the wider and cheaper textiles produced on better looms. Large *houppelande* robes reached the ground at the hem and sometimes the sleeves, and replaced mantles.

1380–1450
NOVELTY AND LUXURY

Many hallmarks of fashion were in place by the late 1400s: novelty, innovation, an element of impracticality, luxury, and—commentators insisted—excessive vanity and social presumption. Sumptuary laws still tried ineffectually to regulate who wore what. English and French head wear was fantastical, large, and varied. Italians were more natural; the Flemish preferred modest linen veils. Like men, women adopted the *houppelande* and other long, full pleated gowns cut from large, circular shapes, belted over a tight underdress that was buttoned or, increasingly, laced down the front. Their long, separate sleeves emerged from under the huge, open outer sleeves. Straight, scooped, or square necklines were low and shaped fashionably high round bosoms, sharply contrasting with the new high collars of outer clothing.

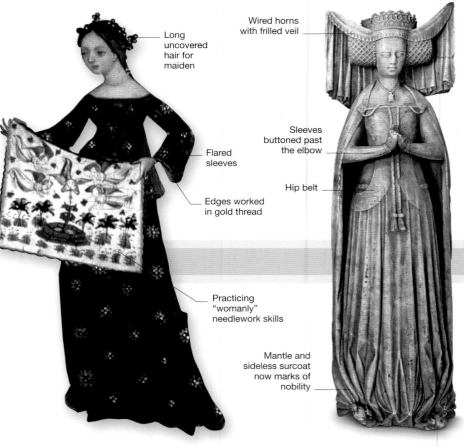

Long uncovered hair for maiden

Flared sleeves

Edges worked in gold thread

Practicing "womanly" needlework skills

Wired horns with frilled veil

Sleeves buttoned past the elbow

Hip belt

Mantle and sideless surcoat now marks of nobility

Italo-Spanish dress Critics complained that necklines were so wide the breasts wanted to leave them. This dress from the 1390s has no belt, Italian style. The pearl-embroidered silk might have been woven locally in northern Italy.

English headpiece In 1417 a chronicler wrote of hats with "horns marvelously tall and broad, with long ears either side." The Countess of Arundel's effigy made in 1415 records this startling fashion.

High horned bun over temples and under frilled linen veil layers

High, narrow belt

Finest fabric The bride in van Eyck's 1434 portrait wears Italian clothing for her wedding in Flanders. The bulk of the fur lining in her wool gown gives a fashionably prominent belly when lifted up.

Fur lining

Long sleeves weighed down with rows of strips dagged (decoratively cut) in cross shapes

Long hem of gown shows sheen of top-quality wool

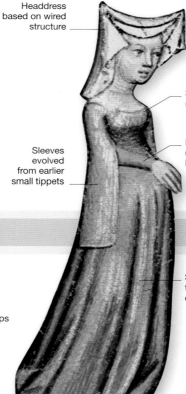

Headdress based on wired structure

Scooped neckline

Sleeves evolved from earlier small tippets

Pink *cote* (underdress) beneath

Skirt less full than that of a noble

French *cote-hardie* This close-fitting outer gown has hanging but not excessive sleeves, and the fabric is plain. The linen veil over modest wired horns shows how normal women modified French court fashion around 1410.

Padded roll forms heart-shaped headdress, worn with linen or silk veil

Open collar

Belt getting wider, under bust

Narrow cuffs

Changing Burgundian styles From the 1430s the *robe* with narrow cuffs replaced the *houppelande*. The high collar, opened in the front and folded down, was the start of the V-neck popular later in the century.

Flemish kirtle All women wore tight-fitting kirtles. This one, from around 1435, is made from squirrel skins with the fur turned inside, seen at the hem. Long, red wool outer sleeves pin on to the short kirtle sleeves. The skirt attaches at the waist, a new construction method.

Braided hair under linen veil

Linen shift visible at neckline

Tablet-woven silk belt

Wool mantle over kirtle

Kirtle

Deep fur hem

Silk textile used on book cover

Cloth-of-gold kirtle

Flemish luxury Van der Weyden's precise 1430s painting captures every detail of this wool gown entirely lined with squirrel fur and pleated through the bust. The lifted hem reveals a glimpse of the sumptuous cloth-of-gold kirtle underneath.

Front of gown laced together

Hair braided under linen veil with frilled selvedges

High girdle is tablet-woven in silk, with gold ends

Plentiful fabric in gown skirt

Popular wide headgear, with hair secured above each temple

Full pleated *pellanda* is Italian equivalent of *houppelande*

Sleeve edges cut into shapes

Sleeves trail on ground

Piedmontese noble This northern Italian allegorical figure wears a huge, cut-sleeved *pellanda* with fur lining over symbolic armor. A chain with leaf pendants is draped around her. Her hat is cut, pearled, and embroidered.

Large fur hat with feathers

Modest-sized sleeves

High, round bust

Long sash of imported coral beads fabulously costly

Golden cote underneath

Houppelande with ground-length trails

Height of fashion A noble French betrothal in the 1410s was an excuse for the finest clothing. This bride's *houppelande* is made of expensive, Italian-made, gold patterned silk.

RENAISSANCE
SPLENDOR

1450–1624

RENAISSANCE SPLENDOR

This was the period when fashion finally moved from draped clothing to fitted garments and the art of tailoring came into its own. Clothes gained structure and became stiffer and more supportive. The first templates for garments that remained modern items of clothing were created: hose with a fitted doublet and outer coat for men, a bodice with a separate skirt for women.

Differentiation in clothing

Clothing now consisted of a greater number of parts including detachable sleeves, under- and overskirts, sleeveless jerkins, and breeches of different lengths. This emphasis on separate parts of the body reflected the new interest in human anatomy that had gripped the natural sciences. The masculine form was enhanced by the latest clothing, with its wide shoulders, prominent codpieces, strong legs, and bellies. Women's clothes emphasized their narrow waists, combining wide shoulders and skirts with a deeply pointed bodice. The garments of different nations or regions showed greater differentiation, and the religious schism between the Catholic church and the reform or Protestant faiths led to the creation of new visual identities for members of the different faiths.

Age of exploration

The Ottoman Empire rose in the near East and southeast Europe, after conquering Constantinople (modern-day Istanbul) in 1453, bringing Islamic might to the region. Through the 16th century, the Spanish empire was the richest and most powerful; it began to wane in the early 17th century as the French became more dominant. This was an age of conquests, exploration, and expansion into the Americas, following Columbus's arrival in 1492. Other explorers ventured around the world opening up sea trading routes around Africa and Asia, crossing the Pacific and discovering new goods to bring back to Europe.

Dominant personalities

New realism and naturalism in painting meant that portraits were much more realistic and could accurately represent individuals and their clothes. Dominant personalities in Europe—Henry VIII and Elizabeth I in England, Philip II in Spain, François I and Henry IV in France, the de Medici dynasty in Florence, and Suleiman the Magnificent in the Ottoman empire—reinforced their position with strong visuals in paintings that portrayed them in fashionable clothes. Ruffs, in particular, became popular. The starching process stiffened cloth and allowed the development of very wide ruffs, and lace became the most luxurious textile to own. In the late 16th century, heeled shoes were invented.

1450–69	1470–99	1500–19
▲ Young man wearing fur	**1470s** Early versions of the farthingale appear in Spain as the *verdugada* or *verdugado*, a bell-shaped skirt stiffened with hoops of cane, or later, willow. Originally hoops are worn on the outer surface of the dress, later they go underneath the overskirt.	**1500–1560s** Men begin layering clothes to give bulk and width, especially at the shoulders, creating a square outline. They start wearing hose to show off their shapely legs, suggesting athleticism.
1450s Sable, lynx, and other exotic furs become fashionable, replacing squirrel furs such as miniver and vair. Ermine remains the prerogative of royalty.	**1476** The new fashion is for slashing garments to reveal the lining or undergarments. Perhaps from the actions of Swiss soldiers following Battle of Grandson in 1476, when they patched tattered clothes with fabrics plundered from dead nobles.	
1450s Women's hair is pulled back from forehead and covered by a caul (small bag worn over a bun at the back of the head) or a crespine (mesh net). Fashionable women shave their foreheads and eyebrows. In warmer Italy, married women wear their hair long, braided, in loose knots, and uncovered.	**1480s** Men start to wear their hair longer. Blonde hair becomes the vogue in Italy for women. Women sit in the sun with their hair spread out on circular disk-shaped hats to lighten it. Chemicals are also used to bleach it.	▲ Wide, square shoulders
1450s Brocade becomes a luxury fabric as weaving techniques improve. The best fabric comes from Italy with Chinese, Indian, and Persian motifs reflecting increased trade with these countries.		**1509** Marriage of Catherine of Aragon to Henry VIII of England starts a trend for geometric black-work embroidery on linen clothing. Designs are inspired by patterns popular in Spain from Moorish culture. ◀ Black-work embroidery
◀ Italian brocade dress	**1490s** Metal pins cost a penny each in Henry VIII's time, so fish bones and thorns are often used for sewing.	**1516** Charles V of Spain unites the Hapsburg territories with Aragon and Castile. Spain becomes the dominant power in Europe. Black clothes with rich decoration are favored.

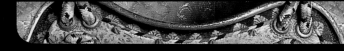

> And I will make thee beds of roses, With a thousand fragrant posies,
> A cap of flowers and a kirtle, Embroidered all with leaves of myrtle.

THE PASSIONATE SHEPHERD TO HIS LOVE, CHRISTOPHER MARLOWE C. 1589

1520–39	1540–59	1560–64	1565–99	1600–20	1621–24

1520
Spanish Conquistadors defeat the Aztecs in Mexico. Cochineal used as a red dye is brought back to Europe.

▼ Collecting cochineal beetles

1560-1600
Men's clothes get narrower on shoulders and longer.

1605
Hemlines go up to show feet, following the introduction of heeled shoes for the rich, hence the expression "well heeled."

1620s
Colored stockings, especially red ones, become popular. The newer style of latchet-closing shoe shows off the hose underneath, and embroidery at the ankle.

1562
English legislate against the wearing of "monstrous and outrageous greatness of hose" after fashion for padding tops of legs reaches ridiculous proportions.

1600s
In lady's wear, the short jacket is introduced. These are initially closed with ribbons, later with metal hooks and eyes. They are worn by all stations of society but the materials depend on rank. Boned bodices cinch in waist and lift the barely covered breasts.

1620s
Surface ornamentation of fabrics is replaced by bright, solid-color satins decorated with rosettes, wide bows, and looped trims. For women, the virago sleeve—full slashed sleeve divided into two puffs at the elbow by a ribbon or trim—comes in.

1540
The codpiece reaches its peak in terms of size and decoration. Designed to cover the gap between the two legs of men's hose, it is padded and shaped to emphasize rather than disguise the genital area.

▲ Pope Pius V wearing his white habit

1566
Pope Pius V is credited with changing the color of the papal robes from red to white, as he would not give up his Dominican habit.

▲ Intricate lacework

1527
Mateo Pagano in Italy and Pierre de Quinty in Cologne publish the first pattern books for embroidery and lace making.

1550s
The chopine, an early platform overshoe, has been popular since the late 15th century. At this time they reach the peak of their height (20 in/50 cm).

1570s
Introduction of the French, or "wheel," farthingale, with a stuffed roll around the hips and a hoop with horizontal stiffeners tied around the waist that makes the skirt stick out from the body.

◄ Reconstruction of a farthingale underskirt

1600–1650
Ruffs are replaced by broad collars of lace. Hats become taller and broader with brims, sleeves get puffier.

► The *Laughing Cavalier* by Franz Hals (1624)

1564
Starching is introduced from the Low Countries and allows for the development of large, stiff ruffs. Starch can be colored yellow or blue to tint the ruff.

1620
English Puritans establish a colony in Plymouth, Massachusetts. Somber colors and tall, black capotain hats are worn; lacings and jewelry are forbidden by Puritans.

1625
Fashionable married women abandon the wearing of a cap and wear their hair elaborately styled, uncovered, or with a hat.

▲ Punched, kid leather and pine chopine from Venice, Italy

1450–1500
THE FASHION SPLIT

By the middle of the 15th century there were marked regional differences in women's dress. The medieval standard one-piece tunic moved toward a broad spectrum of fashions in cut and construction. As garments began to separate into pieces, dressmaking played with the cut of skirts and sleeves newly liberated from bodices, and incorporated folded collars and laced closures. Head wear continued trends from earlier in the century but was becoming spectacularly complex. As the elongated Gothic look disappeared, clothing became softer and wider. Improved weaving technologies continued to increase textile production and make fabrics more affordable, especially for the growing, prosperous merchant classes. In Northern Europe fur remained a vital addition for warmth.

Wulsthaube (German headgear) made of decorative cloth over a large linen roll in fashionable turban shape

End of linen veil

Pleating

Lacing shows linen shift underneath

Cuffs extending over hands

Shift shows through open sleeve seam with buttons

Structured support holds up padded roll

Full, circular skirt attached at waist

Rounded veil Women in Germanic regions kept a more natural soft shape developed from the medieval *houppelande*. Rounded lines appeared in their hats, veils, and necklines. The central panel of pleating gave a neat fullness to the skirt.

HATS AND VEILS

High forehead

Cylindrical hat

Headdresses often emphasized a woman's high, smooth forehead. Many women bleached their hair to a fashionable blonde, or plucked their hairline to create a higher forehead. Cylindrical hats of different lengths were stylish in France, Burgundy, England, and the Low Countries. They were supported by a small cap or wire structure. Wiring and pins were used to attach fine veils of silk or linen over the headdress.

Entirely lined in white fur

Sleeves getting tighter

Belt holds extra fabric in pleats

Streamer connects her to fellow dancer

Long trailing hem

Double cornet headdress The padded roll on this French lady's headdress creates a split effect like a clamshell. Her ball gown shows the shift from a high *houppelande* neckline to the lower V-line one, with less pleating. She could wear another gown over this one.

Long hair tied back

No waistline

Silk and gold textile

Stiffened bands

Split overgown The trend for visible linen undergarments began in Spain. In this portrait from 1482, Isabel of Castile's long, white shift sleeves are pulled from a slit in her outer sleeve. Reinforced horizontal bands help the skirt to stand out—this is the farthingale's origin.

Nearly horizontal hat

Deep collar

Skirt separate at waist

Long, tight sleeves

Silk brocade textile

Gown longer than the wearer—mark of excess

Brocade gown English women tended to wear shorter versions of the tall, continental head wear. Lady Margaret Peyton's gown flaunts expensive, patterned fabric, and her collar is turned back to frame rich jewelry. Wire keeps her veil in a butterfly shape.

Linen veil covering hair

Visible *camisia* (shirt) under dress

Red lacing cord

Gold embroidery

Flowing, loose silk *giornea* (overgown)

Giornea In Italy, looser, natural styles began to be worn. Florentine women of the 1480s wore a long, front-opening *giornea* tunic draped over a laced gown with a natural bustline. The matching sleeves are separate and are tied or pinned to the shoulder.

Hanging sleeves French gowns kept the wide, hanging sleeves of earlier in the century. By 1475 the natural waistline was marked with a sash and the kirtle skirt was revealed.

High forehead

Black hood

Arched neckline and overlapping front opening

Sable fur lining

White silk sash or girdle

Kirtle skirt

Supporting cap

Hair twisted to become part of headdress

Plastron (underbodice) shows at bodice top

Upper and lower sleeves tied together

Front opening held with buttons on skirt

Split sleeves Fashionable women combined many ideas in one ensemble. This French or Flemish lady from just before 1500 wears Italian-style split sleeves allowing the chemise to spill out of her square-fronted gown.

Sleeves tie together and to the shoulder

Patterned underdress visible at bust

Gown entirely lined with fur

Circles cut into sleeve

Heavy fabric

Floor-length skirt

V-neck gown In northern Italian regions such as the city-state of Venice the outer tunic turned into a high-waisted, V-neck gown. Cuts and slashing in sleeves became inventive. In this reconstruction, the shift is decoratively pulled through the holes.

Transparent silk veil

Top of kirtle visible

Wide belt pulled tight

Towering headdress The Burgundian court set a fashion for long, pointed headdresses worn with gowns with high waistlines. The low neckline reveals the top of the kirtle underneath. The style echoed the pointed Gothic architecture.

Skirt extends into very long train

RICH
PANOPLY

The spectrum of Venetian society—and clothing—at the end of the 15th century is displayed here in a rich panorama. The crowds around the Rialto Bridge in 1494 wear an array of styles that reveal something about their position in society. The gondoliers and young men are at the height of fashion, with long curled hair and fantastic displays of *ziponi* (doublets), jerkins, and *camisias* (shirts) bursting from the seams. The *calce* (hose) patterns are particularly varied. Their passengers' dress shows restrained and better-quality versions of these fashions, sometimes covered with looser open robes. On land and crossing the bridge are the patrician professional men, members of guilds and government. They wear *baretas* (small round caps) and *vestas* (long, sober, official gowns) in red or black with a wide-sleeve style called a *dogale*.

Visitors from Islamic lands, who traded with Venice, can be distinguished by their turbans. Two Jewish men are clothed in black hats and Oriental silks. On the balcony are Dominican monks in white and clerical men in red robes under white albs. Few women are out in public, although they can be glimpsed in windows and beating an expensive "Turkey" carpet on the roof. Linen shirts and other items normally hidden from view can be seen drying on roof poles.

> ❝
>
> The sea not only brought the city her prosperity, but ... Venetian painters were inspired to record the dazzling effects of light on the buildings and bridges that line the canals ... the bustle of canal traffic, the gondolas ... and merchant vessels.
>
> **WILL DURANT,** *THE RENAISSANCE*, 1953
>
> ❞

◁ **CLOTHES PARADE BY THE RIALTO BRIDGE**
This detail from Vittore Carpaccio's painting *The Miracle of the Relic of the True Cross* (1494) shows a cross section of 15th-century Venetian society dressed in the fashions of the day.

1450–1500
RENAISSANCE MEN

From the 1480s new broad shapes began to replace the last traces of the medieval in men's clothing. Instead of an emphasis on a long, vertical male figure, the Renaissance man, with his earthier, artistic, and scientific pursuits and a new interest in classical ideas, favored blunt and square forms that expanded sideways. Soldiers' and statesmen's cropped hair grew into the long, natural locks of poets and scholars. Men began to wear collections of clothing as an ensemble and used surfaces, fabrics, and edges as decorative spaces. Places where clothes connected—in seams, the tops of sleeves, and under lacing—revealed layers underneath. Though pleating continued, natural folds reappeared using the elegant drape of circular pieces to great effect.

Wide and square All the elements of a new style were in place by 1490 in France—broad shoulders, flat-toed shoes, copious draping, and a wide neckline. The loose outer gown hides the close-fitting doublet and hose.

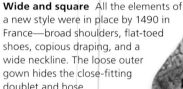

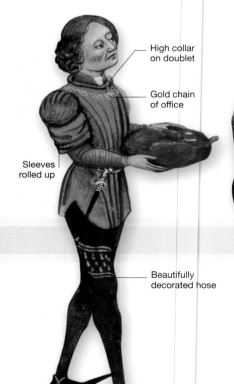

High collar on doublet

Gold chain of office

Sleeves rolled up

Beautifully decorated hose

Short robe, long toes Serving the king at the table was an honor for English lords. This man's sword shows his knightly position. The exaggerated long toes of *poulaine* shoes were very fashionable at court.

Belt with decorated purse

Open sleeves caught with clasps

Intricate silk brocade

Leopard fur lining

Wide-toed shoes

Round cap

Mi-parti (two-part) colored robe

Visible lacing

Sword, dagger, and hunting purse

Mid-length robe

Pantofle slippers with open backs

Hunting livery The two colors in this young Frenchman's robe were probably livery, showing his employment by a lord. The lacing fastening the front was now visible. The collar and sleeves showed a careful cut and fit.

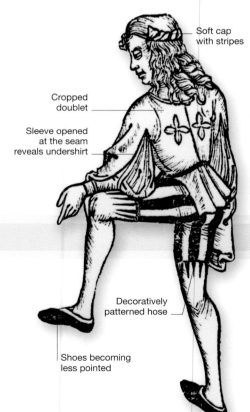

Soft cap with stripes

Cropped doublet

Sleeve opened at the seam reveals undershirt

Decoratively patterned hose

Shoes becoming less pointed

Decorative elements Northern European youths flaunted fashion knowledge by blending new Italian influences such as long, curling hair and a slashed doublet sleeve with local styles. The short doublet was a sign of youth.

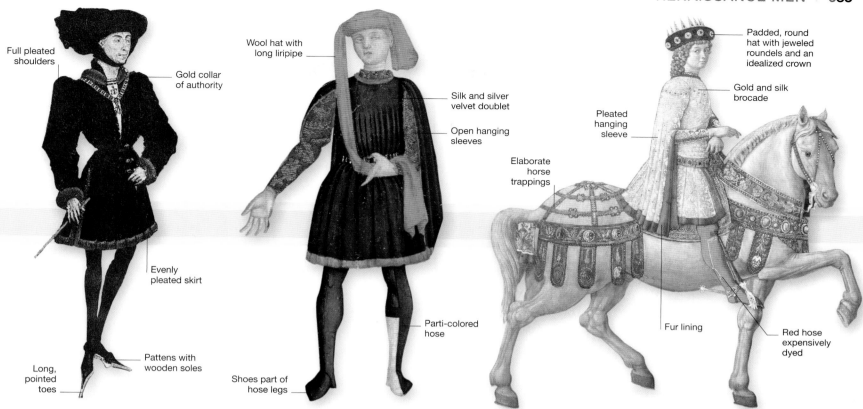

Full pleated shoulders

Gold collar of authority

Evenly pleated skirt

Pattens with wooden soles

Long, pointed toes

Wool hat with long liripipe

Silk and silver velvet doublet

Open hanging sleeves

Parti-colored hose

Shoes part of hose legs

Padded, round hat with jeweled roundels and an idealized crown

Gold and silk brocade

Pleated hanging sleeve

Elaborate horse trappings

Fur lining

Red hose expensively dyed

Black velvet robe Charles the Bold's outfit picked up on the popularity of black through the century. Rich, true blacks were difficult to dye and displayed a subtle expensive quality. His large *chaperon* (hat) was stuffed for shape.

Knee-length robe Sumptuary laws in many cities regulated what people in each social level could wear. This noble Florentine man used his outer gown's open sleeves to flaunt the costly Italian velvet underneath.

The power of gold Lorenzo de Medici, the Magnificent, reflected the power of his Florentine banking family c. 1460 in clothing woven with gold. Even his riding accessories were elaborately wrought and made from gold to reveal his social position.

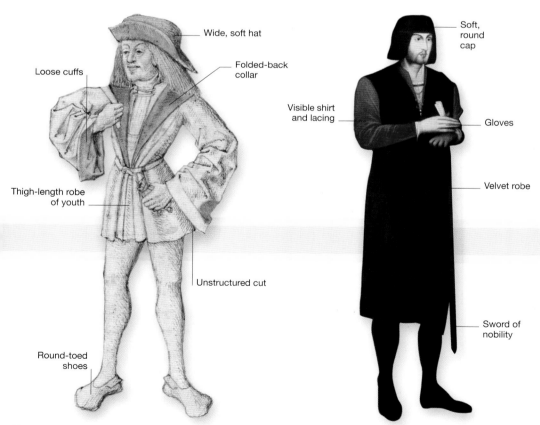

Wide, soft hat

Loose cuffs

Folded-back collar

Thigh-length robe of youth

Unstructured cut

Round-toed shoes

Soft, round cap

Visible shirt and lacing

Gloves

Velvet robe

Sword of nobility

New naturalism English clothing also became less structured and more naturalistic. This man, with his youthful clothing and cheerful expression, embodies the sanguine, optimistic character described in medieval science and medicine.

Royal simplicity By contrast with displays of wealth and excess, a ruler such as Juan II of Portugal chose to dress simply and elegantly. The red silk velvet of his doublet is a valuable textile despite its restrained use.

LIFE CHANGES

As a man moved through each stage of life, his clothing changed to reveal his place in society. Active young men wore short, fitted doublets and robes revealing shapely thighs. In adult maturity, around 25, the hemline started creeping farther down the thigh. By middle and old age hemlines reached the floor. Longer and darker robes enhanced dignity for professional and political men, and for those who did not do manual labor, such as scholars and doctors. The floor-length robes also kept them warm.

1500–1560

FROM DRAPE TO SHAPE

Soft, draped lines began to disappear as the century went on. Women's dress had two main parts: bodice and skirt, and sleeves were often separate, too. The gradual move from clothing that draped over the body to clothing that shaped it was complete. Only outer robes and coats were now waistless. Full skirts widened with gathered and pleated waistlines. Outer skirts were opened up in front to reveal a petticoat or forepart underneath. The Spanish farthingale (a hooped petticoat) created a bell shape and defined the century's silhouette. Bodices became smooth and fitted by adding stiff materials inside. While the torso straightened, sleeves grew larger and more elaborate.

Long hair draped around head

Embroidered breast-band

Black velvet gollar (shoulder cape)

False lining to make puffs of silk

Nonfunctional, pleated linen apron

Tight, vertical pleats in skirt

Heavily pleated skirt The 15th-century obsession with pleating continued in Germanic fashions. This woman's dress is laced open in the front and has an embroidered breastband under her gollar (shoulder cape).

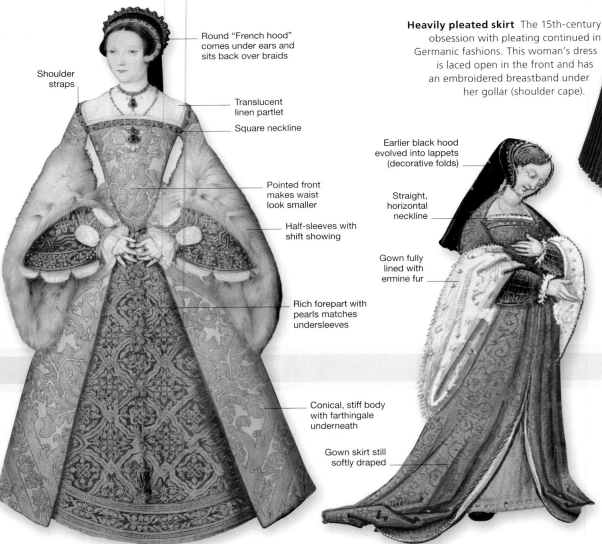

Round "French hood" comes under ears and sits back over braids

Shoulder straps

Translucent linen partlet

Square neckline

Pointed front makes waist look smaller

Half-sleeves with shift showing

Rich forepart with pearls matches undersleeves

Conical, stiff body with farthingale underneath

Earlier black hood evolved into lappets (decorative folds)

Straight, horizontal neckline

Gown fully lined with ermine fur

Gown skirt still softly draped

Triangular shapes Catherine Parr, last wife of Henry VIII, shows off the smooth, triangular shapes achieved by reinforced support beneath outer clothing. The silver-gilt fabric of this gown from 1545 is woven with a large pomegranate pattern.

Fur-lined silk gown The huge sleeves of the Duchesse d'Etampes' 1540 French gown are turned back to reveal an expensive ermine fur lining. While her gown trails on the floor, the kirtle skirt is ankle length.

DEFINED SHAPE

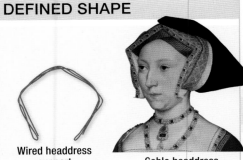

Wired headdress support

Gable headdress

Fashion became architectural as the century progressed. Strong, new shapes distinct from body lines were built over supports that kept the garments taut and straight. The English gable headdress used wire underneath to turn the 15th-century hood into a sharp peak. Spanish women began to wear horizontal willow hoops called *verdugado* (farthingale) under their skirts to make them stand out. Stiffened bodices flattened the bosom, creating an inflexible torso like an inverted triangle.

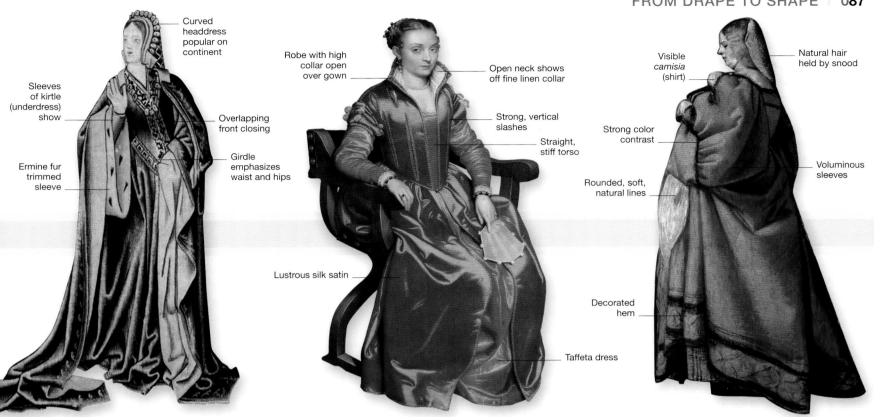

Curved headdress popular on continent

Sleeves of kirtle (underdress) show

Ermine fur trimmed sleeve

Overlapping front closing

Girdle emphasizes waist and hips

Robe with high collar open over gown

Open neck shows off fine linen collar

Strong, vertical slashes

Straight, stiff torso

Lustrous silk satin

Taffeta dress

Visible *camisia* (shirt)

Natural hair held by snood

Strong color contrast

Rounded, soft, natural lines

Voluminous sleeves

Decorated hem

Softly draped dress This Flemish dress from c. 1500 shows the soft, early version of a style that became rigid in form as the century progressed. The torso is natural in shape, and the sleeve cuffs are large. The woman's long mantle (cloak) covers her trailing skirts.

Satin and taffeta The smooth, tight bodice contrasts with the sumptuous, light-catching folds of this Italian dress from c. 1555. The red overgown's short sleeves have fine silk puffs between the panes of fabric.

Gown with large sleeves Even without extra reinforcement, tightly woven silks had a stiffness and body that gave an angular bulk, here painted by Venetian artist Titian.

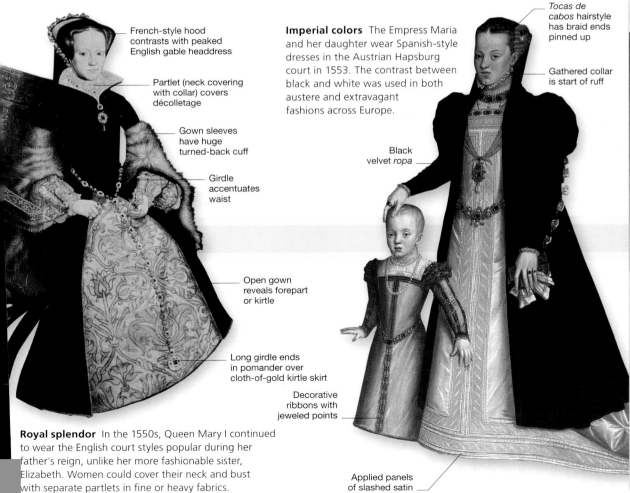

French-style hood contrasts with peaked English gable headdress

Partlet (neck covering with collar) covers décolletage

Gown sleeves have huge turned-back cuff

Girdle accentuates waist

Open gown reveals forepart or kirtle

Long girdle ends in pomander over cloth-of-gold kirtle skirt

Imperial colors The Empress Maria and her daughter wear Spanish-style dresses in the Austrian Hapsburg court in 1553. The contrast between black and white was used in both austere and extravagant fashions across Europe.

Tocas de cabos hairstyle has braid ends pinned up

Gathered collar is start of ruff

Black velvet *ropa*

Decorative ribbons with jeweled points

Applied panels of slashed satin

Royal splendor In the 1550s, Queen Mary I continued to wear the English court styles popular during her father's reign, unlike her more fashionable sister, Elizabeth. Women could cover their neck and bust with separate partlets in fine or heavy fabrics.

LINEN SHIRTS

Beneath every elaborate gown a linen undergarment was worn next to the skin. It was known by many names: English smock, shift, or shirt; French *chemise*; Italian *camisia*; Spanish *camisa*; and German *hemd*. This was an essential layer because linen could be washed and it protected outer garments (which were never washed) from the body. When clothing started to reveal this layer, emphasis on the linen quality and delicate embroidery around the neck and cuffs increased. Sleeves became bigger to create abundant billows emerging from gowns.

1500–1560

NEW MEN IN A NEW WORLD

As conquest, exploration, and wars expanded the known world, men's fashion broadened, too. Clothing expressed an assertive, confident masculinity through bulky layers that increased a man's physical presence. Huge shoulders, broad chests, prominent codpieces, and an emphasis on the thighs all enhanced a sense of the active body. The legs usually peeped out below knee-length skirted robes and jerkins and the newly separate breeches and hose. Clothing complexity increased as linings and shirts burst through deliberately cut and slashed outer garments. Embroidery and lines of braid also helped enrich the surfaces of clothing, largely replacing patterned textiles.

Knit cap

White fur used as contrasting trim

Shovel-shaped beard

Satin doublet with rough cuts

Jerkin with deep, triangular opening and skirt

Broad, domed toes on shoes

Solid, square silhouette Holbein the Younger's 1533 portrait of a French ambassador epitomizes the fashionable solid, rectangular shape. Round puffed sleeves create massive shoulders, while the lines of his cap, skirt, shoes, and spread-out pose all emphasize the horizontal.

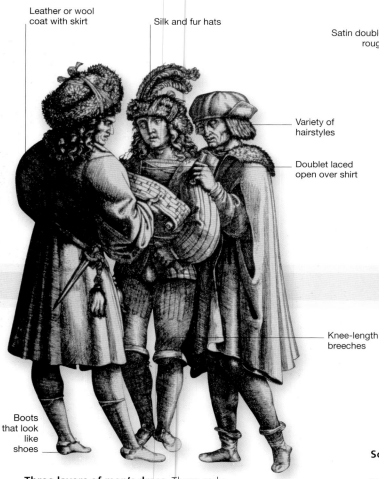

Leather or wool coat with skirt

Silk and fur hats

Variety of hairstyles

Doublet laced open over shirt

Knee-length breeches

Boots that look like shoes

Three layers of men's dress These early 16th-century Italian musicians wear a big-sleeved doublet and hose (center), a bulky coat with a separate skirt cut on the circle (left), and, over the whole, an armhole cloak with fur collar (right).

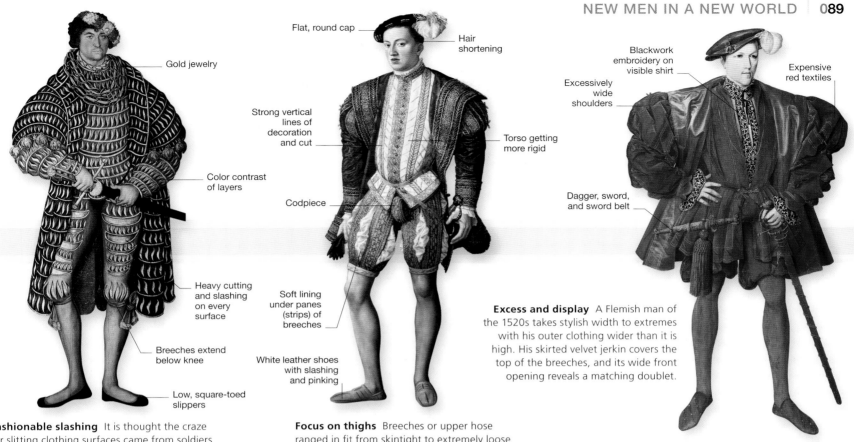

Gold jewelry

Color contrast
of layers

Heavy cutting
and slashing
on every
surface

Breeches extend
below knee

Low, square-toed
slippers

Flat, round cap

Hair
shortening

Strong vertical
lines of
decoration
and cut

Torso getting
more rigid

Codpiece

Soft lining
under panes
(strips) of
breeches

White leather shoes
with slashing
and pinking

Blackwork
embroidery on
visible shirt

Excessively
wide
shoulders

Expensive
red textiles

Dagger, sword,
and sword belt

Excess and display A Flemish man of
the 1520s takes stylish width to extremes
with his outer clothing wider than it is
high. His skirted velvet jerkin covers the
top of the breeches, and its wide front
opening reveals a matching doublet.

Fashionable slashing It is thought the craze
for slitting clothing surfaces came from soldiers
cutting plundered garments to make them fit. In
this 1514 portrait, Henry IV, Duke of Saxony, wears
a whole suit slashed to reveal the inner lining.

Focus on thighs Breeches or upper hose
ranged in fit from skintight to extremely loose
and baggy. By 1548 the jerkin skirts on
Archduke Ferdinand of Tirol had shrunk into
small panes, flaunting the codpiece and thighs.

Doublet
front under
scoop-neck
jerkin

Collar and revers
turned back

As a horse was a sign
of power, horseback
pose suggests leadership
and action

Jewels and feather
in velvet cap

Semicircular
short cloak

Lots of linear
braids emphasize
clothing shapes

Codpiece

Fur-lined
outer coat

Royal fleur-de-lis
emblem

Paned decoration In this reconstruction,
the deep U-shaped jerkin front goes over
a doublet made of fabric panes (strips)
joined by buttons. The sleeves are also
made of panes.

Monochrome monarch Henri II of France,
one of the age's dominant personalities,
exploited the stark drama of black and white,
with severe gold decoration, in a mid-16th-
century portrait of sovereign power.

THE CODPIECE

The origins of the codpiece lie in the triangle
of fabric used to join the two separate hose
legs in the late 15th century when doublets
shortened. Soon padding was added and
ended up as the codpiece—a prominent,
suggestive shape filling the gap between
the legs of the breeches. It soon became a
normal part of male clothing, in style across
many countries and social levels until the
end of the 1500s. Tailors became as
creative with codpiece shapes as with other
clothing details. The codpiece could hide a
pocket or even be used as a pincushion.

COAT, DOUBLET, AND HOSE
SAXONY ENSEMBLE

This unique and extraordinary set of mid-16th-century clothes belonged to Maurice, Elector of Saxony from 1547 to 1553. It is the most complete—and oldest surviving—example of real fashion from the period. The princely ensemble comprises a short, round, pleated coat with puffed and hanging sleeves, a satin doublet, puffed and slashed trunk hose, and chamois or suede hose. Yellow silks accented with black velvet are an extravagant reflection of the heraldic colors of the Saxon state. Using bands of fabric in this way to decorate clothing was fashionable throughout the 16th century. The almost square, imposing silhouette matches exactly with the aristocratic masculine fashions seen in many paintings of the time.

Wide, straight lapels show off applied parallel bands of bias-cut dark velvet

Doublet front curves gently

Doublet sleeves have horizontal bands of silk and large diagonal cuts

All bands edged with silver-gilt cords

Prominent codpiece is made of silk velvet and stuffed into shape

Chamois or suede hose have leather soles and a gusset below the ankle to shape the foot

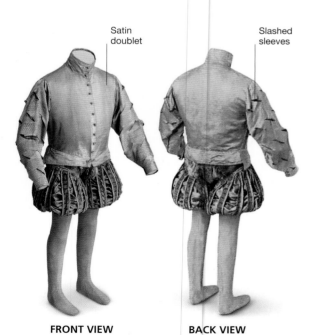

Satin doublet

Slashed sleeves

FRONT VIEW WITHOUT COAT

BACK VIEW WITHOUT COAT

SIDE VIEW

△ **TRUNK HOSE**
The trunk hose are made of panes of silk velvet on the bias, slashed diagonally so the cuts appear straight. Each strip is bound in satin. Inside, pieces of satin are crumpled down to give the fashionable puffed effect.

Large square collar continues from the front and emphasizes the shoulder width

Back of high collar is cut in one piece with the back of the doublet

Hanging sleeves are largely decorative, with armholes halfway down

Coat is nearly a full circle with the width pleated into the shoulders

IN DETAIL

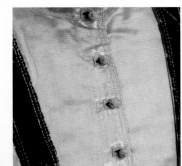

◁ KNOTTED SILK BUTTONS
The buttons closing the front of the doublet are made by wrapping a wood core with a herringbone pattern of silk thread. The shank is very long to raise the decorative part above the strain of the buttonholes, which are stitched in silk thread.

◁ SILK DAMASK
The stunning yellow silk is damask woven: this means the massive, rounded pomegranate pattern is made by contrasting the matte and sheen of two directions of weaving that catch the light differently. It was more expensive than a plain weave.

◁ PUFFED SHOULDERS
By alternating straight strips of black velvet with the damask to form puffs, the shoulders are made bigger. Increasing the volume across the torso was popular in the early 16th century. It added bulk and an imposing presence. Laces on the inside hold up the puffs.

◁ PASSEMENTERIE KNOTS
On the end of the hanging sleeves are cross shapes of Italian passementerie—cord, knot, and tassel work made from silk. The vegetable-dyed colors have faded from the original violet. The pale parts of the knots are entwined with silver-gilt thread to catch the light.

◁ EVEN FOLDS
The elegant hang of the coat is created by deep pleats. In German regions at this time, both men's and women's clothing used huge quantities of round, even pleats. The contrasting color bands form an arresting horizontal against the strong vertical lines.

1450–1624
CUSTOM-MADE ARMOR

While medieval knights wore surcoats over mail or armor, their Renaissance counterparts wanted to show off the splendor of their full swordproof plate. Each suit was unique—reflected in the cost—and increasingly decorated with gilding, inlay, or battle scenes. Since the armor fit perfectly, the substantial weight (about 55 lb/25 kg) was evenly distributed. The knight could move freely and mount and dismount his horse without help—once his servants had undertaken the lengthy task of putting the suit on. The use of full plate armor waned as the 16th century wore on, and handguns replaced swords as the weapon of choice.

Close helmet with visor

Feathered cap

Paned and puffed sleeves

Striped hose

Colors may have distinguished one company from another

Swiss mercenary Highly skilled fighters were greatly in demand as paid infantry troops. Swiss soldiers, like this one in 1530, set fashion trends with their bright, color-coordinated doublet and hose slashed into exaggerated shapes.

Together with the sallet helmet, the bevor (neck piece) offers full head protection

Vulnerable join covered with besagaw (round armpit shield)

Complete head and neck cover

Sections buckled together

Complete protection A knight in full armor did not need to carry a shield. Mail under the plate or sewn into joins covered potentially vulnerable points.

Full suit of armor Made for Sir Thomas Sackville by the Royal Workshop in Greenwich, this steel, leather, gold, and copper alloy suit, c. 1590, weighs a hefty 81 lb (36.7 kg) with its plackart.

Detachable plackart gives extra protection

Gold decoration

Broadsword

Sabatons end at tip of toe unlike 15th-century pointed ones

Made to measure This 16th-century suit of armor was made for Henry VIII when he was past his youthful slimness. Armor was custom made for a snug fit, so it was extremely expensive.

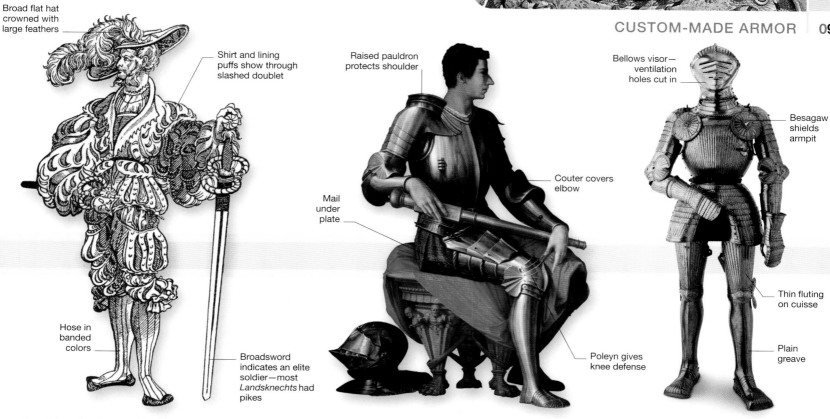

Broad flat hat crowned with large feathers

Shirt and lining puffs show through slashed doublet

Hose in banded colors

Broadsword indicates an elite soldier—most *Landsknechts* had pikes

Raised pauldron protects shoulder

Mail under plate

Couter covers elbow

Poleyn gives knee defense

Bellows visor— ventilation holes cut in

Besagaw shields armpit

Thin fluting on cuisse

Plain greave

Landsknecht German "land servants," c. 1500, probably based their costume on their rival Swiss mercenaries. Their flamboyant dress typified the Renaissance. They wore multicolored hose and slashed their doublets open to reveal their shirts and linings.

Italian armor The rigidity of plate armor provided better defense against swords than medieval mail. In 1534 Alessandro de Medici wears a suit of armor with articulated steel plates that allow him to move his arms and legs.

German full plate armor Visually pleasing as well as functional, this cuirass (breastplate) of 1520 is sharply pulled in at the waist like men's clothing, and fluting imitates pleated material. Mitten-type gauntlets protect the hands.

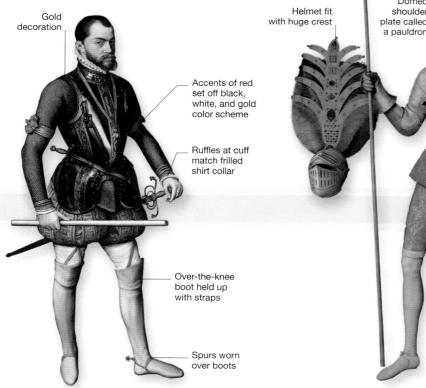

Gold decoration

Accents of red set off black, white, and gold color scheme

Ruffles at cuff match frilled shirt collar

Over-the-knee boot held up with straps

Spurs worn over boots

Philip II of Spain By the late 16th century, full plate armor was less common. Philip confined himself to a gold-embellished cuirass, worn more for ceremony than practical protection.

Helmet fit with huge crest

Domed shoulder plate called a pauldron

White knight Robert Radcliffe, Earl of Sussex, wears English armor designed for tournaments in this painting detail c. 1593. The earl has unprotected legs since fighting often took place over a barrier.

HELMET TYPES

Sallets were typical of northern Europe from the mid-15th century. They fit the head except for a point to protect the back of the neck. Close helmets enclosed the head but were light enough to allow movement. They had full visors, neck, and chin guards and became more ornate as their battlefield function lessened. Jousting helmets had sloping sides to deflect lance blows.

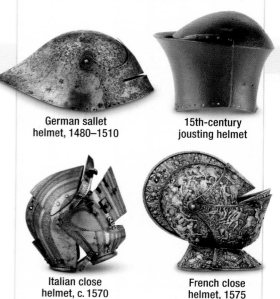

German sallet helmet, 1480–1510

15th-century jousting helmet

Italian close helmet, c. 1570

French close helmet, 1575

1560–1590
ELEGANT FORMALITY

A s the century progressed, so the gradual stiffening of women's dress continued. The increasingly rigid garments needed extra support, and separate boned "pairs of bodies" (stiff undergarments) worn under gowns started to appear—the beginning of stays and corsetry. Linear bands and braids followed the clothing's sharp lines and emphasized its control of body shape. The body's natural lines rarely appeared. The rise and power of the Spanish empire made their severe formality and clever tailoring fashionable, although in many Italian areas a more relaxed, soft look held sway. Ruffs slowly widened and became separate from shirt collars. Labor-intensive lace made its first appearance and became a mark of luxury—similar to velvets or jewels. Necklines were either at bust level or up to the chin. The silhouette stayed triangular with narrow waists ending in sharp points and full skirts. The tops of sleeves of women's dresses started to be styled into puffs, tabs, and rolls. Male and female fashions followed similar trends of adornments, cut, and color.

Spanish *saya* In the 1570s Anna of Austria, Queen of Spain, wore an elegant black *saya* (gown) with white accents and lavish embroidery. The gown's long, pointed sleeves and subtle fit earned Spanish tailors international repute.

High collar with small ruff

Doublet worn underneath

Silver and gold embroidery

ACCESSORIES

The 16th century saw an increase in the variety and adornment of accessories for both men and women. Gloves, made of the finest leather, could be embroidered, and were given as tokens of respect and affection. Fans were popular in hot countries. Linen handkerchiefs were a splendid way to show off the new techniques of needle and bobbin lace. When shoes became visible, their heels and rosettes became equally decorative. Silk and gold ribbons, used in abundance if possible, were also a form of accessory because of their high price.

Low neckline with open partlet

Fashionably blonde hair

Oriental-style veil

Embroidered gloves

Feathered Italian fan

Softer lines This Venetian bride's bodice is rigid and pointed, but her skirt, sleeves, and posture are softer and more relaxed than northern European fashions. Venetian women wore chopines (platform shoes with cork soles) for extra height.

Jeweled aglets (ribbon tips) with silk ribbons

Handkerchief edged with needle lace

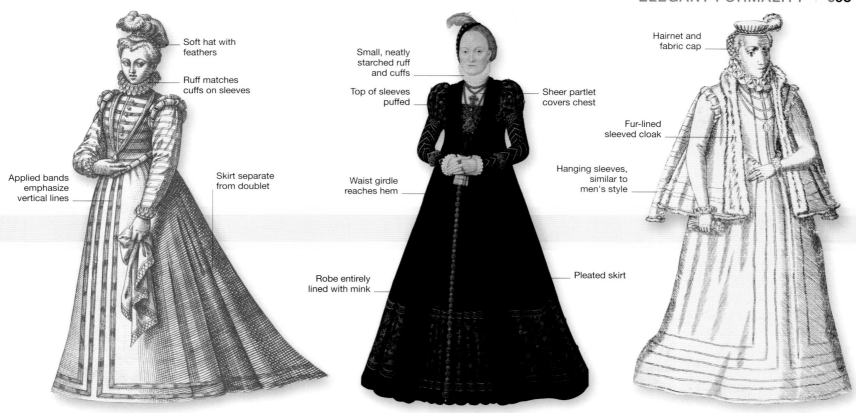

Soft hat with
feathers

Ruff matches
cuffs on sleeves

Applied bands
emphasize
vertical lines

Skirt separate
from doublet

Small, neatly
starched ruff
and cuffs

Top of sleeves
puffed

Sheer partlet
covers chest

Waist girdle
reaches hem

Robe entirely
lined with mink

Pleated skirt

Hairnet and
fabric cap

Fur-lined
sleeved cloak

Hanging sleeves,
similar to
men's style

Masculine style This Flemish ensemble shows how the cut and tailoring of female dress borrowed from male clothing. The doublet has horizontal braid, front buttoning, and shoulder tabs just like a man's.

Saxon Anne, Electress of Saxony, in this painting from c. 1565, wears a short-sleeved fitted robe over a low-necked gown. Her heavy gold jewelry, pleated skirt, and hairnet with cap are typically Saxon.

German woman Other than her head wear, this noblewoman's dress keeps up with fashion in Europe. She wears petticoats without the rigidity of a farthingale. Women below her class or in rural areas dressed in more regional style.

Arched
bodice front

String of pearls

Jeweled
bracelets
and girdle

Silk damask

Cloth-of-gold
petticoat

Curved
French hood

Chemise
shows at
neckline

Typical way of
draping pearls

Sleeves increasing
in size again

Soft folds contrast
with Spanish
severity

Red and gold This sumptuous gown of c. 1575 has an open front over a Spanish farthingale. The short oversleeves could be supported with boning, wire, or wood to create their shape. The sleeves and shoulders are encrusted with embroidery.

Married French noblewoman Mature women covered more of their heads, and widows were totally veiled. This gown's soft, full skirts are lifted above a narrower petticoat. The partlet's open collar is the predecessor of a standing ruff.

HAIRSTYLES

New clothes were costly and time consuming but hair could be changed every day. Another example of the inventive Renaissance love of finery, women's hair during the 16th century was parted in the center, swept over the temples, curled, crimped, arranged over pads to keep the shape, frizzled, bewigged, piled into high peaks, or hidden. In Italy, bleaching hair blonde was particularly popular, as in the drawing of the Venetian woman below. Hair on the back of the head was curled up in braids and became a support for hats and headdresses, attached with pins. Women added jewels, ribbons, and feathers, like the ribbons perched on Anne of Denmark's fluffy mounds of hair.

Venetian woman   **Anne of Denmark**

FASHION ICON

ELIZABETH I

Daughter of Anne Boleyn and Henry VIII, Elizabeth I ruled England between 1558 and 1603. She inherited many of her father's characteristics, including clever use of image and clothing to cement power and excite the adoration of her people. Her wardrobe was legendary, recorded in portraits that publicized the Protestant queen's self-made mythology. Some of her gowns even went on display in the Tower of London during her lifetime to impress foreign visitors. Her shrewdness, intelligence, and ruthlessness made her a political force, just as the magnificence of huge ruffs trimmed with devastatingly expensive handmade lace; enormous embroidered sleeves; and large, structured, bejeweled stomachers turned her into a glittering fashion icon who loved to be admired.

The language of dress

Elizabeth emphasized her tall, slender frame—and her status—with regal headdresses. French hoods and jeweled caps were the perfect foil to set off her flaming red hair. An iconic hairstyle saw her curls twisted over supports to frame her face like a heart with two large puffs on either side. Haloes of pearls and gold outlined the edges of the hairstyle.

Symbolism made Elizabeth's dress and accessories even more compelling. Pearls—worn as long ropes, seed pearls, and pendant drops—were a favorite. As a symbol of purity and chastity they were most appropriate for this Virgin Queen who put her nation before personal happiness. She wears them in almost every portrait from the age of 13, when she was painted wearing sumptuous red silk damask and furs. Her love of fashion, ornament, luxury velvets, damasks, and brocades as well as her use of striking colors finally found expression when she became queen at 25. Elizabeth favored red,

gold, and silver to complement her pure white complexion and ruddy hair color. She adopted black and white as her personal colors—a dramatic background for her jewelry and long, elegant fingers. A poet described her as coming in "like starlight, thick with jewels." Other symbolic items included a phoenix pendant—the fabled bird that rose from the ashes and spoke of the Queen's uniqueness, power, and chastity.

If her dress sometimes appeared overwhelmingly magnificent to foreign tastes, from the 1560s Elizabeth's dominant personality, expressed through clothing, breathed new life into fashion—it was much more staid and darker before her reign. She encouraged her courtiers to dress splendidly—especially the men, who could win her favors with an elegant leg, beautiful clothes, and flattering gifts of gloves, gauzy scarves, and rare jewels.

With such a monarch, 16th-century English people embraced lavish fashions. Although none of Elizabeth's clothing survives, account books unfold luscious descriptions of the queen of fashion's staggering wardrobe.

A royal legacy

Elizabeth's self-fashioning was so successful that she remains an icon in modern times. Her image has been developed in movies and television series and inspired designers. The tight bodices, bold shapes, huge ruffs, and regal aura have fed into the work of fashion designers as diverse as Jean Paul Gaultier, Martin Margiela, and Vivienne Westwood. Westwood, for example, has showcased slashed fabric; large, regal gowns; ruffs, and enormous collars, while many generally "futurist" fashions feature arrestingly angular shapes reminiscent of Elizabethan style.

△ **THE RAINBOW PORTRAIT** c.1600
In this late portrait in mask costume, Elizabeth wears a fantastic headdress inspired by an engraving of Greek women's dress. The eyes and ears painted on her mantle and the jeweled serpent on her sleeve may symbolize fame and wisdom respectively. She holds a rainbow, seen in many of her clothes, perhaps suggesting heavenly ideals.

◁ **DRESS BY ALEXANDER McQUEEN**
The enduring influence of Elizabeth I is clear in this McQueen dress. It features a high neck ruff and sleeves with the built-up shoulder and narrow, trimmed cuff reminiscent of Elizabethan gowns.

TIMELINE

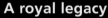

1533 Born at Greenwich, near London

1536 Her mother, Anne Boleyn, is executed. Elizabeth is declared illegitimate. A later Act of Parliament restores her right to succeed to the throne

1558 ▽ Becomes queen. Her coronation robes of 1559 were of cloth-of-gold (fabric woven with gold-wrapped thread) trimmed with ermine, with a tight, pointed bodice

1559 Becomes head of the Church of England, replacing her sister Mary's Catholicism with the Protestant faith

1560s Taking a lead from Elizabeth's delight in clothes, English fashions become more decorated and full of novelty

1580s Inspires English trends for extravagant, exaggerated dress

1581 Knights Francis Drake on his return from a world voyage. Trade links foster the fashion for exotic fabrics and ornament

c.1595 ▽ Embraces all the new fashions, like larger ruffs seen in this gold pound coin

1603 Dies at Richmond, near London

O 1530　　O 1550　　O 1570　　O 1590　　O 1610

1590–1625
FEMALE GEOMETRY

With the onset of the 17th century, every aspect of women's clothes became highly exaggerated—and borrowed heavily from masculine styles. Fashion history's most geometric period created unnatural silhouettes made from straight lines, triangles, and circles. Huge ruffs isolated head from body, or open collars revealed décolletages cut immodestly low. The French farthingale (a wheel-shaped support worn over the hips) made women the widest and squarest they had ever been. It also shortened hems to make feet—in new, heeled shoes—visible for the first time. These skirts marked France's ascent as Europe's fashion leader. Around 1620, a new naturalism appeared and styles relaxed again. By 1625 the long, pointed "bodies" (bodice) had been virtually replaced by a natural waistline, and petticoats took over from farthingales.

Hair in two arches over temples

Neck area covered by partlet

Stomacher

Large sleeves with pinking

Pointed, stiffened bodice

Stiffened open collar

Triangular stomacher In the 1580s as the woman's upper garment (bodice) lengthened and the gown opened, the central space was covered with a triangular piece called a stomacher. It was another surface to embellish.

Stiff petticoat with less fabric

Revealing bust line

Ribbon rosette as decoration

Silk brocade with silver and gold threads

French farthingale

Tightly fitted sleeves like men's doublet

Widest size of double ruff, starched blue

Silk taffeta skirt with gold embroidery

Masculine-style hat with lace

Extended, curved bodice front

Silk petticoat showing

Cartwheel ruff Flemish artist Rubens painted his wife, Isabella Brandt, wearing this huge ruff edged with lace. Ruffs achieved their greatest width in the Low Countries, where starching techniques originated. The low, curved bodice front also became a regional style.

Large, dyed feather fan

French farthingale Anne of Denmark, the English queen, epitomizes women's fashion in the early 17th century with a low, round neck, transparent, lacy collars and cuffs, and carnation-colored accents. The farthingale's tabletop effect has transformed her gown's silhouette.

Skirt's length taken up by farthingale; shoes visible for first time

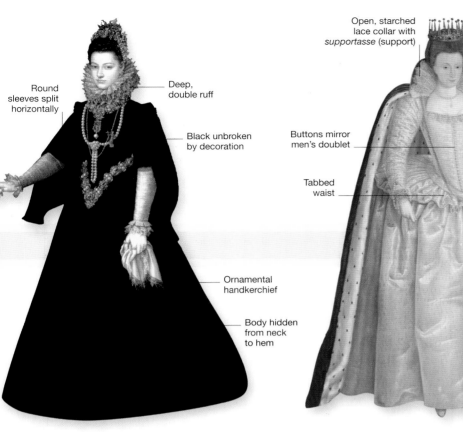

Round sleeves split horizontally

Deep, double ruff

Black unbroken by decoration

Ornamental handkerchief

Body hidden from neck to hem

The triangle's apex In the 1590s Spanish hairstyles rose to a point, completing the triangular effect of the costume. Infanta Isabella Clara Eugenia's high neckline and bell-shaped skirt were a contrast to revealing squarer fashions in neighboring countries.

Open, starched lace collar with *supportasse* (support)

Ceremonial velvet mantle with ermine lining

Buttons mirror men's doublet

Tabbed waist

Elongated bodice

Satin pinked all over

Pinned into shape At the time of this painting in 1605, women's clothing was held together with pins. The Countess of Southampton's ladies would have pinned her gown up over the farthingale, her stomacher to her stays, and her collar open.

SLASHING

Deliberately cutting into textiles was one of the defining features of Renaissance fashion. The slashes could be long and careless, or neatly cut lines that gaped to reveal underclothing. Isabel de Valois's spectacular red wedding dress has slashed sleeves with bound edges. Pinking—cutting zigzag or rippled lines, or making small, neat regular holes—was particularly popular on leather.

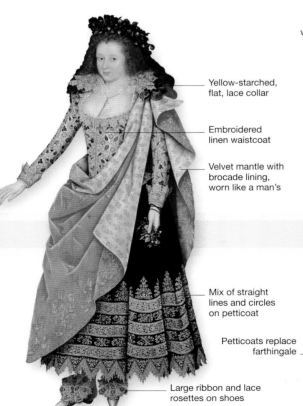

Yellow-starched, flat, lace collar

Embroidered linen waistcoat

Velvet mantle with brocade lining, worn like a man's

Mix of straight lines and circles on petticoat

Petticoats replace farthingale

Large ribbon and lace rosettes on shoes

Smooth lines for a masque The Countess of Hertford has composed an allegorical ensemble from the less formal petticoat and a linen waistcoat, worn over stays to create a smooth torso. Both are elaborately embroidered with stylized forms.

Diadem with white feathers

Ruff, cuffs, and shift show off lace

Waistline nearly at natural level

Italian silk skirt embroidered with gold opens to reveal embroidered petticoat

Embroidered leather shoes

Softening shape This English portrait shows how, around 1620, fashion's inflexibility started to yield. The exquisitely embroidered gown is still linear with pattern on every surface, but is more softly draped, with gathers and curves.

Shoulders and waist lengthened with tabs

Double ruff breaks triangular line

Small-scale motifs

Floor-length, pointed sleeves

Surfaces and angles Spanish dress was slower to change than other nations' fashions. The planes of clothing became even more rigid and angular. Surfaces became smoother and inflexible, showing off the colors, textures, and decoration.

1550–1590
A NEW SUIT

By the late 16th century a "three-piece suit" of doublet, jerkin, and hose with a cloak or robe over the top was worn uniformly by European men. Breeches, trunk hose, and upper stocks were names for trousers in an increasing variety of styles—split-leg garments were definitively male. Although the silhouette moved closer to the rounded lines of the body, careful tailoring and padding helped exaggerate masculine areas such as shoulders, groin, and thighs. Even the most dashing, virile men enjoyed using elaborate textiles and accessories such as earrings, pendants, feathers, and embroidery to express themselves. The dandy and the adventurer coexisted happily; elegant men were expected to dance and write poetry as well as fence, ride, or take a role in politics.

Sleeve puffed at top

Jeweled aglets (tags)

Generous padding and shaping

Gold embroidery

Calf turned out in "making a leg" stance

Slashed white leather shoes were popular

Horizontal braid on doublet helps hold shape

Clean, tailored lines

Leather hat—crown getting higher

Beginning of peascod (padded "pouter pigeon") belly

Separate ruff

Prominent codpiece

Doublet front starting to curve out

Long cloak for weather protection

Clear division between each body part

Small flat cap

Puffed sleeves on outer gown

Braid defines edges

Paned breeches

Tightly fitting silk stockings

Light and shade This portrait of Philip II of Spain shows how the earlier wide shoulders begin to narrow from the 1550s. The dramatic effect of contrasting and extensive gold embroidery enhance his prestige.

Travel wear Water-resistant longer cloaks covered valuable clothing and unprotected legs. Hats kept in warmth and brims deflected rain. This Low Countries gentleman from around 1580 wears a skirted jerkin that nearly covers his breeches.

Spanish style The horizontal lines decorating the doublet of Don Carlos of Spain in 1564 are typical of the Spanish style. Lines of stitching and heavy braid reinforce the shape. His satin cloak has bands of slashed black velvet as subtle decoration.

Elegant posing This Venetian man's counterpoint pose suggests classical grace. Wearing clothes well was as important as the clothes themselves. His entirely black ensemble accentuates his pale legs just as the white collar highlights his face.

Knit cap

Longer beard for older man

Cut hanging sleeve

Older style of coat

Breeches lining drops below knee

Flat shoes

Longer robes As in the Middle Ages, older men tended to wear longer robes and outer garments. This Germanic man of about 1580 wears a short robe and drooping breeches that would have looked dated to fashionable contemporaries.

Cap in local style

Black background sets off gold embroidery

Gold jewelry popular in Saxony

Holding gloves

Complete ensemble In this painting from the mid-1560s, August, Elector of Saxony, has wide embroidered gold bands delineating the edges of his cloak, skirted jerkin, and paned breeches, which emphasize the shapes of his Lutheran clothing. Like Catholic rulers, he favors black.

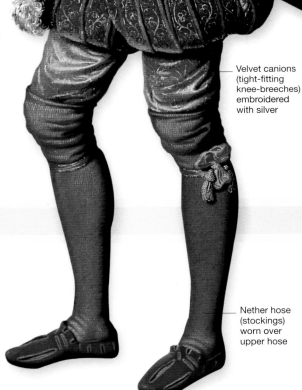

Frayed edges

Figured satin jerkin and doublet

Sleeves cut to natural arm bend

Velvet canions (tight-fitting knee-breeches) embroidered with silver

Nether hose (stockings) worn over upper hose

Statesman in red In this 1560 painting, Italian Gian Gerolamo Grumelli wears red from head to foot, though each element is subtly different. A variety of textiles—satin, velvet, leather—and clever surface embellishment give a distinct look to each part of his body.

Doublet tied under shoulder roll

Small, ruffled collar

Exaggerated hips with stuffed upper hose

Long, slim legs

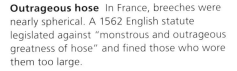

Outrageous hose In France, breeches were nearly spherical. A 1562 English statute legislated against "monstrous and outrageous greatness of hose" and fined those who wore them too large.

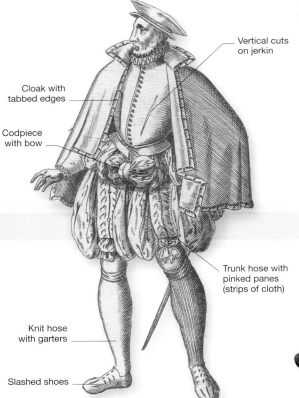

Vertical cuts on jerkin

Cloak with tabbed edges

Codpiece with bow

Trunk hose with pinked panes (strips of cloth)

Knit hose with garters

Slashed shoes

Cutting on every surface This drawing of a German man from the 1570s combines most types of decoratively cut cloth in his ensemble. Slashing was an effective way of adding surface detail and was cheaper than embroidery or braid.

FRIVOLITY AT COURT

Henri III, who reigned as King of Poland-Lithuania from 1573–1575, and of France from 1574–1589, was an elegant, cultured young man who adored clothes and dressing up. He demanded the highest standards of dress from his courtiers, especially the effeminate, frivolous young men in his entourage called *Les Mignons* (Darlings). They plucked their eyebrows, powdered their faces, and adopted feminine accessories such as small dogs and muffs. His mistresses wore the kind of exuberant dress seen in this ball painting. The flat French farthingale, would-be lovers complained, kept men at a distance, as did huge stuffed sleeves. The turned-back fronts of gowns revealed white bosoms above sharply pointed bodices supported by whalebone. Both sexes indulged in luxuries, such as exquisite lace, perfume, and jewelry— Henri was noted for his pearl earrings.

Henri lightened the austere Spanish influence at the French court. Men and women wore such vast starched ruffs that people told courtiers they looked like John the Baptist's head on the platter. From his time as Polish king Henri brought back fuller breeches called Venetians or Polacks, as well as small Polish caps decorated with gems and aigrettes. Once, he galloped through Paris's streets with 30 young men all dressed alike in Italian-inspired pantaloons. Banquets where men dressed as women and vice versa, or spectacular balls where male clothing outshone female, show Henri III's appetite for fun, novelty, pleasure, and flair—the essence of fashion.

> **“**
>
> … exceedingly odious, as much by their foolish and haughty demeanor, as by their effeminate and immodest dress …
>
> **CONTEMPORARY CHRONICLER PIERRE DE L'ESTOILE DESCRIBING THE KING'S FAVORITES, 1576**
>
> **”**

◁ **EVENING BALL FOR THE WEDDING OF THE DUC DE JOYEUSE, 1581–1582**
Henri III is third from the left, wearing black, next to his mother Catherine de Medici. The rare full-length and back views convey all the vivacity of court fashion during his reign.

1590–1624
MALE EXTRAVAGANCE

As the tailor's art improved, the male body took on perfectly straight, rigid lines like those of armor, but created with cloth. Even soft ruffs were straighter, or disappeared in favor of straight collars. The new clothing changed the way people moved. Rigid torso garments with padded areas and exaggerated lines made it difficult to slouch or bend, though clever cutting left the limbs free to help men stride and indulge in manly pursuits such as fighting and riding. Fashionable men and women were equally matched in their ostentatious display of decoration. Both sexes coveted silk stockings, rosettes, ribbons, sashes, jewels, perfumed buttons, and, particularly, lace. Rich men could—and did—pour fortunes into their dress, or seek a fortune at court through the beauty of their appearance and grace in "making a leg." Fashion moved from purely geometric lines to a new relaxed style by the 1620s, as breeches and hair lengthened again.

Tailored geometry James I wears a suit with straight lines achieved by stiffened, tailored clothing. The doublet's buttons emphasize its precise lines, echoed by the cloak and the paned breeches. His square collar replaces the round ruff, and his shoes have the new latchet closing.

Straight doublet front

Hat brim widening

Falling band collar

Padded breeches

Stockings over tight hose

Latchet shoes with rosette

Large lace standing band with *supportasse*

Draped cloak has stiff lining covered with silk

Glove gauntlets match doublet

Deep, needle-lace cuffs

Velvet cloak with imported fur

Striking a pose Men wore their short cloaks in many stylish ways: sideways, upside down, with the sleeves on their necks, or slung over one shoulder. This Burgundian man has a typical swaggering pose and air of active virility.

Round, felt or leather hat with feather

Starched ruff

Pearl necklace

Petticoat breeches

Exaggerated curves and body line

Cloak (with sleeves) worn backward

Silver-gilt garter ends

Silver-gilt lace rosettes

Heeled shoes with rosettes

Huge expense In this 1613 painting by William Larkin, Edward Sackville's entire outfit reveals his wealth and position as the 4th Earl of Dorset. Each separate part of his body is decorated or increased in size. An ensemble like this one could cost as much as a house.

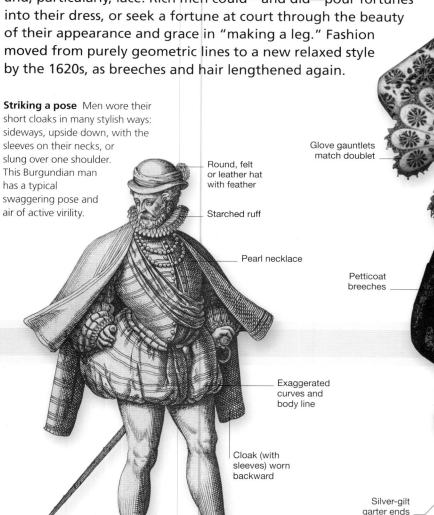

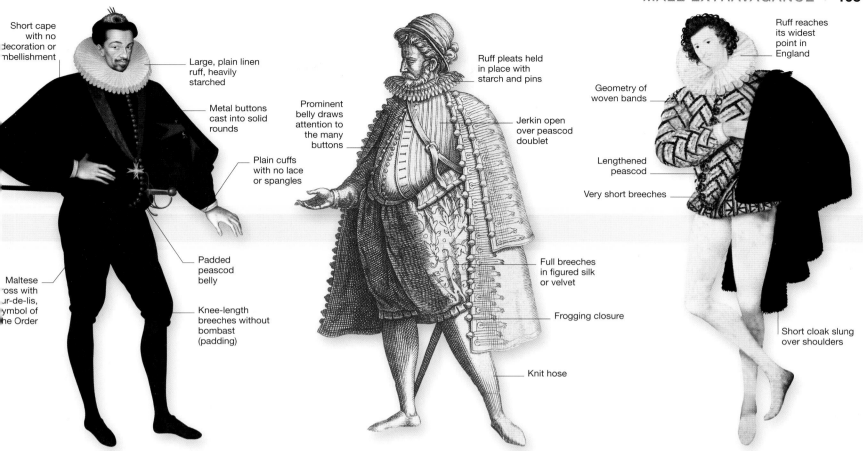

Short cape with no decoration or embellishment

Large, plain linen ruff, heavily starched

Metal buttons cast into solid rounds

Plain cuffs with no lace or spangles

Prominent belly draws attention to the many buttons

Padded peascod belly

Maltese cross with fleur-de-lis, symbol of the Order

Knee-length breeches without bombast (padding)

Ruff pleats held in place with starch and pins

Jerkin open over peascod doublet

Full breeches in figured silk or velvet

Frogging closure

Knit hose

Ruff reaches its widest point in England

Geometry of woven bands

Lengthened peascod

Very short breeches

Short cloak slung over shoulders

Dark majesty King Henri III of France wears the garb of the Order of the Holy Spirit, which he started in 1578. The blue ribbons used to hold the Order's medallion may be the origin of the phrase "cordon bleu" for excellence.

Eastern influences This Frenchman wears longer upper breeches, called Venetians, in patterned fabric. The frogging closures on his robe follow Eastern fashions, sometimes referred to as Polish style in western Europe.

Youthful beauty A fashionable young Englishman displays his elegant legs under very short paned breeches. The artful draping of his sleeved cloak over one shoulder and his careful posture suggest a studied poetic melancholy.

Order of the Garter

Satin suit pinked with holes all over

Stocking tops turned over garters

Courtly style An English courtier shows off his well-shaped legs, part of the taste, grace, and cultured skills essential at court. A man's physical appearance could make or break him, so stylish clothing of excellent quality was vital to success.

TAILORING

In this period, cut, as much as fabric and decoration, became a mark of taste. Skillful tailoring did much to improve the wearer's appearance through fit. Stiffening and padding—a harder shell around a soft core—made the clothed body very different from the natural one. Different materials helped to create rigidity: linen, buckram (stiffened linen cloth), cardboard, and parchment, and various weaves of wool. Stuffing with bran, horsehair, or unspun fleece created large, unnatural shapes.

Pattern books from the 1580s onward reveal the tricks of subtle cutting and economical fabric use. Basic tailors' tools from the period are still used today: measuring stick, chalk, pins, and shears (right).

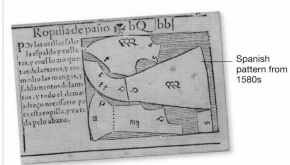

Spanish pattern from 1580s

Juan de Alcega's pattern book

Late 1560s Italian portrait of a tailor

1450–1624
TRADING IN TREASURES

The Renaissance period was an age of expansion. Explorers setting out from Europe discovered "New" worlds in the Americas and improved sea trading routes into Asia. Now fashion became global as luxurious new commodities flooded into the West, and better transportation made them available to wealthy people. Silver, gold, and cochineal beetles for dyeing made the fortune of the Spanish empire. Precious rare materials, such as aloeswood and civet glands for perfumes, and ebony wood, ivory, and ostrich feathers, became more accessible. The explosion in printing also spread knowledge to new audiences, including once-secret apothecary recipes and images of the unfamiliar, exotic inhabitants and fauna of foreign lands.

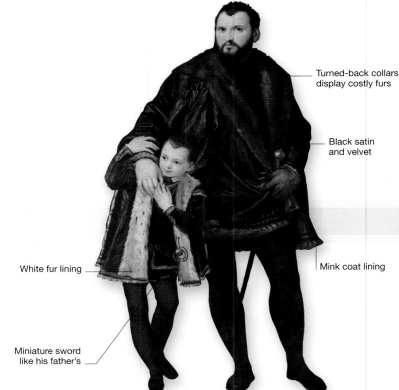

Turned-back collars display costly furs

Black satin and velvet

Mink coat lining

White fur lining

Miniature sword like his father's

Fur-lined cloaks Demand for fur sent traders to Muscovy (Russia) and Africa to source exotic pelts for European customers. With discoveries of new animals such as the beaver in North America, skins for hats were shipped back across the Atlantic.

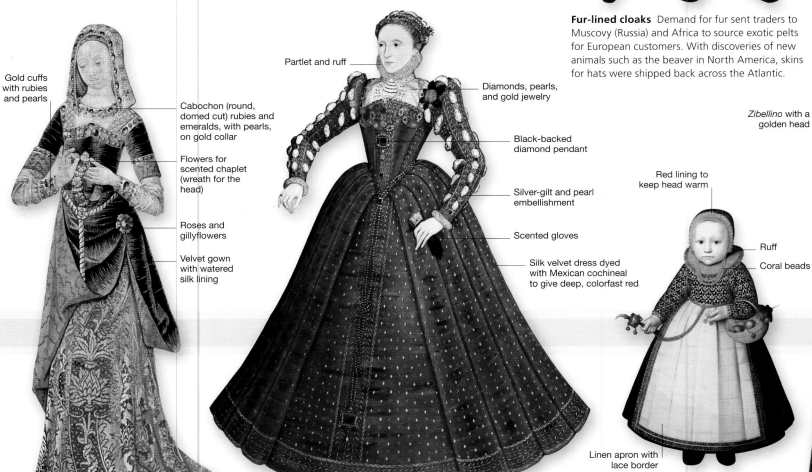

Gold cuffs with rubies and pearls

Cabochon (round, domed cut) rubies and emeralds, with pearls, on gold collar

Flowers for scented chaplet (wreath for the head)

Roses and gillyflowers

Velvet gown with watered silk lining

Partlet and ruff

Diamonds, pearls, and gold jewelry

Black-backed diamond pendant

Silver-gilt and pearl embellishment

Scented gloves

Silk velvet dress dyed with Mexican cochineal to give deep, colorfast red

Zibellino with a golden head

Red lining to keep head warm

Ruff

Coral beads

Linen apron with lace border

Tapestry dyes This woman, from a late 15th-century tapestry, links flowers to create a perfumed chaplet. Her clothes are woven using the finest red dyes from Europe and the Americas to make stable reds. Under her gown she wears a shimmering cloth-of-gold lampas skirt.

Rich red and royal diamonds The world's only known diamond source during the Renaissance was Golkonda in India, and the gems were exceedingly valuable. Queen Elizabeth I, shown here, accentuated her status with copious jewelry, including two large diamonds with black backing.

Coral beads Wealthy families prized coral, from the Mediterranean around Italy and the African coast, as a charm to protect children from illness and the evil eye. The fine quality of this girl's clothing, like that of a miniature adult, shows great expense—especially her silver and ivory rattle.

Lynx lining Veronese's portrait of Countess Livia da Porto re-creates the depth of her lynx fur–lined robe. Over her arm is a *zibellino*—an Italian accessory made from the whole skin of a marten or mink, which was popular around 1551, the date of this painting.

Pearl necklace

Lynx fur lining

Girl dressed in floor-length robe similar to her mother's

Satin coat with embroidery

Gold earring

Cloak worn sideways, also popular in Europe

Layers of bright feathers

European jug

Fabric woven with gold

Deep pleats of silk and gold textiles

New World feathers Indigenous Americans had ways of making intricate pictures and clothing, such as capes, using native feathers. Colonists brought these ideas and materials to Europe and used them in new styles of adornment.

Many ostrich feathers

Hairnet and cap

Gold neck chokers and chains

Sleeve slit at elbow and paned to show off fine linen shirt

Large, tablet-woven silk and gold girdle

Lapdog for warmth, status, and company

Ostrich feathers No expense is spared in the Duchess of Saxony's 1515 ensemble, recorded by Cranach the Elder. African ostrich feathers adorn her hat, heavy gold necklaces with black diamonds crowd her neck, and gold is used wherever possible on her gown.

PEARLS

For the aristocracy, pearls were the most favored jewel during this period. Women wore long strands as necklaces, worked them into their hair, and embroidered them into clothing. Men also wore earrings, brooches, hatpins, and other pearl adornments. Religious vestments incorporated the splendid luster of pearls. They were even crushed in cosmetic recipes to beautify the skin.

Pearls were sourced laboriously from salt-water oysters around India and Arabia. Their mysterious appearance made them highly valuable, with irregular shapes set into great pendants.

1450–1624

SYMBOLISM AND FANTASY

The Renaissance world revolved around emblems, iconography, and allegories, and people delighted in using these symbolic representations in dress. Almost any animal, plant, god, object, color, or foreign fashion could be used metaphorically to say something more than itself. At a time when most people could not read, visual meanings were especially important. Medieval heraldry had established symbols as distinctive badges of houses and families. Personal iconography became a poetic, decorative language using emblems such as knots, phoenixes, carnations, and lilies to show a person's virtues along with other abstract ideas. These could be embroidered or painted on to clothing, or worked into jewelry or armor. Characters from religion and classical mythology were popular allegorical themes, often used to convey hidden moral or political messages. At masques (theatrical court entertainments) and costume balls, costumes were an opportunity to draw on different cultures.

Pictish warrior woman
This naked woman is a fanciful take on classical Greek mythology and Celtic folklore. Tales of the Picts' painted skins inspired the floral tattooing in the contemporary Elizabethan style. Prints spread a mix of accurate and imaginary ideas about foreign or past cultures across Europe.

Pose like a classical statue

Loose, "uncivilized" hair

Fanciful floral tattoos

Spear reflects Elizabethan idea of Amazon tribeswoman

Skin looks like embroidery

Orientalist hat

Sculpted leather mask

Fantasy headdress

Small mask as token disguise

Courtesan showing off beautiful clothes

Harlequin costume with fleur-de-lis and Templar crosses

Puffed sleeves did not exist in normal dress

Exotic tunic and tassels

Bright colors and symbols, probably printed

Overskirt made of fine linen panes held together with buttons

Sword signifies Catherine's martyrdom

Venetian carnival Masquerade balls were a chance to throw off social convention and change roles through disguises. The Italian comedy theater *commedia dell'arte* introduced stock characters like Harlequin and Pantalone as popular costumes.

Holy fantasy dress Artists used inventive imaginary dress in their pictures of female saints, like this c. 1500 Flemish depiction of Saint Catherine. Oriental elements such as drapery and tassels helped conjure an out-of-this world biblical setting.

RED AND BLACK

Color itself was a symbol with complex meanings. The most prized shades were true black and crimson or scarlet. Red denoted power and was used by royalty, nobility, and religious authorities, such as the pope and his cardinals above.

Following 16th-century religious divisions, members of both the Catholic and Protestant churches used black to show their piety, humility, and restraint. But dyeing cloth a deep, rich black was expensive in terms of time and ingredients, so the color was also a fashionable way to show off wealth alongside spiritual values.

Starched lace standing band collar

Gilt braid

Suns, moons, and stars embroidered on panes (strips of cloth)

Embroidered, vivid silk stockings

Silk rosettes

Iconographic suit English courtiers like Richard Sackville, 3rd Earl of Dorset, delighted in playing with symbols on their clothing to send messages about their family, virtues, and political allegiances. Celestial motifs denoting the heavens were popular, like those on Sackville's hose.

Wired silk hoops

Open lace ruff with *supportasse*

Embroidered panels

Painted silk petticoat

The natural world The lustrous petticoat and stomacher of Elizabeth I have been painted with exquisite, naturalistic pictures of plants and animals. Some are mythical, but most are real, indicating the queen's knowledge of the natural world, including strange sea creatures.

Conical hat with silk veil

Long, loose hair

Open robe like a caftan

Soft, flat slippers

Masque costume This unknown lady of the 1590s is dressed as the Persian maiden from Boissard's 1581 costume book. Artists drew on illustrations of exotic costume as a design resource. Boissard's book inspired architect Inigo Jones's famous masque costumes.

BLACKWORK AND EMBROIDERY

As undergarments peeped out from clothing in the 15th century, Italian and Spanish needlework was used to embellish the visible edges. Blackwork is the English name for an embroidery technique using red or black silk thread in geometric, stylized patterns on linen garments for both sexes, such as shirts, smocks, coifs, and caps.

After the idea came to England local needlewomen built on the technique. By the Elizabethan and Jacobean periods, complex twining patterns of naturalistic plants and animals covered outer clothing in a tangle of multicolor designs accented with gold. The exuberance contrasted with the geometric formalism of garments.

1450–1624
PRACTICAL CLOTHING

Renaissance fashion, for the rich, was a riot of silks, velvets, and jewels. However, for the vast majority—peasants working the land, traders, or part of the growing class of the "middling sort" including merchants and landed gentry—garments tended to be less fitted and exaggerated, and better suited to daily life. Linen and wool were staple fabrics—wool could be spun and woven at home. Silk was a rare luxury. As in any era, people wore the best they could afford. Subtle hierarchies of cloth qualities were used to distinguish between coarse, sturdy everyday wear and finer, best garments. Producing fabric was labor intensive, so cutting out the expense and time of dyeing made sense. Clothing styles for the ordinary people changed over time, but slowly, since garments were replaced less often.

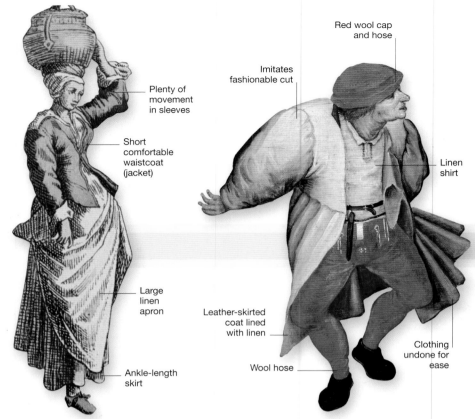

Plenty of movement in sleeves

Short comfortable waistcoat (jacket)

Large linen apron

Ankle-length skirt

Red wool cap and hose

Imitates fashionable cut

Linen shirt

Leather-skirted coat lined with linen

Wool hose

Clothing undone for ease

Waistcoat and petticoat This French peasant from the early 17th century wears a comfortable, practical outfit. She uses linen garments like her shirt and apron to protect her skirt. The thick linen scarf or cap helps stabilize the jar.

Occasion wear Brueghel's cheerful dancing man wears his best red cap and hose for a special occasion. He is dressed in fewer pieces of clothing than nobility, but the cut is not radically different.

USEFUL FABRICS

Holes punched in star shapes

Zigzag pinking cut stops fraying

Leather jerkin

Leather was a practical choice because it was tough, protective, and needed little stitching. Aside from shoes, leather was used for aprons, purses, doublets, coats, and jerkins, like this late 16th-century example for a young man. This jerkin has been pinked and cut with star shapes for embellishment and to make it more flexible. Strong wool fabrics were also popular, often left in their natural color.

Linen cap

Tabbed shoulders

Loose shirt and collar

Linen sleeves

Garment tied around waist

Flat, coarse leather shoes

Old-fashioned hood

Wicker basket

Dark clothes—undyed or dirty

Torn clothing

Ankle boots

Following fashion Musicians wore more fashionable costume than peasants. The tabbed shoulders and paned sleeves of this musician's gown reflect early 17th-century French fashion.

Poor clothing The aging "Everyman" from a painting by Bosch of 1515 wears a drab coat and wrinkled torn hose, with a black doublet and hood, and a traveling basket. His shoes are typical ankle boots fitting the foot's shape.

High hat
with feather

Dark,
cheap dye

No decoration

Shorter-length
coat easy to
move in

Hose falling
down from
walking

Patches and
repairs

Untied pants
showing linen
underwear

Undyed
leather

Shoes without
stylish toes

Fashionable cap
shape in plain linen

Small amount of
expensive velvet

Velvet cuff

Skirt
hooked up
for walking

Wool dress

Tasseled
sash

Red wool kirtle

Hat to
protect skin

Linen veil for
older woman

Mantle

Feathers in
wide-rimmed hat

Linen
collar with
needlework

Turned-back
cuffs

Warm, sturdy,
knee-high boots

Chopines of cork

Rural worker In this picture from the 1570s
the worker's coat still has large shoulders and
a longer skirt similar to styles earlier in the
century. Woven stockings—less elastic than
knit ones—reveal his knees.

Unlaced hose Bosch's figure of c. 1480 reveals
the practice of untying the points connecting
doublet and hose when working. Without elastic,
the ties gave no ease for bending. His leather
doublet is torn at the elbow and has been repaired.

Modest mantle An older woman in the
1570s wears the respectable black mantle
that was used in Spain by many social levels.
Her skirt reveals her stockings and *chopines*
(high platform shoes).

Buttoned coat A Frenchman selling on the
streets in the early 17th century wears a long
coat with wider sleeves. His collar has a stylish
shape with decorative edging. The outfit is a
less elaborate version of contemporary fashions.

Middle-class quality Hans Holbein's
close observation of a young woman's ensemble
suggests quality, not extravagance. Her gown uses
plenty of fabric yet is carefully held up for walking.
Her cap is plain but has elaborate veiling.

1450–1624
OTTOMAN FINERY

The Ottomans conquered Constantinople (now Istanbul) in 1453 and made it the center of a vast empire. Their territory covered most of southeast Europe, stretching to the edges of Austria and Poland-Lithuania, and included Hungary and the Balkans. Clothing in all these areas showed a strong oriental influence in long robes, horizontal fastenings, and turbans. Venetian fashion also drew on Eastern ideas through trade with Byzantium. Muslim Ottomans continued to wear the flowing garments of earlier centuries—a contrast with the growing Western passion for fitted, separate, rigid clothing. Ottoman dress used fewer, simpler garments and depended more on nuances of fine-quality textiles and embroidery than novelties of fashion. The most obviously foreign difference was that women in Eastern areas often wore trousers, while in the West, European split-leg garments were exclusively male.

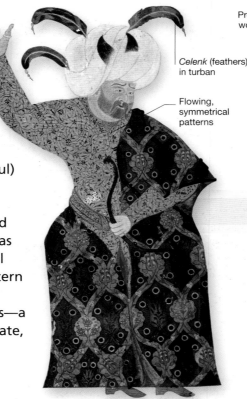

Intricate silks A miniature of Selim II shows off the lavish colors and sinuous patterns of his clothing. Caftans' large surfaces were ideal for showcasing quality textiles, which expressed prestige and power rather than fashionable cut.

- *Celenk* (feathers) in turban
- Flowing, symmetrical patterns

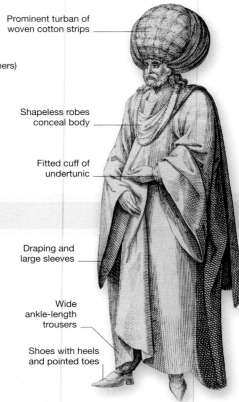

Turbans and loose tunics Turbans were the most significant point of difference between Western and Eastern dress. This Armenian nobleman's draped clothing is in sharp contrast to contemporary tailored fashion.

- Prominent turban of woven cotton strips
- Shapeless robes conceal body
- Fitted cuff of undertunic
- Draping and large sleeves
- Wide ankle-length trousers
- Shoes with heels and pointed toes

TEXTILES

Constantinople had long been a trading center for textiles to Europe. Likewise, Ottoman merchants imported costly silk velvets from Genoa, Venice, and France. Local textile weaving used the stylized, two-dimensional motifs of Islamic art in harmonious repetition and striking color combinations. Venetian Gentile Bellini's painting of a Turkish scribe, made when he visited the Ottoman court around 1480, shows a pomegranate motif and richly contrasting fabrics.

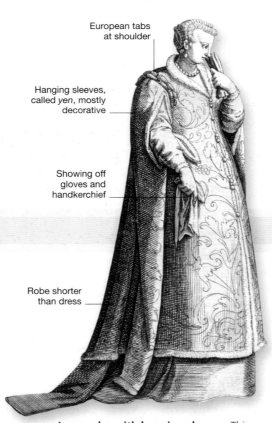

Long robe with hanging sleeves This courtesan from Padua wears a fur-lined brocade robe with central button closure. Elements of Eastern or caftan styles had become usual in European clothing by the late 16th century.

- European tabs at shoulder
- Hanging sleeves, called *yen*, mostly decorative
- Showing off gloves and handkerchief
- Robe shorter than dress

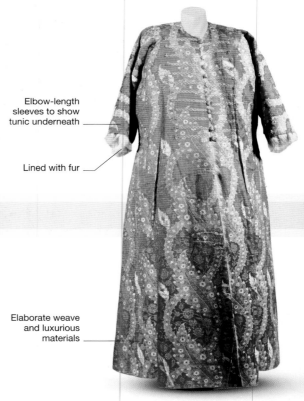

Royal caftan This late 15th-century silk and gold damask caftan belonged to Sultan Beyazid II. Caftan were the main garment worn by Ottoman men and women and eastward into Persia (now Iran) and central Asia. Cut, length, and width varied.

- Elbow-length sleeves to show tunic underneath
- Lined with fur
- Elaborate weave and luxurious materials

Small turban badly tied around fez hat

Russian fur-lined black satin caftan

Silk damask robe

Flat leather slippers

A la turque Around 1617, Rubens painted Nicolas de Raspaigne, a Flemish merchant trading in Constantinople, in garments that are probably genuinely Turkish. The portrait shows the European vogue for wearing oriental dress.

Tall peaked headdress

Long silk or linen veil

Natural waist marked with sash

Fringed scarf

Overgown split at sides

Rhodes blend Ottoman-ruled regions such as Greece mixed clothing ideas from many places. This courtesan wears soft robes but not the trousers and tight caftans of Ottoman women. The artist may have added imaginary touches.

Flat peaked hat

Horizontal frogging

Turkish-style waist sash

Flowing cape

Knee-high boots with heels

Hungarian style A 1577 Dutch costume plate of eastern European peoples shows the strong Turkish influence on clothing in the area. This man displays similar style details to those of Ottoman male dress.

BAROQUE
AND ROCOCO

1625–1789

BAROQUE AND ROCOCO

O pulence, grandeur, heavy ornamentation, and rich colors were the defining characteristics of fashion throughout Europe in the 17th century. No one demonstrated this baroque style to greater effect than King Carl Gustav of Sweden, who wore such a richly decorated doublet at his coronation in 1654 that the fabric beneath the embroidery was completely invisible. The baroque style was set at the royal court in France, where the stiff-bodiced, heavy-skirted court dress known as the *grand habit* was established in the splendor of Louis XIV's Versailles. The fabrics for these stately clothes were produced across Europe, but the French silk industry, centered in Lyon, dominated. Farther afield, the influx of goods from Asia via trading organizations such as the Dutch East India Company, founded in 1602, meant that printed cottons and painted silks from India and China flooded the European fashion market.

Rococo lightness

By the 18th century, there was a move in the decorative arts toward a lighter, more flowing aesthetic known as the rococo, which was reflected in fashion. This could be seen in the curving lines of the silk designs produced by such craftspeople as Anna Maria Garthwaite and the Spitalfields silk weavers in London, many of them Protestant Huguenots who had fled religious persecution in France. Gone was the boned bodice and skirt, to be replaced first by a loose, full-skirted gown known as a mantua, and then by an open robe and petticoat. Men's doublet and hose had disappeared, too, giving way to coat and breeches.

Revolutionary spirit

By about the 1770s, England was setting the principal style in men's dress with the coat called the frock, worn by men for countryside pursuits. This more informal look was taken up in revolutionary America and even in France, the center of fashion, where the revolutionary leaders opted for styles that set them apart from the aristocratic and increasingly isolated Ancien Régime. It was around this time, too, that cottons and muslins traded from the East became the new wonder fabrics, and women's dress took on a softer silhouette.

FASHION EXTREMES
Young fops of the 1770s, nicknamed "macaronis," took fashion to absurd heights, wearing extravagant clothes and towering wigs.

1625–40	1641–70	1671–80

1649
The English Commonwealth is proclaimed, with puritanical Oliver Cromwell at its head. Style in England becomes more subdued as a result.

▶ Oliver Cromwell

1660
Charles II is proclaimed King of England, and a year later Louis XIV assumes personal rule of France—the monarchy is reestablished as the center of European fashion.

▼ Louis XIV, the Sun King

▲ Henrietta Maria, French wife of Charles I of England

1625
Charles I ascends the throne and marries Henrietta Maria of France; she brings the fashions of the French court with her. Meanwhile, black clothes remain popular in the Dutch United Provinces (now the Netherlands).

1666
Charles II introduces the Persian vest and the justaucorps (a style of long coat) to England.

1670S
Louis XIV, to disguise his growing baldness, promotes the fashion of wearing wigs.

1630s
The "bucket-top" boot for men makes an appearance, and strings of pearls become fashionable for women.

1675
Under sumptuary laws protecting local markets, Charles II bans the import of French lace into England.

▶ Bucket-top boots and abundant lace

1681–90 | 1691–20 | 1721–45 | 1746–65 | 1766–74 | 1775–89

1692
Following the Battle of Steenkerque between the French and the allied forces under William of Orange, a new, military-style cravat, the "Steinkirk," becomes popular.

▼ Flower-patterned silk designed by Anna Maria Garthwaite

1728
Silk designer Anna Maria Garthwaite starts work in London.

1748
A craze for costume dress and "masquerade" emerges; in 1748 society hostesses Elizabeth and Maria Gunning attend a ball at Dublin Castle wearing theater costumes.

1775
Grand Tours to Italy are popular with wealthy European men, who go there to study classical antiquity and to experience polite society.

1710s
The sack back dress featuring Watteau pleats, named after a style often depicted in the work of French rococo painter Jean-Antoine Watteau, is popularized.

◄ *Robe à la française* (also known as sack back dress) with Watteau pleats

► Figure at a masquerade, dressed as Pulcinella from the Italian *commedia dell'arte*

1778
King George III of England introduces the Windsor uniform; this starts the lasting trend for royalty to wear liveries, conveying the idea of military discipline and duty.

▼ From the 1770s onward George III preferred to be painted wearing military dress

1685
Louis XIV revokes the Edict of Nantes, forcing large numbers of Huguenots to seek refuge in London. Importing their silk-weaving expertise, these escapees helped found the Spitalfields silk industry.

c. 1718–1719
The Spanish fashion for the pannier (hoop petticoat) spreads to France.

▼ Stiffened hoops held out the upper skirt at the hips

1745
Jeanne Antoinette Poisson, Madame de Pompadour, becomes Louis XV's mistress and exerts tremendous influence on court fashions.

▼ Madame de Pompadour, dressed sumptuously in white silk

1764
The "Spinning Jenny," a machine using multiple spindles for spinning yarn, is invented.

▼ New technology speeds up the production of cloth

1774
Marie Antoinette becomes Queen of France and introduces a series of new fashions.

1774
Georgiana Cavendish marries the Duke of Devonshire; she will become a trendsetter in English fashion.

1686
The importation of chintz is banned in France (and 40 years later in England) to promote the interests of French and English wool mills.

1765
The caraco emerges as a women's jacket style in the 1760s.

► Painted and dyed cotton caraco

1778
The *Gallerie des Modes*, an early fashion magazine, is founded showing details of the styles of the day.

1625–1635

MEN IN LACE

By the mid 1620s, with a new king, Charles I, on the English throne, the heavily padded doublets of King James I's reign (also widely worn in courts across continental Europe) were passing out of fashion. New, longer doublets in plain or subtly patterned silks replaced the tabbed styles made of the heavy woven and embroidered fabrics that were popular earlier in the 17th century. Breeches, too, changed in shape. They became much longer, reaching to mid-calf level, and were worn with soft leather boots rather than decorated shoes. Neckwear such as circular ruffs (held out behind the head by a wire support called a *supportasse* or a pickadil) began to fall out of fashion and give way to extravagant lace collars. The plainer fabrics of the new-style doublet were a perfect foil for such accessories, and this became a boom time for lace makers. Lavish quantities of elaborately patterned lace were used for every accessory, from cuffs and collars to handkerchiefs and boot hose. Flemish bobbin lace was widely available, but the new fashions benefited every lace-making center in Europe.

Wide-brimmed hat

Layered ruff

Lace-edged cuffs

1625

Cape worn on one shoulder

Decorated shoes

Dressed in black Dark clothes were a particular fashion in the Dutch United Provinces (now the Netherlands). Large ruffs made of layers of linen, expertly laundered and pressed, remained popular here long after the fashion had died out in the rest of Europe.

Jacket-style doublet

Long lock of hair tied with ribbon

Sleeves open to cuffs

Wide lace collar

Shoulder hanger for sword

Open sleeves

Wide-topped boots

Lace boot linings

Points at knees

Softly creased boots

Wide collar Deep, scallop-edged lace collars covering the shoulders were fashionable for both men and women in the mid-1630s. Often made of, or decorated with, Flemish bobbin lace, the collars were worked by hand in the finest linen threads.

Bigger breeches In the mid-1630s men's breeches were becoming much fuller, with the fabric drawn in just below the knee with a series of points. The lower sleeves of a doublet were sometimes fully open to show the shirt beneath.

THE DOUBLET

Points

The padded jacket that men wore in the first part of the 17th century was known as the doublet. This garment had several variations in shape and style. The one illustrated here has deep stiffened tabs and is made of figured, paned silk. Doublets were attached to trunk hose (the short, puffed breeches that were fashionable in this period) with points or ties, which held the two parts of the outfit together. The fastenings were called "points" because of the pointed metal ends of the laces. They were often made of silver and gold thread, and added decorative trimming to the doublet.

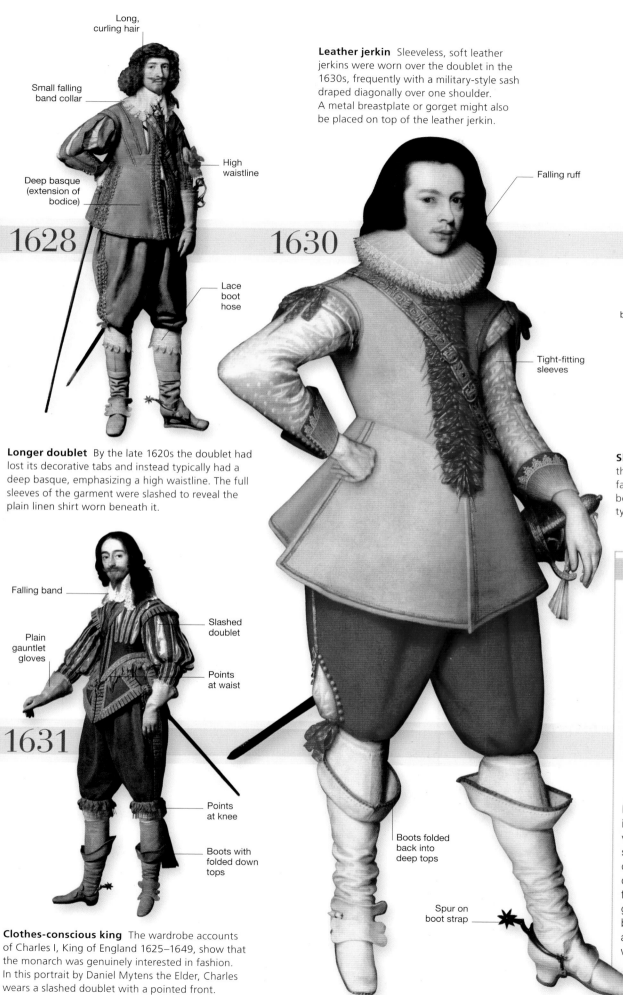

Long, curling hair

Small falling band collar

Deep basque (extension of bodice)

1628

High waistline

Lace boot hose

Longer doublet By the late 1620s the doublet had lost its decorative tabs and instead typically had a deep basque, emphasizing a high waistline. The full sleeves of the garment were slashed to reveal the plain linen shirt worn beneath it.

Leather jerkin Sleeveless, soft leather jerkins were worn over the doublet in the 1630s, frequently with a military-style sash draped diagonally over one shoulder. A metal breastplate or gorget might also be placed on top of the leather jerkin.

Falling ruff

1630

Tight-fitting sleeves

Boots folded back into deep tops

Spur on boot strap

Falling band

Plain gauntlet gloves

1631

Slashed doublet

Points at waist

Points at knee

Boots with folded down tops

Clothes-conscious king The wardrobe accounts of Charles I, King of England 1625–1649, show that the monarch was genuinely interested in fashion. In this portrait by Daniel Mytens the Elder, Charles wears a slashed doublet with a pointed front.

Lace collar covers shoulders

Paned doublet

Long breeches

Funnel or bucket-top boots

Short cloak Decorative rather than functional, the short cloak was often richly patterned. This fashionable gentlemen also wears funnel-topped boots and a wide-brimmed, plumed hat, both typical of French styles of the time.

BUCKLES AND STRAPS

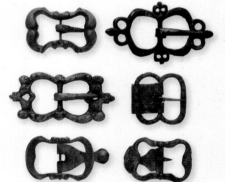

Cast metal buckles

In the 17th century, male accessories included numerous buckled straps worn on various parts of the body. Straps attached spurs to boots; belts and shoulder hangers carried swords; and bandoliers, slung diagonally across the body, held ammunition for firearms. Military paraphernalia such as gorgets (protective collars) and metal breastplates were also attached with straps and buckles. The only place belts were not worn was around the waist, because this destroyed the smooth lines of a doublet attached to breeches with points.

1625–1635
SOFTER SILHOUETTES

Fashions changed relatively slowly in the 17th century; but with the demise of the rigid farthingale petticoat, the trend in the mid-1620s to mid-1630s was toward a more bulky, soft silhouette, and dresses with higher waists and fuller sleeves. During this period, dresses could be made up of three separate parts: a bodice, a petticoat, and a gown over the top (which might be gathered up to reveal the petticoat below). Another style was to wear the gown hanging from the shoulders. As with men's fashion, the ruff gave way to the broad falling collar edged with elegant handmade lace. Only in the Dutch United Provinces (now the Netherlands) was the ruff retained as the neckwear of choice. The fabric used in European fashionable dress in the 17th century was produced in many countries, with silk satins and velvets designed and woven in France and Italy, and linen for shirts and smocks made in the Netherlands and Germany.

Gown worn from shoulders

Large ruff

Puffed sleeves

Old fashioned This lady, possibly a Genoese marchioness, wears the dated style of European royal courts of the late 16th century. The bodice was a separate garment, stiffened with buckram or pasteboard, and sometimes with a central wooden busk.

Separate skirt

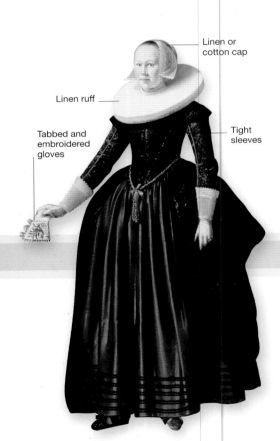

Linen or cotton cap

Linen ruff

Tabbed and embroidered gloves

Tight sleeves

Cartwheel The ruff was a fashion that persisted in the Netherlands in the mid-17th century, while in the rest of Europe it was dying out. It grew ever larger, becoming a cartwheel shape of finely goffered (frilled pleats) linen.

Scooped neckline of bodice edged with lace

Hair worn loose

Conical cuffs

Wide ruff

Ribbon rosette

Feather fan

Apron

Wired standing collar edged with lace

Contrasting tone draws attention to ruff

Trailing hem

Low décolletage Queen Anne, wife of King James I of England, was sometimes portrayed wearing low-necked dresses. For modesty, a revealing neckline could be covered by a linen garment called a partlet, which was stitched to the shift.

Full sleeves A much fuller, elbow-length style was the fashion for sleeves in the later 1620s. They were often paned—made of worked and finished strips of silk fabric—with the puffs separated by ribbon ties and rosettes.

Voluminous silhouette The fullness of the skirt and the puffed sleeves, plus the trailing hems, gave a round shape to women's dress in the 1630s. In the Dutch United Provinces dark colors were popular, worn here with a large pleated ruff.

Sombrero

Gown hangs from shoulders

Petticoat possibly made of wool

Saddle bag, known as an *alforias*

Puffed sleeves

Curled hairstyle

Pearl necklace

High waist

Glossy silk satin

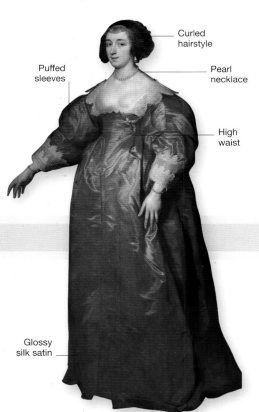

Sombrero The Spanish artist Zurbaran painted this portrait of the 4th-century Saint Margaret of Antioch. She wears the Iberian sombrero, which inspired the fashion for soft plumed hats in the rest of Europe.

Lustrous silk In the 1630s, dresses were made of light-colored silk satins that shimmered in the candlelight. The high-waisted styles often had a low-cut bodice edged with costly lace, which matched the lace on the separate cuffs.

JEWELRY

Gold and gemstone breast ornaments

On formal occasions jewelry—along with lace and rich materials—was one of the most important components of women's fashionable dress. Seventeenth-century paintings and prints show that the "must have" piece of jewelry of the 1630s was a breast ornament, somewhat like a brooch, worn at the center front of the bodice. Portrait painters also showed women wearing two or three necklaces of gemstones; and strings of pearls, too, were a popular choice. Pearls were also worn as drop earrings and as hair ornaments.

1635–1649
DOUBLET AND BREECHES

During this period, France remained the center of fashion. The doublet and breeches were still the main style of dress, often made from matching fabric. Gradually the waistline on the doublet became higher and the fabric tabs below the waist lengthened to create a jacketlike garment, which finished at hip level. The slashed effect remained popular with vertical openings down the front, back, and sleeves of the doublet. Breeches retained a fullness around the seat but were now worn longer on the leg, tapering below the knee and held in around the calf with a band, often decorated with bows. In the mid-1640s doublets and breeches became much shorter, with breeches gradually getting fuller, finishing in a straight line at the knee. Referred to as petticoat breeches, they resembled a skirt and were worn with underdrawers with decorative edging "canions" that hung beneath the hem.

LACE

Lace continued to be a popular accessory for men and women. Originally developed as a scalloped trim on the edging of linen garments, gradually whole cuffs and large collars made of lace became fashionable. Patterns for lace were drawn up on paper and lace makers, often families who handed down the skills, would work with fine linen threads to copy the designs. Lace was a highly valued personal possession—it was extremely costly since it took a long time to make even the smallest piece. The finest lace was produced in Italy, France, and the Flanders area of Belgium, and there was a strong international market for it since it was easy to transport and high in value.

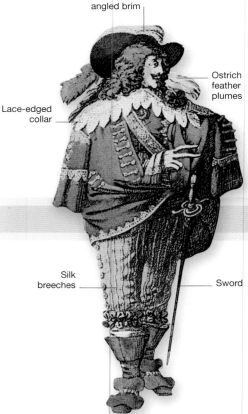

Feather in cap Hats were often decorated with trailing feathers such as ostrich plumes. These were placed on the left side of the hat leaving the right sword arm free to move. Worn indoors, hats were removed before royalty and elders.

Collar extends to edge of shoulder

Boot-hose tops

Butterfly spur leathers

Band collar Made from fine linen and often trimmed with costly lace edging, collars were an important accessory. The earlier ruff style was replaced with the flatter band, which draped softly from a high neckline, and cut straight across the back.

Cloak

Banded decoration on sleeve

Hat with feathers

Breeches

Cup-top boots and boot-hose tops

Boot fashion By the 1630s spurs developed into a leather butterfly shape at the front of the foot, becoming very large and dramatic in size. The top of boots began to widen and were known as cup shapes. By the 1640s these slouched down the leg.

Felt hat with angled brim

Ostrich feather plumes

Lace-edged collar

Silk breeches

Sword

Pelt hat The "sugarloaf" hat with a high crown and narrower brim was popular along with the "cocked" hat, which had a shorter crown and wide brim, worn at an angle. The finest hats were made of beaver pelts imported from North America.

Curled, fringed hair

Trimmed beard and moustache

Scallop-edged lace cuffs and collar

Cup-top boots

Wide-brimmed, angled hat

Lace-edged collar

Cloak

Decorative bow on band securing breeches under knee

Baldrick sash

Shoe rose

Open-sided shoes

Curls and fringes Hair was worn to shoulder length—curled and frizzed with bangs. Wigs were introduced by King Louis XIII, but they did not become popular until the midcentury.

Huge rosettes Shoes with open sides were popular and toe shapes became more square. They fastened with ribbons or decorative rosettes known as shoe roses. The cloak remained essential outdoor wear.

Tall, crowned hat

Doeskin gloves

Ostrich feather plumes

Tall, crowned hat

Linen shirt visible through split sleeve

Short doublet

Butterfly spur leathers

Ribbon rosette decoration

Cup-top boots and boot hose

Spurs

Decorative detail One of the more elaborate accessories were boot-hose tops—decorative, lace edged, or embroidered tops of overstockings. They were also made as separate tops that tied like large cuffs around the top of the stocking.

Doublet rises When doublets shortened in the 1640s it became fashionable for the linen shirt to be visible between the hem and the top of the breeches, often with decorative ribbons around the waist. Decorative lace cuffs remained in vogue.

1635–1649

TAFFETA AND LACE

There was a relative simplicity about women's dress in the late 1630s and 1640s, with everyday styles consisting of a boned bodice and a separate skirt, usually made in soft, draping silks such as taffetas and satins. The look was completed with broad lace and linen collars, or folded kerchiefs worn across the shoulders or as edging to a bodice. Lace cuffs were attached to the sleeve ends of a linen smock that was worn as an undergarment. Hair was worn with the bangs set in thin curls across the forehead, with longer frizzed locks at the side. Henrietta Maria, the queen consort of King Charles I, both set the trends in fashions for women and attracted criticism for her extravagance from Puritan moralists.

COLLAR STARCHING

Fine white linen, deep lace collars, and pleated ruffs meant that skilled laundresses had an important role to play in mid-17th-century fashion, when cleanliness was a luxury. *Gerard's Herbal*, a popular almanac of the time, maintained that the purest and whitest starch was from the roots of the cuckoo pint plant but that it could chap and blister laundresses' hands.

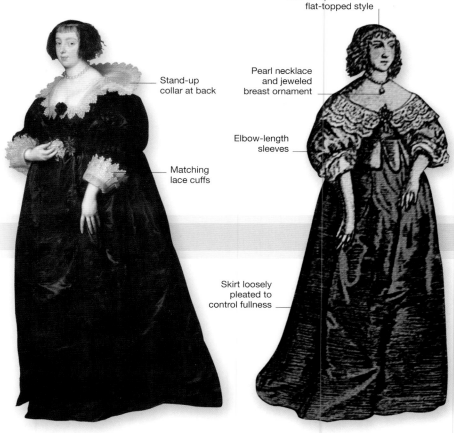

Stand-up collar at back

Matching lace cuffs

Black clothes Dark clothing was fashionable in the Dutch United Provinces (the Netherlands). Large ruffs made of layers of linen, expertly laundered and pressed, remained in vogue here long after they died out in the rest of Europe.

Hair swept back into flat-topped style

Pearl necklace and jeweled breast ornament

Elbow-length sleeves

Skirt loosely pleated to control fullness

High waist By the end of the 1630s women's dress throughout Europe was high waisted. Here, the green silk separate boned bodice has deep tabs, the middle one a curved pointed shape, and is worn over a ruby-red silk skirt.

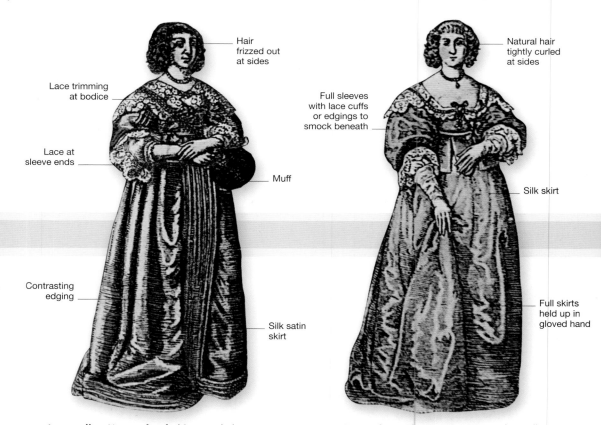

Hair frizzed out at sides

Lace trimming at bodice

Lace at sleeve ends

Muff

Contrasting edging

Silk satin skirt

Lace collar New, softer fashions and glossy silks led to a spectacular rise in the production and consumption of lace. Excellent design skills and sharp business acumen meant that Flemish laces were popular across Europe.

Natural hair tightly curled at sides

Full sleeves with lace cuffs or edgings to smock beneath

Silk skirt

Full skirts held up in gloved hand

Engravings The engraver Wenceslas Hollar was born in Bohemia and worked in London, copying portraits of aristocratic sitters so that the images could be widely sold as prints. This print shows a lady in a boned bodice, worn over a silk skirt.

Hair teased
into small curls
at forehead

Fur tippet over
shoulders

Muff Large fur muffs were a
popular, but costly, accessory to
winter dress in the 1640s. The
muff is worn here with a fur
wrap known as a tippet,
which is draped shawl-like
around the shoulders.

Soft ringlets with
extra hair now at
sides of head

Ribbons and bows
worn in hair

Patterned fabric This long boned
bodice and separate skirt are made
of matching figured woven silk.
While skirts seen beneath
gowns could be embroidered
or patterned, portraits from
the mid-17th century rarely
show patterns on bodices
and skirts.

Fur muff

Silk sash
worn across
one shoulder

Ringlets on
one shoulder

Softly
draping
folds

Longer skirts
coming into
fashion

Trailing hem, with fullness
concentrated on back

Full sleeves with
panes that show
billowing smock
beneath

Topknot
at back of
hairstyle

Length of
draped
fabric

Sloped
shoulders

Sleeves
of smock or
shift beneath

Unadorned fabrics Women's fashions
at the court of King Charles I were stylish
and elegant. Dresses were made of
relatively undecorated fabrics such
as woven silk taffetas and satins,
in colors such as apricot and
soft blues and greens.

Plain-colored
fabric shimmers
as wearer moves

Portrait painters English court artists in the 1630s,
including van Dyck, painted fabric folds and billows
rather than recording stylistic details, which makes it
difficult to date precisely. Hairstyles and accessories,
however, give an impression of current styles.

Full skirts with
trailing hem

FASHION ICON
HENRIETTA MARIA

The daughter of Henry IV of France and Marie de Medici, Henrietta Maria (1609–1669) married Charles I of England in 1625. She had grown up in the French court and imported grace, style, and imperial grandeur, along with a vast trousseau of clothes and jewelry. Immediately her youth, French background, and vivacious personality introduced a new sophistication to court culture, as well as the shock of the new.

Freer fashions

The queen made her mark through her dress sense, which was greatly admired and copied throughout Europe. Severe styles went out. Stiff brocades gave way to shiny, smooth silks, and strong, heavy colors softened. Courtiers often wore the queen's favorite colors, which were orange, blue, gray, peach, yellow, and olive-green. Henrietta abandoned the farthingale, even for formal occasions, and also the fashion for long stomachers that had pressed the farthingale flat in front to fan out behind. Full skirts were instead supported by ornamental petticoats that were visible, since the fashion was to hold up the long overskirts when walking.

Styles were relaxing. Henrietta influenced the move away from the rigid style, ruffles, and flounces of the Elizabethan era. Even ruffs were discarded in favor of wide, low collars, which gradually lowered to reveal a square-cut décolletage. Shoulders grew soft and rounded as the waistline rose, sitting just beneath breast level in the 1630s. Henrietta adopted the *Virago* sleeve, a paned sleeve that was drawn into the arm creating puffs. She replaced stiff hairstyles with a softer coiffure, wearing her hair flat on top but curled in soft ringlets at the side.

Henrietta's fame as a leader of fashion was mainly due to Sir Anthony van Dyck (1599–1641), a Flemish Baroque artist who became the leading court painter in England. Despite flattering his subject, van Dyck captured her regal character, whatever costume she chose to wear. The queen's niece, who knew her aunt only from van Dyck's portraits, was astonished to discover that Henrietta Maria was a very small woman, with crooked shoulders, long, skinny arms, and protruding teeth.

The Queen's passion for dancing, music, and theater heavily influenced her style. Elaborate masques staged by Inigo Jones and Ben Jonson dramatized the ideals of the Stuart monarchy. Sumptuous costumes combined dazzling colors and languid elegance. Her attire when performing on stage outraged Puritans, who considered her choice of clothing to be extremely provocative. One famous outfit had such a low décolletage that her nipples were barely hidden.

Toning down

Henrietta took less interest in fashion as her children and the political situation occupied more of her time and thoughts. The civil war in England in the 1640s brought women's fashion to a grinding halt and women's wear became more subdued in both England and France. High waists were lowered almost to natural level.

Supporters of the monarchy (Royalists) wore detailed and lavish fashions in rich resplendent satins, but the shock of the new was over. Henrietta's husband struggled—and failed—to hang on to the throne. He was beheaded in 1649. Henrietta was a fierce campaigner, raising funds and marshaling royal support, diverting her sartorial brilliance into political and intellectual channels.

△ **TREND FOR PEARLS**
Henrietta introduced fresh new styles into the English court, among them a renewed love of pearls. She proudly wore these symbols of wealth in her hair, around her neck, and as double drop earrings.

SHIMMERING SATIN ▷
Henrietta's high-waisted gown has tabbed skirts and open three-quarter sleeves over full chemise sleeves. Her wide collar is made of lace and pearls, and she wears a ribbon sash.

TIMELINE

1609 Born in Paris, France

1625 The chic young Catholic bride arrives in England. In her first year of married life she wears flounced farthingale skirts and stiff upright collars, before ditching both

◁ **Mid-1630s** Stiff fabrics give way to lighter silks. Colors brighten with oranges and olive-greens. The *Virago* sleeve, gathered in with a ribbon or fabric to create two large puffs, becomes all the rage

◁ **Late 1630s** High collars and ruffs give way to lower necklines

Early 1640s As civil war approaches, fashions get simpler with natural waistlines

1669 Dies near Paris at the age of 60

○ 1610   ○ 1620   ○ 1630   ○ 1640   ○ 1650   ○ 1670

1649–1660

PURITAN INFLUENCE

After King Charles I was executed in 1649, England became a republic called the Commonwealth, with Oliver Cromwell at its head. Cromwell, a Protestant and a Puritan, believed that people should lead pious lives and dress in a plain and practical way. His opponents, the Royalists, supported a return to the monarchy and wore elaborate clothing inspired by French fashion. Cromwell's Puritans based their dress on Dutch traditions, since the Dutch United Provinces (now the Netherlands) was a strongly Protestant country as well as a wealthy, influential one. Many style features associated with this period—such as linen collars covering the shoulders and the widespread popularity of black—are Dutch in origin. Dark clothes with little or no decoration were favored. English Puritans, a branch of Protestants, established a colony in Plymouth, Massachusetts, in what is now the US, in 1620 that would influence all aspects of American culture, including fashion.

"Chaperone" (small soft hood)

Capotaine-style hat with angular crown

Low neckline with lace collar

Softly straggling hair

Long bodice with laced stomacher

Narrow sleeves

1650

Moderately full skirt

Cape worn over one shoulder

Both figures wear high-heeled shoes

Into the Commonwealth At the beginning of this period in England, people were still wearing fashions from Charles I's time. The laced stomacher (front panel) of the lady's bodice and soft-toned color of the man's doublet were both styles from the 1640s.

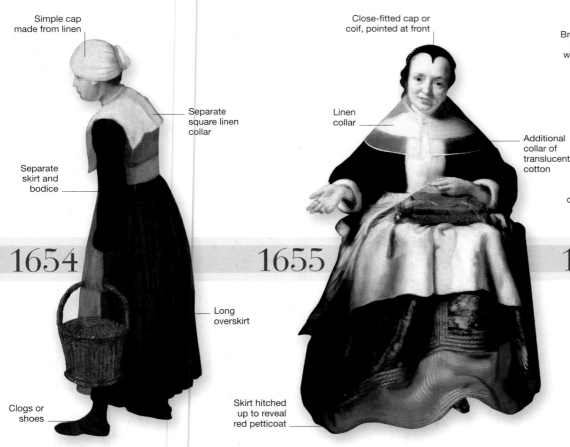

Simple cap made from linen

Close-fitted cap or coif, pointed at front

Broad-brimmed, beaver-fur hat with high crown

Large linen collar covers shoulders

Separate square linen collar

Linen collar

Small linen falling collar

Coif

Separate skirt and bodice

Additional collar of translucent cotton

Dressed completely in black

1654

1655

1657

Long overskirt

Clogs or shoes

Skirt hitched up to reveal red petticoat

Black leather shoes

Luxury trim on petticoat

Dutch servant In a detail from a painting by Jacobus Vrel, this young servant girl wears clothes of linen and wool fabrics, with names like "serge" and "linsey woolsy." These would have been far less expensive than silk and cotton.

Seated woman In this Nicolaes Maes painting, c. 1655, a Dutch housewife mends a linen shirt. Linen was woven in the city of Haarlem, exported widely, and used locally for both clothing and domestic textiles.

Merchant class Artist Pieter de Hooch offers a glimpse of Dutch domestic life in the 17th century. The prosperous couple is dressed in black, but with luxurious details, such as the woman's silver petticoat and laced bodice.

Hat with
high crown

Pointed
linen collar

Lace
cuffs

Breeches
fastened
at knee

Clothing is
largely black

Black shoes,
fastened with
latchets or ties

1651

Oliverian clothing Named for Oliver Cromwell, this man from 1650 wears simpler clothes to express Puritan disdain of worldly splendor. Cromwell's supporters cut their hair close to their heads, giving rise to the term "Roundhead."

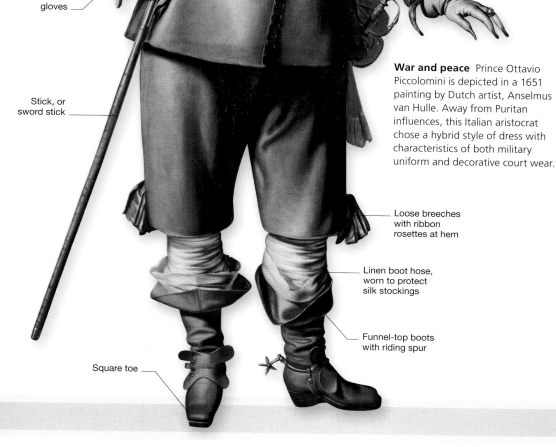

Neat, full bushy
hairstyle

Small, linen
falling collar

Full doublet sleeves with
buttoned slashes to
reveal shirt underneath

Buff-colored
leather jerkin

Gauntlet
gloves

Stick, or
sword stick

War and peace Prince Ottavio Piccolomini is depicted in a 1651 painting by Dutch artist, Anselmus van Hulle. Away from Puritan influences, this Italian aristocrat chose a hybrid style of dress with characteristics of both military uniform and decorative court wear.

Loose breeches
with ribbon
rosettes at hem

Linen boot hose,
worn to protect
silk stockings

Funnel-top boots
with riding spur

Square toe

Linen cap

Linen collar,
completely
covering shoulders

Child's linen
or cotton cap

1658

Long skirt
to the floor

Overskirt hitched
up to show blue
petticoat

Dutch child Another de Hooch detail portrays a servant girl with a small child in simple modest dress. At this time children's clothes were just smaller versions of the outfits worn by their parents.

MILITARY DRESS

The English Civil War, from 1642 to 1651, came with a new style of military dress. Parliamentarian Colonel Hutchinson appeared in the English House of Commons in "a habit which was pretty rich but grave" (a dark doublet decorated with gold and silver points), but ordinary soldiers wore plainer clothes. Buff-colored leather coats were worn by Cromwell's New Model Army and by those involved in conflicts in Europe.

Parliamentarian
felt hat

Baldrick with
sword belt

**Buff-colored leather coat
(worn over doublet)**

1660–1685

OPULENCE RESTORED

With the Restoration of the monarchy in 1660, opulence returned to fashion in England. The *justaucorps* (knee-length coat) took over from the doublet as the main garment in a man's wardrobe. Its body was longer and straighter than the doublet, falling to the knee and closing down the front with small buttons from neck to hem. The lower part of the coat known as the skirt had back and side openings (to allow a sword to poke through). Gradually it became tighter on the waist and fuller at the hem. Sleeves were wide with turned-back cuffs. The waistcoat was worn underneath—it was the same length but narrower in cut than the coat, with long, fitted sleeves. Breeches were still worn full and short to just below the knee, often decorated with bows and ribbon trimmings. By the 1680s breeches became slimmer in fit and fastened at the knee.

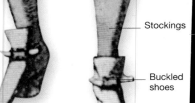

Gold braid galloon hat trimming

Embroidered cuffs

Cane decorated with ribbon rosette

Silk coat

Lace trim

Stockings

Buckled shoes

Wide-brimmed, felt hat

Cloak

Gold braid decoration

Lace cuffs

Ribbon rosette decoration

1665

Canions

Cane

Buckled shoes

Shoes with bow fastening

Breeches Petticoat breeches, known as pantaloons at this date, were falling out of style. Canions—the form of under breeches with elaborate trimmings, which fell below the hem of the petticoat breeches—had been popular in the early part of the century.

Shoulder sash A baldrick—a leather or silk sash—was worn to support the sword. With military dress the baldrick could be used to denote the allegiance or rank of a soldier before the introduction of uniforms.

Shoe buckles Shoes became popular again, taking over from boots. A new style of fastening—the shoe buckle (a square or rectangular metal fastening)—was both decorative and practical. Charles II brought to England the heels and red soles earlier introduced by Louis XIV at the French court.

Hats off The fashion for large, heavy wigs led to men removing hats indoors because it was more comfortable without them. In summer waistcoats (vests) were abandoned for coolness in favor of a coat worn directly over the linen shirt.

1660

Felt hat

Button fastenings

Felt hat

Buckled shoes

Felt hat

Plain linen collar

Garter rosettes add decorative touch

Old and new There was a new fashion for straight-cut tunics worn over a waistcoat (vest). This practical ensemble is part old-fashioned, sleeved mantle, part up-to-the-minute tunic. The broad linen collar resembles lace collars of the time but is plainer.

CHARLES II

In 1660 King Charles II returned from exile in France to take the English throne. He was known for his love of fashionable dress and introduced styles from the French court. In 1666 he introduced a more sober style of dressing of a coat, waistcoat (vest), and breeches in black silk over white. This is seen as the origin of the three-piece suit.

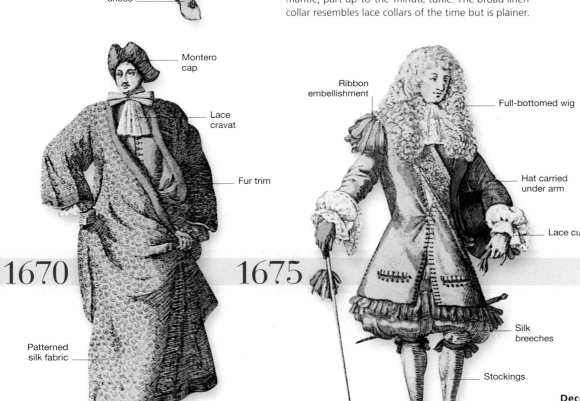

Montero cap

Lace cravat

Fur trim

Patterned silk fabric

1670

1675

Ribbon embellishment

Full-bottomed wig

Hat carried under arm

Lace cuff

Silk breeches

Stockings

Home wear A nightgown was an informal garment worn at home, similar to a robe. Inspired by Eastern styles, it was made from rich silks or decorative printed cottons. A montero—an informal cap with flaps of fur or cloth—completed this look.

Heavy wigs Long, curled, full-bottomed wigs became fashionable. Calottes (small linen caps) were worn beneath to absorb the sweat. France's Louis XIV had a large collection, and Charles II popularized this style in England when he came to the throne.

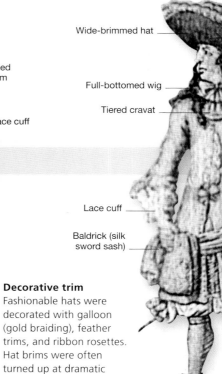

Wide-brimmed hat

Full-bottomed wig

Tiered cravat

Lace cuff

Baldrick (silk sword sash)

Decorative trim Fashionable hats were decorated with galloon (gold braiding), feather trims, and ribbon rosettes. Hat brims were often turned up at dramatic angles. The tiered cravat is made of layers of fine linen overlaid with lace.

1660–1680

BONED BODICE TO MANTUA

The 20 years between 1660 and 1680 saw significant change in women's fashions and in society in general. In England King Charles II reclaimed the throne, while in France King Louis XIV established the Palace of Versailles, re-establishing the monarchy as the center of patronage and high fashion. The evolution of women's clothing saw the slow demise of the dress made up of a boned bodice, a skirt, and gown, and the beginnings of the mantua, a loose gown with an overskirt elaborately draped at the back. New styles demanded different expertise, and women's dress was now made by mantua makers, although more structured garments were still constructed by stay makers and tailors. Women selected fabric and trimmings for dresses, including lace, from visiting drapers, linen and silk merchants, and milliners.

Riding clothes Women wore a particular type of clothing to travel on horseback in the 17th century. A "safeguard" was a loose skirt worn to keep off the dust, and there are also references to women wearing an early style of tailored jacket for riding.

Fashionably high forehead

Elbow-length, tightly set sleeves restrict movement

Dropped waist

Bands of applied lace

1660

Rigid bodice The distinctive round shape of women's dress in the 1660s was achieved by a tightly boned bodice with strips of whalebone inserted into finely stitched channels. Separate sleeves were tied to the garment at the shoulder.

Long, curling hair

Jeweled ornament at breast

Full sleeves

Clothes made of rich silk brocade

Royal gown Queen of France Marie-Thérèse (wife of Louis XIV) wears a boned bodice, and matching skirt and gown (edged with ermine) of the finest woven silk. Her deep collar is of exquisite, Flemish bobbin lace.

Stock tied at neck

Loose jacket of wool or silk

1675

Safeguard

Long lace lappets (decorative flaps), or scarf, pinned to back of hair

Lace-edged sleeve ruffles

Large, painted or printed fan

Gown held up at back

1678

Slender walking cane

Separate skirt, known as petticoat

A new style During the 1670s a full-length gown was worn buttoned across the chest, and open below to reveal the petticoat. The skirts were caught up and draped at the back in a loose bustle arrangement.

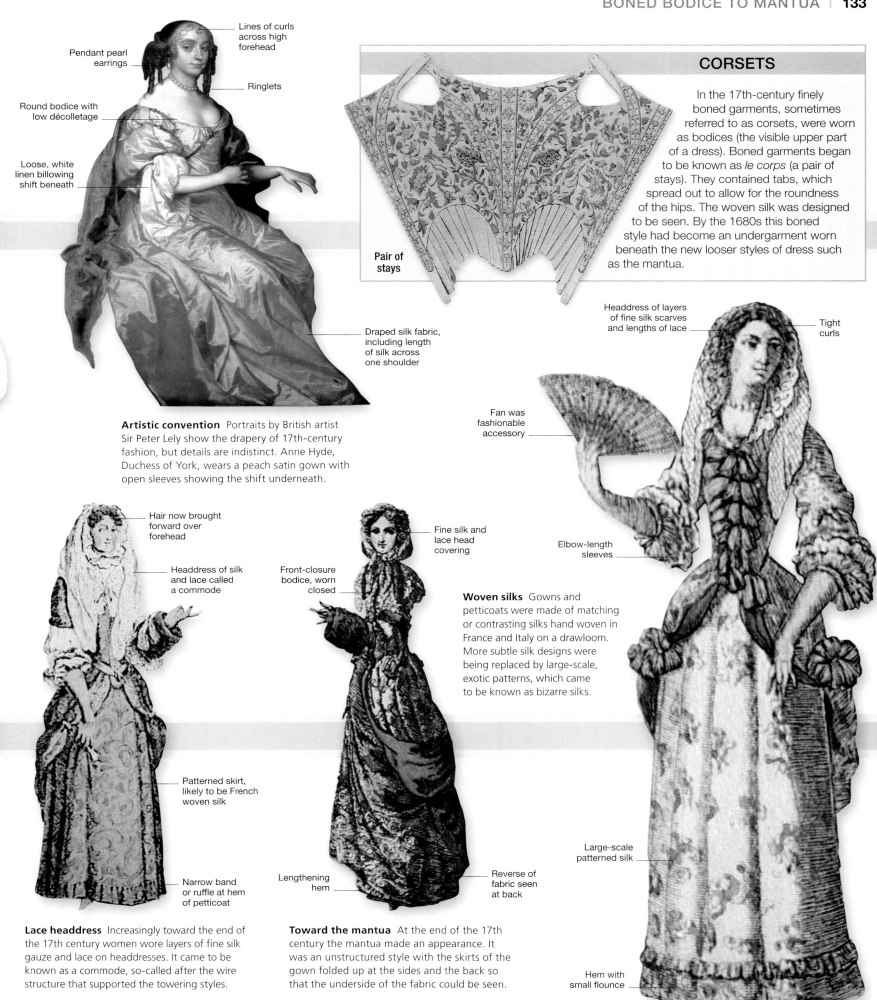

Pendant pearl earrings

Lines of curls across high forehead

Ringlets

Round bodice with low décolletage

Loose, white linen billowing shift beneath

Draped silk fabric, including length of silk across one shoulder

CORSETS

In the 17th-century finely boned garments, sometimes referred to as corsets, were worn as bodices (the visible upper part of a dress). Boned garments began to be known as *le corps* (a pair of stays). They contained tabs, which spread out to allow for the roundness of the hips. The woven silk was designed to be seen. By the 1680s this boned style had become an undergarment worn beneath the new looser styles of dress such as the mantua.

Pair of stays

Artistic convention Portraits by British artist Sir Peter Lely show the drapery of 17th-century fashion, but details are indistinct. Anne Hyde, Duchess of York, wears a peach satin gown with open sleeves showing the shift underneath.

Headdress of layers of fine silk scarves and lengths of lace

Tight curls

Fan was fashionable accessory

Elbow-length sleeves

Woven silks Gowns and petticoats were made of matching or contrasting silks hand woven in France and Italy on a drawloom. More subtle silk designs were being replaced by large-scale, exotic patterns, which came to be known as bizarre silks.

Hair now brought forward over forehead

Headdress of silk and lace called a commode

Fine silk and lace head covering

Front-closure bodice, worn closed

Patterned skirt, likely to be French woven silk

Narrow band or ruffle at hem of petticoat

Lengthening hem

Reverse of fabric seen at back

Large-scale patterned silk

Hem with small flounce

Lace headdress Increasingly toward the end of the 17th century women wore layers of fine silk gauze and lace on headdresses. It came to be known as a commode, so-called after the wire structure that supported the towering styles.

Toward the mantua At the end of the 17th century the mantua made an appearance. It was an unstructured style with the skirts of the gown folded up at the sides and the back so that the underside of the fabric could be seen.

FASHION RESTORED

The Restoration of the English monarchy in 1660 signaled the dawn of a new age of prosperity for the English aristocracy, which was reflected in the fashions of the time. Charles II was self-indulgent and foppish, and his courtiers soon followed suit. Despite their extravagances, English nobles took an interest in charitable causes, such as the one depicted in the painting, *The Tichborne Dole*, opposite, in which the Lord of the Manor in the village of Tichborne distributes bread to the poor. This painting showcases the lavish fashions worn by the noble class, in contrast with those worn by the less fortunate.

The central male figure in the middle ground wears a long and ornate waistcoat, fastened with close-set buttons from throat to hem, underneath a plainer coat. This was one of the many fashions introduced by Charles II. The figure also wears an elaborate lace cravat and a periwig, an indispensable part of wealthy fashionable attire. Shoes are high heeled and square toed.

The two women to his left show female fashions of the day. Their bodices, with a horizontal décolletage, are long, pointed, and fastened in the front with jeweled clasps. They wear full-puffed sleeves to the elbows, and their skirts are gathered at the hips in tight pleats, opening down the front over an ornate petticoat. Their bodice and skirts are joined, but poorer women would wear them separately, in different colors. Skirts were raised—to the toe for court women and to the instep for peasant women. Though the women use stays, the overall effect is one of increasing freedom.

> **"**
> The King hath in Council declared his resolution of setting a fashion for clothes, which he will never alter. It will be a vest, I know not well how, but it is to teach the nobility thrift, and will do good.
>
> **SAMUEL PEPYS,** OCTOBER 8, 1666
> **"**

◁ **THE TICHBORNE DOLE** This scene, painted by Gillis van Tilborgh in 1671, depicts an English festival of charity during the Feast of the Annunciation.

1685–1720
TOWARD THE SUIT

The silhouette of the coat became increasingly exaggerated, worn tight on the waist and flaring to full pleated skirts below. Decorative braiding was applied along the center front closure, pockets, and cuffs. Sleeves became longer and tighter, but cuffs remained large. The waistcoat, still fit close to the body, was now worn shorter than the coat. While the waistcoat front was richly decorated, the back was frequently made of plainer fabric since it was rarely seen. Breeches were worn narrower and closer to the leg, fastening just above or below the knee. They were made from the same material as the coat or from a plain black fabric—the forerunner of the suit. From the 1690s, large ornamental buttons became popular on pockets with decorative flaps and on cuffs as well as forming the front closure. These buttons could be made from decorative metal or from the same fabric as the coat and finished with embroidery.

CLOTHES SELLER

Expensive garments were made to measure, but there were many ways of buying cheaper clothing. Basic garments such as shirts and breeches could be bought in towns and cities from large clothing warehouses, and secondhand garments could be purchased in markets or from clothes sellers. These traders carried their wares around the streets, ready to sell to any interested customers. In order to be able to carry as much stock as possible, this clothes seller wears his hats piled on top of his head, allowing customers to instantly recognize his trade.

Engraving of old cloak and hat seller

Finishing touch This long, flared coat is worn with shoes with a fashionably high tongue. The tongue could be folded over to reveal a colored lining and was often cut into a scallop shape around the edge.

High peaked wig

Decorated pocket flaps

Ostrich feather plumes

Buttons on center front closure

Square-toed shoes with high tongue and matching heel

Tricorn (cocked hat) worn with point to front

Gold galloon braiding on arms

Ornate pocket flap

Buttons are more decorative

Waistcoat worn open to reveal linen shirt

Lavishly embroidered cuffs

Cocked hat The wide-brimmed felt hat was now worn with the brim turned up in three folds to create a style known as a tricorn. Rich gold galloon braiding was added as a decorative trim on the turned-up edges.

Laced breeches Gathered into a waistband, breeches could be adjusted by laces at the center back. They were held up with a tie around the waist, often a decorative sash.

Cocked hat with braid decoration

Lace cravat with bow

Enormous lace cuffs

Gold embroidered edging

Royal attire Louis XIV introduced a style of dress *justaucorps à brevet*—a blue coat with gold embroidery and lined with scarlet. Highly coveted, it was worn by the French royal family and 50 selected courtiers.

Long, curled wig

Fine lace cravat

Silk woven with gold thread pattern

Waist-sash tassels visible below coat

Lace cravat The large, wide collar gave way to a separate necktie (cravat). Costly lace styles were reserved for the most formal occasions, but a steinkirk (long, plain linen cravat) became popular for men and women.

Double peaks The wig's height reached a central point in the 1690s, echoing the shape of the female fontange style. The fullness then divided into double peaks. By 1710 this impractical style was replaced by styles such as the campaign wig—hair tied back in three sections.

Double-peaked, full-bottomed wig

Fine wool becomes popular for coats

Hat carried under arm

High tongue with scalloped edge

Wide cuff with decorative buttons

Leather shoes with turned-over tongue

Suit ensemble The coat, waistcoat, and breeches were now known as a suit. Along with silk, fine wool in blue and brown became popular as it was warm and practical, and could support heavy embellishments.

Garter surrounds shield of St. George

Gold collar with pendant figure of St. George

Garter hat with ostrich feather plumes

Cloak with white silk lining

Order of the Garter Garter robes, for those awarded the UK's highest honor, consisted of a blue velvet mantle, the left shoulder embroidered with the garter encircling the shield of St. George. The buckled, blue velvet garter was worn around the left calf.

1681–1720
MANTUAS AND PETTICOATS

From the 1680s, the mantua became the chief item of women's dress, with a linen smock or shift remaining as the main undergarment. A full-length, coatlike garment with elbow-length sleeves, the mantua was worn over the stiffened bodice and skirt of earlier periods. Closed from neck to waist, the sides and back were folded up and secured at the waistline to reveal the skirt below. To fit beneath the mantua, the bodice had straps instead of sleeves and was formed like a corset. It opened down the center back with a lace closure and was still long and stiffened and cut low on the chest. The petticoat was full and gathered in at the waistline. By the 1690s, the top part of the mantua was worn open to show the bodice. It was filled in with a decorative panel known as a stomacher, which was pinned on to the stiffened bodice beneath.

1684

Curled hair worn loose

Rolled full sleeves of linen smock

Silk nightgown During the Restoration famous beauties were painted in languid poses wearing rich silk casual robes (called nightgowns) over a linen smock. This red silk garment, worn by Charles II's mistress, has decorative fringing and metal clasps.

Gold fringe trim

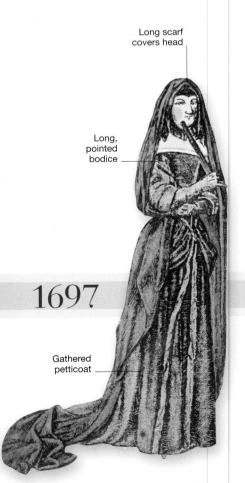

Long scarf covers head

Long, pointed bodice

1697

Gathered petticoat

Riding hood Long scarves were often worn to cover the head outdoors, and riding hoods (hooded cloaks) were also popular. The long, cloaklike fabric shown here may have been used more for effect in a portrait than as a practical wearable garment.

Cone-shaped bodice narrows to waist

Ruby clasps fix cloak to mantua

Mantua drawn back over hips

1709

Textured silk

Ermine-trim cloak

Bejeweled mantua This silver-gray silk mantua, worn by the Duchess of Burgundy, is embellished with rubies and other jewels. Over this she wears an ermine-trimmed cloak of blue and gold brocade, fixed at her shoulders with jeweled clasps.

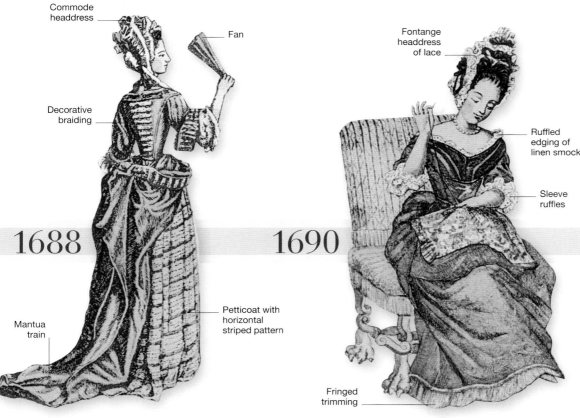

Commode headdress

Fan

Decorative braiding

1688

Mantua train

Petticoat with horizontal striped pattern

Folded train Toward the end of the 17th century the train on the mantua became much longer. The sides were intricately folded and pinned up at the back of the skirt to reveal ever more elaborate linings.

Fontange headdress of lace

Ruffled edging of linen smock

Sleeve ruffles

1690

Fringed trimming

Tall cap The fontange cap was worn flat at the back of the head, rising up high above the crown in layers of lace and ribbon, often supported by a wire-frame commode. It was named after Madame Fontange, who originated the ribbon style.

Hood made from light muslin scarf

Soft calf-leather gloves

1695

Mantua train with contrast lining

Mantua and petticoat By the end of the century the mantua and petticoat were made from matching fabric, with contrasting material used for the lining of the mantua. Petticoats were decorated with horizontal bands of lace or fringing (furbelows).

White silk wrapping gown

Blue drapery adds classical effect

1715

Long full skirt

Wrapping gown An informal robe known as a nightgown or wrapping gown fell loose from the shoulders and was worn over a bodice, petticoat, and linen smock or shift. A popular choice for portraits such as this one, it was seen as a timeless garment.

Cocked hat with feather decoration

Elbow-length sleeves

1720

Riding dress Women's riding habit evolved from male styles of dress, with a coat worn over a waistcoat (vest) and petticoat. The habit was often decorated with metal braiding and frogging (horizontal bands across the front).

STAYS AND STOMACHER

Lacing at center back

Colorful embroidery

Stays

Stomacher

Stays or bodices, still an essential part of women's dress, were made of whalebone stitched between two layers of buckram, a stiffened linen fabric. Bodices were often covered with embroidered silk; a decorated panel, or stomacher, might be worn over the top for further embellishment or contrast.

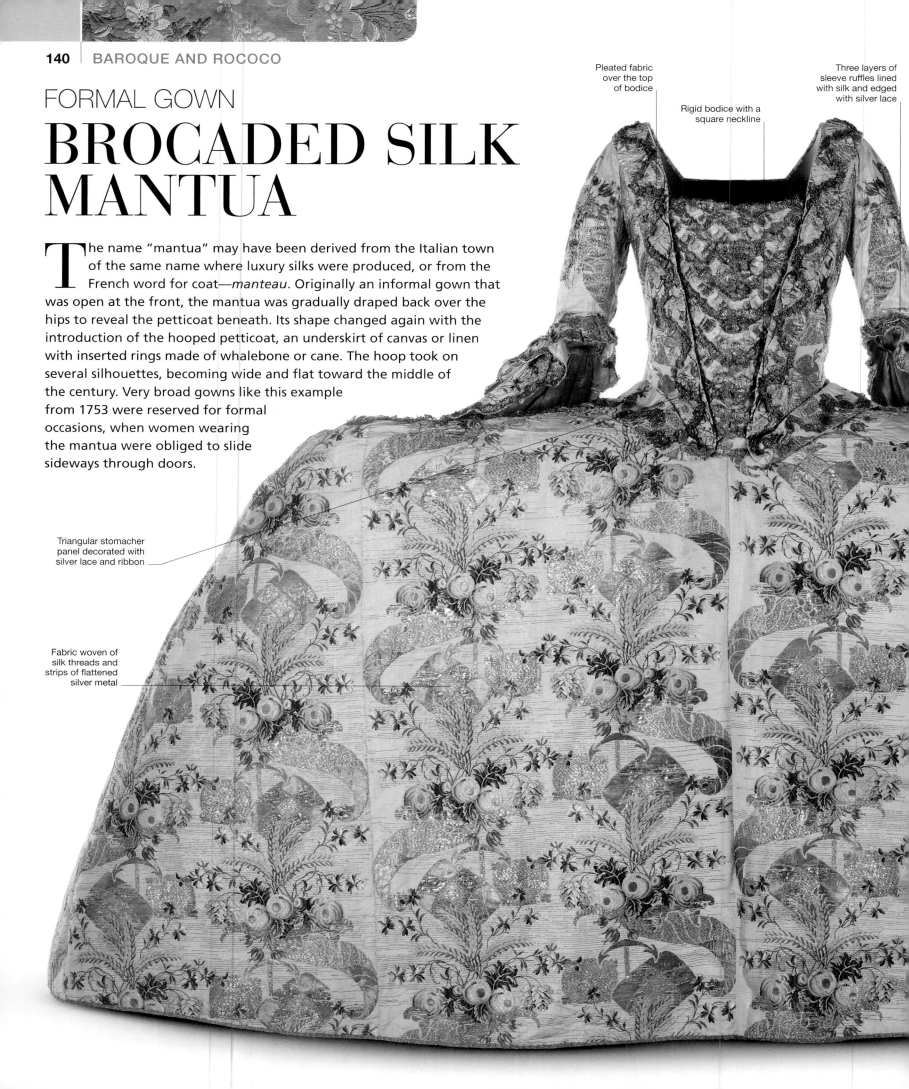

FORMAL GOWN
BROCADED SILK MANTUA

The name "mantua" may have been derived from the Italian town of the same name where luxury silks were produced, or from the French word for coat—*manteau*. Originally an informal gown that was open at the front, the mantua was gradually draped back over the hips to reveal the petticoat beneath. Its shape changed again with the introduction of the hooped petticoat, an underskirt of canvas or linen with inserted rings made of whalebone or cane. The hoop took on several silhouettes, becoming wide and flat toward the middle of the century. Very broad gowns like this example from 1753 were reserved for formal occasions, when women wearing the mantua were obliged to slide sideways through doors.

Pleated fabric over the top of bodice

Rigid bodice with a square neckline

Three layers of sleeve ruffles lined with silk and edged with silver lace

Triangular stomacher panel decorated with silver lace and ribbon

Fabric woven of silk threads and strips of flattened silver metal

BACK VIEW

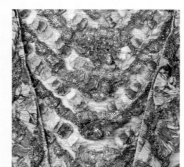

SIDE VIEW

Wide hips created by
the hooped petticoat
worn underneath

**ANGLED SIDE
VIEW**

Skirt constructed
from narrow
widths of fabric
sewn together

IN DETAIL

◁ **STOMACHER**
The triangular piece of fabric worn center front—the stomacher—was first pinned to the stays (a heavily boned underbodice) before the gown was pulled into position and secured with pins. Diamonds might adorn the stomacher on grand occasions.

◁ **CENTER BACK SEAM**
The silk has been carefully pieced together so that the pattern is mirrored on either side of the central seam that runs down the back of the gown. The mantua developed from a loose gown that was originally draped into graceful pleats before these came to be stitched into position. The arrangement of fabric at the back of the waist alludes to earlier incarnations of the mantua gown. These would have had their open skirts swathed toward the back, where a long train was looped up and arranged in pleats.

◁ **SLEEVE RUFFLES**
During the 1740s deep sleeve cuffs were replaced with ruffles, usually worn in three layers. Sometimes a lead weight, the size of a large coin and covered in fabric, was attached inside the bottom of the sleeve to prevent it from riding up.

◁ **BROCADE**
The silk is brocaded, which means that the complicated pattern was woven into the fabric, rather than embroidered onto it. At least 14 different colors and four types of silver thread were used, reflecting the light in different ways and sparkling beautifully in candlelight.

1720–1770

MANTUAS AND OPEN ROBES

Throughout most of the 18th century the basic style of women's dress was the open robe, a garment that was put on somewhat like a modern-day coat. A separate skirt known as a petticoat was worn beneath, and the gap at the bodice covered by a stiffened panel called a stomacher, which was pinned in place to the robe by a series of tabs. The robings (foldback edges of the gown) covered the pin heads. Fashion for the most formal occasions was set at the French court of King Louis XV and copied throughout Europe, particularly the style known as *le grand habit*—a heavily boned bodice, and a separate, richly decorated skirt and train. The mantua, a style of dress that involved folding and draping the sides and the back panel, was also popular and seen at the English courts of the Hanoverian kings.

Open robe This 1738 open robe of lustrous brocaded silk is worn with a separate petticoat over a circular hoop made of cane or whalebone. The robe is open down to the waist over a triangular stomacher decorated with a single bow.

Robings

Stomacher

Engageantes (sleeve ruffles)

Large-scale silk pattern

Separate petticoat

Reproduction lace trim

Buttoned stomacher

Elbow-length sleeves with flounced ends

Rococo robe The undulating lines of the design on this dress silk are characteristic of the mid-18th-century rococo movement in the decorative arts. The robe falls in softer, less formal folds than the exaggerated lines of the heavily hooped dresses.

SHOES

For most of the 18th century women's shoes were made of fabric. Although the material might be patterned dress silk, it was not usual to choose a gown and shoes in matching material. Sometimes separate leather overshoes were worn to protect the fabric shoes. A metal buckle decorated with cut-glass pastes was pinned into the latchets (side straps) to fasten the shoes.

Tip-up, pointed-toe shoe

Lower heel in 1740s

Latchets or straps flap across the vamp (top) of shoe

Woven silk
with large-scale
botanical design

Back panel
turned up

Side panels
draped to
center

Painted
leaf fan

Silver strip and
silver filé thread

Tree of Life
embroidery
of fantasy fruit
and flowers

Open bodice
with gap filled
by stomacher

Silk embroidered
in silver gilt and
colored silk thread

Pleated
sleeves

Separate lace
sleeve ruffles

Train folded
up at rear

Mantua
side
panels

Mantua The mantua was a style left over from the end of the 17th century, and by this date was only worn at the most formal occasions. Technically the mantua is the bodice, but the term is also used for the style of dress.

English court This ribbed silk mantua embroidered with over 11 lb (5 kg) of silver metal thread was worn at the court of King George II in Britain. Side hoops, which gave this exaggerated rectangular shape, were introduced as court dress in the 1740s.

Parading wealth France and England boasted the finest professional embroidery workshops. In the 18th century, dress was a way of parading wealth—everybody knew that your family was rich and important if you wore a costly mantua such as this one.

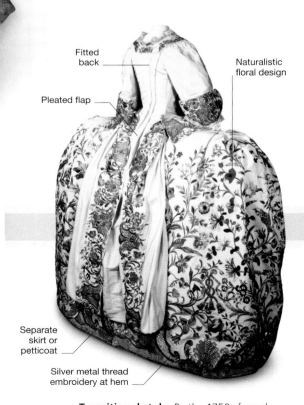

Fitted
back

Naturalistic
floral design

Pleated flap

Separate
skirt or
petticoat

Silver metal thread
embroidery at hem

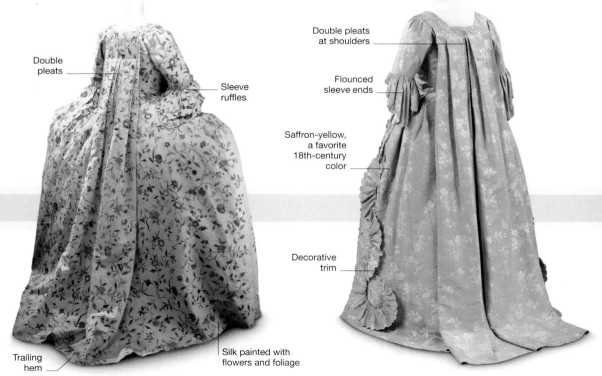

Double
pleats

Sleeve
ruffles

Trailing
hem

Silk painted with
flowers and foliage

Double pleats
at shoulders

Flounced
sleeve ends

Saffron-yellow,
a favorite
18th-century
color

Decorative
trim

Transitional style By the 1750s formal fashions were changing and the draped style of the mantua was replaced by a bodice, which had only a hanging pleated flap from waist to hem. This was the forerunner to the court train.

Hand-painted Chinese silk Robes and petticoats made from painted silk were all the rage in the 1760s and 1770s. Heavily patterned, woven dress silks were going out of fashion to be replaced in part by painted and printed fabrics imported from China and India.

Sack back Originally a nightgown style, the French *sacque* (sack back) became the most fashionable and graceful dress style in mid-18th century England. The double pleats falling from the shoulders gave the distinctive triangular shape.

GOWN AND PETTICOAT
SACK BACK DRESS

The sack back dress, also known as a *robe à la française*, started out as an informal style in France earlier in the 18th century. It came to be the most elegant dress for most of the midcentury throughout Europe and the fashionable world. The sack back could be worn in two ways. The pleats could hang straight down from the back of the shoulders into a slight train. In the alternative polonaise style, the back fabric was tucked up using tapes in the waistband to create fullness at the back. The dress was cut away at the front, and so would have been worn with a triangular stomacher, as well as a matching petticoat. A pair of stays worn under the dress kept the bodice rigid and flat fronted and molded the body into the fashionable cone shape, with a narrow waist widening to the bust.

Dress is cut away (open) at the front

Stomachers were often beautifully embroidered

The robe is worn open to reveal the petticoat

Heavily pleated petticoat

BACK VIEW WITH SKIRT DOWN

SIDE VIEW WITH SKIRT DOWN

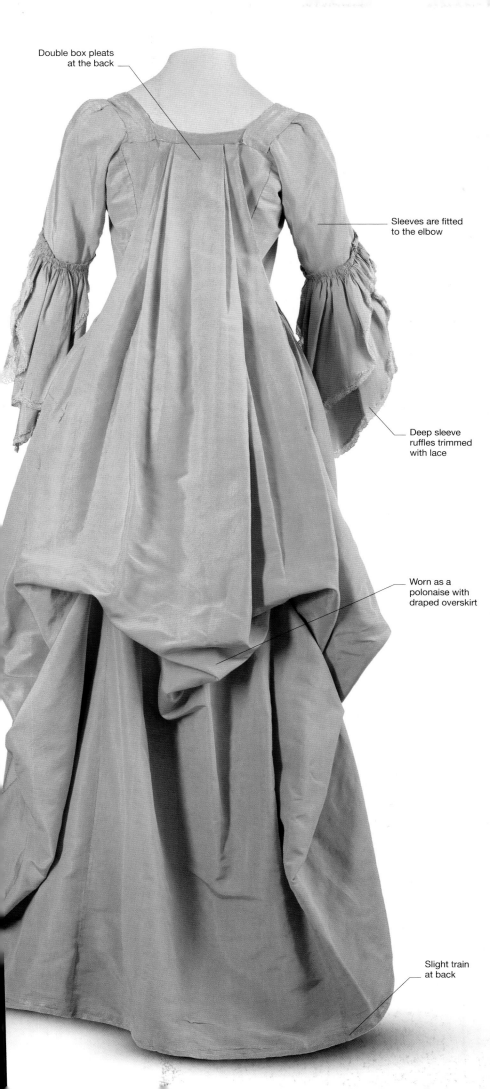

Double box pleats at the back

Sleeves are fitted to the elbow

Deep sleeve ruffles trimmed with lace

Worn as a polonaise with draped overskirt

Slight train at back

IN DETAIL

◁ STOMACHER

Although this stomacher is in poor condition, originally it would have been heavily embellished with colored silk and metallic threads in a floral embroidery design. The stomacher was pinned or stitched onto the stays and could potentially be worn with a range of different dresses.

◁ BOX PLEATS

Deep pleats of silk stitched into the back of the neckline allowed the fabric to fan out over the back of the dress to display the quality and quantity of the silk.

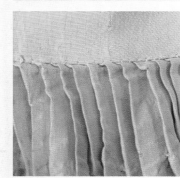

◁ LACE SLEEVE RUFFLES

Sleeves were cut tight to the elbow, and finished with cuffs, which were gathered and hand stitched onto the sleeves in two layers of ruffles. To achieve a light appearance, the ruffles were edged with lace.

◁ CARTRIDGE PLEATING

This type of pleating, in which the fabric is folded in tight pleats, gives a great deal of volume. Cartridge pleats shaped the petticoat to expand from the narrow waistband to the width of the side hoops.

◁ POLONAISE MECHANISM

Tapes sewn into the inside of the waistband could be looped and fastened to create the draped effect known as a polonaise, which added fashionable volume to the skirts. When the dress was worn hanging down, the tapes would dangle freely beneath the skirt.

1778–1789

FRENCH A LA MODE

Toward the end of the 18th century people of fashion looked to France for the latest word on matters of taste in clothing, manners, and cultural trends. But on the eve of the Revolution, the French aristocracy were out of touch with the general population, and it showed in the excesses of their dress. The styles of the age included tightly waisted bodices and draped and padded skirts. Upthrust, corseted bosoms were set off with low, round necklines, often edged with lace. Hair tended to be high-rise and hats were big. The French influence, and exquisite textiles such as Lyon silk, ensured that well-bred ladies were not merely dressed in fine clothes but were themselves sophisticated adornments both in society and at home.

1778

Hair styled in sausage-shaped rolls

Pannier

Puffed bustle

Skirts end at ankle, revealing shoes

High crown

Bright ribbons for decoration

Overskirt trails on floor

Supporting structure Ladies wore very wide skirts supported by a framework of cloth-covered cane hoops called a "pannier." Here, with this vital accessory in hand, a dressmaker hurries to her client.

High hats Women favored big hats with flat brims, tilted to the back or slightly to one side. Underneath this dress is a separate petticoat—the word at this time describing an underskirt that was meant to be seen.

CALASH

Series of hoops to support cloth

Cartoon of calash

To protect their towering hairstyles, women wore a kind of bonnet called a "calash" after the similar hood on a horse-drawn carriage of this name. Usually made of fine silk stretched over hoops made of cane, wood, or whalebone, the calash folded away concertina-style when not in use. No calash was as vast as the caricature seen here, which is taken from a book of illustrations poking fun at 18th-century fashion.

Decoration included feathers, flowers, and ribbons

Natural hair anchored over wire frame, with false hair added

Ruffle detailing on sleeve

Deep flounced petticoat

Hair padded with wool or horsehair to give height

Dress style also known as *robe à la française*

1779

Integral train

Crowning glory Hair was complicated: padded, powdered, curled and rolled, and heavily adorned. Dressed hair was left untouched for months, and "scratchers" were used to deal with itches and vermin.

Sack back Sometimes spelled "sacque back," the term refers to a style of dress with a loose back falling from the shoulders. Generally popular early in the century, by the 1770s the sack back was for court wear only.

Frills and ruffles Flouncy aprons served no purpose—they were purely for decoration. This impractical fashion was inspired by the French Queen Marie Antoinette, who enjoyed dressing up and pretending she was a milkmaid.

Elaborate hairstyle adorned with feathers

Nosegay pinned to bodice

Bodice over back-fastening corset

Dressed down When a lady was at home, getting ready or receiving visitors, she wore a type of attire referred to as "undress." Although the style looks fussy and elaborate, the term meant "relatively informal."

Full, loose sleeves

High hairstyle with side rolls

Linen fichu (scarf)

Cotton gauze apron decorated with pink bows

Short, flounced petticoat

Long, tight sleeves

Soft silk In contrast with the heavy brocades and patterned silks fashionable for gowns in the early 18th century, ladies at this time favored plainer, light, floaty fabrics known as "slight" silks.

Floral headdress and triple-rolled side curls

Matching bracelets on both wrists

Jeweled necklace

Puffed back bustle

1789

Flounced silk petticoat

Swagged overskirt

Ruffled hem

High-heeled shoes made of printed leather or silk

Polonaise On some dresses the overskirt could be lifted up and draped in swags, like a pair of curtains—the effect was called a "polonaise." Although the word suggests Polish origins, the style originated in France.

FASHION ICON
MARIE-ANTOINETTE

When the Austrian-born Marie-Antoinette (1755–1793) arrived in France in 1770, she was handed over to the Bourbon court and stripped naked. Relinquishing her Austrian nationality along with her clothes, she was dressed in a gleaming ceremonial gown. She was to marry the dauphin, Louis Auguste, the future King Louis XVI of France, and give the kingdom an heir. At first she played the dutiful wife, but struggled to fit in with Versailles' rigid idea of royal glamour: vast pannier skirts (undergarments worn wide at the sides, but flat at the front and rear) and whalebone corsets. Friendless, childless, and viewed with suspicion by a hostile French court, she turned to costume as a strategy for survival and to bolster her prestige. One disapproving aristocrat remarked that she had staged a "veritable revolution in fashion."

Extravagance and experimentation

Marie-Antoinette confounded expectations of a royal consort. In a scandalous move, she refused to wear the posture-enhancing corset. After learning to ride, she abandoned the long, flowing skirts of a sidesaddle rider and wore male breeches and a riding coat, drawing swift condemnation. Her mother warned: "If you are riding like a man, dressed as a man ... I have to tell you that I find it dangerous as well as bad for bearing children ..."

In 1774, when her husband Louis XVI was crowned King of France, all eyes were on Marie-Antoinette and her new "pouf" hairstyle. Heavily powdered hair was teased high above the forehead and topped with a cluster of white ostrich feathers. It was a look soon emulated by all of French society.

The queen experimented with eye-catching ensembles. She made weekly trips to Paris to meet the city's most famous designers. Rose Bertin (1747–1813), originally a fabric seller, became her most trusted stylist. In 1780, her provocative *robe à la polonaise*, with a bosom-enhancing bodice and ankle-baring skirt, soon caught on. Instead of having panniers, gowns once again had bunched fabric at the back. Sleeves remained elbow length, but were tight fitting and edged with a frill. The new "Polonaise" style was adopted simultaneously by the French and English courts.

Simplicity and star quality

By the mid- to late 1780s, Marie-Antoinette had changed style completely. She offended her French compatriots by adopting Anglophile fashions, wearing much simpler, lighter dresses. As her look softened, she outraged courtiers by wearing thin, muslin *chemises à la reine* loosely belted at the waist. Without panniers, the fabric molded around the legs. The peasant-girl look was topped with a broad straw hat, tilted at every imaginable angle. It was a trend condemned by French society but soon copied. Through her dress, Marie-Antoinette conveyed total power, a queen who wore whatever she wanted, no matter the cost. Her enemies at court spread rumors of her financial irresponsibility and addiction to fashion, and in revolutionary France her outfits came to symbolize a betrayal of the people. Marie-Antoinette rode to her death in 1793 wearing a brand new white chemise she had secretly saved. A trendsetter whose style had been copied by commoners and courtiers alike, Marie-Antoinette was a queen of fashion to the very end.

△ **THE YOUNG MARIE-ANTOINETTE**
In this portrait painted when she was 12, the Archduchess Marie-Antoinette is shown as perfection personified.

◁ **THE PANNIER GOWN**
The epitome of exaggerated style, the material of Marie-Antoinette's dress is heavily laden with lace. Wide panniers, often up to 12 ft (3.5 m) wide, typified the style of dress required at court when Marie-Antoinette first became queen.

TIMELINE

1770 Brings Austrian fashion to the French court, but is made to wear the traditional corsets and heavy dresses of the royal court

▷ **Early 1770s**
Refuses to wear a corset and dons outrageous androgynous riding habits

1774 Stuns the court with her new "pouf" hairstyle

Late 1770s Her extravagant dresses repeatedly cause a stir

1780 Introduces the much-copied "Polonaise" dress, bringing the "bustle look" back in vogue and baring the ankles

Late 1780s Adopts simple dresses and rustic attire, rebelling against strictures of Versailles

◁ **1788** Poses with her young children in a softer dress, showing her maternal side

○ 1770   ○ 1775   ○ 1780   ○ 1785

◁ **A SUITABLE PORTRAIT** This 1783 portrait, showing the queen clad in silk, swiftly replaced an earlier portrait of her posing in her muslin *chemise à la reine*, which had caused an outcry.

1720–1770
BAROQUE TO NEOCLASSICAL

France was the center of fashion in the 18th century, and dressing well was seen as the cornerstone of an established society. France had the finest textile industries, and throughout the salons of Paris, and Europe, clothes were the visible elements of social standing. It was English country dress, however, that became increasingly important as the century progressed. Fashions changed slowly, but there was an awareness of slight nuances, such as new styles in silk design or a change in the length of waistcoats (vests). The components of men's dress remained constant—an outer garment, waistcoat, and breeches—but the look changed across the century from the heavy baroque through the lighter rococo to the beginnings of the neoclassical. By the end of the period there was a new garment called the frock, which was based on English sporting dress.

Tightly curled Campaign wig

Coat, buttoned just at neck

Deep cuff (boot sleeve)

1725

Waistcoat with long skirts

Cotton or linen stock with lace-edged scarf over the top

Order pinned to coat

Blue sash, an alternative way to wear chivalric orders

Silk coat with matching breeches

Bulky cuffs In early 18th-century Europe there was a baroque heaviness in the style of fashionable menswear, exemplified by the oversized turn-back cuffs on a man's coat, which reached almost to the elbow.

Contrasting waistcoat, with embroidered edges

Natural hair, dressed with one side curl on either side

Black stock, and lace-edged neckwear

Deep turn-back, embroidered cuffs

Longer length waistcoat

Linen shirt with small, frilled cuffs

Small, folded linen stock

Deep cuffs and numerous buttons, fashionable in earlier decades

1750

Black breeches

1760

Red-heeled shoes, worn at court

1762

Matching silk knee breeches

Old style This man wears a bob wig, a style that was going out of fashion at this date. His suit, with its deep cuffs and its coat and waistcoat made of the same wool cloth, is old fashioned.

Summer shades Full suits (matching coats and breeches) in colorful tints were worn as formal dress at European courts, with pink silks and satins a popular summer choice. Men switched to heavier suits of patterned silk velvet in winter.

Grand tour Wealthy men traveled to Italy to study classical antiquity and to experience polite society. An appreciation of fine dressing was part of gracious living. This man wears an embroidered matching silk coat and waistcoat.

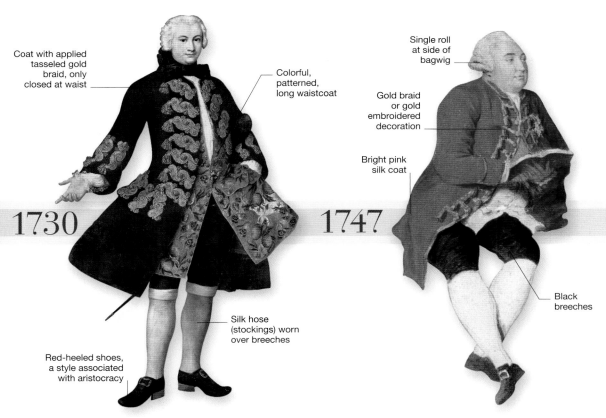

Coat with applied tasseled gold braid, only closed at waist

Colorful, patterned, long waistcoat

1730

Red-heeled shoes, a style associated with aristocracy

Silk hose (stockings) worn over breeches

Revealing skirts The skirts of men's coats were often stiffened with buckram so that they stood away from the body showing the richly decorated waistcoat beneath. Waistcoat panels were woven or embroidered to shape before being stitched together.

Single roll at side of bagwig

Gold braid or gold embroidered decoration

Bright pink silk coat

1747

Black breeches

Bagwig By the 1740s throughout both mainland Europe and the European colonies most men wore a wig. The prevalent style was the bagwig, with a series of rolls at the side, and the tail caught up into a small bag at the back.

Bagwig with two side curls

Close-fitting sleeves

Tricorn hat

Frock with fold-over collar

Natural hair

Tight-fitting sleeves

1765

Side vents, to take a sword, required wear at court

1769

Buff-colored waistcoat and breeches

Turn-down riding boots

Shoes with oval buckles

Tricorn hat A hat was an essential part of a man's ensemble, and the tricorn was the height of fashion in the mid-18th century. As wigs became taller in the 1760s, the tricorn was carried increasingly under the arm.

Sporting clothes Thomas Graham, Baron Lynedoch, who later fought in the Napoleonic wars, was a Scottish country gentleman and a daring rider in his youth. Country dress worn for such sports activities was known as a particularly British style.

WAISTCOATS (VESTS)

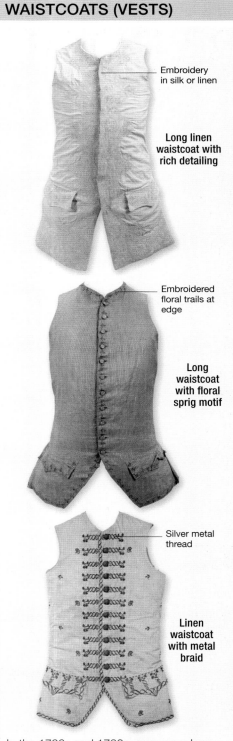

Embroidery in silk or linen

Long linen waistcoat with rich detailing

Embroidered floral trails at edge

Long waistcoat with floral sprig motif

Silver metal thread

Linen waistcoat with metal braid

In the 1720s and 1730s, men wore long waistcoats, and there was a vogue for hand-embroidered white-work styles in white cotton or linen threads on a white linen ground. The mid-18th century saw the start of more color, with delicate naturalistic embroidery in colored silk threads, sometimes with metal thread, around the waistcoat edges and the pocket flaps. There were embroidery workshops throughout Europe, with the finest in France and England. Portraits also show men wearing waistcoats decorated with broad bands of applied braid, giving a military appearance.

1770–1789
MACARONI TO DANDY

The 1770s saw the final flicker of flamboyant male fashion. Earlier in the century, the term "macaroni" had been coined for young men who affected fussy foreign dress and grooming (other labels were "fop," "exquisite," and *élégantes* in France). The name seems to have come from the informal Macaroni Club, made up of young gentlemen back from their Grand Tour, much of it spent in pasta-loving Italy. Then, toward the end of the century, powdered wigs fell from favor and the collared frock coat, based on English sporting dress, became popular. The inspiration for men's fashion had begun to move from France to England, from formal city to relaxed country, and (during the Age of Enlightenment) from the worship of rank to the belief in democracy. This was reflected in simpler, subtler styles—fashionable men of the time, tastefully free from macaroni excesses, were known as "dandies."

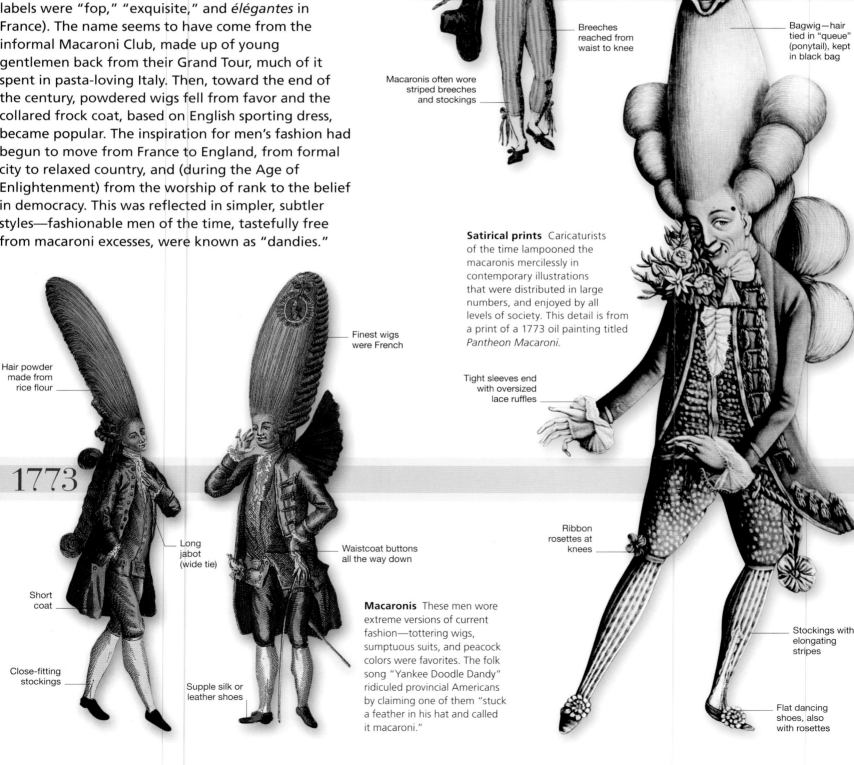

1757

Powdered wig with exaggerated tail

Fall-front breeches For this style, two side flaps buttoned together at the center, across the stomach, then the front panel flapped up over them and buttoned at the waist. This illustration is a caricature of the style, and also of the fussy neckwear in vogue.

Draped, folded linen worn as stock at neck

Breeches reached from waist to knee

Macaronis often wore striped breeches and stockings

Bagwig—hair tied in "queue" (ponytail), kept in black bag

Satirical prints Caricaturists of the time lampooned the macaronis mercilessly in contemporary illustrations that were distributed in large numbers, and enjoyed by all levels of society. This detail is from a print of a 1773 oil painting titled *Pantheon Macaroni*.

Tight sleeves end with oversized lace ruffles

1773

Hair powder made from rice flour

Finest wigs were French

Long jabot (wide tie)

Short coat

Waistcoat buttons all the way down

Close-fitting stockings

Supple silk or leather shoes

Macaronis These men wore extreme versions of current fashion—tottering wigs, sumptuous suits, and peacock colors were favorites. The folk song "Yankee Doodle Dandy" ridiculed provincial Americans by claiming one of them "stuck a feather in his hat and called it macaroni."

Ribbon rosettes at knees

Stockings with elongating stripes

Flat dancing shoes, also with rosettes

1771

Bundle on back is exaggerated bagwig

Turn-back lapels

Short, slim coat, typical of macaroni style

Garter, possibly from a lady

Turn-down riding boots

Turf macaroni This was the nickname of Augustus Henry Fitzroy, 3rd Duke of Grafton and British prime minister (1768–1770). An ineffectual leader who often slept at cabinet meetings, he invested most of his energy in horse racing, women, and fashion.

Soft, round hat with flat crown and broad brim

High linen stock

Riding crop

Plain, large metal buttons

Short, simply striped waistcoat replaces longer, patterned ones

1772

Lace-edged neckwear

Cutaway displays waistcoat

Tricorn hat, still required at court

Pale-colored breeches

Flat shoes with cut-steel buckles

Coat and waistcoat For formal occasions such as court, gentlemen wore elaborate, expensive clothing, usually in the form of a fitted coat and waistcoat—often embroidered finely at the edges, and sometimes matching.

Small, round hat

Wigs would have been itchy—sword makes a handy scratch stick

Flouncy ruffle instead of folded, linen stock

1776

Seals hanging from waistcoat

Outsized rosettes; buttons or small buckles were more usual

Strapped shoes

Hairstyles Although huge wigs, cylindrical side curls, and fussy decoration were widely popular, macaronis exaggerated this style significantly. Swords were often shown in caricatures—as an ironic comment on their effeminate appearance.

Coat cut straight across, without side pleats

Breeches fastened at knee with buttons and buckle

1778

High, baggy riding boots

Romantic hero Goethe's 1774 novel *The Sorrows of Young Werther* inspired "Werther fever"— dressing in the informal, distinctly English country style of its hero. This French version of the English frock coat is slimmer with more decoration.

Hat with cockade (knot of ribbons) and feather plume

Red, stand-up collar

Lace ruffle at chest

1786

Blue jacket with red cuffs that echo Windsor uniform

Tight, turn-down boots

Spurs on ankles

Slim lines The macaronis left one legacy: slim tailoring never went out of fashion. Numerous conflicts in Europe made military dress acceptable as day wear. This outfit resembles the official Windsor (court) uniform designed by King George III.

COAT, WAISTCOAT, AND BREECHES
STREAMLINED COURT SUIT

This man's court outfit from 1780, embellished ornately with a floral theme, is a typical example of a rococo, French-style suit known as the *habit à la française*. Such suits consisted of a coat (*habit*), waistcoat (*vest*), and knee breeches, worn with a white shirt, a jabot frill, ruffled cuffs, and silk stockings. The striking colors, lavish fabrics, and extravagant embroidery continued a trend for bright colors and decoration from the 1600s. Characteristic of the pre-French Revolution period, outfits such as these were typically worn by the 18th-century upper-class man. Suit cloth often came already embroidered—known as *à la disposition*—prior to being made up. The slim, fitted cut of this suit is typical of the later 1700s, with its streamlined, unpadded coat and shorter, sleeveless waistcoat. As the Revolution (1789–1799) approached, stripes became popular—this cut-velvet coat is striped with pink.

Jabot frill at the neck

Narrow-wristed, slim sleeves contribute to the elegant shape

Decorative shirt-cuff ruffles

Embroidery design on one side mirrors that on the other

Narrow, cutaway sides to reveal decorated waistcoat

Breeches dark (once black) velvet patterned with tiny, pink diamonds

Breeches tighter fitting, like coat and waistcoat

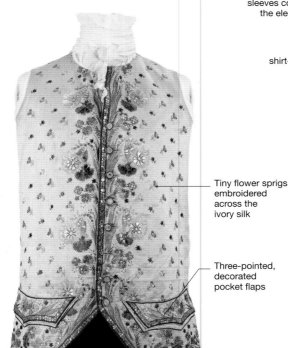

Tiny flower sprigs embroidered across the ivory silk

Three-pointed, decorated pocket flaps

△ **WAISTCOAT**
With its very shallow, cutaway skirt fronts, this distinctive shape is typical of the era. The front section is made of ivory satin richly embroidered with colored silks. The pale color shows off the embroidery and contrasts with the dark coat.

Short stand collar reveals neckwear

Coat fabric is black cut velvet striped with pink

Embellished coat pockets

Back pleats of coattails drape to reveal decorated panels

Short length coat, to the knees

IN DETAIL

◁ **STAND COLLAR**
The short stand collar is a feature that became more popular on men's coats (and waistcoats) from the 1790s. The fully embroidered, stepped, cutaway version on this coat is small and works in harmony with the modestly sized jabot frill. Much taller collars were to become popular.

◁ **COAT CUFFS**
True to later 18th-century fashions, the coat's cuffs, smaller than in previous eras, hug the wrist closely, in keeping with the garment's slim, fitted profile. Their lavish decoration includes sequins, glass flower shapes, and embroidered buttons.

◁ **TAIL TRIMMINGS**
Focusing embellishment around the central division of the coat tails, and in a broad band close to the waist, attracts attention to the neat, elegant cut of the tails and the subtly waisted form of the coat.

◁ **FALL FRONT**
The dark (once black) velvet knee breeches feature the characteristic 18th-century "fall" front. The fall is a panel that closes up toward the waistband with buttons. The buttons here are covered with the same fabric as the breeches, making them more discreet.

◁ **KNEE BANDS, BUCKLES, AND BUTTONS**
A colorful band of floral-themed embroidery sewn over the velvet and tightened with a buckle provides a stylish trim for the bottom of the breeches. The side opening is closed with embroidered buttons and shaped to ensure a snug fit at the knees.

1770–1789

SIMPLER STYLING

Both England and France were instrumental in establishing the look of fashion, which was then followed by the rest of Europe, and farther afield. French fashions were elegant, while English dress was more informal. By the 1770s the collarless coat with bulky side pleats, fashionable since the 17th century, had been replaced by the frock coat, derived from the informal garment worn by English men in the country. There was also a growing informality in women's dress in both England and France, with floating and draped styles of newly available cotton fabrics from the East becoming popular.

High-piled hairstyle sloping backward from forehead

Natural hair and wavy locks denote an artistic sensibility

Linen shirt

1755

Buff breeches, gathered at the back

Knit stockings

Cotton muslin chemise dress with drawstring neck

Leather shoes with flat heels

Loose cloak

Blue ribbon sash at waist, possibly with seal tied at one end

Country dress Self-colored wool outer garments worn with linen shirts, and white silk or cotton knit stockings were typical English country wear in the mid-18th century. This trend for less formal dress would soon inspire fashions throughout the rest of Europe.

Drape of red silk used as artistic backdrop

Muslin neck scarf

Seals hanging from chain at waist

Short leather gloves, held in hand

Round black hat

"The Maid from Bath" A play was written about the beautiful young soprano Elizabeth Linley, the most famous woman in England in the 1770s. She was painted in the very latest fashions.

Hair wildly curled at sides, with single ringlet over one shoulder

Silk gauze or very fine cotton gauze neckerchief tied in large bow

1779

1780

1785

Buff (pale yellow-brown) breeches

Apricot silk dress with green silk sash at waist

Trailing hem

Turned-down riding boots

Flat, slipper-style shoes

Tailored coat Britain was known for immaculate tailoring and the finest wool cloth. The double-breasted style and cutaway skirts of this navy blue wool coat heralded the era of Beau Brummell and dandyism in the early 19th century.

Chemise Fashionable in the 1780s, this garment was the forerunner of later neoclassical dress. The style, a tube of cotton muslin with a drawstring at the neck and sash at the waist, grew popular throughout Europe.

High-heeled shoes

Own hair, rolled into side curl

Frock coat

Contrasting waistcoat (vest) edged with braid

Close-fitting sleeves

1770

Walking sticks were highly fashionable

Boots with turnover tops

Flat straw hat made in Italy or England

Engageantes (sleeve ruffles) of English bobbin lace

Petticoat pleated to take medium-wide skirt hoops

1775

Pleated, pierced, and pinked robings run down length of gown

Walking stick, often of rattan

Tricorn hat

Wide lapels

Double-breasted closure

1778

Shoes with buckles

Frock coat The frock coat was characterized by a folded-over collar, narrow sleeves without a turn-back cuff, and a slim silhouette, often with a curving front. It was a somber-toned wool cloth garment, with blue-black a popular choice.

Chiné robe This sack back style is in the newly popular chiné print. The pattern was printed onto the warp thread prior to weaving, giving a fuzzy effect known in this era as chiné in France and "clouds" in England.

Overcoat Another new style for men in the 18th century (as well as the frock coat), the overcoat, or redingote, was derived from English working men's dress. This French example was worn as a walking coat over a close-cut suit.

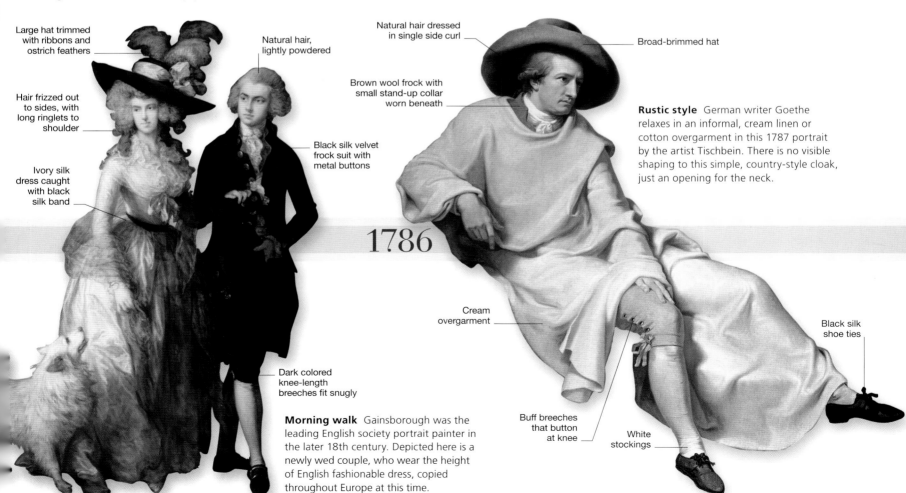

Large hat trimmed with ribbons and ostrich feathers

Natural hair, lightly powdered

Hair frizzed out to sides, with long ringlets to shoulder

Ivory silk dress caught with black silk band

Black silk velvet frock suit with metal buttons

Natural hair dressed in single side curl

Broad-brimmed hat

Brown wool frock with small stand-up collar worn beneath

Rustic style German writer Goethe relaxes in an informal, cream linen or cotton overgarment in this 1787 portrait by the artist Tischbein. There is no visible shaping to this simple, country-style cloak, just an opening for the neck.

1786

Dark colored knee-length breeches fit snugly

Cream overgarment

Buff breeches that button at knee

White stockings

Black silk shoe ties

Morning walk Gainsborough was the leading English society portrait painter in the later 18th century. Depicted here is a newly wed couple, who wear the height of English fashionable dress, copied throughout Europe at this time.

1625–1790
MASQUERADE

Since medieval times, dressing up had been popular all over Europe. In the Middle Ages, masked mummers (traveling actors) performed in village pageants and traveled from house to house in Carnival season, which lasted from Christmas until Lent. During Carnival, the Catholic Church allowed merrymaking and open-air festivities, so bands of masked revelers regularly paraded through the streets. During the Renaissance, people performed set scenes in elaborate processional pageants. By the 18th century, Carnival was celebrated all over Italy, with Venice leading the fashion for lively masquerades (masked balls and entertainments), held at night and lit with flickering candles and torches. This trend soon became popular in France and England, too, possibly because shadows and masks encourage relaxed behavior. The term "masquerade" specifically described dressing as particular characters, but these extravagant events led to the more general practice of displaying wealth and social position by wearing "fancy dress"— formal clothes with small elements of masquerade added.

1650

Hooked nose identifies Pulcinella

Many women, not just nuns, wore wimples in the Middle Ages

Dressed as a monk

Female players, rare in *commedia dell'arte*, usually dressed as figures from the past

Long, medieval-style skirt had to be held up for walking

Commedia dell'arte This comic open-air entertainment, first seen in Venice, may have been connected to Carnival. The traveling players, dressed as stock characters such as Harlequin and Pulcinella, probably performed at early masquerades, providing costume inspiration.

Domino In Venice, a masquerade cloak was known as a *domino*, and this garment came to typify a masked character with an air of intrigue and adventure. During the 18th century, these figures (who could be male or female) were particularly popular in London.

Cloaked characters often wore a white mask, here perched on the typical tricorn (three-cornered) hat

Costumes from Middle Ages popular for masquerades

Pointed hat with a veil

Mask for fancy-dress ball

Full naval-commander costume

Turban headdress

1750s

1789

Costume cloaks were always hooded, black, and voluminous

Shalvar (baggy pants) for Turkish costume

Gown and hooped petticoat fit underneath cloak

Fashionable gown of the period

Sources of inspiration Masqueraders took their costume ideas from varied sources—the exotic cultures of Africa and Asia, the past, political and social scandals, fairy tales, and extreme fashions. For late-1700s fancy-dress balls, guests accessorized their best contemporary clothes and wore a mask.

Black mask (traditionally, Harlequin had a blacked face)

Harlequin Probably the best-known *commedia dell'arte* character, even today, Harlequin is witty, mischievous, clownish, childlike, and nimble. Early Harlequin costumes were sewn together from patches, which was probably the origin of the diamond motif.

Belt over front-closure jacket

Distinctive suit patterned with colored diamonds

Soft, slipperlike shoes

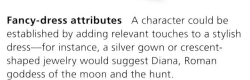

Sugarloaf hat (named after the large cones in which sugar was sold)

Mask with long, crooked nose

Floppy white neck ruffle

Pot belly

Pulcinella Cantankerous rather than clownlike, the Pulcinella character is dwarfish and humpbacked. In Italian, his name means "little chicken." In English he became Mr. Punch in traditional Punch and Judy shows.

High hairstyle threaded with ribbon and feathers

Gold mask

Short train and skirt folded back at sides

Mantua-style dress has separate bodice and petticoat

Deep border of silver fabric at hem

Fancy-dress attributes A character could be established by adding relevant touches to a stylish dress—for instance, a silver gown or crescent-shaped jewelry would suggest Diana, Roman goddess of the moon and the hunt.

Shako (tall military hat)

Short cape worn over one shoulder

Gold braiding on jacket

Short jacket called a dolman

Pants were usually red

High leather riding boots

Hussar Dashing Hungarian soldiers (Hussars) rode fast horses, acted as scouts, and took on dangerous skirmishes. Their youth and courage fired public imagination, and their glamorous uniforms were ideal for costume balls.

LADY WITH A MASK

This print of a portrait by British artist Henry Morland is called *The Fair Nun Unmasked*. In 18th-century England the word "nun" could suggest a prostitute, and the painting is a form of satire. The black veil suits this purpose, since prostitutes of the time often donned religious dress. The veil also suggests an Italian *batua*, a length of black silk that covered the face for masquerades.

TURKISH DELIGHT

Jeanne Antoinette Poisson, better known as Madame de Pompadour (1721–1764), was the powerful mistress of Louis XV of France from 1745 to her death. When she commissioned artist Charles André van Loo to paint her as a Turkish Sultana, Pompadour started a craze for *portrait à la turque*. Exotic Asian culture was already widely popular in France, and *Turquerie,* as the craze was known, permeated all aspects of French art and fashion.

Both women in this picture wear a loosely wrapped turban (Madame de Pompadour's is decorated with her signature rose); a flowing, long-sleeved shift worn over a full skirt with a natural waistline; and on top, a long jacket in rich colors. Pompadour wears an ornate belt with full, baggy silk trousers. She kept several styles of these garments in her wardrobe and enjoyed wearing them in private. Pearls were particularly favored by women at this time, and here, Pompadour has them entwined in her hair, hanging from her ears, and around her neck. Her hair is dressed in a style she helped to popularize, drawn back close to the head in a small bun, from which a few curls fall onto the neck or over the shoulder to decorate the nape.

> 66
> The first piece of my dress is a pair of drawers very full that reach to my shoes. Over this hangs my smock of a fine white silk gauze, edged with embroidery ... The smock has wide sleeves ... the shape and colour of the bosom is very well distinguished through it ...
>
> **LADY MARY WORTLEY MONTAGU,** *TURKISH EMBASSY LETTER,* 1717
> 99

MADAME DE POMPADOUR ▷
This portrait of Madame de Pompadour, *A sultana served coffee by a slave,* was by one of her favorite painters, Charles André van Loo. Painted in the mid-18th century, it shows Pompadour in exotic Turkish attire.

1625–1789

SPORTS DRESS

Men wore tailored coats for country pursuits such as riding, hunting, hawking, and fishing. Often these activities were social and became sports occasions as a result. Special occasions demanded special dress, and so sports dress evolved. Men put on leather boots, breeches, and sometimes a cape or cloak with or without a hood. Women, too, wore tailored coats—for the first time—for riding. Since horseback riding was the main form of transportation, the tailored habit became the principal form of traveling dress, right up to the mid-19th century. Women's tailored jackets and skirts were based on 16th-century garments known as juppes and safeguards—Queen Elizabeth I had these in her wardrobe. For swimming, undergarments and linen caps were worn. A 1675 engraving of the Kings and Queens baths at Bath in England shows women in linen shifts and men topless with linen breeches, all wearing linen caps. The earliest sports to have specific dress were cricket, with *The Sporting Magazine* depicting cricketers in white jackets and breeches in 1793, and golf, for which red jackets were worn.

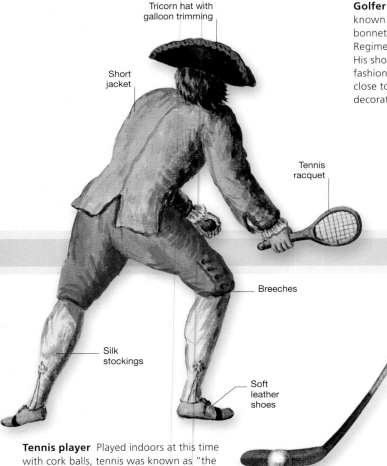

Prince Charlie beret of blue wool with red tuft and band

Powdered wig

Short, wool coat

Red became mandatory for golfers

Tricorn hat with galloon trimming

Short jacket

Golfer This golfer wears a beret known as a Prince Charlie or Scotch bonnet, which was worn by Highland Regiments in the mid-18th century. His shortened version of a fashionable coat has sleeves cut close to the arms and minimal decoration for ease of movement.

Tennis racquet

Breeches

Silk stockings

Silk stockings

Soft leather shoes

Tennis player Played indoors at this time with cork balls, tennis was known as "the sport of kings." Light leather shoes were worn to permit players to move quickly, along with a shorter jacket or waistcoat (vest).

Cocked beaver hat with silver braid trim

Gun

Double-breasted frock coat

Silk stockings

Shooting coat Riding and shooting frock coats worn at this time were shorter than regular frock coats, and often double breasted. The waistcoats were also shorter. The ammunition pouch was held on a leather belt around the waist.

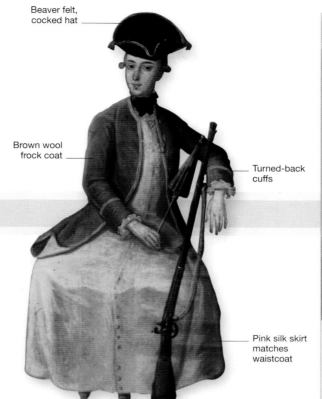

Beaver felt, cocked hat

Brown wool frock coat

Turned-back cuffs

Pink silk skirt matches waistcoat

Tailoring for women This brown wool tailored jacket follows the line of a man's frock coat. It is lined with the same pink silk that makes up the waistcoat and skirt. The wearer finishes her outdoor ensemble with a beaver felt, cocked hat.

CHILDREN AND SPORTS

From the late 18th century, outdoor activities were regarded as an essential pastime for children. Previously dressed as miniature adults, they began to wear less constrictive garments. The skeleton suit consisting of a short jacket and trousers allowed for better movement. For games such as cricket, boys wore a shorter jacket, and girls donned riding habits not only for riding but also for outdoor pursuits such as walking.

Varnished, leather hat with visor

Frock coat, waistcoat, and breeches all of uniform fabric

Silk stockings

Leather shoes

French formality Hunting hats of varnished leather with straight visors were popular in France in the 1750s. The casual approach of English dress for outdoor pursuits contrasted with the more formal uniform styles popular in France.

Straw hat with ribbon embellishment

Silk caraco (thigh-length, waisted) jacket

Matching silk skirt

Informal wear This lady wears a short caraco jacket made of the same silk as her skirt. Around her neck is a cotton gauze scarf known as a fichu. Her fashionable straw hat is worn tilted right over her forehead.

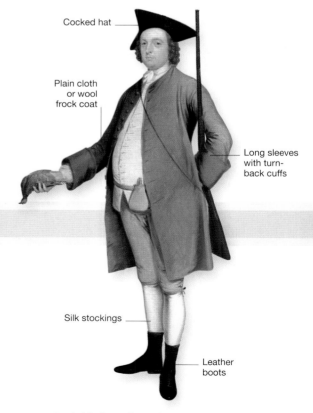

Cocked hat

Plain cloth or wool frock coat

Long sleeves with turn-back cuffs

Silk stockings

Leather boots

Buckskin breeches This gentleman wears buckskin breeches, which became fashionable for outdoor pursuits. Worn with wool frock coats in buff, blue, or black, they were a practical, durable choice. He sports a shooter's leather belt around his waist.

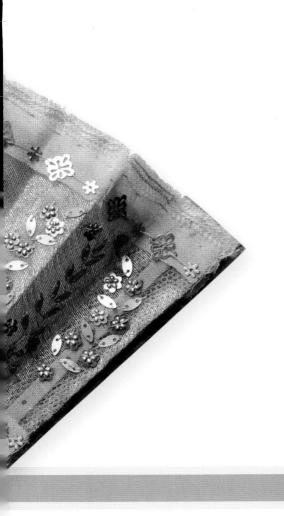

FROM REVOLUTION
TO FRIVOLITY

1790–1900

FROM REVOLUTION TO FRIVOLITY

This was a century of unprecedented and accelerated change. The world's population grew dramatically, and infant mortality was reduced by a quarter due to improved health care and hygiene. The average adult lifespan increased by a decade, and a burgeoning middle class acquired property and possessions, patronized department stores, and indulged in sports activities. Day trippers to national exhibitions and the seaside saw fashionable society men and women at leisure and aspired to their lifestyle—and fashions. Philanthropic reforms, including educational provision, assisted the working classes in seeking to better themselves by working their way up in factories, stores, or "in service." The world was changing rapidly, and the increase in members of the affluent middle classes breathed life into the market for fashionable garments.

On the move

After the Industrial Revolution, there was a major shift from country to town dwelling. Improved transportation systems—railroads, steamships, roads, and bridges—supported trade and allowed ordinary people to travel greater distances. Increased mobility expanded their range of experiences and gave rise to a new sense of worldliness and fashion consciousness. The efficient circulation of newspapers and the advent of mail delivery, as well as photography, the typewriter, telephone, and transatlantic telegraph facilitated long-distance communications. News of national, European, and American politics traveled at greater speed. Fashion information, through magazines and correspondence, could now be readily shared between continents. Fashion was becoming truly international.

A new age

Rapidly evolving politics, economics, technology, and new discoveries affected fashion. Pride in national heroes in Britain spawned the Wellington boot, named after the Duke of Wellington, and the Gladstone bag after Prime Minister William Gladstone. Mechanization of textile processes enabled ever more complex weaves and prints at more affordable prices. A revolution in the home came with the domestic sewing machine and running water, which aided daily washing; most people above the breadline now owned and wore more garments than ever before.

SEASIDE ELEGANCE
Two elegantly dressed women; a color plate in *The Englishwoman's Domestic Magazine*, January 1875.

1790–1800	1801–10	1811–30
1790 The fashion for "dandyism" emerges, championed by socialite Beau Brummell.	 ▲ Napoleon's profile on a coin	**1811** Jane Austen's first novel, *Sense and Sensibility,* is published, and another five novels follow, two of them the year after her death in 1817. A social commentator, Austen's novels include acute observation of her characters' clothes. ▼ Portrait of Jane Austen
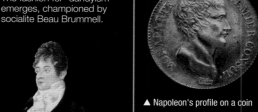	**1804** Napoleon Bonaparte is crowned. During his reign, he puts France at the forefront of fashion innovation and design.	
	1806 *La Belle Assemblée,* a British women's magazine, is published for the first time and includes features on fashion.	**1815** After the Duke of Wellington defeats Napoleon Bonaparte at the Battle of Waterloo, Wellington boots become a popular fashion item.
▲ Beau Brummell in his "daytime ensemble"		
1790 The first design patent for a sewing machine is granted. Within 50 years they are produced and start to be used in factories.	 ▲ Early model of a sewing machine	▼ Mechanized plush loom
1795 Waistlines are raised, paving the way for the development of the empire silhouette and the unabashed neoclassicism of late 1790s fashion.	**c. 1810** British-born Edward Cartwright had patented the first power loom in 1785, but the design was in need of modification. Between then and the early 19th century it underwent improvements, and by 1820 was commonly used in both Britain and the US.	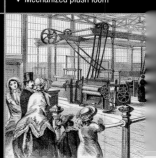

"
Fashion is a form of ugliness so intolerable that we have to alter it every six months.

OSCAR WILDE, 1890
"

1831–50	1851–54	1855–70	1871–80	1881–94	1895–1900

1839
The registration of designs for clothing is established to help protect emerging manufacturers from pirate copies of their goods being made.

1851
American women's rights activist Amelia Bloomer makes the bloomer pants popular.

1851
The Great Exhibition in Crystal Palace, London, attracts millions of visitors who observe displays of fashion and style.

1855
A dotted pattern on fabric is named "polka dot" after the polka, a popular dance.

1859
A new range of dye colors in purple–pink hues are discovered and named magenta and solferino after contemporary battles.

1872
The marcel wave is first developed by hairdresser François Marcel, and remains popular for more than 50 years.

▶ Irons used for creating the marcel wave curling effect

1845
With the arrival of the railroad in the 1840s comes mass travel and clothes designed for travel, leisure, and vacations.

1852
The Englishwoman's Domestic Magazine is published, including advice on needlework from domestic writer Mrs. Beeton.

▼ Bustling Regent Street outside Liberty & Co. department store in London

1882
Oscar Wilde embarks on a tour of America. His "too too and utterly utter" aesthetic fashion style is regularly remarked upon in the media.

1887
Fancy Dresses Described by Ardern Holt is published.

1895
The new artistic style of Art Nouveau influences fashion in the form of simple felt hats, turbans, and clouds of tulle.

▼ Playbill poster shows an actress dressed in Art Nouveau style

1892
The first issue of *Vogue* magazine, founded by Arthur Turnure, is published in the United States.

1892
Viyella (a blend of wool and cotton) is introduced and is popularly used for night wear.

◀ Photography was used for fashionable visiting cards

1854
With the birth of photography comes the "carte de visite," a fashionable visiting card that includes a photograph of the traveler. Immense popularity leads to the publication of the cards of prominent figures, whose fashions are followed.

1869
Dolly Varden costume, named after a character in Charles Dickens's *Barnaby Rudge*, becomes a fashionable look.

1875
Liberty & Co. department store opens in London.

▼ *Dress'd in a Dolly Varden* became a popular song

1848
Known as the "Year of Revolutions" because of the series of political upheavals that take place throughout Europe, prudery reigns supreme and women's skirts are down to the ground.

1900
By the end of the century, high collars, long-line bodices, colored tights, and high heels are fashion must-haves.

◀ Turn-of-the-century fashion looks ahead to the Edwardian era

1790–1800
NEOCLASSICISM

The fashions of the last decade of the 18th century reflected a time of upheaval and change. It brought more informal dress, inspired by country rather than court styles, and influenced by revolutionary fervor in France. Wrapping gowns in striped silk and painted chintzes gave way to printed cottons and plain cotton chemise dresses that could, at last, be washed. Imported Indian muslins and cotton gauzes were popular for neckerchiefs and full-length dresses. By 1800, white predominated. The shape was a neoclassical columnar silhouette, with a simple, high-waisted dress. There was little understructure except for an opaque linen shift and cotton underslip that echoed the shape of the gown, and sometimes half-stays to support the bust. Hand-stitched seams were neat and unobtrusive. Accessories added colorful highlights. Extraordinary features emerged: like the audacious revealing of thighs through flimsy muslins, laced corsets worn on top of dresses, and red ribbon that may have signified veiled support for the revolutionaries.

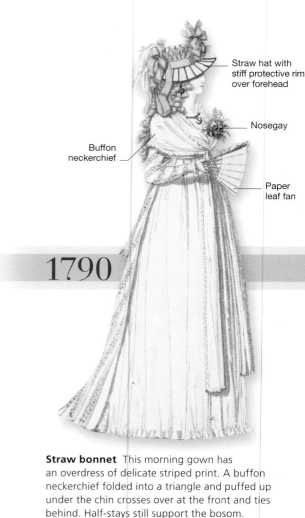

Straw hat with stiff protective rim over forehead

Nosegay

Buffon neckerchief

Paper leaf fan

1790

Straw bonnet This morning gown has an overdress of delicate striped print. A buffon neckerchief folded into a triangle and puffed up under the chin crosses over at the front and ties behind. Half-stays still support the bosom.

Soft cotton gauze and ribbon headdress

Cameo-type jewel to neckline

Fashionable yellow silk or wool overtunic

Satin tabard with ruched trim

Fur tippet with high collar

1799

Trailing tambour-style embroidery

Fringe curls visible

Headdress entwined with ribbon

Laced corset-style bodice

Ribbon hem to overskirt, revealing petticoat

Overtunic embroidery White cotton dresses were fastened with ties, or Dorset (yarn-covered) buttons, and often had drawstring necklines. This sleeveless, trained overtunic is secured on the shoulders, toga-style.

Outer wear Fur muffs added warmth for women suffering for the whims of fashion, as did satin and velvet tabards, and bearskin-fur tippets. Close-fitting head wear covered shorter hair.

Laced bodice Neoclassical meets avant-garde in the dress (left) with external front-laced corset. Accents of color are introduced to the dress (right) through the use of red ribbon trim.

Unpowdered hair with ribbon bandeau

Cloak cord with tassels

Short sleeves for evening

Flat pumps with pointed toe

Ostrich plume headdress

Mass of clustered curls

Attached watch fob

1798

Slight train, for evening

Decorative festooning to hem

English court dress
The abstract embroidered spot motif across this petticoat is remarkably futuristic. The striped silk overdress is trimmed with cording and tassels, and chenille embroidery. Hooped understructures were still worn for the English court up to 1820.

Ostrich feather plumes

Short-sleeved bodice

Long kid gloves

Evening ensemble The high waistline is clearly visible in this 1798 cotton gauze dress. The full-length, sleeved overgarment is cut away and fastened under the bosom. Its dark color could be accentuated with cut steel or Berlin ironwork jewelry.

Classic dress This is the essence of the neoclassical look. The flimsy cotton gauze layers are indicated by the visible outline of a knee. The short Roman-style cloak has tasseled cord ties. Ribbon defines the bosom and high waistline.

SHOES

Striped silk, Italian heel c. 1790

Red leather, tassel c. 1795

Woven silk, ribbon rosette c. 1795

By the 1790s women wore slip-on "sandal shoes" with pointed toes. Heels were getting lower and disappeared by 1800. Italian heels were also all the rage. Pattens were still worn to protect shoes outdoors, especially over painted leather or brocaded silk shoes. Lighter pump-style slippers of kid leather, striped silk, and silk satin were worn indoors.

Those who could afford to, had their shoes made to measure by their shoemaker. However, straights—shoes that were interchangeable, without a left or a right—were usual. Pink and yellow were popular dye colors, and there is a clear Eastern influence in shoes of the later 18th century that complements textiles such as the Indian cottons and Kashmir shawls of the period.

1800–1809
EMPIRE LINES

Fashion magazines produced hand-colored plates for each month, specifying whether a dress was best for morning, afternoon, or evening wear, or designed for a special occasion. In France the so-called Empire line had been fashionable since the 1790s (Napoleon became emperor in 1804). This simple style was inspired by classical Greek and Roman statuary, where figures were draped in fabric with minimal ornamentation. Waistlines were high and skirts had short trains until 1807 when straighter lines were favored. The palette at this time was white or pastel shades, although trim and accessories could add brighter accents. Corseting was unboned but corded corsets separated the breasts and controlled waist and hips with back lacing. Dresses with short sleeves in simple cotton muslin required stoles and capes or pelisses to provide warmth. Some dresses were overlaid with layers of lace and gauze. Gradually, more exotic accessories became available, such as parasols and embroidered shawls from India.

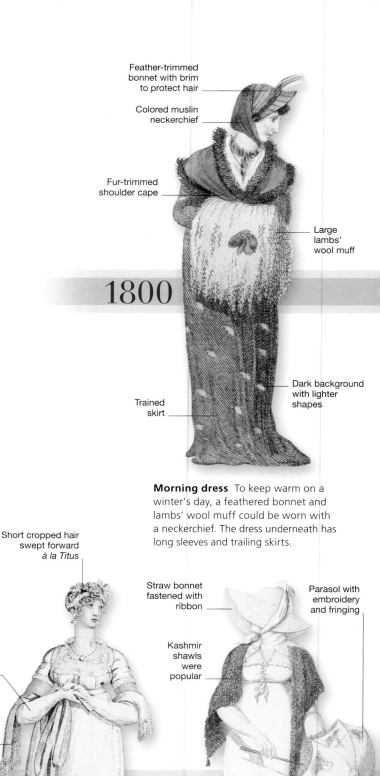

1800

Feather-trimmed bonnet with brim to protect hair

Colored muslin neckerchief

Fur-trimmed shoulder cape

Large lambs' wool muff

Dark background with lighter shapes

Trained skirt

Morning dress To keep warm on a winter's day, a feathered bonnet and lambs' wool muff could be worn with a neckerchief. The dress underneath has long sleeves and trailing skirts.

Cap with bandeau edge

Short-sleeved Empire gown

Ostrich feather on soft cap

High waistline, under the bust

Cloak hangs from shoulder

Short cropped hair swept forward *à la Titus*

Straw bonnet fastened with ribbon

Parasol with embroidery and fringing

Bare arms

Kashmir shawls were popular

Simple stole with lace edging

1805   **1807**

Swans' down boa

Draped fabric creates train

Fabric drapes to floor

Cut without a train

Skirt falls from high waist, without a train

Roman-toga style The influence of classical Roman dress is clear in this softly draped, white muslin dress. The light garment is covered by a cloak worn over one shoulder in the style of a Roman toga.

Grecian This style of dress clings to the body with draping reminiscent of a Grecian statue. The dress is simple with a trained skirt. A feather bonnet and boa lend elegance but very little warmth.

Classical influence Based on an idealized version of a classical Greek statue, this simple gown has very restrained decoration; just lace edging at the neckline and along the hem.

Cotton gown A light cotton gown cut in the high-waisted Empire line required little corsetry. The fabric was so thin and simple that decorative shawls were often worn for warmth and to add color.

Tall hat

Trimmed with braids and tassels

Fabric gathered at back

Folding fan

Short train

Afternoon dress The vertical braids with tiny tassels on this columnar dress emphasize its slender lines. It has elbow-length sleeves and a train, and is worn with a relatively simple, tall hat. Pale colors such as this lemon tint were favored.

Feathered bonnet

Gold earrings and necklace

Net spencer (short cardigan-jacket)

Net overskirt secured at waistband

GETTING DRESSED

A woman of substance required a lady's maid to help her dress, particularly to get her into her corset. In this period, corsets were long-line and unboned, and worn over a linen shift called a chemise, drawers—of linen, cotton, or stockinette—and stockings with decorative embroidery. The maid would then assist with the sleeveless dress, which was filmy and clinging, and put on jewelry as required before helping to curl and pin her mistress's hair under a bonnet or a bandeau trimmed with feathers.

Hair *à la Titus* (short, in a mass of curls) with bandeau

Pelisse is dress length

1809

Pelisse lined with salmon-pink silk

Lace along hem

Long evening gloves

Turbanlike headdress

Slight puff to sleeves at end of decade

Bracelet worn on upper arm

Overdress

Embroidered train of overdress

Embroidery along hem of dress

Embroidered skirt border

Grecian slippers

Pelisse For walking in springtime, a pelisse coat, such as this full-length sleeved version in figured silk, could be worn. The extravagant fringed parasol is pagoda-shaped. The waistline on the dress is now a little lower.

Stronger hues Colors became stronger by 1809, and this green dress is trimmed with bright red ribbon. There is also a contrasting embroidered hem, though the net or lace spencer and overskirt are white.

Gauze for evening This overdress retains its train, an indicator of evening wear. It covers an embroidered cotton gown. There is more decoration from the exotic headdress, pendant, and bracelets.

REGENCY SOCIETY

In the early 1800s, Regency Britain changed from a rural society to an urban, trading one, and London became an important center. A "social season" evolved during the 17th and 18th centuries where the better off divided their year between the high life of London (also Edinburgh and Dublin) and hunting seasons at country residences. Provincial towns and cities boasted Assembly Rooms and theaters for the proliferating middle classes. Social rounds provided chances for young people to parade their looks and fashionable clothes in order to make good marriages.

In this fashionable evening gathering in Bristol in 1817, the young women favor a relatively simple look: a pale empire-line gown with a low, wide neckline, short puffed sleeves, gloves, fan, and modest floral hair ornaments. Frilled and decorated hems and shorter dress lengths had recently gained currency, and diaphanous fabrics such as muslin and gauze, including satin gowns with net overlays, were popular. Maturer and married ladies dressed in stronger colors with fancy head wear.

The gentlemen wear long-skirted frock coats, tall, upright collars, and cravat-style neck cloths. Transitions in menswear are apparent—the man on the right wears black knee-breeches and silk stockings, while the man in the center with a lady on each arm sports loosely cut trousers.

> **"**
>
> What gown and what head-dress she should wear ... became her chief concern ... She lay awake ten minutes on Wednesday night debating between her spotted and her tamboured muslin, and nothing but the shortness of time prevented her buying a new one for the evening.
>
> JANE AUSTEN, *NORTHANGER ABBEY*, 1817
>
> **"**

◁ **THE CLOAKROOM, CLIFTON ASSEMBLY ROOMS, 1817**
Men and women prepared carefully for a social event in Regency England. Artist Rolinda Sharples shows them in the cloakroom of the Assembly Rooms in Clifton, a fashionable area of Bristol.

1811–1820
REGENCY BELLES

Fashions began to move in a new direction, away from the narrow Empire line and into a softer bell shape, with fuller skirts. Though white still predominated, stronger dye colors were reintroduced for outer garments like pelisses and spencer jackets. Upper sleeves gained small puffs, and lower sleeves had longer cuffs. The English waistline had begun to move down a little c. 1808–1814, but this did not last and it sprang back up to a high point when French fashions became accessible again after the Battle of Waterloo in 1815. Pin tucking appeared on skirts as a decorative feature and went on to be used for lengthening and shortening skirts as hemlines changed. Vandyking (zigzag shaping) was a prevalent feature c. 1815–1835 and satin stitch was popular. Original gowns that survive testify to the detail, ingenuity, and fineness of the designs and embroidery.

1810

Short, straight-cut sleeves

Gathered bodice

High waist

Deep hem border on skirt extending into rounded train

Rounded train Fabrics of woven silver tissue, light muslin embroidered with silver foil, and printed cotton with small repeats were popular for evening dresses. The border pattern on the hem, cuffs, and collar coordinates with the main fabric of this gown.

Feminine take on military stovepipe shako hat

Spencer jacket matches hat

1815

Dress with double hem ruffles

Ankles visible

Summer fashion Peace after the Napoleonic wars put a spring in the step of ladies of fashion. There was a buoyancy and frivolity about fashion designs, which began to feature decorative trims and ruffles. A parasol to keep the sun off completed this outfit.

Hair dressed with artificial flowers

Short puffed sleeves

Greek key border motif

Vandyked hem

Evening dress This evening dress with back outlined in chenille or ruffled ribbon demonstrates the ultrahigh waistline that returned from 1815 to 1817. The design, inspired by neoclassical decoration, featured in the April issue of the *Lady's Magazine*, a British fashion magazine.

SHOPPING

Drapers, haberdashers, hosiers, and mercers supplied fine materials like gauze and trimmings for dressmakers and ladies who liked to trim their own dresses and bonnets, or give fashion items as presents. Milliners not only sold caps and ribbons, but also plain white cotton cloth, jaconet (cotton muslin), cambric (linen), sarcenet (silk), and superfine fabrics, gloves, and lace. There were dyers who also cleaned clothes, with ox-gall and fuller's earth. Note the reticule (bag) on the lady's wrist.

Necklace

Long, thin
scarf tied
around waist

Gloves
and fan

Dark
net mesh
overdress

Pumps

1811

High fashion This short-sleeved
evening dress with sash comprises an
overdress with embroidered sequins or
bugle beads in circles and swirls, over a
yellow silk slip.

Cap with
protective
brim

Brown
checked
pelisse

Dark leather
shoes

Fur trim Pelisses of 1811 were worn
to calf length over plain cotton
muslin gowns. This Londoner wears
one with fur trim on the collar fronts
and cuffs.

Tall bonnet

Ruff-style
pleated frill
to chemisette

Cape collar
to pelisse

Decorative
hem to
cotton dress

1814

Costume Parisien This French
pelisse coat has vertical, green,
woven stripes typifying the era.
The higher waistline in Paris
influenced English styling.

JEWELRY

Jewelry was worn extensively for evening.
Parures (sets) were admired, and came in
presentation boxes. This set of necklace,
drop earrings, and brooch of seed pearls on
mother-of-pearl adopts the bunch of grapes
design so beloved of the neoclassical era.
Rings, pendants on chains or ribbons, and
matching bracelets were also worn.
Cameos and engraved gems were popular
as was turquoise, amber, topaz, carnelian,
and other semiprecious stones. Gold and
metal tiaras and bandeaux (headbands) and
tortoiseshell combs were worn on and in
the hair. Bloomed (matte-textured) and
chased (relief-decorated) gold, gilt metal,
and imitation paste diamonds made
fashionable jewelry more affordable.

Seed pearl parure c. 1800–1835

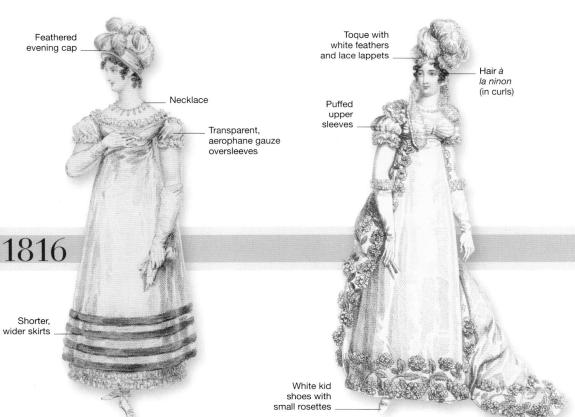

Feathered
evening cap

Necklace

Transparent,
aerophane gauze
oversleeves

1816

Shorter,
wider skirts

Fine net Four horizontal, red silk rouleaux give
weight to this fine net overdress. The underdress
has puffed sleeves and hem ruffles. The delight of a
separate transparent overdress was that it could be
worn over various colors to create different looks.

Toque with
white feathers
and lace lappets

Hair à
la ninon
(in curls)

Puffed
upper
sleeves

White kid
shoes with
small rosettes

Parisian court This dress has a trained overgown of
white satin or silver tissue, with colored foil, point lace,
and kid gloves ornamented with "narrow fluted
quilling of blond" (lace) as described in *La Belle
Assemblée* magazine.

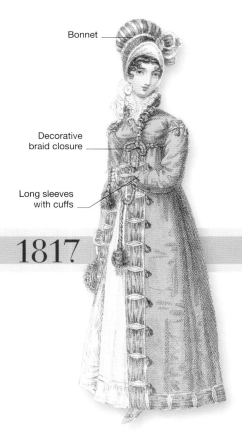

Bonnet

Decorative
braid closure

Long sleeves
with cuffs

1817

Brandenburg-closure pelisse This green
pelisse coat is fastened with brandenburgs
(decorative loops and buttons). Worn below are
a bell-shaped, white skirt, and cambric chemisette
with a layered, pleated frill at the neck.

FITTED, OUTDOOR COAT

REGENCY PELISSE

Made from a pale green silk with a darker contrast trim, this pelisse would have been worn outdoors during the day over a lightweight dress. Dating from c. 1818–1820, it features the high waistline that had been fashionable from the late 18th century. Although the garment retains much of the neoclassical simplicity of earlier years, the additional trimmings—padded collar and cuffs, and slashed mancherons at the shoulder—anticipate the fussier Gothic styling of the years to come. The shoulder detail adds volume at the upper arm, which continued to be an area of focus through the 1820s and early 1830s.

SIDE VIEW

BACK VIEW

IN DETAIL

▽ **MANCHERONS**
The shoulder detail, known as a mancheron, was a popular feature. It takes inspiration from the epaulets of military dress and also reflects the influence of medieval costume. The piped edging is an up-to-the-minute fashion.

Waistband with concealed fastening

Long sleeves taper to cuff

Open front allows for movement

Adjustable bands to tighten at wrist

Shoulder detail, known as a mancheron

Padded collar matches cuffs

a concealed closure beneath its overlap at the front. Edged with braid of twisted metal thread, it looks like a belt.

▷ **CONSTRUCTION**
This detail shows the distinctive diamond-shaped back panel of the pelisse, which is stitched together by hand. Clothes of this time were often meticulously crafted, demonstrating fine needlework skills.

▷ **PLEATING**
The fabric is gathered into the waistband at the back of the pelisse, to add volume and create a soft, bell-shaped skirt. This was a fashionable silhouette for dresses, too, which were sometimes padded to accentuate the shape.

▷ **CUFFS**
Padding, and rolls of wool-padded fabric known as rouleaux, were beginning to be a popular decoration on clothing. These cuffs are padded and hand stitched, to form decorative puffed bands at the wrist.

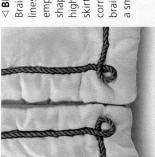

▷ **BRAIDED TRIM**
Braiding follows the lines of the pelisse to emphasize its cut and shape, particularly the high waist and long skirt. To create a neat corner at the hem, the braid is twisted into a small loop.

Long cuffs over knuckles—a feature of 1815–1820 fashion—provide additional warmth

Parasol of layered green silk, with pinked edges

Pale green silk

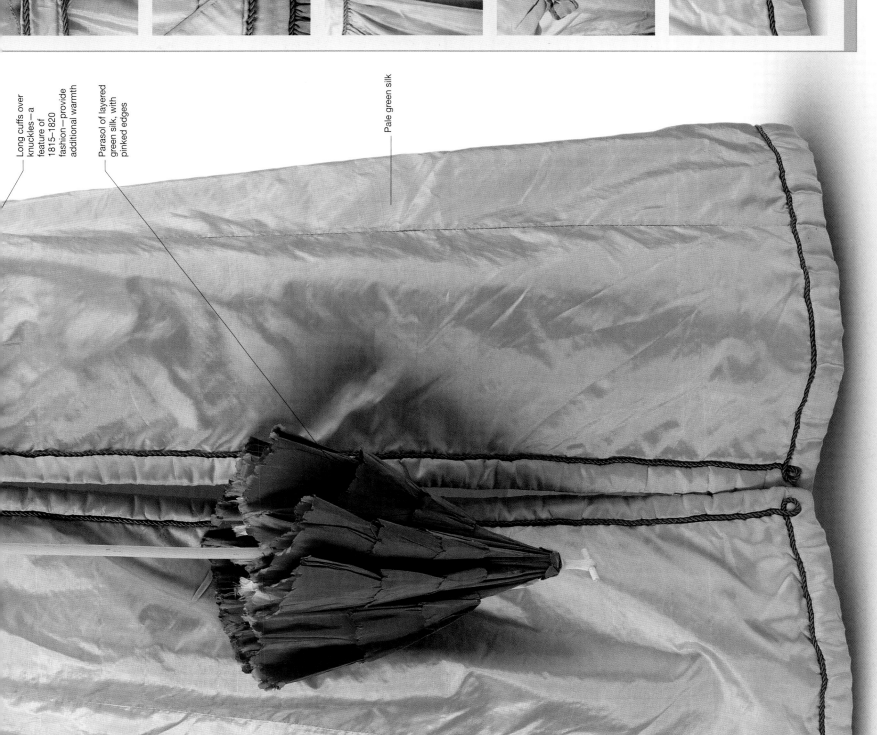

1820–1830

DELIGHTING IN THE DETAIL

The widening and shortening of skirt hems in the 1820s revealed footwear and, on occasion, stockings and ankles. A wide waistband helped to lower the waist, enabling alterations through the addition of a strip of extra fabric under the belt. Piping appeared on bodices and cuffs and persisted until around 1870. Dress bodices were uniformly back fastened, while spencer jackets and pelisses opened at center front. The pelisse evolved into a redingote (literally riding coat). Fashion plate distinctions between outfits for different occasions were not so clear in real life—people adapted what they had. Upon the death of George IV (June 1830), various stages of mourning were shown, as a lavender-gray filter descended on fashion.

HATS AND BONNETS

Hat with feathers

Hat with artificial flowers

The 1820s were typified by elaborate hats and bonnets that revealed faces, and were poised at jaunty side angles. Front temple curls or smooth-parted hair was always visible under light muslin or lawn caps. Head wear was of straw, velvet, or silk on a firm foundation, or fabric drawn across cane or wire. Feathers and artificial flowers on top were balanced by ribbons fashioned into bows and roses under the brim. There were endless variations on a theme, ever more stylish and extravagant. Ribbons of silk gauze were highly prized. Trimmings were often pinned in place, and moved from one hat or bonnet to another.

1824

Matching purple bonnet lined with cerise silk

Cap of embroidered light muslin

Line of decorative, self-covered buttons to sleeve

Travel wear This winter coat is closed with buttons. It has a fur hem (and possibly lining), complemented by a shaggy fur muff. Muffs of bearskin and goatskin were popular, and a useful accessory for traveling.

White crêpe hat with ribbons and feathers

Fine cotton chemisette with vertical tucking and bow

Mourning handkerchief

Low-key decoration of double zigzag and leaves

1830

French gray Mourning dress for the king in July 1830 saw black and white stripes. In August, mourning continued, as here, with French gray afternoon dresses and white cotton trimmings. Sleeves are in "double bouffant" puffed shapes to the wrist.

Black hat with violet ribbons

Elizabethan-style ruff

Fichu-pelerine

Matching wrist bracelets

Overskirt

Short skirt reveals two-tone walking boots

Cording detail This mourning dress is of plain violet fabric, with cording to fichu-pelerine and overskirt. The shoulder line shows cartridge pleating into the gigot sleeves, as the shape evolves and fullness moves down the upper arm.

Center-front
busk panel

Gigot sleeves

Clever use of the
fabric creates
diagonals

1828

Cartridge
pleating

Dual purpose This striped dress could
be worn in the daytime with a bonnet,
and then dressed up with a headdress,
as here, for dinner. The skirt is cartridge
pleated into the waist.

Redingote This walking dress for
summer is a pretty picture of late
Georgian delights. The crosshatch
closure resembles feather quills,
the gigot sleeves are gathered
with piped banding, and
vandyked light muslin is
seen on the Marie-
Stuart under cap and
the collar.

1829

Vandyked
(zigzag-bordered)
chemisette collar

Gold chain
and watch

Matching wrist
bracelets with
carnelian stones

Gilt buckle
to wide belt

Ribbon and
scarf tendrils

White
hat

Lower
sleeve
decoration

Carriage shoes

Vine embroidery This redingote with wide collar
is decorated with meandering vine and grape
embroidery, and ruching. A scarf square is tied
lightly around the neck, and lilylike trumpet flowers
sing out from the hat.

Hat tilted sideways,
decorated with
chains and tassels

Very wide
shoulderline

Tasseled
cord belt

Gothic style A Gothic-style, dark bodice tops
this bell-shaped, white skirt. The back-closure
bodice is probably boned. Although the bodice
is cut low and jewelry is worn, the hat suggests
afternoon rather than evening wear.

Hat with green
ribbon trim

Banded gigot
sleeves

Matching wrist
bracelets

Trumpet
fanning

Dinner dress This vandyked (zigzag-bordered)
bodice forms a wide "V" to the tiny waist. The
dress has asymmetrical, pinked trumpet fanning
along a piped line on the skirt. Its short length
reveals high-laced indoor shoes.

1820–1830
THE EVENING HOURGLASS

Key features of evening wear between 1820 and 1830 were the gradual appearance of very wide puffed sleeves and strong appliqué decoration. At the beginning of the 1820s, dresses were simple and pale, with small puffed sleeves and some decoration around the hem of the full skirt. By the end of the decade, they became shorter and puffed sleeves expanded, balancing the bell-shaped skirt and emphasizing the tiny, corseted waist. Appliqué decoration in self fabric and lattice work created three-dimensional layering on dresses, and realistic flower trimming on dresses was used as well as on hair adornments. Evening dresses had low décolletage necklines, which emphasized a bottle-shaped neck. The bare neck was often unadorned, or sometimes broad necklaces were worn. Hairstyles became elaborate, piled high on the head with sculptural shapes formed of bows and loops adorned with flowers, feathers, and jewels.

1822

Hair adorned with flowers

Puffed sleeves

Hair finely braided and formed into an Apollo knot

Wide décolletage

Embroidered hem decorations

Parisian ball dress Skirts were now softly full. Fashionable materials included "gros de Naples" (Italian silk with a corded surface), and lutestring (a finer and shinier silk).

Elbow-length gloves (slipped down to reveal bracelet)

Floral finials

Hair supported on wire framework

Silk fabric mimics feathers

Worn over a petticoat probably now stiffened with horsehair

Very short hem reveals pumps with ribbon strapping

Appliqué decoration

Ostrich feather on bandeau

Bandeau headdress with pearls

Large jeweled cross

1826

Draped white overskirts

1830

Court dress Underpinned by hoops, this dress was suitable for wearing at court (though hoops were banned by George IV in England). It has a squared décolletage and is accessorized with an elaborate bandeau.

Off-the-shoulder dress This silk dress has lantern-style puffed sleeves. Careful pleating on the bodice tucks into a low waistband. The skirt has a deep lattice overlay with diagonal piping, and ribbon bows.

Tassel trimmings This unusual, silk dress is overlaid with spotted, silk ribbon. It has trellis fringing and plentiful tassels. There is a wide belt and ties and even wider shoulder epaulets.

Hair worn up and curled

Lacy veil

Décolleté with bow trim

Long, diaphanous, gauze scarf

Piping

Heavy hem, embellished with ruching interspersed with flower heads

Padded rouleau band

1824

Ostrich feather hair adornment

Chemisette with ruff collar

Cloak collar

Longer sleeve opening

Turban headdress with feathers

Short puffed sleeve

Back view shows bodice construction

Crescent motifs

Padded rouleau band adds weight to the hem

1825

Hem detailing Layers of ruched fabric on this silk opera dress form a wavy border between a line of piping and padded rouleau, formed of bias-cut fabric filled with wadding to give weight and interest to the hem.

Opera cape This velvet opera cape is lined with wadding and yellow sarcenet (silk) and edged with fur. The double sleeve recalls medieval gowns that had an opening at elbow level for wearing "short."

Dress for religious festival This round gown was worn for a religious festival in France. Though the dress is a relatively straightforward shape, the silver embroidery is dramatic, especially the crescent motifs above the padded rouleau band.

Apollo knot trimmed with flowers

Wide, puffed sleeves emphasize narrow waist

Artificial flowers at waist reflect flowers on skirt

Light, flowing silk skirt over underskirt stiffened with cording or crin (horsehair)

Hemline above ankle

Wide sleeves and full skirt create hourglass shape

Fan made from ivory brisé and tortoiseshell

Ribbon flowers attached to dress

Deep plain hem

Puffed sleeves In a soft-colored silk with cream lace at the neckline, this dress has a shorter hem for dancing. A bold line of appliqué foliage ends with a pretty bouquet. Short sleeves became wider and more gathered by this time.

Ball gown The plain silk of this dress is decorated with garlands of silk roses. The bodice is finely pleated to the waist, emphasized by a wide ribbon. Ribbons were also used for the rose decorations and chenille (a furry yarn) for the leaves.

HAIRSTYLES

Forehead jewel

Feather fronds

Artificial flowers

Curls on temples

The Apollo knot was a hairstyle introduced c. 1826 that gave height and poise to fashionable ladies. To achieve the complex confection, hair was centrally parted and swept up to the crown, where it was styled into braids and looped into bows. Sometimes false hair braids were used as well as wires to help loops stand erect.

FASHION ICON

BEAU BRUMMELL

Routinely dismissed as a shallow fop, George Bryan ("Beau") Brummell was far more than the fashion arbiter for Regency England. The first true dandy, and enormously influential, he helped overturn men's fashions in the early 1800s and pave the way for modern menswear. He also became an archetypal, appearance-obsessed star in a celebrity-crazed age—a phenomenon still familiar today. Brummell developed a close friendship with George, Prince of Wales (the Prince Regent and later King George IV), and became fashion and etiquette adviser to the prince and his court. His influence spread widely both in England and France.

Modern menswear

Said to have been tall and fair, Brummell probably justified his nickname. His fastidiousness means that he is often seen as the instigator of overly fussy fashions, but the reverse is true. Eighteenth-century aristocratic menswear included lavish fabrics, white stockings, ruffles and buckles, three-cornered hats, and fragrance. Fashions were simplifying by Brummell's time, but he cemented and extended this trend, sweeping obvious fussiness aside in favor of somber-colored, elegant restraint.

Brummell's bold simplicity was a take on the English country gentleman's sportswear, and fit with the neoclassical revolutionary spirit of the era. It featured a plain white linen shirt, immaculately bleached and starched; a fitted, pale waistcoat (vest); a short-fronted, double-breasted, swallow-tailed wool coat, dark blue or black; fitted pantaloon pants rather than knee breeches; a white linen neck cloth tied showily (Brummell often fastened it in a "waterfall" of flowing layers); and a top hat. Brass coat buttons were the only gaudy detail. This type of outfit had become standard by the 1820s and '30s, and what Brummell popularized with his pants-jacket-flamboyant neckwear combination was none other than the original modern suit and tie.

Brummell's clean look also included close-cropped curls and a freshly washed face. He rejected fragrance because he washed daily, which was rare in Regency times. Scrupulous personal grooming was part of his code of etiquette, built on poise, excellence, and attention to detail. Brummell had his boots polished with champagne and rejected piles of neck clothes while dressing, until the creases fell in just the right place. One literary caricature based on Brummell suggests he was so fussy about perfect cut that one glover made the hands of his gloves, another the fingers, and a third one the thumbs.

Striking a pose

Dandyism is also an attitude of mind. Brummell affected a studied indifference, as if his simpler look was effortless (this parallels modern "cool" and the Chanel ethos—Coco was called "the female Beau Brummell"). Behind the façade of nonchalance, it took Brummell about six hours to get ready. Attitude was underpinned by expert cut and fit. Thanks to advances in textile-making during Brummell's lifetime, more flexible wool cloth was produced. It made a neatly cut fit much easier to achieve than in previous generations.

Brummel's fashion influence helped to establish London as the center of men's tailoring. His reputation for impeccable quality inspired Charles Worth, Aquascutum, and Tommy Nutter of Savile Row. In attitude and style, the dandy has lived on in Mick Jagger's 1960s and '70s suited look and more recently in Karl Lagerfeld's personal wardrobe.

△ **CURLS AND CRAVAT**
This engraving of a young Beau Brummell was taken from an original portrait miniature. He is not yet quite the peerless dandy, but his cravat is immaculate.

PORTRAIT OF BRUMMELL, 1805 ▷
Robert Dighton's painting shows Brummell in his famous daytime ensemble, complete with tasseled boots.

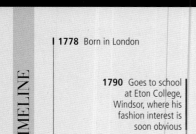

TIMELINE

1778 Born in London

1790 Goes to school at Eton College, Windsor, where his fashion interest is soon obvious

1794–1798 Short military career. Starts to develop as a true dandy

▷ **1799** Influence on men's fashion grows. Sets up Mayfair home, and career as fashion arbiter takes off

1812 Falls out with Prince Regent as a result of his sharp tongue

◁ **1816** Flees to France to escape creditors. Fashion influence on the wane

1835 Imprisoned for debt

1840 Dies in an asylum in Caen in northwest France

○ 1780   ○ 1790   ○ 1800   ○ 1810   ○ 1820   ○ 1830   ○ 1840

SATIRICAL PRINT (c. 1812) Scandalmongers had it that, after the Prince Regent ignored him, Brummell (at left) asked the prince's companion, "Alvanley, who's your fat friend?" The friendship ended. ▷

1790–1839

THE RISE OF THE DANDY

Gentlemen in this period prided themselves on the quality of their wool cloth and the tailoring and fit of their clothes. Earlier interest in elaborate brocaded and embroidered silks disappeared as the upper classes affected a country look. Men's coats were now of fine wool, in rural colors, and developed waist seams from the 1820s. Tailors perfected a range of coat styles for different occasions. Pantaloons and trousers gradually replaced breeches. The riding crop, cane, or umbrella, together with beaver hat, buckskin gloves, and riding boots, were now essential accessories for the man about town. Some of the most exacting Regency dressers, such as Beau Brummell, paid extraordinary attention to every last detail of their appearance. White cotton vests and fine white linen stocks and cravats were a hallmark of their style.

1790

Hair worn long and unpowdered

Hat buckle symbolizes revolutionary sympathies

Patterned vest, cut straight across at waist

Decorative buttons and false buttonholes

Long-line, country-color breeches

Hessians (flat riding boots) edged with red leather

White silk hose

Stylish country look This morning walking ensemble to wear in town is influenced by riding apparel. The coat with standing collar has decorative buttons but slopes sharply away to a swallow tail, fastened with hook and eye.

Ivory silk top hat

Hair in tight curls on temples

Stock and cravat

1828

Heel to shoe

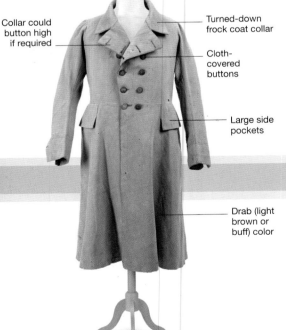

Collar could button high if required

Turned-down frock coat collar

Cloth-covered buttons

Large side pockets

Drab (light brown or buff) color

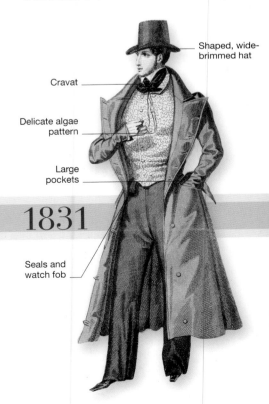

1831

Shaped, wide-brimmed hat

Cravat

Delicate algae pattern

Large pockets

Seals and watch fob

Double-breasted top coat Good-quality wool cloth tailored to fit, as shown here, looked stylish and protected the wearer from severe weather. The top coat was a forerunner of the top frock of the mid-19th century.

Cossack trousers These pegged trousers show Cossack influence. The single-breasted frock coat has puffed upper sleeves, echoing women's sleeve styles. The ruby velvet vest has a roll collar.

Greatcoat This vest with padded chest has a slightly pointed waistline, echoing women's waistlines. Likewise, the greatcoat has wide lapels that emphasize shoulder width, and full coat skirts that make the waist look small by contrast.

Short hair and sideburns

Beaver top hat

Contrasting collar revers

Glimpse of colorful vest below

Leather Hussar boots with V-notch at front

1800

Georgian royal blue The contrasting collar demonstrates the M-notch, which tailors introduced (along with N and V) to ease the intersection of collar with lapel. The white stock and cravat partially encase the chin.

Short, curly hair with side part

High stock and flamboyant red cravat

Shiny beaver opera hat

Jersey weave, cut on cross, single leg seam

Gray spats over slimline, flat pumps

Top hat and tails This dashing Frenchman is a stylish man about town, in evening dress coat, crisp white vest, and skin-tight pantaloons. The tailcoat waist seam aided by chest padding creates a "pouter pigeon" look.

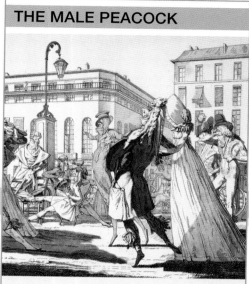

THE MALE PEACOCK

Dandies were the successors of the decadent *Macaronis* and foppish *Incroyables*. They liked to eclipse their female companions with their finery, as shown by this cartoon. The man struts along like a male peacock, walking on tiptoe to make himself look taller and thinner, a gait that indicates extreme pride in his appearance. Dandies spent hours tying their stocks and cravats, wore jewels and perfume, had their hair carefully dressed, and were prepared to be laced into corsets to achieve a small waist. In total, they spent a small fortune on their wardrobe.

Collar now laying flat

White gloves

Walking cane

1832

Slight heel to shoes

Special occasion outfit The dress coat, white vest with a woven or printed abstract floral pattern, together with white stock cravat (made all-in-one), white pantaloons or trousers, and stylish shoes, constituted an ideal wedding outfit.

Silk top hat

Cord edging to collar revers

All-in-one white stock (necktie)

Corded frogging fastening

Walking cane

1836

Heeled footwear

Frock coat with military frogging This coat displays corded frogging for fastening and trimmings. Frogging is a military hussar reference, and reappears later on velvet smoking jackets. The velvet revers lay flat, the waist is nipped in, and the skirts are full.

Decorative jewel fastening shirtfront

Cravat now more similar to bow tie

1838

Stirrups under heeled shoes

Parisian full dress A Parisian gentleman here wears full dress suitable for the opera. Tailcoat, pantaloons, light-colored checked vest and dress shirt, top hat, and dress shoes comprise an outfit of elegant sobriety and restraint.

1790–1840
REGENCY SPORTSWEAR

As leisure time increased in the early 19th century, men took up a variety of sports. Walking tours and excursions, hunting and hawking, angling, and ice skating were all popular pastimes. Riding dress and morning dress were frequently synonymous because riding was considered a morning sport, and any dashing young man would at least pretend an interest. Women's sporting dress mainly comprised riding habits. Women rode side saddle until the end of the century, so skirts were very long by 1840 to ensure their legs were fully covered as they rode. They also wore habits for traveling in open or closed carriages, for walking, and for boating. "Seaside bathing habits" were worn for promenading by the sea but not for immersion. Tailors and the burgeoning ready-to-wear industry worked hard to meet the demand for all the assorted outfits.

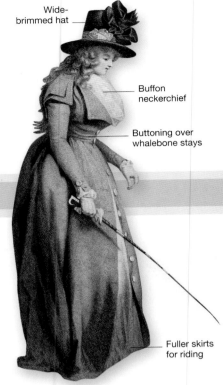

Wide-brimmed hat

Buffon neckerchief

Buttoning over whalebone stays

Fuller skirts for riding

Riding habit Dating from the early 1790s, this riding habit buttons through the skirts like a man's greatcoat, and has large lapels and double shoulder flaps for added protection. Stays pull in at the waist.

Brimmed cap with chin strap

Cravat at the neck

Rust-red frock coat

Coat lining in silk

Riding breeches

Tan leather cuffs

Boots with heels to accommodate stirrups

Hunting wear This style of hunting outfit from 1830 is still seen today. The brimmed hard cap is practical, as is the frock coat with cutaway front—tailored to stay out of the way when sitting astride the horse.

Top hat

Cane with ivory handle

Jacket cut high at front for riding

Tight-fitting pantaloons

Pointed boots

Morning outfit This outfit is a variation on Regency town wear, but the green coat marks it as a morning riding outfit, with tight pantaloons and flexible leather boots.

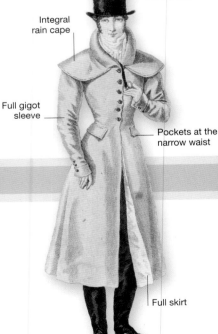

Beaver or felt top hat

Integral rain cape

Full gigot sleeve

Pockets at the narrow waist

Full skirt

Leather boots

Traveling coat A pardessus or overcoat could be worn over a stylish outfit. Superfine broadcloth was popular for such coats. The light color is suitable for summer but the wide shoulder cape will keep off the rain.

Beaver-skin top hat

Neckerchief

Leather gloves

Fashionable riding dress
Brown and dark gray wool riding habits were popular in the early 1800s. This long-sleeved jacket bodice is open to reveal a short-waisted linen "habit shirt," with frilled collar and colored neckerchief.

Skirts skim the floor

Bonnet with decorated crown

Linen ruff collar

Spencer jacket with basque (close-fitting underbodice)

Leather gloves and riding whip

Full skirts ensure modesty at all times

Spencer jacket With ample skirts suitable for riding side saddle, this riding outfit from 1815 would ideally have been made of green merino wool. The spencer jacket with basque may have been a separate garment.

Hair braided around ears, like the young Queen Victoria

Veil attached to top hat

White cuffs of shirt visible

Full skirts for riding side saddle

Royal blue habit
Queen Victoria and Empress Eugénie both rode, and wore habits in this shade of blue. This 1840 habit has a roll collar on the bodice, a white shirt, and brown cravat, echoing the male hunting outfit of the time.

White gauntlet

Wide leather belt with cup for arrows

Tassel to dust off arrows

Gentleman archer The green coat worn by this toxophilite (lover of archery) has a button-through style like a medieval pourpoint (doublet). Belted at the waist, it is worn with a soft-crowned cap and loose trousers.

Peaked cap

Cravat at the neck

Militia-styled jacket

Large carrying pouch

Over-knee gaiters

Waterproofed footwear

Shooting outfit Wildfowling, grouse shooting, and dry shooting required warm underclothing and sensible footwear. Recipes for waterproofing boots featured beeswax, beef suet, resin, and balsam.

RIDING VEILS

Veils appeared intermittently on women's head wear during the 19th century. They were worn with wedding dresses, as part of mourning outfits, for riding, and later, for traveling in open-carriage trains and buses and for motoring. Fine silk net and gauze, cotton muslin, black lace, and silk tulle were all used depending on the occasion. White veils on top hats would waft attractively while ladies rode side saddle. They also had a practical function to offer privacy and protection to the wearer while out in public. Below, the high neckwear and wide shoulder line set off the top hats beautifully, as do the tight curls on the temples.

Front view

Back view

1830–1837

PRINTS AND PATTERNS

A number of recently evolved fashion features came to epitomize the new reign of Britain's King William IV and Queen Adelaide. The gigot sleeve had expanded to its fullest, and a lightly whaleboned corset was back in place. A tiny waistline was prized, with the waist at a more natural level. A small cushion pad sat in the small of the back. Separate pockets returned, and waist petticoats multiplied to support still fuller skirts. Patterned materials, particularly roller-printed China silks, soft cottons, and fine wools, were in vogue. Fashion was becoming accessible for the emergent middle classes, with import tax on silk reduced from 1825 and more ready-made goods available. Articles appeared in magazines to support home dressmaking. Girls were taught needlework skills such as piping and cartridge pleating. They stitched samplers to practice decorative borders and motifs, and alphabets for laundry marking. And they gathered a wedding trousseau in their bottom drawer.

1830

Pink ribbons on hat match belt

Chemisette worn underneath

Lozenge and pleated fan design

Walking boots

Square shawl A printed or woven border in the colors of an English country garden adorns this shawl worn folded diagonally, to wrap round bouffant sleeves. The outfit is completed with white kid gloves and green boots.

Pink bonnet, worn over white lace cap, tied with ribbon under chin

Gilt belt buckle

Gilt jewelry

Pleating of bodice to central busk

1833

Cartridge pleating from waist to allow skirt fullness

Decorative leaf—a variant on vandyking— hides the closure

Bonnet with curlicue

Cloak matches two-toned walking shoes

Roller printing The fabric of this dress is roller printed by the mill-engraving technique, with two-color, wavy lines. More interest is created on sleeves and bodice through clever positioning of the printed material.

Pelisse-robe The pelisse (coat) of earlier decades developed into the pelisse-robe, which now fastened down the front with concealed hooks and eyes. Here, these are covered with decorative bows and tassels.

Rococo cloak Featuring a rococo design on figured material, this cloak with cape is trimmed and lined with darker wool or velvet material. The bonnet picks up the blue of the striped dress worn underneath.

Gray gauze ribbon arranged in star form

Hat of rice straw

Neck chain and lorgnette of jet

Pelerine collar

Ceinture (belt) with corresponding jet buckle bracelets

Broken cone dressing on dress front

Black slippers

Lightweight cotton This light dress is made from jaconet, a lightweight cotton material. The *manche à la Montespan* oversleeve with a large bouffant at the elbow is held by a muslin band. The lower sleeve, embroidered in foliage, forms a ruffle.

Feathers dyed to match dress

Capelike, diaphanous collar across shoulders

Bouffant upper sleeves

Tight-fitting, lower sleeves

Promenade dress This spring/summer afternoon promenade dress has roller-printed, pale turquoise stripes and a meandering convolvulus flower pattern. The range of color gradations with vegetable dyes was improving.

Afternoon dress The diagonal checked pattern on this dress and its V-shaped collar create the illusion of looking up to the sky through a trellis in an arbor. The shirt and bouffant sleeves anticipate the later, ubiquitous white blouse.

Artificial daisies on hat

Collared shirt front with pleating

Bouffant sleeves gathered at elbows

Scarf of russet red wool

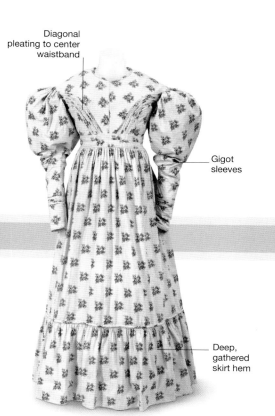

Diagonal pleating to center waistband

Gigot sleeves

Deep, gathered skirt hem

Walking dress Abstract floral weaves and prints on cream-colored sturdy cotton, lightweight wool, or challis silk and wool were popular. Gigot sleeves had a narrow tubular lining, and skirts were stiffened with a cotton lining.

Sleeve plumpers padded with feather down support upper sleeves

Bustle pad worn in small of back

1834

Silk or light muslin over satin was common

Wedding dress White weddings were popular from the early 1800s. The style was a restrained version of fashionable dress. This cream dress would have been worn with a veil of Brussels bobbin lace, orange blossom, and an embroidered linen fichu.

WEDDING SHOES

Ivory-colored shoes and boots like these survive in large numbers. They were usually wedding footwear, kept carefully after the special day, for sentimental reasons and because they would very quickly be ruined or worn out by wearing for ordinary, everyday tasks. Boots of silk, twilled cotton, and kid leather were typical.

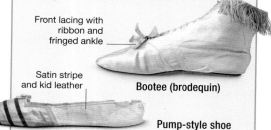

Front lacing with ribbon and fringed ankle

Satin stripe and kid leather

Bootee (brodequin)

Pump-style shoe

1830–1838

TURBANS AND TIGHT LACING

E vening wear at the start of the 1830s had boat necklines that emphasized the champagne-bottle necks that were so admired. Turbans, an Oriental fashion formed of long scarves imported from India, fed the desire for exotic fabrics and an air of mystique gleaned from Romantic and Gothic novels. The turban became a favored style of older ladies for going out to dinner, opera, and parties. These ladies, who had sported bare arms in the neoclassical era, now benefited from transparent oversleeves for evening. From 1835 the neckline drew in, and the sleeve head was pulled down with pleating, which restricted movement. Bodices dipped down slightly at the front and hemlines returned to floor length. Crin (horsehair) was now used extensively in linen petticoats to stiffen them.

Ornate headdress

Bunch of silver wheat

Necklace of hanging pearls, *en girandole*

Lappets of blond lace

1830

Feathered headdress This woman's ornate headdress includes a plume of three ostrich feathers, a gold comb decorated with pearls, and a pearl bandeau that goes around her forehead. Her dress is trimmed with blond lace and a satin rouleau.

STRAPLESS CORSET

Boned corsets cut with triangular gores (panels) under the arm and on the hips created the desired hourglass figure. A center front steel busk and corded panels forced an erect form. Metal eyelets allowed for tighter lacing for a more fitted shape and dispensed with shoulder straps, to suit the wide boat necklines.

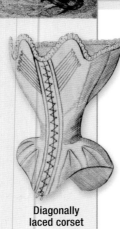

Diagonally laced corset

Ball dress Appliqué bows in zigzag vandyke pattern circle the skirt of this dress. Young ladies in the marriage market were encouraged to adopt each new novelty in fashion, be it the direction of a bow or the exact tilt of a hair comb.

Boat neckline

1831

Lightweight turban with feathers

Ivory complexion was prized

Butterfly-shaped corsage (bodice)

Bouffant oversleeve

Overlayered skirt

Bouffant gown Large bouffant oversleeves and a butterfly-shaped corsage, or bodice, emphasize the impossibly narrow waist of this purple silk evening gown and create an ethereal effect. The expansive turban is worn at an angle.

Vandyking on
corsage (bodice)

Hair comb

Fur-lined cloak
with cape

Wool with
decorative
weave

Lace
headdress

Chain necklace
wound round
several times

Two pockets

Apron is
foil for
embroidery

Matching turban This dress with red, floral
motifs coordinates with the turban and cloak.
Its transparent sleeves are gathered at the
elbow with a muslin band. This outfit would
have been worn to the opera.

Fancy apron The items gathered at and
fastened around a lady's waist—which was still
incredibly small—might now include chemise,
corset, several petticoats, a pair of hidden
pockets, the dress, a belt, and a fancy apron.

Boteh
(pinecone) motif

Fringed scarf
turban interlaced
with ribbon

Hair looped
under ears

Horizontally worn
brooches typical
of 1837–1850

Turban
covers hair

Cheeks
rouged

1837   1838

Trellis
patterning

Deep lace or
embroidered
flounce

Figured
net, or
lace skirt
flounce

Stylized pinecone motif A diaphanous overskirt
covers this plain, ivory silk ball dress. Static images
and surviving garments cannot fully convey the joy
of these dresses in movement, but there is a sense
of the flow of material here.

Modes de Paris This lady wears a long, mantle-
shaped pelerine with turn-down collar, trimmed with
lace. The sleeves of the white dress would be tightly
pleated below the shoulder line and puff out at the
lower arm. A restrained, demure look was evolving.

All-enveloping cloak Under the silk and
velvet cloak, the deep flounced skirt hem may
show off the early use of machine-made lace.
Turbans were soon to be relegated to costume
dress, until a brief revival in the 1870s.

1837–1855

DEMURE DAY DRESSES

From the late 1830s, dresses expanded slowly but surely to ever wider proportions, enveloping the legs and ankles completely. Lower shoulder lines and tighter sleeves restricted the range of upper body movement, as did square shawls folded diagonally and draped around shoulders. Corsets, and often bodices, were stiffened with whalebone and had a long front busk pushing down on the embonpoint (plumpness of the stomach), creating a narrow waist. Full skirts, organ-pleated into the waist, were supported on multiple layers of petticoats, at least one of which was stiffened with *crin*, (from the French for horsehair). Dress skirts began to feature tiers and, by the early 1850s, were embellished with trimmings. The desired look, as shown in these fashion plates from France and England, was meek and submissive. Accessories such as beadwork bags, purses, and parasols were pretty and feminine.

Wide-brimmed bonnet shows curls

Frills add fullness to upper sleeve

1837

Bell-shaped skirt worn over layers of petticoats

Soft silk and wool (challis) shawl with floral print

CHILDREN'S WEAR

Party dress   **Darker overcoat**

Girls at this time were dressed as miniature versions of their mothers, with full dresses worn over two or more layers of petticoats to create a bell-shaped skirt. Young girls' skirts were shorter, however, and revealed pantalettes (linen or cotton leggings tied above the knee), which were edged with lace or pretty embroidery. When outdoors, these light-colored dresses were covered with darker overcoats made from heavier fabrics. Bonnets and gloves were also worn.

Young boys also wore dresses until they were "breeched" (first dressed in breeches or trousers), which was usually when they were between four and eight years old.

Contrast trim Dark plum silk trimming draws attention to the fashionably small waist of this bodice and the fullness of the skirt, which is organ-pleated into the waistband.

Feather trim

Ringlets framed by bonnet

Long fitted sleeves

Dark plum trimming

Slender waist, curving down at the front

1847

Ermine muff

Skirt made from two contrasting tiers

Pastel shades This summer dress in a lightweight fabric is trimmed with pretty frills. It is worn with a pastel yellow sash with matching ribbon and feather trimmings on the bonnet.

Silk bonnet with ribbon ties

Removable muslin collar

Striped shot taffeta This French dress has three flounces with pinked edges, which add volume to the skirt. It is trimmed at the neck and cuffs with white lace or embroidered linen.

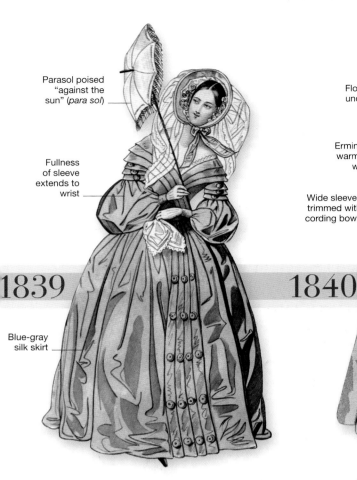

1839

Parasol poised "against the sun" (*para sol*)

Fullness of sleeve extends to wrist

Blue-gray silk skirt

Pleated blue-gray silk The wide V-shaped neckline of this dress is echoed by the pleating over the sloped shoulders, across the front of the bodice, and into the narrow waist. Lace-edged handkerchiefs were popular accessories.

1840

Flowers worn under bonnet

Ermine for warmth in winter

Wide sleeves trimmed with cording bows

Pelisse robe This opulent blue coat, a color popular during the 1840s, is edged with luxurious ermine. Cording bows on the sleeves are matched at the waist by a belt that is finished with decorative tassels.

1844

Spanish lace By this date, Spanish mantilla (veil-like headdress) lace could be machine made. This taffeta dress has generous mantilla-style lace trims.

Headdress has muslin lappet features below the ears

Black lace trim

Deep flounce of lace at hem

Hair is parted in the center

oping shoulder seams restrain arm movement

Cashmere shawls were desirable accessories

1855

Tiered sleeves

Flounced, checked skirt

Tartan flounces This checked dress reflects the popularity of Queen Victoria's new Scottish palace, Balmoral, and the ensuing vogue for tartan. The flounces of the skirt are cut on the bias to create a diamond-shape pattern.

Wedding, confirmation, or party dress The flounced sleeves and skirt with central diaper pattern panel are both trimmed with yellow ribbons and *broderie anglaise*. The hair is outlined with pink ribbon, in Italian style.

BONNETS

Bonnets of fabric or straw were worn outside to keep delicate complexions fashionably pale. They were fastened under the chin with ribbons and decorated with frills, lace, ribbons, silk flowers, and feathers.

The wide-brimmed bonnets of the 1830s were gradually replaced with more closely fitting head wear shaped to cover the cheeks in the 1840s, like the straw bonnet here.

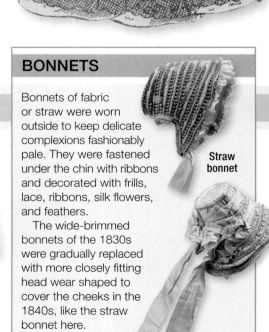

Straw bonnet

Silk bonnet

IMPERIAL OPULENCE

France during Napoleon III's Second Empire (1852–1870) was a place of prosperity, quickly made fortunes, and rampant consumerism. Visitors flocked to see Baron Haussmann's transformation of Paris into a city of grand boulevards, and the theaters, opera houses, and new department stores buzzed with life. The favorite court painter, Franz Xaver Winterhalter, who painted the scene opposite, captured a glittering imperial life, providing powerful public relations for the regime.

At the center of this court life was Napoleon's striking, Spanish-born empress, Eugénie—a leading fashion icon of her day, whose patronage of designer Charles Frederick Worth made him the first real "dictator" of Paris fashion. Eugénie (fourth from the left) wears trimmings in purple, a color she loved. Purple was an expensive natural dye, suitable for royalty, when this was painted in 1855, but just one year later a synthetic dye was made and soon "mauve madness" swept Europe and the United States, fueled by Eugénie's example. The luxuriantly stylish court ladies, shown in tulle, taffeta, silk, muslin, lace, and ribbons, also display the newly fashionable crinolines, which became enormous during the Second Empire. In 1861 one English fashion magazine noted: "The Empress Eugénie['s] petticoats … stood out a great deal: and following her example, all the Paris Ladies are wearing their skirts very wide and ample."

Would you believe that, in the latter half of the nineteenth century, there are bearded milliners … who … take the exact dimensions of the highest titled women in Paris—robe them, unrobe them, and make them turn backward and forward before them?

CHARLES DICKENS, *ALL THE YEAR ROUND*, 1863

◁ **THE EMPRESS EUGENIE SURROUNDED BY HER LADIES IN WAITING**
Winterhalter's painting is in the *fête gallante* style (beautiful people shown in pastoral settings) of 18th-century artist J-A Watteau. Eugénie was fascinated by this period, especially by Marie Antoinette, and some of her outfits incorporated 18th-century features.

1856–1869
CRINOLINES

The new crinoline frame provided relief from wearing multi-layered petticoats, but its buoyancy meant that long cotton drawers were now essential under linens. In the 1860s an oval frame shape evolved and box-pleated skirts gave way to gored panels, which provided a smoother fit over the frame. Bodices and skirts were often separate items, allowing alternate styles of bodice, and front-closure for convenience. With the availability of domestic sewing machines home dressmaking increased, as did the use of copious trimmings. Large frames were abandoned after 1867, skirts trailed and were gathered up internally with ties, forming a soft bustle. Then crinolettes and bustle pads took over.

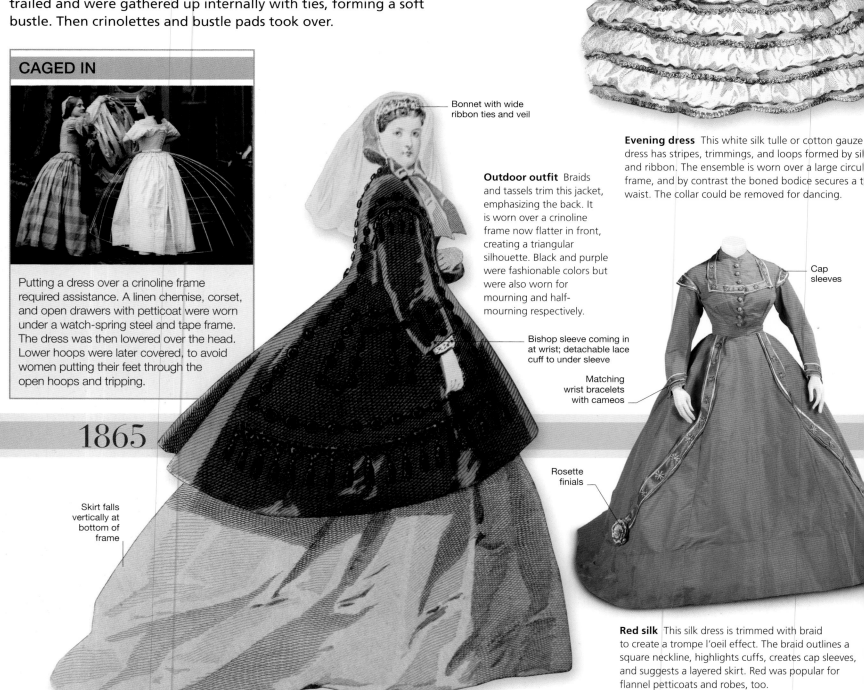

CAGED IN

Putting a dress over a crinoline frame required assistance. A linen chemise, corset, and open drawers with petticoat were worn under a watch-spring steel and tape frame. The dress was then lowered over the head. Lower hoops were later covered, to avoid women putting their feet through the open hoops and tripping.

1859

Hair swept back under cap and streamers

Matching wrist bracelets with cameos

Lace-edged handkerchief

Pagoda-shaped sleeves

Evening dress This white silk tulle or cotton gauze dress has stripes, trimmings, and loops formed by si[lk] and ribbon. The ensemble is worn over a large circul[ar] frame, and by contrast the boned bodice secures a t[ight] waist. The collar could be removed for dancing.

Bonnet with wide ribbon ties and veil

Outdoor outfit Braids and tassels trim this jacket, emphasizing the back. It is worn over a crinoline frame now flatter in front, creating a triangular silhouette. Black and purple were fashionable colors but were also worn for mourning and half-mourning respectively.

Bishop sleeve coming in at wrist; detachable lace cuff to under sleeve

Matching wrist bracelets with cameos

Cap sleeves

1865

Skirt falls vertically at bottom of frame

Rosette finials

Red silk This silk dress is trimmed with braid to create a trompe l'oeil effect. The braid outlines a square neckline, highlights cuffs, creates cap sleeves, and suggests a layered skirt. Red was popular for flannel petticoats and robes, too.

Artificial flowers
on rim of bonnet

Pussycat
bow

0 ft (3 m)
cumference
the hem
s usual

Skirt cut in
gored panels

1861

Snood hair net
and feathered hat

Bow tie echoing
men's style

Pagoda sleeves
over *engageantes*

Functional and
decorative buttons

Double hem
ruffle to skirt

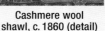

WOOL AND SILK WEAVES

**Cashmere wool
shawl, c. 1860 (detail)**

**Machine-woven silk
daisies (apron detail)**

The range of materials and complex
patterning available to women by 1860 was
extraordinary. The textile industry in Britain
vied with Indian manufacturers to satisfy
increasing demand and changing tastes.
Edinburgh, Crayford in Essex, Norwich,
and later Paisley produced wool shawls.
Huge, double-square, long shawls
were folded in half and then
diagonally draped across the large
skirts. Jacquard looms could
produce wide lengths of woven
silk to look like embroidery that could
be used for dress skirts, and accessories
such as aprons, as here. The subtlety of
color gradation, and accuracy in depicting
specific flowers, are quite remarkable.

Visiting outfit This bodice and skirt has copious
lengths of pleated, black fabric applied by sewing
machine. Pagoda sleeves reveal *engageantes*
(undersleeves) of cotton, cotton gauze, or lace that
were detached for laundering.

Walking outfit *The Englishwoman's Domestic
Magazine* was a fount of fashion advice, and
gave patterns for bodices and coats like this
paletot. Checked fabric was popular, and the
outfit clearly borrows elements from menswear.

Removable
lace collar

Rosette to
separate belt
that covers
join of bodice
with skirt

Square panel
of silk facing

Bishop
sleeves

One of two
bodices that
survive with
this skirt

Skirt worn
over smaller
crinolette frame

Slashed
sleeves

Waistline
now higher

1867

1868

1869

Fringing
and ribbon
decoration

Tartan dress This day dress is of three-color
checked wool: red, pale green, and heather blue. A
horsehair pad supports the back fullness of the skirt.
Velvet rickrack (zigzag) braid trim suggests a collar.
Rosettes were a popular feature in 1867–1870.

Royal blue This silk moiré outfit has separate
bodice and skirt—the front-closure bodice made
getting dressed much easier. Here a small crinolette
frame gives buoyancy and, with the squared bodice
and apron front, anticipates 1870s styles.

Madame Vignon creation The bodice sleeves
on this magenta, silk outfit are slashed in Italian
Renaissance style. The skirt, with mock apron and
peplum overskirt, trails along the ground, and paves
the way for the onset of bustled skirts.

DESIGNER
CHARLES WORTH

Worth's reputation as the father of haute couture—designer-led, custom-fit "high dressmaking"—was well earned. He dominated the Paris scene for the entire second half of the 19th century and made the city the couture capital. Shaping the high-end industry we know today, Worth led a general move in 19th-century Paris away from tailor-dressmakers toward designers whose creations bore their name.

An Englishman abroad

The initial irony was that Monsieur Worth was an Englishman. When family financial problems forced him out to work, he swapped his Lincolnshire home for an apprenticeship at London drapers Swan & Edgar at the age of 13. In 1845 he moved to Paris to Gagelin's, a dress accessories shop where he made a major mark, winning a medal for a stunning embroidered train at the 1855 Exposition Universelle in Paris. By 1858 he had established his own *maison* with business partner Otto Bobergh at 7 rue de la Paix. Worth combined creative, impeccably fitted and made garments with astute business sense, especially the canny cultivation of an aura of exclusivity. With a discreet gilt sign outside, his *maison* featured a series of enticing salons, including a mirrored one with dressed wooden mannequins arranged so that customers would compare their own dress unfavorably.

Against the backdrop of the heady prosperity of Napoleon III's Second Empire (1852–1870), Worth's enterprise flourished. His wife's relentless networking helped. By the 1860s Pauline, Princess Metternich, the wife of the Austrian Ambassador to France was a customer. She introduced him to the fashionable French Empress Eugénie. It was a short step to securing her patronage.

Enduring values

Worth's creations included frothy ball gowns and outfits combining taffeta, velvet, and his beloved Lyon silk, with intricate detailing such as wood beads wrapped in silk thread. Midcentury, his work featured the oversized crinolines for which the man and the era are so well known. He pioneered the flat-fronted, bustle-backed skirt silhouette that took over after the empire fell in 1870. Other innovations included a knee-length tunic worn over a long skirt, the shorter crinoline, ideal for walking, and the *gigot* sleeve popular in the late 1800s—one of many historical (in this case, Elizabethan) influences culled from National Gallery visits during his London years. Worth was first to show whole seasonal collections in advance, to use live mannequins to display garments, and to produce pieces that were copied in France and sold worldwide in addition to exclusive one-offs. Concerned about copyright issues, he pushed for the couture association that is still going today.

After his death in 1895, House of Worth and its values went forward under Charles Frederick's sons, Gaston-Lucien and Jean-Philippe, and beyond, taking in glamorous 1920s cocktail and evening dresses along the way before closing in the 1950s. Worth's influence has been far reaching, from Poiret to Bellville Sassoon to Valentino.

△ **VISITING CARD IN FANCY DRESS c.1860**
Worth had the gift of self promotion and helped turn a trade into an art form. The first male style arbiter with international superstardom, his word was law. Customers deferred to him rather than the other way around.

◁ **DEBUTANTE'S BALL DRESS**
This satin gown with iridescent taffeta is decorated with silk roses and petals and accessorized with an ostrich fan. Worth's efficiency and talent with sumptuous materials made him equal to the task of producing the 1,000 or so lavish gowns that might be needed for just one imperial ball.

TIMELINE

1825 Charles Frederick Worth born in Bourne, Lincolnshire

○ 1820

1838 Starts apprenticeship at Swan & Edgar, London

1845 Takes work with London silk mercers Lewis & Allenby. Moves to Paris to work at dress accessories shop, Maison Gagelin

○ 1840

1851 His designs win prizes at London's Great Exhibition

1852 French Second Empire begins—an era of wealth and lavish dress

1857–1858 Opens his own ladies' fashion business on the rue de la Paix

◁ **1860s** A period of acclaim and success—creates all of Empress Eugénie's evening and state wear from 1864

○ 1860

1870 Second French Empire ends. Splits from business partner Otto Bobergh and continues alone. Prospers with rich American and Russian clients

○ 1880

◁ **1895** Dies in Paris; House of Worth continues under his sons, making dresses such as this, worn by renowned Parisian beauty Countess Greffulhe

○ 1895

ELIZABETH OF BAVARIA, EMPRESS OF AUSTRIA Court painter Winterhalter portrayed many of his royal sitters in Worth dresses, such as this tulle ball gown confection

1870–1879
SOFT BUSTLES AND FISHTAILS

Fashions by the 1870s were softer and more delicate, with pastel coloring and frivolous trimmings and decoration. Bodice necklines were square, with exposed décolleté for evening. Dresses had three-quarter-length sleeves with lace cuffs, or could be sleeveless for evening wear. Aided by the sewing machine (now becoming a desirable acquisition for home use), fabric was draped and layered around the hips, creating an overskirt with apron and panniers that was supported in the small of the back by a straw or horsehair understructure, called a soft bustle. By 1875 colors were deeper, a more streamlined shape was emerging with a smoothly fitted bodice, and the waist and hips were more defined. By 1876 dresses were shaped in a Princess line (with an all-in-one princess petticoat), often with a *cuirasse* over bodice. The upper fullness of earlier skirts had moved lower at the back, forming a fishtail train that was delightful to look at but complex to create and needed skill to manage.

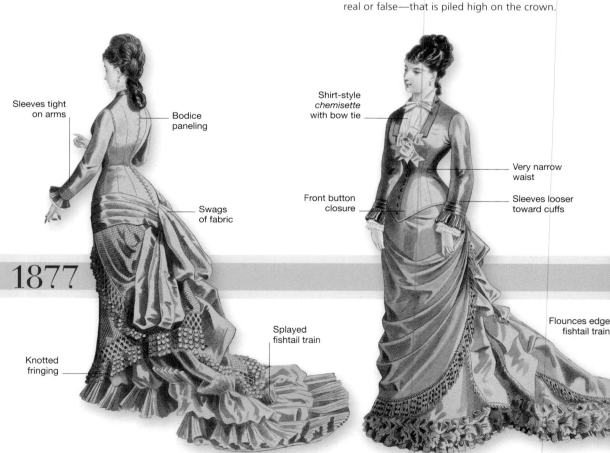

1872

- Small *bergère* (shepherdess) straw hat
- Veil hangs down at the back
- Soft bustle outline
- Pleated trim with contrasting ribbon
- Each tier edged with lace

Wedding dress This triple-tiered main skirt is overlaid with 1770s-style polonaise overskirts, with each layer outlined in a dark trim. The *bergère* straw hat is perched jauntily on hair—real or false—that is piled high on the crown.

SOFT BUSTLES

To support the fullness in the top of the skirt at the back, a framework known as a soft bustle was worn. This could be made from a variety of materials, including meshed horsehair, wadding, and straw, or even improvised with scrunched-up newspaper. The example shown comprises covered watchspring steel, half hoop cording for the lower skirt, moire fabric, and a wavy braided outline along the hem. It fastens at the front of the body with buttons.

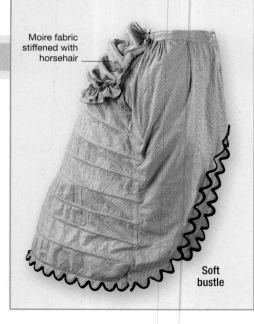

- Moire fabric stiffened with horsehair
- Soft bustle

1877

- Sleeves tight on arms
- Bodice paneling
- Swags of fabric
- Knotted fringing
- Splayed fishtail train

- Shirt-style *chemisette* with bow tie
- Very narrow waist
- Front button closure
- Sleeves looser toward cuffs
- Flounces edge fishtail train

Fishtail train This skirt has copious drapery, which would have hampered movement. The train would swish from side to side as the wearer walked and turned. A ribbon on the train's end could be attached to the wrist to lift the fabric for ease of maneuver.

Cuirasse bodice The *cuirasse* (from the French for armor) bodice helped create a small waist. It was aided underneath by a princess petticoat and back-laced corset, which by now had steels and a front-opening spoonbill busk.

Hat at acute
45-degree angle

Self-colored
silk trim

Decorative
basket

External pocket

Bronze outfit This beautiful bronze-brown
ensemble has a self-colored silk ribbon trim.
The blue buttons and blue hair ribbons
create an unusual color combination with
the bronze, a look specific to 1872–1874.

Simple toque

Decorative
ribbons cover
hook-and-eye
closures

Fitted
sleeves

Kid leather
gloves

Marinière (marine-style)
cuffs

Parasol with
contrasting
lining

Walking suit This olive-green silk outfit has
a long jacket, fitted to the body and flaring
at the hem; the band collar is trimmed with
machine-made cream lace. The paneled
skirt is gathered up at the front.

Hair in French
pleat decorated
with flowers

Sleeveless
bodice

Low
bustle

Evening gown This 1878
dress in blue and white—
colors reminiscent of Chinese
porcelain—has layers of
tulle and lace at the front. It
includes the practical feature
of a dust ruffle that could be
removed and washed.

Cotton
balayeuse
dust ruffle

Train

Artificial flower
decorations

High collar in
contrasting fabric

Traveling dress Ideal for
walking, picnics, or traveling,
this tan outfit of heavy silk and
velvet from 1874 has a darker
collar, cuffs, and underskirt,
and olive fringing.

1874

Beginnings
of a train

Elaborate
ruffles and
ties

Tight-pleated
hem

Drop earrings

Choker with
heart pendant

Asymmetry in the
cross-over fichu
(scarf)-style collar

Bodice
paneling

Artificial flowers
at waist

Deep lace cuff

1875

Ruby red signals
appearance of new
depth of color

Chenille
fringing

Parisian style This up-to-the-minute 1875 design
shows the new style from Paris. The bustle is more
restrained and the fishtail train makes an appearance.
Hips are at their slimmest for 50 years, and skirts are
caught in around the knees, forcing a hobbled gait.

1878

BOOTS AND SHOES

Higher heels began to alter the body's
posture, tipping it forward slightly, which
emphasized the bustle skirts and carried
through to the tilted hat. Heels were small
(1½ in/4 cm) and stocky, and curved inward
at the back. Toes were squared off (as
shown here), rounded, or pointed. Most
boots were black for everyday wear, but
for weddings or balls, ivory satin or fine
kid leather was used. Elastic sides were
popular, using imported rubber, and uppers
were decorated with bows and tassels.

Elastic sides
make boots
easy to pull on

Shoes

Satin could be
dyed different
colors

Boots

MATCHING TWO-PIECE
BUSTLE SKIRT

Consisting of a tightly fitted bodice and long, trained skirt, this two-piece ensemble of striped, apricot silk displays the fashionable silhouette and longer bodice of 1874–1875. Skirts narrowed, and volume shifted to the back to form a bustle. A bustle pad worn under the skirt provided the support. This style of skirt takes its inspiration from the 18th-century *polonaise* and is constructed in a similar way. Tapes attached to inside of the skirt allow it to be gathered up at the back. The wearer could also choose to loosen the tapes and have the skirts long, achieving the look of the alternative back and side views below.

Ruched silk applied to bodice

Concealed hook-and-eye closure

Suede or kid gloves would have been worn

Flat-fronted skirt

BACK VIEW WITH SKIRT DOWN

BACK VIEW WITH SKIRT UP

SIDE VIEW WITH SKIRT DOWN

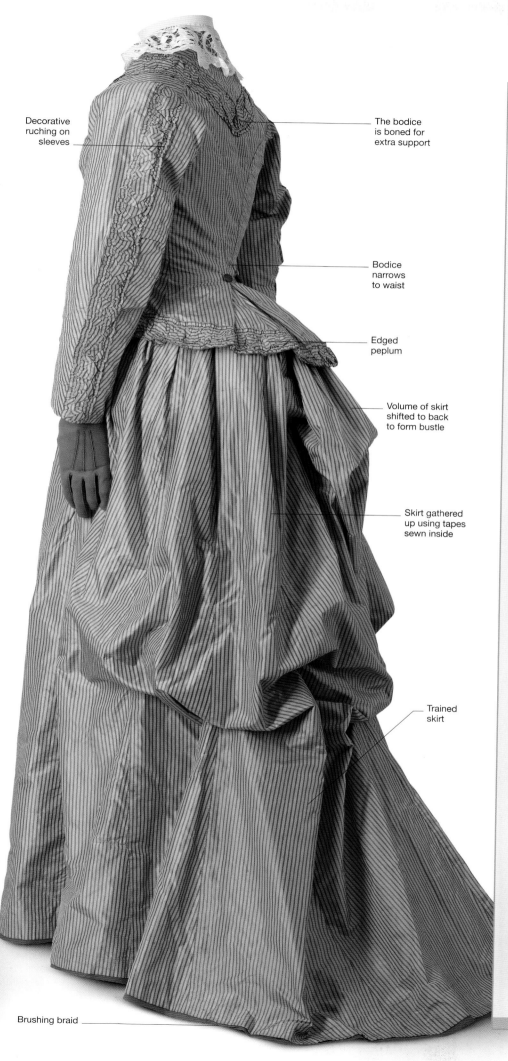

Decorative ruching on sleeves

The bodice is boned for extra support

Bodice narrows to waist

Edged peplum

Volume of skirt shifted to back to form bustle

Skirt gathered up using tapes sewn inside

Trained skirt

Brushing braid

IN DETAIL

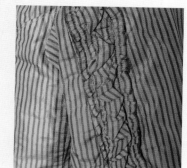

◁ RUCHING TO SLEEVES
Strips of the silk have been ruched and applied as decoration to the sleeves and bodice. The advent of the sewing machine enabled the increasingly complicated decorations and trimmings fashionable at this time. The machine stitching is visible on the sleeves.

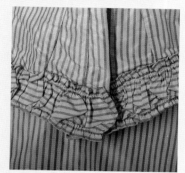

◁ FRONT OF PEPLUM BODICE
The bodice is fastened at the center front with five metal hooks and eyes for a close fit around the narrow, corseted waist. The bodice extends to a short peplum, which is shaped over the hips into a pointed front and finished with a ruched band of fabric.

◁ BUTTON DETAIL
A pair of brown, fabric-covered buttons trim the center back waist and mark the top of two deep pleats, which splay over the volume of the bustle. This simple detail draws influence from masculine tailoring and anticipates women's fashions in the following decades.

◁ POCKET
From the 1840s dresses began to have pockets sewn into the skirt. This skirt has an internal pocket lined with glazed cotton, a durable fabric suitable for holding items. The lining discreetly matches the tone of the dress.

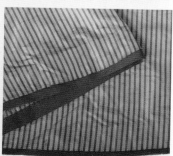

◁ HEM
This contrast binding, which was known as brushing braid, was used to finish the hem of the skirt. It would have helped to strengthen and protect the silk as the train trailed on the ground. The brushing braid could be brushed to remove dust and dirt at the end of the day before the outfit was put away.

1880–1888

THE RISE AND FALL OF THE BUSTLE

By 1880 there was no discernible bustle, and fishtail trains were rejected. Cotton combinations—chemise and drawers—were worn under the main outfit, and were supplemented by knit wool combination garments that combated a series of cold winters. An extremely tight, steel-boned corset secured the small waist that was being increasingly admired and forced a rigid, upright posture. Further boning reinforced the dress bodice. A new bustle shape gradually developed from 1881–1883, this time stiff and angular. From 1883–1887 the bustle grew, and stuck out at right angles, eventually tilting over into a chicken tail feather flourish before disappearing. The majority of garments were now made by sewing machine, and many fabrics were colored with synthetic dyes.

Coordinating bonnet

Triple-layered cape collar

1880

Matching parasol with pom-poms

Fan pleating

French day dress This walking outfit demonstrates superb use of controlled skirt drapery and contrasting trimmings: a neat row of buttons, collar with alternating colors, and discrete fan pleating on the cuffs and hem.

Striped ribbon

Spanish promenade fashion
Contrasting silks and velvets, wools and silks, or light and dark colors were used effectively in exciting combinations, and matching accessories created a smart ensemble. Deportment—a back as straight as a rod—was key to carrying off this style.

Stiff collar

False vest fronts

1888

Balayeuse dust ruffle visible

Feathered cap tied under chin

Deep-dyed colors fashionable across Europe

Long bodice front

Pomegranate motif

Morning dress The pomegranate design on this skirt is particularly identified with Spain. Eiderdown feather petticoats were popular in the cold winter of 1887–1888.

MOURNING

Half-mourning cap

Mourning bonnet

There was a strict etiquette for mourning royalty and relatives. The fashion industry perfected the art of dyeing fabric black, providing copious lengths of black crêpe and bombazine fabrics, ribbons, bonnets, veils, and feathers. Department stores stocked ready-to-wear mourning outfits. Wool cloth was advised since it absorbed light, rather than reflecting it. Half-mourning required gray, white, and purple to be worn in specific time frames.

Victorian mourning dress

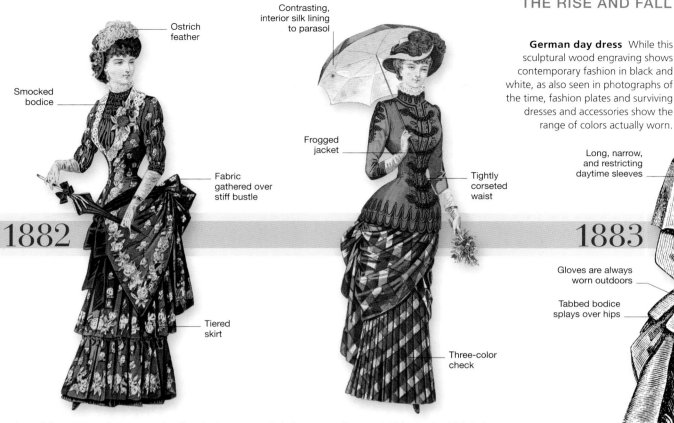

Ostrich feather

Smocked bodice

Fabric gathered over stiff bustle

Tiered skirt

1882

Contrasting, interior silk lining to parasol

Frogged jacket

Tightly corseted waist

Three-color check

German day dress While this sculptural wood engraving shows contemporary fashion in black and white, as also seen in photographs of the time, fashion plates and surviving dresses and accessories show the range of colors actually worn.

Very little flesh shows—only face

Long, narrow, and restricting daytime sleeves

1883

Gloves are always worn outdoors

Tabbed bodice splays over hips

Disposition patterning Attractive floral prints or weaves *à la disposition*—with different patterns in the same colorway, used together—were popular. Forehead fringes appeared in high society, but were disallowed for maids.

Fabric cut on diagonal This checked fabric is kilted to one side. The diagonal stripe effect of the pleated underskirt is striking. Pleats needed careful laundering and ironing. Cleaning the fabric with solvents may have been an option.

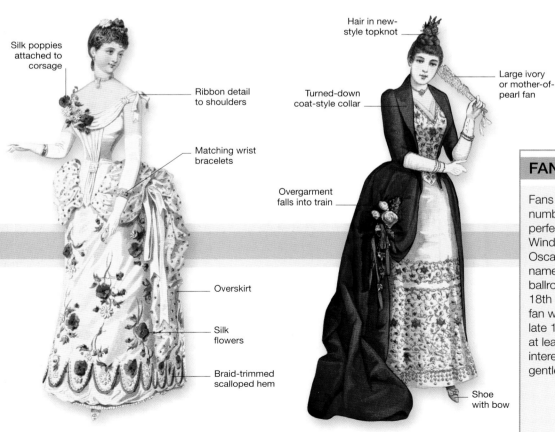

Silk poppies attached to corsage

Ribbon detail to shoulders

Matching wrist bracelets

Overskirt

Silk flowers

Braid-trimmed scalloped hem

Hair in new-style topknot

Large ivory or mother-of-pearl fan

Turned-down coat-style collar

Overgarment falls into train

Shoe with bow

Ball dress This design from Madrid would require a skillful dressmaker to swathe spotted fabric over the hips, attach silk flowers, and make the rigid understructures of whalebone and steel disappear.

Evening dress This Spanish dress and bodice are exquisitely embroidered. The trained overgarment adds warmth and elegance. This fashion plate, along with the three to the left, show the range of styles in Spain in a single year.

FANS

Fans were produced in huge numbers. They were the perfect gift—as was Lady Windermere's fan in the 1892 Oscar Wilde play of the same name—and useful in a warm ballroom or theater. The early 18th century language of the fan was largely lost by the late 19th century, but might at least allow a female to signal interest or otherwise to a gentleman admirer.

Cockade face protector

Fan with mother-of-pearl sticks and guards

1890–1899
HIGH RUFFS AND WASP WAISTS

Women's wear in the last decade of the Victorian era was characterized by high collars, held in place by collar stays, and stiff steel boning in long-line bodices and corsets. Mid-decade, tiny wasp waists were emphasized by the most enormous sleeves and pyramid skirts with smooth fronts, which had pleating concentrated at center back. In mainstream fashions, the ruff, corseting, padded sleeves, and cone-shaped skirts consciously recalled Elizabethan fin-de-siècle styling. Ball dresses were décolleté (had a low neckline), but for day wear barely any flesh was revealed below chin level. Dark colors persisted but were challenged by a lighter palette anticipating Edwardian pinks and creams. Colored stockings and high heels were popular. The use of exotic bird feathers and even whole birds on hats had become such an issue that the Royal Society for the Protection of Birds was founded, to campaign against any but ostrich feathers being used in the future.

1890

Shoulder puffs

Tight-corseted waist

Trained overdress

Gilt and colored bead embroidery on net

Dressed for evening The shoulder puff heralded a new focus on sleeves. Petticoat silks were tin-weighted to make them sit properly, and rustled as the wearer moved. Here, delicate embroidery, worked on fine net or gauze, overlays the skirt.

CAPES

On trend: red and black

Moleskin and feathers

Satin and velvet

Short, boxy capes replaced the 1880s dolman capes, once the bustle had disappeared. Silk brocade was popular for opera wear, to cover décolletage, and might be trimmed with jet, French jet (glass), lace, appliqué, braid, fur, or feathers. For day wear, wool cloth capes trimmed with braid or appliqué detail coexisted alongside traveling jackets and full-length coats. They were certainly easier to wear over the large, leg-of-mutton sleeves of 1893–1896. Black and red were the most fashionable colors.

Leg-of-mutton sleeves

Crescent "Diana" headdress

Wasp waist

1895

Hourglass shape Warp-printed chine silk gives this outfit a particular luster. Enormous, leg-of-mutton sleeves, bows along skirt seams, a defined V shaping to the bodice, and "Elizabethan" ruff typify the fin-de-siècle style.

Veil

Pleated blouse front

Spotted fabric for paneled skirt

1896

Summer blouse and skirt This veiled hat would have been secured with decorative hat pins that pierced into the top knot of swept-up hair. The ruff encouraged good deportment, always required in Victorian women.

Lace above bodice

Shoulder fanning

Lace appliqué

Wide-brimmed hat with flower trim

Leg-of-mutton sleeves

Cutaway "dress coat" detailing

1893

Straw bonnet decorated with birds' wings and artificial flowers

High neck for day wear

Lawn ruffle

Repeat flower print

Umbrella

Tiered skirts

Daytime visiting This dress is clearly made all in one. The horizontal drapery masks subtle hook-and-eye side closures. The skirt is given decorative treatment with lace appliqué. Lace also adjoins the high, stiff collar.

Businesslike A new tailored style appeared in mainstream fashion, made in wool cloth. Here, masculine vest, stiff collar, and triple braiding add up to a stylish look.

Leg-of-mutton sleeves narrow from elbow

Puffed-out center panel

Stylish high collar

Overcape

Double row of buttons

1898

1899

Satin skirt fully lined with pink taffeta

Pink satin These sleeves are leg-of-mutton shape and the gored skirt has box-pleated fullness at the center back. The high-necked bodice, trimmed with black velvet, jet, and lace, is attached to the skirt with hooks and eyes.

Traveling This skirt has characteristic 1890s detailing in its diagonal trim, and the checked overcape has echoes of an epaulet shape in its squared shoulder line. The wool cloth cape is lined with fur.

Spring afternoon dress The Edwardian era is near, and the straight-fronted corset is now in evidence. This dress is made of delicate printed silk, linen, or light muslin, with lawn ruffles, and a wonderful tiered skirt design.

BODICE AND SKIRT

RECEPTION DRESS

This elaborate house dress, designed by American couturier Kate R. Cragmile in 1891, reflects the change in women's fashionable dress from the exaggerated bustle of the 1880s to the rounded hourglass shape of the 1890s. The dress features broad shoulders on leg-of-mutton sleeves, a very narrow waist, and a skirt gently widening to the hemline. The contrasting colors and textures of deep velvet and light-catching silk damask emphasize a tiny waist, while the vest and overdress show the influence of late 18th-century masculine tailoring.

SIDE VIEW

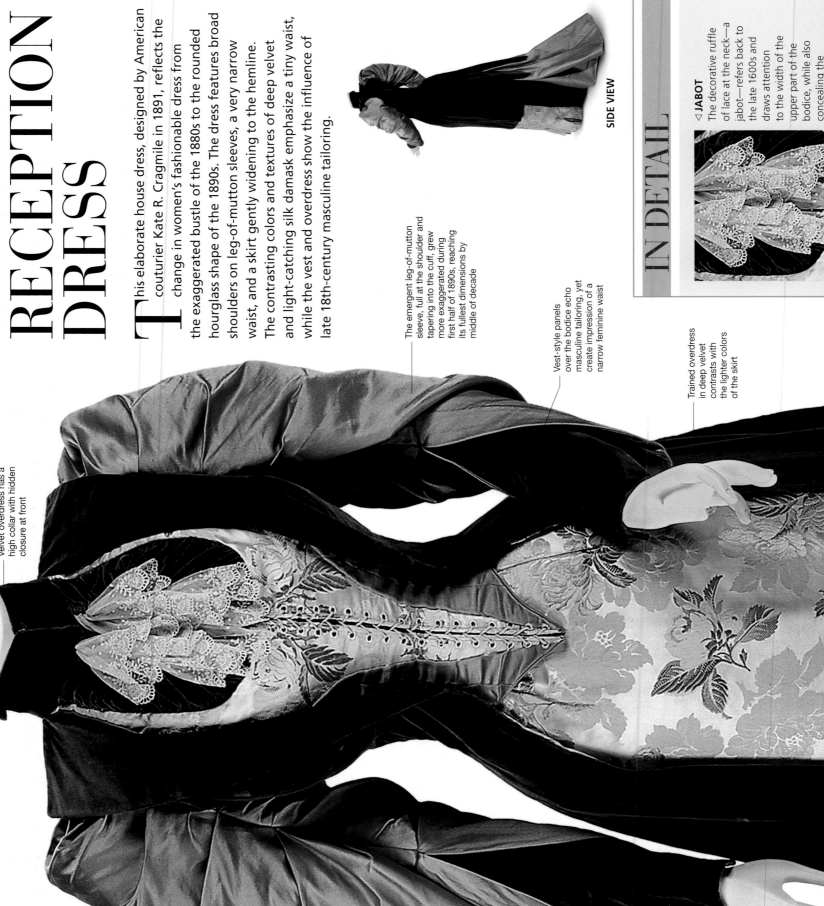

Velvet overdress has a high collar with hidden closure at front

The emergent leg-of-mutton sleeve, full at the shoulder and tapering into the cuff, grew more exaggerated during first half of 1890s, reaching its fullest dimensions by middle of decade

Vest-style panels over the bodice echo masculine tailoring, yet create impression of a narrow feminine waist

Trained overdress in deep velvet contrasts with the lighter colors of the skirt

IN DETAIL

◁ **JABOT**
The decorative ruffle of lace at the neck—a jabot—refers back to the late 1600s and draws attention to the width of the upper part of the bodice, while also concealing the dress closure.

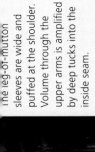

...he leg-of-mutton
sleeves are wide and
puffed at the shoulder.
Volume through the
upper arms is amplified
by deep tucks into the
inside seam.

▽ **DAMASK SILK**
The patterned silk
dress fabric is a complex
weave combining a
damask self-colored
pattern of silver-gray
roses overlaid with
a brocade of more
colorful roses in green
silk and gold thread.

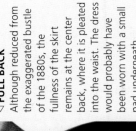

◁ **FULL BACK**
Although reduced from
the exaggerated bustle
of the 1880s, the
fullness of the skirt
remains at the center
back, where it is pleated
into the waist. The dress
would probably have
been worn with a small
pad underneath.

▽ **SMALL TRAIN**
A fairly short gathered
train of golden silk
adds length at the back
of the dress, and is
framed by long velvet
panels resembling
a man's tailcoat.

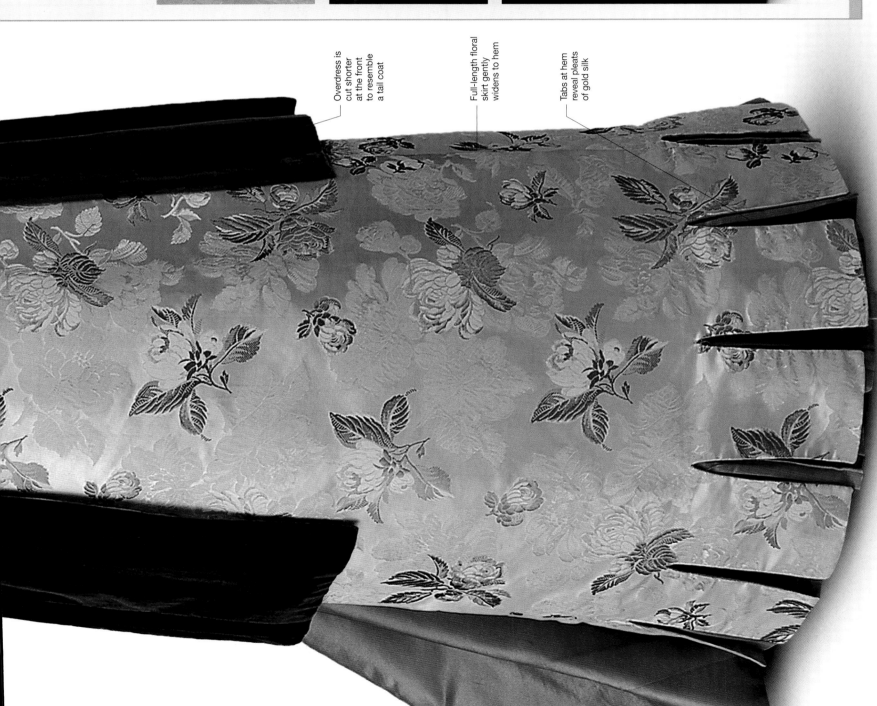

Overdress is
cut shorter
at the front
to resemble
a tail coat

Full-length floral
skirt gently
widens to hem

Tabs at hem
reveal pleats
of gold silk

1840–1900
FORMAL WEAR FOR MEN

Gentlemen's formal dress became more somber in shape and tone in the mid-19th century. The three-piece suit emerged in the 1860s, although it was still years away from becoming a uniform of business respectability. Fibers for all garments were still natural, but advanced machinery made more intricate weaves and color combinations possible. The sewing machine helped the ready-made trade, while tailors' manuals with patterns for varying styles of coat proliferated. In leisure wear, there were color combinations and contrasts to delight: embroidered accessories, an intriguing glimpse of luxurious lining fabric, or a jaunty pair of striped, checked, or plaid trousers. Stylish items of day wear—top hat, cravat, and pantaloons—became reserved for formal wear, while bowler hats and ties supplanted them for day. Fall-front trousers gave way to fly fronts.

Stovepipe hat

Fine wool cape

Quilted cape Lambs' wool quilting kept a gentleman warm when going to the opera or paying an evening call. The contrasting silk lining shows off fine hand stitching. Top hats were of beaver, felt, or silk.

Dress suit

Leather gloves

1845

Top hat lends stature

Sleeves echo women's full bishop sleeves

1868

Buff-colored trousers contrast with dark coat and vest

Morning coat This coat and vest set is highlighted by light-colored trousers. Heavy tweeds and worsted wools, used here, were the materials for winter, replacing the stout twilled linen drill and cotton nankeen trouser fabrics of summer.

Heels add a few inches to height

FAVORS 1840–1870

Figured, checked, or embroidered with ribbon work, decorative wool and silk vests added an accent of color to a man's outfit. Brides-to-be might embroider them in canvas work for their grooms. While the fronts were decorative, the backs, covered by a jacket, were of plain cotton with an adjustable strap.

Figured fabric

Flower garden embroidery

Woven check

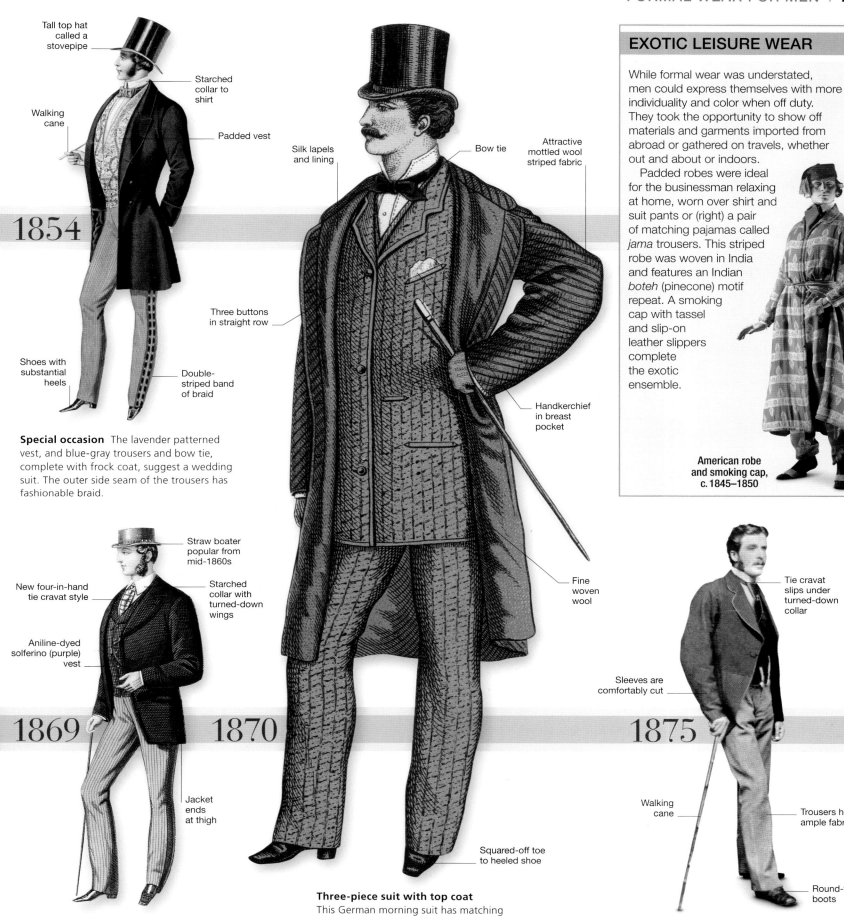

Tall top hat called a stovepipe

Starched collar to shirt

Walking cane

Padded vest

1854

Shoes with substantial heels

Double-striped band of braid

Special occasion The lavender patterned vest, and blue-gray trousers and bow tie, complete with frock coat, suggest a wedding suit. The outer side seam of the trousers has fashionable braid.

Silk lapels and lining

Bow tie

Attractive mottled wool striped fabric

Three buttons in straight row

Handkerchief in breast pocket

Fine woven wool

EXOTIC LEISURE WEAR

While formal wear was understated, men could express themselves with more individuality and color when off duty. They took the opportunity to show off materials and garments imported from abroad or gathered on travels, whether out and about or indoors.

Padded robes were ideal for the businessman relaxing at home, worn over shirt and suit pants or (right) a pair of matching pajamas called *jama* trousers. This striped robe was woven in India and features an Indian *boteh* (pinecone) motif repeat. A smoking cap with tassel and slip-on leather slippers complete the exotic ensemble.

American robe and smoking cap, c. 1845–1850

Straw boater popular from mid-1860s

New four-in-hand tie cravat style

Starched collar with turned-down wings

Aniline-dyed solferino (purple) vest

1869

1870

Jacket ends at thigh

Squared-off toe to heeled shoe

Lounge jacket The lounge jacket emerged around 1859 and was well established as lounging or morning wear by 1869. Light-colored trousers increasingly indicated casual dress, as did the straw boater.

Three-piece suit with top coat
This German morning suit has matching tailored reefer jacket, trousers, and vest, with an overcoat in dashing bronzed tan, a dye color favored in the 1870s. The materials are of superb quality and the fit is expert.

Tie cravat slips under turned-down collar

Sleeves are comfortably cut

1875

Walking cane

Trousers have ample fabric

Round-toed boots

Lounge suit jacket This jacket is worn with a tie cravat, velvet vest, and light-colored trousers. The jacket edges are turned and stitched; earlier jacket edges were left raw with firmly woven and milled cloth.

むめつぼ

CULT OF BEAUTY

After 250 years, Japanese isolation from the West during the Shogun era ended, and the impact on Western fashion, art, and culture was swift. Inspired by the display of Japanese art at the International exhibition of 1862, members of the Aesthetic movement (1862–1900) with its "cult of beauty" embraced all things Japanese. E. Desoye opened a store of Japanese curios in Paris, and in 1875 Arthur Lazenby Liberty sold Japanese goods at his store, Liberty and Co. on Regent Street, London, alongside a comprehensive range of fabrics and artifacts from the Far East.

Japanese prints based on conventionalized forms of the natural world, such as flowers, birds, dragonflies, and butterflies, along with free-flowing garments, appealed to the bohemian style makers of London, in particular Aesthetes such as Oscar Wilde and his wife Constance. Fashions such as classic Greek gowns or "Athenes," Japanese kimonos, Indian pajamas, and embroidered coats from China and Japan created an immediate contrast with the established, traditional Victorian dress of corsets, crinolines, and bustles, and a restricted and structured silhouette. At the Divan Japonais nightclub in Paris, fans and silks festooned the walls, and customers were attended to by waitresses dressed in kimonos. In 1876, Claude Monet painted his wife wearing a kimono in a painting entitled "La Japonaise."

66

One should either be a work of art, or wear one.

OSCAR WILDE, 1894

99

◁ **JAPANESE BEAUTIES**
Facsimile of a chromoxylograph by Wilhelm Greve after Katsukawa Shunsho, 1776.

1870–1900
SPORTSWEAR FOR THE NEW WOMAN

Women's day wear was adapted for sports from archery to croquet and boating to tennis, while still preserving a fashionable waistline, sleeve shape, and skirt fullness. Drawers worn under petticoats enabled freedom of movement without fear of embarrassment. Knit underclothing such as Dr. Jaeger's sanitary underwear, available from the mid-1880s, cotton combination garments that avoided bulky waists, and specifically designed sports corsets were a boon. The breathable cotton-mesh fabric Aertex was invented in 1888, and less restrictive corsets were made that incorporated this mesh to allow better air flow. Women supporters of the Pre-Raphaelite and Aesthetic movements had already stopped wearing corsets and wire understructures. While the new woman spurned fancy fabrics, burgeoning department stores sold silk brocades and plush velvet gowns in joyful colors, and society women found themselves with an abundance of choice.

Contrasting trim

Dress worn over crinolette frame or soft bustle

Looped-up apron skirt

Copious gathering made easier with new sewing machines

Dust ruffle for muddy walks

Bustle dress This sensible wool dress in brown, c. 1870–1875, was suitable for country walking, traveling, croquet, archery, and picnicking, all popular female pursuits. Going-away outfits were often of a similar style and color.

ARTISTIC AND AESTHETIC

Women in artistic circles, such as the Pre-Raphaelite muse Jane Morris, flouted rigid dress conventions, pioneering a freer style. Dress reform societies also campaigned for healthier, less structured forms of dress. Their dress styles recalled medieval (pre-hooped skirt) days. They borrowed relaxed styles such as the early sack back, in which fabric fell unfettered from nape to hem.

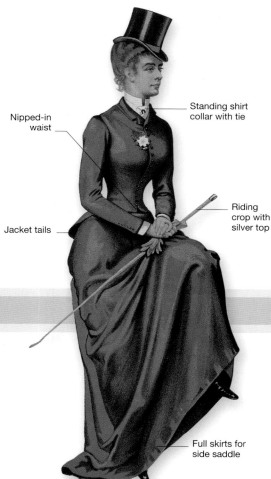

Nipped-in waist

Standing shirt collar with tie

Riding crop with silver top

Jacket tails

Full skirts for side saddle

Riding habit Made of soft wool, this jacket has a long row of tiny buttons to fasten tightly over a corset. Riding tails sat neatly upon late 1880s bustles. The top hat perches high on the crown on frizzed hair.

Stylish ribboned straw boater

Leg-of-mutton sleeves

Squared tennis racquet

Tight corseting

Gored skirt

Lawn tennis dress Although earlier tennis dresses (c. 1875–1885) had aprons with pockets for the balls, this 1897 fashion advertisement for the new season offers little concession to sports. *Punch* magazine joked that women should have a handicap.

Hat with
stuffed bird

Tailored
jacket

Silk cummerbund
defines waist

Gored skirt
has fullness
at the back

Apt "racing
green" choice
of color

The races Dress for spectator sports evolved as a relaxed version of day wear, in sympathetic fabrics and colors, c. 1890. The focus on large hats on race days continues to this day.

Contrasting bow

Striped under
bodice

Draped
overskirt

Skirt
pleating

Sleeves for
bicycling follow
fashionable shapes

Wool jacket
worn over
wasp-waist
corset

Bifurcated
skirt (split into
two parts)

Matching
gaiters

Bicycling suit This tailored jacket was worn with a modest patented bifurcated skirt, for ease when bicycling, c. 1896–1898. More daring knickerbockers were also worn by some women. Cycling gaiters and a veiled boater would complete the outfit.

Braided
sailor stripes

Separate
belt

Bloomer-style
leggings
resemble
knickerbockers

Bathing dress Sailor suits influenced bathing dress, hence the sailor collar and stripes. This wool serge garment, c. 1900, is an all-in-one, like combination undergarments. There may have been a modesty skirt originally.

Nautical Blue and white striped fabrics as well as children's sailor suits gave a nautical flavor to dress, and were worn for regattas, yachting, boating, and seaside promenading. The draping and soft vertical pleating over the bustle of this dress from 1885–1888 suggest informality.

Dark straw
boater

Leg-of-mutton
sleeve

Gored
skirt

Walking suit Tailored by the French designer Jacques Doucet, this no-frills linen suit, from c. 1894, reflects a move toward the sobriety of men's suits. Women now joined men in hill walking and mountain climbing.

1837–1900
MEN OF ACTION

W hile men's suits settled into sobriety and uniformly dark coloring, their leisure wear for sports and country pursuits became more flamboyant and revealing. Garments were adapted for the purpose of health-oriented exercise, using stretchy materials such as jersey knit. Drapers who supplied cloth and ready-to-wear shirts began to focus increasingly on sportswear for pursuits such as tennis, boating, mountaineering, and golf. Men wore plus fours for golf from the 1860s. From the mid-century French companies and Britain's Aquascutum and Burberry developed lined, twilled cotton fabrics for waterproof outerwear for the "huntin,' shootin,' fishin'" fraternity. Shepherd plaid, a black-and-white check, was popular in the 1890s. Sports clubs and activities brought industrialists, military men, artists, and writers together, in pursuit of healthy bodies to fuel the mind. J. M. Barrie, author of *Peter Pan*, even had his own cricket team from 1887.

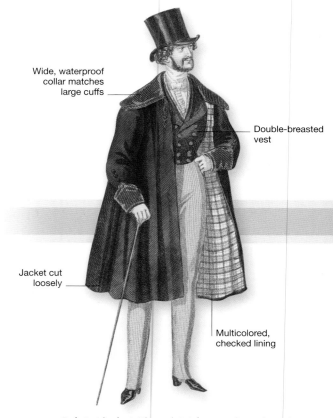

Wide, waterproof collar matches large cuffs

Double-breasted vest

Jacket cut loosely

Multicolored, checked lining

Paletot jacket The paletot for men hung loosely from the shoulders and was sleeved. Checked and tartan wool linings, as in this example of c. 1838, provided warmth for country clothing. They later became a fashion statement.

Side parting fashionable 1865–1870

Lightweight shirt

Flat shoes

Felt hat with curled brim

Lounge or Norfolk coat worn open to reveal high-buttoning vest

Breeches often worn with buttoned leather gaiters

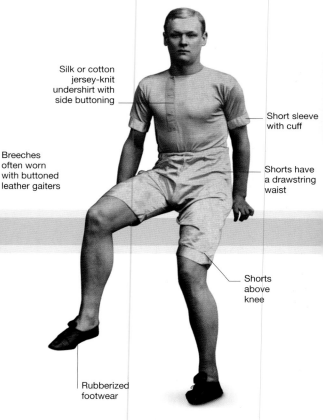

Silk or cotton jersey-knit undershirt with side buttoning

Short sleeve with cuff

Shorts have a drawstring waist

Shorts above knee

Rubberized footwear

Tennis clothes "Whites" were established for tennis and cricket as early as the late 1860s. This tennis outfit consists of a lightweight linen jacket, now called a blazer, with trousers, cotton shirt, and a cap.

Cycling suit The Earl of Albermarle, president of the National Cyclists' Union, rides a tricycle, c. 1880. He wears a wool three-piece suit consisting of single-breasted jacket, vest, and breeches that finish just below the knee.

Team sports Men undertook football, rugby, and rowing in variations of undershirt and drawers. This sportsman, c. 1890, may be a member of Cambridge University's rowing team. His short-sleeved undershirt precedes the T-shirt.

Hunt dress This British cloth hunting jacket of 1868 is buttoned high with five buttons and teamed with breeches of Bedford cord. Hard hats (jockey caps) and club buttons were also worn for the hunt. Cravat pins bore images of hounds.

- Top hat
- Patterned silk cravat
- Red worn for hunting
- Whip was an essential accessory
- Top boots

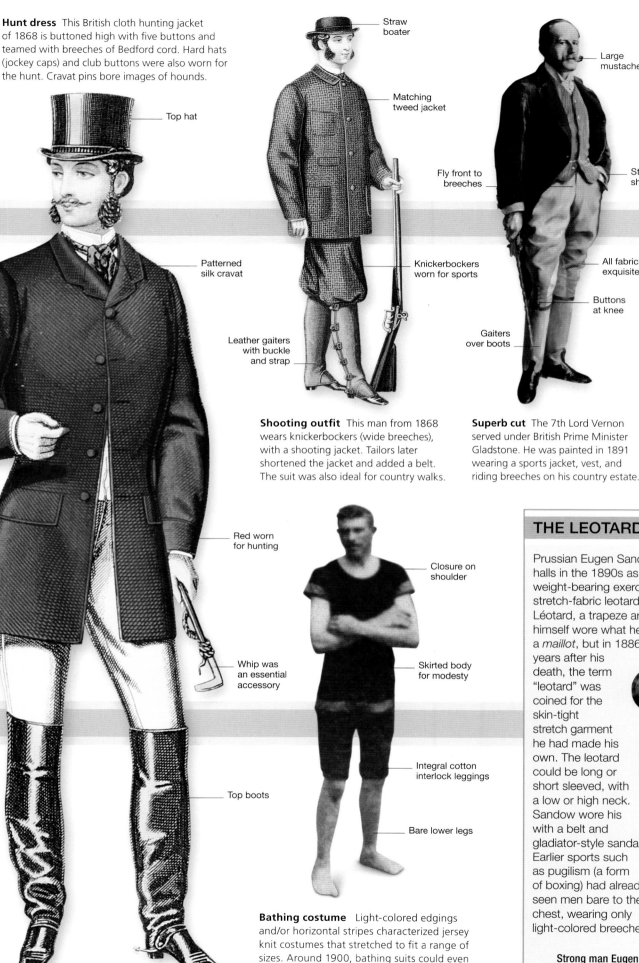

- Straw boater
- Matching tweed jacket
- Fly front to breeches
- Knickerbockers worn for sports
- Leather gaiters with buckle and strap

Shooting outfit This man from 1868 wears knickerbockers (wide breeches), with a shooting jacket. Tailors later shortened the jacket and added a belt. The suit was also ideal for country walks.

- Large mustache
- Starched shirt cuff
- All fabrics exquisite
- Buttons at knee
- Gaiters over boots

Superb cut The 7th Lord Vernon served under British Prime Minister Gladstone. He was painted in 1891 wearing a sports jacket, vest, and riding breeches on his country estate.

- Wide-brimmed hat shields face from sun
- Blazer jacket and vest over shirt and tie
- Breeches button at knee
- Riding boots

Riding gear for Japan This man, c. 1890, wears linen, which was cool, lightweight, and washable. London's Army and Navy Stores supplied outfits to British expatriates.

- Closure on shoulder
- Skirted body for modesty
- Integral cotton interlock leggings
- Bare lower legs

Bathing costume Light-colored edgings and/or horizontal stripes characterized jersey knit costumes that stretched to fit a range of sizes. Around 1900, bathing suits could even be rented on the beach.

THE LEOTARD

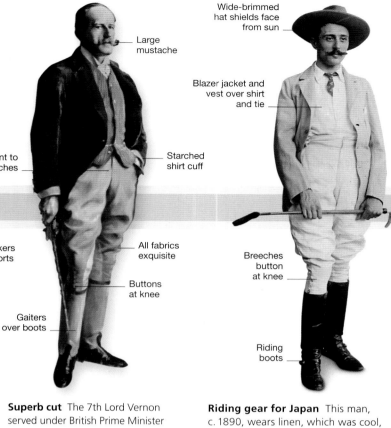

Prussian Eugen Sandow became a celebrity of British music halls in the 1890s as a bodybuilder, extolling the virtues of weight-bearing exercise on the physique. He wore only a stretch-fabric leotard. The garment was named after Jules Léotard, a trapeze artist. Léotard himself wore what he called a *maillot*, but in 1886, some years after his death, the term "leotard" was coined for the skin-tight stretch garment he had made his own. The leotard could be long or short sleeved, with a low or high neck. Sandow wore his with a belt and gladiator-style sandals. Earlier sports such as pugilism (a form of boxing) had already seen men bare to the chest, wearing only light-colored breeches.

Strong man Eugen Sandow

1800–1900
THEMED COSTUMES

Themed costume parties enabled the late Georgians and Victorians to have fun with dressing up. Like a game of charades, partygoers had to guess who their fellow guests were dressed as. Esoteric costumes absorbed influences from history, mythology, theater, literary characters, and the Orient, reworked by dressmakers in imaginative and extravagant ways. Some partygoers wore costumes that family members had brought back from abroad, or retrieved treasured ancestral outfits from the attic. Others were inspired by sources such as Arden Holt's 1887 catalogue of *Fancy Dresses Described*, which was sold through Debenham and Freebody's, the department store. These featured themed costumes as diverse as a foppish *Incroyable*, a witch, and a hornet. Natural materials such as beetle wing cases and butterfly wings, and even live fireflies in net bags, were used to create a suitable macabre or exotic atmosphere.

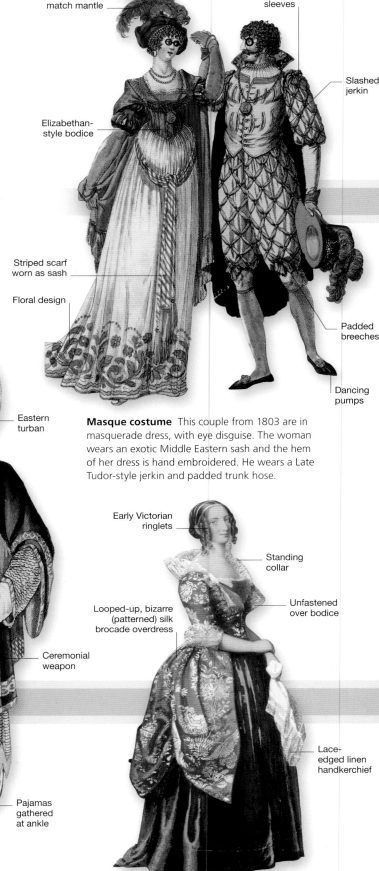

Feathered headdress to match mantle

Checkered, padded sleeves

Elizabethan-style bodice

Slashed jerkin

Striped scarf worn as sash

Floral design

Padded breeches

Dancing pumps

Masque costume This couple from 1803 are in masquerade dress, with eye disguise. The woman wears an exotic Middle Eastern sash and the hem of her dress is hand embroidered. He wears a Late Tudor-style jerkin and padded trunk hose.

ROYAL DRESSING UP

England's 1897 Devonshire House Ball was themed around allegorical or historical costume pre-1820. The Duke of York went as the 3rd Earl of Cumberland, with embroidered Genoa velvet pourpoint, sleeves, and mantle; steel gorget (plate armor collar); crimson velvet trunks; high boots; and felt hat with three feathers. The Duchess was Marguerite de Valois, in pale blue satin, with a Medici old lace collar, and copious pearls and diamonds.

Eastern turban

Neck scarf

Patka (waist sash)

Ceremonial weapon

Pajamas gathered at ankle

Buskin-type boots

Middle Eastern This 1830 figure wears a Persian-style, knee-length vest of metal thread over a white lawn shirt and under a rich blue tunic trimmed with gold braid. Vandyking (zigzag borders) often indicated a themed costume in the 19th century.

Early Victorian ringlets

Standing collar

Looped-up, bizarre (patterned) silk brocade overdress

Unfastened over bodice

Lace-edged linen handkerchief

Antique brocade The Eglinton Tournament of 1839 was a romantic extravaganza with medieval jousting and banquets. This lady, shown in her costume for the Scottish event, wears a Queen Henrietta Maria-style dress with a silk brocade overdress.

Cavalier hat
with feathers

Reticella lace
collar and cuffs

Male costume This figure from 1834 is dressed as Charles I, as seen in portraits by Anthony van Dyck. The open-sleeved doublet reveals a linen shirt. It is worn with a cloak and knee-breeches.

Petticoat
breeches with
yards of ribbon

Lace-trimmed
boots over
white hose

Skullcap with
devilish horns

Slashed jerkin

Archetypal
devil's cloak

Spiked horns on
headdress

Snake
necklace

Gilt corsage
with devil mask

Double layer
of stiff, pleated
underpetticoats

Train of heavy,
spotted, looped-
back fabric

Skintight,
Tudor-style
hose

Slashed
leather shoes

Ribbon
and feather
headdress

Powdered wig
like those of
c. 1775–1780

Laced
stomacher

Open gown
with petticoat

Matching
fabric puff
and trim

An amalgam An 1831 fashion plate shows a late 18th-century-style costume. It combines the 1760s open gown with petticoat and the early 17th-century-style bodice with a wide neckline and lace collar, which also mirrored fashions of the early 1830s.

DOLLY VARDEN STYLE

This look mimicked the 18th-century *bergère* (shepherdess) style, with its straw bonnet and looped-up polonaise skirt over a quilted petticoat. Dolly Varden was a coquettish character in Charles Dickens's *Barnaby Rudge,* published in 1841 but set in 1780. This music sheet cover depicts a woman in a Dolly Varden style costume.

G. W. MOORE'S GREAT SONG.
DRESS'D IN A DOLLY VARDEN.

G. W. MOORE.
ORIGINAL CHRISTY MINSTRELS, St JAMES'S HALL.

Dolly Varden

Diablesse This 1885 French costume for a female devil is dictated by contemporary fashion, with its tight corseting, bustle-shaped skirt, and high heels. The short petticoat length revealing the calves was extremely daring.

Mephistopheles The devil character in Goethe's *Faust* is the inspiration behind this French costume. The look was popularized by Sir Henry Irving, who played him in a similarly vivid red costume at the Lyceum Theatre in London from 1885–1888.

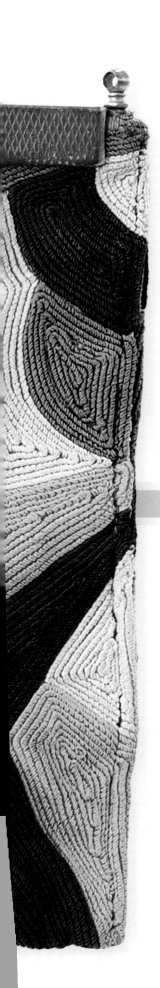

LA BELLE EPOQUE AND THE JAZZ AGE

1901–1928

LA BELLE EPOQUE AND THE JAZZ AGE

Simplification, and in particular the idea that "less is more," governed the development of fashion in the early 20th century. The old way of dressing was only abandoned after a final extravagant flourish, which found shape in Paul Poiret's colorful Orientalist designs and Lucile's gossamer creations. The beginning of World War I accelerated the trend toward less restrictive clothing, as many women became used to wearing practical uniforms. After the war, the popularity of elaborate hairpieces and many layers of flimsy fabric diminished in favor of practical, shorter skirts and sweaters. The figure of the static, hourglass woman was being replaced by the energetic, boyish "flapper." Always on the move—either dancing the night away or racing around in an automobile—the new style represented youth, fashion, and fun.

The suntan era

Men and women increasingly revealed their bodies, as clothes shrank and became less structured. The fashionable set went to Palm Beach and Malibu in the US, or the Riviera in France, to acquire a suntan and to flaunt their beach pajamas and summer suits. Different outerwear also meant changes to previously restrictive undergarments—fewer pieces of less-rigid underwear became possible. New designers were particularly adept at picking up the trend toward increased movement and practicality in fashion. French designers Chanel and Patou both started their Houses just before World War I, and promoted clothes for the active woman, in which knitwear featured prominently.

New icons

Royalty and aristocracy still played a significant role in setting trends. In Britain, Prince Edward initiated and popularized new styles. Following his investiture as Prince of Wales in 1910, the 16-year-old heir to the throne soon became a major fashion icon, accelerating the move toward less structured garments. He also popularized the use of garments such as Fair Isle knitted vests and plus fours off the golf course. With the rise of Hollywood during the second decade of the century, movie stars such as Douglas Fairbanks, Rudolph Valentino, and Louise Brooks began to supplant high-society figures in setting trends.

1901–03

1902
J.C. Penney, the American retail magnate, opens his first department store in Wyoming.

c. 1903
The straight-fronted corset, also known as the swan-bill, S-bend, or "health corset," is popular from the turn of the century until the 1910s. It forces the torso forward and makes the hips protrude, removing pressure from the abdomen and creating an S-shaped silhouette.

◄ A straight-fronted corset worn under the dress provides the distinctive S-shape silhouette

1904–07

▲ Women work in a factory that makes rayon underwear

1905
Artificial silk made from viscose (known as "rayon" after 1924) is first sold commercially in the UK. It reaches the US in 1910.

1906
Madame Paquin introduces the empire-waist dress in imitation of the fashion of the Regency period.

1908–10

1908
Mannequin parades are introduced at the House of Lucile in London, and become very popular.

1909
Bobbed or short hair for women is introduced to Paris fashion.

1910
Mariano Fortuny patents his pleating and dyeing process. His long, clinging sheath dresses, known as Delphos, are made with a single, vibrantly colored piece of silk. Devotees include stars such as Eleanora Duse, Isadora Duncan, Cleo de Merode, and Liane de Pougy.

1910
Paul Poiret designs a range of loose-fitting, Orient-inspired dresses, paving the way for modern dress.

▼ A Paul Poiret creation designed for a costume party

> 66
> The designers have forgotten that there are women inside the dresses … Clothes must have a natural shape.
>
> COCO CHANEL, 1928
> 99

1911–13 | 1914–16 | 1917–19 | 1920–22 | 1923–25 | 1926–28

1913
The first modern brassiere is patented by New York socialite, Mary Phelps Jacob. Old-fashioned corsets are no longer suitable to wear under new lighter, less formal garments.

1913
The tango arrives in most European capitals. Jean Paquin designs gowns to be worn for dancing the tango, which are shown during "dress parades" at popular "Tango Teas" held in London.

▼ Tango shoes are designed with crisscrossing straps

1913
Coco Chanel opens a boutique in the French seaside resort, Deauville.

▼ The Chanel logo soon becomes established

CHANEL
PARIS

▲ *The Munition Girls* by English painter Alexander Stanhope Forbes

1914
World War I begins, ushering in an era of darker colors and simple cuts. Women take over men's jobs, accelerating the trend toward practical garments.

1914
Burberry is commissioned to adapt army officer's coats for the trenches. The trench coat is born.

▶ Print advertisement for military clothing made by Burberry

1915
Fashion magazine *La Gazette du Bon Ton* shows full skirts with hemlines above the ankle. They are called the "war crinoline" by the fashion press, who promote the style as "patriotic" and "practical."

1917
Invented by Giden Sundback in 1913, the zipper is finally patented in 1917. It is first used for closing rubber boots in the 1920s.

1920
The 19th Amendment to the US Constitution gives women the right to vote. Some believe that the women's rights movement affected fashion, promoting androgynous figures and the death of the corset.

1920
The Prohibition Era begins in the US, but is largely ignored by fashionable young men and women of the time. "Flappers" dance the night away to jazz tunes at illegal speakeasies.

1922
Howard Carter and George Herbert, 5th Earl of Carnavon, discover the tomb of Ancient Egyptian ruler Tutankhamun. Fashion designers are inspired to use motifs from ancient cultures in their creations.

1923
The Broadway show *Runnin' Wild* includes the popular tune "The Charleston." It becomes a dance craze, requiring low-waisted dresses with fullness at the hemline to kick up the heels.

1924
The diplomatic visit of Edward, Prince of Wales to the US popularizes a kind of short breeches for men—plus fours.

◀ Plus fours were four inches longer than the traditional knickerbockers worn by men

1925
Fashion designers make up a large number of the artists who display their luxury wares at the "Exposition Internationale des Arts Décoratifs et Industriels Modernes" in Paris, which gave art deco its name.

1926
The ideal haircut for showcasing cloche hats—the fashionable Eton crop—is first mentioned in *The Times*. It is popularized by Josephine Baker, an African American expatriate singer, dancer, and entertainer, who becomes an overnight sensation at the *Folies Bergère* music hall.

JOSEPHINE
BAKER

▲ Stylized poster portrait of fashion icon Josephine Baker, by Jean Chassaing

◀ Dancing the Charleston in cloche hat atop Chicago's Sherman Hotel

1901–1914
SUITS FOR CITY GENTLEMEN

The turn of the century did not herald major changes to the three-piece suit, although some styles were gradually replaced or began to be used for different occasions. For the day the black frock coat with its long, straight skirt, worn with black trousers, was the most formal option. It was followed by the cutaway frock ("morning coat" in the UK) with its sloping front, which could be worn with matching or contrasting trousers. The lounge suit, originally country wear, was now worn in town. In the evening options gradually expanded as "tails" (tailcoats) were joined by tuxedos (tail-less dinner jackets), at first only considered appropriate for informal dinner parties. More formal attire demanded the stiff collar, available in several shapes. Men had a wide choice of accessories including canes, umbrellas, a variety of hat styles, cravats, bow ties, watch chains, and tiepins.

1901

Frock coat A young Winston Churchill wears a single-breasted black frock coat with customary silk-faced lapels. His top hat and cane indicate this is a formal outing—they were beginning to be associated only with special occasions.

- Silk top hat
- Dark bow tie
- Double Albert watch chain
- Trousers of same material as coat

ROYAL FASHION LEADER

King Edward VII had become a male fashion icon when he was still Prince Albert of Wales, popularizing the Norfolk jacket, the Homburg hat, and the Albert watch chain. The king also lent his name to double-breasted frock coats, which he preferred. The unusual closure shown here might have had more to do with his increasing girth than with any fashionable considerations.

- Silk top hat
- Tiepin
- Large flower for buttonhole
- Waisted silhouette
- Cane
- Contrasting white sock

Morning coat The very dapper Lord Chesterfield wears his morning coat with white vest, shirt with high stiff collar, striped cravat, and prominent buttonhole (the flower worn on the lapel).

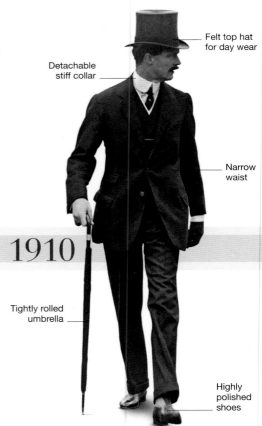

1910

- Felt top hat for day wear
- Detachable stiff collar
- Narrow waist
- Tightly rolled umbrella
- Highly polished shoes

Lounge suit Unusually the Duke of Roxburghe wears a lounge suit, rather than morning coat, to call at Buckingham Palace. A waistcoat slip, a stiff cotton strip attached to the neckline of his vest, gives the illusion of a second vest worn beneath.

Bowler or derby hat

Mustaches slowly went out of fashion

Striped shirt with stiff wing collar

Fine pinstripes

Binocular case

1906

Narrow trousers with front crease

At the races Major Loder's binocular case indicates that he is at the races. The racehorse owner sports a double-breasted pinstripe suit, yellow vest, and cravat. A handkerchief tucked nonchalantly in his breast pocket and a cane complete his ensemble.

Relatively low, silk top hat

Stiff wing collar

Unusual color for vest

1909

Frock coat

Tapering trousers

Half boots

Blue vest This gentleman wears a top hat, frock coat, and gray-striped trousers with front crease and cuffs. Stiff wing collars were the correct choice for frock coats, but gentlemen could choose between cravats or bow ties.

Fedora was a new hat shape

New suit Toward the end of the first decade suits had a high waist and flared out toward the hips. Jackets were long and trousers narrow to display fancy shoes and socks. This suit was advertised by the Parisian *High Life Tailor*.

Notched lapel

Stiff collar with round edges

Black top hat with grosgrain ribbon

Stiff shirt front

Silk lapel

Shiny, black top hat

Opera cape with deep lapels

Cane, held casually

1913

Trousers with front crease

Front crease

Cane

Trousers taper toward ankle

Pumps (heel-less shoes) would normally be worn

Black pumps worn with black silk stockings

Cuffs

Tailcoat The somewhat ill-fitting tailcoat of this American gentleman suggests that it might have been borrowed for a special occasion. Black vests were an alternative to the more customary white until the middle of the century.

Evening wear This idealized version of a suave gentleman in evening wear shows him correctly accessorizing his tailcoat with a white vest, white bow tie, a large opera cape, top hat, cane, and gloves.

Dainty shoes

1901–1914
SPORTS AND COUNTRY

G arments initially developed for sportswear were often modified or appropriated for mainstream fashion. The most popular example from the male wardrobe were knee breeches of various widths and shapes called either knickerbockers, apparently after the garment worn by 17th-century Dutch settlers in America, or plus fours that extended 4 in (10 cm) below the knee. Before World War I, knee breeches were rarely seen away from the shooting ground or the golf course. Now they formed part of suits worn in town. Other garments that were used for sports were cardigans for tennis, cricket, and baseball as well as increasingly for leisure wear, and thick, wool sweaters seen on motorcyclists and skiers. Wool sweaters were also popular with fishermen—work wear being another source for fashion innovation. Sportswear remained modest, however, and the male body was mostly hidden except at the beach where male swimsuits became increasingly revealing, although they did not shrink into mere trunks until after World War II.

Tweed This gentleman sports a Norfolk jacket, made fashionable by the Prince of Wales in the 1860s. A popular part of golf attire, it was originally developed for shooting. It was always single-breasted, with box pleats in the front and back, and a belt or half-belt.

Flat cap

Formal wing collar

1900

Front box pleat

Patch pocket

Knickerbockers

Thick, wool socks

Leather golf shoes

Leather cap, worn with goggles

Thin shoulder straps

Thick, wool sweater

Gauntlets

Lower part often in two layers

1909   1911

Long, leather gaiters

Wool swimwear The marathon swimmer S.S. Nichol wears an all-in-one swimsuit, probably made of heavy, machine-knit wool, which lost its shape when wet. Nonprofessional male bathers usually wore short trousers with a separate tank top.

Leather gaiters The British racing driver Oscar Godfrey poses with his motorcycle during the British Motorcycle Race Club Trials at Brooklands, England. He wears very long gaiters (leg coverings that fasten over his shoes and stretch up to his knees), probably over knickerbockers.

Flat cap

Loden jacket with practical pockets

Thick socks worn over knickerbockers

Special cycling boots

Knickerbockers For athletic pursuits, such as cycling, knickerbockers were acceptable wear, but a shirt and tie were still required. Vests could be dispensed with. Other markers of casual dress were the flat cap and wide belt.

Bowler-shaped hat with feather decoration

Short trousers, probably own design

Knee-length wool socks

Sturdy hiking boots

Loden Franz Joseph I, Emperor of Austria, wears a jacket made of loden—a thick, waterproof, wool cloth. Originally used by peasants, similar jackets, usually fastened with horn buttons, are still popular particularly in southern Germany, Austria, and the Tyrol.

Cricket style Other than the cuffs on his pants, and maybe their high waist, there is not much in Frank Tarrant's cricket gear that suggests it is from the early 20th century. A personal touch is provided by the use of a tie as a belt.

Peaked cap with coat-of-arms of the county of Middlesex

Soft shirt collar

White flannels

Cuffs

SPORTS AND COUNTRY | 227

1905

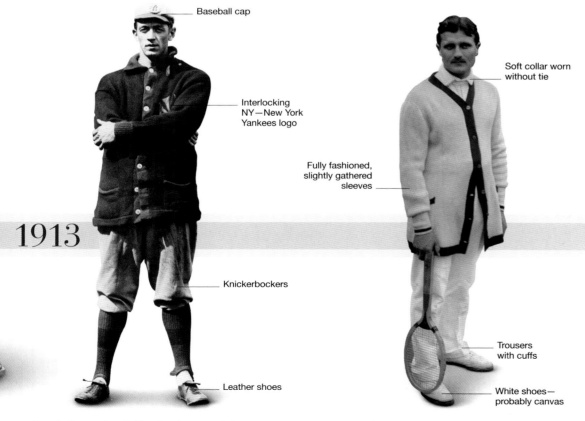

Baseball cap

Interlocking NY—New York Yankees logo

Knickerbockers

Leather shoes

1913

Baseball cap Ray Caldwell, a famous pitcher for the New York Yankees, is shown in practice wear: knickerbockers, a roomy, wool cardigan, and a peaked cap. His gaiters might have been in his team's color.

Soft collar worn without tie

Fully fashioned, slightly gathered sleeves

Trousers with cuffs

White shoes— probably canvas

Cardigan Otto Froitzheim wears a long, white cardigan edged in a contrasting color during the tennis world championships in France in 1913. This kind of outfit would not be seen off the tennis court until after World War II.

SKIING

This 1904 poster for a French resort demonstrates that the vogue for skiing depended on direct trains from Geneva and Paris. Initially skiers wore multiple layers of everyday clothes. It was inconceivable that women would wear anything else but skirts. Specific clothing for the sport was developed only after the war.

Chamonix ski poster, 1904

1900–1914
SIMPLER SILHOUETTES

While the period between 1900 and World War I saw a great transformation in women's silhouettes, certain aspects were slow to change. The fashionable, wealthy lady was still expected to change outfits several times a day, and her body continued to be molded into the desired shape by rigid corsetry. There was, however, a gradual shift from a curvy, hourglass figure—with its emphasis on a tiny waist—toward a more tubular outline. The practical tailor-mades (suits) that had been introduced in the previous century remained fashionable and heralded the move toward simpler garments. Turn-of-the-century ribbons and lace, and ruches and pleats were slowly discarded to reveal not only a more pared-down style but also women's feet.

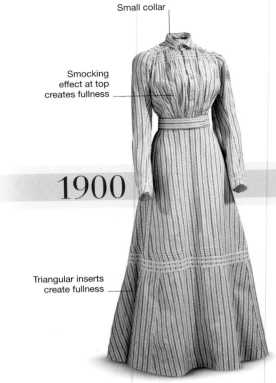

Small collar

Smocking effect at top creates fullness

1900

Triangular inserts create fullness

Shirt and waist This striped cotton skirt and waist (blouse) might look relatively informal but would have been worn over body-shaping undergarments to produce a narrow waist. The vertical pleats of the blouse create fullness around the bust.

LINGERIE

Flimsy, soft, and highly decorated chemises and camisole-and-underpants combinations were worn underneath rigid constructions that molded the body into the fashionable shape. The flat-fronted corset induced the "S-bend" with the upper body pushed forward while the hips were thrown back. Corsets left the busts largely unsupported so that bust bodices and a variety of bust improvers had to be enlisted to create the fashionable, impressive "monobosom."

Toward the end of the first decade corsets slid down the body, shortening above the bodice and lengthening below. Gradually, women were allowed to stand upright again.

High lace collar

Lapels

Mannish tailoring

Sleeve cuffs decorated with button

1908

Wrap skirt effect

House of Creed This French house began as a tailoring business in London in the 18th century and specialized in riding habits and tailor-mades. This suit shows the move away from the S-shape silhouette toward a more tubular outline.

Hat with oversized bow decoration

Open-collared blouse

Single button fastening

1910

Long columnar skirt

Skirt with narrow pleats

Ship shape For travel aboard a liner, two young Americans wear loosely fitted jackets with straight skirts. This new look was more comfortable and practical than the narrow-waisted dresses of the preceding years.

Straw hat with ribbon and ostrich feather trimming

Fans still popular and very large

Lace decoration

1902

Narrow skirt ends in short train

French day dress This confection accentuates the fashionable S-bend posture and emphasizes the narrow waist and "monobosom." While the skirt is relatively plain, the bodice remains elaborately decorated.

Promenade dress Although the V-shaped ruffle of the bodice mimics the low décolletage of evening dresses, this delicate creation covers the entire body. It was made by the House of Drécoll, which was opened in Paris in 1905.

Straw hat worn at jaunty angle

Ruffles give the illusion of elbow-length sleeves

Fabric insert for fake décolletage

1905

S-bend

Parasols helped to conserve fashionable pale complexion

Soft hat with plumage

Deep turned-back cuffs

Long gloves stretch to elbow-length sleeves

Jacket hemmed to hip length

1913

Slim-fitting skirt

Shoes or boots with Louis heel

Pour le Matin This tailored French morning suit for spring 1913 features a prominent high waistband and asymmetric button fastening. The skirt takes the newly fashionable slim column shape, narrowing to the ankles.

Hat with feather

High lace collar

Sash made of same fabric as blouse

Skirt loose around hips

Narrow knee area

Flowered silk

Shoe buckles reminiscent of 18th century

New silhouette This ensemble was recommended for vacation traveling wear. The skirt is relatively loose but narrows toward the hem where it allows a glimpse of the wearer's shoes and stockings—a new focus for decoration.

HATS AND SHOES

While some women favored small, modest hats, others wore huge creations decorated with ribbons, flowers, and feathers. Hats floated on elaborate coiffures created with the aid of transformations (hair pieces). With these lavish trimmings, occasionally incorporating entire birds, large hats had to be kept in place with long and often highly decorated hat pins.

Hat ribbon echoes bow at neck

Straw hat

Ostrich feather trim

Hat with feather

For day wear, women could choose between practical and sturdy laced or buttoned ankle boots and shoes. Heels returned to a manageable height and were usually of the curved "Louis" heel type. Straight-sided, stacked leather "Cuban" heels became popular toward the end of the first decade.

Ankle boot with Louis heel   **Buttoned ankle boot**

Laced shoe

1901–1916
WOMEN IN ACTION

Until World War I, women's sportswear followed the fashionable silhouette and included garments that could also be worn in other contexts. The "tailor-made" (a suit), and the shirtwaist (simple blouse) and skirt combination were often adapted for sports. For bicycling, hiking, and fencing, women could wear divided skirts or bloomers, provided they covered their legs with high, laced-up boots or gaiters. Sportswear usually had minimal surface decoration and was often paired with a manly cravat and flat cap. Even when playing tennis or bicycling, women wore corsets, but these were often smaller and more lightly boned than usual. The knee-length dresses worn over bloomers for bathing gradually became shorter, but continued to be worn with dark stockings.

Leg-of-mutton sleeves

Divided skirt gathered below knee

Tennis Dora Boothby, winner of the ladies' singles title at Wimbledon in 1909, is wearing a corset with her white shirtwaist and flared skirt. White canvas shoes were popular for tennis with men and women.

Tie often worn by female tennis players and golfers

Bicycling The divided skirt is the only really practical part of this bicycling outfit from just before the turn of the century. Shorter corsets were sometimes worn for sport.

Veil drawn back from face

Naval captain's cap

Marine telescope

Very narrow waist

Sleeves follow fashionable silhouette

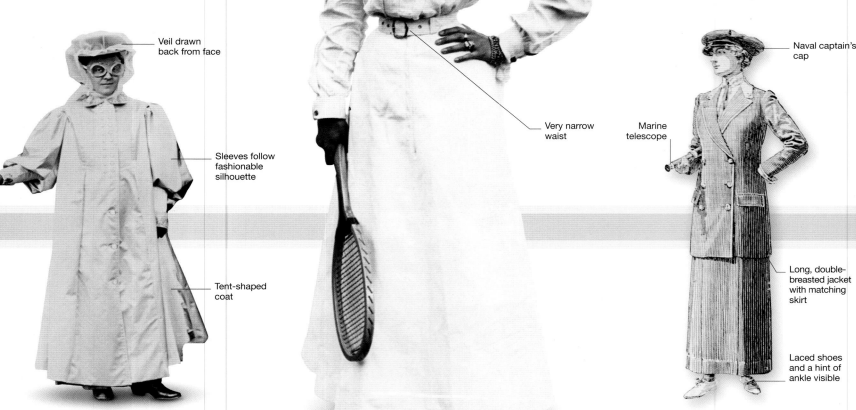

Long, double-breasted jacket with matching skirt

Tent-shaped coat

Laced shoes and a hint of ankle visible

Motoring Most early cars were open, and to travel comfortably the entire body and face needed protection. Clothing included a long coat of light-colored fabric called a duster, goggles, and motoring bonnets or veils to shield the face.

Yachting The English firm of Burberry supplied a variety of clothes for women and men for summer and winter sports. The relatively short skirt of this yachting gown, worn with a manly tie and flat cap, reveals practical footwear.

Wide straw hat
with feather trim

Chatelaine
attached to
waist belt

Quiver to
hold arrows

Archery This dress is minimally adapted for sports.
The archer wears a leather guard on her left hand
and has attached a chatelaine (decorative hook)
to her belt. Archery accessories, including a brush
to clean the arrows, hang from the chatelaine.

Hunting
whistle

Waterproof cloth
was often used

Double-breasted
closure for added
wind protection

Hunting whip with
hook to open gates

Hunting This figure is taken from an advertisement
for H. J. Nicoll of London's Regent Street for its
"world famous wrap coats." These warm, long over
garments were useful for walking, carriage driving,
the races, and hunting.

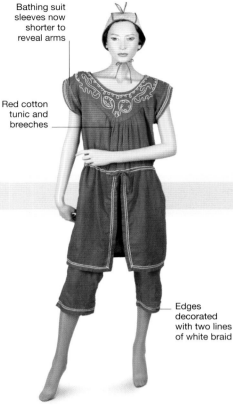

Bathing suit
sleeves now
shorter to
reveal arms

Red cotton
tunic and
breeches

Edges
decorated
with two lines
of white braid

Bathing Most bathing suits were navy blue,
but occasionally lighter and brighter colors were
used. Black stockings and bathing shoes were
usually worn along with breeches or knee-
length bathing dresses.

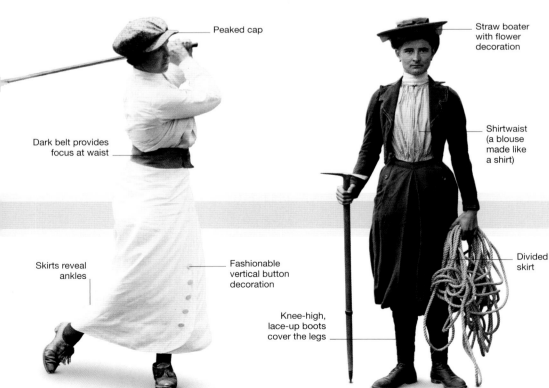

Peaked cap

Dark belt provides
focus at waist

Skirts reveal
ankles

Fashionable
vertical button
decoration

Golfing The white shirtwaist, usually worn with
a tie, was popular with female golfers. Here, it is
accessorized with a tweed cap and kilties—shoes
with a fringed tongue that covers the lacing and
keeps out water.

Straw boater
with flower
decoration

Shirtwaist
(a blouse
made like
a shirt)

Divided
skirt

Knee-high,
lace-up boots
cover the legs

Hiking Mountaineering became fashionable
after the mid-19th century. This practical
tailor-made suit has a divided, rather than the
more customary floor-length, skirt. It is worn
with a shirtwaist underneath.

Toques (brimless
hats) were worn
at an angle

Mackinaws often
had a check or
tartan pattern

Muffs were
a popular
accessory

Detachable
skates attach
to boots

Skating This suit from the American department
store Sears Roebuck is made of mackinaw, a dense,
water-repellent, wool cloth. The ensemble is cut
along fashionable lines, which, by 1916, had
become more suitable for physical exercise.

1900–1914
EVENING AND TEA GOWNS

Ladies of the Edwardian era (1901–1910), whether young or old, bared their décolletage and upper arms when wearing evening dresses, but encased their lower arms in long evening gloves. Sumptuous fabrics such as silk satin, damask, and chiffon, usually in light, soft colors, were decorated with lace, rhinestones, and spangles, often highlighting a part of the body or the face. The gowns' many layers made them difficult, if not impossible, to put on without help. Often made of materials that could easily be damaged, evening wear required decorous deportment. Tea gowns had emerged in the 1880s and continued to be a popular choice for receiving guests in the afternoon. The gowns were often made up of many layers of soft, light fabrics that were flattering but utterly impractical.

THE GIBSON GIRL

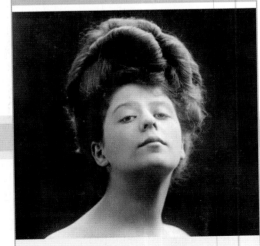

In the 1890s, the American illustrator Charles Dana Gibson drew tall, slender-waisted, confident young women with layers of softly waved hair piled high on their heads. The "Gibson Girl" set an almost unobtainable beauty standard for the next two decades. The actress Camille Clifford (above) won a competition to find a living version of Gibson's creation.

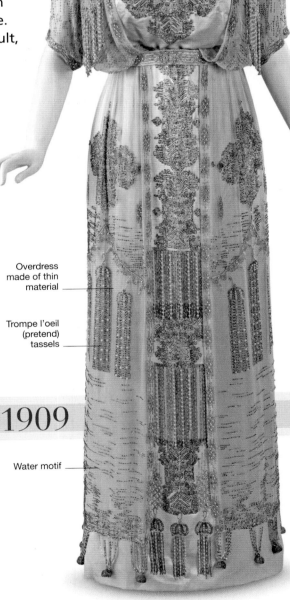

1909

Overdress made of thin material

Trompe l'oeil (pretend) tassels

Water motif

Empire line Both the silk underdress and a fine outer layer are embroidered in colored beads arranged in linear motifs that emphasize the statuesque feel of this gown. The three-dimensional tassels would move sensuously with the wearer.

Silk chiffon

Short lace sleeves

Asymmetric décolletage

1900

Shining, pink, silk satin

Satin gown This evening gown by the French House of Worth is embroidered with beads and rhinestones in a motif of ears of corn. Lace and chiffon soften the edges around the low décolletage and bare arms.

Décolletage softened with lace or chiffon

Embroidered peacock

Printed peacock fabric used for sleeves

Thin, gauzy fabric for overskirt

1910

Entire peacock printed on skirt

Peacock dress The blue and green of the printed and embroidered peacock's body and feathers in this dress are picked up in the waist sash, sleeve ends, and deep hem. The dress was bought in the little-known House of Weeks in Paris.

1906

Deep lace ruffle covers upper arms

Very low décolletage

Skirt extends into short train

Floral embroidery

Slimmer lines Toward the end of the first decade dresses become higher waisted and slimmer, as in this design for a French House of Paquin evening gown. Embroidery or lace trimmings were essential.

1907

Modest décolletage typical of tea gowns

Narrow sleeves ruched at front

Sash

Silk gown

Three-dimensional linen lace

Short train

Tea gown Worn indoors for afternoon tea, these gowns were usually made in light colors and soft fabrics, as seen in this magnificent example by the French House of Doucet. These garments went out of fashion around 1918.

Elbow-length sleeves

Lace with flower pattern

Asymmetric bodice

Long train with tassel decoration

Cut suggests underdress made entirely of lace

Pink damask The loop attached to the train is slipped over the wrist to lift the gown during dancing. The lace echoes the floral pattern of the damask. A local English dressmaker may have made this dress.

1913

Flower at waist provides focus

Drapery emphasizes hips and knees

Dinner gown The longer sleeves and absence of embroidery and other surface decoration, other than the fabric's pattern, mark this as a dinner, rather than an evening, gown. The skirt is split to aid movement. The new shape is very evident here.

1914

Red feather hair decoration

High waist

Overskirt of thin, stiff fabric

Very narrow skirt

Shoes are now visible

Robe du soir The French magazine *Gazette du Bon Ton* presents an idealized version of a Paquin evening gown. It shows the hallmarks of the new style: high waist, slimline but relatively loose, split skirt, and short "lampshade" overskirt.

FASHION AND THEATER

London couturier Lady Duff-Gordon dressed actresses—such as musical comedy star Gertie Millar (above)—both on and off the stage. Duff-Gordon, who owned the House of Lucile in London, favored slit skirts and low necklines. She used copies of dresses worn on stage to open a Paris branch of her House of Lucile Ltd. in 1910.

A LIFE OF LEISURE

The early 1900s was a time of contradiction: on one hand was rapid technological change, the rise of motorcars, and female emancipation; on the other, a golden glow of romantic, hedonistic nostalgia enjoyed by the leisured classes. The latter view still defines the Edwardian era for many, and it was captured perfectly by contemporary fashions.

Edward VII's love of extravagant pleasure set the age's tone, with rounds of lavish balls, country-house parties, travel, and athletic pursuits. England's expanding middle classes, upwardly mobile due to the Industrial Revolution, aped this upper-class lifestyle: garden parties, tea on the terrace, picnics, regattas, the races—all requiring suitable outfits. For women, pastel colors were de rigueur, as was sumptuous lace, *mousseline de soie* (gauzelike fabric), silk chiffon, tulle, crêpe de Chine, ribbon trimmings, and any frilly, lacy detailing. Huge hats bobbed with great feathers or silk flowers. Long, wavy hair was fastened around pads for luxuriant fullness, and the parasol was an essential accessory. The fashionable female shape, created by corsetry, was also luxuriant: a large, low, forward-thrust "monobosom," a wasp waist, and full hips from which a bell-shaped skirt, narrower than Victorian styles, fell gracefully. High necks and long sleeves were worn in daytime, with bodices and necklines infilled with lace or light fabric. Male fashions served as a simple, sober foil. Frock and morning coats were joined by lounge suits worn with crisp collar and cuffs, hats, and umbrella or cane.

> Society tottered through the last of the pre-War parties, waved tiny lace handkerchiefs, and carried elaborate parasols until the War came with its sweeping changes.

LUCILE, LADY DUFF GORDON, LEADING EDWARDIAN-ERA LONDON COUTURIER, IN HER MEMOIRS, *DISCRETIONS AND INDISCRETIONS,* **1932**

FASHIONABLE PURSUITS ▷
The man's binocular case suggests these Edwardians are at the races. Ascot, Derby, Longchamps, and Auteuil almost served as catwalks and the less well-to-do went to these racecourses not only to bet but also to gape.

1900–1920
ANTI-FASHION

Transforming women's clothing into something more practical, timeless, "aesthetic," or all three, had been the aim of dress reformers since the 1850s, albeit without much success. Despite the introduction of specialized clothing for some physical activities, many women at the beginning of the 20th century still wore restrictive clothing and, if they could afford it, changed their wardrobe frequently according to fashion's demands. Artists and designers in several countries tried to change this state of affairs. While they proposed different solutions, their designs had common features. Corsets, seen as the root of all evil, were generally abandoned; dresses often had a high, relatively loose waistline, while voluminous sleeves and skirts allowed greater freedom of movement. Prominent surface decoration incorporating the swirling lines and motifs of Art Nouveau—or based on patterns derived from Ancient Greece, the Renaissance, or Byzantium—was a common theme.

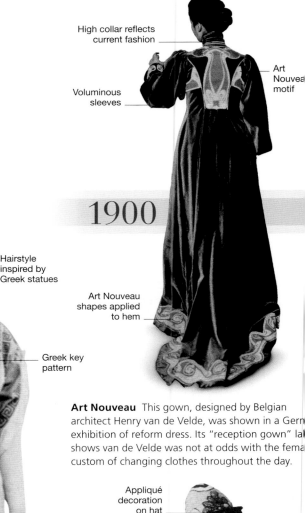

High collar reflects current fashion

Art Nouveau motif

Voluminous sleeves

1900

Art Nouveau shapes applied to hem

Art Nouveau This gown, designed by Belgian architect Henry van de Velde, was shown in a Germ[an] exhibition of reform dress. Its "reception gown" la[bel] shows van de Velde was not at odds with the fema[le] custom of changing clothes throughout the day.

Hairstyle inspired by Greek statues

Greek key pattern

High, loose waistline worn without corset

Abundance of fabric

Grecian The American dancer Isadora Duncan was fascinated by Greek culture. Her gowns inspired by, but not replicating, ancient Greek clothing enabled her to dance more freely. Off the stage Duncan wore mainly fashionable dress.

ANNA MUTHESIUS

In 1903, German concert singer, and wife of a well-known architect and writer, Anna Muthesius published a book entitled *Das Eigenkleid der Frau (Women's Own Dress)*.
Muthesius believed that dress should express the individuality of the wearer, and she urged women to break free from the fashion dictates of Paris and develop their own taste. Only then would they be able to make suitable sartorial choices and design clothes to suit themselves, using aesthetically pleasing textiles and patterns.

Appliqué decoration on hat

High wais[t]

Stole in complementary pattern

1910

Bergfalter pattern used in two colorways

Wiener Werkstätte Koloman Moser was one of the founders of the art collective Wiener Werkstätte (Vienna Workshop). Moser designed the fabric for this dress, which is cut looser than the current fashion.

High, pleated collar

Very high waist

Geometric pattern

Bell shape

1913

Narrow skirt

Pattern Austrian designer Eduard Josef Wimmer-Wisgrill founded the fashion department of Weiner Werkstätte. His design reflects a move toward a tubular form. The use of different patterns and colors strengthens the effect of stacked-up geometric shapes.

High-necked blouse in complementary design

Swirling Art Nouveau pattern

Bishop sleeves

1903

Wide, flaring skirt allows movement

Long sleeves

Artistic reform The Munich artist Elisabeth Winterwerber designed this outfit using Art Nouveau motifs. Its softer lines are a direct contrast with the S-shaped corseted dresses of the period.

Yoke in black and white triangle pattern

Collar in chessboard pattern

Necklace designed by Josef Hoffman

Several layers of ruffles on sleeves

1906

Skirt falls straight to seam

Trained skirt

Austrian revolt Defying the prevailing fashion, Viennese couturier Emilie Flöge wears a loose gown designed by her partner, the Austrian painter Gustav Klimt. A Wiener Werkstätte necklace accessorizes the gown.

Shoulder falls naturally

Wide arm holes

1915

Contrasting silk lining

Large peacock feather pattern

Liberty The London department store Liberty & Co. had been associated with aesthetic dress since the 1890s. This dramatic evening gown shaped like a kaftan is made of "hera," one of the most well-known Liberty prints.

Wide scoop neckline with drawstring encased along inside edge

Belt of matching silk with silver metallic stencil of trailing oak leaves and dots

1920

Pleats fall like a Greek column, worn without a corset

Full-length dress sweeps floor

Mariano Fortuny The Spanish designer's trademark dress was the Delphos, a simple column of finely pleated silk, inspired by Greek clothing. Mme. Condé Nast, Isadora Duncan, and Lilian Gish were photographed in his gowns.

1914–1918
WARTIME WOMEN

World War I accelerated the trend toward less restrictive and decorative day wear as many women became accustomed to wearing practical uniforms or work wear. The loss of male workers to the armed forces meant that women were employed as railroad porters, bus drivers, train conductors, window cleaners, and even welders. Women also became members of voluntary forces, which were organized and dressed along military lines, such as the "land girls" who worked in agriculture or helped with cutting wood. Most of these occupations came with their own uniforms, though these often had to be bought. Some garments, such as the "British Warm" greatcoat worn by officers during World War I, was adopted as fashionable wear by both men and women.

FOOTWEAR

The war had a big impact on fashion, changing the way women perceived themselves and how they were seen by others. Many more women were now doing manual work, requiring practical, durable clothing such as pants and sturdy, sensible footwear. Women needed shoes and boots that were comfortable enough to wear all day, and strong enough to withstand the elements. British shoemakers Clarks produced boots that were waterproof as well as "dainty." The low heel and welting made them practical, while their narrow fit and neat eyelet closures kept them feminine.

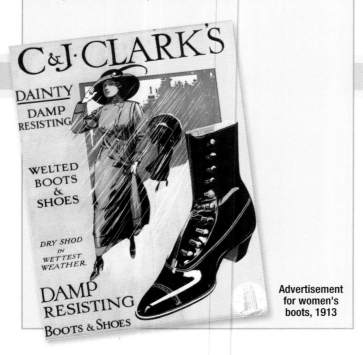

C&J·CLARK'S

DAINTY
DAMP
RESISTING

WELTED
BOOTS
&
SHOES

DRY SHOD
IN
WETTEST
WEATHER

DAMP
RESISTING
BOOTS & SHOES

Advertisement for women's boots, 1913

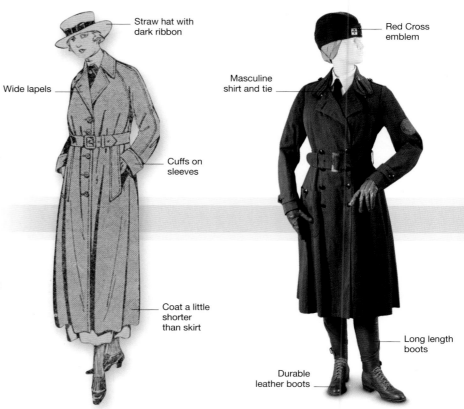

Straw hat with dark ribbon

Wide lapels

Cuffs on sleeves

Coat a little shorter than skirt

Trench coat Versions of the belted officer's coat became part of many women's uniforms. For motoring, or as part of the work wear of the "land girls," the coat was shortened to just above the knee.

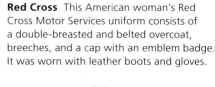

Red Cross emblem

Masculine shirt and tie

Long length boots

Durable leather boots

Red Cross This American woman's Red Cross Motor Services uniform consists of a double-breasted and belted overcoat, breeches, and a cap with an emblem badge. It was worn with leather boots and gloves.

Draped hat

Detachable fur collar

High waistline

Wide skirt

Pointed boots

Russian look The revival of the full skirt at the end of 1914 pleased petticoat makers. Russian influences remained and knee-length tunics as well as fur-trimmed "Cossack" coats were "quite the stylish thing" for women outside the workplace.

Hat with brim

Belted tunic with large pockets

Lace-up knee boots

Dark-colored jodhpurs

Land Army Wearing durable jodhpurs and sturdy boots, this member of the British Women's Land Army is one of about 33,000 females who worked on the land during the war, all requiring practical and durable garments.

Brim fastened on one side

Stand-up collar

A-line skirt

High leather boots

Bus conductor Wartime uniforms for women, like this worn by a London "clippy" (a bus conductor) often incorporated shorter skirts or jodhpurs. To maintain modesty, they were usually worn with high boots or puttees.

Practical brimmed hat

Wide shoulders

Button to fasten collar together

Wide hem gives stiffness

Fine leather lace-up boots

Motor Corps The original Abercrombie & Fitch, a New York retailer of sporting goods, supplied so-called "Lightning Liz" with her Motor Corps uniform. The skirt could be exchanged for breeches when she needed to scramble around truck engines.

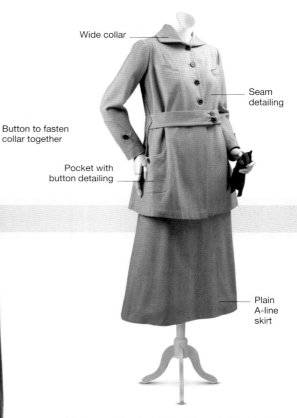

Wide collar

Seam detailing

Pocket with button detailing

Plain A-line skirt

US wear The simple detailing of this American wool suit is reminiscent of women's wartime uniforms. The buttoned half belt at the waist recalls the "British Warm," and clever seaming provides some surface decoration.

WARTIME FASHION

The cover girl of *The Gentlewoman* wears the uniform of a US male soldier: campaign hat with pinched crown, issue shirt with large pockets, breeches, and puttees (a bandage covering for the lower leg). After the US entered the war in April 1917, US women took part in military service, though their uniforms usually included skirts.

"Miss 1918"

Buttoned up to the neck for good coverage

Head scarf tied like a turban to protect hair

Long coveralls worn over day wear

Coveralls Working with explosives was hard, dirty, and dangerous. These munitions workers from Kent dress in full-length coveralls and head scarves to protect their clothing and hair from factory dust and dirt.

1914–1923
TOWARD THE NEW WOMAN

The new woman of the 1920s with her bobbed hair and knee-length dress emerged gradually. The evolution to the modern female silhouette took around ten years and started just before World War I. Maybe the most fundamental change was the gradual revelation of the lower part of women's legs, which put a new emphasis on shoes and, more importantly, on stockings. Flesh and soft pastel colors replaced the dark stockings of the previous age and were made of real or very shiny artificial silk. Equally noticeable was a change in the fashionable ideal: the statuesque, shapely, mature woman was replaced by her bosomless, hipless, thighless, much younger sister. Waistlines rose and dropped, finally settling around the hips. The new silhouette and less rigid clothing necessitated different kinds and fewer items of underwear.

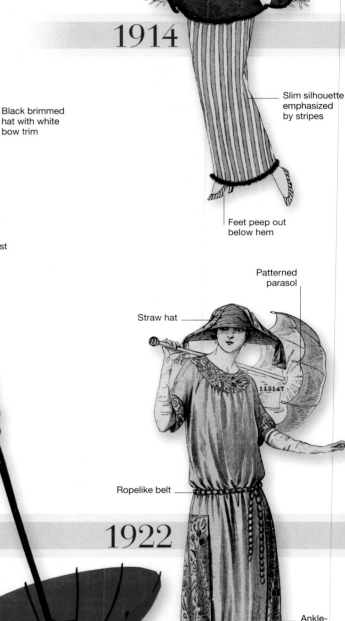

Two-part ensemble
This blouse is made of ratiné, a loosely woven fabric with a knotty surface. The tight hat hiding most of the wearer's hair foreshadows the hairstyle and cloche hats of ten years later.

Striped front panel

Embroidered belt

1914

Slim silhouette emphasized by stripes

Feet peep out below hem

Black brimmed hat with white bow trim

Flat chest

Sash tied at one side

1921

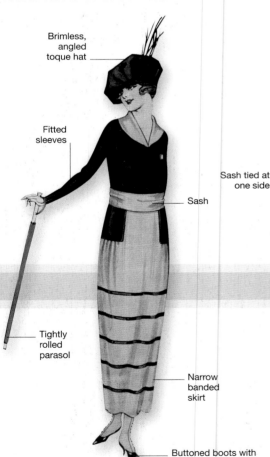

Brimless, angled toque hat

Fitted sleeves

Sash

Tightly rolled parasol

Narrow banded skirt

Buttoned boots with black galoshes

Patterned parasol

Straw hat

Ropelike belt

1922

Ankle-length skirt

French pattern Almost no traces of the hourglass figure ideal remain. The simple cut of this dress would have made it easier for dressmakers to replicate than previous more elaborate confections. The use of only two muted colors creates visual interest.

Lower waist This simple, striped dress has a Peter Pan collar and matching cuffs. A few darts in the side seam, just above the low waist, allow for a small bust. The black and white of the hat are echoed in the two-tone, lace-up shoes.

La mode simple This French pattern for a summer dress was practical and easy to make. Side skirt panels of patterned fabric make the simple shape more interesting. The same fabric is used to edge the neck and sleeves.

1916

Military-inspired frogging

Wide-brimmed hat with matching trim

Blouse cuff

Tightly rolled umbrella

Marshall & Snelgrove This taffeta suit from a London department store echoes the shape of the uniforms worn by female bus conductors during World War I. The hat still features the large crown popular before the war.

1918

Embroidery detail

High waist emphasized by belt

Flaring, practical skirt

Wide, ankle-length skirt

Journal des Demoiselles The French *Magazine for Young Women* shows an elegant yet practical dress design. The collar could be attached to a chemisette—a biblike, fake blouse that did not increase bulk.

1919

Brimless toque in contrasting color

Buttons possibly for decoration

Belt

Skirt narrows toward hem

Fashion statements There were several ways to enliven the basic silhouette just after the war. Here, drapery and deep pockets add width to the hips. Other options were a short lampshade overskirt or a skirt composed of deep ruffles.

1923

Deep green velvet

Smocking provides fullness for bust

Bishop sleeves made of different panels

Deep hem

Russian influences After the 1917 Bolshevik Revolution, many Russians fled to Paris where some found work as embroiderers. The collar, sleeves, and hip area of this velvet day dress are embroidered with motifs found in Russian folk dress.

Cloche hat with dyed ostrich feathers

Straight neckline

Large bow at low waist

Fashionable strapped shoes

Modern woman The American magazine *Elite Styles* specialized in patterns for women's and girls' clothing. The flat-chested, narrow-hipped modern woman could easily slip on this colorful dress and face the day.

BLOUSES

Pullover blouses, like these two examples from a 1922 pattern book, were popular in the early 1920s. Those intended to be worn over the skirt usually had a band, sash, bow, or other feature at the low waistline. Women could choose from a variety of necklines to complement their jacket or cardigan. Nautical styles remained in favor, blouses with sailor collars being advertised as "middies" in the US after the shirt of the midshipman.

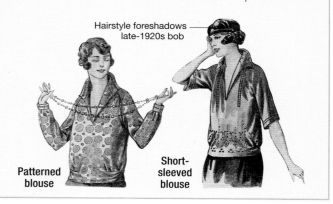

Hairstyle foreshadows late-1920s bob

Patterned blouse

Short-sleeved blouse

> Whenever I sign a garment with my name, I consider myself as the creator of the masterpiece.

PAUL POIRET

DESIGNER
PAUL POIRET

Known as *Le Magnifique* in Paris and the King of Fashion in the US, Poiret (1879–1944) was said by *The New Yorker* (1927) to have "helped to change the modern retina." This brew of descriptions underlines three aspects of the man who dominated Parisian and international fashion in the 1910s—a theatrical Orientalism, a new talent for branding and promotion, and a blending of clothes with avant-garde art. Poiret started auspiciously, working for two leading turn-of-the-century *maisons*: Jacques Doucet, then House of Worth. When he opened his own Parisian couture house around 1903, he set about overturning Belle Epoque fashion values. European women had been enslaved to a corseted waist, more or less, since the Renaissance. From 1903 Poiret set out to free them from the petticoat, and then the corset, in favor of looser, leaner lines. Although others, such as Madeleine Vionnet, also endorsed corset-free fashion, Poiret stole the limelight with vigorous self-promotion.

Draping by design
With a new silhouette came Poiret's fresh take on structuring garments. He replaced classic 19th-century pattern-dependent tailoring with an inspired draping of fabric and let garments hang from the shoulders. Between 1906 and World War I, Poiret experimented with bold shapes inspired by a more natural female form and his own take on oriental luxury. Beginning with the svelte, empire-waisted lines of his startlingly simple Directoire garments, recalling French styles of the late 1700s and early 1800s, he pushed aside the subdued Edwardian palette, and added striking colors and exotic turbans. The year 1910 saw hobble skirts, so narrow at the ankles that walking was almost impossible. The next three years brought harem pants, followed by a minaret or lampshade tunic

shape in colorful beaded and fur-trimmed silks and chiffons. Confucius cloaks, kimonos, cocoon coats, and African kaftans were popular shapes.

Fusing fashion, theater, and art
A sense of theater was integral to Poiret's work, the oriental costumes of the Ballets Russes in productions such as *Schéhérazade* (1910) being a major influence. Poiret's lampshade tunic appeared in his costume designs for an Orientalist play called *Le Minaret*. Placing his young wife, Denise, in the audience at the Paris premiere of the play in 1913, dressed in a similar garment, was a mark of Poiret's genius for promotion. Poiret showed women how to make their fantasies into daily reality. Famed for lavish events—such as a Persian-themed costume party entitled "The Thousand and Second Night" (1911), co-hosted by a Poiret-dressed Denise—the business-savvy Poiret is often credited with inventing the glitzy fashion launch. Under Poiret's influence, fashion became part of a total artistic lifestyle. An enthusiastic painter himself, Poiret collaborated with artists such as Raoul Dufy and Erté, elevating clothes to an art form. He founded a decorative arts school in 1911, worked in interior design, and pioneered the couturier perfume business.

Nicknamed the Prophet of Simplicity by *Vogue* in 1913, there is irony in the fact that Poiret was undone by modernism. He was dismayed by the androgynous 1920s *garçonne* look and Chanel's love of black over color. Although the 1920s saw his business in dire straits, he remains a towering fashion influence on designers such as Proenza Schouler, Prada, Hussein Chalayan, and Rei Kawakubo.

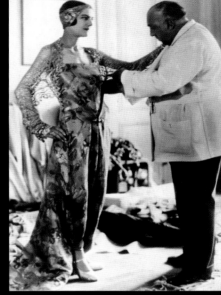

△ **NEW WAYS OF WORKING**
Poiret painstakingly fits a house model, draping fabric directly onto the body and cutting material in straight lines. Despite the lean simplicity, his look was sensual, elegant, and feminine.

◁ **EMPIRE LINES**
A Directoire-style evening dress from 1910, in forest-green and ivory-striped silk and black silk chiffon. This neoclassical columnar shape was revolutionary in the age of the corseted S-curve. Collar and cuffs are made from a traditional French cartridge-pleated linen bonnet, while the high waistline is caught with the folkloric brocaded ribbon that Poiret adored.

TIMELINE

1879 Born in Paris	
1898 Starts work for Paris couturier Jacques Doucet, and creates an early stir	
1901 Joins the House of Worth, Paris, under Gaston Worth	
c. 1903 Founds his first fashion *maison* on rue Auber, Paris	
1906 Launches the simple, empire-line Directoire Revival look and begins the liberation from corsetry	
1910 Designs hobble skirts—an impractical, Orient-led fashion	
▷ **1911** La Perse coat, in silk and fur, features fabric designed by Raoul Dufy. Harem pants appear	
▷ **1913** Iconic Poiret lampshade-minaret shapes launched	
1922 Beaded, Oriental-type evening dresses in hot Poiret colors	
1929 Closes his fashion business	
1944 Dies penniless in Paris	

○ 1900   ○ 1910   ○ 1920   ○ 1930

◁ **MADAME POIRET, 1919** Denise Poiret was her husband's muse and most effective advertisement—her naturally slim figure promoted his designs perfectly.

1909–1926
ORIENTALISM

In the summer of 1909, the Ballets Russes (Russian Ballet), the company formed by impresario Sergei Diaghilev, first performed in Paris with great success. Shows in other European cities followed over the next 10 years, and everywhere the bright colors of the ballet's sets and costumes made a huge impact—"exotic" features such as turbans and harem pants were adapted for fashionable dressing. While Paul Poiret claimed to have used bright colors before the Ballets Russes, the French couturier, the so-called Pasha of Paris, is most associated with this trend. Poiret continued a long tradition of using motifs from Middle Eastern and Asian cultures in Western design that went back at least as far as the Renaissance. During the 19th century, North Africa and Japan were prominent sources of inspiration and continued to be in the 20th century. Ideas of which countries belonged to the "Orient" changed over time, but they were usually associated with a richer, freer, and more sensuous way of life.

1909

Dark velvet band at neck

Flower made of gathered silk

Narrow hem conforms to contemporary silhouette

Japonism The cut of this evening mantle by the House of Worth is reminiscent of a kimono and shows the enduring influence of Japan. The original founder's son Jean-Philippe, who ran the House of Worth after 1895, had studied painting, an art form in which Japonism was all the rage.

HARLEM DANCER

The identity of the woman in this 1925 photograph—titled *Dancer*, taken in Harlem in New York City—is unknown, but she is wearing a costume similar to a Ballets Russes design. Dyed ostrich feathers tower over a headdress perhaps inspired by traditional Persian dress. Other than the baggy pants, her outfit is heavily embroidered with beads and spangles.

Diadems and headbands were fashionable for evening wear

Fur trim

See-through sleeves

1914

Split skirt with tiny train

Lamp-shade tunic After his famous Persian costume party, Paul Poiret created one of his best-known designs—a tight "hobble" skirt and a lamp-shade tunic held out with wire. This diaphanous example is edged with black fur.

"Aigrette" or tufted feather decoration

Hat similar to popular tricorn shape

Fashionably long necklaces

Chinese shoes with upturned toes

Pagoda The tiered tower design from Asia was imitated in Western architecture, interior design, and fashion. The outfit depicted in French designer Etienne Drian's fashion plate might have been costume, but certain features also appeared in fashionable gowns.

Hat alludes to Russian folk dress

Feather decoration

Dyed ballet shoes

Bodice decorated with spangles

1911

The Firebird Tamara Platnovna Karsavina danced the title role in Igor Stravinsky's ballet *The Firebird*, a huge success when launched in Paris in 1911. The costume is by Léon Bakst, who worked on many Ballets Russes productions.

Fashionable turban

Costume In 1911 Paul Poiret organized a costume party with the theme "The One Thousand and Second Night" to promote his new designs. This opulent creation foreshadowing the use of "lamp shade" overskirts was worn that evening.

Fabric encrusted with beads in various shapes

Embroidery from head to ankle

Gold lamé

Skirt held out by wire

Harem pants

Bold, abstract patterns in colored embroidery

Shawl collar in machine-made lace

Large hand-embroidered buttons

Silk chiffon lining visible through net panel

1912

Opera coat Attributed to Poiret, this garment shows a range of influences, both in cut and finish. The loose wrap-over shape and wide sleeves resemble a kimono, while the embroidery is inspired by Middle Eastern architecture.

Leather cloche inspired by Egyptian hairstyles

Vermilion, chestnut, and gold embroidery

1923

Black, silk velvet panels

Tutankhamun After the discovery of the Pharaoh's tomb in 1922, elements that were believed to be part of Egypt's culture appeared in dress and jewelry. Poiret's afternoon dress is embroidered with hieroglyphic motifs.

Batwing sleeves

Gold print

Cord belt

Short train falls from shoulders

1926

Renaissance Italian designer Maria Gallenga is often compared with Venetian-based Fortuny over her choice of colors, fabrics, and techniques. Hand-stenciled velvets reminiscent of Renaissance fabrics were made into a dress shape evocative of the Middle Ages.

1920–1929
ROBES DE STYLE

In stark contrast to the streamlined dress of the "modern woman" with its straight lines, often emphasized by geometric decoration, a much softer and more romantic silhouette survived beyond the late 1910s. The most prominent feature of this feminine style was a very full skirt that sometimes required support by the means of side-hoops—stiff understructures shaped like small baskets and worn over the hips. The Paris couturier Jeanne Lanvin is most associated with this type of dress, which was particularly suitable for younger ladies. The so-called *robe de style* was inspired by 18th-century gowns and was more forgiving than androgynous 1920s shapes. The vast expanse of the skirt provided a large, blank canvas that could be filled with embroidery, artificial flowers, lace, and feathers.

DOLLY SISTERS

The Hungarian-born twin dancers Roszika and Janszieka Deutsch were known less for their stage act than for their matching outfits, often provided by Jean Patou, and their spectacular private lives acted out on the French Riviera, in nightclubs and casinos. The ostrich feather skirts of their windmill costumes echo the *robe de style* silhouette.

Cinderella The French House of Douillet was known for attention to detail and exquisite evening wear. Andre Marty illustrated this evening dress called *Cendrillon* (Cinderella), which combines soft lace, a colorful band at the hips, and large blocks of austere black.

Waist at natural level

1920

Short overskirt

Lace skirt with black apron feature

Tulle band softens neckline

Spangled streamers provide movement

Low waistline

Embroidered roundels

Peacocks In the center of the roundels decorating Lanvin's evening gown, two embroidered peacocks face each other, surrounded by beads, pearls, rhinestones, and spangles. Embroidered tulle decorates the neck and hem bands.

Simple neckline

Silk appliqué leaves

1924

Fall leaves The French couture house Mybor employed artists to create designs for their clothing. Silk fall leaves, their veins emphasized with pieces of lamé, are attached to triangular panels that fall to the hem of this skirt.

Hair put up to create proto-bob

Thin shoulder straps

Diagonal eats below waistline

Diaphanous overskirt

1922

Flower decoration at hem

For the dance This *robe à danser* by the French House of Worth combines a dress shape that foreshadows the 1950s with its wide, see-through overskirt that allows movement on the dance floor and gives the ensemble a *robe de style* air.

Straps edged in red

Appliqué velvet flowers

Lamé Fabrics using metallic yarns were popular in the 1920s. Lanvin used gold lamé for this gown decorated with three-dimensional flowers made of painted velvet. The color red appears in the edging of the straps and hem.

Jolibois Lanvin called this gown *Prettywoods*, probably an allusion to the types of flowers embroidered on it. Soft, plush *chenille* (French for caterpillar) yarn has been used for the decoration.

Chenille embroidery in contrasting colors

Slightly waisted bodice

Blue silk taffeta

Wide skirt

Matching scarf

Crescent shapes

Waist and skirt lower at the back

1928

Feathers This evening gown by the French House of Louiseboulanger is adorned with feathers that would have emphasized the wearer's dance moves. Individual filaments of, probably, dyed ostrich plume have been knotted together to form longer strands.

Train emanates from shoulders

Tulle embroidered with metallic thread

Low, rounded neckline

Silk ribbon flowers

Floral basket design, typical of Boué sisters

Uneven hem echoes decoration

Historical influence The shape of this gown by the French Boué sisters, and the flowers arranged in garlands, hark back to the 18th century. The silhouette is supported by an underslip that includes two rows of boning just below the hips.

FANS

Ostrich feathers in natural color

The 1920s probably saw the last flowering of the fan as a fashionable evening accessory. Restaurants and nightclubs used printed paper fans for advertising, and perfume companies doused them in scent. Large fans made of ostrich feathers were particularly popular since the plumes could be dyed any color—to match or contrast with the wearer's outfit. As here, ostrich feathers were also used in their natural colors.

DESIGNER
COCO CHANEL

Credited with inventing everything from the suntan to the little black dress, "Coco" Chanel (1883–1971) was one of a number of designers, including Jean Patou, who set the tone for informal womens wear. She was a towering fashion figure, expertly anticipating the post–World War I spirit, representing the modernist woman, and adding weight to many trends. Her 1920s and 30s women's wear developed a cleverly "simple" look that chimed with the sober functionalism of wartime clothes. It embraced relaxed Chanel suits in jersey and tweed, as well as streamlined shift chemises and the LBD (Little Black Dress), costume jewelry, wide-bottomed trousers, and signature accessories.

Capitalizing on her own boyish figure, Chanel embraced the less constricted approach, creating clothes that were comfortable and easy for "new" women to wear. Her own appearance — and lifestyle—personified modernist ideals, providing powerful publicity and giving her an enduring, iconic status.

Making the right connections

After a hard start in life, support from wealthy male admirers helped Chanel establish a Parisian millinery business in 1910, followed by shops in the fashionable beach resorts of Deauville and Biarritz. She began experimenting with menswear styles and making women's garments from jersey, a soft, easily draped fabric. By 1919 she had a booming business in Paris.

The 1920s established her staple range of pullovers and loose or cardigan jackets, short skirts, and simple blouses. There were fancier dresses for evening but still with a lean, stylish simplicity. Acclaim followed. Practicality and comfort were key to Chanel's relaxed mode—encapsulated in the sensibly placed pocket, for example. More importantly, Chanel clothes spoke of youthful effortlessness, so different from prewar styles, but with high price tags; her market was the leisured wealthy.

Chanel promoted an often muted palette of gray, black, white, and navy, and fed a major craze for beige. Enlivening additions included gilt buttons and gilt-chained bags, as well as costume jewelry, which under her influence became not just acceptable but desirable. She pioneered mixing real gems with fake ones—artificial pearls were a favorite.

Closing her couture house during World War II, Chanel (then in her 70s) relaunched herself in 1954. Her reinvented simple skirt suit with braid-trimmed collarless jacket was an enormous success, especially in the US, where Jackie Kennedy Onassis was a high-profile 1960s fan of the boxy ensemble and pearls. Chanel's enduring appeal is thanks partly to loose lines that suit a wide variety of women and partly to her beautifully perfectionist finish, while her separates have promoted the all-important concept of the mix-and-match, investment capsule wardrobe.

Reinventing the look—Lagerfeld

Chanel was still overseeing her collections when she died, in her 80s, in 1971. The couture house continued, and in 1978 the first prêt-à-porter (ready-to-wear) line was launched. In 1983 Karl Lagerfeld became head of design, raising the brand's profile globally and promoting cult use of the Chanel logo. That he found so many fresh ways to mine Chanel concepts proves that Coco had tapped into a timeless purism. Many designers have drawn on her approach, from Claire McCardell to Betty Jackson.

△ **TIMELESS ALLURE**
Effortless chic and an air of enduring youth came naturally to Chanel and were key elements of the clothes she designed.

◁ **THE CLASSIC SUIT**
Still going strong in the 21st century, the Chanel suit with its collarless jacket, relaxed style, and easy-to-wear fabric is instantly recognizable.

TIMELINE

1883 Born Gabrielle Bonheur Chanel, in Saumur, France

1910 Opens hat shop in Paris

◁ **1918–1919** After running shops in Deauville and Paris, moves shop to 31 rue Cambon, Paris, selling ensembles and separates. It remains there today

1921 Launches her fragrance Chanel No. 5

◁ **1930** Goes to Hollywood to design movie costumes for United Artists stars, such as Gloria Swanson, and evening dresses

1939 Closes her couture house

1953–1954 Relaunches and reinvents prewar ideas to produce a classic collarless suit for the modern age

1971 Dies in Paris, age 87

1983 Karl Lagerfeld takes over Chanel haute couture (1983) and prêt-à-porter (1984)

○ 1880   ○ 1910   ○ 1920   ○ 1930   ○ 1950   ○ 1970   ○1980

TAILS Chanel ma

1920–1929
THE NEW KNITWEAR

In the late 1910s, women began to wear cardigans and long sweater tunics, mainly for sports or resort wear. Coco Chanel famously donned a long jersey sweater on the Normandy beach as early as 1913. This knit textile had previously been used only for underwear but Chanel fashioned it into coats and suits. Knitwear was the perfect fit for the active, modern woman, personified by the French tennis ace Suzanne Lenglen who patronized Chanel's rival Jean Patou. While not everyone could afford his patterned sweaters—with matching accessories—cheaper versions were available for the mass market. Knit cardigans, tunics, short coats, or entire knitwear ensembles were easy to put on, comfortable to wear, and survived transportation in a suitcase to the Riviera or the Alps.

JEAN PATOU

In the Paris of the 1920s and early '30s, the dashing Jean Patou was as famous and successful as Coco Chanel. Often credited with the invention of the knit sweater and swimsuit, and sportswear in general, the couturier dressed sports stars, actresses, and dancers such as the Dolly sisters and Josephine Baker. The French tennis champion Suzanne Lenglen, a major popularizer of *la mode sportive*, here models a long, belted tunic sweater with zigzag bands on sleeves and hem; a pencil-pleated, white crêpe de Chine skirt; and a fashionable felt cloche hat. Patou also designed the daring short-sleeved cotton attire Lenglen wore on court.

Suzanne Lenglen

Hair cropped short

1922

Plain wool sweater

Twisted cord belt

Simple tote bag

On vacation For her spring vacation this stylish woman has accessorized a hip-length tunic sweater with a twisted belt. The white of her plain skirt is picked up in her hat, Peter Pan collar, long gloves, and two-tone strapped shoes.

White scarf to match dress

Skirt hemmed to knee

1927

White, lace-up pumps

Plain, black wool jersey

Black, satin cuffs

Finely pleated jersey skirt

Stylish sportswear This young woman steps off the court in style, wearing a tennis dress of white crêpe de Chine with a knee-length pencil-pleated skirt. Her simple silhouette is fashionably slimline.

Jersey Coco Chanel's perfect "little black dress" is in fact made in two parts from one of her trademark materials: wool jersey. The unlined skirt, attached to a deep waistband, is paired with a short sweater edged with satin.

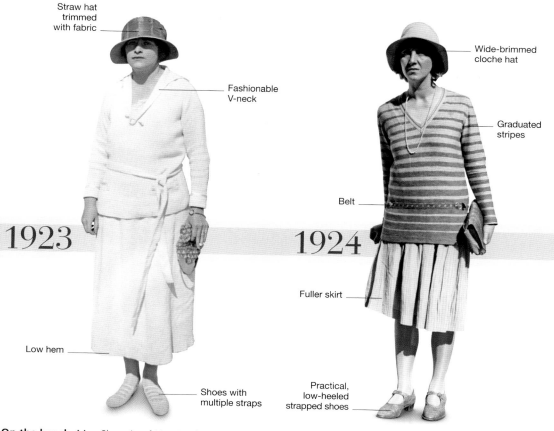

1923

Straw hat trimmed with fabric

Fashionable V-neck

Low hem

Shoes with multiple straps

1924

Wide-brimmed cloche hat

Graduated stripes

Belt

Fuller skirt

Practical, low-heeled strapped shoes

1925

Fitted cloche hat

Leather clutch bag

Flat sandals

On the beach Mrs. Sherwin of New York wore an all-white outfit while on vacation in Palm Beach, Florida. Hip-length tunic sweaters were usually worn with matching or contrasting belts, often fastened to one side.

Graduated stripes The explorer Violet Cressy-Marcks could scarcely be more fashionable. She wears a simple hip-length, V-neck sweater with a short, full skirt, accessorized with a belt, long necklace, and clutch bag.

Zigzag The simple shape of this knit ensemble shows off its dynamic striped design in colored wool. The button-front closures on both garments provide an easy-fitting, versatile outfit.

1928

Neat cloche hat

Geometric designs

Fabric corsage

Strapped shoes with button fastening

1929

Fake buttons on insert

Pattern created through seams

Ornamental belt buckle

Skirt hemmed just below knee

Side pleats

Cardigan suits These ladies wear fashionable knit jersey ensembles by Wilson's of London, inspired by the casual chic of leading designers Chanel and Patou. Long cardigans are layered over simple sweaters, teamed with pleated jersey skirts.

Simplicity This deceptively simple, British going-away outfit has geometric seams to create a pattern, pleated side panels in the skirt that allow movement but keep the straight line, and a collar facing that echoes the V-neck insert.

KNITWEAR

The "knitted wear" available from Gorringes, the London department store, in 1924 was declared "suitable for the smartest occasions." All the styles incorporate a low waist and are patterned, some models reflecting the vogue for ornamentation based on eastern European traditional dress. While the top left model is wearing a patterned cardigan for golf, the other styles were clearly suitable for more than just sportswear.

1924 Gorringes advertisement

1920–1929
RISING HEMS

Victor Margueritte's scandalous novel *La Garçonne*, published in 1922, describes the transformation of a young woman into the "tomboy" of the title. The androgynous, youthful look came to represent the decade, though not every woman could carry it off. Thankfully there were several styles to choose from, as long as they had a low waist. Hemlines rose and dropped at least twice, skirts being at their shortest around 1927. The gowns' straight silhouettes were often broken up or emphasized by geometric decoration, and different colors could be used for the top and bottom halves. Fuller skirts remained in fashion, becoming more prominent when hemlines were lower. The tight, bell-shaped cloche hat with its diminishing brim became universally popular and indicated that its wearer's hair had been cut fashionably short, but hats with wide brims also remained in vogue.

Soft line The straight outline of this outfit is softened through the use of fluid fabrics, pleating, layering, and pattern. Many trademark accessories of the 1920s are displayed: the small hat, the long necklace, and the strapped shoes.

Hat decorated with flowers

Fur shawl

Patterned blouse worn over the skirt

Sash is part of blouse

Pleated skirt

Low strapped shoes

1920

LINGERIE

While women could choose from a bewildering array of undergarments, they all served one purpose: to reduce or entirely remove any curves that even vigorous dieting could not eliminate. Brassieres had been introduced the previous decade but now shrank into a flattening band. Underpants remained large and could also be attached to camisoles. Artificial or real silk, crêpe de Chine, and georgette in pink, peach, apricot, or brighter colors such as cyclamen (pink) replaced white cotton. Edgings and inserts were made of lace. Corsets were still used but now often took the shape of girdles compressing the hips with and without the help of elastic.

Lace trim

Artificial silk or rayon, popular fabric for lingerie at end of decade

Elasticized waist

Rayon slip and underpants

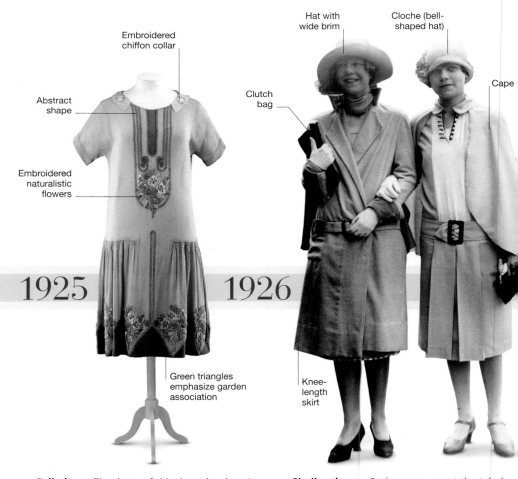

Embroidered chiffon collar

Abstract shape

Embroidered naturalistic flowers

Green triangles emphasize garden association

Hat with wide brim

Cloche (bell-shaped hat)

Clutch bag

Cape

Knee-length skirt

1925

1926

Folk dress The shape of this short day dress is a mixture of the simple tubular silhouette and the more voluminous *robe de style*. The colors and style of the embroidery might have been derived from the traditional dress of eastern Europe.

Similar theme Both women sport the tubular silhouette with a low waistline and hem just below the knee. Variations are provided by the use of different outer garments, shoes with and without straps, and different hat styles.

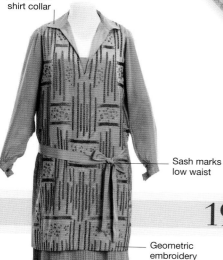

1922

Hat with
small brim

Fur shawl
collar

Small handbag

Hemline
rises up

Wrapped up The clever use of two
different fabrics meant that this wrap
coat could be mistaken for a skirt and
jacket combination. Fur was a popular
material for outerwear in the 1920s but
has been used here for just the collar.

V-neck and
shirt collar

Sash marks
low waist

Geometric
embroidery

Finely pleated
underskirt

Day couture The long sleeves and open shirt
collar of this creation by the French couture
house Goupy mark it as a day dress. The silk and
metallic thread embroidery in geometric patterns
imply luxury or a special occasion.

1923

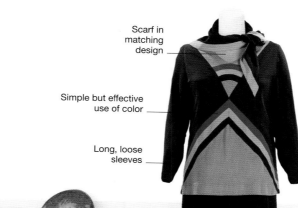

Scarf in
matching
design

Simple but effective
use of color

Long, loose
sleeves

Colored
band at
hem

Art deco Unlike much of the
clothing of the previous decade,
this day dress is easy and fast to slip
on, perfect for the active, modern
woman. The matching scarf softens
the straight lines of the decoration.

Low V-neck

Smaller
pattern
on sleeve

Asymmetric
decoration

Sash marks
low waistline

1928

Short skirt In 1927–1928, dresses
were at their shortest, sometimes
rising almost above the knee. This
outfit incorporates several 1920s
trademarks: dress made to look like
separate top and skirt, sash, low
V-neck, and geometric decoration.

Matching
shoes

SHOES

Strapped shoes had been worn in the
previous decade but became one of the
defining trademarks of the 1920s. Women
could choose between tie shoes closed with
a bow, shoes with single or multiple buckled
straps, or so-called sandals with T-straps.
Strapless pumps and dress shoes remained
in vogue including the Cromwell, which had
a high tongue reminiscent of 17th-century
footwear. Laced shoes derived from men's
styles such as the Gibson, Derby, and Oxford
were also available. These usually featured
straighter and lower heels than strapped
shoes and pumps. Fringe brogue shoes were
recommended for the country.

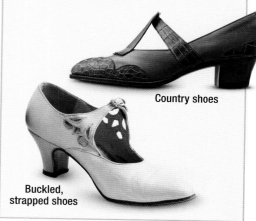

Country shoes

Buckled,
strapped shoes

Straw hat with
brim to shade
from the sun

Sleeveless,
simple top

Bands in
matching color

Fashionable
strapped shoes

Summer dress Not everyone wore tubular
slip-on dresses all the time. This summer dress
has a voluminous skirt but is still fashionably
short. Stockings were an important accessory
and always had a high sheen.

INTO THE JAZZ AGE

During the Roaring Twenties, women's clothes became a powerful expression of the modernist approach to all forms of art. Many old attitudes were swept away by World War I, and with them the long skirts and waist-cinching corsetry of the early 1900s. Such constrictions were unsuited to the vital, active wartime roles women took as land workers, drivers, and machine operators. By the 1920s, more women could vote, and more entered the professions. They drove, smoked, drank cocktails, and worshipped screen stars such as Clara Bow. Dress became relaxed and strikingly simple.

One key aspect of the modern woman's look was *pour le sport*. Clothes developed for physical activity left their mark on fashion, while sports itself helped to achieve the stovepipe silhouette. Women hankered after the image of *La Garçonne* (Bachelor Girl or Tomboy) from the 1922 novel by Victor Margueritte. Hair was bobbed or cut into the "Eton crop" and hugged by cloches, waists abandoned or dropped to the hips, and chests flattened.

Believing that clothes should be casual and easy to wear, and borrowing from men's garments and sports and leisure fabrics, Coco Chanel and Jean Patou took a fashion lead. Their plain sweaters; short, pleated skirts (hemlines rose to the knees by the mid-1920s); and use of soft wool jerseys allowed free movement and won immediate international success. Everyday clothes featured unstructured jackets, hip-length sweaters, and simple blouses and skirts. By night, drop-waisted, full-hemmed dresses allowed flappers another important freedom—to dance the night away at jazz clubs.

> Fashion is not something that exists in dresses only. Fashion is in the sky, in the street, fashion has to do with ideas, the way we live, what is happening.

COCO CHANEL

◁ **POUR LE SPORT**
Models seated in the back of a luxury yacht showcase the fashion of the day with linen jackets, pleated skirts, and berets or cloche hats.

1923–1929
ROARING TWENTIES

Despite the brevity of their reign, knee-length evening gowns sprinkled with beads and paillettes are probably the main garments associated with the Roaring Twenties. Hems moved upward during 1923, peaking just below the knee a few years later—only to inch toward the ground again almost immediately. As sleeves were abandoned, women invested in safety razors and tried out the new deodorants. The French designer Jean Patou remarked that it was "the taste for dancing" that determined the line of evening gowns. It also influenced their decoration— beaded fringes and feathers attached to thin crêpes and georgettes swayed to the rhythm of the Charleston and Black Bottom. For a few years everything glittered: real diamonds or rhinestones decorated tiaras, bandeaus, and detachable heels. Anticipated by pointed hems and trailing shawls attached at the waist or shoulder, the long evening gown returned by the end of the decade; the dancing was over.

False eyelashes now available

1925

Slip-on design

Low waist accentuated with belt

Geometric patterns above hem

Layers Evening dresses of this period often consisted of two garments. Here, a silver lamé foundation shines through the lace fabric of the overdress. The entire gown is covered in tiny red and pink bugle beads.

Multicolored embroidery

Black edging

1927

Shawl falls from shoulders to give longer hem at back

Pointed hem This dress marks the transition stage between the short, straight evening dress and the longer gowns of the end of the decade. Around front, the neckline turns into a low V at the back, where shawls of transparent fabric hang from the shoulders to below the hemline.

Matching shoes

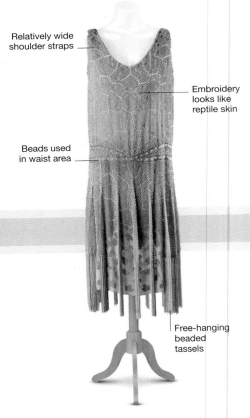

Relatively wide shoulder straps

Embroidery looks like reptile skin

Beads used in waist area

Free-hanging beaded tassels

Reptile English-born couturier Edward Molyneux created this unique dress. A variety of beads are used to make the fabric appear as if made from snakeskin. Long, triangular inserts emanating from the skirt underneath the hips end in beaded fringes.

Waist not marked

Scalloped hem

Chiffon The deliberately asymmetric hem of this chiffon dress is echoed in the irregular embroidery consisting of a semiabstract floral design. This beaded pattern seems to be expanding, which gives the appearance of movement.

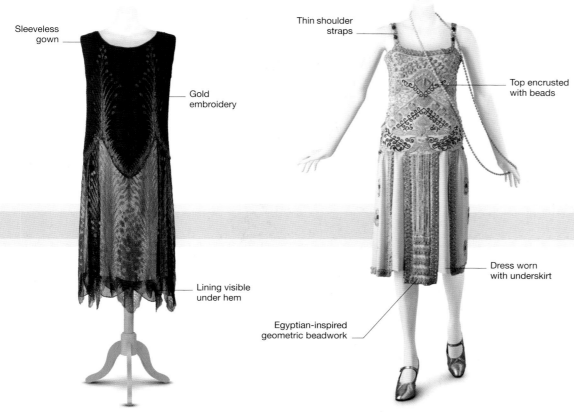

Sleeveless gown

Gold embroidery

Lining visible under hem

Thin shoulder straps

Top encrusted with beads

Dress worn with underskirt

Egyptian-inspired geometric beadwork

Gown made of chiffon

Clear beads form rings

Red foulards attached to waistband

Black underdress visible

Irregular hem

Slip-on Most evening gowns in the 1920s did not have any closures and were just slipped on. This dress is embroidered all over in gold. Its peach-colored chiffon lining is used as a decorative feature and shines through below the waist.

Egyptian style Popular interest in archaeology led to the use of shapes and colors that were inspired by artefacts and imagery of ancient cultures. The architectural nature of the embroidery here would have given the wearer a statuesque air.

Beadwork This transparent chiffon gown is embroidered with black and clear beads. The black underdress, visible underneath, has narrow shoulder straps. Foulards (scarves) of red gauzy material attached to the waist soften the straight silhouette.

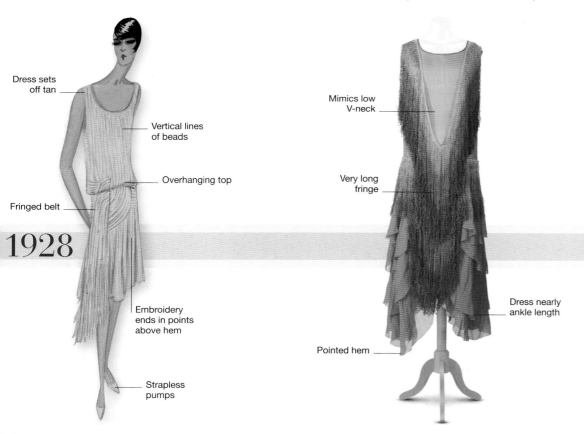

Dress sets off tan

Vertical lines of beads

Overhanging top

Fringed belt

1928

Embroidery ends in points above hem

Strapless pumps

Mimics low V-neck

Very long fringe

Dress nearly ankle length

Pointed hem

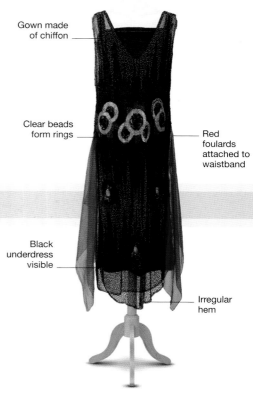

STRAPPED PUMPS

Evening dresses were worn with closed sandals or strapped pumps in a variety of materials, including fabric and metallic leathers. The quest for decoration and ornament extended to shoes: leather was tooled (stamped or painted), and fabric was embroidered with beads, spangles, and rhinestones. Some manufacturers even offered separate heels ornamented with rhinestones that were laid in geometric shapes into a celluloid base imitating mother-of-pearl. These heels could be attached to different pairs of shoes.

Green brocade shoe

Gold leather shoe

Glow worm The name given to this design, *Ver Luisant* (glow worm), might allude to the iridescent beads with which it is covered. The top is embroidered with beads in vertical lines that give way to swirls below the waist, finishing in a fringed sash.

Shades of red This bright red chiffon gown has several rows of deep flounces below the hips. It is decorated with layers of two types of deep fringing in lighter to darker shades of pink and coral.

BEADED EVENING WEAR

DANCE DRESS

This iconic evening gown, designed by the London company Reville and Rossiter c. 1925–1928, has all the hallmarks of a Jazz-era "flapper dress." Popular features were thin, fluid textiles like this cream silk chiffon, deep V-necks, and a dropped waist. This tubular, slip-on dress falls straight from the shoulders and has little shaping. Geometric motifs in embroidery, silvery beading, rhinestone studs, and fringing grab the attention—elements that would create a spectacular display on the dance floor.

SIDE VIEW

BACK VIEW

IN DETAIL

▽ **CAPPED SLEEVES**
Small, capped sleeves trimmed in silver and rhinestone studs were typical of the period. The new revealing style not only showed off bare arms but also encouraged women to experiment with the

Row of silver and rhinestone studs

Panel of scrolled beadwork down the front elongates torso

Delicate silk chiffon in soft ivory color

Short cap sleeves showed off dancers' arms

V-neckline emphasized by embroidered and beaded band

Silver glass bugle beads

Triangle of black silk covered with beads draws attention to the dropped waist

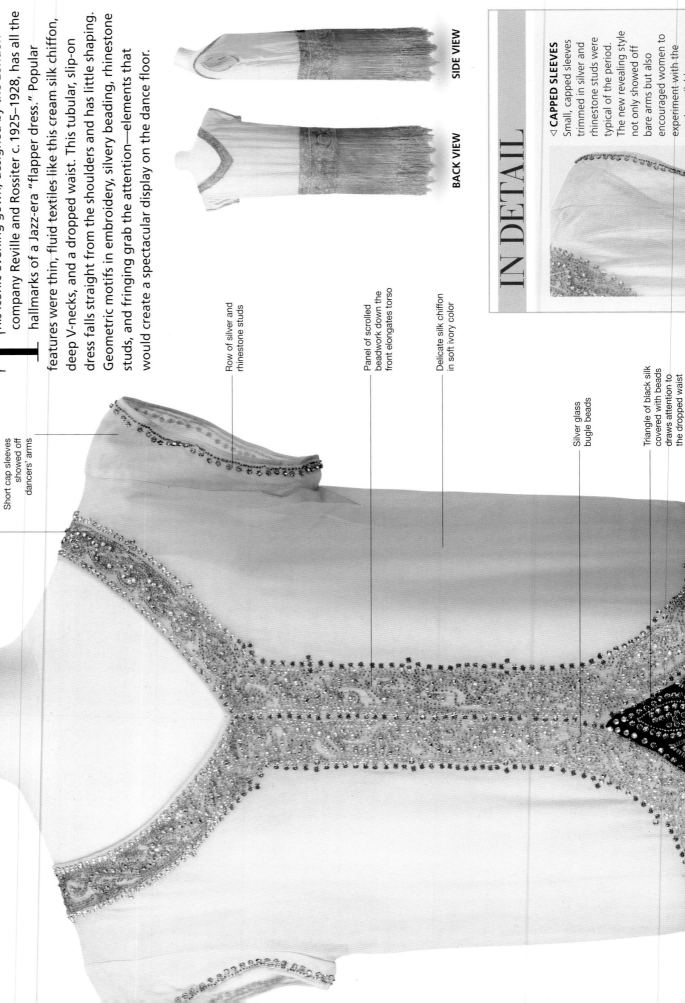

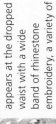
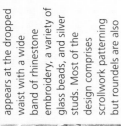

appears at the dropped waist with a wide band of rhinestone embroidery, a variety of glass beads, and silver studs. Most of the design comprises scrollwork patterning but roundels are also a feature.

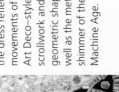
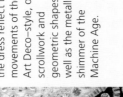

△ **INFLUENCE OF ART**
Beadwork patterns on the dress reflect the art movements of the time: Art Deco–style, organic scrollwork and geometric shapes, as well as the metallic shimmer of the Machine Age.

△ **FRAGILE BEADING**
The density of the beadwork weighs heavily on the delicate, silk chiffon fabric. This helped to maintain the straight line of the dress, though it also took its toll on the fragile material, especially during dancing.

△ **FRINGED HEM**
The fringed skirt is created from ornate silk tassels. Tightly wound threads are covered with beads and the ends wrapped in silver wire. The tassels are hung at a variety of lengths to mimic feathers.

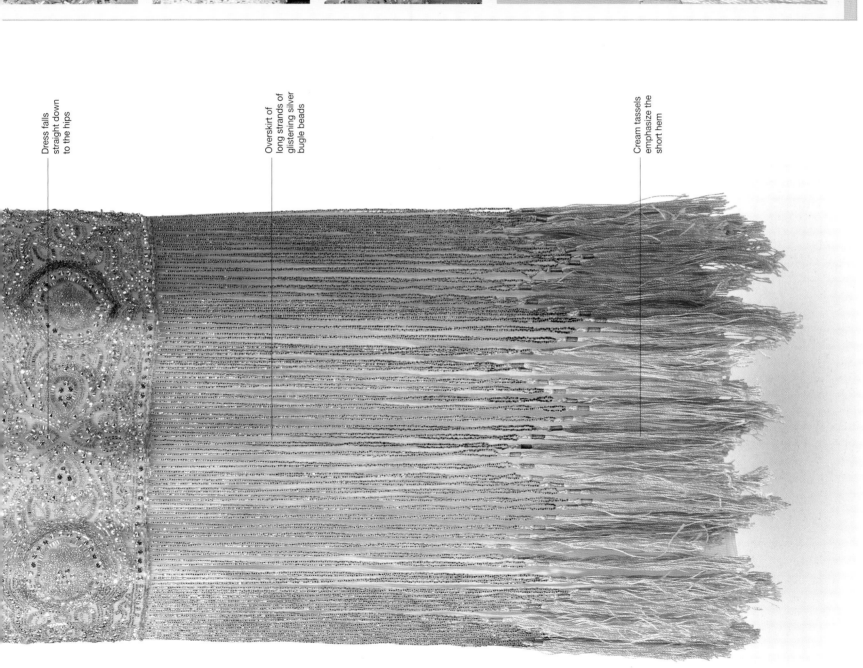

Dress falls straight down to the hips

Overskirt of long strands of glistening silver bugle beads

Cream tassels emphasize the short hem

1920–1929
AT THE BEACH

For centuries, respectable women had feared the effects of the sun, but now that fashionable clothing exposed more skin, men and women entered the "suntan era." If the real thing was elusive, sunlamps, suntan stockings, and suntan powder could be used to achieve the desired complexion. Alabaster skin once denoted a life free of outdoor work; now it signified an indoor life of office or factory drudgery. From 1922, wealthy sun seekers and those wanting to try their luck in one of the Grand Casinos could board the luxurious Blue Train in Calais at 1 p.m. and arrive on the Côte d'Azur the next morning. These novel pursuits provided opportunities for sartorial invention—revealing bathing suits cried out for a practical cover. The "divine sloppiness" of beach or Lido pajamas became so irresistible that in 1933 the Riviera resort of Juan-les-Pins was christened "Pajamapolis," a tag that equally could have been applied to Malibu or Palm Beach.

Thin shoulder straps

Contrasting belt

Block of color

1923

Cool bathing The wealthy stockbroker E. F. Hutton, owner of the largest private sea-going yacht of the era, shows off his tanned physique in the typical, fashionably striped and belted one-piece male bathing suit of the 1920s.

Collar in contrasting satin

Short sleeves leave arms exposed

Pants loose at top

1926

Satin ankle bands

Strapless pumps

Lido wear The sandy beach of the Venetian Lido island gave its name to seaside resorts and pools, as well as fashionable beachwear. These pajamas of royal blue georgette feature a collar, tie, and facings of contrasting jade satin.

Striped bathing suit underneath

Contrasting cuffs and lapels

1927

Wide pants

Patterned shoes

Palm Beach The riotously patterned beach pajamas of Mr. Kenneth B. Van Riper of New York are a far cry from formal wear, but they do feature adorned side seams also found on tuxedo or dinner suit pants.

PARASOLS

While at the beach, parasols provided shelter from the sun and wind, as well as being stylish accessories. At this time, bold printed fabrics were often chosen, in silk or its newly popular synthetic alternative, rayon. Asian parasols, that were made from varnished paper and decorated with exotic designs, were also fashionable at seaside resorts across Europe.

Striped silk

Floral print rayon

Cap reminiscent of previous decade

Fashionable headband

Rompers This novelty outfit, paraded on the beach of New Jersey's Atlantic City, did not catch on but foreshadowed a later trend. Rompers met a need for a loose pants ensemble that could easily be slipped over a bathing suit.

Beach pajamas The wearer of these beach pajamas apparently, and not entirely surprisingly, caused a sensation in Palm Beach. The large floral pattern, tasseled cords, and unusual shoes all contributed to the startling effect of the pajama outfit.

Decorated tiepin

Very narrow waist

Bathing suit

1924

Pants gathered at hem

Canes remained fashionable

Shoes tied around ankle

White summer shoes

Summer suit Seasonal heat in the French resort of Deauville demanded a lightweight suit. Probably showing far too much cuff to be respectable, this gentleman has accessorized his soft-collared shirt with a dark tie and a tiepin.

Fashionable turban

Easy-to-wear wrap top

Geometric pattern

Wide pants legs

1929

Very wide pants legs

Deep hem band

Bold stripes

Special beach shoes

Wrap top The flamboyance of beach and lounging pajamas inspired dressmakers and fashion designers. Here, the black and orange color blocks of the wide pants are picked up in the geometric pattern of the wrap top.

SPORTSWEAR

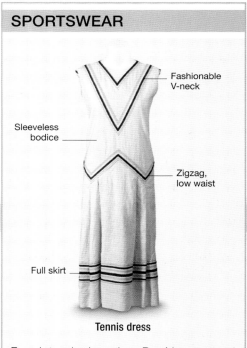

Fashionable V-neck

Sleeveless bodice

Zigzag, low waist

Full skirt

Tennis dress

French tennis champions René Lacoste and Suzanne Lenglen both influenced sports fashion. The turbaned Lenglen inaugurated the short, sleeveless sports dress, while Lacoste went on from his tennis career to establish *La Chemise Lacoste* in 1933, which sold tennis whites, as well as golf and sailing clothes, of his own design.

1920–1929

SETTING STANDARDS

Although there were no major additions to the vocabulary of men's formal wear in the 1920s, the move toward increasing informality continued in that decade. The constant changing of rules could cause anxiety and embarrassment. In the casinos of French resorts or at the dinner tables of ocean liners, a dinner suit or tuxedo was now considered appropriate when previously only full dress would have done. The tail or dress coat remained a must for an evening spent at the opera, a ball, or a formal dinner party where it provided the perfect foil for colorful, sparkling evening dresses. Frock coats could still be seen on city streets but mainly worn by older men. Magazines and etiquette books were prescriptive about what was considered good form, but those wealthy, famous, or good-looking enough such as Hollywood stars were granted a certain sartorial license.

ARROW COLLAR MAN

This advertisement for collars and shirts bearing the American Arrow label sets almost unobtainable sartorial and physical standards. The stiff, white shirt front, wing collar, and white bow tie draw the eye to the typically chiseled feature of J. C. Leyendecker's creation. White carnations were the recommended buttonhole for full dress, although gardenias were also accepted. The illustration highlights the close fit of full dress, emphasizing the chest and confining the waist.

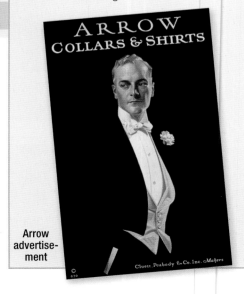

Arrow advertisement

At the opera Full dress consisted of tail coat, white vest, stiff bosom shirt with wing collar, and white bow tie. Black top or opera hat and black patent leather boots or pumps completed the ensemble. Overcoats were a must, even in summer.

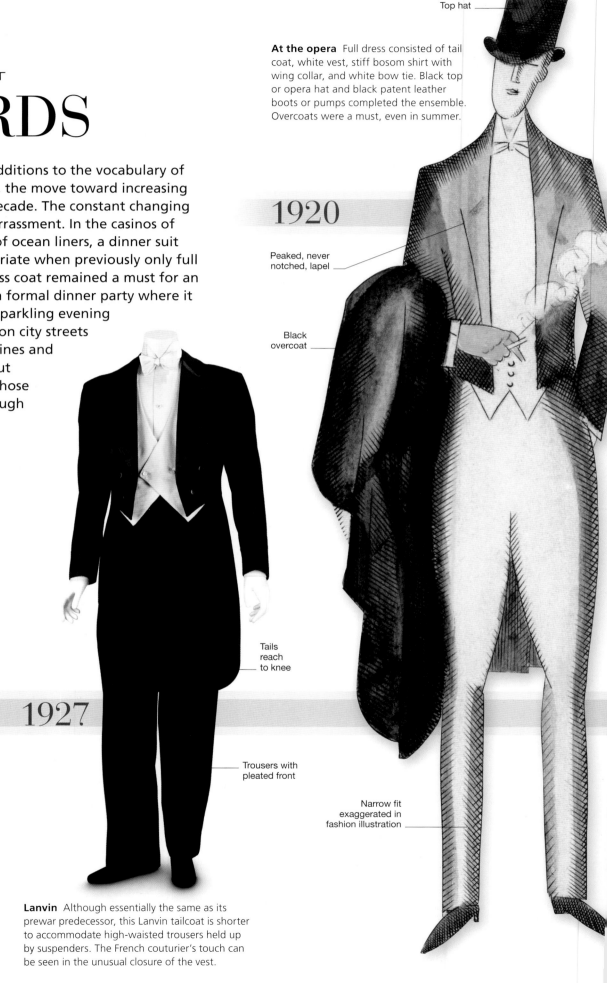

Top hat

1920

Peaked, never notched, lapel

Black overcoat

Tails reach to knee

1927

Trousers with pleated front

Narrow fit exaggerated in fashion illustration

Lanvin Although essentially the same as its prewar predecessor, this Lanvin tailcoat is shorter to accommodate high-waisted trousers held up by suspenders. The French couturier's touch can be seen in the unusual closure of the vest.

1924

Silk top hat with black ribbon

Ascot cravat with tiepin

Gloves had to be worn or carried

Coat edged with narrow braid

Moderately tapered legs

Father of the bride This cutaway coat with braided edges, white vest, and gray worsted trousers with black and white stripes are the correct attire for a Philadelphia wedding. It had to be worn with a four-in-hand, Ascot cravat, or black bow tie.

1925

Sometimes gray top hats were worn

Peak lapel

Four-in-hand is simple, most usual tie knot

Gray trousers with black and white stripes

Light-colored spats

At the races Yasuhito, Prince Chichibu of Japan, sports a morning coat, matching vest, striped trousers, turn-down collar, and four-in-hand tie. According to one writer, shoes should never be worn with a top hat unless with spats.

1926

Silk top hat

Sloping shoulder line

Wing collar and bow tie

Rounded-off front

Long cane with tasseled ribbon

Trousers with small check

Hollywood George K. Arthur is dressed as Madame Lucy, the flamboyant gay couturier in the 1926 film *Irene*. This might account for the unusual pairing of black dinner jacket with checked trousers, normally teamed with a morning coat.

Silk plush top hat

Double round collar

Morning coat The US Secretary of the Navy, Charles Francis Adams III, wears a black morning coat with matching, single-breasted vest, and striped trousers. A top hat and stylish, leather Oxford shoes complete his formal look.

Very high turn-down collar

Customary pocket handkerchief

Homburg hat

1929

Front crease

Business suit Alfred P. Sloan, Jr., the president of General Motors, is in a relaxed variation of semiformal wear. After 1925 a dark, single-breasted business suit became known as a Stresemann in Germany after the country's foreign secretary.

Sloping shoulders

Front cut square

Black boots

Opening of parliament What looks at first glance like a frock coat is in fact a double-breasted Chesterfield, the correct overcoat to wear with a morning coat. The matching vest is worn with a white slip just visible near the four-in-hand.

1920–1929
SUITS FOR ALL

In 1922, one fashion critic declared that the lounge suit had become "the almost universal utility dress for men," but this did not mean that sartorial distinctions had become extinct. Differences in the quality as well as the quantity of suits a man owned remained. A suit could be bought ready-to-wear or secondhand, but many men still "bespoke" a suit from their tailor or had it made to measure. Many appreciated the English cut promoted by London's Savile Row tailors, but others preferred the less fitted and softer American "sack suit," or the more overtly fashionable shapes provided by the French *tailleur*. Suit fabrics became lighter, particularly for summer—as demonstrated by the cloth used to make "Palm Beach" suits in the US. This affected male underwear and slowly undershirts worn with cotton shorts replaced the earlier "union suit" (all-in-one undergarment). Toward 1930, the high-waisted suits of the early part of the decade made way for a straighter silhouette.

1920

French style This suit advertised by the Paris tailor Barclay has a close-fitting, waisted coat with slanted hip pockets and peaked lapel. The ankle-length, tapering trousers focus attention on the black boots worn with spats.

Homburg with dark ribbon

Stiff turndown collar

Belted overcoat

Tapering trousers with front crease

Large shawl collar

Wide legs with deep cuffs

Raccoon The American football idol Harold "Red" Grange wears a comfortable-looking tweed suit with a three-button jacket. Coats made of the fur of the North American raccoon were hard-wearing and recommended for driving.

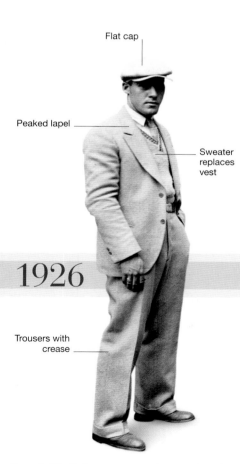

Flat cap

Peaked lapel

Sweater replaces vest

1926

Trousers with crease

Casual "Red" Grange wears a low-cut American sack suit with little or no shaping around the waist and natural shoulders. The sportsman's V-neck sweater, tucked into his belted trousers, and flat cap denote informality.

Panama hat

Sports shirt with soft collar

1924

Cuffs

White summer shoes

Seaside "White flannels," trousers made of light, brushed wool cloth, were recommended for summer, whether staying at the Riviera or an English seaside town. Flannels were worn with belts, rather than suspenders.

Homburg with rolled brim

Straight flap pockets

1925

Light-colored spats

Dark umbrella

Double-breasted By mid-decade the suit was less fitted and worn with slightly wider trousers. Sir Arthur Conan Doyle wears his double-breasted suit with a soft collar shirt and club tie. The light color of the homburg hat is echoed in the spats.

Stiff bowler hat

Four-in-hand tie

Race club badge attached to buttonhole

Boots worn instead of shoes

Front crease

The races The meaning of a lounge suit could be transformed by the choice of hat and shirt. This Yorkshire race goer pairs a light, double-breasted suit with a starched collar and a relatively formal bowler hat.

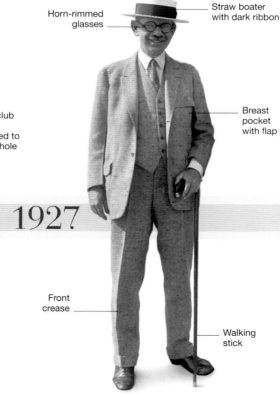

Horn-rimmed glasses

Straw boater with dark ribbon

1927

Breast pocket with flap

Front crease

Walking stick

Florida beachwear Marcus Lowe, vice president of Metro-Goldwyn Pictures, wears a lightweight "Palm Beach" suit for a day at the beach. He sports a boater, which remained fashionable for summer wear throughout the decade.

HATS AND SHOES

Men in the 1920s could choose from a variety of hat shapes that had all been introduced in the previous century. Other than the top hat, lounge suits could be worn with every hat type. The bowler, also called derby or coke, was the most formal, followed by the homburg, a stiff felt with a center crease and rolled brim. The trilby and wider-brimmed fedora, both named after literary characters, were everyday city hats, while the boater or other varieties of straw hat were for summer or the beach.

Bowler hat

Felt trilby

Straw boater hat

Shoes had gradually replaced boots since the turn of the century. These were mainly of the lace-up Oxford type and had to be matched to the rest of the outfit and the season. Dark business suits were worn with black or tan shoes, but in summer shoes of white leather or cotton duck accessorized white flannels or Palm Beach suits. Toward the end of the decade two-tone shoes became all the rage.

Box calf sandal

Two-tone Oxford

Tan Oxford

1919–1928
MODERNISM

Some artists-turned-fashion creators were inspired by the past. Others, spread around Europe and in postrevolutionary Russia, looked toward a variety of futures and created clothes for the new world. Aleksandr Rodchenko in Russia and Thayaht in Italy developed an early form of the functional overall, and Hungarian Laszlo Moholy-Nagy customized existing work wear. The Italian Futurists' love of speed and movement found expression not only in their art, but also in bright, one-off clothes with abstract patterns. Varvara Stepanova and Lyubov Popova designed textiles based on universal shapes to rationalize mass production in Russia. In Paris the Russian-born Sonia Delaunay also used geometric forms in bright colors but in the service of the moneyed few. That the straight silhouette of the 1920s lent itself to decoration with regular lines and shapes occurred to creative people besides artists, and similar designs could be found outside elite fashion.

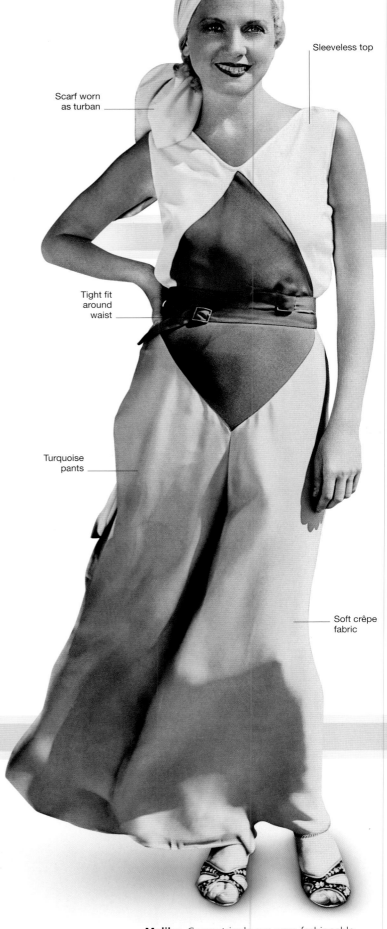

Scarf worn as turban

Sleeveless top

Tight fit around waist

Turquoise pants

Soft crêpe fabric

Worn with open white collar

Practical pockets

Adjustable length

TuTa In 1919 the artist and designer Ernesto Michahelles not only adopted the name Thayaht but also designed the TuTa, an early example of an coverall. The soft lines created by this "universal garment" followed those of the body.

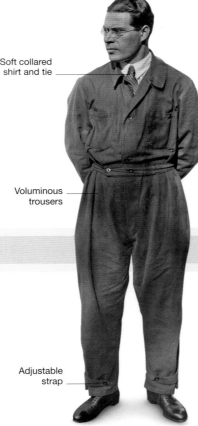

Soft collared shirt and tie

Voluminous trousers

Adjustable strap

Work suit Between 1923 and 1928 the Hungarian Moholy-Nagy was a teacher at the German Bauhaus school. Its aim of fusing crafts and fine arts was echoed in his *Arbeitsanzug* (work suit), presenting the artist as craftsman.

Malibu Geometric shapes were fashionable farther afield than Europe, as demonstrated by the silk crêpe beach pajamas worn by Lilyan Tashman. "Hollywood's best-dressed star" allegedly owned a million-dollar wardrobe.

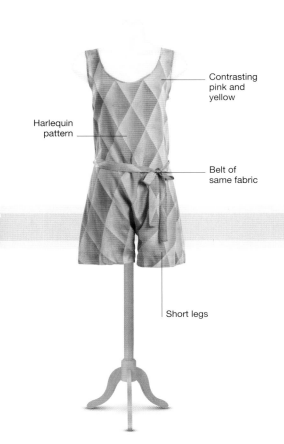

Contrasting pink and yellow

Harlequin pattern

Belt of same fabric

Short legs

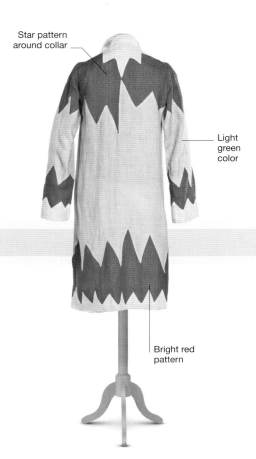

Star pattern around collar

Light green color

Bright red pattern

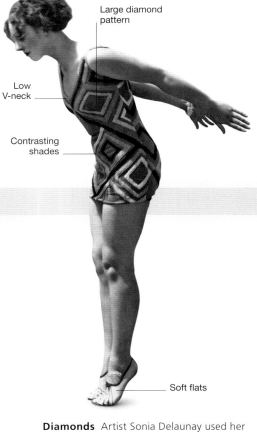

Large diamond pattern

Low V-neck

Contrasting shades

Soft flats

Harlequin The Standard Oil heiress Millicent Rogers liked the fabric of this creation so much that she acquired a second one in yellow and gray. A practical slip-on garment, it was probably made for wearing at the beach or by the pool.

Sawtooth The decoration on the back of this linen coat by Sonia Delaunay is deliberately asymmetrical. While the coat's cut is simple, the aggressive jagged-edged shapes separating the light green central parts supply drama.

Diamonds Artist Sonia Delaunay used her bold, geometric, abstract patterns on many textiles and garments, including swimsuits. In this example, light blue silk is embroidered in red, white, and green diamond shapes.

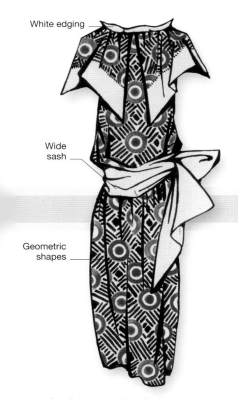

White edging

Wide sash

Geometric shapes

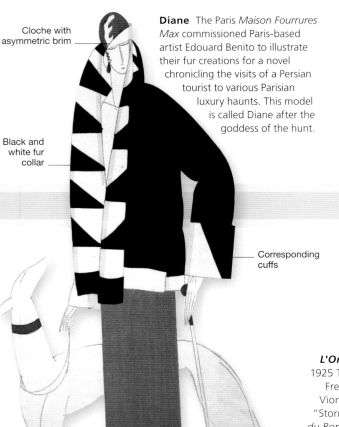

Cloche with asymmetric brim

Black and white fur collar

Corresponding cuffs

Diane The Paris *Maison Fourrures Max* commissioned Paris-based artist Edouard Benito to illustrate their fur creations for a novel chronicling the visits of a Persian tourist to various Parisian luxury haunts. This model is called Diane after the goddess of the hunt.

Low waist

Rectangular shape of dress echoed in pattern

Productivism In 1921 the Russian artist Lyubov Popova turned away from the easel and focused her attention on textile design. The straight-lined geometric forms of her fabric patterns contrast with the more fluid shapes of her dress designs.

L'Orage Between 1919 and 1925 Thayaht designed for the French couturier Madeleine Vionnet, here illustrating her "Storm" dress for the *Gazette du Bon Ton*. The simple lines of the garment are enlivened by graduated geometric shapes.

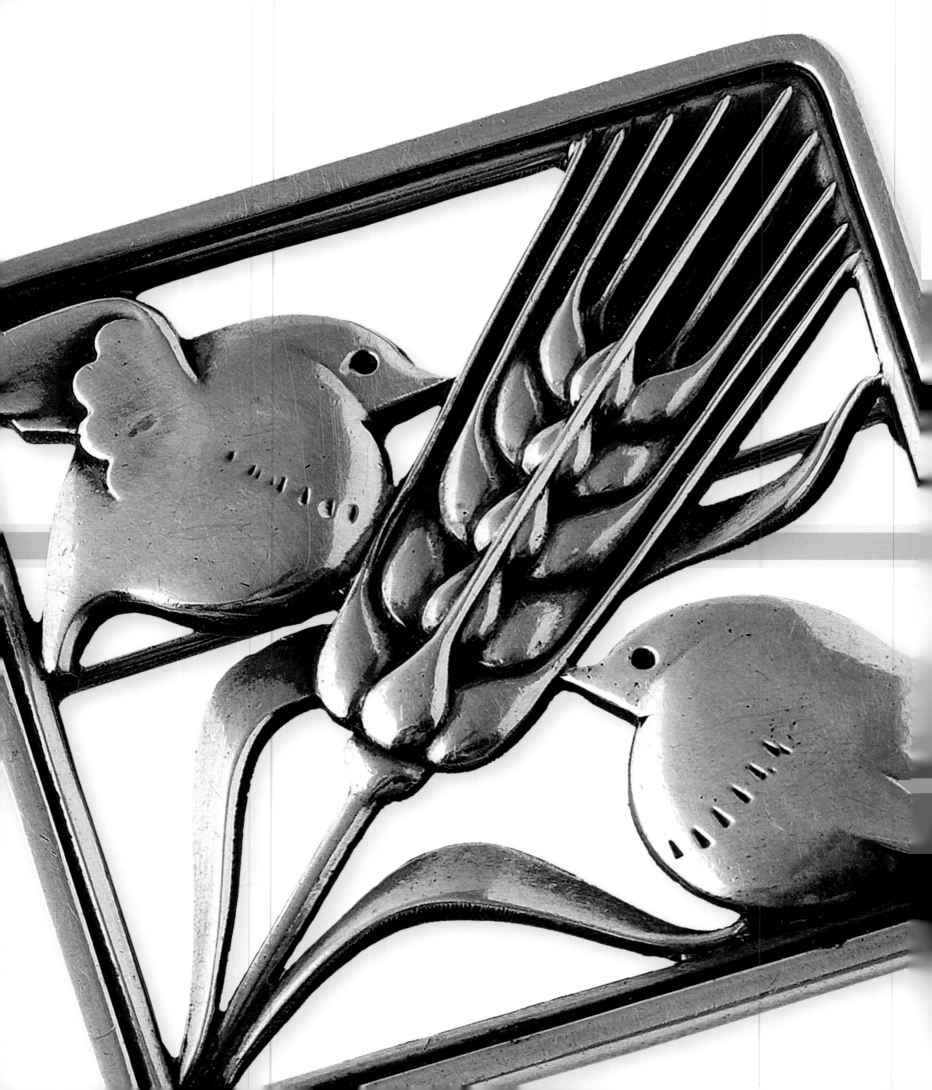

FROM GLAMOUR
TO UTILITY

1929–1946

FROM GLAMOUR TO UTILITY

The Wall Street Crash in the fall of 1929 brought the Roaring Twenties to an abrupt halt. Hemlines dropped suddenly while waistlines rose to a little above the natural waist—the reign of the youthful flapper was truly over. "Austerity day wear" for women was angled and slim fitting, with wide shoulder pads and calf-length skirts. During the day, the slimline silhouette was broken up and softened with clever seaming, belts, novelty buttons, deep cuffs, and pussy bows. In the evening, the focus shifted from legs to plunging backs with designers such as Lanvin, Mainbocher, and Chanel producing shimmering, floor-length dresses.

Fashion at the movies

During the 1930s, New York ready-to-wear designers developed a new style that seemed to embody the nation's values. Their practical approach resulted in easy-to-wear pieces that could be adapted to different occasions by mixing and matching. At the opposite end of the scale, Hollywood designers Adrian, Walter Plunket, and Travis Banton created glamorous outfits for stars such as Jean Harlow, Joan Crawford, and Marlene Dietrich. These Hollywood styles were arguably the biggest influence on fashion in the 1930s. Out of reach for most, patterns and pared-down versions were available for those of less lavish means. Hollywood stars Fred Astaire, Cary Grant, and Gary Cooper set impossibly high standards for male beauty and elegance. The look became a best seller on both sides of the Atlantic, and many bought their suits in London's Savile Row.

Effects of the war

The start of World War II in 1939 brought an end to lavish, excessive designs. Many countries established a rationing system, trying to prevent the waste of scarce resources and ensure a fair distribution of garments. Decorative features such as excessive pleating and lace were abandoned, leading to simplified styles that constituted a kind of civilian uniform. Paris retained a skeletal couture industry after the invasion in 1940, but the rest of the world was cut off from French fashion dictates. New US fashions emerged and some hoped that French couture's sometimes excessive use of fabric and decorations had been banished forever, but this was not to be.

US WOMEN'S ARMY UNIFORMS, 1940s
Three women model, from left to right, officer's winter uniform, officer's summer uniform, and auxiliary private's uniform.

1929–30

1930
As fashion becomes more conservative, dresses are generally styled with a lower hemline.

▼ Depression hits, hemlines fall

1931–32

1932
Flying Down to Rio pairs Fred Astaire and Ginger Rogers for the first time. Astaire was an impeccable dresser on and off the screen, favoring suits made on London's Savile Row.

1932
The movie *Letty Lynton* by MGM, starring Joan Crawford, begins a craze for padded shoulders in the US.

◄ Joan Crawford in *Letty Lynton*

1933–34

◄ Astaire's elegant style

1934
The word "brassiere" is gradually shortened to "bra" through the decade. According to a survey by *Harper's Bazaar*, "bra" is the most commonly used expression among college women for the brassiere.

1934
Women's sports clothes become briefer than ever. Bathing suits are slashed and backless, and shorts begin to be seen on the tennis court.

▼ First shorts at Wimbledon

It's no longer smart to be chic … The new mode is casual, bold, chunky and realistic.

VOGUE, 1936

1935–36

1937–38

1939–40

1941–42

1943–44

1945–46

1935
Italian-born Elsa Schiaparelli opens her first designer Boutique at 21 Place Vendôme, Paris, France.

▲ A pair of nylon stockings

1935
Nylon is invented by Wallace Carothers at DuPont's research facility. It is used as a substitute for silk in many different products.

1936
Edward VIII abdicates the throne of England. His American mistress, Mrs. Wallis Simpson, is dressed by Mainbocher for their wedding.

◄ Mrs. Wallis Simpson's wedding dress

1936
As more women take on paid employment, daytime looks are tailored and angular, with square epauleted shoulders, frogging, plumed hats, low heels, and gauntlet gloves.

1937
The Spanish designer Cristóbal Balenciaga opens his couture house in Paris. He'd had boutiques in Spain since 1918.

▲ *Gone with the Wind*

1939
Gone with the Wind is released, picking up brilliantly on the air of insecurity and emphasizing a feminine, romantic note in fashion that would not be seen again until Dior's New Look in 1947.

1940
Ties become wider, with bolder patterns that range from art deco designs to tropical themes.

◄ Hand-painted tie

1939
England and France declare war on Germany in September 1939. Clothes have to be practical. *Vogue* patterns are now for pants for volunteer drivers. Sweaters become the basis of most looks; skirts are long and full.

▲ Rosie the Riveter

1942
Rosie the Riveter is the star of a song that praises the American women working in factories. Her much-admired practical image has her dressed in a blue coveralls, hair concealed underneath a red spotted scarf.

1943
The Zoot Suit riots explode in Los Angeles, California. White sailors and marines take umbrage at young Mexican-Americans wearing suits that use large amounts of cloth.

Wartime pamphlet ▶

1944
Rationing becomes severe, and where economies in designs can be made, they are. Fabrics are cheap and cuts are sparing.

1944
A highly visible, military presence provides inspiration for designers during wartime. Civilian fashion seeks to emulate the uniform of servicemen and women.

▼ American GIs in Paris, 1944

1946
The first Paris collections after the war foreshadow Dior's New Look of 1947.

▲ Slim-cut herringbone suit

1930–1939
AUSTERE TIMES

The Wall Street Crash forced the frivolous single girl of the 1920s to grow up and take life more seriously. The new silhouette was long and lean, emphasized by hemlines several inches below the knee, vertical seams, and slanting pockets. Perhaps in empathy with those actually on the breadline, anything round or full was abhorred, and women were all sharp angles and hipbones, their outlines sometimes softened by fur collars and cuffs. Linings or facings in contrasting colors, large pussy bows, belts, buttons, and deep cuffs were popular decorative features. Floral patterns were still fashionable for summer, while checks and plaids became particularly popular toward the end of the decade. Clutch bags, as slimline as their wearers, were held in hands sheathed in gloves with spiky gauntlets. Hair was worn close to the head in a permanent wave, at first still covered by close-fitting cloches and later adorned by a tiny hat worn at a jaunty angle.

Collar and cuffs Astrakhan (from a young lamb), fox, and other furs were often used for cuffs and, sometimes detachable, collars. Seams were used for decoration. Gloves and hats remained indispensable accessories for the fashionable woman.

1931

Fur shawl collar

Deep fur cuffs

Zigzag seaming

Inverted pleats

MISS MODERN

Aimed at the unmarried working girl, *Miss Modern* was a "sixpenny," a cheap monthly British magazine first published in October 1930. Its ideal reader, shown here on the cover, was not afraid to check her makeup and adjust her hat in public using the mirror inside the flap of her fashionable clutch bag. The business girl could add to her stylish wardrobe using the free pattern for an "ideal office dress" inside the magazine.

Miss Modern
magazine cover

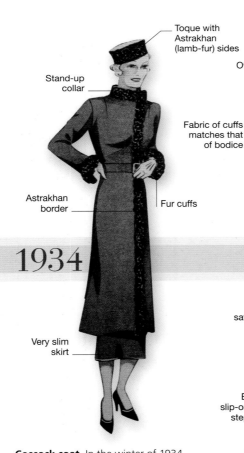

Toque with Astrakhan (lamb-fur) sides

Stand-up collar

Astrakhan border

Fur cuffs

Very slim skirt

1934

Oversized bow

Fabric of cuffs matches that of bodice

Black satin skirt

Black slip-ons or step-ins

Cossack coat In the winter of 1934 every stylish woman was said to hanker for a Russian Cossack coat. Underneath, a blouse with cross-over fronts and a straight skirt were recommended.

Satin This "Sunday night" dress is constructed of a high-waisted skirt of black satin and a bodice of palest pink lamé. Gathered loops at the neck are made to look like a large bow.

1932

Hat had to be worn on one side

Belt with metal buckle

Very slight flare

Hem below knee

Neat cloche hat

Stand-up collar

White cuffs with notch

Slightly flaring skirt slims hips

Bolero with crescent-shaped seams

Hat worn at an angle

Tartan belt

Hidden inverted pleat

Strapless pumps

Lace yoke extends with sleeves

Skirt falls in folds

Sharp angles This modern take on the trench coat is provided with feminine touches such as metal buttons, ornamental cuffs, and contrasting lapel facings in blue leather.

Sober elegance The white facing of the lapels, pockets, and cuffs emphasize the diagonal lines and jagged edges that so often appeared in women's clothing in this decade.

Tartan Two vertical seams highlight the long lines of this dress of white wool jersey. Green and black *écossais* (Scottish) fabric was used for the yoke, puff sleeves, and belt.

Satin and lace The crêpe satin of this gown is draped at the waist to form a belt that turns into a small basque (skirt) on one side. Buttons above the bust and on the hips emphasize the asymmetric cut.

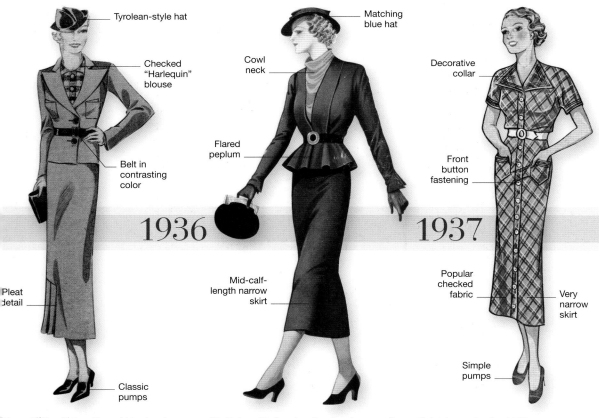

Tyrolean-style hat

Checked "Harlequin" blouse

Belt in contrasting color

Pleat detail

Matching blue hat

Cowl neck

Flared peplum

Mid-calf-length narrow skirt

Decorative collar

Front button fastening

Popular checked fabric

Very narrow skirt

Simple pumps

Classic pumps

1936

1937

Versatility This suit could be made with plain or fur lapels and worn with or without its cape and vest. The blouse was worn untucked at the waist to keep the hips looking slim.

Stylish suit Gracing the front page of Spanish magazine *Moda Practica*, the jacket of this stylish navy suit has a full peplum, which flares over the hips to contrast with the slim line of the skirt.

Shirtdress In the 1930s many women still made their own clothes at home. The pattern for this simple, practical shirtdress came with a copy of *Woman's Own* magazine.

SHOES

The 1930s saw a range of shoe and heel shapes to choose from, particularly toward the end of the decade. Shoes with straps were gradually replaced with strapless opera pumps for everyday wear. "Sandals" (pumps with one or more straps) nevertheless continued to be worn in the summer and for dancing. Piping in a contrasting color or metallic leather was often used for decoration. Shoes with higher vamps, referred to as "slip-ons" or "step-ins," and lace-up styles, usually called Oxfords, were practical daytime choices. Wedge heels and open-toe styles heralded the 1940s.

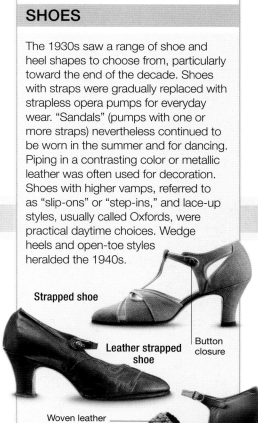

Strapped shoe

Leather strapped shoe

Button closure

Woven leather

Early 1930s sandal

1930–1939
SHIMMERING GOWNS

At the end of the 1920s the relatively brief reign of the short evening dress was over. The fashionable sipped cocktails in long, figure-hugging gowns that sometimes left little to the imagination. Frequently cut along the lines of swimwear, dresses were often precariously suspended from the thinnest of shoulder straps and left the backs of their wearers completely exposed. Shiny, fluid fabric—such as satin and lamé—was cut on the bias and manufactured into confections that clung to the body. If dieting did not have the desired effect, women could buy foundations made of the new "tu-way stretch" materials to achieve the all-important smooth, unbroken line. Women stepped out in whites, off-whites, silver, gold, and shades of apricot, peach, and salmon—if they were not wearing black.

1933

Inventive piecing of upper sleeves

Tight drapery across waist

Lamé dress American designer Jessie Franklin Turner used lamé to great effect in this bias-cut evening gown, making the wearer look as if sprayed with liquid metal. Unusually, the dress has long sleeves but still exposes glimpses of the upper body.

Now slightly tarnished, fabric would have been much brighter originally

1937

Shoulder straps form long shawls

Belt of same material

Asymmetric embroidery on skirt

Silver spangle embroidery

Fashionable apricot The base color of French designer Jeanne Lanvin's evening dress is accentuated with silver sequin embroidery. The simply but elegantly cut dress is made of a synthetic material, which was used even in couture houses.

1938

Two wide shoulder straps

Very low back

Graduated lengths of silk thread form fringe

Scallop arcs increase in size toward hem

Silk fringing It looks as if widening bands of fringing have been applied to this clinging rayon dress by French designer Madeleine Vionnet. Closer inspection reveals that individual silk threads have been sewn on to the dress; each forms two drops of fringe.

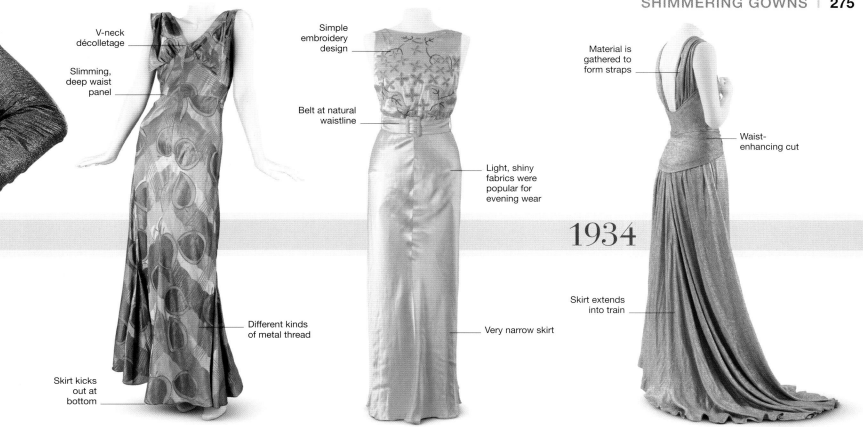

V-neck décolletage

Slimming, deep waist panel

Different kinds of metal thread

Skirt kicks out at bottom

Simple embroidery design

Belt at natural waistline

Light, shiny fabrics were popular for evening wear

Very narrow skirt

Material is gathered to form straps

Waist-enhancing cut

1934

Skirt extends into train

Modernist pattern The relatively simple cut of American designer Elizabeth Hawes's evening dress ensures that the focus is on the modernist pattern of the fabric. The large falling leaves accentuate the movement of the flaring skirt.

Fluid material The cut and material of this English dress would have necessitated the right kind of underwear. The gown bears no label but the simple embroidery design suggests that it might have been made by a local dressmaker.

Revealing cut The cut of this dress by French designer Coco Chanel would have highlighted the wearer's fashionably bronzed back and arms. Gathered and draped in front and hugging the waist, the gown's skirt flares out below the hip.

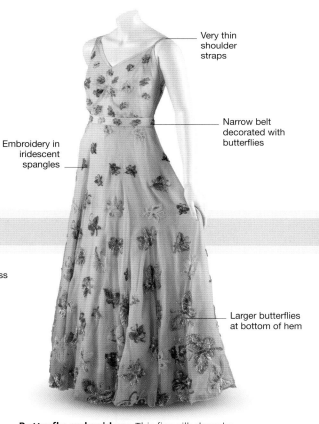

High neckline with bow detail at back of neck

Bows accentuate breasts

Bows grow larger toward hem

1939

Lamé underdress shines through

Very thin shoulder straps

Embroidery in iridescent spangles

Narrow belt decorated with butterflies

Larger butterflies at bottom of hem

Cap-sleeved overdress The overdress of Madeleine Vionnet's design is made of very fine black lace decorated with black bows. The shimmering silver lamé underdress, with a halter neck and very low back, could be worn on its own.

Butterfly embroidery This fine silk dress by French designer Mainbocher is embroidered with butterflies in iridescent spangles, which grow larger toward the hem. The dress would have been worn over a flesh-colored slip.

JEAN HARLOW

When Howard Hughes's movie *Hell's Angels* was released in 1930, 19-year-old Jean Harlow became an international star. Harlow popularized the white evening gown, and by bleaching her hair weekly completed the look and had an indirect influence on the sale of peroxide. American designer Adrian (Gilbert Adrian) created gowns for Harlow's role in *Reckless* (1935, above), accentuating her body with clinging, bias-cut dresses made of light-reflecting materials.

1930–1944
CLASSICISM

In September 1930, the French magazine *L'Officiel de la Mode* observed "a tendency toward classicism and pure Greek lines" in the latest collection of the Paris fashion houses, singling out Vionnet as having been "decidedly" influenced by Greek art. In the previous decade, appreciation of ancient styles had found expression in the use of patterns such as the meander or the Greek key. The return to long evening gowns in the 1930s enabled couturiers to transform their clients into Greek or Roman statues. The look of original garments from the classical period had been a matter of chance coupled with the wearer's skill for drapery. Neoclassical gowns were more structured—the drapery and folds more controlled—drawing attention to the body underneath. The use of fluid fabrics such as silk jersey or satin, asymmetry, and decorative borders were trademarks of this new line. White and off-white governed this style, but black, and occasionally brighter colors, were also used.

MADAME GRÈS

In 1933 Germaine Krebs began to create clothes under the assumed name of Alix Barton. She changed her name again when she opened the House of Grès in Paris in 1942. Having trained as a sculptress, Mme Grès liked to drape her pleated evening gowns on a model or stand. She often used silk jersey, which molded itself to the wearer's body, for her neoclassical designs. Her success continued until the 1980s.

Gathered shoulders

Symmetrical décolletage

Fabric drawn together at waist

1931

Figure-hugging top

Three bands create "Greek" shape

Narrow pleats below waist

Skirt very wide at hem

Pleating It is not surprising that dieting was much discussed in the 1930s, since evening dresses of this decade focused attention on the body while providing little support. This skirt's width is created by narrow pleats fanning out.

1937

Slightly trained

Alix Barton Silk or wool jersey was a favorite material of Alix Barton (later known as Madame Grès), which she used to create gowns reminiscent of Ancient Greek dress. The drapery is often held together by drawstrings, ties, or girdles.

Smooth top

Cape or shawl at back

Metallic leather decoration

Slim skirt

Leather accents This dress's classical feel is created through very clean lines and the belt's gold and silver pattern. The scrollwork is made of metallic leather, a material French designer Lanvin experimented with in the mid-1930s.

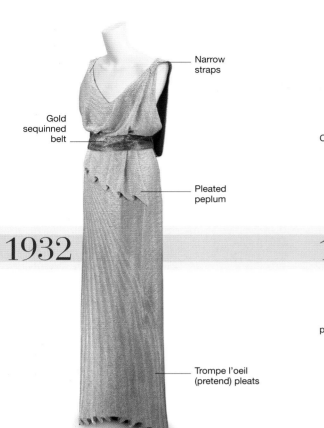

1932

Narrow straps

Gold sequinned belt

Pleated peplum

Trompe l'oeil (pretend) pleats

Pink and gold French designer Patou's tulle evening dress is covered in pink and gold glass bugle beads, creating the illusion of drapery and folds. The shape of the gown is reminiscent of the Greek peplos that gave its name to the peplum (short overskirt).

1934

Brooch in shape of branch

Central ruching

Soft fabric, probably jersey

Long scarf falling from shoulder

Scarves Trailing pieces of fabric, often attached to the shoulders, were a common feature of neoclassical dresses. The statuesque silhouette of this *Dove* evening gown by the English company Motley is emphasized by the brooch and the model's hairstyle.

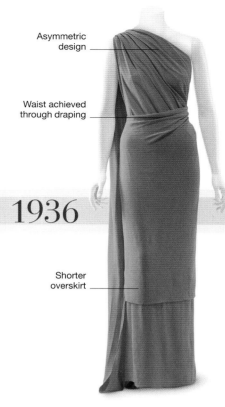

1936

Asymmetric design

Waist achieved through draping

Shorter overskirt

Simple drapes White and black were common colors for neoclassical dresses, but Madeleine Vionnet chose a deep orange for this pared-down design. Fabric gathered at one shoulder is draped over the bust while falling to the floor at the back.

Abstract embroidery

Pleating below bust

Embroidered tendrils

1938

Softly draped, flared skirt

Scrolls Unlike the evening gowns of the 1920s, neoclassical dresses were usually only sparsely embroidered so that the sculptural lines were not broken. The halter neck of this gown is reminiscent of a pectoral (crescent-shaped) necklace.

Asymmetric top

Tight overdress

1944

Finely pleated skirt

Beaded border on shawl and overdress

Ancient Rome The Hungarian-born American designer Eta Hentz transformed the loose and more accidental drapery of Ancient Rome into an evening gown that left little to chance. This neoclassical silhouette is supported by a decorative border.

BRASSIERE

First patented in 1914, it was during the 1930s that the brassiere (a term in use at least since the early 20th century) came into its own. Rather than compressing the bust, it now provided lift, support, and separation. Kestos developed a brassiere with two formed cups. The brand name derived from the Greek *cestus* or *cestos*, the magic girdle or belt of the goddess Aphrodite. Kestos also developed special brassieres for low-backed evening dresses.

Kestos brassiere

The brassière that gives you 'line'

You need the unerringly beautiful Kestos contour to do full justice to lovely knitwear.
Through nearly thirty years of changing fashion Kestos has gone on moulding an unchangingly perfect contour. There is a range of models and a choice of materials. The prices are modest as befits an essential item of everyday wear

KESTOS. REGD.   KESTOS LIMITED, MADDOX HOUSE, REGENT ST., LONDON, W.I. (Wholesale entry)

Kestos advertisement

LIVING SCULPTURES

In the short period of peace between the two world wars, designers turned to the classical era of ancient Greece and Rome. To those reeling from the horrors of World War I, classical antiquity stood for a golden time of proportion, pared-back beauty, purity, and a life-affirming appreciation of the human body.

French fashion designer Madeleine Vionnet (1876–1975) created her women's wear shapes of the 1930s from the drapery and perfect body forms of classical statues. Her twin concerns were fabric and the body. Famous for her genius with the bias cut, she draped fluid materials such as silk crêpe to create simple, loosely structured day wear and dramatic evening wear with minimal sewing and embellishment and without corsetry or petticoats. Her garments clung sensuously, shocking her customers. Early 1920s dresses with pointed drapery resemble the Greek peplos, while a dress from 1918–1919, which hangs from the shoulders with an uneven hemline and cowl neckline, recalls the *chlamys* and *chiton* from ancient Rome.

> **"** She made a Greek dress in a way the Greeks could never have imagined; there was nothing archaic about her lines. Everything Vionnet created had a cling or a flow, and women dressed by her were like moving sculptures. **"**
>
> CECIL BEATON

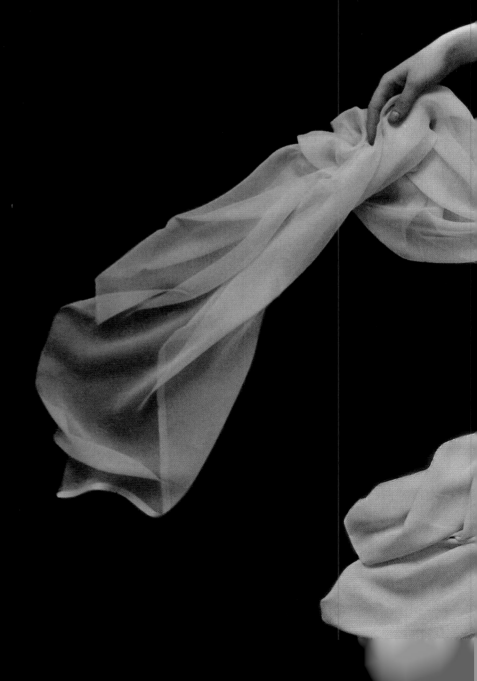

THE CLASSICAL MUSE ▷
This photograph by leading photographer George Hoyningen-Huene, c. 1931, shows Sonia, Vionnet's favorite model, looking like a graceful dancing figure from a Greek vase in her pale silk crêpe romaine pajamas and long scarf. The model had to lie down for the photographer to achieve the desired effect.

1928-1939

PARED DOWN AND SPORTY

Sports continued to play a part in pushing fashion forward, although women did not take up new sports during this period. "Form follows function" was the guiding principle for clothing worn for physical activities. This usually meant partial or complete abandonment of ornament, which resulted in a pared-down and modern look. Particularly in America, the term sportswear became common not just for clothes worn for tennis or golf, but also for resort wear designed for travel and leisure, and for casual but stylish clothing for town and country. The aviatrix Amelia Earhart designed a range of sportswear for American department stores. Pajamas—ensembles incorporating wide-legged pants—continued to be a fashionable choice for the beach and on the yacht, and provided scope for innovative designs.

FOR THE YACHT

Sailing for pleasure was a relatively new phenomenon, requiring a special set of clothing. Etiquette books and magazines advised planning so that all occasions were covered. This advertisement for Clarks shoes was probably intended to appeal to the aspirational shopper.

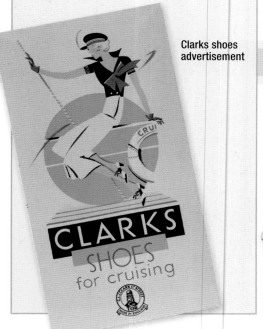

Clarks shoes advertisement

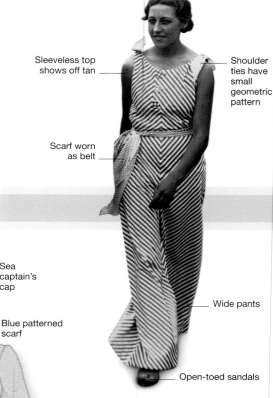

Sleeveless top shows off tan

Shoulder ties have small geometric pattern

Scarf worn as belt

Wide pants

Open-toed sandals

On the beach The English aviatrix Amy Johnson Mollison wore beach pajamas for a party in 1933. She and her husband had just flown nonstop to the US, surviving a crash-landing in Connecticut.

Sea captain's cap

Blue patterned scarf

Tight-fitting sweater

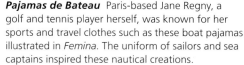

Pajamas de Bateau Paris-based Jane Regny, a golf and tennis player herself, was known for her sports and travel clothes such as these boat pajamas illustrated in *Femina*. The uniform of sailors and sea captains inspired these nautical creations.

Leather helmet

Masculine tie

Short leather trench coat

Tight jodhpurs

High, lace-up leather boots

Air-sportswoman To keep out the cold, aviators customarily wore leather clothing. Amelia Earhart, here photographed in 1928 before crossing the Atlantic, reportedly slept in her first leather jacket for three days to make it look worn.

Cloth cap

Cable-knit sweater

Hockey The goaltender of the Wiesbaden Women's Hockey Club, Germany, surveys the field during a match in 1936. Thick wool sweaters were worn by both sexes for a variety of sports, including cricket and skiing.

Leather gloves

Pants for women had side closures

Leg guard

Peaked cap with ear flaps

Suit made of red wool

Low belt echoes fashionable line

Adjustable sleeves

Narrow pants

Skiwear In the absence of special fabrics, ski clothes were usually made of wool. Elastic bands were attached to pant legs to prevent them from riding up. A matching turtleneck sweater with red stripes at the cuffs, neck, and waist completed this ensemble.

Visor

Golf blouse

Inverted pleats to ease movement

Lace-up shoes

Golf Lady Nancy Astor, the first female member of Parliament, seems to have worn shoes resembling Scottish ghillies when playing golf. In this 1933 photograph she is wearing a golf blouse, sensible pleated skirt, and visor.

DRIVING GLOVES

Gloves for driving incorporated gauntlets for practical reasons but they also began to appear as a decorative feature in fashion accessories. That this hand-sewn pair was intended for driving rather than everyday wear is indicated by the strap with which the gloves could be buttoned closely around the wrist. In a period when hand signals were still used for indicating, the reflective triangle was functional. Black and white were popular colors for women's gloves in the 1930s.

Contrasting stitching

White leather used for back of hand

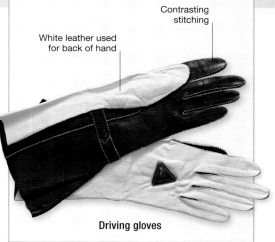

Driving gloves

HEALTH AND BEAUTY

In 1930, Mary Bagot Stack founded the Women's League of Health and Beauty. Her daughter, Prunella, became the poster girl of the league with its motto "Movement is Life." The league organized several performances of exercise routines en masse—one occasion involved 5,000 women. The official exercise uniform consisted of black satin shorts and a sleeveless white "waist" (blouse). Apparently members were advised to shave their armpits and to use deodorant.

1931–1944

RELAXING THE RULES

On the slopes, the tennis court, and the yacht the sartorial rules governing men's clothing in the city could be stretched or even abandoned. The move toward lighter fabrics continued, increasing the emphasis on the body underneath. In summer, gray, white, beige, or striped flannels (trousers made of a light wool fabric) were popular. In England their cotton or linen equivalent—white ducks—were supposed to be paired with a blue blazer only. The sport coat had emerged in the late 19th century when it could be seen in rowing clubs. Team blazers could be brightly colored, striped, or have contrasting edging, and often displayed a crest or insignia on the breast pocket. The polo shirt, despite its name, was originally worn for tennis and golf and had been around for at least a decade, but now became ubiquitous.

Polo shirt

Sport coat

Tennis rackets

Athletic shoes with rubber sole

Tennis The dark V-neck of tennis legend Fred Perry's white sweater is just discernible underneath his sport coat with club crest. A white, open-neck polo shirt completes the ensemble.

Long scarf

Cable-knit pattern

Legs exposed

Lace-up sports shoes

Boat race President of the Cambridge University crew for the annual boat race in 1937, this gentleman wears cotton sports shorts. He keeps warm with a thick cable-knit sweater and wool scarf.

Flat cap for country wear

Riding coat

Binoculars case

Riding breeches

Tight riding boots

Derby day Spectators of the steeplechase at Derby Racecourse usually dressed more formally than this gentleman. His riding breeches and boots, long-skirted riding coat, and flat cap suggest he might have owned a horse or stable.

Blazer with wide stripes

Front crease

Sandals

Beachwear In 1935, *Country Life* announced that "men can get away with more in the way of colorful beachwear." This thought might have been behind Orson Welles's choice of a striped blazer and jersey top, light trousers, and sandals.

Sikh turban

Narrow blazer with club crest

Wide-legged trousers

Pointed shoes

Punjabi prince The trousers worn by the dapper Raja Ravi-Sher Singh of Kalsia, India, at Croydon Aerodrome are almost wide enough to qualify as "Oxford bags." The Raja's slim frame is emphasized by his tight, single-breasted sport coat.

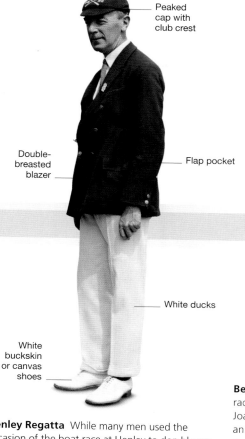

Peaked cap with club crest

Double-breasted blazer

Flap pocket

White ducks

White buckskin or canvas shoes

Henley Regatta While many men used the occasion of the boat race at Henley to don blazers in colors or stripes that declared their allegiance to a club or country, this gentleman opted for white ducks and a double-breasted blue blazer.

Cloth cap

Racing goggles

Plush or fur material

Knickerbockers

Patterned socks

Before the race German racing driver Heinrich Joachim von Morgen wears an informal attire of tweed cap, buttoned sports jacket, and knickerbockers, appropriate for a box at the Nürburgring race track.

Open collar

MDRP favored artificial silk

Waterproof fabric

Lightweight, wide shorts

Lace-up shoes

Health and comfort The Men's Dress Reform Party (MDRP) was founded in London in 1929 to rail against restrictive clothing. During a Dress Reform competition a male model poses in a waterproof jacket and shorts.

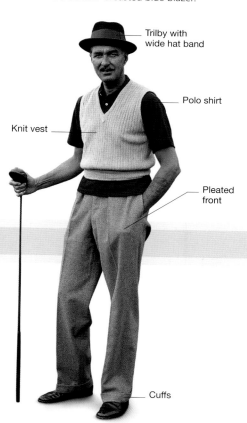

Trilby with wide hat band

Knit vest

Polo shirt

Pleated front

Cuffs

Golf *Life* magazine in 1938 declared Charles Munn, who made his money from greyhound tracks, "Palm Beach's most eligible bachelor." Here, Munn replaces the more customary plus fours with wide trousers with cuffs.

JAEGER

The London company of Jaeger had promoted wool clothing since the late 19th century. After the Prince of Wales championed the distinctive Fair Isle pattern, golf pullovers became a staple of the sports wardrobe. Both men in this advertisement wear their pullovers with shirt and tie. Matching golf hose (knee-length knit socks) were also available.

Jaeger advertisement, c. 1936

TWEED THREE PIECE

PLUS FOURS SUIT

Made popular in the 1920s by the British Prince of Wales (later King Edward VIII), plus fours (baggy breeches) had first appeared at the beginning of the century. Named for the number of inches they fell below the knee, and roomier than the more traditional knickerbockers, plus fours were respectable enough by the 1930s to be worn outside their natural environment—the golf course. This suit by Couch & Hoskin, London, is of checked tweed in brown, beige, and gray. The pattern matches exactly at every seam, a mark of good tailoring.

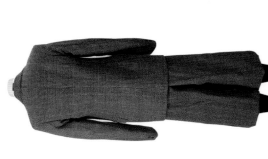

BACK VIEW

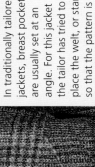

SIDE VIEW

Three button closing on jacket

Waist-level pockets with flaps

IN DETAIL

▽ **BREAST POCKET**
In traditionally tailored jackets, breast pockets are usually set at an angle. For this jacket the tailor has tried to place the welt, or stand, so that the pattern is not interrupted.

Slightly sloping shoulders

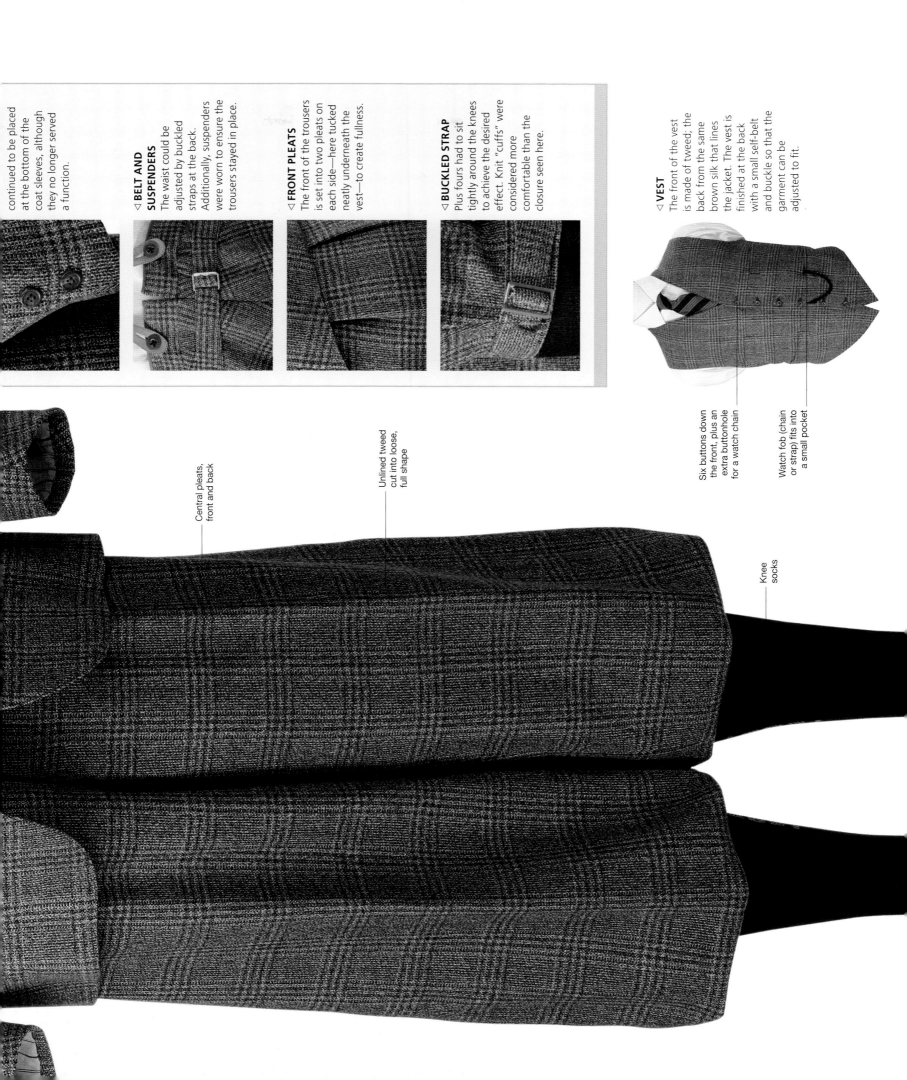

continued to be placed at the bottom of the coat sleeves, although they no longer served a function.

▽ **BELT AND SUSPENDERS**
The waist could be adjusted by buckled straps at the back. Additionally, suspenders were worn to ensure the trousers stayed in place.

▽ **FRONT PLEATS**
The front of the trousers is set into two pleats on each side—here tucked neatly underneath the vest—to create fullness.

▽ **BUCKLED STRAP**
Plus fours had to sit tightly around the knees to achieve the desired effect. Knit "cuffs" were considered more comfortable than the closure seen here.

▽ **VEST**
The front of the vest is made of tweed; the back is made from the same brown silk that lines the jacket. The vest is finished at the back with a small self-belt and buckle so that the garment can be adjusted to fit.

Central pleats, front and back

Unlined tweed cut into loose, full shape

Six buttons down the front, plus an extra buttonhole for a watch chain

Watch fob (chain or strap) fits into a small pocket

Knee socks

FASHION ICON

EDWARD VIII

△ STYLISH SUITING
This photograph from around 1936, the year of Edward's abdication, shows him in a draped suit with notched lapel, a tabbed shirt collar, and a boldly patterned handkerchief in his breast pocket.

GOLFING GEAR ▷
This iconic portrait, painted by William Orpen in 1927, highlights Edward's famed love of Fair Isle sweaters and large plus fours, which helped to bring casual sportswear into everyday dress.

Edward VIII's reign as British monarch may have been brief, but he left a lasting imprint as a fashion icon. After abdicating in 1936 to marry US divorcée Wallis Simpson, the Duke of Windsor became one of the international leaders in men's fashion and was largely responsible for the rise of casual menswear in the 1930s.

Dressing down

Charming, youthful, good looking, and with a slight frame, the blond prince was an ideal model for a revolution in tailoring. The early 1930s saw the introduction of a new style of suit that became known as the "English drape," characterized by a loose-fitting cut in the jacket, with a full chest and a defined waist. This relaxed style was promoted by Savile Row tailor Anderson & Sheppard, and Edward soon adopted this less stuffy approach. Many of Anderson & Sheppard's other high-profile clients, such as Fred Astaire and Gary Cooper, emulated the prince's style by sporting the pioneering casual look he popularized.

Edward's promotion of casual style also led to the rise of lounge suits, which increasingly superseded more formal attire from the 1920s. By the 1940s, a sweater was often worn in place of a vest. The Fair Isle sweater, previously worn only as sportswear, was widely adopted as casual wear. He also helped to promote wearing plus fours off the golf course.

Among Edward's other style statements were tweed sports jackets; low, two-tone or brown suede shoes; chalk-striped wool fabrics; bold patterns and colors,such as checked and plaid suits (including the Prince of Wales check); and belts rather than suspenders, a practice drawn from American style.

Colors, collars, and cuffs

Edward's trendsetting role extended to evening wear. His casual style included wearing double-breasted tuxedo style jackets rather than tailcoats. His love of midnight-blue evening wear also caught on, while other jacket favorites included longer hems, and lapels that extended all the way down to the bottom buttons; he preferred four buttons to the usual six.

Edward is further credited with having popularized a number of details in men's formal attire, such as tab collars, nonstiffened shirt cuffs for evening wear, cuffs on trousers, soft collars, and striped ties. The wide "Windsor" tie knot was named after him, as was the "Prince of Wales" or "Windsor" collar, widely cut to accommodate the knot.

The face of men's fashion

Edward's impact on men's fashion spread well beyond his contemporaries. His checked and plaid suits were a likely influence on the postwar American fashions for plaid sport coats and checked shirts.

More recently, designers such as Tom Ford have been inspired by his elegance and admiration for tailoring. Other innovators emulate the way in which Edward subverted and adapted traditional styles: Hedi Slimane's emphasis on a slender silhouette, Lucas Ossendrijver's loose-fitting suits, and Thom Browne's conscious revival of 1930s style through bold prints and cropped trousers, to name just a few.

More than any other factor, however, it was Edward's questioning of the conventions of male dress, along with his desire to adapt clothes to the needs of the wearer, that left a mark on men's fashion that has lasted from the 1920s to the present day.

TIMELINE

1911 Invested as Prince of Wales at Caernarfon Castle

1914 Begins his service in the army at the start of World War I

1918 Returns home at the end of World War I

▷ 1923 Cuts a dashing figure in riding outfit with double-breasted coat and leather boots

1936 Ascends the throne as King Edward VIII in January. Abdicates in December the same year

1931 Meets Wallis Simpson for the first time at the house of Lady Furness

1937 Marries twice-divorced American Wallis Simpson

1940 Installed as Governor of the Bahamas, a post he holds for five years

1945 Wallis and Edward return to Europe

1957 Gives a heart-shaped Cartier brooch with the couple's initials engraved on it to Wallis on their 20th wedding anniversary

▷ 1960 Publishes his book, *A Family Album*, charting the changes in royal life and fashions through history

○ 1910   ○ 1920   ○ 1930   ○ 1940   ○ 1950   ○ 1960

MOVIE STAR LOOKS Edward, pictured with his wife Wallis, displays his love of color and bold statement in his wide, bright trousers; patterned shirt, tie, and socks; and two-tone shoes.

1930–1940
THE ELEGANT MALE

Just as the female body had become toned and tanned during the 1920s, so the male physique had also been modified into the new ideal shape of wide shoulders, prominent chest, and narrow hips. If wholehearted participation in outdoor sports had failed to produce results, then his suit might do the trick. The master of the flattering cut was the London tailor Frederick Scholte, who distilled three characteristics of the uniform of the Household Cavalry—narrow waists, wide shoulders, and roomy armholes—into what came to be known as the "London cut." First popularized in the US by the Prince of Wales, this was soon followed by Hollywood celebrities, who began to displace the British aristocracy and upper class as fashion icons. Double-breasted coats, peaked lapels, and striped suiting were popular, since they further helped to achieve the desired athletic silhouette.

1930

Gray "topper" with dark hatband

Narrow tie knot, known as a "four in hand"

Tightly rolled umbrella

Striped trousers

Derby Day In the 1930s, morning coats would rarely have been seen on city streets but were still worn at the races. Here, Sir John Buchanan-Jardine has chosen a double-breasted waistcoat (vest) with a shawl collar to wear underneath his coat.

SUITS FOR WOMEN

In a famous scene from the 1930 film *Morocco*, Marlene Dietrich, playing a nightclub singer, performed in a black tailcoat. Dietrich also wore suits offscreen, and her studio exploited her style. Publicity photos showed Dietrich in a gray suit with black turtleneck sweater and beret, and the star turned up for a film premiere in a tuxedo. Dietrich's preference was said to have started a trend, but formal trousers for women did not really catch on.

Felt homburg

White, linen vest

Cuffs

Lounge suit Conservative politician Anthony Eden was a fashion leader. His trademark outfit was a white linen waistcoat (vest) worn with a lounge suit and his favorite silk-brimmed homburg hat, which became known as the "Anthony Eden."

Long, pointed shirt collar

Only one button closed

1936

Front crease in trousers

White canvas or buckskin shoes

White suit Born in Corsica, singer Tino Rossi performed in clubs on the French Riviera before moving to Paris in the 1930s. White suits were usually for resort wear, and were accessorized with white or tan and white shoes.

1933

White handkerchief

Double-breasted jacket

Creased trousers

Honeymoon suit Newlywed Lord Furness is dressed for a honeymoon trip in his private airplane. He wears a stylish double-breasted jacket with peaked lapels; the black carnation buttonhole may be a symbol of mourning.

1935

Butterfly bow tie

Trousers pleated at top

Mess jacket For a short period during the 1930s the tailless "mess jacket" became an alternative for the white dinner jacket in hot weather. This fashion was borrowed from military "mess dress" (formal evening wear).

Homburg hat

Peaked lapels

Flap pockets

White flannels with front crease

Reefer jacket Prince Arthur of Connaught, Queen Victoria's grandson, shows how to wear this jacket correctly. All three buttons should be closed when there are no "show" (purely decorative) buttons at the top.

1940

Stiff-fronted dress shirt

Double-breasted jacket

Front crease

Dinner jacket suit The double-breasted dinner jacket was considered slightly more informal than the single-breasted variety. It usually had shawl lapels that could be faced with gleaming satin instead of silk.

Wing collar

White bow tie

Enlarged sleeve head

Made for dancing The tails worn by the always dapper Fred Astaire in the film *Top Hat* (1935) are said to have been made by the Savile Row tailors Kilgour French & Stanbury. The coat's sleeve head was enlarged to facilitate Astaire's dance moves.

Pleated-front trousers

Lace-up dance shoes

1917–1935
BERLINER CHIC

In 1929, the writer and translator Franz Hessel published observations made during walks in Berlin. He remarked that the sight of young women in "well-fitted clothes and little hats oozing a lock of hair" should be enough to convince anyone that "Berlin is well on the way to becoming an elegant city." The many *Konfektion* (ready-to-wear) manufacturers based in Berlin had long transformed the dictates of Paris into clothes displaying the famous Berliner chic. While the "golden twenties" lasted—from around 1923 to 1929—Berlin became a magnet for artists, writers, and performers such as Josephine Baker who appeared with *La Revue Nègre* in 1925. Audiences flocked to the theaters, watched productions of the Berlin-based UFA—Germany's largest movie company—in thousand-seater cinemas, and gaped at synchronized chorus lines. Entertainment of a different kind could be found in Berlin's many gay and lesbian clubs, including the Eldorado where transvestites mingled with members of Berlin's high society.

KaDeWe

KaDeWe advertisement

Kaufhaus des Westens (Department Store of the West), or KaDeWe, was and still is one of Berlin's leading retail establishments. Opened in 1907, its 120 departments housed smaller shops. The owner hoped to satisfy the desires of Berlin's high society. This poster advertises *Lindener Samt* (velvet from Linden)—a high-quality cotton velvet.

1917

Dark stage makeup

Short skirt made of feathers or fringe

Thick tights

Dance shoes

Dance Valeska Gert first appeared on the stage during World War I. In her grotesque dance performances she parodied themes such as ballet, boxing, and prostitution. Her costume foreshadows the silhouette of the *robe de style* of the 1920s.

Ostrich-feather sash

Asymmetric hem

Strapped shoes of metallic leather

Ostrich feathers This 1925 evening gown created by the Berlin fashion house Jacob Hobe is modeled by a look-alike of the surrealist muse Lee Miller. Ostrich feathers dyed in a matching color floated around the wearer while dancing.

Wide-brimmed hat

Matching scarf

1927

Dark silk stockings

Theatrical cane

Modernism Berlin-style elegance found a home in other European capitals. In 1927, Marlene Dietrich appeared on the stage in Vienna and also found time to appear in the silent movie *Electric Café*. Here, she models a modernist day ensemble.

The Berlin look This couple, from a 1920 sheet-music cover, is dressed in the height of fashion. She wears a long jersey top over a very short skirt, while he has belted his trench coat at just the right height and brushed his hair back aviator style.

Soft toque

1920

ong jersey top with hem in contrasting color

Short, pleated skirt

Fox neckpiece

Dark stockings

Narrow trousers

Wide-skirted trench coat

1925

Ornamented bandeau

Ostrich-feather fan

Asymmetrical dropped waist

Tiered skirt

Skirt lower at back

Window shopping This mannequin, displayed in a draper's shop window, perfectly conveys the fashionable silhouette and showcases popular accessories of the period, such as the long pearl necklace and the ostrich-feather fan.

Soft, wavy hairstyle

Shoulder straps and belt encrusted with jewels

Feather boa

1935

Fluid fabric

Lamé German actress Brigitte Helm's choice of shimmering lamé might be related to the title of the science-fiction movie *Gold*, in which she starred in 1934. Metallic fabrics like lamé draped over the body and caught the light on camera.

CHORUS LINE

In 1924 Eric Charell, director of a large theater in Berlin, produced his first revue. Much of its success was due to the appearance of the famous Tiller Girls from London, who dazzled audiences with their synchronized movements. Troupes danced in identical costumes such as these skimpy ensembles with short hemlines, playful top hats, and tap shoes. One critic wrote that "the rhythm, the lightness, the exactness are electrifying."

1930–1944
ROMANTIC NOSTALGIA

There seems to be a limit to the amount of modernity and restraint fashion can endure. *Robes de style* (with loose bodices, dropped waists, and full skirts) had preserved prettiness and the traditional idea of femininity throughout the 1920s. Now diaphanous concoctions trimmed with an abundance of frills, ruffles, and lace became popular with those too young, too old, or not streamlined enough to squeeze their bodies into an unforgiving lamé or satin sheath. Adrian's design for Joan Crawford playing Letty Lynton in the eponymous 1932 film is widely credited with starting this trend. Deflated versions of the gigantic ruffled sleeves of the star's dress of white *mousseline de soie* (a thin fabric made of silk or rayon) remained fashionable until the end of the decade, and even crept into Walter Plunkett's costume designs for *Gone with the Wind* in 1939. Britain's Queen Elizabeth gave her royal seal of approval when she wore her famous "White Wardrobe," a series of romantic gowns based on Winterhalter paintings during a state visit to Paris in 1938.

1932

Diaphanous sleeve ruffles

High waist

Ruffles grow deeper toward hem

Shoes of metallic leather

Debutante look This high-waisted gown of Devonshire silk net in love-in-a-mist blue would have been considered more appropriate as evening wear than a clinging dress for a young, unmarried woman.

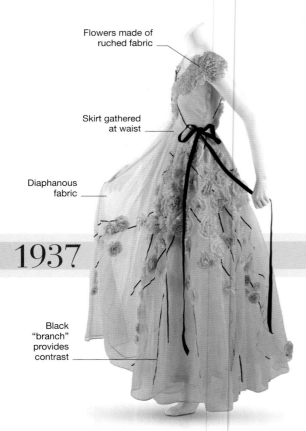

Flowers made of ruched fabric

Skirt gathered at waist

Diaphanous fabric

1937

Black "branch" provides contrast

Flower trail French designer Lanvin opted for a more sophisticated romanticism avoiding puff sleeves, ruffles, or lace. The prettiness of the flowers in different shades of pink that seem to be encircling the wearer's body is counteracted by the use of black for the tendrils or branches.

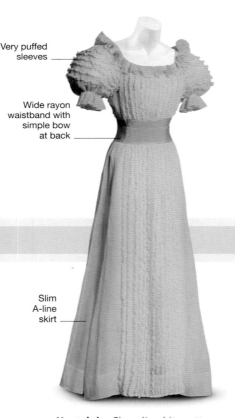

Very puffed sleeves

Wide rayon waistband with simple bow at back

Slim A-line skirt

Nostalgia Chanel's white cotton evening dress, with its slim silhouette, puffed sleeves, and low neckline, is reminiscent of Edwardian fashion. Narrow rows of delicate ruching add to the nostalgic feel of the 1937 design.

Velvet band collar

"Faggotted" seams (fabric joined with decorative stitches)

Fragility French designer Vionnet has not only used a lingerie technique for some of the decorative seams of this gown, but also a color that was fashionable for delicate underwear. The covered décolletage, elbow-length sleeves, and wide skirt contradict this association.

Deep
V-neck

Lace ruffles
form short
sleeves

Hip area is
kept slim

1932

Skirt flares
out toward
hem

Black swan French designer Chanel did not just create simple jersey gowns. The heightened prettiness of this dress, covering the wearer's body entirely in lace, is toned down by keeping the midriff silhouette simple and using black.

Sequins decorate
bodice and skirt

Gathered
tulle for
a soft,
romantic look

Gently
gathered
collar

Full,
translucent
sleeves

Organza is
lightweight and
semitransparent

1939

LETTY LYNTON EFFECT

This outfit was created by Paramount Picture's star designer Travis Banton, and modeled by the actress Lilyan Tashman. The lace jacket with its ruffled sleeves and apronlike front is a clever take on Joan Crawford's Letty Lynton gown, injecting the right dose of romanticism into a sharp, uncompromising white sheath dress.

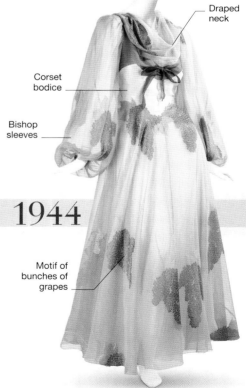

Draped
neck

Corset
bodice

Bishop
sleeves

1944

Motif of
bunches of
grapes

Victorian This embroidered tulle gown was photographed for the high-end Texan department store Neiman Marcus in 1939. Sequins encircle the skirt to create a tiered appearance, evoking the Victorian charm of a Winterhalter painting.

Organza Made from layers of delicately printed silk organza over fine netting, this meticulously crafted evening gown by Madeleine Vionnet has an ethereal beauty. Full sleeves of translucent panels and a gently gathered collar enhance the romantic style.

Contrasting shapes American Charles James created this gown for the socialite and fashion icon Millicent Rogers. The corsetlike bodice contrasts with the diaphanous silk draped softly at the neck and gathered at the wrists.

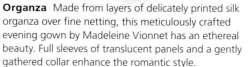

1935–1945
DREAM DRESSES

Surrealists tried to trick the subconscious into revealing itself by using methods influenced by the writings of Sigmund Freud: free association, dream analysis, and automatic writing. Seeking to achieve freedom from rationality, much of the output of this loose, Paris-centered group of artists, writers, and filmmakers had a dreamlike quality. Ordinary objects were taken out of their natural environments and plunged into new ones, creating a world "beyond realism." Many surrealists were fascinated with disguise and costume dress, and some were directly involved in the creation of fashionable clothes and imagery. Man Ray's fashion and advertising photographs were published in *Vogue* and *Harper's Bazaar*. Salvador Dali, Alberto Giacometti, Meret Oppenheim, and Jean Cocteau all collaborated with Elsa Schiaparelli on designs of clothes and accessories. Startling juxtapositions and the use of motifs from other contexts could be found in the work of several couturiers in the late 1930s and early 1940s, and surrealism continues to influence fashion today.

SURREALIST ACCESSORIES

Handbags and hats in particular lent themselves to the surrealist treatment, since they did not have to fit to the human body. These telephone and champagne bucket bags were made by Anne Marie of Paris, a store based in the Parisian Hotel Meurice in the late 1940s. Possibly the most famous surrealist accessory was a hat in the form of a high-heeled shoe turned upside down. It was based on a sketch by Salvador Dali and featured in Elsa Schiaparelli's 1937–1938 Fall/Winter collection.

Handbags

1937

Worn with underslip

Wide straps

Belt in lobster red

Dali lobster print

Silk organza and horsehair

Lobster Salvador Dali had incorporated lobsters into his work a few years prior to his collaboration with French designer Schiaparelli. Cecil Beaton photographed Wallis Simpson in one of the few copies of this dress, not long before her marriage to the Duke of Windsor.

Bands extend from sleeves

Skirt flares out below hip

Cross-over drapery

1939

Fabric printed with masks

Short fishtail

Masks Jean Cocteau designed the fabric for this dress by US-based Charles James, incorporating portraits of himself and his lover—actor Jean Marais. Cocteau denied the influence of surrealism on his work, but his movies, in particular, have surrealist qualities.

Puff sleeves

Cuffs

Contrasting ribbon feature

Horses printed on fabric

Pants worn underneath

Horses Lounging pajamas were in some ways the successors of the tea gown and could be worn for receiving guests at home. The rearing horses give a fantasy flourish to this witty example by the American designer Elizabeth Hawes.

Crin lace (horsehair net)

Puff sleeves

Slim skirt

Butterflies look as if pinned

Butterflies Dali often used symbols of transformation and change in his work, including caterpillars and butterflies. This wide-meshed "crin lace" worn over Schiaparelli's dress is reminiscent of a butterfly net.

Feathers The French House of Lanvin is not generally associated with surrealism. But the pattern of the fabric of this evening gown featuring outsize feathers tumbling to the hem, as well as the surprising name Fusée, give it a dreamlike quality.

1938

Some feathers are embroidered in red

Fine cartridge pleats

Exaggerated shoulders

Bones outlined in "trapunto"

Decoration ends at elbow

Silk crêpe fabric

Very narrow skirt

Skeleton Part of Schiaparelli's 1938 *Circus* collection, this dress is the result of another collaboration with Dali. Trapunto (stuffed technique) quilting is used to create raised shapes, resembling a human spine, ribs, and leg bones.

Printed fabric

Wide shoulders

1944

Dress provides dark background

Stallion Hollywood designer Adrian was a fan of Schiaparelli. He used textiles by Dali in some of his creations and transformed this simple black column of a gown with a menacing-looking Roan Stallion.

Boat neck

Shoulder pleats

Appliquéd decoration

1945

Colors picked up at hem

Elephant Jo Copeland's dinner dress with its appliquéd elephant and turbaned rider is faintly reminiscent of Schiaparelli's 1938 *Circus* collection. Copeland also made reference to fellow American Adrian in this design.

"
Dress designing, incidentally, is
to me not a profession but an art.

ELSA SCHIAPARELLI
"

DESIGNER
SCHIAPARELLI

Courageous and highly original, Italian-born Elsa Schiaparelli was one of the leading designers of the 1930s. Like her rival Coco Chanel, "Schiap" did not have any couture training, which seems to have made it easier for her to disregard sartorial conventions. Observing the trend toward sportswear while living in the US in the early 1920s, Schiaparelli started off with practical knitwear that already displayed her determination to inject humor into fashion. The sign outside her first establishment at 4 Rue de la Paix in Paris displayed *Pour le Sport* underneath her name, later to be joined by *Pour la Ville* and *Pour le Soir*—for the city and the evening.

Art and inventions

Schiaparelli was interested in art from a young age and published a selection of poetry as a teenager. She was not the only designer to work with artists but her collections seem to bear a more obvious trace of the influence of collaborators such as Jean Cocteau and Salvador Dali.

Like the surrealists, Schiaparelli enjoyed shaking up tradition and introduced fabric and other items into new and unexpected contexts: she used tweed for evening wear, waterproofed taffeta for raincoats, and fashioned hats into the shape of shoes and lamb cutlets. Buttons brought out particular spurts of inventiveness, and they appeared in the shape of animals, such as fish and butterflies, as well as chessmen, lollipops, and even miniature trapeze artists.

Excited by anything new, Schiaparelli worked with enterprising fabric manufacturers such as Charles Colcombet and was happy to use synthetic textiles such as rayon and nylon, and even cellophane and Rhodophane, a transparent plastic. At the same time the designer had a long-standing working relation with Lesage, the

famous Paris embroidery firm dating back to the mid-19th century. Schiaparelli was one of the first fashion designers to realize the creative potential of zippers, although, as she admitted, "King Button still reigned without fear at Schiap's," at least before World War I.

Stars of the stage and screen loved this mixture of practicality and flamboyance, and Schiaparelli counted Katherine Hepburn, Joan Crawford, Greta Garbo, and Marlene Dietrich among her clients, not forgetting Wallis Simpson, the future Duchess of Windsor.

Daring to be different

Schiaparelli delighted in wearing head-turning creations herself, remembering in her 1954 autobiography that before World War II, "People were not afraid of being different." Her clients had to have a similar attitude. When tennis star Lily d'Alvarez appeared at the Wimbledon tournament in 1931 wearing a Schiaparelli divided skirt, there was a public outcry.

Schiaparelli's signature color was a shade of magenta which she called "shocking pink," and in 1937 her perfume *Shocking* was packaged in a bottle shaped like the film star Mae West's torso. Schiaparelli introduced themed collections and in the late 1930s was inspired by music, the circus, astrology, and even shopping. Her *Cash and Carry* collection for the spring of 1940 featured large pockets.

After World War II ended, the "hard chic" look of the 1930s was replaced by ultra-feminine styles, which did not suit Schiaparelli's particular brand of creativity. While her star no longer shines as brightly as in her own lifetime, Schiaparelli's irreverent take on fashion was later emulated by Moschino and Jean Paul Gaultier.

△ **THE DIVIDED SKIRT, 1935**
Schiaparelli models one of her own creations, a *jupe-culotte* (pants-skirt), in London's Hyde Park. Considered appropriate resort wear, this kind of garment probably raised eyebrows being paraded on city streets.

◁ **THE TEARS DRESS**
Designed in collaboration with Dali for the *Circus* Collection in 1938, the textile for this evening dress and matching veil was printed to look as if it was torn, apparently revealing the shocking pink lining.

TIMELINE

1890 Born in Rome into a conservative family of aristocrats and intellectuals

1913 En route to London, attends her first ball in Paris in a blue and orange ball gown she made herself

1922 Returns to Paris where Poiret encourages her to design clothes

1919 Moves to New York where she mixes with an arty crowd including Man Ray, Marcel Duchamp, Francis Picabia, and his wife Gaby

1932 Wears slim evening dress of white crêpe with red velvet bolero in Saint Moritz, further popularizing the short evening jacket

1927 Launches her first collection of hand-knit sweaters and opens her first store at 4 Rue de la Paix a year later

▷ **1941** Moves to New York for duration of World War II. Returns to Paris in 1945 and continues to shock with new twists on evening wear

◁ **1935** Moves business to 21 Place Vendome (the "Schiap Shop"). Collaborates with artists Salvador Dali, Alberto Giacometti and, for this piece, Jean Cocteau

1954 Stops designing and publishes her autobiography *Shocking Life*

1973 Dies in Paris

O 1890   O 1920   O 1930   O 1970

◁ **A TOUCH OF THE UNUSUAL** This 1930s black crêpe dress with small turtles printed at the neckline was one purchased by Wallis Simpson. A striking black straw pole bonnet tops the outfit.

1939–1945
WOMEN IN WARTIME

During World War II, about 400,000 women joined the US army and nearly half a million women served in the British armed forces; an even greater number was involved in voluntary services. An attractive uniform could work as a recruiting tool and the blue double-breasted jacket and skirt of the British Women's Royal Naval Service (WRENS) was considered especially becoming. In contrast, *Life* magazine remarked that the "Women's Land Army is unpopular because of the drab costume." Ladies of means had uniforms made to measure at Austin Reed and Moss Bros; others had to alter and adjust the standard issue. Regulations not only governed dress—members of the Women's Auxiliary Air Force had to ensure that their hair was cut or coiffed so that it did not touch their jackets. Some services tried in vain to ban makeup, but this proved difficult to enforce.

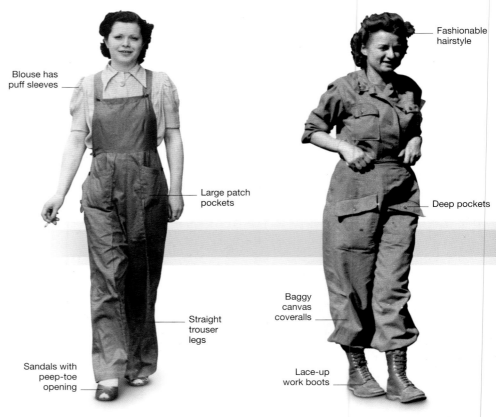

Blouse has puff sleeves

Large patch pockets

Straight trouser legs

Sandals with peep-toe opening

Overalls This young woman might have chosen her outfit because cotton overalls did not use up any of her rationing coupons. She has swapped her work shoes for peep-toe sandals.

Fashionable hairstyle

Deep pockets

Baggy canvas coveralls

Lace-up work boots

Coveralls Going about her wartime occupation, this woman sports heavy-duty coveralls and solid leather boots. Despite the masculine clothing, she maintains her femininity with her carefully styled hairdo.

KNITTING

Knitting pattern

Women were urged to assist in the war effort by knitting gloves, scarves, gum-boot stockings, knee caps, and chest protectors for "our boys in the forces." The scarcity of wool meant that knitters were encouraged to unpick their old garments. In the US, the Red Cross issued pamphlets with patterns and instructions, and was responsible for the distribution of the knit items. America's first lady, Eleanor Roosevelt, addressed a "Knit for Defense" tea in New York, and was frequently photographed knitting.

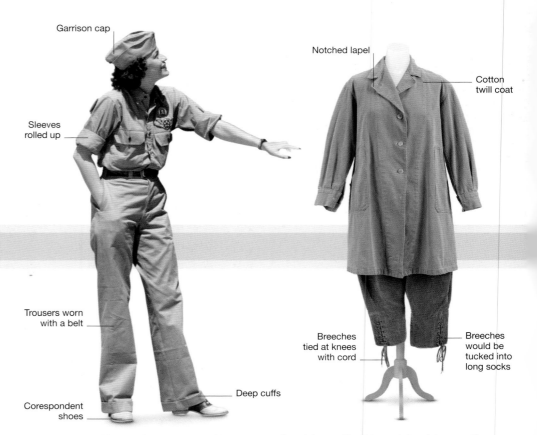

Garrison cap

Sleeves rolled up

Trousers worn with a belt

Corespondent shoes

Deep cuffs

Summer uniform This woman working in a US Naval Base in Texas wears a uniform similar to that of a US army private. The outfit is made from cotton khaki. Women's trousers usually closed at the side.

Notched lapel

Cotton twill coat

Breeches tied at knees with cord

Breeches would be tucked into long socks

Land Army The Women's Land Army uniform included corduroy or whipcord breeches and long-sleeved, cotton twill coveralls worn with brown brogues and tan knee-length socks. Recruits also wore a green V-neck sweater, tan shirt, and tie.

Felt Tyrolean-
style hat

Field
Service
cap

Canvas haversack
with ground sheet
attached

Water bottle
in cloth carrier

Skirts hang just
below knee

High-heeled
pumps

"Ammo Boots"
worn with short
canvas gaiters

ROSIE THE RIVETER

Out of patriotism, necessity, or because new opportunities became available, a very high number of women entered the workforce during the war. In the US, "Rosie the Riveter," from a well-known song, became a potent symbol of the new working women who were employed as welders and riveters on air bases. In Britain, all women between 19 and 40 had to register at their local Labour Exchange after March 1941. They were asked to choose from the women's services, civil defense, farming, or industry. At its peak, in 1943, over 80,000 women were recruited into the Women's Land Army.

Real-life
"Rosie"

CWAC cap

Hair worn in
"Victory roll"

White shirt
and tie

Brass
buttons

Canvas
shoulder bag
with leather
strap

Notched
lapel

Stripes and
"curls"

Sari
replaces
skirt

Skirt hangs
16 in (40 cm)
off the ground

Brown
stockings

Soldier's sweetheart The man is in his British Army combat uniform (P-37 or pattern 37). The pattern was based on skiwear of the time. His girlfriend's coat has fashionably wide shoulders and a swing skirt. She wears a small-brimmed hat—hats did not require coupons.

Army corps The uniform of the Canadian Women's Army Corps (CWAC) consisted of a drab-colored baratea (fine wool) jacket and skirt worn with a khaki drill shirt, brown necktie, and canvas bag.

WRINS The Women's Royal Indian Naval Service based its uniform on that of the WRENS, their British equivalent. However, instead of a skirt, they wore a sari with a slightly longer jacket, white shirt, and tie.

KHAKI TUNIC AND SKIRT

WOMEN'S LEGION

This khaki uniform was worn by a volunteer in the Women's Legion, working alongside ARP (Air Raid Precaution) wardens in England in World War II. The corps was founded by the Marchioness of Londonderry during World War I and at its peak had more than 6,000 members working directly with the army in catering and transportation. During World War II, Legion members continued to act as drivers for the military and run canteens and support victims in the aftermath of bombing raids.

△ **LEGION RECRUIT**
Legion officer Sybil Davis wears the corps' badges on her lapels and cap, and has leather gauntlets for driving.

SIDE VIEW

BACK VIEW

IN DETAIL

▽ **SHOULDER FLASH**
All ranks other than officers wore shoulder flashes bearing the words "Women's Legion." Officers wore a narrow red braiding below their rank badges.

Collar is unpinned

Service stripes on sleeve

Fitted long-line tunic flares from the waist and skims the hips

...bearing the Legion letters was retained for buttons on the epaulets and pockets, and closing the tunic or jacket.

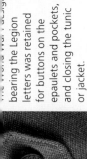

▽ **SHIRT AND TIE**
Civilian coupons were needed for the shirt and tie. Jewelry and handbags were not permitted and only a minimum of makeup was allowed.

▷ **POCKETS**
Notebook pockets had to be worn flat; slouching with hands in pockets was forbidden.

▷ **LEATHER BELT**
The broad belt has equipment loops and a stud and keeper to hold the end in position.

▽ **SMART TAILORING**
Side and back vents shape the tunic and allow freedom of movement. Members were required to wear full uniform correctly when working in the corps, and to maintain a "smart alert bearing" at all times.

A-line skirt

Neutral stockings

Leather brogues with a low heel

Regulation hemline ends 14in (35cm) above the ground

1939–1946
MENSWEAR ON CIVVY STREET

American General Limitation Order L-85 and Britain's austerity regulations had a greater effect on women's fashion than on men's. Menswear features such as patch pockets, "fancy backs," pants cuffs, and the buckles on vest adjusters were abandoned, but this did not make much difference to the wide-legged, long-coated silhouette. More important were wartime shortages, which played their part in the demise of different suit types for different occasions. Even before the war, an ample wardrobe had been beyond the reach of most men. Now demobilized servicemen were issued with one "civvy" suit only, and opinion differed on whether the, usually, good-quality cloth made up for the poor fit. Clothes-conscious youth cultures began to emerge—the male Latinos of Los Angeles and the *Petits Swings* or *Zazous* of occupied Paris used fabric-consuming drape shapes, wide peg trousers, and low-slung key chains to signal their disaffection.

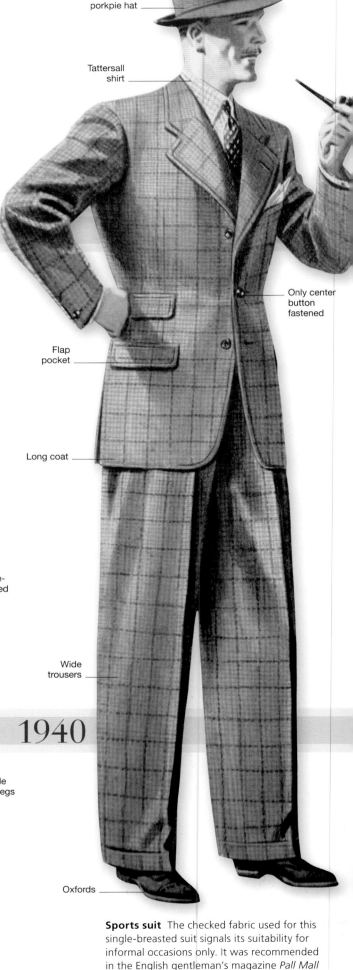

Snap brim, porkpie hat

Tattersall shirt

Only center button fastened

Flap pocket

Long coat

Wide trousers

Oxfords

Sports suit The checked fabric used for this single-breasted suit signals its suitability for informal occasions only. It was recommended in the English gentleman's magazine *Pall Mall Fashions* for Fall/Winter 1940.

SPIVS AND WIDE BOYS

The origin of the word "spiv" applied to a salesman is unknown, but the similar term "wide boy" could come from a penchant for thickly striped suits, generous lapels, or wide, showy ties. A British phenomenon, spivs waited on street corners, especially in London's East End, for business that would come their way. The spiv of wartime cartoons wore his suits double-breasted, his soft hat angled, and his mustache neatly trimmed.

Workingman's cap

Wide lapels

Double-breasted jacket

Pinstripe cloth

Very wide trouser legs

Light-colored shoes

1939

1940

Parisian casual The flat cap and slightly ill-fitting suit, worn with a sweater instead of a vest, by this young French civilian in the first year of the war suggest that he is a man of slender means.

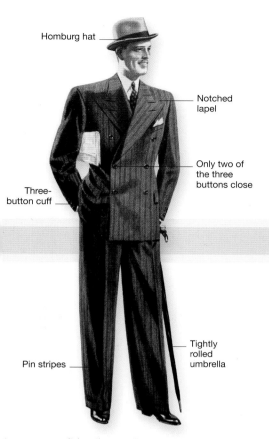

Homburg hat

Notched lapel

Only two of the three buttons close

Three-button cuff

Pin stripes

Tightly rolled umbrella

1941

In town English tailors traditionally called a single-breasted jacket a lounge coat and a double-breasted jacket a reefer coat. This example was described as a "two-button (show three) D.B. Reefer Suit," appropriate for city wear.

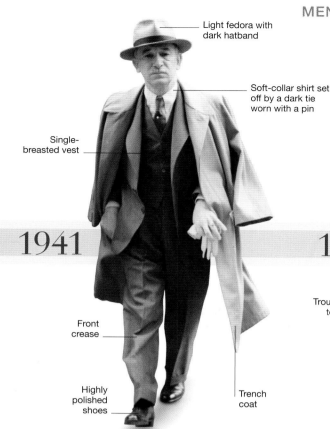

Light fedora with dark hatband

Soft-collar shirt set off by a dark tie worn with a pin

Single-breasted vest

Front crease

Highly polished shoes

Trench coat

Muted elegance The always dapper Eduard Beneš, President of Czechoslovakia in exile, arrived at his London offices wearing a long-coated, three-piece lounge suit underneath a trench coat.

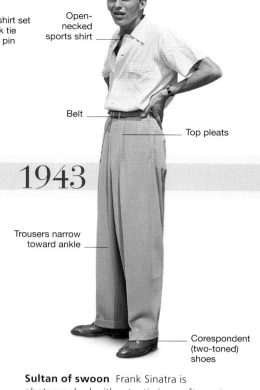

Open-necked sports shirt

Belt

Top pleats

Trousers narrow toward ankle

Corespondent (two-toned) shoes

1943

Sultan of swoon Frank Sinatra is photographed without a tie in a soft sports shirt, wide-cuffed peg trousers, and corespondent shoes. For suits, he favored big knots when wearing four-in-hand ties.

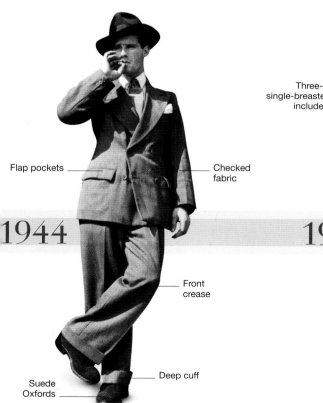

Flap pockets

Checked fabric

1944

Front crease

Deep cuff

Suede Oxfords

Wide boy The clothes and the attitude of this young Londoner nonchalantly smoking display several "wide-boy" characteristics: a double-breasted suit, a hat worn at a rakish angle, and a wide tie.

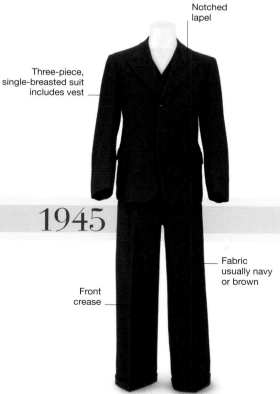

Notched lapel

Three-piece, single-breasted suit includes vest

1945

Front crease

Fabric usually navy or brown

Demob suit When a British soldier had completed his wartime service he had to report to a demobilization center to be processed for civilian life. His gear was exchanged for a three-piece, single-breasted or two-piece, double-breasted suit.

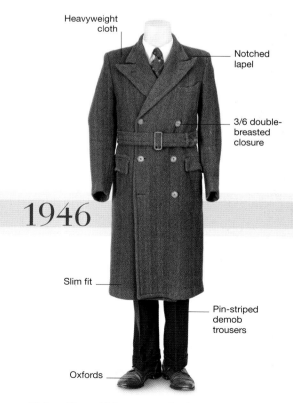

Heavyweight cloth

Notched lapel

3/6 double-breasted closure

Slim fit

Pin-striped demob trousers

1946

Oxfords

Ulster "Demob" boxes contained a coat usually of the raincoat variety. This belted Ulster, a sporty take on a traditional style, was popular in the 1940s. Double-breasted versions required more fabric than utility coats.

1939–1945
FASHION ON RATION

In March 1941, the British government imposed austerity regulations limiting the amount of materials as well as features such as pleats and buttons that could be used in a garment's production. In June of the same year rationing was introduced to ensure clothes were allocated fairly. Ration books were issued, and set numbers of coupons had to be presented when buying clothing, cloth, footwear, and yarn for knitting. More specific guidelines were applied to garments produced as part of the Utility Clothing Scheme. Clothes marked with the distinctive CC41 (Civilian Clothing 1941) label had to adhere to government-set quality standards and were price controlled. In May 1942, members of the Incorporated Society of London Fashion Designers were asked by the Board of Trade to contribute designs to a utility range to persuade women that austerity could be chic. British *Vogue* declared that the new silhouette, "straighter, trim and businesslike," was the only one to follow.

Long-sleeved jacket

Hat worn at jaunty angle

Flap pocket

Darted for fitted waist

Gored skirt

1939

Hemline just below knee

Short and full This *Vogue* pattern was published just as Britain declared war against Germany. The shortness of the skirt remained a feature of wartime clothing but its fullness was soon to become a thing of the past.

AUSTERITY SHOES

Leather was needed for army purposes, so an alternative material for shoe soles had to be found. Wood soles could be bought coupon-free, but were disliked because they were stiff and noisy to walk in. Split wooden soles attached by a leather hinge were an attempt to solve the problems. The traditional Bavarian walking shoe, the *Haferlschuh*, provided the inspiration for a widely produced style that incorporated side lacing and piping in contrasting colors. On the footwear front, women were seen to be at a disadvantage since their shoes tended to wear out more quickly than men's. There were complaints that women were using all the family's coupons.

Hinged wooden sole

Utility lace-up

Puff shoulder

Fair Isle pattern knit from used wool

Only two box pleats allowed per dress

Moygashel Crease-resistant moygashel, an artificial fiber made from a viscose/polyester blend, was used for this dress. Patterned knitwear made use of many short lengths of wool, obtained by unraveling old garments.

Contrasting edge

Wide shoulders

Large clutch bag

1943

Deep hem

Leather pumps

Ready-to-wear When first asked to design for the ready-to-wear company Berketex, London couturier Norman Hartnell refused, believing it would harm his status. He later changed his mind and designed stylish utility dresses.

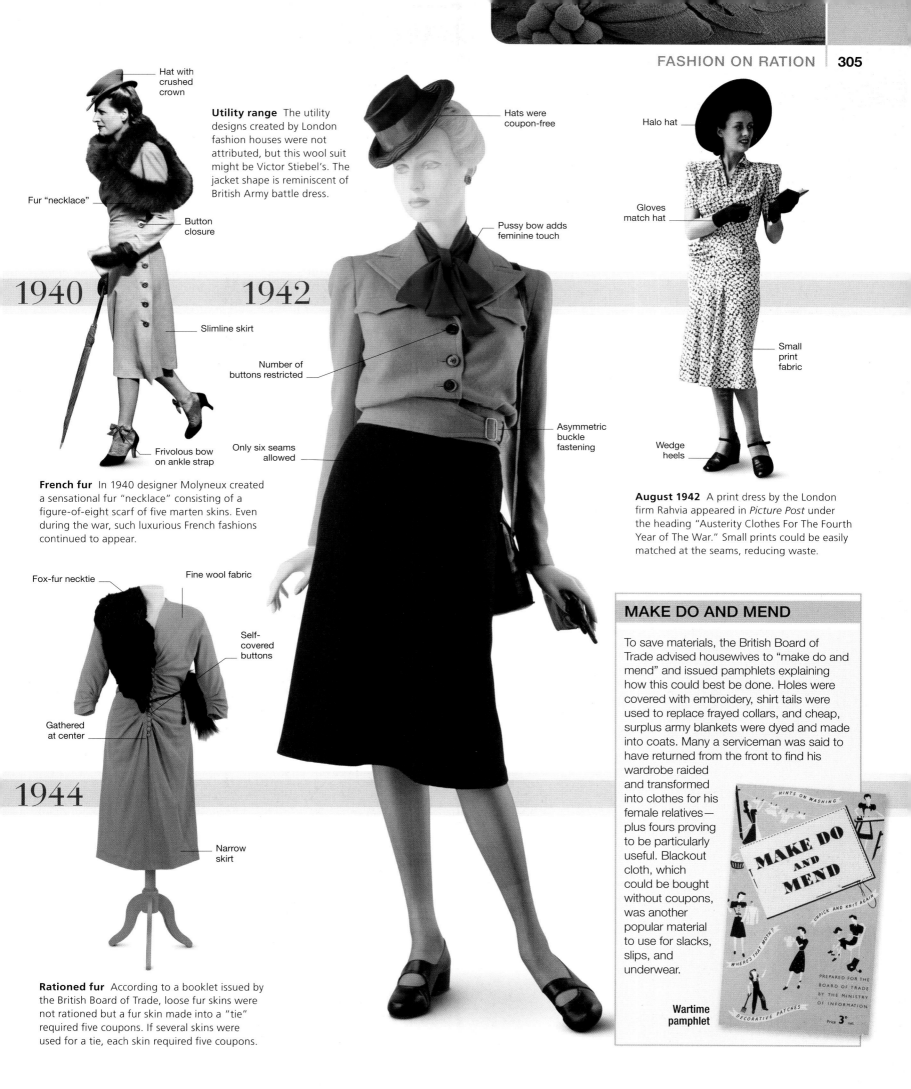

1940

Hat with crushed crown

Fur "necklace"

Button closure

Slimline skirt

Frivolous bow on ankle strap

French fur In 1940 designer Molyneux created a sensational fur "necklace" consisting of a figure-of-eight scarf of five marten skins. Even during the war, such luxurious French fashions continued to appear.

1944

Fox-fur necktie

Fine wool fabric

Self-covered buttons

Gathered at center

Narrow skirt

Rationed fur According to a booklet issued by the British Board of Trade, loose fur skins were not rationed but a fur skin made into a "tie" required five coupons. If several skins were used for a tie, each skin required five coupons.

1942

Utility range The utility designs created by London fashion houses were not attributed, but this wool suit might be Victor Stiebel's. The jacket shape is reminiscent of British Army battle dress.

Hats were coupon-free

Pussy bow adds feminine touch

Number of buttons restricted

Only six seams allowed

Asymmetric buckle fastening

Halo hat

Gloves match hat

Small print fabric

Wedge heels

August 1942 A print dress by the London firm Rahvia appeared in *Picture Post* under the heading "Austerity Clothes For The Fourth Year of The War." Small prints could be easily matched at the seams, reducing waste.

MAKE DO AND MEND

To save materials, the British Board of Trade advised housewives to "make do and mend" and issued pamphlets explaining how this could best be done. Holes were covered with embroidery, shirt tails were used to replace frayed collars, and cheap, surplus army blankets were dyed and made into coats. Many a serviceman was said to have returned from the front to find his wardrobe raided and transformed into clothes for his female relatives—plus fours proving to be particularly useful. Blackout cloth, which could be bought without coupons, was another popular material to use for slacks, slips, and underwear.

Wartime pamphlet

HINTS ON WASHING

MAKE DO AND MEND

UNPICK AND KNIT AGAIN

WHERE'S THAT MOTH?

DECORATIVE PATCHES

PREPARED FOR THE BOARD OF TRADE BY THE MINISTRY OF INFORMATION

Price **3°** net.

STYLED BY HOLLYWOOD

Hollywood became a big fashion influence in the 1930s. Movie-going was a major hobby and alluring movie outfits provided escapism from the Depression and the war in Europe. Animal prints flourished after the *Tarzan* movies; while bias-cut, satin, Jean Harlow-style evening wear and Katharine Hepburn's casual look found numerous admirers.

A white frothy confection stole the show in the 1932 movie *Letty Lynton*. Worn by Joan Crawford, the gown's huge sleeves helped popularize the padded-shoulder line, promoted by Schiaparelli, of the 1930s and '40s. New York department store Macy's was said to have sold thousands of copies. The *Letty Lynton* gown was designed by legendary Hollywood costumier Adrian (Gilbert Adrian, 1903–1959); other influential contemporary Hollywood designers included Edith Head, Travis Banton, and Walter Plunkett. For *The Women* (1939), a hit movie about Manhattan socialites (shown here), Adrian gave each central character a distinct look. The movie was shot in black and white but with a short Technicolor fashion-show sequence featuring avant-garde Adrian designs that caused a stir. Small, jauntily angled hats like those worn by the cast became very popular in the US at this time, while Adrian's pill box, slouch, and trench coat styles were already much copied from Garbo movies. His square-shouldered look for Crawford (right) became a popular 1930s and '40s silhouette.

Hollywood's ascent in the fashion industry was helped because designers had to create outfits that looked ahead of the trend by the time the movie was released. The fashions were then copied by retailers and American design started to move away from Paris—"historical" couture styles of the 1930s, for example, borrowed from Hollywood costume.

> 66
>
> We, the couturiers, can no longer live without the cinema any more than the cinema can live without us. We corroborate each other's instinct.
>
> **LUCIEN LELONG,** 1935
>
> 99

MOVIE FASHION PARADE ▷

In this still from *The Women* (1939), cast members, including Norma Shearer (seated, white hat), Joan Crawford (standing, extravagant plumes), and Rosalind Russell (knitting), are shown outfits at a high-end fashion house.

1935–1944
AMERICAN READY-TO-WEAR

Following the invasion of Paris in June 1940, the rest of Europe and the United States were cut off from French couture for four years. During the previous decade, American fashion designers had begun to develop a distinctive style, focusing on easy-to-wear, modern clothing as opposed to the elaborate and elite confections of Paris. Practicality was one prominent characteristic, and resulted in the use of easy-care fabrics, adaptable styles, and capsule wardrobes with elements that could be interchanged. The need for simplicity required by mass production was not seen as a hindrance but was used to advantage. The work of New York-based, ready-to-wear designers was promoted as symbolic of American values such as democracy, pioneer spirit, and a pragmatic approach to life. The creations of made-to-measure designers such as Valentina and Adrian, who continued in the couture tradition, were less aligned with national identity.

1935

Tyrolean-style hat

Hair in neat waves

Wide inset mimics blouse and jacket

White cuffs

Slim silhouette

Stylish day shoes

Luncheon wear High society continued to wear different types of clothing at different times of day. This dress by Mme. Clayton of New York is being modeled during a fashion benefit luncheon at New York's luxury Versailles Restaurant.

ON FIFTH AVENUE

The recognition of home-grown design talent in America depended heavily on the Fifth Avenue department store Lord & Taylor, particularly the promotional activities of Dorothy Shaver, who became the store's vice president in 1931. In 1932, at the height of the Great Depression, a series of window displays featured the work of New York designers rather than the manufacturers they worked for. A year later a press release extolled the output of what was called "The American Designers' Movement," and in 1938 the store inaugurated the annual $1,000 Lord & Taylor American Design awards. In 1945 the store launched another campaign to promote "The American Look," a phrase they also copyrighted.

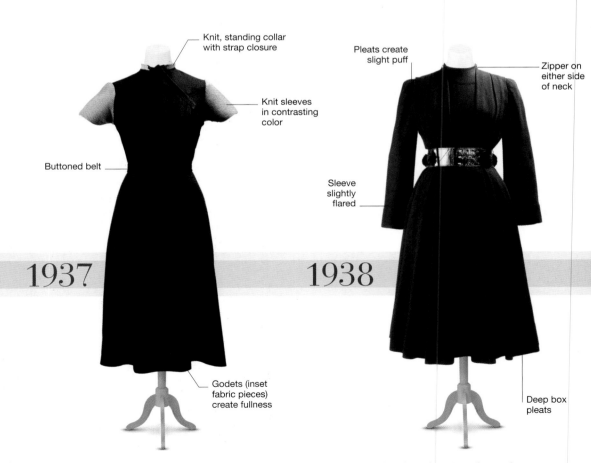

Knit, standing collar with strap closure

Knit sleeves in contrasting color

Buttoned belt

1937

Godets (inset fabric pieces) create fullness

Contrasts This witty design by Claire Potter incorporates a knit collar and sleeves. Although Potter was known as a great colorist, she used a pared-down palette for this dress. Her designs emphasized the figure.

Pleats create slight puff

Zipper on either side of neck

Sleeve slightly flared

1938

Deep box pleats

Slip-on style This pleated version of one of Claire McCardell's most famous designs, the "Monastic" is made of open-weave wool. Zippers on either side of the neck allow the dress to be slipped on; a wide belt provides the shape.

Straw beret

Stand-up collar

Off-white silk blouse

Long coat and skirt

Velvet trim

Simple lines Designer Helen Cookman produced good-quality, ready-to-wear lines and was known for her tailored clothes and tweeds. The simple line of this ensemble is underlined by the use of velvet trim in strategic places.

Halter neck (cut low at back)

Dart below bust

Denimlike fabric

Contrast stitching

Deep patch pockets

Hem below knees

Soft tricorn hat

Bishop sleeves

Metallic trim

Belt trim adds interest

Skirt slightly flared

Hemline well below knee

Smart casual The simple design of this green knit dress is enlivened by the metallic fastening at the collar and the belt. Described as a "sports dress," it would have been regarded as stylish casual wear for town and country.

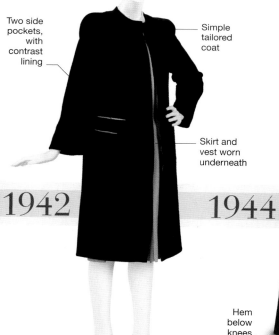

Two side pockets, with contrast lining

Simple tailored coat

Skirt and vest worn underneath

1942   1944

Coordinating separates This 1942 ensemble by Vera Maxwell includes a bloomer playsuit, skirt, vest, and tailored coat, all made from artificially produced fabrics developed by American companies.

Vacation clothes Claire McCardell designed this practical resort-wear ensemble for Townley Frocks. The skirt and halter top could be interchanged with shorts and a slip-on blouse. McCardell liked to use practical, easy-care fabrics like "everfast cotton."

FOOTWEAR TRENDS

Before the war, Paris not only dictated fashionable silhouettes but was the source of inspiration for accessories. American shoe manufacturer Delman—founder of one of the top footwear brands in the US—opened a design studio in Paris, so that he could keep up with the latest trends in shoes. The designs he brought back to sell in America during the 1930s had the added fashion credibility of being Paris models.

Parisian influence was lost during the war, but made a comeback toward the late 1940s. At this time Italian shoe design also started to gain fashion credence with the production of light, elegant sandals with slimmed-down heels. The two pairs of American shoes illustrated below show the influence of the new European designs, featuring cutaway sections that reveal more of the foot, and higher, slimmer heels than in previous years.

Peep toes   **Cutaway sides**

1943–1946
COMPETITIVE COURE

Commenting on the Paris Spring Collections of 1945, American *Vogue* noted "a very slight tendency toward the longer skirts, Balenciaga, Lelong, and Rochas showing them a bit more below the knee." The supremacy of French couture had been challenged during World War II, with Norman Hartnell claiming that London fashion designers had given "the home product a stability and elegance which hitherto was possessed by Paris alone." After the Liberation of Paris in August 1944, the fight for the place at the top of the fashion tree and the search for a new silhouette began. French designers did not waste time and soon dispatched their latest outfits to cities in Europe and the US. In London, the 1946 Britain Can Make It exhibition showcased 5,000 goods destined for export, including ready-to-wear and couture clothing, which were seen by almost 1.5 million visitors. In October 1945, *Life* magazine declared that "New York custom dresses are high fashion." But could the US and Britain resist the lure of Paris chic?

1943

American style This soft wool coat by ready-to-wear designer Monte-Sano strikes a bold silhouette. The width of fabric over the shoulder pads is gathered into deep folds at the waist and forms an extremely full skirt.

Simple, black head scarf

Extremely wide, padded shoulders

Belted waistband

Double-breasted closure

UTILITY CLOTHING

1944 advertisement

Austerity Regulations, which had simplified the female silhouette, were lifted in England in 1946, but clothes rationing continued for another three years. Utility clothing had ensured that good-quality garments were available to all at modest and regulated prices, and was not phased out until 1952. This 1944 advertisement for the utility range of the London ready-to-wear company Jaeger shows the wide shoulders and short skirts typical of the war years; the narrowing waists and the slight flare of the skirt on the right are pointers to the future.

1946

Square shoulders

Fitted waistband

Crescent-shaped clutch bag with wide strap

Gathering over hips for a fuller skirt

Dark gloves

Braided "crown"

Skirt just below knee

Spring fashions Despite being part of the Spring Utility collection, this dress shows a more balanced and feminine silhouette than earlier in the decade. The slight gathering into the skirt increases emphasis on the waist and hips.

V-necks Despite cloth shortages, very wide shoulders became fashionable toward the end of the war. These two outfits are variations on a theme: V-necks, narrow waists, skirts with pleats on either side of a flat front, and dark accessories.

Herringbone pattern

Seams used for shaping and emphasis

Narrow skirt with box pleats

Charles James The complex seams of this herringbone wool suit by US-based Charles James emphasize the outfit's silhouette and accentuate the nipped-in waist by approaching it from the sleeves. The central button draws further attention to the waistline.

1945

Cossack-style hat

Wide shoulders

Sleeves narrow toward wrist

Hem just below knee

Balenciaga The straight shoulders and boxy silhouette seen in England in the war years were not so prominent in Paris. The narrow waist and the full upper sleeves of Balenciaga's wool coat, plus a large hat, introduce drama.

Hat with tall crown

Collar in contrasting fabric

Cinched-in waist

Vanity case

Peep-toe, sling-back sandals

Wide shoulders Having made the first transcontinental rail trip from Los Angeles to New York, this passenger disembarks in style in a wide-shouldered jacket with a narrow waist, slim skirt, and a spotted veil.

THEATER DE LA MODE

In 1945, French couturiers staged what *Harpers Bazaar* called "a luxurious puppet show" to collect funds for war survivors and to revive the French fashion industry. Each house donated up to five outfits, as well as accessories, to dress more than 170 fashion dolls. After a debut in Paris in March 1945, shows followed in London, Leeds, Copenhagen, Stockholm, and Vienna before the mannequins arrived in New York in May 1946, now clad in the latest spring/summer collection. While they had been traveling a fashion revolution had occurred.

Tuxedo front

Full skirt

Peep-toe sandals

Balmain The first postwar Paris shows caused both indignation and admiration. Luxuriously full skirts, as seen in Pierre Balmain's coat and candy-striped dress, stood in contrast to the dire circumstances in which many Parisians still lived.

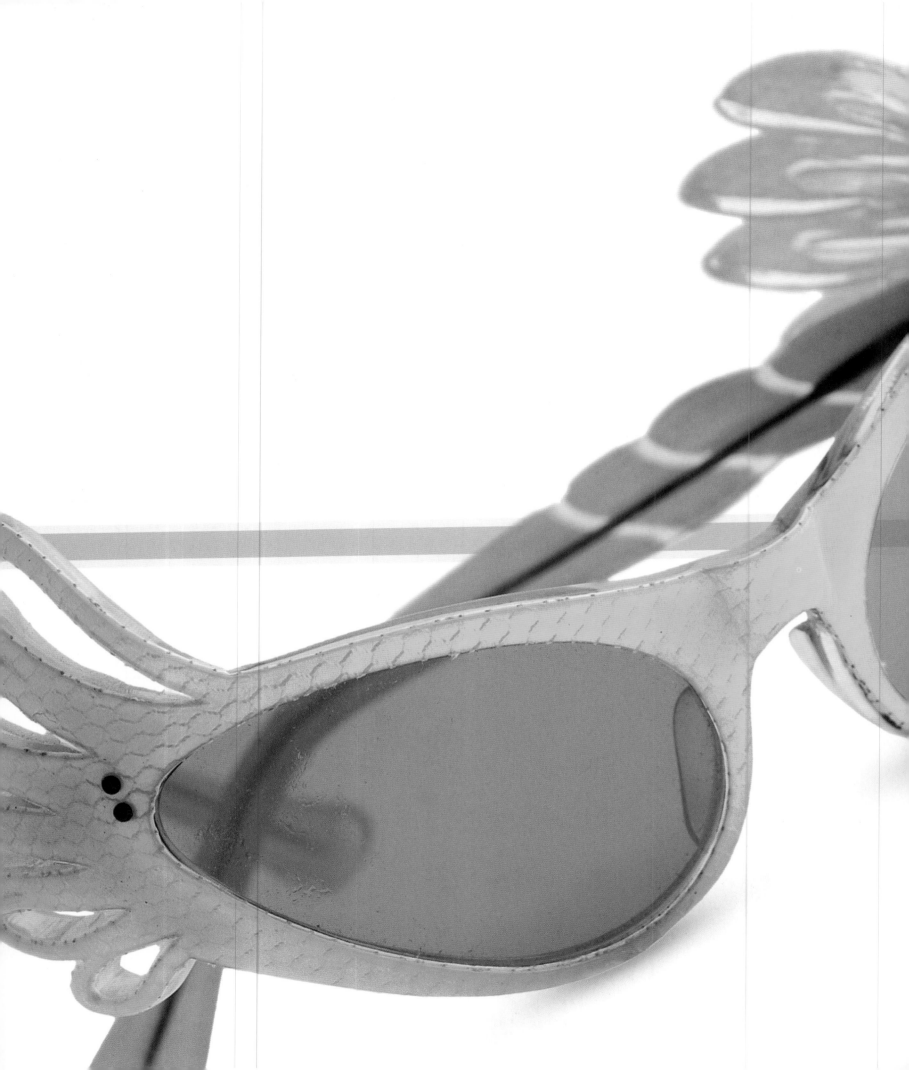

OPTIMISM
AND YOUTH

1947–1963

OPTIMISM AND YOUTH

Most of Europe faced a long period of recovery following World War II, but France's fashion industry resurfaced quickly, with the Chambre Syndicale ensuring that the Paris couture houses could open and show collections. On a cold February day in 1947, Christian Dior showed his *La Corolle* collection, sowing the seeds of glamour and creating the basic shape of fashion for the next decade. In Britain, clothes rationing lasted until 1950, but Mayfair couturiers such as Hardy Amies produced their version of Dior's "New Look" for English women eager for new styles in a drab postwar world.

Europe and America

Buyers from North America traveled to Paris to secure toiles (mock-ups of garments) to reproduce "Paris Fashions" in the major department stores back home. In Hollywood, costume designers including Helen Rose and Edith Head were inspired by the styles coming from Paris, and produced their own versions, including the ice-cool, elegant clothes worn by stars like Grace Kelly in Hitchcock's *Rear Window*. There was a connection between Italian style, traditionally excellent for knitwear and printed silk, and American fashion, perhaps through the GIs stationed in Italy during the war, perhaps through mass emigration to the US. Designers in both countries, such as Tina Leser and Claire McCardell in America and Emilio Pucci in Italy, produced stylishly casual clothes, as opposed to the more formal feel of French and British fashion. This easier approach to dressing struck a chord, particularly with younger women.

New consumers

Against the backdrop of an uncertain world haunted by the Cold War and an insidious nuclear threat, young people developed their own culture. A new term was coined—"the teenager"—and they wanted clothes just for themselves. There was a new breed, too, of cultural hero or role model, men like Elvis Presley who wore leather flight jackets and other military surplus, and young men wanted to look like him. Work wear and denim blue jeans also crossed boundaries and became fashion wear for both young men and young women.

COSTUME DESIGNER
Edith Head designed costumes for movie stars including Gloria Swanson, Janet Leigh, and Grace Kelly. She won the Oscar for Best Costume Design eight times.

1947 · 1948–50 · 1951–52

1947
Princess Elizabeth of Great Britain marries Lieutenant Philip Mountbatten; her Norman Hartnell wedding dress is the main topic of conversation.

◀ Academy award

1948
The 21st academy awards introduces an award for Best Costume Design.

1949
Dorothy Shaver, president of Lord and Taylor department store, launches a line of casual but elegant sportswear dubbed "The American Look." It is based on an earlier advertising campaign featuring designs by Claire McCardell, Clare Potter, and Bonnie Cashin.

1950
Father of the Bride, starring Spencer Tracy and Elizabeth Taylor, is released. The lace wedding dress worn by Taylor in the movie is considered one of her most iconic looks.

▼ Elizabeth Taylor in *Father of the Bride*

▲ Christian Dior

1947
Dior shows his first collection, immediately named "The New Look" by American fashion editor Carmel Snow, putting Paris back on the fashion map.

1951
American disc jockey Alan Freed popularizes the term "rock 'n' roll." New teen styles emerge linked to the music, such as "Teddy boys" and prom dresses.

▲ Rock-'n'-roll-style, poodle skirt

1952
Jack Kerouac publishes *On the Road*, which inspires a generation of beatniks who wear slim-fitting, black clothes, berets, and dark glasses. Audrey Hepburn's *Funny Face* in 1957 further popularizes the style.

▶ Original scroll manuscript for *On the Road*

1952
Balenciaga shows the sack dress, an early stylistic move toward looser-fitting garments, which appear in the late 1950s and '60s, and include cocoon coats and shift dresses.

66

Fashion is not frivolous. It is part of being alive today.

MARY QUANT, FASHION DESIGNER, 1960s

99

1953–54	1955–56	1957–58	1959–60	1961–62	1963

1953
Coronation of Queen Elizabeth II, and London couturiers including John Cavanagh, Victor Stiebel, and Mattli make ball gowns for guests at coronation balls and dances.

1955
Rebel Without a Cause is released, launching its star, James Dean, as a style icon for the rising youth culture. His death a year later cements his legendary status.

◀ *Rebel Without a Cause* poster

1953
The Wild One is released; Marlon Brando's representation of disaffected youth popularizes blue jeans and leather jackets.

1953
Pierre Cardin shows his first collection in Paris.

1957
Jailhouse Rock, starring Elvis Presley, marks the spread of rock-'n'-roll style.

▼ Scene from *Jailhouse Rock*

▲ Brunette Barbie in brocade dress and coat (available 1959–1964)

1959
Debut of Barbie doll, marketed as a "Teen-age Fashion Model."

▲ John F. Kennedy is sworn in while Jackie Kennedy, wearing a gray coat by Oleg Cassini paired with a pillbox hat and fur muff, looks on

1961
John F. Kennedy becomes president. His wife, first lady Jacqueline Kennedy, soon becomes a fashion icon.

1954
Easy-to-wash and easy-to-dry nylon twinsets advertised in British *Vogue* fashion magazine.

1955
Stiletto heels are popular by the mid-1950s, aided by new technology. Ultrathin, ultrahigh steel heels could sustain great pressure in comparison to wood heels.

1961
Fur coats are much sought after because they are seen as a status symbol. Movements in the following decades protest vigorously against the wearing of fur.

◀ Full-length fur coat with shawl collar and wide cocoon shape

1963
The Beatles make their first national TV appearance. Their identical haircuts became a popular look among young men on both sides of the Atlantic.

▼ "Beatlemania" takes hold and the group's look is widely copied

1955
Mary Quant opens her influential store, Bazaar, in London.

1962
The Sidney Janis Gallery in New York exhibits works by contemporary American pop artists and the "Nouveau Réalisme" movement in a groundbreaking show called the "International Exhibition of the New Realists."

◀ Mary Quant's store on the King's Road

1956
Movie star Grace Kelly marries Prince Rainier of Monaco in a religious ceremony, wearing a lace wedding dress designed by Helen Rose.

1958
The youthful Yves Saint Laurent shows his first collection at Dior—*Trapeze*—after Dior's death in 1957.

1959
Lycra, also known as spandex or elastane, is invented. It revolutionizes performance sportswear and then fashionable dress.

1947–1955
THE NEW LOOK

Two years after the end of World War II, French haute couture designer Christian Dior introduced the New Look. The silhouette he defined had its beginnings in the late 1930s, but during the war its development was put on hold until couturiers started showing again in 1944. Other designers were also working on similar skirt shapes but the fashion media credited Dior with the inception of the New Look. Dior's collection—his first—marked a change from the shapes of the previous decade. Before and during the war a square-shouldered and boxy utility suit, which saved on fabrics during rationing, was prominent. The New Look collection, launched in February 1947, included rounded or sloped shoulders; a tiny, nipped-in waist (achieved via a short corset and other undergarments); padded and rounded hips; and a very full skirt with heavy pleating. Extra fabric and a slip helped to create the skirt's fullness.

Rounded shoulder

Nipped-in waist

Padded hips

1947

Pleated full skirt

New Look defined The design that started it all, this *Bar Suit* of 1947 by Dior defined the silhouette of the 1950s. Carmel Snow, American editor of *Harper's Bazaar*, called the collection the "New Look" and the name stuck.

Demure dressing
French couturier Jacques Heim designed this New Look–inspired dress in 1950. Less flamboyant than his colleagues, Heim designed couture that was both utilitarian and ladylike for clients. He also launched a line aimed specifically at a younger clientele.

Silk grosgrain bodice with faux-pearl button fastening

Padded hips

Box pleats for fullness

1950

Round red buttons

Accentuated waist

Rounded shoulder line

Sculptural wasp waist

1952

Fabric released from pleats

Ankle-strap sandals

Casual elegance

Matching red shoes

NEW LOOK UNDERWEAR

Those re-creating the New Look style utilized separate undergarments to create the ideal silhouette. Short corsets, girdles, brassieres, or waist cinchers proved to be the basis of fashions during this period and helped women to achieve this hyperfeminine look.

The Spencer "Spen-support"

American day wear This 1950s shirtwaist day dress from Los Angeles was like those typically worn by the American housewife. It is of simple red and white cotton gingham, and includes a plastic belt and a necktie of matching fabric.

Luxury fabric Dior's New Look collection of 1947 also included *Chérie*, this blue silk taffeta dinner dress. The skirt is made of a full width of fabric, from selvage to selvage, much of which is used to pad the hips.

Luxurious
materials

Sequins
and lace

Refined
tailoring

1948

Floral
motifs

Spanish style This exquisite cocktail dress by
Spanish designer Cristóbal Balenciaga utilizes
the New Look silhouette to great effect. The
toreador-like black lace in floral motifs over
deep red silk references the bullfights of Spain.

Lavender
print

Emphasis
on hips

1955

Full
skirt

Feminine florals In 1953 Dior began to use
bold floral patterns in his New Look dresses,
and other designers quickly followed suit. Susan
Small, a British ready-to-wear firm, created this
beautiful floral-print party dress in 1955.

Coordinated
accessories

Silk shirtwaist

Full, gathered
skirt

Cocktail-length
wedding dress

Formal
sandals

The well-dressed wife
American designer Anne Fogarty is
best known for her 1959 book, *Wife
Dressing: The Fine Art of Being a
Well-Dressed Wife,* and for her love of
simple New Look–style shirtwaist dresses,
such as this wedding dress from 1955.

PRINCESS MARGARET

An early adopter of the New
Look, Princess Margaret
began wearing this style
in 1948 in the form of a
suit designed for her by
the famed British designer
to the royal family, Norman
Hartnell. At each formal
appearance, her
wardrobe reflected
the style of the
day. She grew
to be recognized
for her elegant, refined,
and timeless dress
sense, and quickly
became an iconic
fashion figure.
She is pictured
here arriving in
Trinidad in 1955.

Sharp,
tailored
details

Wide pleats

Tailored French designer Hubert de Givenchy
created this tailored New Look suit in 1955 for
actress Leslie Caron to wear on stage. The skirt is
of alternating pleats of silk moiré and wool, and
the narrow-waisted jacket has off-center buttons.

Simplicity, good taste, and grooming are the three fundamentals of good dressing.

CHRISTIAN DIOR

DESIGNER
CHRISTIAN DIOR

French designer Christian Dior's revolutionary "New Look" dominated women's wear from the late 1940s to the mid-1950s. Suddenly, waists were cinched in and tiny, busts high and prominent, shoulders soft and sloping, and skirts longer than before and voluminous. Dior's hourglass look revived stiffened bodices and crinolines, and used lavish quantities of expensive fabric. After the plain, boxier styles of World War II, this return to extravagance and the femininity of the past was perplexing to some, but others found it refreshing and alluring.

In his earlier years, Dior had studied political science and had also helped run two art galleries, but in 1935 he began selling fashion illustrations to newspapers and to designers such as Robert Piguet. By 1938, he was Piguet's assistant designer. At Piguet's, Dior produced round-hipped, narrowing "amphora" dresses, which reappeared later. He attracted much attention with a *Café Anglais* outfit for Spring 1939, featuring a houndstooth wool dress with a tight-fitting top and full skirt.

Looking to the past
Dior's next fashion post (1941–1946) was at the House of Lucien Lelong—first alongside fellow assistant Balmain, then as principal designer. Here, while making costumes for the film *Le Lit à Colonnes* (1942), set in the later 1800s, Dior's research into period fashions and tailoring techniques fired his imagination.

Dior opened his own house in 1946, thanks to the backing of textile producer Marcel Boussac. His first collection, for spring 1947—one line named *Corolle* after its inverted petal shape and featuring the iconic *Bar* suit—was called the "New Look" by *Harper's Bazaar* editor Carmel Snow. So began ten years in which the diligent, fastidious, and shyly modest Dior was at the fashion world's pinnacle, bringing Paris-centered haute couture back after a period of US-style ascendancy. Rita Hayworth, Margot Fonteyn, and Princess Margaret were among many glittering devotees, and in 1957 Dior accounted for over half of all Paris haute-couture sales.

Changing shapes
After a string of collections, Dior's Spring 1953 *Tulip* collection featured flowery colors and patterns, and a series of looser silhouettes. The "H" shape (1954) narrowed and flattened with an accent across the hips, while spring 1955 saw "A-line" suits influenced by men's tailoring and flaring from the shoulder; fall's "Y-line" brought tapered skirts and emphasis on shoulders. Other style-setting trademarks included sumptuous evening dresses, dramatic "coolie" and "cartwheel" hats, ropes of pearls, standaway collars, princess-seamed dresses, half-belts on jackets and coats, and stoles. Blue, gray, white, pink, and red were favorite colors. Eastern touches were seen in tunic dresses and cheongsams (straight dresses with stand-up collars and a side split). Dior's styles later loosened into forms such as the *vareuse* (peacoat).

After Dior died in 1957, his young assistant, Yves St. Laurent, took the reins, followed by Marc Bohan, Gianfranco Ferré, John Galliano, Raf Simons, and Maria Grazia Chiuri. Dior's success stemmed in part from his brilliance at what today is known as marketing, and that flair for product promotion is as much his legacy as his New Look. While at the top for only about a decade, the influence of his still-thriving, multi-product global brand has been enormous, and he has been a major inspiration to designers from Christian Lacroix to the Marchesa label.

△ **TRADEMARK STYLE**
Dior was kind, conscientious, and loved by his employees. He is seen here in 1957 with one of his models, who wears a superbly styled Dior suit.

◁ **DIOR FOR EVENING**
A stunning take on the hobble skirt in gleaming satin, this model was presented at Dior's Fall/Winter 1959 show. Self-fabric roses clutch the dress above the knees, creating a full, bloused effect.

TIMELINE

1905 Born in Granville, Normandy

1935 Starts career as a fashion illustrator

1938 Hired as Robert Piguet's assistant designer. Begins to develop Dior look

1941 Takes post at Lucien Lelong; later made principal designer

1946 Founds own fashion house in Paris

▷ **1947** Presents first collection, soon to be dubbed the "New Look"

1953 Launches *Tulip* collection, with floral patterns

1957 Dies at Montecatini, Italy

1996 John Galliano, first Englishman to run a French couture house, leaves Givenchy to become Dior's artistic director

2012, 2016 Raf Simons becomes artistic director, followed by Maria Grazia Chiuri

◁ **2009** Galliano holds triumphant Spring/Summer show

1900   1930   1940   1950   1990   2000

◁ **ICONIC DIOR** The hat, the nipped-in waist, and the full skirt all add up to the "New Look" of 1947.

ANTIQUE LACE
WEDDING DRESS

There was a vogue for ballerina-length wedding dresses in the mid- to late 1950s, often made of or incorporating lace. This dress, created for an English wedding in 1960, shows an evolution in style from one fashion icon to the next. In the heady optimism of the 1950s, Grace Kelly–style dresses like this one—with tiny waists, luxurious full skirts, and copious lace—were copied widely. Lace production stopped during World War II, and afterward it was sought after obsessively. The neat tailoring reflects the style of an emerging fashion icon, Jacqueline Kennedy, who became the first lady in 1960. Made of heavy ivory silk, the gown was designed by Christina Ciapella working with the bride, Margaret Carter. Ivory was a sophisticated color choice in the 1960s, and the scooped neckline showcases the antique lace collar.

▷ **ACCESSORIES**
The bride's accessories included cream leather shoes and a tiny brown feather hat with a veil.

VEIL

SHOES

SIDE VIEW

Stiffened collar

Lace was often removed from an earlier garment and incorporated into a wedding dress because it was an heirloom or, as here, a gift to the bride

Darts at the elbow narrow and shape the lower sleeve

Three-quarter-length sleeves with lace-trimmed "wedding points"

Waist sits just below natural waistline

Skirt falls in heavy, unpressed box pleats

Collar stands clear
of the dress

Dropped
waistline
falls into
a deep V

IN DETAIL

◁ BACK CLOSURE

A fashionable long zipper runs down the back of the dress from the deep, curved V of the neckline. The plunging V of antique lace, and the inverted V of the dropped waistline at the back, mirror the shape to gorgeous effect. The back of a wedding dress is particularly important since this is what the guests see during the ceremony.

◁ LACE COLLAR

The front of the dress is completely plain other than the embellishment of a deep band of 19th-century lace, thought to be a type of Brussels lace called "Duchesse." It was donated to the bride by an elderly friend. Reusing lace and other fabrics has a long tradition to do with the expense of textiles as well as the sentiment attached to them.

◁ BOAT NECKLINE

The stiffened lace at shoulder height is cut wide to flatter the neck and shoulders, and creates the illusion of a cap sleeve, popular on wedding dresses at the time.

◁ SIDE SEAMS

A perfect hourglass shape is produced using two sets of princess seams at each side of the bodice, running from the waist to the bust and armholes, with another two seams at the back ending at shoulder-blade height. The dropped waist lengthens the body.

◁ BOX-PLEATED SKIRT

The skirt falls just below the knee, its width gathered into wide box pleats. Petticoats with Vilene (a synthetic stiffener) help to create the shape.

1950–1959
THE COCKTAIL HOUR

With the hard times of World War II behind them, the growing middle class of the 1950s started to respond to the dawn of a new age and live their lives in different ways. Cocktail parties, often held at home, were part of the changing world. The appropriately named cocktail dress, along with a veiled cocktail hat and gloves, were the requisite attire for such gatherings. The formal, mid-calf length dresses of luxurious materials such as velvets and brocades were meant to be worn between the hours of six and eight in the evening. French designer Christian Dior first coined the term "cocktail dress," and his New Look silhouette defined its romantic style with a tight bodice and full skirt emphasizing the waist. But cocktail dresses were not restricted to the bouffant skirt, and many designers experimented with the narrower sheath style.

Demure neckline

Silk grosgrain

Machine-embroidered roundels

1950

Strapless bodice

Feminine side bow

Wide, flared skirt

Summer dress French designer Pierre Balmain created this dress for the *jeune fille* (young woman). Its light color, simple silhouette, and Swiss embroidery imply the innocence of youth. A layered slip with a heavily boned bodice creates the ideal shape.

Gathered skirt

White silk taffeta

Dotted net yoke

Fitted bodice

Gathered net

1955

Extends below knee

Brown and purple-lilac print

Dior's A-line Dior was inspired by intersecting diagonals for his 1955 Spring/Summer collection, and he aptly named it the A-line. This short evening dress from that collection includes a cross-over drape bustier with a gathered skirt creating a bowknot.

Little black dress For this 1955 dress, Madame Grès—a French couture house headed by Germaine Émilie Krebs (also known as Alix Barton)—was inspired by the veiled cocktail hat. Spotted net is draped into an elegant side bustle.

1951

Layered, scalloped bodice

Tightly tailored

Stiff silk organza

Loose pleats at skirt

Strapless silk Jean Dessès, a Greek designer born in Egypt, drew inspiration from his travels. He designed this delicate silk organza dress for Princess Margaret in 1951. A wavelike bodice and the sea-blue color suggest Dessès was inspired by the ocean.

1953

Ties on shoulder

Snug waist

Influential Fath French fashion designer Jacques Fath designed this stunning silk and wool cocktail dress in 1953. A well-known name in the Paris couture industry, his designs appealed to the international, younger woman.

SHOES

Open-toed, grosgrain shoe

Gold kid peep-toe sandals

Not surprisingly, short cocktail attire placed emphasis on the exposed foot and ankle, requiring an elegant shoe. The high-heeled, generally pump, quickly became the icon of the decade and was soon adopted by Hollywood starlets like Jayne Mansfield and Marilyn Monroe, who furthered its sexy image. Gold kid peep-toes, such as those seen here from 1951, were an alternative.

1957

Long, fitted bodice

Froufrou skirt

Accordion pleating and rosettes

Froufrou Inspired by both Spanish flamenco dress and ballet costumes of the day, French designer Pierre Balmain created this extravagant cocktail dress in 1957 for the modern young woman. The taffeta and tulle are edged with satin ribbon.

Boned bodice

Silk ribbon around waist

Overskirt cut away at back to reveal petticoat slip

Frilled net gives bustle effect

Layered net Created for Lanvin by Spanish-born, but Paris-based, designer Antonio Castillo, this dress has its own built-in slip. Black net with white felt spots covers layers of silk taffeta, net, and gauze.

1958

Strapless sheath and wrap

Wraparound bodice and skirt

Bold floral print

Narrow skirt

Sheath dress This 1958 sheath dress with matching wrap in a pink and green floral motif was created by British manufacturer Rodney Dresses. It is an example of an alternative skirt shape acceptable for the cocktail hour.

POSTWAR PERFECTION

Cecil Beaton's 1948 photograph of stunning evening gowns by leading American couturier Charles James encapsulates the heady optimism and return to glamour of postwar New York. Wartime closures of French *maisons* and tight postwar travel budgets had turned influential US magazine editors toward homegrown design. A vibrant scene of high society and fashionable clubs, along with a rapidly strengthening economy, gave American designers a further boost. New York had become a rising fashion location.

Evening wear in the late 1940s and 1950s by designers such as Dior, Balenciaga, and Balmain reveled in copious fabric and the glamorized, old-fashioned feminine ideal. English-born James, widely considered the only true US couturier, was said to have inspired Dior's New Look silhouette, the ultimate antidote to wartime utility.

James was an obsessive perfectionist, best known for dressing socialites in fabulously expensive, dramatic gowns. These intricately constructed sculptures, fabricating a perfect postwar woman, were art forms in their own right. James used boning and multiple layers of silk, satin, taffeta, and tulle to build 19th-century-influenced gowns with expressive shapes and complex seaming, spiral draping and wrapping, asymmetric features, light-catching materials, and differently colored layers that flashed as the wearer glided across a room. Totally self-supporting, these hourglass garments tightly molded and defined the torso, before exploding into vast skirts reminiscent of butterfly and swans' wings or four-leaved clovers.

> ❝
>
> America's greatest couturier, the world's best and only dressmaker who has raised it from an applied art to a pure art form.
>
> **CRISTOBAL BALENCIAGA ON CHARLES JAMES**
>
> ❞

◁ **"HIGH-SOCIETY" TABLEAU**
Poised *Vogue* models imitate a high-society scene in an elegant, neoclassical New York interior. Narcissistically checking themselves in mirrors or touching their fashionably showy jewelry, they are more like statues than real women, representing subtle variations of a feminine ideal.

1950–1957
COUTURE GOWNS

Typically worn to balls and grand occasions by the wealthy elite, haute couture evening gowns were the ultimate expression of couture house art. They were bold and dramatic, and intended to draw attention to the wearer. Designers used the finest fabrics and the most intricate techniques to create them. Best known were French designers Christian Dior, Pierre Balmain, and Hubert de Givenchy; Spanish designer Cristóbal Balenciaga; and the American-based Charles James. While based on a runway model, a gown could be customized to the needs of a client for a specific event. The New Look silhouette emphasized the hourglass figure, with its narrow waist. Married women wore strapless gowns but young unmarried women wore gowns with straps or capped sleeves. Skirts were usually full, though the columnar sheath also grew popular.

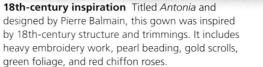

1950

- Strapless
- Wrapped bodice
- Natural waist
- Flowing sash
- Ankle-length skirt

Fit and flare This Cristóbal Balenciaga gown shows the dramatic flare expected of haute couture evening wear. Often inspired by his native Spain, his design draws on the bullfighting tradition with a sash over an intricately embroidered columnar skirt.

1955

- Covered shoulders
- Cowl neckline
- Slightly flattened bust
- Fullness at back
- Ankle-length skirt

Heavy brocade Hubert de Givenchy, who trained under Balenciaga, designed this evening dress. Using a heavy silk matelassé brocade in emerald green, Givenchy's design elements include a draped cowl neckline and a slightly dropped, sloping waistline.

- Sweetheart bodice
- Fitted waist
- Cream satin

18th-century inspiration Titled *Antonia* and designed by Pierre Balmain, this gown was inspired by 18th-century structure and trimmings. It includes heavy embroidery work, pearl beading, gold scrolls, green foliage, and red chiffon roses.

- Princess seams
- Copper colored roses
- Slight train

Taffeta gown Cuban-born American designer Luis Estevez created this gown. After training in Paris at the House of Patou, Estevez returned to the US to start his own label, which sold at department stores such as Bergdorf Goodman.

1953

1954

Bare shoulders

Cross-over bodice

Tight waist

Wide skirt

Ankle length

Velours de Lyon (black velvet)

Heavy understructure

White duchess satin

Clover hemline

Matching bolero

Silk organza

Flowers, beads, and sequins

Floor length

Reveal and conceal This strapless black gown uses a peekaboo bodice treatment, further emphasizing the décolletage. Made of silk taffeta, the full skirt reveals a section of light pink underskirt below a see-through net panel.

Clover gown Charles James created his Four-Leaf Clover gown for Mrs. William Randolph Hearst, Jr. to wear to the Eisenhower Inaugural Ball. His background in architecture and his tendency toward sculptural, highly controlled silhouettes are evident here.

Custom couture Christian Dior designed this gown, *La Ligne Muguet*, based on his runway model *Belle de Nuit* for socialite Gloria Guinness. Intricate handwork, including beading, metallic embroidery, and ribbon work, emphasizes the luxury of his couture work.

1957

Strapless

Folded bustline

Wild silk organza

Draped overskirt

Geometric hemline

Strapless and youthful

Petticoat slip adds width

Full-length gown

Gathered skirt

Flounces and bustles Victor Stiebel, a South African–born British designer, referenced historical elements with this gown. The blue and white striped silk taffeta underskirt includes a knee-high flounce and the draped overskirt has a slight bustle.

Stripes Frank Usher, an important ready-to-wear design firm in the UK during the 1950s, created this extravagant strapless evening gown in 1957. Horizontal stripes in a delicate pink accentuate the high-waisted bodice and daring décolletage.

ACCESSORIES

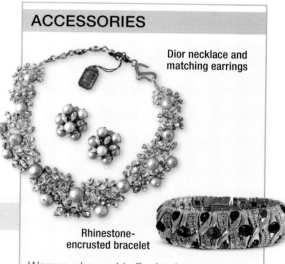

Dior necklace and matching earrings

Rhinestone-encrusted bracelet

Women who could afford to buy expensive couture gowns usually had real jewels—including diamonds, emeralds, and rubies—to go with them. Pearls were popular, too, either in single strands, or combined with other elements in statement pieces such as the 1959 pearl necklace and earrings seen here. For those without real gems, there was costume jewelry. Manufacturers such as Vendôme created striking costume jewelry using artificial stones and imitation metals. The bracelet shown above is embedded with rhinestones in emerald-green, ruby-red, and clear crystal.

DESIGNER
BALENCIAGA

A private man, monastically dedicated to the pursuit of perfection, Cristóbal Balenciaga let his dramatic, fluid clothes speak for him. Although lauded less than Dior, he anticipated aspects of the New Look, headed the most exclusive Paris *maison* in the immediate postwar era through the 1950s, helped create 1960s garment shapes, and most importantly invented a totally new silhouette for women.

Balenciaga had a legendary talent for cut, seaming, and finish. He understood how fabric draped and how the stiff materials he loved dictated sculptural shapes. Born in a fishing village in Basque Spain, the young Balenciaga absorbed a great deal from his mother, a dressmaker to local wealthy women. In his early teens, a local aristocrat, who later became both patron and client, helped him secure a superior tailoring apprenticeship.

The move to Paris

By his early 20s, Balenciaga had a boutique in the fashionable Spanish seaside resort of San Sebastián. Branches in Madrid and Barcelona followed as he became Spain's leading couturier. The Spanish Civil War triggered a move to Paris, where by 1937 he established himself in style at avenue Georges V. Soon after Balenciaga arrived in Paris, the city hailed him as a major presence. He created a series of distinctive shapes, often waistless and loose, that magically seemed both independent of the body and in harmony with the female form. The mature women who made up a large part of his wealthy clientele found his clothes especially flattering.

His first runway show referred to the Spanish Renaissance, and his collections drew on his country's culture and past. He put bustles on evening gowns. The 1939 hourglass Infanta gown sprang from Velázquez's paintings. The traditional female dress and religious vestments of Spain, and other Spanish artists such as Zurbarán, inspired dramatic dark garments. Bolero jackets and capes echoed toreadors' outfits, while short-fronted, long-backed garments recalled flamenco dresses.

Down to essentials

Balenciaga pared down his elegant lines in the 1950s. His partly tight, partly loose garments, such as jackets with a fitted front and billowing back, introduced around 1951, created a revolution in fashion. His straight, loose sack dress (1957) prefigured simple 1960s shapes. There were also flounced, trapezoid baby doll dresses with wide waists (1957 and 1958), balloon jackets and skirts, cocoon coats, and empire-line gowns. Standaway collars lengthened the neck, big buttons added bold detail, and seven-eighths-length sleeves revealed women's bracelets. Sleeves were an obsession. Balenciaga remade any, sometimes on the wearer, that did not lie perfectly. He was adept at tricky dolman-style sleeves, cut as a piece with the garment body.

The 1960s brought bold experiments with fabric. Balenciaga developed a stiff silk called silk Gazaar with Abraham's fabric house and also used transparent materials and plastic rainwear. He further refined the linearity that now dominated fashion. Despite producing some of his most exciting work in this decade, Balenciaga was perhaps out of step with new mass-market values and he closed his couture house in 1968. After a stagnant period and acquisition by Gucci, his love of shape lives on with Nicolas Ghesquière's designs for the Balenciaga brand. Courrèges and Ungaro, both Balenciaga apprentices, and Givenchy, were all influenced by their mentor. So were Mila Schön, with her expert tailoring, and Oscar de la Renta, with details like sash bows on evening gowns.

△ **CRISTOBAL BALENCIAGA 1927**
Dubbed the "Picasso of fashion" for his artistic innovations with shape and form, Balenciaga was among few couturiers capable of making a haute couture garment from scratch himself.

◁ **EVENING DRESS 1946**
Balenciaga loved and understood material, hence his cleverly draped gowns like this one, reminiscent of flamenco costume. Black, red, and pink were favorite colors.

TIMELINE

1895 Born in Guetaria, Spain

1917 Establishes first dressmaking business in San Sebastián

1936–1937 Civil war prompts move to Paris. Shows first collection for Fall 1937

1939 Introduces *Infanta* silhouette

1947 Creates more voluminous Barrel line

1950s ▷ Designs extravagant evening gowns. Introduces rollaway collars, slim tunics, and sack dresses

1960s Experiments with bold shapes, wool capes, plastic rainwear, and transparent fabrics

1968 Designs Air France uniform. Fashion house closes. Balenciaga retires

1972 Dies in Valencia, Spain

1997 Fashion house fortunes revive when Nicolas Ghesquière is made design principal

2006 ▷ Actress Nicole Kidman wears Balenciaga at the Academy Awards in Hollywood

2001 Gucci Group buys Balenciaga brand (now ready-to-wear)

○ 1920   ○ 1940   ○ 1960   ○ 1980   ○ 2000   ○ 2010

◁ **ASYMMETRIC JACKET 1950** The sweeping curve of the front, emphasized by bold buttons, narrows to a cinched-in waist, with big pockets at the hips

1948–1954
FEMININE FORM

Tailoring for women was one of the strongest trends in 1950s fashion. Stylish two-piece suits with architectural shapes and sculpted lines reflected the sophistication and modern aspirations of the times. From the mid-1930s, tailoring had become an important part of the female wardrobe, partly inspired by military wear and partly dictated by a need for practical garb for women who worked outside the home. In the 1950s, designers exploited tailor's techniques to help create an idealized feminine form. Innovators such as US-based Charles James and Spanish Cristóbal Balenciaga injected fresh ideas into suiting and framing the body. Jackets were typically rounded at the shoulder, rather than square and padded, and were tightly fitted through the bodice to shape a small waist before flaring out to accentuate the hips. Skirts hit mid-calf and were either pencil slim or very full.

Trim waistline echoes "New Look"

Slanted pockets at hip add volume

Full A-line skirt shape

1948

Neat pleats This gray worsted suit by British designer Hardy Amies retains the influence of Dior's 1947 New Look silhouette. Amies adapts the full-skirted shape into a sharp tailored suit with the use of a panel of narrow pleats.

HATS

Cartwheel hat with silk edging

Beret with quill-like feather

Bird-topped tricorn by Maud et Nano, 1951

Toreador style with hail-spot veil

In the 1950s the mark of a well-dressed woman was her hat. For day and evening, small hats were in vogue, especially pillbox, cloche, or beret styles, although cartwheel shapes were also worn. The popularity of the cocktail hour led to fanciful creations that added drama to an outfit. These often sat toward the back of the head to prevent flattening the carefully coiffed hair. Hats were almost always adorned with veils, feathers, birds, fruit, flowers, or other whimsy.

Black buttons match braid detail

Understated tailoring

1952

Toffee-colored wool

Precision tailoring This suit by British designer Charles Creed is simple but exact in cut and construction. Decoration is kept restrained with inset bands of black braid and small loops, repeated at the back of the skirt.

Short, wide sleeves for pairing with long gloves

Wide, rounded collar

Oversized buttons add drama

Flared jacket hem slims the hipline

1953

Lightweight wool suit US designer Norman Norell partnered with Anthony Traina to set up the Norell-Traina label. Their designs were elegant yet relaxed, like this 1954 ensemble of a slim, straight skirt and half-sleeve jacket.

Navy and white lends conservatism

Tight bodice emphasizes hourglass shape

Bracelet-length sleeves add elegance

Notches allow for full skirt

Chic gray Christian Dior displays both his dressmaking and tailoring skills in this gray wool ensemble, in which the focus is entirely on the upper body. An intricately paneled and draped jacket is set off against a plain, slim skirt.

Cross-over front with three-button closure

Hairline wool adds texture

Jacket wraps the body

Long, slim skirt

1950

Demure suit Worn to Ascot, this 1948 design creates a demure impression with its shawl collar, bow, grosgrain trim, and pleated skirt. The nipped-in waist and full skirt echo Dior's New Look.

Full, stiffened skirt with pleats

Slender lines The jacket of this hairline-striped wool suit by US designer Adele for Fall/Winter 1952 is cut short to reveal the tiny waist. Dolman sleeves and diagonally set hip pockets emphasize the model's shape.

Double-breasted, collarless jacket

Hand-embroidered silk blouse

Narrow, nipped-in waist

Narrow, mid-calf-length skirt

Neat collar extends into scarflike flourish

1954

Straight skirt has kick pleats at back

Parisian chic Despite the rise of fashion houses outside Paris, the city held on to its fashion credibility. Here, Audrey Hepburn starring in the 1954 film *Sabrina* plays a girl transformed into elegance by two years spent in the capital.

Curves This beautifully tailored wool suit by British designer Lachasse demonstrates an eye for detail. Following the line of the darts, flared panels sewn into the jacket bodice fall in layers over the hips to emphasize the sculpted curve.

1947–1962
A GOOD COAT

Not for several decades had the coat been as important for women as it was in the years after World War II. Uniforms influenced fashion, especially the military trench coat, which was adopted for civilian wear as much by women as by men. This popular trend was bolstered by Hollywood screen queens: Marlene Dietrich, Lauren Bacall, Ingrid Bergman, Ava Gardner, and Katharine Hepburn all famously wore trenches in movies during this period, to glamorous effect. The right coat was a key element for achieving a polished, "tied-together" look. It was vital that the outer garment was just long enough to cover the hem of the dress or skirt underneath. Since wartime shortages of materials decreased, coats became ever more luxurious. Furs, in particular, took off and for many women a mink coat was the ultimate status symbol of the era.

Hourglass shape Following Christian Dior's New Look of 1947, there was a change in the female silhouette, seen to some extent in these coats made the same year. They are sculpted to fit the body and sharply define the waist.

Turban-style hat

1947

Shoulders still broad

Fur accessories are "in"

Mid-calf hemline

Asymmetric draping of skirt

Shoes becoming more pointed at toe

Color-coordinated pumps

Large collar

Double-breasted closure with matching buttons

Deep, turned-back cuffs

Tie belt creates shape

1951

Hat worn with decorative brooch

Short cape

Contrasting button closure

Hemline just below knee

Shoes match buttons and brooch

1952

Winter warmer Made from a thick wool cloth, this belted coat was a sensible choice for women during the 1950s. The tied belt draws the coat in at the waist to give a full-skirted silhouette that reflects dress shapes of the time.

Short cape German model and winner of Miss World 1956, Petra Shurmann wears an ensemble of skirt, jacket, and cape from the department store Defaka. Her matching red gloves, hat, and handbag complete the outfit.

Hats become a statement accessory

Fur trim on shawl collar

Double ring of fur on sleeve adds luxury

Peplum (ruffle)

Revival In the late 1940s, and into the 1950s, designers echoed the shape of the redingote, or frock coat, of the 18th and 19th centuries. The new style was formfitting with a nipped-in waist, long flared skirt, and padded hips.

1948

More fabric needed for very full cut

Small, neat collar

Bracelet sleeves

Collar in astrakhan (lamb skin)

Large black buttons complement collar

1950

Smocklike cut

Loose lines A swing coat allows for fuller styles worn underneath—ideal for wearing over the big skirts of the 1950s. Unstructured cuts like this one use decorative touches to add punch.

Wide shawl collar

Broad tie belt

1961

Wraparound style

1962

Flared hemline balances narrow shoulder

JACQUELINE KENNEDY

At the beginning of the 1960s, Jacqueline Kennedy, stylish wife of President John F. Kennedy, was a significant influence on fashion. Her neat, youthful appearance made her a role model for women who rejected some of the more radical clothes of those years. The first lady favored dress and coat ensembles for day wear, usually worn with matching hat, handbag, and shoes, and often all in shades of white or a single color. American designer Oleg Cassini created Mrs. Kennedy's White House wardrobe. His coats characteristically featured straight lines, a mandarin or stand-up collar, deep patch pockets, large self-cover buttons, bracelet-length sleeves, and a hem finishing just below the knee.

Jacqueline Kennedy: style icon

Status symbol This fur coat from the early 1960s has a fuller cocoon shape with a broad shawl collar and wide tie belt. Many women dreamed of owning a fur coat because it symbolized glamour, femininity, and success.

Leopard spots Animal prints were in vogue for the well-dressed woman of the era. Designers favored real leopard for elegant clothes and accessories. Here, the thick pile of the skin lends structure to Paulene Trigère's banded swing coat.

1949–1959
WIVES AND MOTHERS

The postwar era saw advances in textiles and technology. Wash-and-wear fabrics appeared in the early 1950s, reducing time-consuming laundering. Mass manufacturing, and the end of rationing in the UK, made a wider range of clothes available. At the same time, women were plunged back into traditional roles as homemakers. Glossy magazines advocated that women should look well turned out at all times, even when doing the housework. The housedress was especially significant since so much time was devoted to tasks in the home, at least for the majority of women who were not in paid employment. A typical day might include three hours of housework and an hour making the evening meal. For daily shopping trips into town, a more stylish, fitted, dress was recommended.

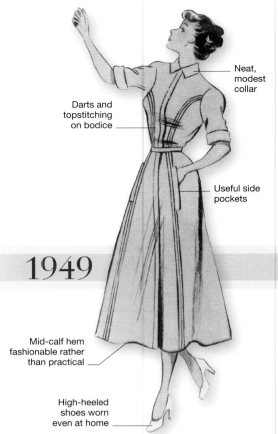

1949

- Neat, modest collar
- Darts and topstitching on bodice
- Useful side pockets
- Mid-calf hem fashionable rather than practical
- High-heeled shoes worn even at home

Pretty in pink Doing housework did not have to mean looking dowdy. As this illustration from French magazine *Votre Mode* shows, the aim was to look stylish and feminine in the home. "A housedress for elegant and practical women," the caption noted.

HANDBAGS

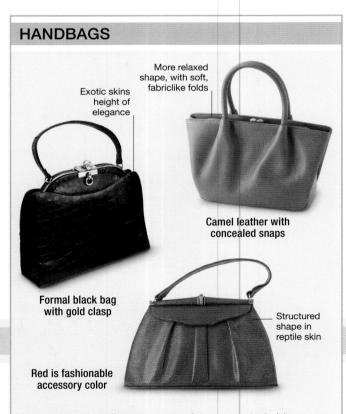

- Exotic skins height of elegance
- More relaxed shape, with soft, fabriclike folds
- **Camel leather with concealed snaps**
- **Formal black bag with gold clasp**
- Structured shape in reptile skin
- **Red is fashionable accessory color**

A neat, boxy handbag was one of the most desirable accessories a woman could own. It was usually carried in the hand or in the crook of the arm so that it would not interfere with the line of a dress or suit. The bag generally held a wallet, compact and lipstick, handkerchief, small notebook and pencil, and possibly a pair of sunglasses, and had inside pockets for accessories such as gloves.

The height of luxury was a handbag that matched the shoes, though in reality few could afford more than one good bag. Handbags were engineered with a frame and gold-tone clasps at the top to enable a firm and secure closure that also looked stylish.

- Cross-over bodice
- Bow detail draws eye to waist
- Slimmer silhouette
- Sateen is in vogue

Day dress Samuel Sherman's UK dress company, Sambo, became known for its floral cotton dresses. This style shows the slimmed-down lines, sateen fabric, and bigger, bolder prints that characterized the mid-to-late 1950s.

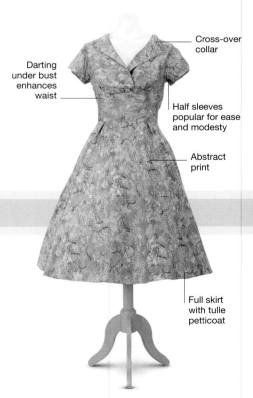

- Cross-over collar
- Darting under bust enhances waist
- Half sleeves popular for ease and modesty
- Abstract print
- Full skirt with tulle petticoat

Abstract prints The talking point of the 1950s was the new art movement, abstract expressionism. Jackson Pollock in particular influenced fashion and interiors. Fabric designers created prints for uses from dresses to curtains.

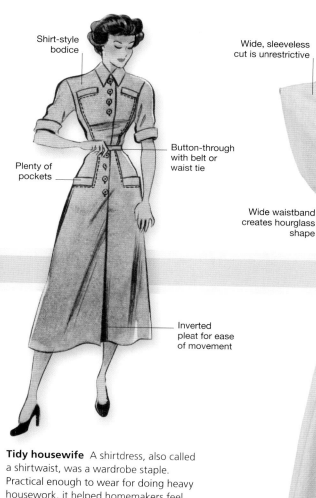

Shirt-style bodice

Plenty of pockets

Button-through with belt or waist tie

Inverted pleat for ease of movement

Tidy housewife A shirtdress, also called a shirtwaist, was a wardrobe staple. Practical enough to wear for doing heavy housework, it helped homemakers feel both comfortable and neat.

Strapless bodice made modest with bolero

Slightly high-waisted to show off full skirt

Bolero hem lines up precisely with waistband

Pink and gray, a chic combination

Stylish day out A dress from British ready-to-wear maker Horrockses was considered the ultimate in daytime chic in the 1940s and '50s. The brand, known for its fine-quality cottons and cheerful prints, was famously worn by Queen Elizabeth II.

Wide, sleeveless cut is unrestrictive

Stand-up collar with small tie

Rows of tucking add shape

Wide waistband creates hourglass shape

Cotton pique (weaving style) is crisp and cool

1950

1953

Style and comfort American sportswear designer Claire McCardell is remembered for her beautifully made, practical clothes, which filled a gap in the market for stylish, comfortable day wear. This ivory cotton summer dress displays the purity of line for which she was known.

Boat neckline with rolled edge

Wide self-belt is fashionable

Big patch pockets serve to replace apron

Metallic embroidery lifts plain dress

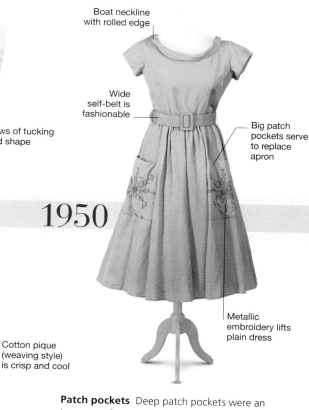

Patch pockets Deep patch pockets were an important feature of a housedress or casual day dress. They held essential domestic items such as clothespins, diaper pins, or a notebook and pen for shopping lists.

CHAIN-STORE CHIC

In the US, department stores such as J.C. Penney had spread to the new suburban shopping malls by the mid-1950s. These dresses from the company's 1959 catalogue were made from a new cotton-rayon called cotron.

Catalogue advertisement, 1959

1950–1961
RESORT WEAR

The prosperity of the 1950s brought the concept of leisure to the mainstream. It was no longer just the wealthy who had time and money to take vacations; and since air travel became less exclusive, more people ventured abroad. The upper class had mastered the art of dressing for travel and leisure long ago, and now the middle class embraced the idea. Responding to a burgeoning market, the fashion industry produced a new category of clothing known as resort wear, comprising diverse ranges of vacation clothes and accessories. Although "resort" implied a casual look, people dressed up, if in more colorful and revealing clothes than for everyday life. That meant playsuits, beach dresses, bathing suits, and coordinating cover-ups for women, and matching swim shorts and short-sleeved shirts for men. Vivid fabrics, including Hawaiian florals, Indonesian batik, and animal prints, were widely used. Tropical-themed accessories were an important part of the look.

MEN ON VACATION

It was not only women who liked colorful leisure clothes. When men took time off, they usually opted to break out of the conservative attire of the 1950s workplace and embrace flamboyance. Men's short-sleeved shirts and coordinating swim shorts were sold in an array of patterns and colors, often with a tropical motif.

1950s advertisement

Swimsuit construction creates hourglass figure

Patch pockets

Matching beach coat Abstract fabrics were big news in fashion from the late 1940s through to the 1950s, and this pairing uses them to great effect. An elastic cotton swimsuit is partnered with a terry cloth robe in a complementary print.

Underwiring and padding shape at bustline

Support in bottom keeps tummy flat

Sun top

Blouse

Practical cut combined with pretty print

Separate skirt

High-waisted bikini Brigitte Bardot helped to make the bikini popular when she posed in one at the Cannes Film Festival in 1953. This design, in a charming foliage and floral print, is typical of the era, with plenty of support built into the bikini top.

Separates Summer wear comprising matching separates—such as skirts, sun tops, blouses, and shorts—was fashionable on the beach. The various elements of this 1956 striped outfit could be bought one piece at a time.

Hourglass silhouette As with foundation garments, swimwear used rubber elastic fibers, underwiring, boning, stretch tummy panels, and padding to create a smooth, structured look—whether a black bikini in the guise of a French maid's uniform, or a demure one-piece.

Frilled bikini top shows off bust

Apron offers modesty but adds sex appeal

Exaggerated ruffles for fun

Classic sweetheart neckline

Smooth lines thanks to new rubber technology

Halter neckline common for swimwear

Shirred midriff creates shape

Girl's one-piece Surface textures and effects were popular in the 1950s, thanks to new manufacturing processes and affordable synthetic fabrics. Ruffles and shirring transform this child's swimsuit into a special garment.

Loose-fitting, see-through top

Bold pattern

Minimal skirt

Platform soles

Braids, for girlish effect

More natural bustline

Form-fitting capri pants

Casual ballet flats

Hooded top Then, as now, summer weather was unpredictable. This hooded beach top from the mid-1950s provided a quick cover-up for swimmers and sunbathers if the weather turned chilly.

Head turning Confidence would have been needed to parade on the beach in this striking outfit, modeled in 1952. Both the top and the tiny matching skirt, worn over a bikini, are see through.

All about sex By 1961, when this photo of Brigitte Bardot was taken, resort clothes were more relaxed. The emphasis was now on youthfulness, freedom, and raw sex appeal.

ACCESSORIES

Maintaining a polished appearance was a priority for the 1950s woman, so fashion companies produced resort accessories. For sunseekers there were cover-ups, costume jewelry, raffia, straw and cotton beach bags, hats, shoes, and sunglasses to coordinate with their outfits. Because hairdos were carefully coiffed, a bathing cap was de rigueur; designers had fun with it, turning a mundane piece of sports gear into a decorative display adorned with rubber petals, spikes, scalloping, and ruffles.

Peach sunglasses

Sunflower sunglasses

Peep-toe mule

Out of the water, women wore large straw hats, especially lamp-shade styles, often decorated with embroidered raffia flowers and fruit. Sunglasses had been mass-produced since the late 1920s, but after World War II, when UV technology improved and air force pilots made the aviator style sexy, they were sold in a variety of novel shapes. Pointed and winged frames were especially popular. When it came to footwear, there were espadrilles (part of a craze for all things Spanish), Japanese-style wooden slides, carved mules inspired by Polynesian crafts, and rubber flip-flops, which really took off after the Korean War when returning soldiers brought them back as souvenirs.

1950–1955
CASUAL AND POLISHED

After years in military uniform, men were back in civilian clothes, and now wanted to indulge themselves a little and dress in a more relaxed style. Clothing makers adapted to the new mood. From the late 1940s, generously cut, double-breasted jackets were teamed with wide-leg trousers, often pleated and with a center crease and cuffs. In Britain, tailors in London's prestigious Savile Row launched a Neo-Edwardian look that harkened back to a time of luxury. Shoulders followed a more natural line, rather than being padded, and jackets in expensive fabrics were cut for a slimmer fit. Italian menswear makers pioneered lightweight suiting using fine fabrics such as silk—the perfect balance between casual and polished. The shorter, sportier-looking continental jacket was very popular in the late 1950s. All shades of gray were fashionable, especially in flannel pinstripe.

1950

Black bowler hat

Handkerchief in breast pocket

Single-breasted vest

Leather briefcase

Loose, wool trousers

Business suit In the city of London, menswear retained formal dress codes. This gentleman wears a tailored, dark wool three-piece suit and bowler hat – a look little changed from the 1850s.

Shawl collar popular until late 1950s

Relaxed trouser style

Dressing up The tuxedo, or dinner suit, first worn in the late 1800s, was very much in vogue during the 1950s, when men's clothing included formal wear for most evening occasions.

Hat an essential accessory

Fashionable thin black tie

Tie clips all the rage

Slimmer-line trousers

1952

White cotton formal shirt

Leather gloves add gravitas

Polished brogues

Homburg

Natural shoulder line

1954

Creased trousers dominate the decade

Natural shoulder line

Slim cut with three buttons

Turned-back cuff

Contrasting, rather than matching, trousers

Work style On the West Coast of the US and in Europe, suits became less formal, even for the businessman. A softer, slimmer jacket was preferred, along with a slightly tapered trouser leg.

Executive US ambassador to Moscow George Frost Kennan wears a finely pin-striped, double-breasted gray flannel suit—typical attire for the prudent, mature "company man."

Old and new A debut design from Christian Dior's menswear line, launched in 1954, this suit harkens back to the Edwardian era, but details such as the cropped vest give it a fresh spin.

Neo-Edwardian This jacket and trouser ensemble typifies the New Edwardian tailoring of the 1950s. The brown wool jacket is cut on a long line, with a slightly waisted effect.

Short "boyish" haircut

Greased hair with brushed-up forelock

Jazzy bow tie

Peaked lapel

Light-colored suiting for casual look

Long-line jacket

Draped trousers

Conservative pin-striped flannel

Suede shoes

1955

HATS AND SHOES

Single crease in crown

Brown Homburg

Stiff, slightly upturned brim

Black Homburg

The hat was the key accessory. Not until the late 1950s was it acceptable for men to go bareheaded. Along with the revival of Edwardian fashions in the early 1950s came the Homburg hat, first popularized in Britain by King Edward VII. Other favored styles included the fedora, as famously sported by Humphrey Bogart, the bowler, and the porkpie. Brims were generally narrower than in previous decades.

For the more conservative man, the shoes of choice were Oxfords, brogues, and loafers, though gradually toes became more pointed. Among the younger generation, desert boots, sneakers, and "winklepicker" ankle boots were the norm.

Plain, durable leather

Mid-brown shade was popular

Laces of same color

Classic Oxford style

Double act Hollywood's favorite comic duo wears classic styles of the mid-1950s. While funnyman Jerry Lewis pairs a light-colored, single-breasted suit with a patterned bow tie, his foil, Dean Martin, opts for a more sober, double-breasted, pinstripe look.

1950–1959

HIPSTERS AND TEDDY BOYS

Two distinct, mainly male, style tribes, hipsters and teddy boys both dressed in ostentatious suits to rebel against the social order. The original hipsters were African Americans who emulated the lifestyle and clothing of "bebop" jazz musicians of the late 1930s and early 1940s. Their fashion uniform was the zoot suit, consisting of high-waisted trousers with a baggy leg that tapered dramatically to a narrow cuff, and a long, generously cut jacket with a wide lapel and padded shoulders. It was usually worn with a gold watch chain, a broad-brimmed felt hat, and two-tone or pointed shoes. Across the Atlantic, teddy boys were working-class London teenagers, listening to American rock 'n' roll but usurping the Edwardian suit revival on Savile Row to invent their own style. They wore flamboyant, Edwardian-cut jackets with vests, string ties, and pegged trousers. Teddy girls mixed these masculine elements with feminine accessories.

Greased hair shaped into forelock

Cotton overcoat

Drainpipe trousers cuffed at hem

Duster coat The teddy boy style spread across Britain, drawing on what was available locally. This young man, photographed in Derbyshire in 1957, wears a simple coat more suggestive of working-class utility than Savile Row tailoring.

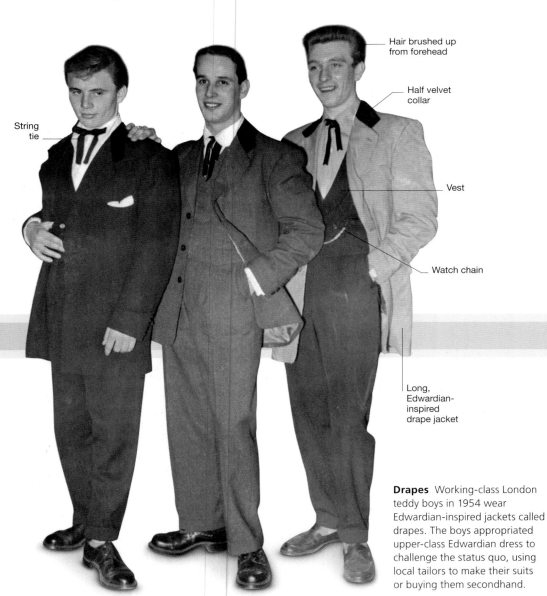

Hair brushed up from forehead

Half velvet collar

String tie

Vest

Watch chain

Long, Edwardian-inspired drape jacket

Drapes Working-class London teddy boys in 1954 wear Edwardian-inspired jackets called drapes. The boys appropriated upper-class Edwardian dress to challenge the status quo, using local tailors to make their suits or buying them secondhand.

High-collared white shirt with string tie

Voluminous jacket with piping

Cropped tapered pants that expose white socks

Ballet flats

Style mix A 17-year-old teddy girl poses in 1955. Teddy girls were British adopters of American teen basics such as jeans and ballet flats. They mixed them with clothing styles from the Edwardian and Victorian eras.

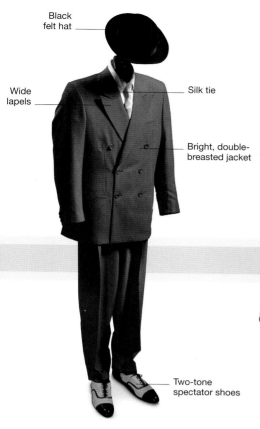

Black felt hat

Wide lapels

Silk tie

Bright, double-breasted jacket

Two-tone spectator shoes

West Indian style The zoot suit spread from the US to the Caribbean, where the local men interpreted it in brightly colored cloth. West Indian migrants to Britain in the 1950s brought the style with them. This modern re-creation recalls the snappy fashion of that time.

Suspenders hold trousers under ribs

Satin handkerchief

Two-tone shoes

Clownlike trousers pegged at ankles

Exaggerated shape This sharp zoot suit is inspired by the exuberant jazz singer Cab Calloway in the 1943 movie *Stormy Weather*. Political activist Malcolm X once described this look as "a killer-diller coat with a drape shape, reat-pleats, and shoulders padded like a lunatic's cell."

Floppy silk cravat

Wide lapels

Crisp, white dress shirt

Jacket reaches to tips of extended fingers

High-shine shoes

Fingertip jacket The drape was a more conservative version of the zoot suit. It had a shorter jacket, as in this 1994 reproduction by Chris Ruocco Tailors, London. Suspenders or a thin leather belt held the trousers high on the waist.

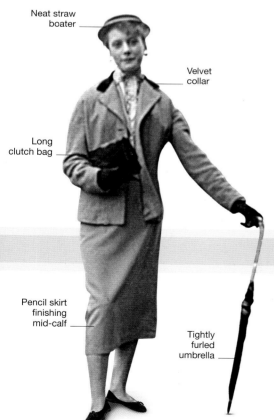

Neat straw boater

Velvet collar

Long clutch bag

Pencil skirt finishing mid-calf

Tightly furled umbrella

Accessorized This teddy girl wears a jacket borrowed from the teddy boys with its loose shape and velvet collar. She carries the signature teddy girl accessories of a clutch bag and an umbrella.

SHOES

Two-tone leather shoes

Crêpe-soled brothel creepers

Hipsters wore spiffy, thick-soled shoes that were often shiny, made of exotic skins, or two-tone, harkening back to the jaunty, off-duty style worn by the wealthy man of leisure in the 1920s. Pointed shoes, historically a sign of status, were also popular. Shoes were worn to attract attention, never to blend with the suit. Teddy boys adopted chunky, crêpe-soled, suede "brothel creepers" to ground their look. Alternatively, they sported stylish leather Derbys with thick soles.

THE YOUTH
REVOLUTION

This iconic image from the movie *The Wild One* (1953) turned the brooding Marlon Brando into a poster boy for young people feeding off postwar restlessness and aching to escape the polite conventions of 1950s society. His blue denim jeans and zipped black leather jacket would become universal casual wear. In the movie, Brando plays the leader of a motorcycle gang. When asked what he's rebelling against, he drawls, "Whaddya got?" The movie caused a scandal.

Two years later, James Dean, playing a troubled young man in *Rebel Without a Cause* (1955), created a similar look— blue jeans, white T-shirt, boots, and a leather or windbreaker jacket (including the red Harrington windbreaker in *Rebel*)—that continues across the decades. Such looks were subversive not just because they were associated with "working" clothes or hoodlums, but because they were social levelers—these were styles worn by movie stars that most people could afford.

Brando became an identity-marker for the teenager—a notion that had barely existed prewar—and for teenage fashions. Increased 1950s prosperity, and the rise of advertising and mass consumerism, helped to celebrate youth while also giving teenagers something to rebel against.

> 66
>
> He pulled on his big leather motorcycling jacket and went out to his bike. They met at a café called Nick's. It was a working men's café in the daytime, quite ordinary, but at night it was different. It acquired for them at least an excitement and glamour.
>
> **GILLIAN FREEMAN,** *THE LEATHER BOYS*, 1961
>
> 99

◁ **A REBEL WITH MANY CAUSES**
Seminal youth-culture movie *The Wild One* (1953), starring Marlon Brando, spawned many biker movies and biker-influenced looks.

1949–1959

BIRTH OF THE TEENAGER

Up until the late 1940s, most young people left school before the age of 16 to start work or join the military. In the 1950s, families were better off, and young people stayed at home longer, but this new generation looked for a way to assert their independence—by dressing differently. Denim companies targeted teens with the new drainpipe jeans, and rock 'n' roll stars such as Eddie Cochran and Elvis Presley fueled demand. When Marlon Brando wore jeans and a leather jacket in *The Wild One* in 1953, teens found a new fashion uniform in which to rebel. Many youth style tribes originated in the US, including bobby-soxers in poodle skirts, and Beats in bohemian black. But there were also teddy boys, teddy girls, and rockers in the UK; the *Kaminari zoku* (Thunder Tribe) in Japan; and bodgies and widgies in Australia, to name a few.

SILHOUETTE SHAPERS

After the slender silhouette of the 1930s, Christian Dior's New Look of 1947 brought back the bouffant petticoat. Interestingly, what began as a high fashion look was appropriated by teenage girls in the 1950s. Layers of tulle underpinned cinched circle skirts, which were paired with a fitted cardigan, ankle socks, and flat shoes. Dance was the catalyst for the obsession with starched petticoats (crinolines). As girls danced the jive and jitterbug, crinolines showed off their moves, and also preserved their modesty. The newly invented bustier was equally important in creating an alluring silhouette.

Starched to achieve full shape

Petticoat with bustier

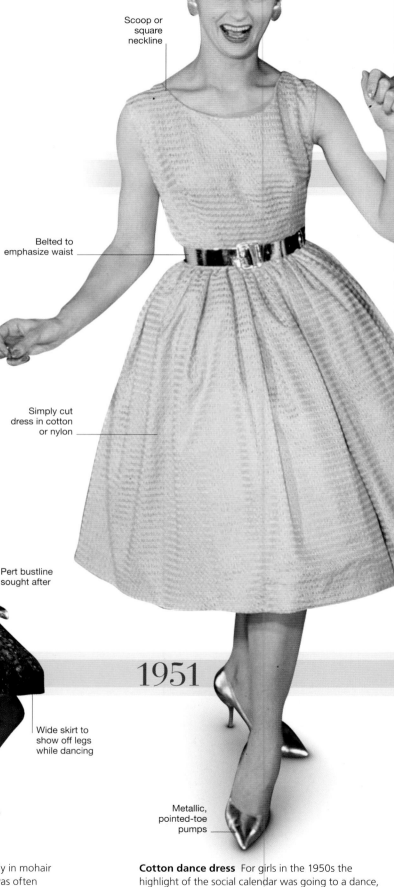

Scoop or square neckline

Belted to emphasize waist

Simply cut dress in cotton or nylon

Pert bustline sought after

Cardigan essential

Wide skirt to show off legs while dancing

Stiletto heels are invented, though few teens wear them

1951

Metallic, pointed-toe pumps

Sweater girl The cardigan, preferably in mohair or angora, was a must-have item. It was often worn buttoned at the back, which emphasized the bust and created the sweater-girl effect made famous by Hollywood sex symbols.

Cotton dance dress For girls in the 1950s the highlight of the social calendar was going to a dance, whether a prom or an informal event held by the school or community. New music styles and dance crazes made these occasions constantly exciting.

American-style checked shirt

Black sweater

Hair tied back with scarf

Suspenders reference the 1930s origins of the jitterbug

Slightly high waistline

Three-quarter sleeve blouse

1949

1950

Full circle skirt supported by starched crinolines

Bare legs and no socks somewhat shocking

Wrap skirt reveals legs

No jeans yet for most French teens

White ankle socks

Unisex sneakers

Left Bank cool American teen style was much admired in France, where young people developed their own take on it. The jitterbug, introduced to Paris by American soldiers in 1945, became a dance craze. These students show off their moves in a Paris nightclub in 1949.

High school style Although uniforms were not required at American schools, teen girls developed their own—the skirt, either full or pencil shaped finishing just below the knee, and sweater or fitted top. Pants and jeans were forbidden.

Long, swept back hair

Turned-up collar

Flattop haircut

Casual plaids are popular

Patterned, short-sleeve shirts are everyday wear

Red jacket symbolizes protest and passion

1955

1958

Jeans with cuffs

Worn-out, Western-style jeans

Biker boots

Heavy, black leather boots look tough

Rebel role model James Dean's portrayal of an anguished teen in *Rebel Without a Cause* was an enormous influence on fashion. His jeans, boots, and form-fitting white T-shirt with slightly rolled sleeves became a uniform for disaffected youth worldwide.

Denim revolution Teen style revolved around dressing down, and attracted the disapproval of adults. These boys wear jeans, which were not allowed in school. Like denim, short-sleeved shirts and plaids were popular because they appeared ultracasual.

WRANGLER

Seeking out a mainstream market, work-wear maker Blue Bell Overall Company launched the Wrangler brand in 1947 with jeans tested and endorsed by professional rodeo cowboys. This tough yet glamorous association was part of the Wrangler appeal to teens. Designed to look good, as opposed to simply being functional, Wrangler's slim "body fit" jeans were a hit. Eventually adults and children were wearing them, too—the start of America's love affair with all things denim.

Wrangler advertisement

1950–1960
SPORTS STYLE

In the 1950s, more and more people became involved in all types of sports activities, whether it was tennis and bowling, baseball and skiing, or golf at the country club. Even if they were not participating in physical pursuits, people wanted to look as though they were aspiring to a wholesome image. Hollywood reflected the mood: when Katharine Hepburn starred in *Pat and Mike* (1952) as a champion athlete, she created a sensation with her athletic figure and stylish, sporty wardrobe. After wearing pants and shorts out of necessity during wartime, post-war women adopted casual wear that offered slimmer, feminine designs in new stretch fabrics. Clam diggers, capris, stirrup pants, jodhpurs, and culottes gradually replaced mannish slacks.

Fur adds luxurious touch to hood

Lightweight snow jacket

Jacket fitted to show off waist

Chalet chic As designers experimented with fabrics, skiwear became lighter, yet was just as warm. Items such as stirrup pants and down jackets also made their way into everyday life.

Black, white, and red fashionable

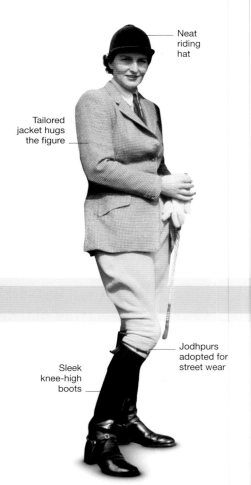

Neat riding hat

Tailored jacket hugs the figure

Sleek knee-high boots

Jodhpurs adopted for street wear

Equestrian elegance Olympic rider Mary Marshall wears formal riding attire here. Even those who had never ridden copied the equestrian look, lured by the lean lines and aristocratic associations. Avid horsewoman Grace Kelly helped set the trend.

Glossy, waved hair

Polo-style knit in pastel shade

Feminine, full mid-calf skirt

Classic bowling shoes

Bowling beauty Bowling was all the rage in the 1950s. Advertisements targeted women, and US manufacturer Capezio launched a range of bowling shoes with a campaign featuring high-society ladies. Women wore full skirts and fitted sweaters.

Raglan sleeves

Fur collar

Narrow, belted waist

Full circle skirt

White lace-up skating boots

Skating style New synthetic fibers developed during the decade allowed for practical, comfortable sportswear. This young figure-skater's outfit follows the fashionable silhouette, while giving greater ease of movement.

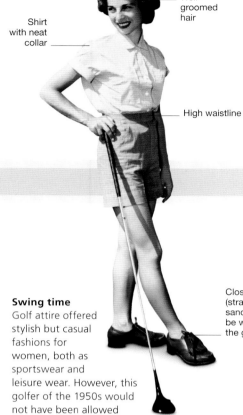

Well-groomed hair

Shirt with neat collar

High waistline

Closed shoes (strappy, open sandals could be worn off the green)

Swing time
Golf attire offered stylish but casual fashions for women, both as sportswear and leisure wear. However, this golfer of the 1950s would not have been allowed to wear such brief shorts while she was on the green.

Small stand-up collar

Form-fitting jacket

Stylish, all-white ensemble

Track pants replace traditional breeches

Glamorous pursuit Fencing, with its skillful, balletic moves and dashing, pants-wearing women, has long inspired fashion and sportswear designers. Here, Bress Aboularia models her practice wear for the French women's fencing team in the 1950s.

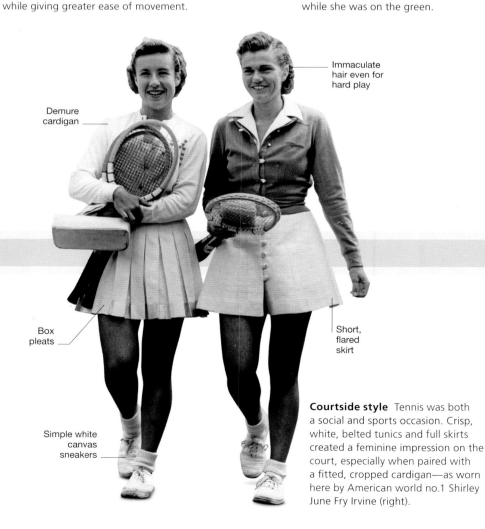

Immaculate hair even for hard play

Demure cardigan

Box pleats

Short, flared skirt

Simple white canvas sneakers

Courtside style Tennis was both a social and sports occasion. Crisp, white, belted tunics and full skirts created a feminine impression on the court, especially when paired with a fitted, cropped cardigan—as worn here by American world no.1 Shirley June Fry Irvine (right).

CHEERLEADING GLAMOUR

Cheerleading is an American phenomenon that began in the late 1800s as an activity for boys, but by the 1950s had become dominated by girls. In an era that prized athleticism, cheerleading provided an outlet for girls, who had limited choices when it came to school and college sports. The uniforms were considered the height of teen glamour—knee-length skirts (that had crept shorter by the 1960s), letter sweaters, bobby sox with saddle shoes, and the all-important pom-poms, originally made of crepe paper and then of water-resistant vinyl in the mid-1960s.

SWINGING SIXTIES TO
GLAM ROCK

1964–1979

SWINGING SIXTIES TO GLAM ROCK

The fashion revolution of the 1960s changed the way that women dressed. There was a seismic shift toward youth—dubbed a "youthquake"—and women were no longer expected to dress in middle-aged, tweedy suits as soon as they grew up. Young London designers led the way and took their funky fashions to the US. "Paraphernalia," a new boutique in New York, sold British modes, with branches opening across the country. Society was becoming less formal with the invention of the contraceptive pill as reflected in the phrase "The Permissive Society." The new mood in fashion was slowly changing the more traditional areas of society: famously, model Jean Shrimpton attended the Gold Cup horse race in Australia in 1965, an annual society event, wearing a skirt 5 in (12.5 cm) above the knee.

Bright new future

The swinging sixties was a time of optimism and belief in the future—with the development of Concorde in Britain and France airplanes traveled faster than the speed of sound, and the space race between the US and the USSR reached a climax when US astronauts stepped onto the surface of the moon. This dynamism and modernity were mirrored in fashion at all levels, from the energetic action shots of new British fashion photographers such as John Cowan and David Bailey to the metallic and plastic fabrics used by French designers including Michele Rosier and Paco Rabanne.

Counterculture

With the continuing war in Vietnam, the Watergate scandal in Washington, D.C., and the three-day week to conserve electricity in Britain, the bright optimism fizzled out as the sixties became the seventies. An impetus to go "back to nature" was reflected in the nostalgic romanticism of Laura Ashley printed-cotton dresses and colorful, hand-knit garments by designers such as Kaffe Fassett. Fashion entered a fantasy era from glam rock through to ethnically inspired collections such as Yves Saint Laurent's Chinese and Russian collections and Kenzo Takada's bright prints. Opting out became most extreme toward the end of the 1970s when entrepreneur Malcolm McLaren, inspired by American groups such as the New York Dolls, formed British punk band the Sex Pistols. The group wore ripped and torn T-shirts with curt slogans such as "Destroy" and "Anarchy."

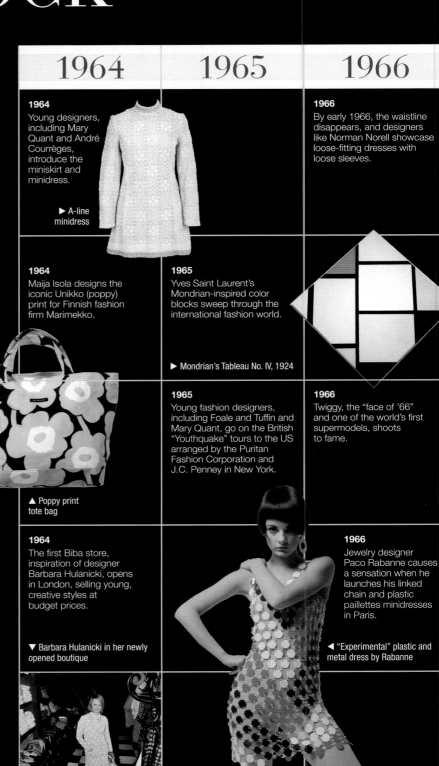

1964

1964
Young designers, including Mary Quant and André Courrèges, introduce the miniskirt and minidress.

▶ A-line minidress

1964
Maija Isola designs the iconic Unikko (poppy) print for Finnish fashion firm Marimekko.

▲ Poppy print tote bag

1964
The first Biba store, inspiration of designer Barbara Hulanicki, opens in London, selling young, creative styles at budget prices.

▼ Barbara Hulanicki in her newly opened boutique

1965

1965
Yves Saint Laurent's Mondrian-inspired color blocks sweep through the international fashion world.

▶ Mondrian's Tableau No. IV, 1924

1965
Young fashion designers, including Foale and Tuffin and Mary Quant, go on the British "Youthquake" tours to the US arranged by the Puritan Fashion Corporation and J.C. Penney in New York.

1966

1966
By early 1966, the waistline disappears, and designers like Norman Norell showcase loose-fitting dresses with loose sleeves.

1966
Twiggy, the "face of '66" and one of the world's first supermodels, shoots to fame.

1966
Jewelry designer Paco Rabanne causes a sensation when he launches his linked chain and plastic paillettes minidresses in Paris.

◀ "Experimental" plastic and metal dress by Rabanne

"

The fashionable woman wears clothes.
The clothes don't wear her.

MARY QUANT, FASHION DESIGNER, 1960s

"

1967–68   1969–70   1971–72   1973–75   1976–77   1978–79

1971
Halston, considered by American socialites as the best evening wear designer, is given the "Winnie" (women's wear award) at the Coty American Fashion Critics' Awards.

1975
Italian designer Giorgio Armani founds his own label.

1976
The comedy crime drama *Charlie's Angels* makes its debut on US television. The three female leads are celebrated for their hairstyles and individual fashion choices.

▶ Charlie's Angels: Kate Jackson, Farrah Fawcett, and Jaclyn Smith

1967
American fashion designer Geoffrey Beene presents his sequined football jersey evening gowns, following his ball gowns in gray flannel and wool jersey shown the previous year.

1972
Japanese designer Kansai Yamamoto designs costumes for David Bowie's Ziggy Stardust tour.

▶ Bowie's Ziggy Stardust stage costume

1968
The rock musical *Hair* opens on Broadway and in London's West End, making Marsha Hunt a star and proclaiming "black is beautiful."

▼ Recording of *Hair* with original Broadway cast

▲ Jimi Hendrix's hippy style at Woodstock

1969
The Woodstock festival takes place in New York state, and is seen as a defining moment of the "hippie era" and '60s counterculture.

1972
British designer Bill Gibb holds his debut fashion show at the Oriental Club, London. His romantic clothes include printed leather skirts and colorful knits.

1977
Ralph Lauren styles Diane Keaton's wardrobe in Woody Allen's film *Annie Hall*, launching numerous copycat looks of baggy linen pants and crisp white shirts and ties for women.

▲ Plaque honoring Perry Ellis on New York's Seventh Avenue

1969
The US lands the first men on the moon, after space exploration earlier in the decade, which inspires space-age fashion looks.

▼ Astronaut Pete Conrad stands on the surface of the moon beside the US flag.

1975
London punk band the Sex Pistols play their first gig at Saint Martin's College of Art.

1978
Perry Ellis founds his own line, showing American sportswear, clothes with loose tailoring, long lines, and oversized sweaters.

1968
The first Ossie Clark for Radley collection is shown at Chelsea Town Hall.

▶ The Sex Pistols' Johnny Rotten in concert

1964–1969
MINI MAGIC

The miniskirt spearheaded a fashion revolution, and the minidress came along hot on its heels. This one-piece was easy and versatile for young women to wear, with the basic A-line design flattering all shapes and sizes. Its very simplicity meant it could be dressed up or down. From minimal cuts and block colors to powerful patterns and pop-art prints, the dress could be as everyday or daring as the wearer wanted. Real trendsetters experimented with bold fabrics, such as metallic PVC and shiny rayon. The straight lines of the minidress silhouette left room for accessories to share the limelight. Matching handbags and shoes became a popular way to enhance and accentuate outfits. With the invention of tights, women were able to wear shorter hemlines while maintaining their modesty.

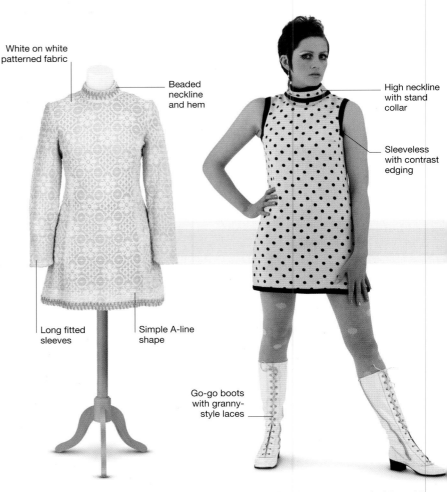

White on white patterned fabric

Beaded neckline and hem

Long fitted sleeves

Simple A-line shape

High neckline with stand collar

Sleeveless with contrast edging

Go-go boots with granny-style laces

All in white This striking minidress from the 1960s boasts a crisp cut and a neat finish. The collar and hem detail breaks up the block white that was popular at the time. Long sleeves and a loose-fitting waistline present a casual, youthful look.

Polka-dot dress Worn with shiny white go-go boots, sleeveless minidresses were a hit on the dance floor, because they gave women freedom to move. The basic shape of this minidress lets the polka-dot pattern take center stage.

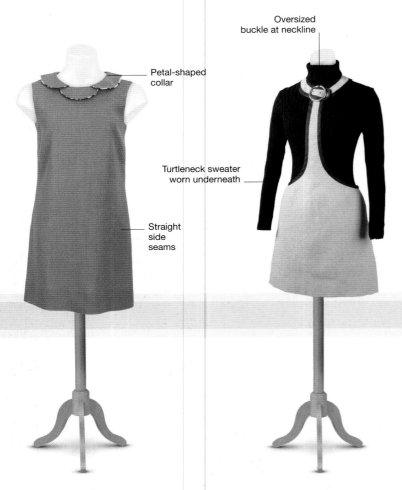

Petal-shaped collar

Oversized buckle at neckline

Turtleneck sweater worn underneath

Straight side seams

Pretty in pink Similar to a minidress but sleeveless and slightly longer, the shift dress—an unwaisted design that grew out of Balenciaga's sack style of the 1950s—was also favored during the 1960s. This classic shift dress is made from a vibrantly dyed linen, with a printed, backed collar.

British belter This outfit by Mary Quant demonstrates her creativity as a designer. Half-dress, half-skirt, the deep cutaway sides and large buckle fastening at the halter neck are both innovative and playful.

POP ART

During the 1950s, a new artistic movement called pop art took off in the US and Britain. Using images from advertising and popular culture, artists and designers made statements on the fleeting and disposable nature of postwar society. American artist Andy Warhol led the pop-art revolution, creating designs inspired by iconic products and famous faces.

This Souper Dress pays homage to Warhol's Campbell's Soup prints, with the distinctive label multiplied into a repeating silk-screen design. The simple shape of the minidress was an ideal blank canvas to showcase Warhol's prints. And fashion provided the perfect medium for discussing themes of capitalism and commerce, art and the everyday.

Dress made of cellulose and cotton

The Souper Dress

Smoky eye
makeup

Oversized collar

Contrasting collar
and front closure

Sailor style The nautical
nature of this dress by French
designer André Courrèges was
on trend in the 1960s. A smart
cut in navy and white with
a slightly longer hemline
produced a more sophisticated
finish for an older wearer.

False
pocket
flaps

Two-tone
floral print

Longer hemline
than most
minidresses

Mellow yellow These
minidresses by French
designer Michèle Rosier
for Pierre d'Alby show two
fashionable outfits typical
of the decade. Bright blocks
of color are matched with
chunky jewelry and
block-heeled shoes.

BAGS

Though handbags are a fashion staple for
most women today, it was not always the
case. After World War II when money was
scarce and practicality was important,
many women made do with whatever was
available. It was in the 1960s that handbags
first became a fashion statement.

Created from a variety of materials
including leather, plastic, and PVC, this
new generation of handbags featured
zippers, frames, locks, fasteners, and
handles. Popular designs were finished
with fake animal-skin prints, psychedelic
patterns, and eye-catching candy colors—
often chosen to match a dress, hat, or coat.
The three bags below are in keeping with
the clean lines of fashionable dress during
the 1960s.

American pink, faux snake
skin Eton bag

Matching
hose

Yellow,
low-heeled
shoes
with straps

Ronay bag of faux
pony skin

Ronay bag of faux
leopard skin

FASHION ICON
TWIGGY

London model Twiggy, born Lesley Hornby, shot to fame in 1966, her face imprinted on the decade. London youth fashions dominated the world and Twiggy was the ideal international ambassador and one of the first supermodels. The teenager's girlish, twiglike figure; short hair; wide, darkly lined and long-lashed eyes (with extra lower lashes painted on her skin); freckles; and innocent expression added up to a waiflike gamine look that spoke to ordinary young women.

The mini-girl in the mini-era

Twiggy—from her existing nickname Twigs—was an unlikely icon at just 16 years of age. She was short for a model, at 5 ft 6 in (1.68 m), with a silhouette and appearance totally different from the curvier, sophisticated models of the day. Her look was a striking version of the mod—a crucial youth-cult link.

Admiring a photograph of the young girl sporting a striking crop on the walls of a London hair salon, *Daily Express* journalist Deirdre McSharry asked to meet her. Soon Twiggy was splashed across the paper as "The Face of '66." That same year saw her in a *Vogue* shoot and, by the following year, she had her own line of dresses and was a top international model, managed by boyfriend Justin de Villeneuve. Throughout 1966 and '67 she was featured in magazines such as *Vogue* and *Elle,* in France, the UK, and the US. Legendary US *Vogue* editor Diana Vreeland championed Twiggy and gave her career a powerful boost.

Much has been said about Twiggy starting the trend for superthin models. But she has countered that she was very young when she began modeling, ate heartily, was naturally skinny, and disapproves of size zero.

Twiggy's status as one of the era's most photographed people helped to promote many of the main fashion trends of the 1960s. Her short hair and underdeveloped figure made her perfect for the little boy/little girl look that revolutionized fashion from Europe to North America and through to Australasia. The look included the baby-doll style and pale stockings of London designers such as Jean Varon and Gina Fratini, and the work of younger Parisian designers such as Pierre Cardin and Emmanuelle Khanh. Twiggy modeled countless variations of the all-important simple '60s mini-shift, including Yves Saint Laurent's landmark 1967 *African* collection, which featured revealing shift dresses made from raffia, shells, and wood beads. She was the first model to design her own range of clothing, and her line included dresses in trendy psychedelic coloring.

Twiggy's big-eyed innocence was echoed in fashion illustration, particularly in the catalogues for Biba, whose clothes she modeled. And her cropped, boyish look brought back 1920s and '30s influences— such as flapper dresses and male-style suiting— in the 1960s and '70s. All this took just four years. She retired from modeling in 1970 to focus on acting and singing, reinforcing 1920s fashions further by appearing in Ken Russell's movie *The Boy Friend*, released in 1971.

Promoting the mature woman

While following a varied subsequent career in music, acting, and TV, Twiggy maintained links with the fashion world, including designing clothes. Later modeling included a key role in a high-profile Marks & Spencer women's wear campaign from 2005 onward, as well as a broader role as an advocate of stylish clothes for mature women.

△ **MOD HAIRCUT**
Few women could carry off hairdresser Vidal Sassoon's severe five-point cut as well as gamine-faced Twiggy. Her crop hairstyle became an integral part of the mod look of the 1960s.

ANDROGYNOUS TREND 1968 ▷
Twiggy is best known for modeling ultra-feminine baby-doll dresses. But she was equally at ease in traditional menswear adapted for women's fashion.

1949 Born Lesley Hornby in Neasden, northwest London

1965 Meets hairdresser Nigel Davies, who renames himself Justin de Villeneuve and becomes her manager

◁ **1966** Launches modeling career and advertises her Twiggy Dresses clothes line for teenage market. Voted British Woman of the Year

1967 The Twiggy Phenomenon causes a stir in New York and Twiggy appears on cover of US *Vogue*

▷ **1969** Cast in Ken Russell's movie, *The Boy Friend*, released in 1971

1970 Retires from modeling

2005 Takes part in the first Marks and Spencer women's wear ad campaign featuring women of different ages. Becomes a judge on TV's *America's Next Top Model*

2009 Featured in exhibition *The Model as Muse: Embodying Fashion* at New York's Metropolitan Museum of Art

O 1960   O 1970   O 2010

THE CHILDLIKE LOOK In 1966, Twiggy epitomized the trend for mini-shift dresses teamed with pale stockings and t-strap shoes. ▷

" The Cockney Kid with a face to launch a thousand shapes ... and she's only 16!

DAILY EXPRESS, February 23, 1966
"

1964–1969
MINICOATS AND SKIRTS

With the fast-paced social scene of the swinging sixties came daring developments in fashion. The introduction of the mini mid-decade saw women wearing skirts that finished above the knee for the first time since the 1920s. Hemlines continued to rise, encouraged by the designs of Mary Quant and John Bates at Jean Varon, reaching a high of the mega-micro, 8 in (20 cm) above the knee. This controversially skimpy style was greeted by the older generation with raised eyebrows, but for young fashionistas the leggy look was an expression of a new freedom. Skirts were simple and neat but in bright, head-turning colors. Coats were similarly thigh skimming, challenging the established notion that women should cover up their bodies. The iconic miniskirt left a lasting legacy, with designers returning to the shape again and again, beyond the 20th century and into the 21st.

MARY QUANT

British designer Mary Quant (1934–) launched her "London look" for the youth culture emerging in the capital. She created unique designs for the teenage market, including the micromini, and showcased them in the windows of her famous Chelsea boutique, Bazaar. The style was soon popularized and became mass produced, with sales spreading across Europe.

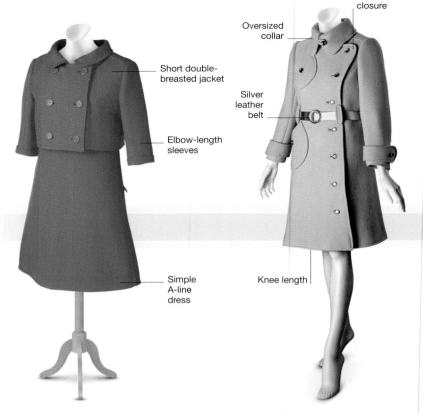

Short double-breasted jacket

Elbow-length sleeves

Simple A-line dress

Asymmetric front button closure

Oversized collar

Silver leather belt

Knee length

Block color In 1964, French designer André Courrèges included the new short style in his collection. This minidress and matching jacket in bright orange wool typifies the minimalist cut of his designs.

Asymmetric detail This simple wool coat, from 1967, shows Courrèges's flair for subtle subversion of a traditional cut. The design features large patch pockets on the diagonal, and a metallic leather belt and buttons.

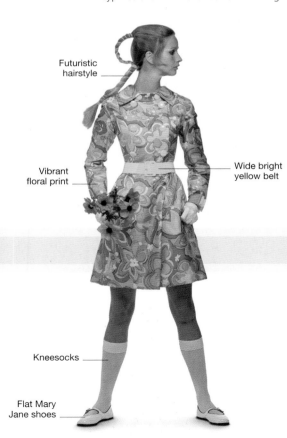

Futuristic hairstyle

Vibrant floral print

Wide bright yellow belt

Kneesocks

Flat Mary Jane shoes

In Vogue This bright floral print coatdress by New York's Originala fashion house was photographed for *Vogue* in 1968. The design features double-breasted button details, a large collar, and a contrasting belt in the style of a raincoat.

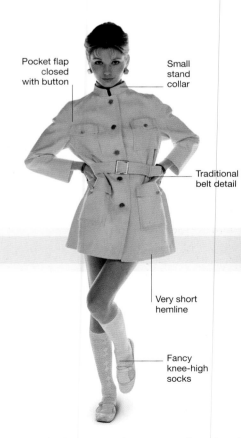

Pocket flap closed with button

Small stand collar

Traditional belt detail

Very short hemline

Fancy knee-high socks

Belted raincoat This waterproof coat by US company Weatherbee put a modern twist on the traditional raincoat, first produced in the 1820s. Here, it is worn with white knee-high socks and Mary Jane shoes.

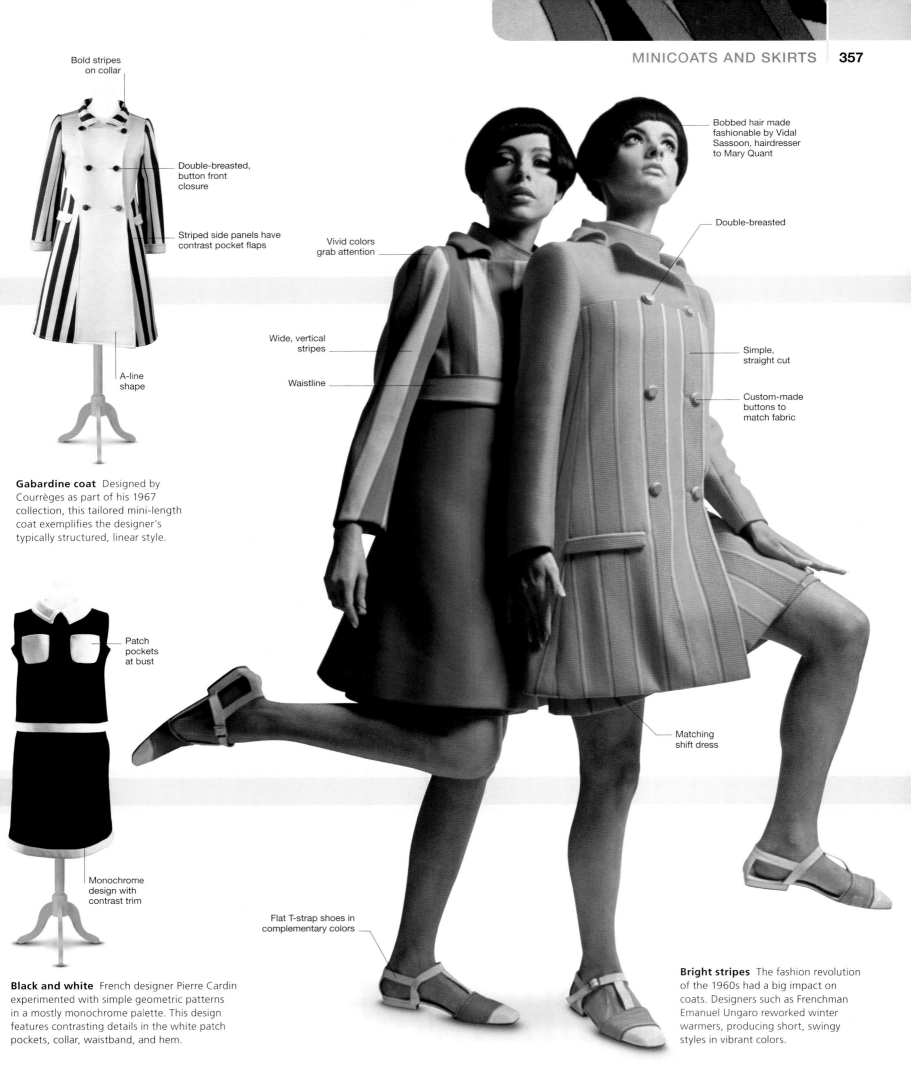

Bold stripes
on collar

Double-breasted,
button front
closure

Striped side panels have
contrast pocket flaps

A-line
shape

Gabardine coat Designed by
Courrèges as part of his 1967
collection, this tailored mini-length
coat exemplifies the designer's
typically structured, linear style.

Patch
pockets
at bust

Monochrome
design with
contrast trim

Black and white French designer Pierre Cardin
experimented with simple geometric patterns
in a mostly monochrome palette. This design
features contrasting details in the white patch
pockets, collar, waistband, and hem.

Vivid colors
grab attention

Wide, vertical
stripes

Waistline

Bobbed hair made
fashionable by Vidal
Sassoon, hairdresser
to Mary Quant

Double-breasted

Simple,
straight cut

Custom-made
buttons to
match fabric

Matching
shift dress

Flat T-strap shoes in
complementary colors

Bright stripes The fashion revolution
of the 1960s had a big impact on
coats. Designers such as Frenchman
Emanuel Ungaro reworked winter
warmers, producing short, swingy
styles in vibrant colors.

ANYTHING GOES

The sixties were optimistic, upbeat, and occasionally turbulent. The new mood of freedom and rampant individualism was reflected in fashion. Younger designers in Britain such as Mary Quant and John Bates, Marion Foale and Sally Tuffin, Caroline Charles and Jean Muir, and also those in France, including André Courrèges, Emanuel Ungaro, and Pierre Cardin, had all been experimenting with more youthful styles for young women who no longer accepted that they had to dress like their mothers. From such beginnings the miniskirt was born in 1964. Hems rose swiftly, until by 1967 styles were thigh high. Stockings with garters could no longer be worn, and so manufacturers developed all-in-one tights, or pantyhose as they were then known.

In fashion once an extreme is reached then a reaction sets in. The miniskirt could get no higher, so designers brought out new skirt lengths: first of all the midi, followed by the more enduring maxi. At the same time the miniskirt still survived, and pantsuits, turtleneck sweaters, and hipster jeans—part of a "unisex" trend—were being worn. By the end of the decade it was a case of anything goes.

> **"**
> Once only the Rich, the Establishment set the fashion. Now it is the inexpensive little dress seen on the girls in the High Street. These girls ... are alive ... looking, listening, ready to try anything new ... they represent the whole new spirit ...
>
> **GEORGE MELLY,** *REVOLT INTO STYLE*, 1972
> **"**

◁ **CHANGING TIMES**
Fashion in the 1960s was evolving at breakneck speed, as demonstrated by the breadth of styles modeled at the opening of Just Looking, one of the numerous boutiques that mushroomed on Carnaby Street and the King's Road, London.

1960–1969
INTO THE SPACE AGE

The 1960s was the decade of space exploration, sparking vivid imaginings about what the future might be like. Fashion was quick to take up the themes—Pierre Cardin's *Space-Age* collection in 1964 began the trend—which continued into the 1970s—with Paco Rabanne, André Courrèges, and Rudi Gernreich soon following suit. The look included metallic or shiny cloth along with synthetic fabrics such as clear and colored plastics, PVC, vinyl, and acrylic. Simple geometric shapes, A-line silhouettes, miniskirts, unisex styles, and bright colors created futuristic ensembles that appealed to the growing youth market.

Matching chain mail headdress

Short-sleeved dresses appealed to young generation

Geometric shapes linked with chain

Bare legs were a necessity with chain mail dresses

The new armor Spanish-born French designer Paco Rabanne applied his love of jewelry design to dressmaking. He became well known for chain mail dresses, which linked plastic or metal geometric pieces together. Model Karin Jensen wears this example from 1968.

Futuristic acrylic visor recalls astronaut helmets

High-necked collar

Blue plastic miniskirt

Circular motifs were common

Tights in various colors were popular, as well as black

Built-in booties

Modern geometry Designed in 1967 by Italian-born French designer Pierre Cardin, this black and blue plastic ensemble paired with a visor is modeled by actress Raquel Welch. An instigator of space-age fashion, Cardin often focused on circular, and other geometric cutouts, and straps.

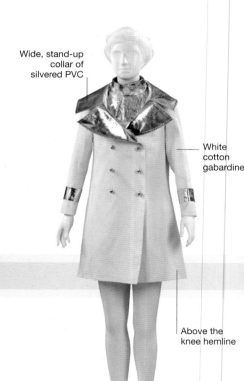

Wide, stand-up collar of silvered PVC

White cotton gabardine

Circular motifs were common

Above the knee hemline

Metallic plastics Englishman John Bates, an early proponent of the miniskirt, designed this wedding ensemble for fashion journalist Marit Allen in 1966. Bates created the double-breasted coat with wide lapels, using shiny metallic polyester and PVC.

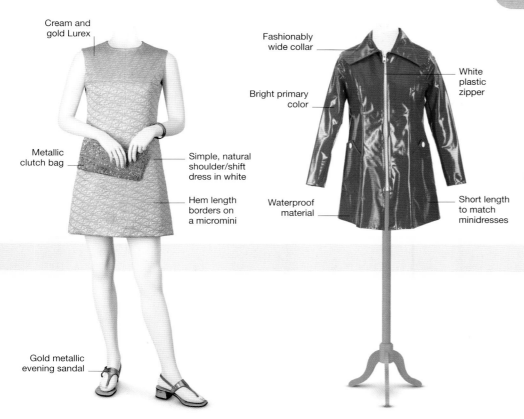

Cream and gold Lurex

Metallic clutch bag

Simple, natural shoulder/shift dress in white

Hem length borders on a micromini

Gold metallic evening sandal

Fashionably wide collar

Bright primary color

White plastic zipper

Waterproof material

Short length to match minidresses

Space-age luxury This Lurex minidress epitomizes the use of new materials and the glamorous effect they produced. Lurex yarn creates a woven fabric made with aluminum, gold, or silver, producing a shiny, manageable surface with a touch of luxury.

Practical design A red PVC, wet-look raincoat of simple design fits well within the new disposable consumer society, where plastic items were not made to last. Pierre Cardin and Mary Quant created similar designs, for the needs of futuristic women.

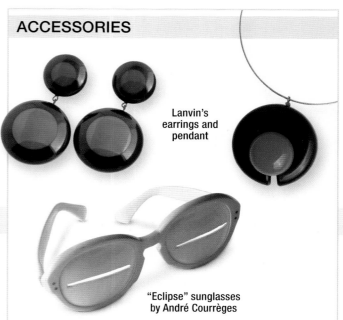

ACCESSORIES

Lanvin's earrings and pendant

"Eclipse" sunglasses by André Courrèges

While older women continued to wear precious and semiprecious jewelry, younger women often opted for plastic or acrylic jewelry and accessories. Bright colors and bold geometric shapes, such as jewelry by the French design house Lanvin, complemented the mod style, while mass production made them affordable. Couture designers created innovative and clever accessories from new materials, too, such as these sunglasses (above) of soft, lightweight plastic.

Geometric zigzag pattern

Contrasting vertical stripes

Empire waist emphasizes a youthful figure

Skirt ends mid-thigh

Sharp revers

Metal accessories and jewelry

Bouffant hair

Plunging neckline

Cut-away armholes

Plastic, knee-high go-go boots with low heel

Colorful Dutch-boy wigs

Contrasting yoke and collar

Two-piece boxy suit with large metallic buttons and trim

Short skirts revealing much of the legs

Youthful flat shoes and pulled-up socks

Shiny sequins Designers such as Yves Saint Laurent, André Courrèges, and Pierre Cardin frequently used highly reflective sequins in contrasting geometric patterns, producing evening dresses that sparkled under the lights.

Science-fiction fashion The 1960s saw a number of space-age movies, including Kubrick's *2001: A Space Odyssey* and *Barbarella*, which starred Jane Fonda (shown). Costume designer Jacques Fonteray and fashion designer Paco Rabanne made good use of futuristic-looking materials and sex appeal.

Youthful look This pair of two-piece suits designed by Frenchman André Courrèges in 1969 illustrates his forward-thinking designs. The A-line miniskirts paired with both square and rounded jackets show his use of structure as a focal point.

1960–1969
EVENING SELECTION

In contrast to the rigid social constructs of 1950s evening attire, the 1960s offered a variety of elegant choices for going out. Gowns could be long or short, even mini for the young and hip. They could be highly trimmed and decorated, or plain—solid or print. Pants were worn as formal evening wear by the daring. For gowns, A-line silhouettes, empire waists, and undefined bodices were popular, though some soft shaping was also in use. Materials for elaborate surface decoration ranged from feathers and jewels to beads and faux fur. Many designers created evening clothes in bright colors or black and white patterns. Popular designers of the decade included French designers Hubert de Givenchy and Yves Saint Laurent, as well as the youthful British designer Jean Muir of Jane and Jane, and Italian designers Emilio Pucci and Valentino.

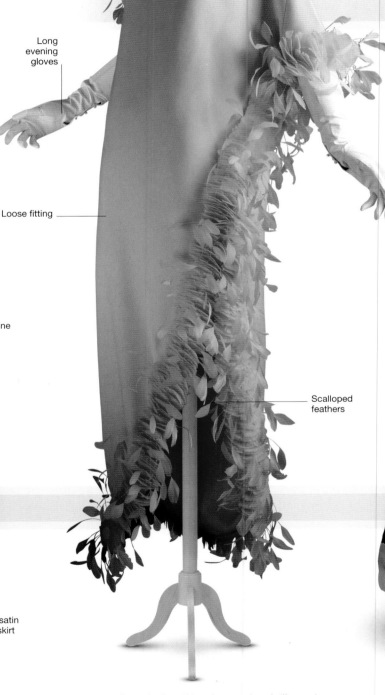

Exposed shoulder

Long evening gloves

Loose fitting

Scalloped feathers

Painted silk jersey

Bold geometric pattern

All-in-one cut

Wide legs

Pants dress The end of the 1960s saw an increasing interest in pants. This 1968 evening pants dress by Italian designer Emilio Pucci, in one of his signature bold patterns, references maxi dresses—also popular at the time.

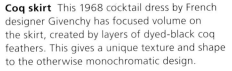

Sleeveless

Wide neckline

Black silk crêpe

Black satin underskirt

Coq skirt This 1968 cocktail dress by French designer Givenchy has focused volume on the skirt, created by layers of dyed-black coq feathers. This gives a unique texture and shape to the otherwise monochromatic design.

Feathered trim This salmon-colored silk evening gown from Givenchy's Fall/Winter 1968–1969 collection is trimmed along each hem with feathers. They give the dress an added sense of movement and flow, and also a touch of drama.

Oversized floral corsage at waist

Transparent sleeves

Very low back

Floral print This beautiful silk chiffon evening gown, created by American designer Geoffrey Beene in 1969, demonstrates the move away from sharp tailored fashions, toward a softer, more romantic silhouette at the end of the decade.

Long, full skirt

Bold, poppy print

1920s styling

Rayon crêpe

Tubular shift

Pleated frills

Adventurous length

Evening minidress Youth-focused British designer Mary Quant created this simple evening minidress for her *Ginger Group* collection in 1967–1968. The bottom is full and the high-waisted line is slightly baby doll.

Dramatic high neck

Short sleeves

Hand-stitched feathers

Trailing feathers

Bird of paradise In 1969, French designer Yves Saint Laurent created this confection of bird-of-paradise feathers and beige silk organza. The feathers are untreated and make the dress uniquely airy and dramatic.

Rounded neckline

Pointed waistband

Taffeta lined

Cocktail dress Designed for Princess Stanislaus Radziwill in 1969 by Italian designer Valentino, this short, velvet cocktail dress features heavy rhinestones embroidery and openwork braid on the cap sleeves and waistband.

HANDBAGS

Women's bags of the 1960s were typically made of leather, alligator, or other animal skins in envelope or pouch shapes with short handles or straps and metallic closures. Everyday bags were usually in neutral colors—especially black—in order to coordinate with a variety of ensembles. Younger women experimented with bags made of nontraditional shapes and materials, such as clear Lucite box bags. An evening bag was usually a small envelope clutch, made to match the evening dress.

Rosenstein evening bag

Pucci velvet handbag

Gucci clutch bag

Judith Leiber evening bag

Faux crocodile bag

DESIGNER
BIBA

△ **BOUTIQUE QUEEN**
Barbara Hulanicki, the genius behind Biba, listened closely to her customers' needs and personally chose every item sold in her shop.

FASHION ON A SHOESTRING ▷
For originality at budget prices, Biba led the way for a decade. This dress-and-pants combination is from a 1967 collection.

L ess a label, more a way of life, the influential Biba brand of the 1960s and '70s blazed a trail for young, hip fashion and the affordable boutique. Biba's 1960s stores were a major democratizing force in a fashion world where the options were haute couture, trendy but pricey stores like Mary Quant's, or somewhat dull "grown-up" wear.

Mail-order origins
Biba was a marriage of Polish-born fashion illustrator Barbara Hulanicki's design genius and her husband Stephen Fitz-Simon's business savvy. In 1963, the couple started a mail-order clothes catalogue of Hulanicki designs that became the Biba Postal Boutique—named after Hulanicki's sister. After a pink gingham dress and head scarf was featured in the *Daily Mirror* they sold 17,000 units.

In 1964, the first Biba shop opened in Kensington, West London, and expanded rapidly, moving twice into bigger premises by 1969. Biba was a new kind of oasis, where friends met and shopped amid a unique, faded Victoriana created by low lighting and eclectic clothes hung from hatstands and piled on to antique furniture. Vibrantly patterned minidresses rubbed shoulders with feather boas, hats, lingerie, and accessories. All garments were originals, and were cheap and creative; limited runs ensured enormous lines to snap up the latest offerings.

Personal vision
Hulanicki's visionary mix of Victoriana, art nouveau, 1920s–'30s art deco, Hollywood decadence, and pop culture ensured that Biba quickly gained an international reputation. Biba

girls were independent and spirited but looked like big-eyed "dolls," with long, thin limbs and a flat chest. The distinctive Biba garment was cut with narrow, inset shoulders and high, body-lengthening armholes, with tight, narrow sleeves. Nostalgic "granny" prints and somber berry, plum, and rust tones became signatures, as did smocks, huge floppy felt hats, and the skinny, chunky-heeled, squarish-toed "Biba boot" in canvas or suede—loyal fans bought several pairs in different colors.

Sophisticated styles were appearing by the late 1960s, including bias-cut, silky '30s-style dresses, cowl necklines, and pants with panel features. Biba added children's and men's clothes, evening wear, and household goods.

Moving up and out
In 1973, the "Big Biba" department store—seven opulent floors selling Biba-branded goods ranging from furniture to baked beans—opened in the suitably art deco premises of a defunct department store on Kensington High Street. Here, celebrities such as David Bowie sipped tea on a roof garden complete with pink flamingoes, as comfortable as the student crowd. Big Biba attracted a million visitors a week, but a gathering British recession hastened its closure after just over two years, and the dream came to an end.

Biba changes hands
The Fitz-Simons moved on to other ventures abroad and the Biba name was sold, the brand resurfacing in other hands. In 2006, Bella Freud designed a short-lived collection, and in 2009/10 Biba lines were launched in two mainstream chain stores. Items included a rose-print mini-shift with bell sleeves and a vampish feather cape—true to Biba's origins, but at higher-end prices.

TIMELINE

1936 Barbara Hulanicki born in Warsaw, Poland, and raised in Palestine then the UK.

◁ **1964** First Biba shop, selling clothes and head-to-toe accessories, opens on Abingdon Road, Kensington, London

1963 Launch of mail-order catalogue that become Biba Postal Boutique

1969 Move to first large shop on High Street Kensington

◁ **1966** Biba dresses in line with fashion of the time

▽ **1970** Biba cosmetics rolled out nationally; become Hulanicki's most successful line

1971 Menswear introduced

1973–1976 Short life of the "Big Biba" department store; Biba business declared bankrupt

2006–2010 Biba relaunched, out of Hulanicki's hands; stores feature new Biba collections

○ 1930   ○ 1960   ○ 1970   ○ 2000

PARTY-STYLE BIBA Hulanicki brought runway glamour to mainstream buyers—in 1969 it was sequins and stripes. ▷

1967–1970
MENSWEAR GOES POP

Movers and shakers from the pop charts took the fashion world by storm in the 1960s. Designers used famous faces and fleeting fads to influence and inspire their clothing collections, with the result that music and menswear went hand in hand. Top of the charts was British band The Beatles, the ultimate mods of music. Their revolutionary style, including longer hair and matching suits, was reflected in the fashions adopted enthusiastically by young men on both sides of the Atlantic. Clothing lines grew at the same rapid rate as fan bases. Continental creations favored by well-known actors and models were also manufactured for the mass market. The admiration and adulation that greeted the arrival of new style icons on the music scene, including the Rolling Stones, The Who, and The Animals, was unprecedented. More and more mainstream stores opened, encouraging young men to spend their hard-earned cash on replica clothing that paid homage to their heroes.

Military-style coat and hat

Coordinated, bright colors

Thick overshirt

Handlebar moustache

T-shirt and scarf worn under jacket instead of shirt and tie

Ethnic-inspired shoes

Beatlemania The impact of Liverpudlian pop group The Beatles was huge. The "Fab Four" dominated the music charts and, as Beatlemania took hold, their fashion choices influenced a generation.

KING OF CARNABY STREET

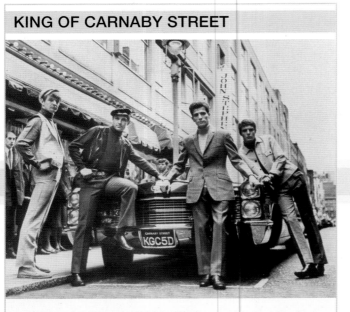

In 1957, John Stephen (1934–2004) arrived in London from Glasgow and started work as an assistant in Carnaby Street's Vince boutique, the first men's clothing store to open in this trendy area. Here, he was inspired to build on the growing demand for modern menswear and also unisex styles, which resulted in his chain of influential stores opening across the capital. Stephen is seen here (second right) posing with models on his beloved Carnaby Street.

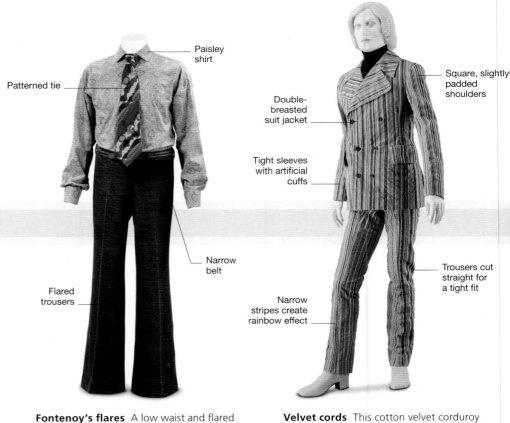

Patterned tie

Paisley shirt

Narrow belt

Flared trousers

Double-breasted suit jacket

Square, slightly padded shoulders

Tight sleeves with artificial cuffs

Trousers cut straight for a tight fit

Narrow stripes create rainbow effect

Fontenoy's flares A low waist and flared legs were popular developments in men's trousers at the end of the 1960s. This on-trend pair made of synthetic jersey was produced by French fashion house Fontenoy.

Velvet cords This cotton velvet corduroy suit is made from a furnishing fabric produced by the American manufacturer Hexter. Lined with silk, it pairs a double-breasted jacket with hipster trousers.

Brocade in floral
turquoise design

Turtleneck

Pocket
zipper

Patent-
leather belt

Off-center
zipper

Patent-
leather
boots

Cardin jersey Part of a collection
put together by English photographer
Sir Cecil Beaton, this wool jersey tunic
is by French designer Pierre Cardin. It
features a longer length and a stylish,
off-center zipper closure.

Loose-fitting
suit

TIED UP

The trendiest sixties suit was unlikely to
impress if the accompanying tie was not
up to snuff. Italian designer Emilio Pucci
(1914–1992) spotted the commercial
opportunities for vibrant ties and produced
a range of original geometric and abstract
designs to enliven and transform men's
fashion. Although Pucci's silk ties were
classically cut, they were transformed by
his creative use of color and became
an instant success.

Pucci printed silk ties

Fabulous Fish This sensational suit was
devised by British designer Michael Fish.
The lurex brocade jacket revives an Art
Nouveau design, while the corded-silk
closure and beaded tassels are inspired
by Victorian men's jackets.

"Mop top"
hairstyle

Fake fur
vest

Sash

Tunic top
with flared
sleeves

Belt

Harem-style
pants

Tight-fitting
pants

Flared trousers
in matching
turquoise

Trailblazers As pop stars
donned ever more daring designs,
young men copied them by
experimenting with fashion. Fake
fur, wild patterns, and feminine
colors were all up for grabs.

Pants
gathered
at ankle

Cowboy
boots

1964–1969
THE NEW DANDIES

After World War II, the accepted norm for menswear was a double-breasted, three-piece suit, heavy in fabric and loose in fit. With dark blue, gray, or brown as the usual options, and pinstripe the only pattern around, young men simply followed suit. But by the 1960s it was not only women who were revolutionizing their wardrobes. As popular culture took over music and fashion, men also discovered a whole new range of style options. Suits sharpened up their act in subtle ways that had major aesthetic impact. Collars became longer and larger, while belts and ties grew wider. Slimmer fits were now popular, as tailored, single-breasted jackets and tighter pants showcased the male form. Color and pattern came in to the alarm of the more conservative. But for a generation of gentlemen finding their fashion feet, it was time to get suited and booted, and ultimately to suit themselves.

Beau Brummell influence Two rock bands of the 1960s named themselves after the Regency dandy as men again became as fashion conscious as women. This young man strikes a pose in his sharp suit accessorized with gloves, cane, and breast-pocket handkerchief.

1965

Contrasting collar color

Accessories for men

Fitted box jacket

Slim-fitting pants

Low-heeled stylish shoes

Matching shirt and tie

Suit in contrasting color

Button detail on jacket arm

Savile Row's quality tailoring

Flattering fabric

1968

Narrow collar

Silk turtleneck shirt in classic black

Front zip fastening

Slimmer-fitting suit

Fabric in mottled gray and white

Fresh with finesse Designed by tailor Blades, this suit is an example of what happened when the freshness of Carnaby Street's clothing met the finesse of Savile Row's tailoring. Roy Strong wore it while he was director of the National Portrait Gallery.

Relaxing the rules The 1960s saw the arrival of more informal dress codes. Teamed here with a silk turtleneck shirt, this casual suit by H. Huntsman & Sons has a noticeably slimmer fit in the pants and modern tailoring on the jacket.

1966

- Tailored suit jacket
- Tighter fit on the leg
- Matching white shoes

Stylish suit Double-breasted suits, with tight-fitting sleeves and lower legs, made in fabric that was light in both color and weight, such as this brought traditional menswear up to date.

1967

- "Highwayman" collar
- Purple bow tie adds color
- Flared wrist on the suit jacket
- Frock coat with extended lines

Dapper delight This suit is a classic from Carnaby Street, London's fashion center during the 1960s. The long frock coat, tall "highwayman" collar, and striking bow tie result in a truly dapper design that pays homage to 19th-century dandyism.

- Hair grown over the ears
- Shirt worn open at the collar
- Fitted pants with creased front

Mismatched suit This young London mod experiments with color and pattern in his combination of oversized tweed jacket and bright red drainpipe pants. A pale shirt and white shoes keep the look casual.

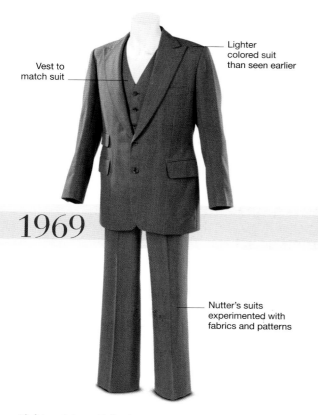

1969

- Vest to match suit
- Lighter colored suit than seen earlier
- Nutter's suits experimented with fabrics and patterns

Lighter stripes Trained on Savile Row, British tailor Tommy Nutter produced high-end fashion suits in the late 1960s for big names including the Beatles. This bespoke suit was designed by Nutter in the same year he opened his own shop.

SETTING UP SHOP

As trendy boutiques such as Hung On You started opening up around London in the 1960s, shopping became a popular pastime for young men. Savile Row was too expensive for most followers of fashion, and these smaller stores sold cheaper and often funkier alternatives. With male models posing inside the stores, wearing the latest creations from up-and-coming designers, trends were set and styles explored in the brave new world of men's fashion.

DESIGNER
YVES ST. LAURENT

A giant of 20th-century international fashion, French designer Yves Saint Laurent dominated the 1960s and '70s. He deftly juggled street style and traditional tailoring, revolutionized the female wardrobe by popularizing women's pants, and raised the status of ready-to-wear clothes.

After winning an international fashion competition, a teenaged Saint Laurent studied fashion in Paris. Having seen some of his sketches, leading legend Christian Dior hired the prodigy as an assistant.

Fashion's *enfant terrible*

When Dior died, in 1957, Saint Laurent became Dior's creative head, and at 21 the world's youngest couturier. His first solo collection was *Trapeze* (1958)—short, trapezoid dresses that swung from narrow shoulders and echoed his mentor's A-lines. However, his rebellious "beatnik" collection (1960), inspired by a love of Paris's Left Bank clubs and jazz bars, sparked criticism. Appalled by the collection's streetwise black turtlenecks and leather biker-style jackets, Dior acted swiftly when Saint Laurent was drafted into the army in 1960 and replaced him with Marc Bohan. After his discharge from the army, Saint Laurent successfully sued Dior for unfair dismissal and set up his own *maison*, showing his first collection in 1962.

Early collections featured peacoats and smocks—more high-end reinventions of street style. The 1960s brought the shock of the cross-gender *Le smoking* tuxedo suit for evening wear, as well as making pantsuits a daily womens wear staple; variants included knickerbockers and culottes. Saint Laurent's love of art exploded in the mid 1960s: color-block dresses (1965–1966) inspired by Mondrian's paintings and the *Pop Art* collection (1966).

From hippies to disco

By the late 1960s, Saint Laurent had shown his famous safari jackets and suits for women (and men), thigh-high boots, controversial see-through blouses, and an *African* collection (1967) inspired by ethnic motifs. He pioneered the referencing of other cultures and was the first designer to feature African and Asian runway models, his multicultural interests greatly influencing hippie fashions. There were dresses featuring exotic feathers (1969–1970), and patchwork fur coats, alongside glamorous evening gowns. His 1940s-inspired, square-shouldered *Libération* collection (1971) offended some with its reminders of German occupation but made a huge mark on the 1970s. The watershed *Opéra-Ballets Russes* collection (1976) offered "peasant chic." Mixing larger shapes and gemlike colors, its luxurious notes chimed with the growing hedonistic US disco scene and helped define 1980s couture.

The empire changes

Through the 1980s and '90s Saint Laurent consolidated both his classic styles and an empire embracing fragrances, cosmetics, home linens, accessories, the all-important ready-to-wear lines and stores, and stylish menswear. In 1999 Gucci bought the YSL ready-to-wear line and made Tom Ford its designer (1999–2004). Ford paid homage to many YSL classics, while his successor, Stefano Pilati, favored a sharp chic. Hedi Slimane, former designer at Dior Homme, took over in 2012.

Saint Laurent closed the couture business and retired in 2002. His promotion of the timeless classic remains a major legacy, while YSL motifs crop up constantly in the collections of younger designers, such as the tuxedo styles of Stella McCartney.

△ **YSL**
Yves Saint Laurent outside his first London boutique in the late 1960s. Couture's "bad boy" was much influenced by Paris's Left Bank scene and used the name Rive Gauche for all his boutiques and ready-to-wear collections.

◁ **PANTS REVOLUTION**
Until Saint Laurent dared to change everything, women were sometimes refused entry to restaurants for wearing pants. This glamorous suit featured in his 1979 Spring/Summer collection.

TIMELINE

1936 Born in Oran, Algeria

1957–1958 At 21 takes over at Dior, when Christian Dior dies. Presents A-line *Trapeze* look at successful first collection

1962 Launches own fashion house

▷ **1965–1966** Creates much-copied "Mondrian" color-block dresses. First Rive Gauche boutique opens in Paris

1971 *Libération* collection reinvents a big-shouldered 1940s silhouette

1976 *Opéra-Ballets Russes* couture-peasant collection hits front page of *New York Times*

▷ **1998** Dress worn at opening of the YSL Room at the National Gallery, London

1999 Sells YSL to Gucci

2008 Dies in Paris

○ 1930   ○ 1960   ○ 1970   ○ 1990   ○ 2000

◁ **TIMELESS STYLING** Saint Laurent made elegant but wearable clothes for women. These styles are from a collection shown in Paris in 1973.

1964–1979
WOMEN WEAR THE PANTS

Stemming from the unisex fashions by futuristic designers such as Pierre Cardin and André Courrèges, fashionable women began wearing pants in the 1960s and '70s. The sexual revolution and "women's lib" meant that women were taking greater strides to enter the workforce, and as a result they borrowed more from men's fashion. French designer Yves Saint Laurent (YSL) first created his sleek but controversial *Le Smoking* tuxedo suit for women in 1966, and continued to create androgynous styles each season. The look slowly became more widely accepted as an alternative to skirts and dresses. In 1971, YSL was inspired by 1940s clothing, incorporating this look into pantsuits and jumpsuits alike. Other designers quickly followed his example. The hippie flower power movement brought in faded denim jeans with wide hems, and the advent of disco encouraged sleek, figure-hugging suits with wide, bell-bottomed pants for both men and women.

1965

Glamorous hairdo

Youthful bangs

High-waisted trousers

Tunic shirt

Wide trouser hems

Tapered to bell-bottoms From the beginning, pants were worn by younger women as a part of the growing youth culture. This group from 1965 shows the variety of styles. As the decade progressed, pants evolved, including more fitted styles and more flared pairs.

AND MEN WEAR THE HEELS

Starting in 1967, designers began to bring back the platform shoe for both men and women, a look that had last been popular in the 1940s. British musical performers such as Elton John and David Bowie quickly adopted the look as a part of a new "male peacock" and psychedelic movement in men's fashion. The examples here are of modest leather styles and heel height, but some platforms were as high as 6–7 in (15–18 cm) and made of wildly imaginative materials and textures such as cork, textured fabric, rope, and even leather-covered plastics or wood. Platform shoes and boots went well with a pair of bell-bottoms.

Platforms paired with bell-bottoms

Men's 1970s leather platform shoes

Cotton jacket in primary colors

1970

Nylon jersey crêpe

Slight flare

Belted tunic blouse

Long sleeves

Machine embroidery

Art Deco motifs

Matching trousers

1973

The acid test Bright colors and simple motifs bridged the gap between 1960s and '70s design. Marimekko, a Finnish design firm, led the way by creating bold floral prints similar to this stylized daisy-print jacket with acid-yellow trousers.

Floral motif British designer Janice Wainwright created this black pantsuit embroidered with floral Art Deco motifs—a typical detail of her work from this period. She continued to focus on simple silver-thread embroidery through the 1970s.

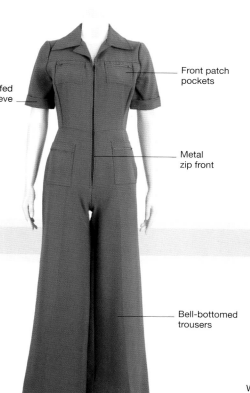

1967

- Dramatic cat's-eye makeup
- Jabot blouse and black silk bow tie
- Alpaca dinner spencer jacket
- Sleek tailored leg
- Slight flare

High-fashion trousers French designer YSL presented the women's tuxedo suit, *Le Smoking*, and it soon became the signature piece of his collection. YSL became well known for empowering women with the option to wear men's styles.

- Modern tailored jacket
- Romantic textile design
- Similar to upholstery fabric

1974

- Wide flare with turn-up

Feminine print Designed in 1974 by Warsaw-born Barbara Hulanicki for Biba, the British boutique, this cotton floral pantsuit combines a traditional pink and green cabbage-rose print, reminiscent of furnishing fabric, with a contemporary design.

- Front patch pockets
- Cuffed sleeve
- Metal zip front
- Bell-bottomed trousers

Jump into the future Continuing the interest in outer space and the future that began in the 1960s, the '70s jumpsuit had ties to futurism and popular science fiction of the era. It became the ultimate in stylish leisure wear, due to its utilitarian functionality.

JEANS

Levi's had been around for 100 years, but by the 1960s they had become the uniform of youth. Hippies wore faded and bell-bottomed jeans, often customizing them as a part of the anti-fashion movement. "Second skin" or figure-hugging jeans were high waisted to emphasize long legs. The first "branded" jeans were introduced by Gloria Vanderbilt and Calvin Klein and were widely worn by the fashionable elite, such as Bianca Jagger and Jacqueline Kennedy Onassis.

Levi's advertisement

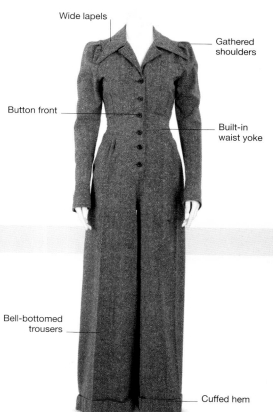

- Wide lapels
- Gathered shoulders
- Button front
- Built-in waist yoke
- Bell-bottomed trousers
- Cuffed hem

War influence This gray tweed jumpsuit from Stirling Cooper is a variation on the boiler suit worn by women factory workers during World War II. Inspired by 1940s style, the suit's wide lapels and bell-bottomed trousers are typical of the 1970s.

FLOWER POWER

Preaching love, peace, and freedom, the hippie movement was a vocal and articulate subculture. Hippies first emerged in 1967 in San Francisco's Haight–Ashbury district, but the trend was soon adopted around the world. They not only took issue with the lifestyle of their parents, but also with racial inequality, sexual discrimination, and civil rights. Protest was at the heart of the movement, in particular against the US involvement in the Vietnam War (1965–1973).

Hippie dress conveyed new beliefs: peace, interest in other cultures, and experimentation—especially with psychedelic drugs; bright clothing patterns attempted to reflect the LSD experience. The trend was anti-fashion and individuality was the key. Clothing, often secondhand, was customized with patchwork, embroidery, and appliquéd designs. Rustic imagery and celestial symbols reflected the strong pacifist and back-to-nature sentiments. The ethnic look dominated: shaggy Afghan coats, fringed suede jackets, caftans, head scarves, and lots of beads. Patterns were psychedelic, and where possible fabrics were natural. Skirt lengths dropped to the floor in swaying maxis, though the mini was still worn, and flares and bell bottoms were in style for pants. American blue jeans were no longer the preserve of the working class, and denim was worn by nearly everyone. The clothes and hairstyles of Indian and African American communities were also incorporated. The fashion for unisex blossomed, and clothes were gender neutral with couples often wearing the same outfits.

> 66
> Today, nothing is out, because everything is in. Every costume from every era is now available to everyone.
>
> MARSHALL MCLUHAN, *HARPER'S BAZAAR*, 1968
> 99

BIRTH OF THE HIPPIE ▷
Hippies spreading flower power in Haight-Ashbury, San Francisco, in 1968. Bright, patterned dresses were influenced by Indian fabrics and psychedelic experimentation.

1970–1979
LONG PRINTED DRESSES

In the 1970s, short skirts were replaced by long, loose A-line dresses. Reminiscent of dress lengths in Victorian times, these "floor-skimmers" wowed with flower power patterns, paisley prints, feminine fabrics, and softer shades. The new decade saw young women embracing peace, love, and freedom in a clear rejection of the warring nations and corrupt capitalist societies dominating the news around the world. The shift toward idealistic notions of harmonious living was best reflected in carefree, natural attire. The ethnic styles of non-Western cultures, especially Indian clothing and fabrics, visibly influenced the dresses of the hippie movement. Styles also reflected a romantic, nostalgic view of the past, recalling the countryside or Victorian aesthetics. Many women opted for tie-dyed creations or floral patterns, personalizing their dresses and jewelry with decorative beads and tassels, and adding printed head scarves and turbans. In the 21st century maxi dresses made another appearance, as long lengths became fashionable again.

Turban

Floral leather motifs

Leather streamers with plastic tubing

Silk lining

Full-length skirt

Skirt of many panels

Pop star production Made by British designer Bill Gibb in 1972—who was synonymous with the maxi-length print trend—this dramatic maxi was worn by UK pop princess Sandie Shaw. It is made of printed cotton, and trimmed with leather and plastic.

WEDGES AND PLATFORMS

While many hippies preferred to pair their long dresses with bare feet for an entirely natural look, designers were stepping up a gear with ever more exciting shoe styles. From bulky boots to strappy sandals, young women and men had an abundance of choice with the variety of shoes both available and on trend in the 1970s. For practical purposes, heels stayed low, but when dressing to impress, wedges or platforms were the chunky choice, adding inches to leg lines. Despite medical advice that these high heels were dangerous, young women put their best foot forward, creating more statuesque silhouettes than ever before.

Low-heeled lace-up boots

Wedge-heeled clogs

Platform open-toed sandals

Rich red and green colors

Extended V-neckline

Sheer, loose-fitting sleeves

Feminine fabric

Clark's creations Flamboyant British designer Ossie Clark was renowned for his flowing dresses in beautifully soft fabrics. Looking to Hollywood's glamour girls for inspiration, his lavish designs flattered the female form.

Cream, tan, and mint floral print

Matching turban

Fitted shirt

Paneled skirt

Contrasting black background

Fabric of choice Silk was another popular fabric during the 1970s. This striking ensemble consisting of a shirt, skirt, and turban in matching silk was crafted by Italian designer Pancaldi & B. in 1976.

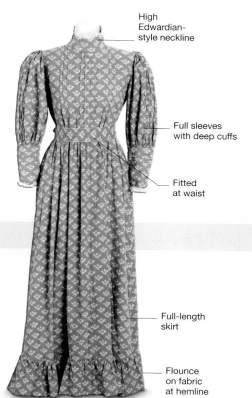

High Edwardian-style neckline

Full sleeves with deep cuffs

Fitted at waist

Full-length skirt

Flounce on fabric at hemline

Floaty florals When Welsh designer Laura Ashley shifted from furniture coverings to feminine clothing, her signature style was defined. Pretty floral prints in natural cotton or pinwale corduroy resulted in classic romantic dresses.

Contrasting print halter-neck strap

Blue and green flower print

Contrasting brighter colors in lower panels

Uneven hemline creates floaty finish

Halter-neck hit Empire-line halter-neck dresses were the ultimate in hippie chic. This 1974 example has a deep scoop at the back, but it is the pattern that catches the eye. The floral print has contrasting paisley panels sewn into the handkerchief skirt.

Quilting feature

Satin in three colors

Circular skirt in three layers

Stitching satin British designer Zandra Rhodes produced a series of textiles, called Knitted Circles, with motifs taken from knitting and embroidery stitches The distinctive motifs are seen on this silk screened caftan-style dress.

Frilled short sleeves

Square neckline

Cinched waistline

Full skirt

True blue A nod toward Laura Ashley's style, this Indian print design in dark blue is fitted to accentuate the waist. The square neckline and flared short sleeves give the suggestion of a child's Victorian pinafore.

Satin yoke and collar

Satin-covered buttons

Loose sleeves frilled at elbow

Strawberry-print crêpe de Chine

Berry best Inspired by Ossie Clark, this strawberry-print dress flatters the female form while showing just a hint of flesh around the neck and bodice. The wraparound skirt ties at the back with a matching sash waistband.

SOFT SUEDE DAY DRESS

JEAN MUIR CLASSIC

By the mid-1970s, British designer Jean Muir (1928–1995) was at the height of her success. This knee-length, navy, suede dress is typical of her fluid, timeless clothes: subtly detailed and made from a natural fabric that hangs beautifully to emphasize the female shape, its construction enhancing the wearer's movements. Unlined, the dress is gathered at the neck in a soft frill. It has a beaded tassel decoration and a belt that can be tied at the front or back. In trademark Muir style, the skirt has two rows of hand-punched eyelets in a dot and teardrop pattern that is repeated around the armhole and on the belt.

Topstitched seams

△ **TASSELED HAT**
The hat, custom-made to accompany the dress, is decorated with a matching tassel and topstitched seams. Muir frequently used neat, machine over stitching on her clothes; it was usually the only decoration needed.

Softly flared skirt

SIDE VIEW

BACK VIEW

IN DETAIL

▽ **DRESS LABEL**
Muir launched her own label in 1966. From the beginning her name was associated with ageless classics, always flattering, and beautifully feminine.

Topstitching adds subtle detail

Soft frill across the top of the bodice

Belt sits naturally on the waist

With the unlined suede worked like woven or knit fabric, the intricately constructed dress is gently gathered at the top of the bodice to create a soft neckline.

▽ TASSEL DECORATION

Being particularly careful with her use of accessories and decoration, on this dress Muir has added a suede tassel with beads—a small nod to 1970s fashion.

▽ BACK BUTTONING

Muir loved beautiful buttons and used handcrafted ones on many of her clothes. Here, she places a four-button placket on the rear of the dress to close the bodice.

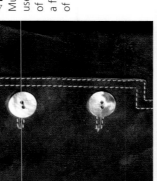

▽ TIE BELT

The butter-soft suede belt can be tied loosely at waist level, either at the front or back. Small, punched eyelets, matching those on the dress, add subtle decoration.

▽ HEM

The heaviness of the suede gives the dress a sculptural quality. Muir's trademark, hand-punched detailing, used on the skirt, was dubbed "brogueing" by the press.

1970–1979
STYLISH CASUALS

Even dressing down involved staying stylish in the 1970s. Simple cotton, versatile polyester, and comfortable jersey were ideal fabrics for everyday wear, but it was handcrafted knitwear that had the fashion-conscious in a tizzy. Knit and crochet garments in bright colors and geometric patterns not only kept women warm but also meant they were in fashion. At this time, color coordination became possible as mix-and-match collections of separates grew to be commonplace in boutiques and stores. In these one-stop shops customers could get entirely matching outfits without having to rummage around for similar pieces. Those on a tight budget could buy balls of wool and knit or crotchet a whole new wardrobe for themselves. For winter days, women opted for chunky cardigans, wool skirts, jersey tops, and pinafore dresses to look impressively in style with the very minimum of effort. But it was not only fashion designers coming up with the goods—anyone could follow a crochet or knit pattern and create their own clothing.

Black, knit hat

Circular, turned-down collar

High waist

Two-tiered skirt

Woven black stripes

Chorister costume Designed in 1971 by British designer John Bates, this ensemble was named for its similarity to choirboy dress. The tweed maxi dress was worn with a plain-weave rayon blouse, with stiffened, circular collar and cuffs.

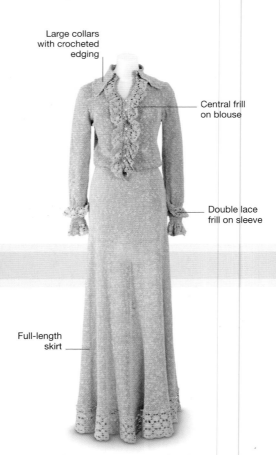

Large collars with crocheted edging

Central frill on blouse

Double lace frill on sleeve

Full-length skirt

Lacy confection This crocheted outfit by British knitwear designer Mary Farrin comprises a stylish matching skirt and blouse. Both are crafted from a slub-textured yarn, including intricate, heavy lace detailing around the sleeves, buttons, and hemline.

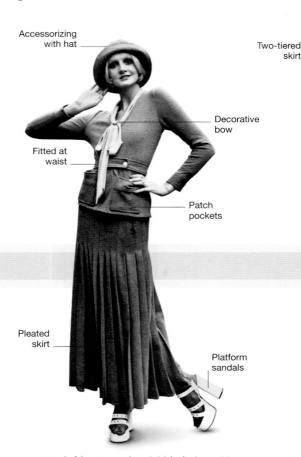

Accessorizing with hat

Decorative bow

Fitted at waist

Patch pockets

Pleated skirt

Platform sandals

Maxi skirt Legendary British designer Mary Quant was the creator of this popular look. The pale blue blouse with an oversized bow is coupled with a silky blue, pleated maxi skirt. The hat and platforms set the 1970s seal.

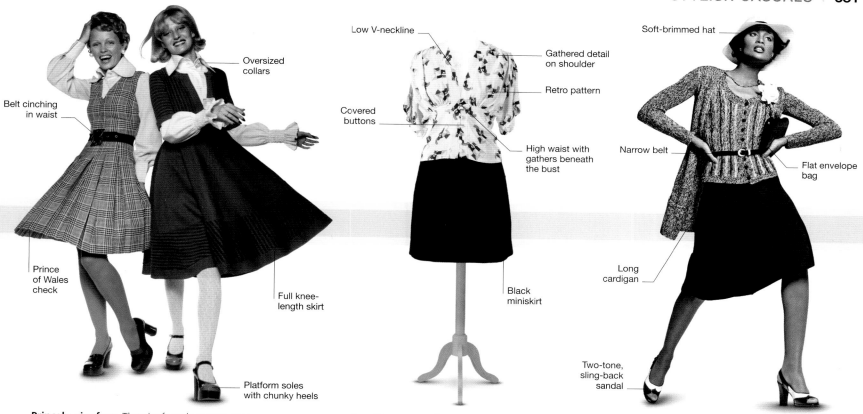

Oversized collars

Belt cinching in waist

Prince of Wales check

Full knee-length skirt

Platform soles with chunky heels

Low V-neckline

Gathered detail on shoulder

Retro pattern

Covered buttons

High waist with gathers beneath the bust

Black miniskirt

Soft-brimmed hat

Narrow belt

Flat envelope bag

Long cardigan

Two-tone, sling-back sandal

Princely pinafore The pinafore dress was easy to wear because of its apron style and full skirt. The example from 1972 (left) by John Bates uses a Prince of Wales check. The choice of blouse worn underneath influenced the overall look.

Bus Stop top A classic miniskirt was a versatile wardrobe staple, making the top the focus. This crêpe de Chine blouse by popular British 1970s fashion chain Bus Stop combines distinctive colors with a flattering, feminine fit.

Model knits One of the first black models, America's Beverly Johnson is seen here in 1974 working a cotton-knit cardigan, matching button-front tank top, and pleated wool skirt by American designer Bill Blass.

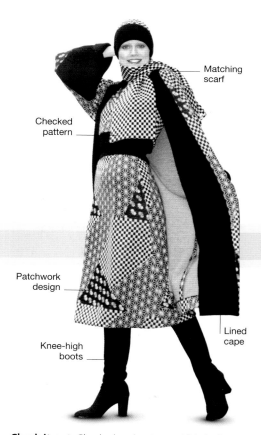

Matching scarf

Checked pattern

Patchwork design

Knee-high boots

Lined cape

Flattened collars

Tie-front bow belt

Vertical stripes

Knee-length skirt

Knee-high boots

MASTERY OF MISSONI

Check it out Checked and patterned fabrics brought casual wear to life, as seen in this 1975 outfit. Though the everyday styles prioritized being warm and comfortable, eye-catching prints breathed new life into the basic designs.

Sharp stripes London Fashion Week in 1975 featured a range of on-trend knitwear designs. The latest winter warmers introduced powerful patterns and contrasting colors, such as this striped knit jacket and matching skirt.

Founded in 1953, Italian fashion house Missoni was the center of knitwear, designing everyday clothing in cotton, linen, rayon, silk, and wool. Bright, colorful patterns were the company's trademark, reflected in this outfit from 1975, which consisted of a herringbone weave head scarf, striped top, and maxi skirt. Even the bed linen around the model in this image is made from Missoni's distinctive fabric.

1970–1979
STAGE, DANCE, AND PARTY

The 1970s was about fantasy, escapism, and new fabrics, expressed in exuberant colors and prints and experimentation with style. Big stars were shining bright in outfits that went all out to impress. Chart toppers and celebrities donned the finest fabrics to create luxurious looks that were a photographer's dream. Classy, full-length figure huggers battled with short, sparkly halter necks and hot pants for center stage. Lycra, satin, and velvet were the fabrics of choice, while feathers and sequins added extra sparkle. Designers went to town creating showstoppers, knowing that an outfit could make or break an up-and-coming artist. As innovative styles were worn, new fashion icons were born. Young people copied their idols, putting on the glitz in cheaper imitations.

AGE OF ACCESSORIES

Dresses and suits were set off by a variety of on-trend accessories. With the penchant for luxurious soft fabrics, many were made of suede, velvet, and fake fur, including hats and handbags. Belts were also tightening their fashion grip as unusual chain versions cinched in waists and accentuated outfits.

Newsboy cap

Hot pants and chain belt

Long-strapped shoulder bags in materials such as sleek satins, crushed velvets, and colored leather were a must-have for young women. Art Deco inspired bags were styled with ornate decorations and artificial jewels. Straps ranged from narrow chains to chunky leather, while buckle and zipper closures finished the look.

Gold bag by Judith Leiber

Decorative bag

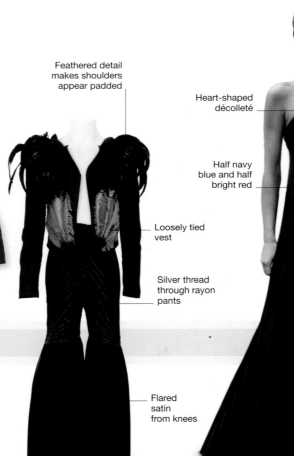

Feathered detail makes shoulders appear padded

Loosely tied vest

Silver thread through rayon pants

Flared satin from knees

Fancy feathers Theatrical influences turned some clothing into costumes. British designer Carol McNicoll here mixes fine fabrics, using feathers to showcase the shoulders, flared satin to add originality, and a colorful vest to break up the black.

Matching turban

Heart-shaped décolleté

Half navy blue and half bright red

Long, pleated skirt

Full-length, green, pleated skirt

Lettuce-leaf hem

Parisian gown The Parisian House of Torrente used bold color blocking in bright red and navy blue silk crêpe for this pleated gown that both reveals and conceals. The addition of a matching turban creates a striking look from head to toe for summer '73.

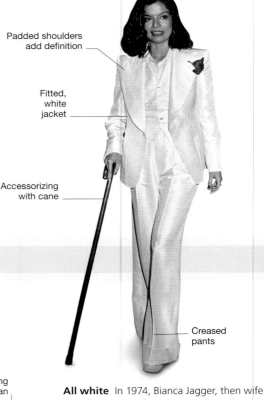

Padded shoulders add definition

Fitted, white jacket

Accessorizing with cane

Creased pants

All white In 1974, Bianca Jagger, then wife of Rolling Stones front man Mick Jagger, wore a dazzling white satin pantsuit by US designer Roy Halston Frowick. Halston-inspired outfits were popular at Studio 54 in New York and parties in 1970s London.

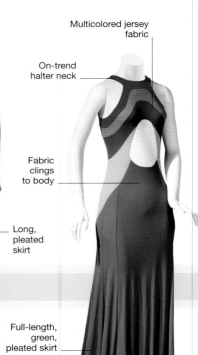

Multicolored jersey fabric

On-trend halter neck

Fabric clings to body

Long, pleated skirt

Full-length, green, pleated skirt

Lettuce-leaf hem

Rainbow dress African American designer Stephen Burrows's passion for both strong colors and comfortable, jersey-style materials are seen in this evening dress from 1973. Bands of colors are seamed carefully around a white, oval center.

Slightly flared
A-line shape

Diamond
design
covers
dress

Machine-
embroidered,
sheer chiffon

Deep neckline,
revealing almost
entire chest

Velvet
shoulder
straps

Acrylic
lozenges
decorate
suit

Laces
close waist

Wide
flared
pants

Twisted, purple
head scarf

Single
sleeve

Pink fur
wrap

Close
fit at
waistline

Matching
scarf

Shimmering sequins This 1972
halter-neck minidress by British designer
Georgina Linhart was perfect for nights
at the disco. It is made of light and
flexible chiffon and covered with
iridescent sequins.

Jumping Jack Flash Worn by
Mick Jagger on stage in 1972, this
flashy jumpsuit by British designer
Ossie Clark is an unusual mix of
fabrics. Velvet, Lycra, acrylic,
and metal all combine in what
is truly glam-rock garb.

Pendant
necklace

Low
neckline

Vibrant
dyed hair

Wide
sleeves
gather
into slim
cuff

Distinctive,
striped
pattern

Tight fit
around
torso

Flared,
satin pants

Shorter-length
pants

Stage suit Rod Stewart wore this
slinky, white suit in 1975 while on
a US tour with his band the Faces.
The legendary rock star has a
fashionable, mullet hairstyle and
wears bell-bottoms and a blouselike
shirt in shimmering satin.

Starman's stripes Pop star David Bowie
was fearless when it came to fashion.
He experimented with makeup, hair dye,
hairstyles, and clothing throughout the
1970s to the delight of his fans. This
unisex, striped top and pants pushed
fashion boundaries.

Supreme style A passion for
purple was evident in singer Diana
Ross's choice of gown here. Worn
in 1975 for a photo shoot, the
elegant shape and feminine fit of
this design by Mahogany ensured
she looked every inch the star.

THE DESIGNER
DECADES

1980 ONWARD

THE DESIGNER DECADES

In the modern age, fashion designers have become celebrities, and fashion weeks and couture shows part of the news cycle. Designers repeatedly push boundaries, finding ever more theatrical and experiential ways to present their collections, from machines spray-painting models' dresses at Alexander McQueen's Spring/Summer 1999 show to a blast-off rocket at Chanel for Fall/Winter 2017. The power of the brand, from Armani to Burberry, has become international—designers' names sell products. Calvin Klein's fragrances, for example, sell an aspirational lifestyle, and his underwear line in the 1990s was so famous that the garment became known simply by the designer's name.

Inclusive fashion

Fashion has made strides to become more inclusive in the modern era, to reflect modern society. Toward the end of the 20th century, signature looks from style tribes—from rappers to surfers—became increasingly mainstream, as fashion designers took influence from the street and reworked styles, and the mass-market followed the trend. In the new century, fashion started to bring diversity into the mainstream. So Winnie Harlow, who "just happens to have vitiligo," took her place on equal footing with fellow models, while amputee Jack Eyers walked for Teatum Jones in a show that mixed menswear and womens wear on the same platform. Fashion embraced gender fluidity, too, with looks by menswear designer Craig Green worn by women in 2015. Multiculturalism also started to be placed center stage. For example, H&M, the second largest fashion retailer in the world, featured a Muslim woman wearing a hijab in promotional material.

Instant fashion

Communication became truly global with the invention of the internet and social media. Fashion, too, became more international, with production shifting from Europe and North America to Asia, and fashion weeks taking place throughout the world, from Ghana and Pakistan to Mexico and New Zealand. The cycle of increased production and consumption from the 1990s onward led to the success of high-street, mass-market stores such as Zara and Victoria's Secret. After the financial crisis of the later 2000s, budget clothing retailers such as Primark and Walmart experienced a boom in business and they, along with the explosion of online shopping sites, have sped up the way that fashion is consumed. However, an increasing awareness of "fast fashion," and of the effects of the fashion industry in general on our world, has led to an acceleration of ethical fashion, with designers Vivienne Westwood and Stella McCartney leading the charge for change.

1980–81

1981
Lady Diana Spencer marries Prince Charles. She wears an ivory silk wedding dress designed by David and Elizabeth Emanuel. It sets the fashion for wedding dresses for at least the next 10 years.

▶ Diana's wedding dress had puffed sleeves and a 25-ft (7.5-m) train

1981
Music Television (MTV) is born and brings pop-star style to a global audience.

▲ MTV brought star style to popular consciousness

1981
The first episode of the US TV series *Dynasty* airs and helps to popularize power dressing and shoulder pads.

▼ The cast of *Dynasty* set 1980s fashion trends

1982–84

1983
Jean Paul Gaultier launches his *Le Dadaïsme* collection, which includes his signature corset.

1984
Polo Ralph Lauren flagship store is built in New York City.

1984
Donna Karan International is established.

1984
The first London Fashion Week takes place, produced by Lynne Franks. BodyMap's shows both shock and wow with their highly innovative use of print and lycra club wear worn by models of all shapes, sizes, and ages.

▶ Bold black and white design by BodyMap

1985–88

1985
With her jangling jewelry, lace, black mesh vest, and hair bows, Madonna in *Desperately Seeking Susan* becomes a style icon for many women throughout the world.

1985
Dolce & Gabbana's first women's collection is presented in Milan.

1988
Anna Wintour becomes editor-in-chief at American *Vogue*.

▶ Anna Wintour

1988
Zara, the Spanish fashion retail chain, begins its international expansion, signaling the beginnings of "fast fashion."

> Power dressing now is designed to let the woman inside us come through.

DONNA KARAN, 2006

1989–90

1989
Prada launches its women's ready-to-wear collection, bringing its designs to a wider audience.

▲ Madonna's conical "bullet bra" is an enduring fashion icon

1990
Madonna creates a fashion sensation when she wears the notorious Jean Paul Gaultier corset during her *Blonde Ambition* world tour.

1990
Vera Wang opens her own design salon in New York, featuring her trademark bridal gowns.

1990
Fashion models become increasingly successful and recognizable; the age of the supermodel begins.

1991–94

1991
Vivienne Westwood wins the British Fashion Award for Designer of the Year.

► Vivienne Westwood with her muse, model Sara Stockbridge

1991
Rifat Ozbek's all-white *New Age* collection is launched. It is viewed as a backlash against the 1980s and a spiritual new dawn for fashion at the beginning of a new decade.

1991
Nirvana release their "Smells Like Teen Spirit" single, which is a big influence on "grunge" style.

1992
Marc Jacobs wins the Council of Fashion Designers of America's award for Women's Designer of the Year. He is later dismissed from Perry Ellis for designing a "grunge" collection.

1994
Tom Ford becomes creative director of Gucci.

1995–99

1995
Friends actress Jennifer Aniston debuts "the Rachel" haircut. It is copied around the globe.

1997
The Fendi Baguette bag emerges. It is the first of the designer "it-bags" and becomes an overnight sensation.

1997
Italian fashion designer Gianni Versace is murdered outside his Miami Beach home; his sister Donatella Versace becomes head of design at Versace.

1998
First airing of HBO television show *Sex and the City*, featuring the lives of four sassy New Yorkers, including fashion-obsessed character Carrie Bradshaw. The series ran until 2004.

◄ Differing styles helped define the *Sex and the City* characters

2000–08

2003
The first season of reality contest *America's Next Top Model* premieres on US television.

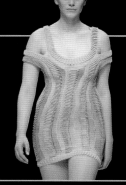

2004
The group Designers Against AIDS is launched to promote awareness of the disease. Designer Marc Jacobs and clothes store H&M go on to collaborate with the charity.

2005
The Istanbul Cevahir Shopping Center opens. It is the largest mall in Europe and the sixth largest in the world.

2008
First Lady Michelle Obama wears a dress by Jason Wu at the Inaugural Ball for President Barack Obama.

2009–17

2009
Mark Fast helps highlight the diversity of the female form when he sends three plus-size models down the catwalk during his show at London Fashion Week in September.

◄ Laura Catterall showcases Fast's figure-hugging designs

2010
Kate Middleton and Prince William announce their engagement. She wears an Issa London sapphire dress, which sells out within minutes. The following year she marries Prince William in a bridal gown designed by Sarah Burton for Alexander McQueen.

2010
Burberry Prorsum's first live-streamed catwalk show launches the trend for using the internet to bring the experience of high-end shows (and shopping) to an audience watching on their phones.

2016
British *Vogue* celebrates its 100th anniversary, and Edward Enninful becomes editor—the first male and first black incumbent of this leading post in fashion.

► Enninful strongly advocates for more diversity in fashion

2017
The Women's March on Washington, D.C., the day after President Trump's inauguration sees thousands of protestors worldwide wearing knitted and handcrafted pink pussy hats as a unified visual statement.

◄ The pussy hat pattern was downloaded over 100,000 times

2018 ▷

▲ Meghan Markle's white wedding dress

2018
British designer Clare Waight Keller at Givenchy designs the wedding dress worn by Meghan Markle to marry Prince Harry at St. George's Chapel, Windsor.

2019
Karl Lagerfeld dies, age 85, after 36 years as head of fashion house Chanel, which he transformed into a global super brand.

1985 ONWARD
SPORTSWEAR

Although there is a long history of sports garments crossing over into mainstream fashion—late-18th-century tailored riding suits, for example—the fitness boom of the 1980s was the catalyst for a major crossover of sportswear into fashion. As the fitness center became a social scene, exercise garb became stylish. At the same time, designers were experimenting with fabrics normally used for activewear. In 1980, American designer Norma Kamali created a collection entirely in gray fleece jersey; in 1984, American Donna Karan popularized the stretch bodysuit, and Tunisian-born Azzedine Alaïa designed Lycra dresses—a fashion revolution. Women's bodies were now shaping the clothes, rather than clothes shaping the body. Beyond the body-conscious trend, other sportswear styles have infiltrated fashion over the past few decades. The celebrity status of football and basketball players, coupled with a trend toward casual dress, has made athletic gear, especially footwear such as sneakers, desirable. More recently, women demanded clothes that would take them from yoga, Pilates, or running to shopping trips, coffee with friends, or even to work. This gave rise to "athleisure" clothes that are as fashionable for going out as working out.

SNEAKERS

The obsession with sports footwear as fashion goes back to 1972, when Nike launched the Cortez, which became the sneaker for the style-conscious in the newly emerging hip-hop music scene. Then, in 1984, when women wore sneakers with their suits to travel to work, Gucci became the first luxury brand to design a sneaker. But this was nothing compared with the buzz around the 1985 launch of the Nike Air Jordan I. Adidas followed in 1986, when their Superstar sneaker was made famous by hip-hop group Run-DMC. Over the past few decades, the big athletic brands have gathered a fan base of "sneakerheads," willing to spend a lot. Eager to create hot-selling sneakers, too, luxury brands began collaborating with "cool" people to create expensive trainers with street cred; for example, Louis Vuitton teamed up with Kanye West in 2009.

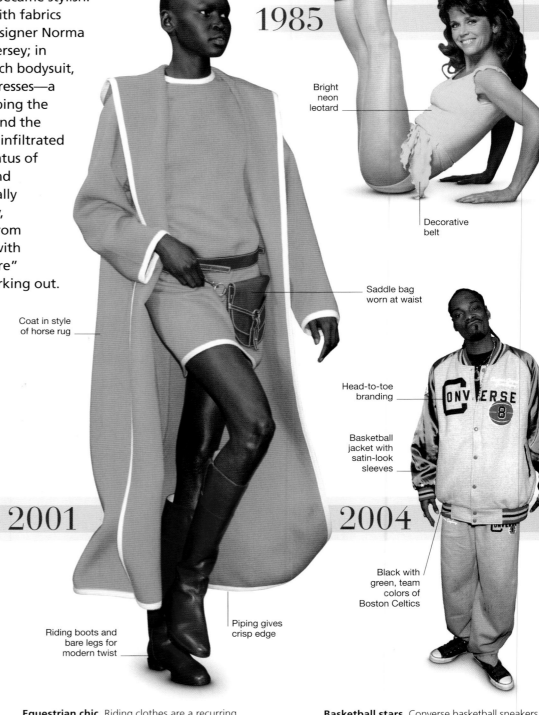

Jane Fonda's workout Jane Fonda was one of the personalities credited with spreading the aerobics craze and changing the idea of exercise clothes. She released a bestselling book, video, and line of leotards and accessories (such as leg warmers) that became part of mainstream fashion.

Two-tone leg warmers

1985

Bright neon leotard

Decorative belt

Saddle bag worn at waist

Coat in style of horse rug

Head-to-toe branding

Basketball jacket with satin-look sleeves

2001

2004

Riding boots and bare legs for modern twist

Piping gives crisp edge

Black with green, team colors of Boston Celtics

Equestrian chic Riding clothes are a recurring source of inspiration. US designer Michael Kors' Fall/Winter 2001 collection included jodhpur-style pants and quilted field skirts, creating a new way of dressing based on active sportswear.

Basketball stars Converse basketball sneakers were first manufactured around 1908. From the 1980s, the sneakers became a fashion item, worn by hip-hop and rap stars, including Snoop Dogg, who used them as his trademark style.

Classic French beret

Highest quality stretch fabric

Structured underwear

Crop tops make look sexy

Shoulder tattoo

1991

Sleek ski-wear fit

Tracksuit bottoms popularized by hip-hop culture

High heels

1995

Fit fashion Always designing for a figure-conscious fit, Azzedine Alaïa created this leopard-print bodysuit for his 1991 show. Modeled by Naomi Campbell, it was an elegant Parisian take on body-conscious dressing for the woman who worked hard for her physique and wanted to show it.

Track stars Pop stars adapted designer sportswear and took it to a wider audience. British group All Saints wore tracksuit bottoms and sneakers as a kind of uniform in the mid-1990s, and girls around the nation copied their style.

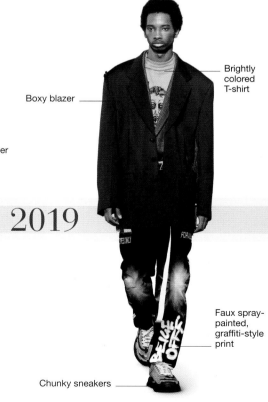

FLASHDANCE

When Jennifer Beals leapt across cinema screens in the 1983 movie *Flashdance* as steelworker-cum-dancer Alex Owens, she sparked a passion for dance-wear-inspired fashions. Slouchy, off-the-shoulder gym sweats and ripped T-shirts are still referred to as "the *Flashdance* look."

Produced in candy colors

Personalization with embroidered text

Fitted around hips and buttocks

Blouson jacket in tech fabric

Long-sleeved underlayer

Fabric lets skin breathe during workouts

Boxy blazer

Brightly colored T-shirt

2017

Mesh inserts show skin

Straight leg to fall over sneakers

Trainers to match

2019

Faux spray-painted, graffiti-style print

Chunky sneakers

Juicy tracksuit Juicy Couture's hooded tracksuit, launched in 2001, made casual clothes sexy. By 2003 it had become ubiquitous. Sales soared when Madonna was photographed wearing a customized version.

Beauty and function Adidas by Stella McCartney is a long-running collaboration and the ultimate sports-fashion fusion. McCartney uses high-quality stretch materials for peak performance, but adds her own desirable details.

Underground label DJ and designer Virgil Abloh, founder of high-end street label Off-White, was appointed creative director of Louis Vuitton menswear in 2018, but still runs his own brand. His Fall/Winter 2019 menswear collection reinterpreted street basics.

DESIGNER
VIVIENNE WESTWOOD

△ **FASHION REVOLUTION**
Rebel fashion visionary Vivienne Westwood wears a signature plaid bondage suit in 1977. Working alongside Malcolm McLaren, her look became the uniform of the punk movement.

GLAMOROUS ANARCHY ▷
Westwood's Spring/Summer 2012 collection, inspired by China, mixed in corsets, lace, brocade, and ticking-stripe bedspread fabrics, and dramatic makeup to glorious effect.

One of the most admired British fashion designers, Vivienne Westwood has played a key role on the British and international fashion stage for over three decades. Westwood began designing in 1971 when she opened her first store, Let It Rock, on the King's Road, London, with partner Malcolm McLaren (1946–2010). She looked to the past for inspiration and sold teddy boy clothes reflecting delinquent youth culture, moving on to biker-inspired gear with black leather and zippers. Rebranding their store Sex (1975), they advertised their ambition to bring sexual experimentation and fetish to London streets. The store soon became synonymous with punk, heavily promoted by McLaren's new band, the Sex Pistols. The look was aggressive and anarchistic. Sweaters had holes in them, and safety pins pierced cheeks and lips. T-shirts were slashed, and emblazoned with provocative images, studs, and slogans. The bondage look became integral to the punk genre, using leather and rubber. In particular, pants were adorned with bondage straps and chains.

The romantic look

As punk fashion became absorbed into the mainstream, Westwood explored the essence of Englishness and sexual politics. Drawing again on historical costumes, she devised a new range of clothes that formed the basis of her first runway collection (1981).

The *Pirate* range was adopted by musicians labeled the New Romantics, who embraced the baggy pants, frills, billowing shirts, and lavish colors that were inspired by 18th-century men's clothing. The *Savage* collection (1982) gravitated toward a tribal look, with rough, distressed fabrics and exposed seams, while *Buffalo Girls* (also known as *Nostalgia of Mud*) garments

of 1982–1983 were made from combinations of twisted, oversized asymmetrical cuts of layered material, inspired by Third World cultures.

Body-shaping design

The corset emerged as a key element, along with other body-shaping pieces such as the crinoline, bustle, and towering shoe. While in Italy in the mid-'80s, Westwood developed the Mini-Crini, featuring shortened 19th-century-style crinolines teamed with tailored jackets—the antithesis of 1980s masculine power dressing. She later combined the style with traditional British fabrics such as Harris Tweed and Scottish tartans. Her *Anglomania* collection (1993–1994) ran with the theme with mini kilts, gowns, newly created tartans, and tweeds. Westwood said, "I am never more happy than when I parody the British in the context of a classical perspective." Designs constricted posture and movement and emphasized the hips. Underwear became outerwear, with bras worn over dresses.

Westwood's *Café Society* collection (1994) was a new take on the hourglass silhouette. Collaborating with her partner Andreas Kronthaler, bustles were made from cushions and cages, voluminous dresses had long trains, and busts were padded. Famously, platform shoes were extremely high. She later became inspired by the costumes in paintings by French artist Jean-Antoine Watteau (1684–1721), creating sumptuous, strapless gowns made of silk taffeta.

By the end of the 1990s, Westwood was firmly established as one of the most important designers in the world. She launched a fragrance line and opened new labels. Despite being made a Dame of the British Empire in 2006, her clothes are still subversive. Rooted in the classics, Westwood remains unflinchingly cutting edge.

TIMELINE

1971 Westwood and partner, Malcolm McLaren, open their London store Let It Rock

1976 The Sex Pistols play their first gig wearing Westwood designs

1981 Her first runway show, *Pirate*, borrows heavily from history and inspires the look of the New Romantics

1982–1983 *Buffalo* and *Punkature* are shown in Paris to critical acclaim. Her innovative designs are widely copied

1989–1991 Appointed Professor of Fashion at Vienna Academy of Applied Arts. Shows first menswear collection in Florence

◁ **1993** Designs her own tartan and tweed for *Anglomania* collection. Includes staggeringly high platform shoes

1994 The British Fashion Council names Westwood designer of the year as she launches her new Red Label

1996 Vivienne Westwood Man is launched, and she opens stores in London, New York, Tokyo, and Milan

◁ **2011** The Spring/ Summer menswear collection sets the trend for a relaxed informal style with plaid trousers

○ 1970   ○ 1980   ○ 1985   ○ 1990   ○ 1995   ○ 2000

LAYERED AND ASYMMETRICAL Westwood's 2010–2011 Red Label collection draws inspiration from tapestries and old country houses for an eco-warrior look with strong makeup. ▷

1980–1989
MUST-HAVE LABELS

After the anti-fashion 1970s, when casual and street clothes gained prominence, it seemed inevitable that the role of the designer would stage a revival. During the 1980s, not only was interest focused increasingly on high fashion, but also on the designer as a personality. The names of some designers became synonymous with their iconic pieces: Italian Gianni Versace for his perfectly fitting cocktail dresses in metallic colors; Frenchmen Christian Lacroix for his puffball skirt and rose prints, and Jean Paul Gaultier for his cone bra; and the German Karl Lagerfeld for the classic Chanel suit updated in jewel colors with a flamboyant dash. Some of the influential 1980s designers continue to the present day.

1982

Sleeves are constructed to sit at right angles

Wool printed with rubberized, ancient erotic motif

Button under bust draws in fabric

Large pocket with Greek key design inside flap

1983

Strong shoulder line interrupted with show of body

Distorted captain's hat in gold gauze

Thigh-high slit and gold tassels

White and gold become ultimate marriage of 1980s

History After the furor of punk designs Vivienne Westwood produced a number of inventive collections in the early 1980s that established her as a mainstream force. This piece is part of her *Savage* collection.

New look French designer Thierry Mugler created a new way of dressing for women in the 1980s, using a strict cut and precision lines to enhance, and contrast with, natural body curves. This nautical look is from Spring/Summer 1983.

1985

Puffed shoulder line and tapered sleeves

Elizabethan-style evening dress

Royal blue, satin, V-shaped bodice

Covered buttons and pin tucks

Flared, silk-satin skirt

Distorted leg-of-mutton sleeve creates broad shoulder

Dark denim with gold, asymmetric zipper

Victorian-era hourglass silhouette

Demi-couture take on street fashion

1987

Signature rose motif on headpiece

Sheer bodice with sequin bustier

Front bustle, or pouf, as hand warmer

Unexpected color combination of brown and black

Evening fantasy In the "greedy" 1980s most women could not afford luxury brands, but there were many mid-priced designers creating stylish clothes. Vera Mont was one such British label, which focused on party dresses and bridal wear.

Body-conscious engineering Tunisian-born Azzedine Alaïa was one of the most influential designers of the 1980s. Women loved his formfitting clothes because they were a kind of internal corset to hold and flatter the wearer.

Extravagant couture Despite being the youngest couturier in 1986, Lacroix's look drew on old-world luxury. His designs brimmed with historical references, and were executed with gorgeous fabrics and a sense of coquettish charm.

Scarlet cashmere cloak evokes the 1920s

Reminiscent of Paul Poiret's style

Wrapped torso

Skirt is draped with side pouch

1988

Seducing with luxury From his graduation show of 1984, British designer John Galliano impressed fashion editors and buyers with his romantic yet daring vision and refined tailoring skills.

Haute couture attention to detail

Padded shoulders

Aluminum mesh drapes like silk

Asymmetric hemline and trailing silk bow

Black silk bindings

The glamour of Versace One of Versace's most talked about innovations was his dresses of aluminum mesh, which he fashioned into figure-hugging forms as if from silk.

Cultural mash-up with various ethnic textures

T-shirt under corset dress breaks rules

Emphasis on breasts

1989

Trademark silhouette with nipped-in waist

Color mix challenges notion of good taste

Antibourgeois Inspired by his Parisian roots and his interest in crossing boundaries between the genders, Gaultier created clothes that challenged preconceptions about how people dress, and about their sex, age, and ethnicity.

PRINCESS DIANA

As a member of the royal family, Diana, Princess of Wales, used the clothes that she wore to project an image and to promote British fashion. She turned to David and Elizabeth Emanuel for her wedding dress in 1981, followed by Belville Sassoon the same year for a romantic, off-the-shoulder gown, one of 70 outfits made for the princess by David Sassoon. As she became more confident, she went to Bruce Oldfield for a vivid blue, one-shouldered dress to wear to a fashion show in 1982. Perhaps her closest designer relationship was with Catherine Walker, who created more than 1,000 pieces for the princess.

Sash emphasizes slim waist and sets off full skirt

Belville Sassoon's 1981 fairy tale gown

Bold Catherine Walker print dress, 1988

Bruce Oldfield gown, 1985

" I think the way people dress today is a form of artistic expression … Take Jean Paul Gaultier. What he does is really art.

ANDY WARHOL, 1984

"

DESIGNER
JEAN PAUL GAULTIER

Dubbed the *enfant terrible* of fashion, French designer Jean Paul Gaultier catapulted onto the scene of the late 1970s, upending the status quo with his unconventional, and often humorous, avant-garde creations. Gaultier had no formal training as a designer. He started his career in 1970 as an assistant at Pierre Cardin, and then, in 1976, he scraped together funds to set up a new label for women.

His first collection included a studded leather jacket paired with a tutu. Gaultier derived inspiration from movies, music, and street culture, showing a deep appreciation of multiculturalism. He loved London, attracted by the look of punk, and iconic figures such as James Bond. His first thematic collection (1979), full of miniskirts and leather pants, brought him international attention. Gaultier went on to turn the classic idea of Parisian chic on its head. He introduced elements that became Gaultier staples: the navy-and-white striped Breton fisherman's sweater and the reconstructed trench coat.

Gender bender

In 1983, Gaultier launched the *Dadaiste* collection, establishing what would become a signature outfit: the corset. Reworking an object of female suppression, he turned it into a symbol of feminine power. (The pop star Madonna later wore Gaultier's most famous creation, a beige corset, for her 1990 *Blond Ambition* World Tour.) Gaultier jumped into menswear in 1984. Men had been reportedly buying Gaultier women's jackets because of the fabrics he used and the clever cut. Seizing the moment, Gaultier produced a sensational runway show where men wore see-through skirts and women smoked pipes. Gaultier continued to play with the idea of men in skirts through the 1980s and '90s, offering a variety of styles, including kilts, sarongs, tunics, and maxi skirts. He became famous for using unconventional models such as older men, full-figured women, and heavily tattooed models, and played with gender stereotypes. A master tailor, he used details such as metal-tipped collars and extended shoulder lines to create a flattering shape, demonstrating a supreme appreciation of cut, form, and beautiful fabrics.

Further inspiration

Gaultier's interest in pulling together different cultures continued. His fall collection of 1993, inspired by the traditional apparel of male Hasidic Jews, was typically controversial. His profile was further raised, especially in America, when he turned his hand to costume design, creating clothes for such movies as Luc Besson's *The Fifth Element*, Peter Greenaway's *The Cook, The Thief, His Wife and Her Lover*, and Pedro Almodavar's *Kikaa*.

Brand name

In 1997, disappointed not to be chosen as the new head designer at the House of Dior, Gaultier launched his first couture collection to critical acclaim. From a strapless denim ball gown to a feather and seashell dress, he has created clothes that mix outrageous features with high-quality tailoring. The Jean Paul Gaultier brand now includes jeans, eyewear, accessories, jewelry, ties, perfume, and shoes. Gaultier may have been fashion's bad boy, but he has become one of the most respected designers in the world.

△ **SHARP TAILORING**
Gaultier has become world famous for his exemplary couture skills. Here, he wears two of his signature pieces: a beautifully tailored tuxedo jacket worn over a classic Breton striped top.

◁ **GREEK CHIC**
Inspired by other cultures, Gaultier based his 2006 Spring/Summer couture collection on ancient Greek mythology, dressing some of his models as goddesses, with wide puffed trousers, surprising cutouts, and soft pleats.

TIMELINE

1952 Born Arcueil, France	**1980** The *James Bond* collection makes a strong aesthetic statement with leather, miniskirts, and beautifully tailored silhouettes	◁ **1990** Madonna's *Blond Ambition* World Tour grabs international headlines with Gaultier's conical bra and corset	**1994** ▷ Spring/Summer show features tribal-style models and clothing	**1997** Launches women's haute couture, Gaultier Paris. Designs the costumes for Luc Besson's *The Fifth Element*	**2003–10** Creative director for Hermès
	1976 Launches first women's label at the *Palais de la Decouverte* in Paris and earns the title *enfant terrible*	**1985** Introduces skirts for men in his *And God Created Man* collection	**1993** Launches *Chic Rabbis*, inspired by Jewish Orthodox apparel	**2000** Receives prestigious International Award from the Council of Fashion Designers of America	**2012** Member of the jury at the Film Festival in Cannes
○ 1950	○ 1970	○ 1980	○ 1990		○ 2000

◁ **FINE FEATHERS** This striking Hecate coatdress from Gaultier's *Les Surrealistes* Autumn/Winter collection of 2006 features a rooster on the sleeve.

1980–2012

A POWERFUL MESSAGE

The idea of using clothes to convey status is as old as civilization, but fashion historians point to the 1980s as the pinnacle of power dressing. As more women entered traditionally male-oriented work environments, they found it advantageous to dress as though they were in command, and sure of their sexuality. This meant jackets with heavily padded shoulders, vibrant colors, big hairdos, bold accessories, and shoes with pointed toes and spiked heels. Throughout the decade, TV series such as *Dallas* and *Dynasty* influenced women's wardrobes. These shows projected images of rich, confident women wearing jewel-toned suits with sharp shoulder lines, extravagant dresses, and larger-than-life jewelry. From the 1990s onward, designers such as Calvin Klein and Giorgio Armani developed a low-key, less "costumey" style for working women. Neutral tones, expensive fabrics, and minimal lines sent a subtler message about competence and capability.

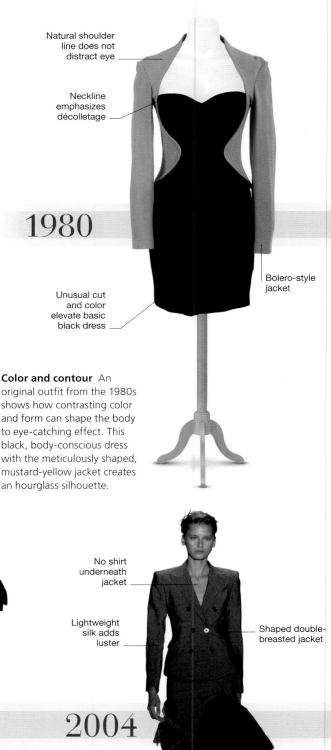

1980

Natural shoulder line does not distract eye

Neckline emphasizes décolletage

Bolero-style jacket

Unusual cut and color elevate basic black dress

Color and contour An original outfit from the 1980s shows how contrasting color and form can shape the body to eye-catching effect. This black, body-conscious dress with the meticulously shaped, mustard-yellow jacket creates an hourglass silhouette.

GIORGIO ARMANI

Italian designer Giorgio Armani's luxurious, softly tailored clothes in neutral tones have been in vogue for more than 30 years. Since establishing his own label in 1976, he has become renowned for making business attire for both sexes more youthful and relaxed, yet still giving the wearer a look of authority and glamour. His preference for simplicity has significantly influenced contemporary fashion.

Soft felt beret

Long-line jacket

1990

Wide-legged, tailored pants

Crossover style One of the most significant trends for working women was Giorgio Armani's soft, elegant tailoring. As in this 1990 outfit, he feminized men's styles, made them in luxurious fabrics in neutral colors, and fashioned a long, lean silhouette.

No shirt underneath jacket

Lightweight silk adds luster

Shaped double-breasted jacket

2004

See-through kick panels in skirt reveal most of legs

Strappy high heels

Sexy suiting American designer Donna Karan built her brand with clothes intended to make a woman feel strong, sensual, and comfortable. Here she puts a sexy spin on the traditional, gray flannel suit, with revealing, transparent panels in the skirt.

Pearl earrings

Sensuous velvet

Elaborate hair is a balance of soft and strong

Romantic shirt

Cropped tux shows off waist

Pencil skirt demure, but reveals knees

Bow on court shoes

Corporate charm Dominican-born Oscar de la Renta brought romantic outfits to the office in the 1980s. The model wears a gray flannel skirt, black velvet jacket, and white silk and lace blouse.

Striking white beret

Football-type shoulders

White collar detail recalls Puritan ethos

1983

Natural fabrics

Belt and fashionable peplum emphasize waist and hips

Flat, no-nonsense shoes

Bold scale Oversized garments were the first part of the 1980s look. Subverting the dress of Puritans—known for their work ethic—French designer Claude Montana created impact in 1983 with massive swagger, rather than showing off the body.

Hat adds polish and height

Covered neckline is restrained

Short, slim skirt elongates legs

Conservative shoe style but sexy heel height

Commanding attention The Duchess of Cambridge's outfit is a perfect example of modern tailoring, designed to draw attention to her slim figure and height and to emphasize both her authority and glamour.

2012

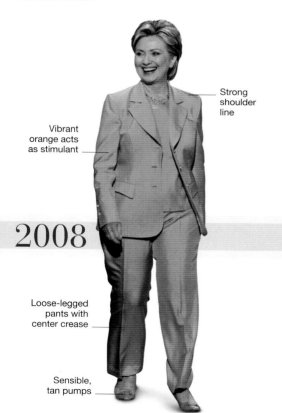

Vibrant orange acts as stimulant

Strong shoulder line

Loose-legged pants with center crease

Sensible, tan pumps

2008

Pantsuit power In the world of male-dominated politics, Hillary Clinton has opted to wear a pantsuit with masculine tailoring but one important difference: color. Her outfits come in bold, bright, head-to-toe colors that stand out on TV.

Ruffled blouse adds softness

Neutral palette ideal for the workplace

Neat fit on jacket

Flattering cut on pants

Statement shoes

2010

Career mode In the 1990s, German designer Jil Sander used expensive fabrics and flattering tailoring for women who wanted to look professional and feel confident. Here Japanese actress Tyoko Yonekura promotes the sellout Jil Sander-Uniqlo collaboration.

WOOL MIX TWO-PIECE
POWER SUIT

The "executive look," which first found expression in the 1970s as part of the working woman's wardrobe, matured by the mid-1980s into "power dressing." This outfit, by French designer Thierry Mugler, combines a sharply accentuated, shoulder-padded jacket with a feminizing short skirt. The single-breasted jacket, in orange worsted wool and polyester mix, is fitted at the waist and rounded on the hips. The pencil skirt is knee length, straight, and made of black wool. The increasingly high profile of women in the workplace was reflected in their wardrobes. Suits were tailored, but used softer dressmaking padding to structure the shoulders than in traditional men's suits. Accessorized with bold costume jewelry and stiletto heels, the look spoke of confidence and power.

Straight line across the shoulders

Close-fitting skirt ends above the knee

BOLD AND BRIGHT
Thierry Mugler tailors his suit to create a stylized feminine archetype: square shoulders, cinched waist, and full hips. Typically crafted in strong colors, this ensemble appeared thoroughly modern in its day. The short, buttock-hugging skirt invited attention but defied anyone to touch.

SIDE VIEW

High, stand-up collar

Shoulder pad holds shape

Sleeves taper to a point with a vent

IN DETAIL

◁ **HIGH COLLAR**
A stand-up collar runs seamlessly into a neckline that closes high above the breast before continuing down in a long, crisp sweep to the top press-stud. This suggestion of femininity is partly offset by the masculine look of the padded shoulders.

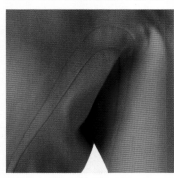

◁ **RAGLAN SLEEVES**
The jacket has strong lines that are softened with raglan sleeves. To achieve the right shape, an oval shoulder pad runs along the shoulder and into each sleeve.

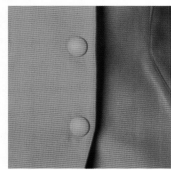

◁ **FASTENINGS**
The jacket closes via three fabric-covered snaps that run down the center front; below the closures the jacket flares into a soft V-shape.

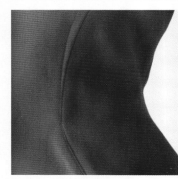

◁ **SIDE PANELS**
Beautifully curved side panels accentuate the cinched-in waist at front and back. The shape is overtly female, implying that the wearer is conscious of her body.

◁ **POCKETS**
Taking his inspiration from the hourglass silhouettes and corsets of the 19th century, Mugler added two welt pockets just below the waist, styling them to curve with the natural shape of the hips. Topstitching lends sophisticated decorative detail.

1973 ONWARD
JAPANESE STYLE

Although Japanese designers Hanae Mori and Kenzo Takada were showing in Paris in the 1970s, it was Issey Miyake who brought the avant-garde movement to the fashion capital in 1973 with his radical approach to dress, a melding of art and science. Kansai Yamamoto made his Paris debut in 1975 with designs inspired by kimonos and kabuki costumes. In 1981, Rei Kawakubo and Yohji Yamamoto shocked fashion editors and buyers with oversized proportions, disregard for gender, and predominant use of black. Yamamoto was interested in purity of form and the interaction between body and fabric, while Kawakubo's focus for her Comme des Garçons label was on deconstruction, breaking down clothes and putting them together in unexpected ways. Kawakubo's protégé Junya Watanabe has forged his own look using techno materials and inventive construction.

ISSEY MIYAKE

One of the foremost textile innovators in fashion history, Issey Miyake established the Miyake Design Studio in Tokyo in 1970 to produce experimental garments. "I try not to fear radical things," he has said, and this is evident in the way he has pushed the boundaries of what clothes can be. Although his designs have sometimes appeared as sculptural objects, most of his retail range is practical. His *Pleats Please* line, for example, is a series of pleated tubes and flat shapes that come to life on the wearer and can be worn in numerous ways.

1973

Concentric circles mimic samurai archer's target

Cut as a full circle of fabric

Wide-legged pants balance oversized proportions above

Sculptural spectacle Kansai Yamamoto is considered the father of contemporary Japanese fashion. He interpreted traditional arts and dress in striking ways to create modern clothes, as seen in this outfit inspired by a samurai fire warden cape.

Hat is also scarf

Knit dress falls over body loosely

Shoes based on lacquered Japanese geta (sandals)

1985

Cape cardigan cut on circle can be layered

Tonal hose and unisex boots

Wearable art Although his clothes use fabrics and cuts that have resulted from sophisticated processes and experimental techniques, Miyake seeks to make his designs easy to wear. This 1985 ensemble based on simple, loose shapes is an example.

1989

Pockets at side

Dress flares out from yoke

Angular asymmetric band

Alternative vision Dubbed the poet of black, Yohji Yamamoto uses the occasional bright detail or piece for impact. The uneven band of orange in this dress creates visual dynamism.

Hand-knit sweater with randomly placed holes

Oversized cuffs

Padded cotton jersey skirt

Asymmetric lines

1982

Flawed beauty For her Fall/Winter 1982 collection for Comme des Garçons, Kawakubo presented this black knitwear that looked moth-eaten—her idea of modern lace. All-black was typical of Kawakubo's 1980s designs.

Rustic hat with straw folded like fabric

Plain white tank top gives modern look

Apron-style peasant skirt hangs from single band

1984

Deconstructed work wear By restricting the color palette in her early collections to black and neutrals, Kawakubo focused the eye on construction and shape. This design features an unstructured jacket with distorted lapels.

Florals mixed with graphic prints

Color clash In contrast to the somber, minimal approaches of Rei Kawakubo and Yohji Yamamoto, Kenzo injected a blast of color and pattern into his collections. His ready-to-wear shows were inspired by the ethnic patterns of Africa, India, and Asia. One of his signatures was clashing floral prints.

Voluminous pants inspired by Egyptian clothing

Patchwork of different denims

Playful oversized straw hat

Removable cape and train

1999

Billowing skirt with stiffened hem

Poetry in motion Yohji Yamamoto has always taken a dark, romantic view of fashion, finding beauty in flaws and mistakes. He prefers working in black, to show off the proportion and volume of his designs. His Spring 1999 collection had a wedding theme.

Doll-like makeup

Padded dress with ridged outer seams

Cutaway dress bodice attached to shirt

2008

Swirling asymmetric ruffles

Culture clash Kawakubo's free-wheeling creative approach is clear in this outfit from her Spring 2008 collection, which is a mash-up of clown costume, circus-girl frills, tribal prints, and men's tailoring.

Full ballerina-style skirt

2019

Platform high-top trainers

Romantic rock chic After training under Rei Kawakubo at Comme des Garçons, Junya Watanabe began designing for his own label. He is often influenced by street wear, taking items such as jeans, and deconstructing and reconstructing them—in this case into a 19th-century crinoline.

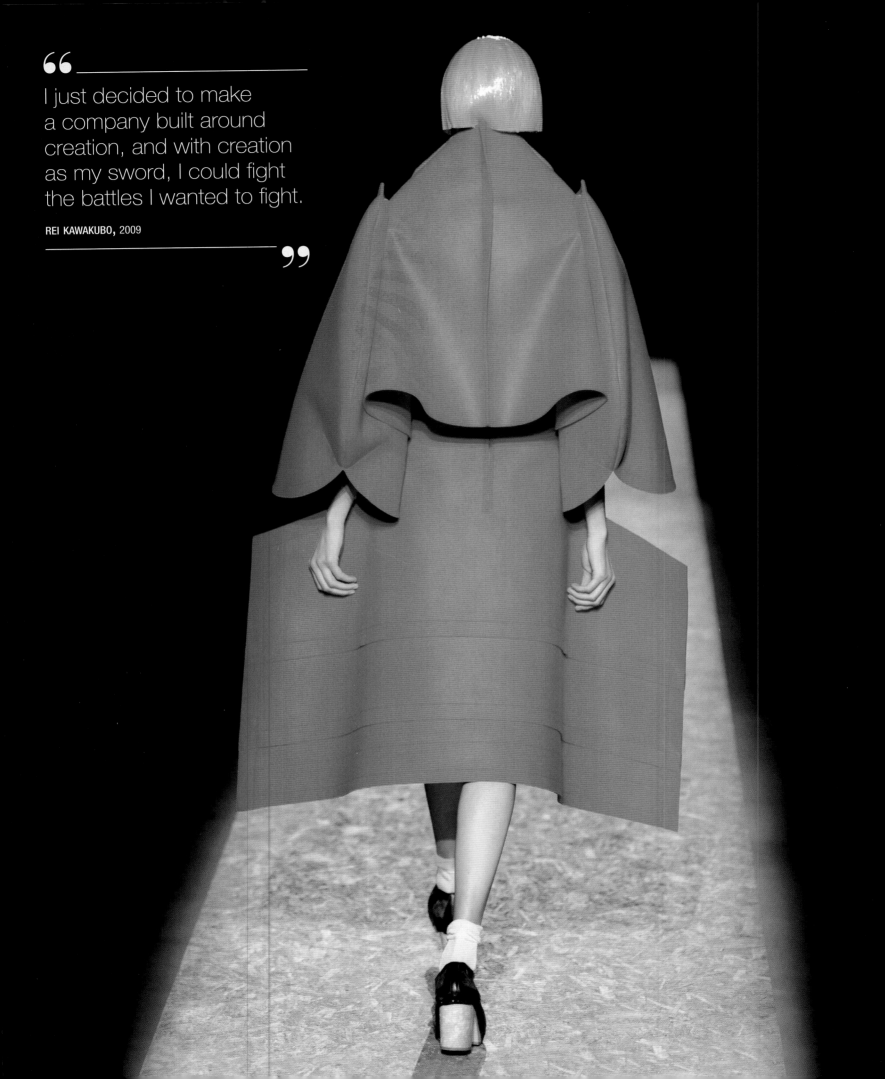

> I just decided to make a company built around creation, and with creation as my sword, I could fight the battles I wanted to fight.

REI KAWAKUBO, 2009

DESIGNER
COMME DES GARCONS

Spanning four decades, the label Comme des Garçons is unique, set apart from any other within the fashion industry. Created by Japanese designer Rei Kawakubo, the company was established in 1973 and has been attracting interest and controversy ever since.

Kawakubo began her career in advertising in the 1960s, and was a self-taught designer. After launching Comme des Garçons, she opened her first boutique, solely for women, in 1975. The late 1970s and early 1980s saw an expansion into menswear; in 1978 a men's line, Comme des Garçons Homme, was added to the label.

The "poverty" look

After moving to Paris in 1980, Kawakubo showed her designs there the following year, to howls of outrage. All the ideals of Western womanhood in the 1970s and '80s—beauty, charm, sex appeal—were missing. Instead, the press reported loudly on the "post-Hiroshima" look of poverty and destruction. The clothes were deliberately tattered and torn, and the collection featured a great deal of black—shape and construction being more important than color. Comme des Garçons (meaning "like the boys") was the opposite of what women were meant to look like.

Kawakubo criticized the very concept of fashion. Her clothes were more like sculpture than couture. She challenged the prevailing silhouette, cleverly using fabric to create a different aesthetic of revealing and concealing. Her second collection, shown in Paris for Spring/Summer 1983, featured drab colors in rough fabrics and garments full of holes. It promoted a new "beggar" look of beauty in destitution, again challenging Western concepts of glamour.

Awards and criticism

Despite initial criticism, by the mid-1980s Comme des Garçons was well on the way to international fame. In 1985 Kawakubo held her first show in the US, and the following year she won a Fashion Group International Award. Comme des Garçons' branding became synonymous with art-house magazines and cutting-edge photography that almost pushed the clothes into the background, adding to their air of mystery.

For Spring 1992, Kawakubo showed garments that looked like the paper patterns of clothes rather than the clothes themselves. In 1995 she roused fierce criticism from Jewish groups for showing male models with close-cropped hair wearing striped pajamas; and for Spring 1997, she sent outfits with bulbous padding down the Paris runway, genuinely shocking an audience that thought it had seen it all before.

More surprises

Kawakubo favored surprising venues and unexpected collaborations. In 2004, for example, she began to roll out a series of "guerrilla" pop-up stores in locations away from traditional fashion capitals. These outlets, which included one in an old bookstore in Berlin, were run on small budgets and were intended to be short-lived. Comme des Garçons also collaborated with the huge mainstream retailer H&M on a ready-to-wear collection, which was released in the fall of 2008 to great critical and consumer acclaim.

Kawakubo continues to confound her critics (and also her admirers), for instance, designing a dress for the fashion doll Barbie, which formed part of Comme des Garçons' *Jingle Flowers* collection.

△ **PRIVATE ICON**
Although often at the center of controversy, Rei Kawakubo has always preferred to stay out of the limelight and is rarely photographed or interviewed. Her trademark look, seen here, comprises a basic black uniform and hair styled in a severe, blunt bob.

◁ **ALL-WHITE**
Kawakubo's Spring/Summer 2012 collection featured full-skirted white dresses worn with short boots.

TIMELINE

1942 Rei Kawakubo born in Tokyo

1967 After early career in advertising, Kawakubo starts work as a freelance designer

1973 Comme des Garçons established as a company

1981 First collection shown in Paris

◁ **1984** Spring/Summer collection features Comme des Garçons' signature deconstructed look

1986 Kawakubo wins Fashion Group International Award

▷ **1997** Spring/Summer collection continues to challenge conventional fashionability with padded clothing

2004 First of "guerrilla" pop-up stores opens in Berlin

2008 Launch of collection in collaboration with mainstream retailer H&M

○ 1940   ○ 1960   ○ 1970   ○ 1980   ○ 1990   ○ 2000

BRIGHT This vibr

1976 ONWARD
STYLE TRIBES

There have always been fashion gangs who dress in a similar way to express a shared identity—mods with their US army parkas in the 1960s, for example, or punks with ripped jeans and fishnets in the 1970s. But in the 1980s, the idea of style tribes really took hold. Style tribes are groups that tend to be associated with a particular place. Members often share the same taste in music, and their way of dressing has DIY elements to set them apart from the mainstream. In the UK there were the flamboyant New Romantics who were inspired by the style of swashbuckling pirates—pop star Adam Ant and designer Vivienne Westwood were role models. In 1987, rave culture took hold in London when Acid House music and the drug MDMA (ecstasy) were transplanted from Ibiza—the smiley face became their emblem. Across the Atlantic, hip-hop and rap gave birth to new style tribes among African Americans, who wore heavy gold "bling" jewelry and pristine sportswear—such as hoodies, puffer jackets, and status sneakers—and their look heavily influenced contemporary menswear across the board. Many of the pre-21st-century style-tribe looks were male-led, with women adopting feminized versions of the signature style. In the 21st century, style tribes have multiplied and include Burberry-clad chavs and Kardashian-clones, who slavishly copy the looks of the Kardashian clan they see on reality TV and Instagram, and followers of cult labels such as Bathing Ape and Supreme.

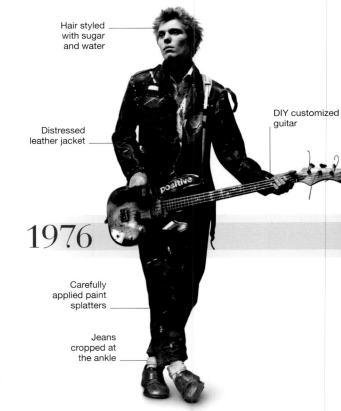

Hair styled with sugar and water

DIY customized guitar

Distressed leather jacket

1976

Carefully applied paint splatters

Jeans cropped at the ankle

Punk style Bassist Paul Simonson of punk band The Clash was recognized as the most stylish of the group. He helped shape punk fashions with his attitude: you had to make people scared of you so they would leave you alone.

FLY GIRLS

While male rappers have held the limelight since the 1980s, a sub-culture of female rappers—known as "Fly Girls"—emerged in the boroughs of New York City in the 1970s. Their style was athletic and sexy, and their signature pieces included satin tracksuits, bodysuits, big earrings, and street wear, such as extra-large jeans, borrowed from the boys. The first all-female crew, Sequence, debuted in 1979 and others followed, including Roxanne Shante, who wore oversize denim jackets with chunky gold earrings, and Queen Latifah with her snapback caps and sneakers. These acts paved the way for later female rap artists such as Salt N Pepa, Missy Elliott, Eve, and Stefflon Don. The word "fly" is slang for someone stylish or cool, and so the term "fly girl" was used for these stylish and bold women.

Knitted tam, with Rasta colors, to hold "dreads"

Denim on denim

Unhemmed jeans

Leather utility boots

Rasta cool The Rastafarian movement began in 1930s Jamaica but was not well known until the 1970s when Rasta Bob Marley became famous. His style influence can be seen in dreadlocks; the Rasta colors red, green, and gold; and denim on denim. Punks also picked up on elements of the style.

Spiked, black hair shows punk legacy

Peekaboo hair covers face

Sheer lace bodice

1984

Long, velvet skirt fitting for romantic heroine

Goth glamour The goth aesthetic came together in London club "The Batcave." Both men and women wore clothes inspired by Victorian mourning garb and Bram Stoker's *Dracula,* and it was not long before this movement took to the streets. Today, courtesy of Camden market, the look is still very much in evidence.

1979

Shiny tonic suit

Skinny tie

Tight, cropped pants

Dr. (doc) Martens shoes

Mod style The Specials were one of the leading British ska bands of the late 1970s and early 1980s, fusing punk energy with Jamaican ska that was sped up to a danceable beat. They wore 1960s rude boy clothes, including slim-cut suits, porkpie hats, and Fred Perry shirts.

1981

Frilled full-sleeved shirt

DIY frayed fabric ties

Pirate-style boots

Antmania Adam Ant was a symbol of the New Romantic subculture but saw himself as a post-punk, styled as both dangerous and romantic. He dressed in flamboyant clothes inspired by 18th-century military uniforms and wore warrior makeup.

Customized Victorian-style top hat

Layered, distressed details

19th-century walking stick

Fantasy-inspired platform boots

1990

Long hair

Leotard top

Denim shorts, preferably cut-off Levi's 501s

High-tops for dancing

Rave scene As police cracked down on illegal rave parties, Acid House returned to nightclubs, in particular the Hacienda Club in Manchester, UK. Fluorescent leggings, high-top sneakers, and bicycling jerseys were the best clothes for dancing all night long.

2012

Sunglasses

Heavy chain with large cross

Expensive, chunky watch and ring

Baggy, dark denim jeans

Brand-new sneakers

Hip hop Sean "Diddy" Combs, aka Puff Daddy, became a fashion icon through his career as a hip-hop star. With support from Tommy Hilfiger and US *Vogue* editor Anna Wintour, he launched the Sean John clothing line in 1998, which brought together music culture and street fashion.

2017

Steampunk The big girls' (and boys') version of playing dress-up, steampunk and cosplay bring fantasy fashion and science fiction into the real world. Steampunk is a mash-up of punk and the clothing of the late 19th century, a time when steam power was the new technology.

1990 ONWARD
MINIMAL AND CONCEPTUAL

In the wake of 1980s power dressing—which emphasized clingy styles, bold color, exaggerated silhouettes, and embellishment—consumers in the early 1990s seemed to tire of fashion, and the industry struggled to lure them. New notions of anti-fashion emerged, with designers paring down the look and using a plainer color palette—the Japanese avant-garde designers had already made all black acceptable during the 1980s. It was a different way of dressing and it appealed to women with professional jobs and busy working lives. It was a time, too, for deconstructivist designers like Martin Margiela and Ann Demeulemeester in Belgium, and Hussein Chalayan in England—all of whom took an intellectual approach to fashion, stripping clothes back to first principles as part of their design aesthetic.

Neat, swept-back hair

Almost-invisible straps

Ultimate neutral US designer Calvin Klein varies his collections subtly each season, often sticking to a color palette of gray, beige, and black. His 1997 Spring/Summer collection made gray fashionable with luxurious fabrics and shiftlike dresses, paired with bare legs.

Two-tone gray with asymmetric seam

1997

Fitted but not clingy, with shine to add interest

Sharp rectangular outline obscures body shape

Classic trench detailing

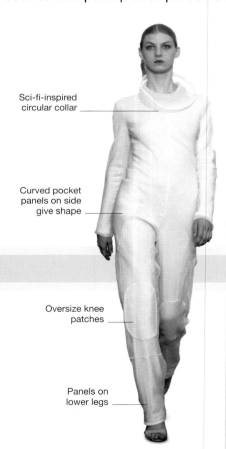

Sci-fi-inspired circular collar

Simple ruffled strap on one side

Exaggerated puff sleeve on other side

Curved pocket panels on side give shape

2000

2011

Starched white fabric

Oversize knee patches

Panels on lower legs

Tiered skirt constructed from wood

Simple pumps

Futuristic jumpsuit The millennium was on Austrian Helmut Lang's mind when he created this take on a spacesuit for his 1999 Fall/Winter collection. The silk organza is layered over easy-give cotton and silk jersey to beautiful effect.

Experimental reduction In Hussein Chalayan's 2000 Fall/Winter collection, the designer pushed the boundaries of everyday dress. In this example, he merged fashion and furniture by morphing a coffee table into a skirt.

Subversive style Belgian designer Martin Margiela reinvented the classic trench coat in his Spring/Summer 2011 collection. The fabric is stretched over a two-dimensional rectangular frame to completely obscure the body beneath.

Dress designed to fall off one shoulder

Loosely draped but showing body's form

Use of fine-quality fabrics

Extra-long, asymmetric hemline

All-white Known for her androgynous, sensual clothing cut in innovative ways to drape and elongate the body, Flemish designer Ann Demeulemeester uses black and white every season. This is a Spring/Summer dress for 1997.

Underpinned by sporty-style tank dress

Sheer layer is slightly draped for movement

1999

Fun color; pared-back fashion is not always neutral

Ankle-wrap shoes reduced to basic function

Sheer color For his 1999 Spring/Summer show, Helmut Lang layered sheer, colored fabrics over white to create dressy sportswear that was hailed by fashion editors as sleek, desirable, and having commercial appeal.

Swim-cap-style headwear with futuristic visor

Mesh gloves

Full skirt drawn in at waist helps create hourglass silhouette

Denim dress looks like an artist's shirt

"Painting" created from laser-cut jacquard with embroidery and applique

2015

Hinged frame integrated into skirt

Simple, polished Oxford shoes

Wearable art Viktor and Rolf's Fall/Winter couture show brought art to life as, in front of an audience, the designer duo placed paintings on their models, before unfastening them and hanging them back onto the wall to create an impressive art gallery for the show's finale.

Breezy, voluminous caftan

2017

Sun-ray stripes in gleaming silk

Laced up biker boots with thick soles

Theatrical dressing Inspired by the 60 costumes he created for the Palais Garnier, whose opera opened the night before his Spring/Summer show, Gareth Pugh's sun-themed collection was full of drama and his signature sculptural and experimental aesthetic.

High-shine leggings

Signature tabi (split toe) shoes

Conceptual tailoring Under John Galliano since 2014, the fashion house of Maison Margiela continues to push the boundaries of clothing design and mix sharp tailoring with bold, eccentric influences from the street.

1990 ONWARD
VINTAGE IN VOGUE

The idea of putting old clothes together to create a new look became popular during the 1990s grunge scene, when army surplus gear and flannelette shirts from thrift shops were wardrobe staples. By the 2000s, the dressed-down hobo look of grunge had evolved into boho—short for bohemian, referring to a group of 18th-century French artists who lived cheaply but with great style. Fashionistas prided themselves on finding bargain designer pieces from past decades. Suddenly it was more stylish to have a vintage Chanel jacket than a new one. Summer music festivals became a stage for dressed-down vintage looks, such as shorts and rain boots teamed with a hippy poncho from the '60s or a '70s T-shirt. As women trawled thrift shops, markets, and upmarket second-hand boutiques, fashion houses such as Dior and Gucci delved into their archives for inspiration from the past.

GOODWOOD REVIVAL

ROW 4
ROW 5

Some lovers of retro clothing make it part of their lifestyle. The Goodwood Revival Festival in England attracts thousands of people in 1950s dress—mostly original and worn as it would have been back then. Women wear colorful dresses with full skirts in bright prints, or pencil skirts with tight sweaters, accessorized with pointy-toed pumps, red lipstick, and immaculately done hair.

1993

Messy hair with streaks

Charms and chains

Luxurious sheepskin coat

Basic white T-shirt

Fedora

Flannelette shirts reference original grunge wear

Square-toed biker boots

Thrift-shop aesthetic The grunge style that emerged from Seattle mixed second-hand and new, but distressed, clothes. Marc Jacobs picked up on the trend and recreated it for Perry Ellis and his own label.

Feminine full skirt

2012

Hem finished mid-calf

New classics During his time as head designer at Christian Dior, Raf Simons took classics from the label's past collections and reinvented them for the modern woman. He used elements from Dior's famous New Look collection of 1947, which created an hourglass figure with rounded shoulders, shaped bust, small waist, and full skirt.

Pointed kitten heel pumps

Diamond earrings

Fitted straight bodice

2016

Decorated with sequins

Ruffled hem

Vintage star Amal Clooney, human rights lawyer and wife of George, is one of several celebrities who choose to wear vintage gowns on the red carpet. For the 2016 Berlin International Film Festival, she wore a 1981 Yves Saint Laurent dress.

Makeup from the
night before

Tailored,
Victorian-style
waistcoat

Slouchy '70s-
style bag

2005

Very short
shorts

Hunter
Wellington
boots

Glastonbury chic Kate Moss set the standard for festival dressing, mixing a rock and roll vibe with classic English country Wellington boots and a fitted waistcoat. Her ability to coordinate pieces from different eras created a carefree effect.

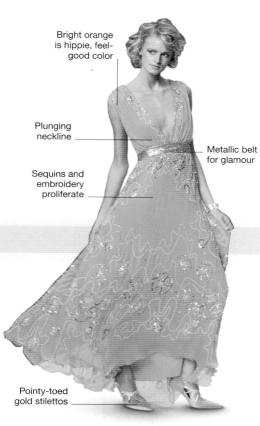

Bright orange
is hippie, feel-
good color

Plunging
neckline

Metallic belt
for glamour

Sequins and
embroidery
proliferate

Pointy-toed
gold stilettos

Boho designers Matthew Williamson and Alice Temperley are cited as boho-chic designers. Williamson's floaty dresses feature butterflies and embroidery, while Temperley, whose dress is shown here, is cast as the English eccentric.

Long, layered
locks

Shrugged-
on cardigan

Multiple gold
necklaces

Dress in
floaty fabric

Hippie deluxe Sienna Miller helped make boho-chic one of the major fashion trends of 2005–2006. Her typical boho uniform was a flowing dress, lots of jewelry, a slouchy jacket or knit, and a cross-body bag.

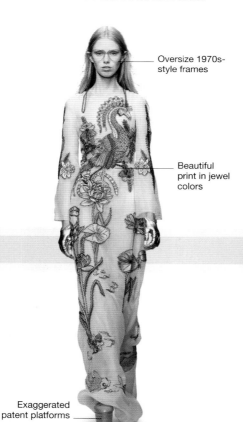

Oversize 1970s-
style frames

Beautiful
print in jewel
colors

Exaggerated
patent platforms

Reworking the brand Gucci returned to the past to become one of the hottest brands, thanks to new creative director Alessandro Michele. He built on the brand's tradition of floral printed scarves, reworking them into new patterns and clothing styles.

Knitted corset-
style top

2017

Delicate lacelike
details

Grounded with
chunky boots

Drawing on tradition The vintage revival made people more aware of the craftsmanship that existed before the modern era of mass-produced, factory-made clothing. Sarah Burton created a romantic Fall/Winter 2016 collection for Alexander McQueen using traditional Shetland knitting.

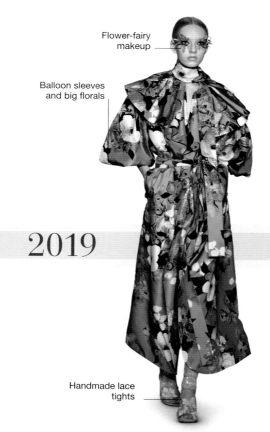

Flower-fairy
makeup

Balloon sleeves
and big florals

2019

Handmade lace
tights

Couture resurgence Valentino's creative director Pierpaolo Piccioli made couture chic again with a rich, flower-themed collection full of color and luxurious fabrics. Some dresses took over 1,000 hours to make by hand, and used more than 65 yards of fabric.

2000 ONWARD
STATEMENT DRESSING

The point of stepping onto the red carpet has always been to make a fashion statement. But these days it is also seen as a stage for making personal statements—about sexuality, about equal rights, about not conforming—and it does not have to be on a red carpet: any big event with paparazzi in attendance will do. Rebellion on the red carpet dates back decades. In 1986, after Oscars organizers urged female guests to stop wearing pantsuits, Cher turned up in a midriff-baring, bondage-style jumpsuit. Fast-forward to 2018 when Kristen Stewart took off her high heels and walked barefoot on the red carpet in protest at the Cannes Film Festival rule that women should not wear flats. The same year, hundreds of celebrities at the Golden Globes wore black to support the Time's Up movement against sexual harassment.

2000

Plunging swimsuit bodice

Wrapped like a beach sarong

Sheer silk skirt with colorful bamboo print

Long train adds a formal touch

2001

3-D swan head around neck

Nude body stocking underneath

Layered tulle ballerina skirt

Tropical vibe Jennifer Lopez wore Versace to the 2000 Grammy Awards, reflecting the growing importance of designers' resort collections. Her dress prompted so many internet searches that Google decided to develop its image-search feature.

Carnival fashion Bjork rejected any ideas of looking elegant in this tutu—a joking reference to animals on a merry-go-round. Despite topping the worst-dressed lists for the 2001 Oscars, the dress by Marjan Pejoski became iconic.

SHOW-STOPPING SHOES

Manolo Blahnik

In the early days of Hollywood, the stars turned to Salvatore Ferragamo, Charles Jourdan, André Perugia, and Beth Levine for fantastic red-carpet footwear. In the 1990s a new generation took over. Credited for show-stopping heels are cult labels Christian Louboutin, Manolo Blahnik, and Jimmy Choo. Now designers Nicholas Kirkwood and Sophia Webster are creating chic shoes, too.

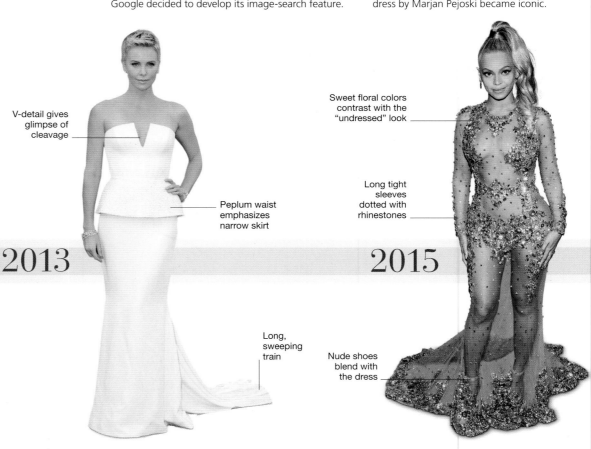

V-detail gives glimpse of cleavage

Peplum waist emphasizes narrow skirt

2013

Long, sweeping train

Sweet floral colors contrast with the "undressed" look

Long tight sleeves dotted with rhinestones

2015

Nude shoes blend with the dress

Brand ambassador As the advertising face of Christian Dior, Charlize Theron of course wore the label to the 2013 Oscars. The simplicity of her white two-piece couture gown, combined with her pixie haircut, projected modern femininity and reflected the brand values of Dior.

Pretty naked Appearing to wear only strategically placed flowers, Beyoncé stole the limelight at the 2015 Met Gala. A sketch of the dress by Givenchy Haute Couture, posted on Twitter beforehand, built anticipation.

2002

No jewels to detract from dress

Embroidered leaf design covers bust

Asymmetric waist softens join between bodice and skirt

Skirt appears to be falling off the hips

Slender skirt with train

Dressed or undressed? Halle Berry's dress, by Lebanese designer Elie Saab, is provocative and demure at the same time. The see-through bodice hints at Berry's sexuality and shows off her athletic physique, while the majestic skirt adds a sense of dignity.

Beaded at sides and neck

Soft gathered, draped waist

2018

Full, fluid skirt with silvery hem

Queen of green Known for promoting ethical fashion, Livia Firth wore a vintage Laura Biagiotti dress from 1981 to the Green Carpet Awards at Milan Fashion Week in 2018—an event that promotes the idea of recycling existing clothing.

Matching hat and purse in meat

2010

Made from raw beef steak

Ripped fishnet tights

Wedge boots bound with layers of meat

Red carpet rebel Now in the Rock and Roll Hall of Fame in the US, Lady Gaga's dress by LA designer Frances Fernandez was reportedly made from 12 pieces of thinly sliced steak, which took a month to specially prepare. The star said the dress symbolized standing up for your rights and not conforming.

Quietly political Lupita Nyong'o selected a dress by Elie Saab Couture for her appearance at the 2018 Baftas, where stars chose to wear black in support of the Time's Up movement promoting sexual equality. Her dress projected strength with warrior-style details.

Natural, braided hair

Gold braid on velvet adds shine

Time's Up badge on shoulder strap

Gladiator-style breastplate

DESIGNER
ALEXANDER MCQUEEN

One of the most important British designers of recent decades, Alexander McQueen reintroduced tailoring to fashion with his sharp suits and frock coats and brought new technology into couture. With a creativity that drove forward his quest for the new, he also reinvented the fashion show. "You've got to give them an extravaganza!" was his philosophy. At first unsettling, by the time of his untimely death at 40, McQueen's shows had become theatrical events.

East End beginnings

Born in 1969, Lee Alexander McQueen was the son of a London cab driver and the youngest of six children growing up in Stratford, East London. Encouraged by his mother, a teacher, the young McQueen showed an early interest in fashion design, and at 16 enrolled as an apprentice cutter and tailor at Anderson and Sheppard, then tailors to HRH Prince of Wales. Legend has it that the teenage McQueen wrote obscenities in the linings of suits for the prince and other clients; what is certain is that he showed an extraordinary aptitude. After 18 months he had mastered the "forward" (a perfectly made test jacket), then learned to cut trousers at Gieves and Hawkes, and finally historical costumes at Angels and Bermans costumiers. Moving into high fashion, he became a cutter for the avant-garde designer, Koji Tatsuno and for Milan-based designer Romeo Gigli.

In spite of a lack of certain requirements in art, McQueen was accepted to the MA Fashion course at Central St. Martins, London. His degree collection *Jack the Ripper Stalks His Victims*, featuring bustled jackets, papier-mâché appliqué, and his own hair incorporated into linings, caught the attention of stylist Isabella Blow, who became McQueen's supporter and advocate. McQueen immediately began showing under his own name. His "bumsters" (low-rise pants) at his second show *Nihilism* scandalized many, revealing the cleft in the models' buttocks, at the same time as elongating the torso and shortening the legs. This was a totally new idea, which launched a decade of low-slung, pelvis-hugging pants in mainstream stores. His shows became must-see events, made on a tiny budget with a dedicated team. *The Birds* (Spring/Summer 1995), held in an unoccupied warehouse, was based on Hitchcock's eponymous movie and, with the theme of road kill, featured tire prints on dresses and corsetier Mr. Pearl with his 18" (46cm) waist in McQueen women's wear. Iconoclastic and transgressive, it was a fashion moment that blew away the cobwebs.

History and nature

Skilled tailoring, revealed in the frock coats, suits, and jumpsuits that were signature McQueen, coupled with meticulous research enabled the designer to realize his extraordinary ideas. Shows like *Highland Rape* (1995), based on historic border conflicts, were testimony to McQueen's fascination with the past and his ability to make it modern, cutting tartan on the bias and updating body-molding corsets. He was also inspired by nature, using feathers, skin and bones, and even live falcons in his shows. McQueen's tenure as head designer at Givenchy was not always a success, given its essentially genteel French signature, but he went on to find the creative freedom he craved at the Gucci Group. The designer was multilayered in his talent and vision, and his later own name collections, *Horn of Plenty* in 2009, and his final show, *Plato's Atlantis* in 2010, raised questions about the future of the planet and man's careless approach. His label continues under the creative directorship of Sarah Burton, designer of the Duchess of Cambridge's wedding dress.

△ **TAILOR AND CRAFTSMAN**
McQueen was awarded British Designer of the Year four times. He was presented with a CBE and voted by CFDA (Council of Fashion Designers of America) International Designer of the Year in 2003.

◁ **PLATO'S ATLANTIS**
This dress from McQueen's final collection shows his skill in print and art and his love of the environment.

TIMELINE

1985 Begins his apprenticeship at Anderson and Sheppard, Savile Row, London

1989 Employed as a cutter of historical costumes at Angels and Bermans, London

1990 Worked as a cutter for designer Romeo Gigli in Milan

1992 *Jack the Ripper* graduation collection at Central St. Martin's College, London

1993 Bumster pants unveiled at *Nihilism* show

1996 & 1997 UK designer of the year

◁ **1997** Brown ponyskin jacket with impala horns on shoulders from *It's a Jungle Out There*

2001 ▷ *Voss* dress with black ostrich feathers

2003 International Designer of the Year awarded by CFDA. Presented with CBE by HRH The Queen

2009 *Horn of Plenty* show

2010 *Plato's Atlantis* — final collection focuses on future of the planet. McQueen's death

2011 *Savage Beauty* retrospective exhibition of McQueen's work at The Met, New York

○ 1985   ○ 1990   ○ 1995   ○ 2000   ○ 2005   ○ 2010

◁ **BIRD-PRINT SILK, *HORN OF PLENTY* SHOW, WINTER 2009** McQueen revisited his love of birds in his penultimate collection.

DIVERSITY IN FASHION

In May 1966, the first African American model appeared on the cover of British *Vogue*. Her name was Donyale Luna and she challenged the biased portrayal of beauty as all-white. But change happened slowly. US *Vogue* had its first black cover girl, Beverly Johnson, in the August 1974 edition. In Britain the next black model on a *Vogue* cover was Gail O'Neill in 1986, followed by Naomi Campbell a year later. By that time, the African-born model Iman and Jamaican-born Grace Jones had become regulars in the pages of *Vogue* and on the catwalks for Yves Saint Laurent and Thierry Mugler. Other steps toward diversity included 70-year-old Daphne Selfe being cast to walk at London Fashion Week in 1998, and Alexander McQueen casting amputee Aimee Mullins in his show for Spring/Summer 1999.

More recently, Kelly Knox, who was born missing a left forearm, modeled for Teatum Jones in the opening show of London Fashion Week and fronted a campaign for Primark, while plus-size model Ashley Graham has appeared on the cover of *Vogue* and walked for top labels including Michael Kors and Dolce & Gabbana. In 2016, transgender model Hari Nef walked the runway for Gucci, and was given control of the brand's Snapchat for fashion week. Models on social media have changed the business of casting: as they connect directly with the public and give them influence, agents and editors are no longer making isolated decisions. With 4.2 million Instagram followers Winnie Harlow, who as she herself says "happens to have vitiligo," which creates contrasting coloration of her skin, is proof that the fashion-buying public supports models who celebrate their differences. And at the 2016 Vetements and Balenciaga shows, the audience immediately criticized the use of all-white models by posting their negative comments on social media. Gradually, the fashion industry has realized that the consumers who buy clothes and accessories want to see models who reflect the diversity of the world we live in.

> **"**
>
> ## All our differences are part of who we are, but they don't define us.
>
> **WINNIE HARLOW,** MODEL, 2018
>
> **"**

◁ **RUNWAY REGULAR**
Since her 2014 debut at London Fashion Week, Winnie Harlow has appeared on numerous runways. Here she walks for Julien MacDonald in 2019.

1998 ONWARD
ETHICAL FASHION

The buying decisions made daily by fashion shoppers have the power to create a cleaner, fairer world—this is the point behind the ethical fashion movement, which urges consumers to choose things that are made without exploiting workers and without polluting the environment. Over the past decade, big fashion chains have become experts at filling stores with cheap, fun fashion that changes every week. But if clothes are cheap, someone has been paid cheaply to make them, and consumers are more likely to throw them away to make way for new things each season. A report by the Ellen MacArthur Foundation showed that a truckload of clothing is wasted every second across the world, and that the fashion industry does more damage to the environment every year than international flights and shipping. Designers such as Katharine Hamnett and Stella McCartney have committed to ethically produced fashion, and industry groups have taken action to stop the waste. The British Fashion Council, for example, launched a "Positive Fashion" challenge, asking stores and designers to agree to reduce waste and recycle more. Consumers can help by buying recycled or upcycled clothes, buying locally made things, and buying fewer but better quality clothes.

Activist-designer Katharine Hamnett's "Choose Life" slogan

Anti-nuclear "Clean up or die" slogan

Dress composed of 20 organic cotton T-shirts

1998

Ball-gown skirt

Recycling rules Eco-fashion represents the industry's environmental conscience, emphasizing sustainability in an era of conspicuous consumption. British designer Gary Harvey created this 1998 dress from T-shirts that he recycled from Katharine Hamnett's 1984 collection.

KATHARINE HAMNETT

Famous for her 1990s slogan T-shirts, British designer Katharine Hamnett has built her business on the Buddhist ideal of making a living without harming anyone or anything in the natural world. For example, her T-shirts are made from organic cotton that is grown using rainwater and natural compost from animal droppings. They are made in a factory that uses renewable energy and does not waste power. Since most of her buyers are in Europe, she has her clothes made in Europe, which means less environmental damage caused by transportation, too.

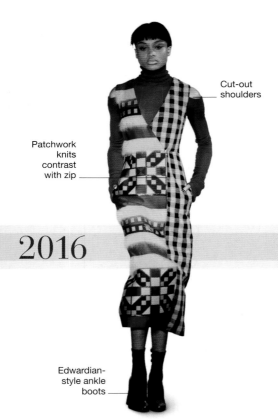

Cut-out shoulders

Patchwork knits contrast with zip

2016

Edwardian-style ankle boots

Natural wool Catherine Teatum and Rob Jones often work with wool, a natural fiber, for their label Teatum Jones. For Fall/Winter 2016, they were inspired by an historic wool mill near Teatum's family origins in Ireland, using wools of different textures in lean, Edwardian silhouettes.

Military-style camo jacket

See-through knit top

2017

Satin skirt with utility apron

Patch pocket and Velcro

Combat boots

Brilliant recycling Christopher Raeburn's graduation show in London in 2006 was a womens wear collection remade from old military uniforms, an idea he reworked for Fall/Winter 2017. His brand is built on the idea of "Remade, Reduced, Recycled."

2013

- Green face symbolizes the environment
- T-shirt with climate change map
- Bright, optimistic colors
- Camo print to match revolutionary spirit
- Fitted waist
- One-shoulder, ruched dress
- Synthetic faux leather
- Long tailored trousers

Buy less, choose well The message at Vivienne Westwood's Red Label show for Spring/Summer 2013 was to think about the environment when you choose what to buy. The designer used her fashion show to encourage shoppers to support climate revolution by purchasing fewer things.

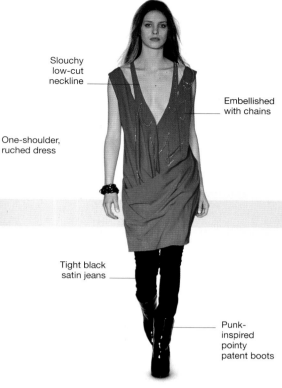

- Slouchy low-cut neckline
- Embellished with chains
- Tight black satin jeans
- Punk-inspired pointy patent boots

Ethical and elegant One of the first high-fashion ethical brands, Edun was set up by Ali Hewson and her husband, U2 lead singer Bono. The range of clothes and accessories is made in Africa, using African artists, producers, and craftspeople. For 2013 Fall/Winter, the theme was punk glamour.

2018

- Metallic dress from recycled plastic
- Eco-friendly tote bag
- Hybrid pumps made from discarded shoes

New fabric technology Passionate about the environment, London-based Vin + Omi developed new eco-textiles for their first collection in 2018. Materials included thread made from melted-down plastic drink bottles and fabrics using plastic sourced from ocean clean-up projects.

Animal-friendly fashion Since 2001, Stella McCartney has aimed to make her collections ethical and environmentally friendly, while at the same time building a successful business. She is a vegetarian, and this is reflected in her collections—for Fall/Winter 2018 she used environmentally friendly faux leather and fur.

2019

- Strong-looking, gray-haired model
- Organically produced linen
- Patchwork of black and white graphic prints
- Flats for walking

Designing a better world Maria Cornejo aims to reduce any waste from producing her Zero + Maria Cornejo label. For Spring/Summer 2019 she used regenerated material from garbage sites and produced more than 80 percent of her collection locally in New York City to reduce the brand's carbon footprint.

2010 ONWARD
THE NEXT GENERATION

In recent years, fashion has moved in new directions to meet the desire of consumers for individualistic looks. No longer satisfied with the big-brand labels, and suffering from "It" bag and logo fatigue, women went on the hunt for fresh looks and original ideas. It was up to a new generation of designers to woo women back to fashion. Alexander Wang, for example, has shown how street cred and savvy design can make millions with a global empire based on grunge meets downtown, while Phoebe Philo's uncompromisingly modern stance at Céline made the once-dowdy label one of the hottest of the early 2010s. Fashion has always thrived on new ideas, and as bored shoppers have gone cold on many mainstream brands, retailers have adapted by commissioning limited-edition collections, such as Eytys x H&M, Halpern x Topshop, and JW Anderson x Converse. Even online retailers have picked up on the trend with exclusive styles from designers. Meanwhile, luxury houses have reinvented themselves with the help of creative talent drawn from the next generation.

VICTORIA BECKHAM

After more than a decade in the industry, Victoria Beckham has shown that the most valuable part of her fashion brand is her own identity— a hard-working mother with a famous husband and four children, all of whom are fashion-show front-row (FROW) regulars. She wears her own clothes, and has evolved with her market. Starting with a small range of jeans and eyewear in 2006, Beckham moved on to the world of high-end ready-to-wear in 2008. Initially skeptical, the fashion press have given rave reviews, and her collections, shown first in New York and now in London, have been a commercial success. Beckham has also mastered Instagram, and astutely uses her lifestyle to strengthen her brand.

2010

Hair painted white

All white looks fresh

Shoulder reminiscent of Chinese armor

Deconstructed tailoring

Gold slashes evoke duct tape

Lace embroidery inspired by Qing Dynasty

Shoes are part of brand

Cool kid US designer Alexander Wang, who fuses casual elements with laid-back tailoring and sporty separates, is admired for being in tune with the needs of the modern customer. He has successfully built a global brand, while remaining edgy.

Tasseled details appeared throughout Fall/Winter 2012 collection

Hot pink, draped satin shows dressmaking mastery

Young cosmopolitan Manhattan-based Taiwanese-Canadian Jason Wu designs luxury sportswear and beautiful evening dresses, like this one from Fall/Winter 2012 modeled by Cara Delevingne. First Lady Michelle Obama chose four of his dresses in 2008 to wear to public events.

Meticulously tailored and tapered sleeves

Wide, notched waistband with buttoned tab

Subtle use of white to shape the torso

Same print also covers shoes

Print master With a talent for abstraction and precise construction, London-based Erdem Moralioglu creates romantic clothes with a contemporary edge. His innovative prints place dense patterns next to empty zones, often with deliberate asymmetry.

The minimalist British designer Phoebe Philo describes her style as "contemporary minimalism." Whether taking her inspiration from cars, buildings, or handicrafts, Philo's collections for French brand Céline were strong, sensible, and chic. This design is from Fall/Winter 2011.

White turtleneck is base

Fabric mimics car upholstery

Laser cutting creates sharp edges

Pants inset with leather stripe

Tapered hem above flat loafers

2011

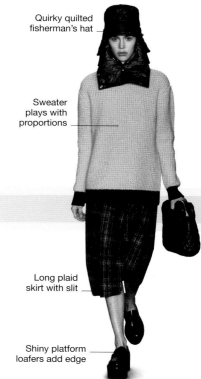

Red ruffle at neck adds modernity

Blush pink is subtle and feminine

Black stripe with ruffles mixes pretty and bold

2012

Fire-engine red platform shoes toughen look

The sophisticate Serbian-born designer Roksanda Ilincic is best known for her elegant dresses. Working in silks, satins, and velvets, she often draws on the 1970s and 1980s to create polished, structured pieces, as here for pre-Fall 2012.

Quirky quilted fisherman's hat

Sweater plays with proportions

Long plaid skirt with slit

Shiny platform loafers add edge

The matchmaker Irish-born JW Anderson mixes a playful approach, tailoring skills, and apparently opposing forces to great effect. This often means the juxtaposition of masculine and feminine, kinky and elegant, as here for Fall/Winter 2012.

Face painted as cross of St. George, England's patron saint

Strapless bodice with serrated top

Black drinking straws

Skintight fingerless gloves

2015

Natural "real"-looking model

Neon colors inspired by techno ravers

Hand-smocked waistband

2017

Ballerina-style tulle tutu

Dark materials After appearing in a fashion talent TV show, Gareth Pugh went on to launch his own label in 2006. He experiments with form and volume, often using unexpected materials such as rubber and plastic. His 2015 Fall/Winter collection was themed around women ready for battle.

Military-style riding boots

Playful princess Molly Goddard's signature look is girlish oversize dresses adorned with frills, often in pretty colors. But there is also a punk element to her designs—she layers dresses over trousers, exaggerates feminine details, and always puts her models in flat shoes or boots.

Head scarf

Head-to-toe floral prints

Lined with contrasting geometric print

Clashing floral tights

2018

Trademark print Richard Quinn loves prints and dramatic volume, and his ability to mix them together is one of his skills. His Spring/Summer 2018 show was famously attended by Queen Elizabeth II, who gave him an award for his contribution to fashion.

A NEW ERA

The idea that fashion should be as intelligent as other technology, such as smartphones and laptops, is gradually becoming reality. Fabrics specially designed to help keep the body warm or cool are now common in gym and sports clothes, and 3-D printing has been used to make accessories such as shoes and sunglasses. But other technologies are now emerging. Google and Levi's worked together on a jacket for cyclists—the wearer can swipe, tap, or hold the left cuff to change music tracks or answer their phone while riding. In the UK, Lauren Bowker launched a range of accessories that change color when the temperature or light changes—a tote bag that is red in winter, blue in summer, and green in spring, for example. And the Diffus bag is wired with tiny solar panels, providing power to charge a mobile phone. The Emel + Aris coat has adjustable temperature settings, thanks to built-in heat panels, which the wearer can turn up or down using a switch inside the coat. Digitsole has developed M-Cube, a shoe inner sole with sensors for collecting health data about the wearer such as their body temperature, heart rate, and posture while walking—the stored information can then be used to identify any potential health problems and help fix them. Although wearable technology like this is still at the experimental stage, it might soon revolutionize what we wear and how we wear it.

> " Everybody could have their body scanned and order clothes that fit perfectly. "
>
> IRIS VAN HERPEN, DESIGNER, 2013

◁ **TECHNOLOGY AND ROMANCE**
For Fall/Winter 2018, Iris van Herpen used laser cutting and a special liquid coating on silk organza to imitate the movement of birds' wings.

3,000 YEARS OF
WOMEN'S WEAR

From ancient civilizations to the present day, women's dress has been shaped not only by personal taste but by economic, political, and technological developments. As the centuries passed, new trade routes introduced exotic fabrics and adornments from distant lands, while the rise and fall of monarchies overturned dress styles and inspired new ones. Major agents of change included advances in technology, from loom to sewing machine, and from natural cloth to man-made fabrics such as Lycra. Against this backdrop sits self expression: in the 1920s boyish shapes and shorter skirts celebrated new-found personal freedom; in the 1980s padded shoulders and tailored suits symbolized female power in a male-dominated workplace. Today the global fashion industry promotes a rapid turnover of styles that cross all national boundaries.

Ancient Greek chiton (reconstructed) fastened at the shoulders

Mid-14th Century Surcoat (reconstructed) worn over *cote-hardie*

1830s Cotton day dress with full gigot sleeves and a flounced hem

1850–1854 Printed day dress with a bell-shaped skirt and pagoda sleeves

c. 1888 Bustle dress with tailored jacket and waistcoat (vest)

1902 S-bend dress with pigeon-pouter chest and hips pushed back

1910–1912 Lace bodice and skirt with sash to emphasize the narrow waist

1940s Utility dress cut to waste as little fabric as possible

1940s Checked dress showing width at the shoulders, worn with head scarf

1950s Day dress and matching bolero jacket, with full skirt over net petticoats

1950s Printed dress with fitted waist and pencil skirt, in a vibrant floral fabric

1960s Minidress hemmed well above the knee, worn with white go-go boots

14th–15th Century Italian gown (reconstructed) with hanging sleeves

1470–1500 Italian gown with a high waist and deep V-neck

1581 Chambermaid wearing a full skirt over a hooped farthingale

1750 Robe à la française of blue silk brocade in a floral pattern

1799 Day dress in the classical style, with very high waist and columnar skirt

1922 Green dress with a dropped sash waist and V-neck collar

1920s Day dress in printed chiffon with a knee-length flounced skirt

1930s Floral print dress cut on the bias with matching smocked bolero

1934 Afternoon dress with boat neck detail and belted waist

1937 Checked dress with the long, lean silhouette of the decade

1960s–1970s Belted shirt dress with red trim and buttons

1976 Silk ensemble with floor-length skirt and matching head scarf

1980s Black dress with shoulder pads, worn with black tights and stiletto heels

1994 Gingham dress worn with heavy black lace-up shoes

2005 Boho outfit of tiered skirt and layered jersey tops

3,000 YEARS OF
MENSWEAR

Since ancient times male clothes have been used as a declaration of social distinction. Every historical age has had its own sartorial codes, either imposed by law or by social pressure—once it was the exact color of toga that mattered; today it is likely to be the label on a pair of designer jeans that counts. One of the most widespread and enduring items of male clothing is the suit, which from the 19th century onward gradually evolved from various jacket-and-pants combinations worn in earlier periods. In the 20th and 21st centuries conventions of male dress have been subverted by youth and subcultures, and alternative notions of taste and acceptability for menswear are well established. However, for business wear and formal occasions, the suit remains the preferred item of male clothing.

c. 1187–1064 BCE Egyptian priest in a long-sleeved pleated robe

509 BCE–476 CE Suit of armor (reconstructed) with leather cuirass

1690 Restoration justaucorps (close-fitting coat) worn over waistcoat

1760 Nobleman wearing a silk coat with matching pants, and a cravat

18th Century Coat and breeches (reconstructed) with ornate vest

1832 Shooting outfit of green morning coat and fitted black pants

1854 Frock coat and trousers worn with a blue embroidered vest

1940s Tan jacket and gray trousers worn over knit sweater

1954 Teddy boy wearing long jacket with drainpipe trousers and a string tie

1963 Double-breasted suit by Pierre Cardin, worn with fedora hat

1968 Mr. Fish suit of striped corduroy, worn with a black turtleneck sweater

1973 Belted jacket with pointed collar and zip pockets, worn open

1343 French tunic with hanging tippet sleeves, worn with wool cloak

Mid-15th Century Tunic (reconstructed) with fur trim

1490–1510 Jerkin (reconstructed) worn over a doublet of fabric panes

1581 Nobleman's dress consisting of doublet, full breeches, hose, and cloak

1646 Cavalier in doublet, breeches, baldric (sash), and bucket-top boots

1890 Morning suit with cutaway coat and vest, and striped trousers

1908 Suit worn with gray vest, bowler hat, and cane

1930s Three-piece suit of tweed jacket, vest, and knickerbockers

1931 Pinstripe suit with double-breasted jacket and wide-leg trousers

1940 Drape suit with wide-leg trousers and loose-fitting jacket

1984 Green linen jacket as worn in *Miami Vice*, with white linen trousers

1985 Double-breasted cropped jacket worn with sleeves rolled up

1998 Gray suit with long jacket, worn by Will Smith over dark shirt and tie

2006 Trench coat and jeans worn by Pharrell Williams, with collar and tie

2012 Black suit and brown satin tie worn by designer Tom Ford

400 YEARS OF
WOMEN'S SHOES

From the towering chopines of 16th- and 17th-century Europe, to 18th-century embroidered silk slippers and 1930s dazzling rhinestone sandals, these diverse shoes from the past 400 years indicate much about the status of the women who wore them. It was quite usual at certain periods, such as the 18th and early 19th centuries, for women's shoes to be made of fabric rather than leather, perhaps because their wearers spent a large part of their time indoors. In the 21st century slender stiletto heels by designers such as Christian Louboutin, Manolo Blahnik, and Jimmy Choo are "must-have" accessories—possibly worn only on special occasions.

1600 Venetian chopine overshoe made from kid leather, with punched decoration, silk overlay, and pine sole

1750s Mule slipper of white and gold striped and figured silk, with a kid-leather sole and shaped heel

1790–1800 Leather shoe in pink, with cream bow trim and faint striped pattern, made in England

1810 English boot made from pale yellow kid leather, with laced front closure and yellow ribbon bow

1905 Austrian dress shoe made from kid leather, with a metal-studded and cutout design over the vamp

1918 Ribbon tie shoe in oyster glacé kid, with ribbon tie and cutout detail, designed and made by Bally of Switzerland

1926 Walking shoe of two-tone calf leather and crocodile skin, with wood heel and tab styled like a golf-shoe flap, made by Bally

1970s Platform sandal made from blue corduroy with a rubber sole

1950s American sling-back shoe of brown suede and reptile skin, with a high heel and front platform

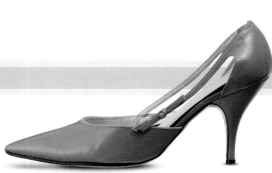

1960s Leather pump of mustard-yellow imitation leather, with pin heel, pointed toe, and cutout sides

1660s–1670s English forked-toe slipper made from silk, embroidered with silver thread and lined with kid leather

1725 English tie shoe of white linen, with red decoration and heel

1725–1750 English latchet-buckle shoe made from green silk, with embroidered design on the vamp and decorative trim

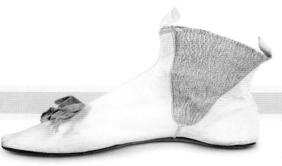

c. 1860 English wedding boot of white kid leather, with expanding ankle and decorative ribbon rosette at the toe

1860s Ankle boot made in England from red leather, with side lacing and a black heel

c. 1880 French mule slipper, with a kilim-weave fabric vamp, decorative gathered-ribbon edge, and low, fabric-covered heel

1930s Evening shoe of painted fabric in a floral design, with cutout detail, and gold kid-leather heel and ankle strap

1938 Evening sandal made from white satin encrusted with rhinestone and lined with gold kid leather

1940s Suede shoe made in the US, with cutout vamp, high heel, and elastic side straps

1980s Stiletto heel made from leather with a metallic silver finish and an almond-shaped toe and low-cut vamp

1993 Platform shoe by Vivienne Westwood, in patent leather with ribbon laces

2008 Heeled sandal by Jimmy Choo, in black snakeskin-effect leather with silver decoration and stiletto heel

200 YEARS OF
WOMEN'S HATS

Toward the end of the 18th century wide, flat shepherdess hats were popular, being overtaken in the early 1800s by bonnets, which remained fashionable for decades. Hat styles during the Victorian and Edwardian eras were extremely varied, ranging from small toques to huge confections of flowers, feathers, and even entire birds. Until well into the 20th century most women, regardless of social status, did not think of leaving the house without a hat. Today millinery has a place in high fashion, with hat designers pushing creative boundaries to ever greater levels of innovation and drama.

1800 Shepherdess hat with silk crown and flat straw brim

c. 1880 Velvet hat in bottle-green, trimmed with a gold and green patterned grosgrain (ribbed) ribbon, and cream and black feathers

1896 Blue bonnet of silk-covered straw, trimmed with black ostrich feathers

c. 1910 Straw hat with wide brim, velvet facing, and silk rose decoration around the crown

1916–1918 Summer hat made from cream-colored embroidered net, decorated with two silk flowers and lined in silk

1940s Black felt hat trimmed with a wide satin ribbon and feather in the brim

1940s Velour hat in burgundy, with turned-up brim and felt flowers

1941 Crêpe hat in blue, with leaf and berry decoration

1950s Velvet hat with a net veil and decorative beading

1960 Round hat of pale pink silk with an upturned scalloped brim, by Givenchy

c. 1965 Soft cap by Simone Mirman, with panels of white leather and striped jersey

1970s Summer hat of cream-colored linen with brown floral appliqué patches and lining

1970s Newsboy cap of turquoise crushed velvet, with peak and button trim

1818–1823 Turban-style evening hat with woven silk decoration

1840s Straw bonnet with feather trim

1850s Straw bonnet with silk lining, lace trim, and floral appliqué

1870s Straw hat trimmed with bands of black ribbon and velvet flowers at the back

1920s Cloche hat of black cellophane straw on brown silk, with ribbon and rosette decoration

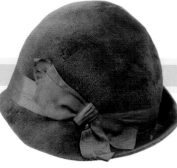

1929 Cloche hat of taupe-colored felt with a matching grosgrain (ribbed) ribbon trim

1930s Straw hat in a natural color with woven black trim and flower decoration

1938 Woven seagrass hat by Elsa Schiaparelli, with grosgrain band and metallic insects

1950s Tea hat of turquoise brushed felt, shaped into leaves around the head

1950s Red beret made from felted wool, with long feather decoration

1960s Cocktail hat of plastic feathers mounted on an elastic net base

1960s Petal hat designed by Dolores, London, and covered with small pink fabric flowers

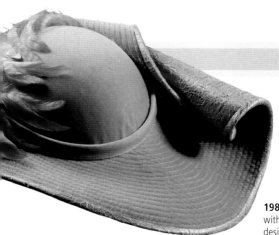

1982 Lilac velvet hat with orange feathers, designed by Stephen Jones

2000s Trilby hat of woven mottled straw, with striped silk ribbon band

2000 Sculptural leaf hat designed by Philip Treacy

2006 Fascinator designed by Jane Corbett

200 YEARS OF
BAGS AND PURSES

Before the end of the 18th century, women kept their valuables under their skirts in a girdle pouch, or a pocket tied around their waist. By the 1790s, when dresses became slim and columnar, pockets were replaced by reticules (small decorative bags carried in the hand), to avoid spoiling the line of the dress. Since then myriad styles have evolved, from the exquisitely beaded evening bag to the exorbitant designer "It" bag.

17th Century Purse with raised embroidery in colored silk and metal threads and sequins

1919 Silver finger-purse engraved with arabesques

1920s Beaded handbag with a filigree frame and a chain strap

1915 Silk clutch embroidered with Oriental design and imitation-jade-encrusted filigree frame

1920 Beaded bag of silver and gold beads with rhinestone paste decoration

1940s Suedette (fake suede) bag with pleated central panel and brass clasp

1940s Red snakeskin bag with clasp opening and gilt-metal hardware

Early 1950s Lucite handbag in light blue with a clear lid and handle, designed by Charles S. Khan

1950s Pleated box purse with a mirror attached inside, designed by Bienen-Davis

1970s Evening bag of brushed gold over metal, with coral decoration, designed by Judith Leiber

1970s Tote bag of woven cotton with a psychedelic pattern, and leather handles and trim

1980s Envelope clutch designed by Diane Love, with sequins in a trellis design

1980s Chainmail bag by Paco Rabanne, made of black leather and linked aluminum disks

Late 18th Century Silk reticule lined with satin and decorated with embroidered floral motif

Early 19th Century Beaded miser's purse with rose decoration

1887 Framed plush bag lined with kid leather, with appliqué flowers and a padded handle

19th Century Basket bag of woven reed with painted bird decoration

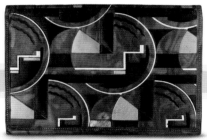

c. 1925 Art deco bag of tooled leather, stained in brown and black, and lined with silk

1930s Beaded bag with curling-thread motif, designed by Josef Hand

1930s Alligator-skin handbag with brass hardware, decorated with alligator feet

1930s Black calfskin handbag by Nettie Rosenstein

1950s–1960s Leopard-print bag with gilt metal clasp, designed by Ingber

1960s Hermès *Kelly* handbag in black calfskin, named after Grace Kelly

1960s Plastic clutch with metal frame and clasp, and fabric lining

1960s–1970s Waterfall-front handbag by Pucci, with gold strap

1985–present Hermès *Birkin* bag in orange leather, named after the actor Jane Birkin

1980s Backpack of black crocodile skin with a white metal clasp and adjustable straps

1990s *Manhattan* bag by Louis Vuitton, in brown leather with gold monogram pattern

2007 Tote bag by Anya Hindmarch, designed to discourage excessive use of plastic bags

300 YEARS OF
SHAPING
THE BODY

Across the centuries, fashion's changing forms and silhouette have been founded on undergarments. From the 16th to the 18th century stays and bodices (or a pair of bodies), stiffened with whalebone, were used to create a cone-shaped torso, with narrow waist and raised bust. In the 18th century these garments became known as a pair of stays, and then in the 19th century, in an adapted form, as corsets. The corset reshaped women's bodies—from the high-waisted neoclassical look to the hourglass ideal. In the 20th century, structural underwear in the form of girdles and foundation garments of elastic fabric helped to smooth female outlines, while underwired bras and bustiers lifted and supported the bust.

1710–1720 Boned bodice embellished with colored embroidery

18th Century Stays stiffened with strips of whalebone, laced at the front

1880–1895 Corset for a fashionable hourglass silhouette, closed at front

1885–1895 Steel-boned corset with steel spoon-shaped busk (flat front panel)

1895 Corset with low, flat front for pushing the hips back

1940s Girdle made from elastic panels, shaped to wear around the waist

1950s Bustier with silk and lace panels, and decorative bow, underwired for support

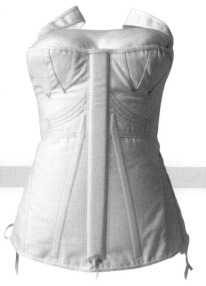

1825 Long corset (reconstructed) to support the bust and cover the hips, laced at the back

1875 Corset (back view) cut shorter at the back, to accommodate a bustle

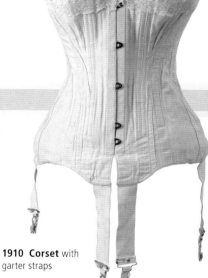

1895–1900 Corset (back view), laced at the back through metal eyelets

1910 Corset with garter straps

1960s Girdle with sprigged floral print and garter straps

1996 Bustier by Rigby and Peller, London, decorated with black lace

SUPPORTING SKIRTS

After the advent of the farthingale in the mid-16th century came a succession of skirt shapes and styles for women. These changing silhouettes were achieved with the support of hooped understructures, such as panniers and crinolines, or with layer upon layer of padded and stiffened petticoats. Hooped supports had the advantage of being much lighter and, as construction technologies advanced, held larger and larger skirts, which were at their widest during the 1860s.

Bum roll (replica)

1750s This robe à la française would have been worn over panniers or hoops, to support the wide skirts.

Fabric draped over back

Farthingale (replica)

c. 1550 Farthingales and bum rolls were worn under skirts from 1545 to the 1620s. Bum rolls, fastened around the waist and tied at the front, gave added volume at the hips.

Hoops worn over hips

Panniers

1860 The cage crinoline, made from hoops of steel, was much lighter than the layers of petticoats that preceded it.

Crinoline

Skirts reached their widest in the 1860s

Crinolette

Bustled overskirt

1872–1874 Crinolettes, or half-crinolines, were made from half-hoops of steel. They acted as bustles, a fashion that first gained popularity in the early 1870s.

ILLUSTRATED
GLOSSARY

Included in this glossary are a series of key terms, organized alphabetically, that relate to the history of fashion and dress. Date ranges are given for each term, with a "▷" indicating that the garment or technique continues to the present day. Glossary entries that appear within the text are italicized.

NATIONAL DRESS

Panels on the following pages examine examples of traditional dress from around the world. Key elements of the national costume are defined in the glossary.

— Cowboy hat

— Bandana

— Chaps

American cowboy
Cowboy hats and *denim* have been linked to cowboys since the 19th century, and their popularity persists today among ranchers in the US and Canada.

A

ACCESSORIES Items such as hats, gloves, and jewelry that are worn or carried to complete an outfit.

ACCORDION PLEATS A series of narrow, evenly spaced *pleats* with alternating raised and recessed edges, allowing the garment to expand or flare with movement.
19TH CENTURY: SEE P.323

ACETATE A light, *silky* synthetic fiber made from cellulose, obtained from wood pulp; invented in Germany.
19TH CENTURY ▷

ACID WASHING A technique often used on *denim*; involves washing garments together with pumice stones that have been soaked in chlorine, which gives the fabric a worn, mottled look.
1980s ▷

ACRYLIC A synthetic fiber made from a petrochemical product and used like *wool*; trade names include Acrilan, Courtelle, Orlon.
1940s

AESTHETIC DRESS Style inspired by historic dress (following from *Artistic dress*) and Eastern clothing such as *kimonos*; involved use of natural fabric dyes and of traditional or nature-inspired patterns; see also *Liberty print*; *Paisley*.
LATE 19TH CENTURY:
SEE PP.212–214, 336–337

AGLETS, AIGLETS Metal sheaths used at the end of the ties that join *hose* to a *doublet*; now refers to the sheaths at the end of shoelaces.
13TH CENTURY ▷: SEE PP.71, 94

AIGRETTE Feather plume or feather-shaped ornament for head wear.
LATE 18TH–EARLY 20TH CENTURY

AKETON Quilted *tunic* worn under armor for comfort and protection.
13TH–15TH CENTURY: SEE P.69

ALB Ankle-length vestment of white *linen* with long sleeves and a cord tied at the waist; worn by Christian clerics and monks in many churches.
MEDIEVAL ▷: SEE P.57

À LA DISPOSITION Term used for a design printed or embroidered on, or woven into a fabric so it can be made up into a specific garment.
1850s ▷: SEE P.205

ALBERT COLLAR A detachable *stand collar* fastened to a man's shirt by a button at the back.
1850s–EARLY 20TH CENTURY

A-LINE A triangular dress shape created by Christian Dior (see also *H-line*, *Y-line*), or generally a dress or skirt flared like the sides of an "A."
MID-1950s ▷: SEE PP.319, 455

ALOHA SHIRT Traditional Hawaiian shirt for men, with short sleeves and made from colorful fabric; can be worn as business wear in Hawaii but casual wear on the mainland.
1930s ▷

ALPACA Fine, soft fiber obtained from the alpaca (a South American relation of the llama) and woven or *knit* like *wool*.

ANDROGYNOUS STYLE Adoption of masculine *jackets*, pants, and suits by women, notably Marlene Dietrich and Katharine Hepburn in the 1930s and Patti Smith in the 1970s.
1930s ▷: SEE PP.288, 372–373

ANGORA (a) Name of the goat whose fleece is used for *mohair*; (b) light, *silky* fiber from the Angora rabbit, used like *wool*.

ANILINE DYE The first form of synthetic dye; mauveine, one of the first, was discovered by British scientist William Perkins, who used it to make the color mauve; also notably used to make the colors purple, magenta, pink, and green.
1850s ▷

ANORAK A hooded *jacket* originally made of animal skin or waterproofed cloth, and worn by the indigenous peoples in Greenland and Canada; now refers to a hooded, weatherproof *jacket* usually made of synthetic fiber with synthetic or down insulation; see also *Parka*.

APPLIQUÉ Decorative technique in which cutout fabric shapes are sewn on to a larger piece of fabric or garment to form a design.
SEE PP.180, 207, 236

ARAN Style of *knitwear* originating among families in the Aran Islands off the Irish coast; made from undyed *wool* featuring raised patterns such as *cables* and twists. Also known as a Fisherman knit *sweater*.

ARGYLE PATTERN Scottish pattern comprising diamond shapes in two or more colors; made popular by golfers, now common on *sweaters* and socks.
1920s ▷

ARISAID Long *plaid* cloak worn by women in the Scottish Highlands and Islands, fastened by a brooch and a belt.
TRADITIONAL

ARMSCYE The armhole of a garment into which a sleeve is sewn.

ARMY SURPLUS Military clothing that was surplus to requirements and sold on to the public, such as *duffle coats* and *bomber jackets*.
1940s ▷

ART DECO An artistic style that emerged in Paris in the 1920s, the name deriving from the 1925 Exposition Internationale des Arts Décoratifs; it influenced many areas of art and design, including fashion, and featured streamlined shapes inspired by aerodynamic machines, and geometric designs.
MID-1920s–LATE 1940s: SEE PP.253, 258–259

ARTISTIC DRESS Quasi-medieval style adopted by female followers of the Pre-Raphaelite artists; featured flowing, loose, high-waisted dresses.
1840s–c.1900: SEE P.214

ASTRAKHAN Lambskin from the Astrakhan region of Russia; also woven fabric resembling *lambskin*.

AUTOMOBILE COAT Also known as a motoring coat, a garment worn in early (open) cars to protect against wind and cold; made of leather or cloth with a thick lining; see also *Car coat*.
LATE 19TH CENTURY ▷: SEE P.230

AYLESHAM *Wool* or *linen* cloth made at Aylesham in Norfolk.
13TH–14TH CENTURY

B

BABY DOLL Style of night wear comprising a short, sheer nightdress, frequently having an empire waist and often worn with short panties; inspired by the 1956 film *Baby Doll*.
1950s ▷

BABY DOLL DRESS A very short minidress, with an empire waist and flared skirt.
1960s ▷: SEE P.329

BACK BREADTH Tailoring term for the overall width of the two back pieces of a coat, at waist level.

BALACLAVA *Wool* covering for the head and neck that leaves the face exposed; first worn by military personnel during the Crimean War.
1850s ▷

BALDRICK Belt worn across the body from shoulder to hip, from which a sword or drinking horn was hung.
13TH–17TH CENTURY: SEE PP.123, 129

BALLERINA SKIRT Full, calf-length skirt with several layers of light fabric, inspired by classical ballet costumes; especially popular in the 1950s.
MID-20TH CENTURY ▷

BALLET FLATS Shoes with a flat heel and a short *vamp*, resembling the slippers worn by ballet dancers.
1950s ▷: SEE P.340

BALLETS RUSSES Avant-garde dance company, led by Sergei Diaghilev; their striking, sensuous costumes, inspired by traditional Russian, Eastern, and Ancient Greek styles, still have a significant influence on fashion today.
EARLY 20TH CENTURY: SEE PP.244–245

BALL GOWN A long dress made from *silk* or other luxury material, short-sleeved or sleeveless, with a fitted, low-cut *bodice* and a full skirt.
EARLY 19TH CENTURY ▷: SEE PP.181, 198–199, 326–327

BAND A shirt collar; main types were the standing band (a flat, starched collar) and the falling band (a collar that was turned down); see also *Stand collar*, *Stand-fall collar*.
16TH–17TH CENTURY

BANDANA A handkerchief, typically with a white pattern on a red or blue ground, often folded diagonally and worn around the neck or head.
18TH CENTURY ▷: SEE P.434

BANDEAU Fabric headband first worn by women as decoration, but today commonly used in sports; also refers to a strapless *bikini* top.
EARLY 19TH CENTURY ▷: SEE PP.169, 180, 291

BANGLE A rigid band of jewelry, wide enough to be slipped over a hand or a foot.
LATE 18TH CENTURY ▷

BANYAN Originally a loose-skirted outdoor coat; the term was later used for a long housecoat for men, also known as an Indian gown, and made from *silk*, *linen*, or *cotton*.
c.1650–19TH CENTURY: SEE P.131

BASEBALL CAP Soft cloth cap with a visor at the front, first used in baseball but now generally popular as an item of casual wear.
MID-19TH CENTURY ▷: SEE P.227

BASQUE Originally a long, close-fitting *bodice*; today a hip-length item of *lingerie* with *boning* and *brassiere* cups; see also *Bustier*.

BASTING Joining fabric pieces temporarily with large running stitches before permanent stitching.

BATEAU-NECK Also called a boat neck, a shallowly curved neckline extending almost to shoulder width.
1920s ▷: SEE PP.295, 335, 451

BATIK Technique possibly originating in Java, but used widely across the world, in which hot wax is applied to parts of a cloth in a pattern; the cloth is then dyed, the wax-coated areas resisting the dye to produce the design; sometimes known simply as "wax" in African countries.
SEE PP.457, 460

BATWING SLEEVE See *Dolman sleeve*.

BAUDEKIN An expensive decorated *silk*, some types having a *warp* of gold thread and a *weft* of *silk*.
MEDIEVAL

BEATNIK STYLE Style inspired by intellectuals in Paris and the Beat generation in San Francisco; featured black *turtlenecks*, *berets*, and for women, black *leotards* with black skirts and stockings and flat shoes.
LATE 1940s–1960s: SEE PP.380–381

BEAVER (a) Beaver fur, used for gloves; (b) a *wool* fabric with a raised *nap*, used for overcoats; (c) a *felt* including beaver fur, used for high-quality hats.
MEDIEVAL ▷: SEE PP.128, 162–163

BELL-BOTTOMS Style of pants fitting closely at the hips but with widely flaring lower legs, originally worn by sailors; see also *Flares*.
1960s: SEE PP.366–367, 372–373, 382–383

BELLOWS POCKET A type of *patch pocket* with sides that could expand; commonly used on *Norfolk jackets*.
1890s ▷: SEE P.453

BELL SLEEVE In women's garments, a sleeve that fits closely from the shoulder to the mid-forearm and then flares widely to the wrist.
1850s ▷

BELLY PIECES Shaped pieces of pasteboard, or *linen* reinforced with *whalebone*, sewn into the front of a *doublet* to support the abdomen.
c.1620–1670: SEE PP.118–119

BERET A soft, circular *wool* or *felt* cap, sometimes worn tilted to one side; originating in the Basque country of France and Spain, it is now worn worldwide.
20TH CENTURY ▷: SEE PP.396–397, 445

BERTHA COLLAR A wide, deep collar of *lace* or *silk*, attached to a dress with a low *décolletage* and extending over the shoulders.
1840s–1920s: SEE P.142

BESPOKE Made to order and custom-tailored for an individual; see also *Tailor-made*.
19TH CENTURY ▷

BIAS The diagonal across the *grain* of a fabric, at 45 degrees to the *warp* and *weft*; cutting on the bias can enable a garment to stretch.
MEDIEVAL ▷: SEE P.446

BICORN A wide-brimmed hat with the brim turned up at the front and back, often with a slight peak at the front and adorned with a rosette or cockade.
18TH–EARLY 19TH CENTURY

BIKINI Two-piece women's bathing suit resembling a *brassiere* and underpants, invented in 1946 by French engineer Louis Réard.
1946 ▷: SEE PP.336–337

BISHOP SLEEVE In women's garments, a sleeve made from light fabrics, widening from the shoulder and gathered into a *cuff* at the wrist.
19TH CENTURY ▷: SEE PP.196–197, 241, 458

BLACK WORK *Embroidery* worked in black *silk* thread to form geometric or scrolled designs, often used on collars and *cuffs*.
c.1510–1630s: SEE P.109

BLANKET CLOTH Heavy *wool* cloth with a raised finish, commonly used for overcoats.
19TH CENTURY

BLAZER Originally a man's *jacket* for boating, now a classic semiformal *jacket*, widely used in school or adult uniforms.
1890s ▷: SEE PP.217, 283–284, 448

BLOCK PRINTING Method of printing fabric, in which one or more colors are applied to fabric using carved wood blocks, each color needing a separate block.

BLOOMERS Baggy *knickerbockers* worn by women for cycling and other sports; also loose, knee-length women's underpants; invented and named after Mrs. Amelia Bloomer.
1851–MID-20TH CENTURY: SEE P.215

BLOUSE A *smock*-like *cotton* or *linen* garment originally worn by working men, or a light, soft shirt for women.
EARLY 19TH CENTURY ▷: SEE P.241

BLOUSON A waist-length, loose-fitting men's *jacket* with elastic or drawstring hem and *cuffs*, used in sports, military, and casual wear; see also *Bomber jacket*.
1950s ▷

BOA A long, round-ended *tippet* made of feathers or fur.
19TH CENTURY ▷: SEE PP.178, 291

BOATER Stiff straw hat with flat-topped crown, straight brim, and hatband of *Petersham*, or *grosgrain* ribbon, for casual summer wear.
19TH CENTURY ▷: SEE PP.211, 214–217

BOAT NECK See *Bateau-neck*.

BOBBIN LACE An openwork fabric made by braiding and twisting together a number of threads held on bobbins.

BODICE The upper part of a garment, especially a dress, between the shoulders and the waist.
15TH CENTURY ▷: SEE P.139

BODIES, PAIR OF An under bodice of two parts joined at the sides, padded, and stiffened with *whalebone*, wood, or steel.
16TH–17TH CENTURY: SEE P.98

BODKIN Formerly a long, ornate hair pin; today refers to a blunt needle used for threading ribbon, tape, or elastic through a *casing*.
16TH CENTURY ▷

BODY COAT Tailors' term for the coat part of a suit, as distinct from an *overcoat* or *topcoat*.
19TH CENTURY ▷

BODY STOCKING A stretchy body covering like a *leotard*, but also covering the legs to the ankles; also known as a unitard.
MID-1960s ▷

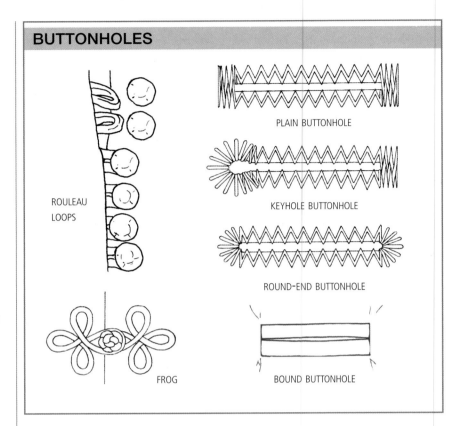

BUTTONHOLES

ROULEAU LOOPS

PLAIN BUTTONHOLE

KEYHOLE BUTTONHOLE

ROUND-END BUTTONHOLE

FROG

BOUND BUTTONHOLE

BOLERO A very short-cropped, decorative, open *jacket* for women, often worn with a dress; inspired by traditional Spanish men's *jackets*.
MID-19TH CENTURY ▷: SEE PP.273, 335, 396

BOLO TIE Also known as a bootlace or shoestring tie, a very narrow necktie comprising a length of cord or braided leather with decorative metal *aglets* secured with an ornamental clasp or slide; worn as part of *cowboy style* or *Teddy-boy style*.
1940s ▷

BOLT Industry standard unit in which rolled cloth is manufactured and supplied, comprising a specific length and/or width.

BOMBACHAS Baggy pants gathered at the ankle, worn for horseback riding in Argentina and Uruguay.
EARLY 19TH CENTURY ▷: SEE P.441

BOMBAST Fibrous material such as *cotton*, horsehair, *wool*, or rags, used to pad out parts of a garment such as the *trunk-hose* or sleeves.
16TH–17TH CENTURY: SEE P.105

BOMBAZINE *Twilled* fabric with a *silk warp* and *worsted weft*, first used undyed and later dyed black for mourning apparel.
16TH–20TH CENTURY

BOMBER JACKET *Blouson*, usually leather, originally worn by US Air Force crews, now generally adopted as casual wear.
1940s ▷

BONDAGE STYLE A style associated with punk and other youth cultures, featuring clothes embellished with straps, chains, and studs.
LATE 1970s ▷: SEE P.404

BONGRACE A flat, rectangular, stiffened head covering extending over the forehead at the front and down to the shoulders at the back; also refers to part of a *French hood*.
16TH–EARLY 17TH CENTURY

BONING Strips of whalebone, or later flexible steel or plastic, added to garments, especially bodices and corsets, to help them stay up and support shapes; see also *Basque*, *Corset*.
16TH CENTURY ▷: SEE PP.432–433

BONNET Originally a soft head covering, but later a women's hat with a brim only at the front.
MEDIEVAL ▷: SEE PP.178, 193

BOOT CUT A style of pants with a straight-leg fit from waist to knee and a slight flare below the knee to ankle.
1990s ▷: SEE P.451

BOSOM FRIENDS *Wool*, fur, or down pads fit to the bosom for warmth and as bust enhancers.
LATE 18TH–EARLY 19TH CENTURY

BOUCLÉ A term for a fabric *knit* or woven using looped or rough-textured *yarn*, giving a knobbly appearance.
LATE 19TH CENTURY ▷

BOWLER A hard *felt* hat with a rounded crown and a narrow brim rolled up at the sides, worn for horse riding and later as stylish headgear.
1850s ▷: SEE PP.227, 265

BOX COAT (a) Heavy, caped overcoat typically worn by coachmen; (b) loose-fitting coat popular in the 1930s and '40s, with a boxy shape and squared, padded shoulders.
LATE 18TH CENTURY ▷

BOXER SHORTS Loose-fitting *cotton* shorts with an elastic waistband, worn by men as underpants; based on the shorts worn by professional boxers, which allow free movement.
1940s ▷

BOX PLEAT A flat *pleat* created by two folds facing toward each other and pressed flat.
LATE 19TH CENTURY ▷: SEE PP.145, 452

BRAID Strands of ribbon or cord interwoven to form a narrow strip, often used as an edging for garments.
MEDIEVAL ▷: SEE PP.176–177

BRAIES Baggy medieval underwear worn under *tunics*; stockinglike *hose* were attached to the braies; as *tunics* became shorter and slimmer, the braies became shorter and more fitted.
MEDIEVAL: SEE P.72

BRASSIERE Women's undergarment worn to support the bust; many types have underwiring to give extra support and shape; usually abbreviated to bra.
EARLY 20TH CENTURY ▷: SEE P.277

BREASTPLATE A piece of plate armor worn over the front of the torso to protect the chest.
MEDIEVAL ▷: SEE PP.69, 92–93

BREECHES In medieval times, the upper part of men's long *hose*; later, men's fitted pants ending at the knee.
14TH CENTURY ▷: SEE PP.88–89, 154

BRETON SHIRT Originally worn by fishermen in Brittany, a long-sleeved garment like a *T-shirt*, with a *boat neck*, and traditionally with navy and white stripes.
MID-19TH CENTURY ▷

BRIAL Spanish *tunic* made of expensive fabric such as *silk brocade* or *silk* with gold thread; laced down one side.
12TH–14TH CENTURY

BRISTOL DIAMONDS A type of rock crystal found near Bristol in south-west England and used as imitation diamonds in jewelry.
17TH–19TH CENTURY

BROADCLOTH Fine *wool* cloth with a *twill weave* and a smooth *face*; an economic staple in England and Flanders in medieval times.
MEDIEVAL ▷

BROCADE Luxury fabric woven with *silk* and often including silver or gold threads, with an extra *weft* added to create a raised pattern.
MEDIEVAL ▷: SEE P.141

BRODERIE ANGLAISE *White work embroidery* featuring floral motifs created from pierced holes bound with *satin stitch*; often used to adorn underwear.
17TH CENTURY ▷

BROGUES Durable leather shoes with punched-leather decoration.
LATE 19TH CENTURY ▷: SEE P.301

BROTHEL CREEPERS *Suede* shoes with *crepe rubber* soles, first worn by soldiers in World War II, and then adopted as part of *Teddy-boy style*; they gained the name "brothel creepers" from the soldiers' habit of wearing them to visit nightclubs.
1940s ▷: SEE P.341

BUCKLED WIG A man's wig with horizontal rolls of hair above or around the ears.
18TH CENTURY: SEE PP.150–151

BUCKRAM Fine *cotton* or *linen* often stiffened, and used in the 19th century for making women's hats.
13TH–19TH CENTURY

BUCKSKIN Leather made from deer hide, used for gloves and at one time for *breeches*; also known as deerskin.
15TH CENTURY ▷

BUFF COAT A durable military coat made from buffalo or ox hide; later adopted by civilians.
16TH–17TH CENTURY

BUGLE BEADS Small tubular beads, which can be smooth or faceted, used to adorn women's clothes.
19TH CENTURY ▷

BUNDHOSEN *Breeches* that finish just below the knee, with a lacing or a buckle closure at the hem; traditional in German-speaking countries.
MEDIEVAL ▷

Deerskin dress

Moccasins

Shoshone woman, Idaho
Dress of the Shoshone people is frequently made of animal skin that is ornately embellished with natural motifs using beading and *embroidery*.

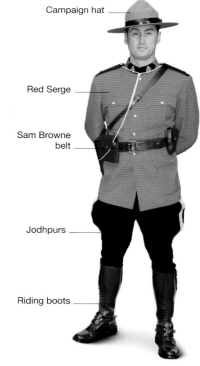

Campaign hat

Red Serge

Sam Browne belt

Jodhpurs

Riding boots

"Mountie" in ceremonial garb, Canada
This man wears the uniform of the Royal Canadian Mounted Police, who are distinguished by their scarlet Red Serge belted *tunic* with gold buttons.

Mexican mariachi in traditional dress
The typical dress worn by charros, similar to American cowboys, is today most frequently worn by mariachi musicians and consists of an ornate suit and *sombrero*.

- Sombrero
- Traje de charro

Maya woman, Guatemala
The *huipil* is the most distinctive element of Central American indigenous dress. Some women also wear a kaperraj on the head, which doubles as a carrier bag.

- Kaperraj
- Huipil
- Corte

BURNOUS Long, hooded *wool* cloak traditionally worn by North African men; also a women's evening wrap made of *cashmere*; see also *Djellaba*, *Jebba*.
17TH CENTURY ▷

BUSK A flat piece of *whalebone*, wood, or metal used to stiffen the front of a *corset* or *stays*; wood busks were often hand-carved and decorated with initials or hearts.
16TH–EARLY 20TH CENTURY

BUSKINS Knee-length boots worn by both men and women made of cloth or later of leather, worn for riding or traveling.
14TH–LATE 17TH CENTURY

BUSTIER Item of *lingerie* combining a *brassiere* and a *camisole*, reaching from the bust to the waist, often with *boning*; see also *Basque*.
1830s–1900s: SEE P.344

BUSTLE Metal frame or padded shapes worn under a woman's dress at the back to support the top of the skirt; see also *Grecian bend*, *Tournure*.
1830s–1900s: SEE PP.200–205, 432–433

BUTCHER'S BOY CAP See *Newsboy cap*.

BUTTON BOOTS Short, lightweight boots fastened up the outside of the ankle with buttons; worn by both men and women.
1890s–EARLY 20TH CENTURY

C

CABLE KNIT A *knitting* technique in which some stitches are crossed over adjacent ones to create a braided effect; notably used in *Aran knitwear*.
19TH CENTURY ▷: SEE P.281

CAFTAN see *Kaftan*.

CAGE PETTICOAT Dome-shaped structure used to support a wide skirt, and consisting of *whalebone* or wire hoops joined by bands of tape; see also *Hoop crinoline* and *Petticoat*.
1850s–LATE 1860s: SEE PP.196–197, 432–433

CALICO A lightweight, finely woven cotton printed with a small floral motif; also, a UK term for a heavier-weight muslin.
17TH CENTURY ▷

CAMBRIC A high-quality *linen*.
16TH CENTURY ▷

CAMEL HAIR Undyed hair from camels, or a wool fabric dyed to imitate the color, usually light beige or tan in color; used to make coats.
LATE 17TH CENTURY ▷

CAMI-KNICKERS An item of *lingerie* combining a *camisole* and loose tap pants; later known as a *Teddy*; see also *Baby doll*.

CAMISOLE An item of *lingerie* that covers the upper body and is held up with thin *spaghetti straps*.
1820s ▷

CAPRI PANTS Close-fitting, mid-calf-length pants for women.
1950s ▷: SEE P.337

CAPUCHIN A soft hood with a deep cape and a colored lining; also called a riding hood, it was worn outdoors and for traveling.
16TH–LATE 18TH CENTURY

CARACO A thigh-length women's *jacket*, fitted at the waist or with *box pleats* at the back; some styles were a little longer in the back than in the front.
MID-18TH–EARLY 19TH CENTURY: SEE PP.117, 163

CAR COAT A thigh-length coat worn for traveling; less bulky than the early *automobile coats*.
1940s ▷

CARDIGAN A *knit jacket* closed with buttons or a zipper, originally worn by soldiers in the Crimean War, but now worn widely by both men and women.
LATE 19TH CENTURY ▷

CARGO PANTS Loose-fitting pants for men and women, with large pockets on the legs, based on pants worn by US military personnel in World War II; now widely worn as casual wear.
1950s ▷

CARTRIDGE PLEATING Tiny, soft, evenly spaced *pleats* used to gather a large amount of material into an *armscye*, waistband, or *cuff*, without adding bulk to the seam.
MEDIEVAL ▷: SEE PP.145, 452

CASHMERE A fine, soft fabric made from goats' *wool* and originally imported from Kashmir; see also *Pashmina*.
18TH CENTURY ▷: SEE P.197

CASSOCK Closed, ankle-length *robe*, with long sleeves and low, *stand-up collar*; usually black; worn by clerics, lay people and choir members of various Christian churches.
13TH CENTURY ▷: SEE P.57

CATSUIT A close-fitting, stretchy one-piece garment for women, combining a zippered *bodice* and tight pants.
1960s ▷

CAVALRY TWILL *Worsted* or *rayon twill* with a diagonally ribbed surface; originally used for cavalry in World War I, but now used for men's smart-casual pants.
1914 ▷

CHAMMER A sleeved gown for men, made from luxury material and worn open at the front.
LATE 14TH–EARLY 19TH CENTURY

CHAMOIS Soft, cream-colored leather, made from the skin of the Chamois goat or from *sheepskin* or lambskin, used for gloves.
16TH CENTURY ▷

CHAPERON Medieval men's hat; originated as a hood with integrated short cape that could be rolled up and fastened; evolved into a padded circlet with scarflike attachment.
MEDIEVAL: SEE PP.72–73

CHAPS Leg covering, often leather, which is buckled over pants to protect them while horse riding.
MID-TO-LATE 19TH CENTURY: SEE P.434

CHASUBLE Colorful, richly decorated outer garment worn by priests, bishops, or archbishops in the Christian Church for Eucharist service or Mass.
4TH CENTURY ▷: SEE PP.36–37, 57

CHECKED A pattern made by crossing stripes of different-colored *warp* and *weft* to create squares, or a similar pattern printed on to cloth.
15TH CENTURY ▷: SEE PP.205, 210, 273, 381

CHELSEA BOOTS Slip-on ankle boots for men, made of leather with elastic sides.
1840s ▷

CHEMISE A *linen* undershirt, first worn by both sexes but later used as a woman's undergarment.
MEDIEVAL ▷: SEE P.87

CHENILLE A velvety cord used in *embroidery*, weaving, or *knitting*, made from *silk* with a tufted surface; a soft, textured fabric made from synthetic chenille *yarn*.
LATE 17TH CENTURY ▷

CHEONGSAM Chinese women's dress of *silk* or *satin*, close fitting, with a *mandarin* collar, and with slits at both sides; now worn worldwide.
1920s ▷: SEE P.461

CHESTERFIELD A knee-length, *single-breasted* or *double-breasted* overcoat for men, with a back vent but no side vents or waist seams, and sometimes with a *velvet* collar.

CHIFFON A sheer, delicate fabric, usually of *silk* or *rayon*, woven with twisted *yarns* to give a slightly grainy surface, used for women's clothes.

COLLARS

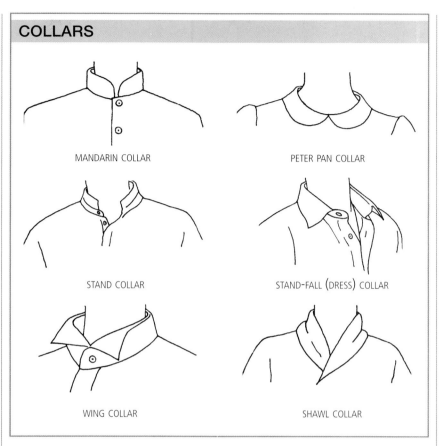

MANDARIN COLLAR

PETER PAN COLLAR

STAND COLLAR

STAND-FALL (DRESS) COLLAR

WING COLLAR

SHAWL COLLAR

CHINOS *Cotton twill* pants for men and women; originally khaki and worn by US servicemen, later popular as casual wear and for the *preppy style*.
1940 ▷

CHINTZ Glazed *calico* with bright, often floral, prints, first imported from India, and used for women's clothing.
17TH–18TH CENTURY: SEE P.221

CHITON Garment worn in Ancient Greece, comprising a large rectangle of *linen* draped around the body, held at the shoulders with brooches and under the bust with a *girdle*.
c. 480–323 BCE: SEE PP.24–25

CHLAMYS A *wool* cloak or short mantle worn in Ancient Greece, first by soldiers and later for general use.
c.480–323 BCE: SEE PP.24–25

CHOKER A decorative band or ribbon worn around the throat by women,
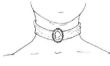
usually for evening wear, and often adorned with jewelry; popular in Victorian times.
LATE 19TH CENTURY ▷: SEE P.201

CHOLI For Indian women, a fitted *bodice* worn under a *sari*.
SEE P.462

CHOPINES Overshoes worn in Spain and Italy by women, consisting of a toe cap and a raised sole of cork or wood; often decorated with paint or gilding.
15TH–17TH CENTURY: SEE PP.111, 426

CHUBA A long *sheepskin* coat worn in Tibet; popular in *hippy style*.

CIGARETTE PANTS Close-fitting, tapered pants for women, similar to *Capri pants* but longer.
1950s ▷: SEE P.452

CLIPPING In dressmaking, cutting slits or *notches* in the edge of a seam so material will fit curves or corners.

CLOCHE Close-fitting hat for women, with a slightly flared brim giving a bell shape; especially fashionable in the 1920s.
1908 ▷: SEE PP.273, 429

CLOTH OF GOLD / SILVER A rich fabric of *silk* or *wool* interwoven with threads or strips of gold or silver.
MEDIEVAL: SEE P.75

COCKTAIL DRESS A semiformal, long or short dress for women, in luxury fabric such as *silk* or *satin*, worn for early-evening parties.
1920s ▷: SEE PP.322–323

CODPIECE Initially a flap at the fork of men's *long hose* or *trunk hose* to shield the crotch; in the 16th century codpieces were padded and projected from the *hose*.
15TH–17TH CENTURY: SEE PP.88–90

COIF Close-fitting *linen* cap for men, or *linen* undercap for women.
MEDIEVAL–19TH CENTURY: SEE PP.61, 128

COIFFE A cap worn by Breton women, typically of *linen* or *lace*, and usually white; can be tied under the chin or pinned to the hair.
MEDIEVAL ▷: SEE P.442

COMBING Preparation of *wool* or *cotton* to remove the shorter fibers and make the long fibers lie parallel, before spinning; used to produce *worsted yarn* or "combed *cotton*."

COMMODE Originally a name for a wire framework covered with *silk* or *lace* to form a tall headdress for women, and then the term for the headdress itself; later commodes had long *lappets* that hung down to the shoulders or were pinned up.
17TH–18TH CENTURY: SEE PP.133, 139

CONVERSE "CHUCK TAYLOR" ALL STAR® A brand of basketball sneakers with a high top, canvas upper, and rubber sole, named "All Star" after the logo, and "Chuck Taylor" after 1920s basketball star Chuck Taylor, an ambassador for the brand; now globally popular, especially with young men and women.
1917 ▷

COPE A full cloak cut as a semicircle and worn by clerics of various Christian churches.
MEDIEVAL ▷: SEE P.57

CORDED SILK Heavy *silk* with raised ribs on the surface; see also *Rep*.
19TH CENTURY

CORDOVAN Fine Spanish leather, originally made from horse hide, used for gloves and shoes.
MEDIEVAL ▷

CORDUROY A *cotton* fabric with a soft *pile* forming parallel ridges of varying widths known as wales (for example, wide wale and pinwale).
1918 ▷

CORK SHOE Shoe worn by both men and women, with a wedge-shaped cork sole; often worn for swimming.
16TH CENTURY ▷

CORNETTE The long tail of a hood; also refers to a type of *wimple* made of starched white cloth, folded up into two "horns" (cornes in French).
MEDIEVAL

CORSAGE The *bodice* of a woman's dress; also a small bunch of flowers pinned to a woman's bust or shoulder, or worn on the wrist.
19TH CENTURY ▷: SEE PP.190, 205, 363

CORSELETTE A women's *corset* with *boning* and laces that pull in the wearer's waist, giving a curvy, "wasp-waisted" shape; made popular as part of Dior's *New Look*.
LATE 1940s ▷: SEE P.316

CORSET A supportive undergarment for women, comprising a sleeveless, boned *bodice* worn under clothing and covering bust to hips.
LATE 18TH CENTURY ▷: SEE PP.133, 190, 432–433

COSSACKS Men's pants with tapering legs, *pleated* at the waist, and with drawstrings at the ankle or straps under the instep.
1814–c.1850: SEE P.184

COSTUME An outfit worn for a specific event or for theatrical performance, or worn by a particular ethnic group; sometimes used for a woman's outfit of *jacket* and skirt.
1800 ▷

COSTUME JEWELRY *Accessories* made with inexpensive materials such as paste, glass, or *rhinestones* to imitate gems, or "base metal" colored to resemble gold or silver.
1930s ▷

COTE Long garment worn over the *chemise* and under the *robe*, by both men and women.
14TH–15TH CENTURY: SEE PP.72–74

COTE-HARDIE A close-fitting, hip-length overgarment for men, or an overgarment for women with a close-fitting *bodice* and sleeves and a wide, full skirt.
14TH–15TH CENTURY: SEE PP.62–63

COTHURNUS An Ancient Greek boot worn for hunting, with thick soles and reaching to mid-calf; also used as part of costumes for Greek and Roman actors in tragedies.
ANTIQUITY

COTTAGE BONNET Simple, close-fitting straw *bonnet* with the sides projecting beyond the wearer's face.
1808–1870

COTTON White, downy fiber from the bolls (seed capsules) of the cotton plant (genus *Gossypium*), and fabric woven from it; first used in the Americas and Asia, and one of the most widely used fabrics today.
5000 BCE ▷

COTTON GAUZE Thin, loosely woven cotton, originally from India, popular for clothing in the 1960s and 1970s; called *muslin* in the UK.
1960s ▷

COUCHED WORK A decorative technique in which threads are laid on the surface of a fabric and then secured with small stitches of another thread.
11TH CENTURY ▷

COUTURE From the French for "sewing," the creation of high fashion, often custom-made, clothing for women; see also *Haute couture*.

COVERT COAT A short overcoat for men, with a fly front and *vents* in the side seams, originally for riding but later adopted generally.
1880s ▷

COWBOY BOOTS Sturdy riding boots, usually mid-calf height and with a *Cuban heel,* often with ornate embroidery on the side; originally worn by North American cowboys.
MID-19TH CENTURY ▷

COWBOY HAT Wide-brimmed hat with tall crown; made from *felt*, straw, or leather; first worn by working cowboys in the US; John B. Stetson is credited with making the first.
MID-19TH CENTURY ▷ SEE P.434

COWBOY STYLE A casual style of dress based on the work clothes worn by US cowboys, such as *jeans*, *cowboy boots*, and *bandanas*.
1950s ▷

COWL NECK A large, softly draped collar seen on women's *sweaters* and dresses.
1920s ▷: SEE PP.326, 451

CRAVAT A neckcloth for men, said to have originated in Croatia, today made from patterned fabric (usually *silk*), with a *pleated* section to go around the neck and tucked into the open neckline of shirt.
LATE 17TH CENTURY ▷: SEE PP.136–137, 184–185

CRÊPE A thin, gauzy fabric in which the fibers are twisted before they are woven to give greater elasticity; types used today include crêpe de chine (*silk*) and crêpe georgette (*silk*, *rayon*, or *cotton*).
17TH CENTURY ▷

CUFFS

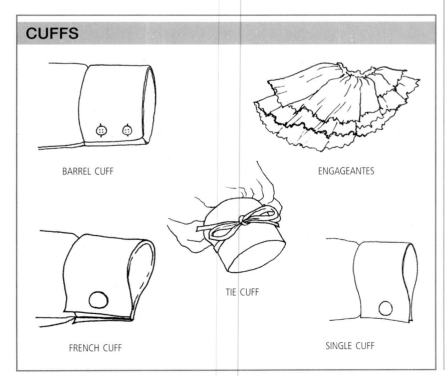

BARREL CUFF

ENGAGEANTES

TIE CUFF

FRENCH CUFF

SINGLE CUFF

CREPE RUBBER Natural rubber used to make soles of shoes or boots, as it is lightweight and gives protection against heat and wet; crepe soles usually have a rough, crinkled surface; see also *Brothel creepers*.
1920s ▷

CRESPINETTE Hairnet worn by aristocratic women of Northern Europe; woven from gold, silver, or *silk*; also called crispine or caul.
13TH–14TH CENTURY: SEE PP.64, 74

CREW NECK A round, close-fitting neckline on a shirt or *sweater*.
20TH CENTURY ▷ SEE P.451

CRINOLETTE An undergarment that marks the transition between the *cage petticoat* and the *bustle*; has a flat front and half-hoops at the back.
c.1868–1873: SEE P.433

CRINOLINE (a) See *Cage petticoat*; (b) a fabric made from horsehair mixed with *cotton*, used to make stiff under-*petticoats*.
1829 ▷: SEE PP.196–197, 433

CROCHET WORK A technique for making fabric or *lace* by working *yarn* (or thread) into loops and chains, using a hooked needle (*crochet* is French for "hook").
19TH CENTURY ▷ SEE P.380

CROPPED Term used for a garment cut shorter than the usual length.
17TH CENTURY ▷ SEE PP.332, 389, 397

CROSS CLOTH A triangular piece of cloth worn over a *coif*, with the longest edge over the forehead.

CRUSHED VELVET *Velvet* with a crumpled *pile*.
20TH CENTURY ▷

CUBAN HEEL A medium-high heel for shoes or boots, with a tapered back edge; see also *Cowboy boots*.

CUFF The part at the end of a sleeve, sometimes thickened or turned back.
15TH CENTURY ▷

CULOTTES Divided skirt worn by women, which looks like a skirt but functions like pants, first used for riding horses or bicycles.
EARLY 20TH CENTURY ▷: SEE P.297

CUMMERBUND A wide pleated sash worn around the waist, particularly as part of men's evening dress.
17TH CENTURY ▷: SEE P.215

CUTWORK (a) Also known as *dagging*, the slashing of a garment border to make decorative shapes; (b) decoration made by cutting holes and filling in the spaces with needlework.
14TH CENTURY ▷: SEE P.72

D

DAGGING Decorative technique whereby a dagge (pattern) is cut into the edge of sleeves or hems; popular in medieval times.
MEDIEVAL–15TH CENTURY: SEE P.74

DALMATIKON A long, T-shaped Byzantine garment with wide sleeves and slits up each side.
300 CE ▷: SEE PP.36–37

DAMASK A fabric of *silk*, *linen*, or *wool* in which a monochrome design is created by the contrast between the face and reverse of the satin weave and can be seen on both sides.
MEDIEVAL ▷

DART A stitched fold on the inside of a garment piece, to create shape or to give a closer fit.

DASHIKI A loose, colorful pull-on shirt traditionally worn by men in West Africa, now worn worldwide, particularly by African-Americans.
1960s ▷

DECK SHOES Nonslip shoes, also called boat shoes or top-siders, with rubber soles, quick-drying uppers, and a lace around the top; some types are similar in style to *moccasins*.
1935 ▷

DÉCOLLETAGE A low-cut neckline on a woman's dress.
1890s ▷: SEE PP.180–181

DECONSTRUCTIONISTS A group of designers who challenged traditional concepts of fashion by ripping clothes, leaving raw edges on garments, and making clothes from items such as gaffer tape.
1980s ▷: SEE PP.401, 406

DEEL Mongolian *robe* with high collar; cut in one piece and worn wrapped across the body and tied with a *silk* sash.
13TH CENTURY ▷: SEE P.459

DEERSTALKER A *tweed* cap with ear flaps tied at the crown, for men to wear during country pursuits.
1860s ▷

DELPHOS DRESS Greek-inspired style of women's dress created by designer Mariano Fortuny; made of thin, finely *pleated silk* weighted down with glass beads at the sides.
c.1907–1950s: SEE P.237

DEMI-GIGOT SLEEVE A style of sleeve that is full from the shoulder to the elbow and tight on the forearm; see also *Gigot sleeve*.
1820s; ALSO 1891

DENIM A *cotton twill* fabric made with one colored thread and one white thread, used to make work clothes such as *jeans*.
17TH CENTURY ▷: SEE PP.339, 345, 373

DERBY SHOES Sometimes called Blücher shoes, a style of men's lace-up leather shoe in which the shoelace *eyelets* are situated on flaps attached to the top of the *vamp*.
20TH CENTURY ▷

DESIGNER LABEL A label bearing the name or logo of a major designer; this may also be displayed on the outside of a garment as a sign of quality or a badge of status.
LATE 20TH CENTURY ▷

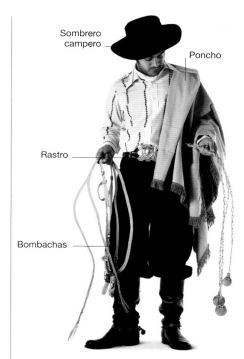

Argentinian cattle herder
South American gauchos dress to accommodate a rugged lifestyle. *Ponchos* are carried and serve as cloaks in cold weather or saddle blankets when riding.

Sombrero campero
Poncho
Rastro
Bombachas

Aymará woman, Bolivia
Traditional Aymará dress, or cholita dress, includes a full, tiered skirt and a felt hat, similar to a *bowler hat*. This hat style was first introduced to Bolivia in the 1920s.

Felt hat
Pollera

Bearskin —

Kilt —

Sporran —

Spats —

Royal Scots Dragoon Guard
Many regiments of the British Army wear uniforms based on traditional Scottish dress. This Guard wears Queen Elizabeth II's personal *tartan*, Royal Stewart.

Coiffe —

Embroidered bodice —

Tavancher —

Woman from Pont l'Abbé, France
Costume from Brittany is distinctive for its use of fine *lace*, especially in *coiffes*. There is an impressive variety of these caps, each village having its own unique style.

DEVORÉ A *velvety* fabric on which some areas of the *pile* have been burned away with chemicals, so that the remaining pile forms a pattern.
LATE 19TH CENTURY ▷

DHOTI A long, *cotton* loincloth traditionally worn by Indian men.
SEE P.462

DIAMANTÉ UK term for *rhinestones*.
19TH CENTURY ▷ SEE PP.258–259

DIAPER A fabric woven so that the surface shows a diaper pattern of interlocking lozenge or diamond shapes when the light catches it.
15TH CENTURY ▷

DIFFUSION LINE Also known as a Bridge collection. A clothing line produced by a high-profile designer at a moderate price.
20TH CENTURY ▷

DIMITY A lightweight *cotton* fabric with some of the *warp* threads standing out to form fine cords.
18TH CENTURY ▷

DINNER JACKET A man's *jacket* for formal evening wear, often with *silk*-faced or *satin*-faced *lapels*; also known as a tuxedo.
1890s ▷ SEE P.289

DIRECTOIRE STYLE Neoclassical style of dress for men and women, popular in France at the end of the 18th century and briefly revived at the end of the 19th century.
18TH–19TH CENTURY SEE P.156

DIRNDL Traditional style of dress for women in Austria and southern Germany, including a lace-up *bodice*, a full, gathered skirt, and an apron.
SEE P.446

DJELLABA Long, hooded *wool* robe traditionally worn by men and women in northwest Africa.

DOGTOOTH See *Houndstooth*.

DOLLY VARDEN BONNET A wide-brimmed *bonnet* with wide ribbons that are tied under the chin.
1880s–EARLY 20TH CENTURY SEE P.219

DOLMAN SLEEVE A loose-fitting sleeve cut as part of the *bodice*; often used on women's *sweaters*; popular in the 1980s; see also *Batwing sleeve*.
1930s ▷ SEE P.458

DONKEY JACKET Short *wool* work *jacket* for men, often with *PVC* on the *yoke*; popular with students and radicals from the 1950s onward.
20TH CENTURY ▷ SEE P.448

DOUBLE-BREASTED A garment, usually a coat or *jacket*, with overlapping panels at the front and two vertical rows of buttons.
18TH CENTURY ▷ SEE PP.289, 366, 448

DOUBLE-FACED A term for a fabric with a finish on both sides (two "right sides"), so usable on either side.
19TH CENTURY ▷

DOUBLET A close-fitting padded *jacket* worn over the shirt, usually by men; doublets could have a buttoned front; see also *Pourpoint*.
14TH–LATE 17TH CENTURY: SEE PP.90–91, 118

DRAINPIPE PANTS Very close-fitting, straight-legged jeans or casual pants first worn by men in the 1950s and later adopted by women.
1950s ▷ SEE P.340

DRAPE SUIT Men's *three-piece suit* with a loose cut through the shoulder and *armscye*, light padding, a narrow waist, and wide sleeves, creating a V-shape silhouette.
1930s ▷ SEE PP.286–287

DRAWERS An undergarment for the lower body, usually made of *linen* or *cotton*.
15TH CENTURY ▷ SEE P.171

DRAWN-THREAD WORK A fabric decoration in which some *warp* and *weft* threads are removed and the remaining threads are sewn to form a pattern; see also *Pulled-thread work*.
16TH CENTURY ▷

DRESS CLOTHES Formal garments for men, particularly for evening, such as the *tailcoat*.
19TH CENTURY ▷

DRESS REFORM Various initiatives taken in Europe and North America, associated with suffrage movements, to make clothing more comfortable and practical, especially for women; see also *Bloomers, Culottes*.
MID-19TH CENTURY–1940s: SEE P.283

DRILL Sturdy *linen* or *cotton twill* used for summer clothing. Also preferred for *corsets*.
18TH CENTURY ▷

DR. (DOC) MARTENS Lace-up walking boots with a high top and air-cushioned sole, worn by skinheads and other youth subcultures; see also *Grunge, Punk style, Skinhead style*.
1960 ▷ SEE PP.404–405

DROP WAIST A waistband that sits lower than the natural waist of the wearer, fashionable for women's dresses during the 1920s.
1920s ▷ SEE PP.240–241, 252–255

DUCHESSE A heavy, luxurious *satin* with a lustrous sheen.

DUCKS Pants made from coarse white *linen* or *cotton*, often worn in hot climates and by sailors.
19TH CENTURY

DUFFLE COAT A coarse *serge* coat first made for the British Royal Navy, later adopted by students and activists; often fastened with *toggles*.
MID-19TH CENTURY ▷

DUPATTA Long scarf, often in sheer material, traditionally worn with women's *shalwar kameez*, draped around the shoulders or head.

DUTCH BOY CAP A man's peaked cap, usually of *wool* and with a flat, circular crown; originally worn by fishermen in Europe, and later popular with youth and left-wing subcultures such as bikers.

DYE Natural or synthetic substance used to color a fabric; see also *Aniline dyes*.
SEE PP.38–39

E

EASING Technique for joining two fabric edges of slightly different lengths, in which the extra fullness on the longer edge is evenly distributed along the seam; more subtle than *gathering*.

EMBROIDERY Decorative stitching applied to a fabric, using materials such as *silk*, *wool*, and metal thread.
SEE P.109

EMPIRE LINE A term used for women's dresses in the early 19th century, featuring a high-waisted *bodice* and long, slim skirt.
c. 1800–1820 ▷: SEE PP.170–171

ENGAGEANTES A French word for *ruffles*, especially detachable ruffles worn at the *cuffs* by women.
LATE 17TH–MID-19TH CENTURY: SEE PP.142, 157

EPAULETS Ornamental shoulder pieces originally worn on *jackets* as part of a military uniform; now also a term for detachable shoulder pieces with insignia of rank, worn by members of the armed forces and other uniformed personnel such as pilots.
18TH CENTURY ▷

ERMINE The winter fur of the ermine (stoat), which is white with a black tip, and in medieval Europe was a symbol of high status.
MEDIEVAL ▷: SEE PP.86–87, 192–193

ESPADRILLES Canvas shoes with twisted rope soles, and sometimes laces, first worn by Spanish peasants but now popular as summer shoes.
1920s ▷

ETHNIC DRESS Traditional clothing from certain ethnic groups that has been adapted for Western fashion, such as the *poncho* or the *caftan*, or *harem pants*.
1950 ▷

ETON COLLAR A large, stiffly starched, detachable *white* collar, notably worn by students of Eton, a prestigious British school.
19TH CENTURY ▷

EYELET A hole made in a garment for ribbon or laces to pass through, often with the edges strengthened by stitching or metal rings.
MEDIEVAL ▷: SEE P.63

F

FACE, OF FABRIC The "right side," the surface that faces outward on a finished garment; see also *Double-faced cloth*.

FACING Attaching a strip of fabric or binding to a raw neckline or other edge of a garment, to give a neat enclosed seam.

FAGGOTTING (a) Joining of two fabric pieces by a network of stitches; (b) *drawn-thread work* in which some threads are removed and the rest tied in bundles to form a pattern.

FAILLE A soft *silk* or *rayon* fabric with a slight luster and a *ribbed weave* creating a textured feel.
1860s ▷

FAIR ISLE A traditional *knitting* style from Fair Isle in the Shetlands, with bands of repeating motifs in various colors or natural fleece tones.
1860s ▷: SEE PP.286, 304

FARTHINGALE An underskirt with wicker, *whalebone*, or rag hoops sewn in to hold a top skirt in a particular shape; see also *Spanish farthingale*, *Wheel farthingale*.
LATE 15TH–MID-17TH CENTURY: SEE PP.432–433

FASCINATOR
A delicate head ornament made from materials such as feathers and net, derived from the cocktail hats of the 1960s.
1970s ▷: SEE P.429

FASHION PLATES Mass-produced illustrations showing the general features of new fashion styles; used until the advent of photography.
17TH–EARLY 20TH CENTURY

FEDORA A *felt* hat with a crease along the crown and two "pinches" at the front, first worn by women but now a classic style for men.
1890s ▷: SEE PP.225, 303

FELT A fabric made from *wool* and/or fur matted together by heating, moisture, and friction.

FEZ Also called a tarboosh, a red *wool felt* cap with cylindrical or conical sides, and a flat crown, frequently with a tassel, traditionally worn by Muslim men in Turkey and North Africa.
SEE PP.113, 453

FIBER Strands of *cotton*, *silk*, or other natural or synthetic substances that are twisted into *yarn* or *felted* to make fabric.

FICHU Worn by women, a triangle of *muslin* or *linen* draped over the shoulders and loosely knotted at the bust or tucked into a low neckline.
EARLY 18TH–EARLY 20TH CENTURY: SEE PP.147, 178

FILLET A thin headband of *linen* or gold, or a headband of *satin* with pearls for evening wear.
MEDIEVAL ▷: SEE PP.49, 61, 64

FISHNET Open-*weave* material used for women's stockings and tights.
LATE 19TH CENTURY▷

FLAMENCO DRESS Ankle-length dress with a low neckline; fitted *bodice*, waist, and hips; and frilled skirt; traditional in Andalusia, Spain; derived from local Romani dress.
EARLY 19TH CENTURY ▷: SEE P.329, 445

FLANNEL *Wool* fabric with a plain or *twill weave* and a slight *nap* on both sides.
MEDIEVAL ▷

FLANNELETTE A *cotton* fabric like *flannel*, with a *nap* on one or both sides; also called cotton flannel.
1870s ▷

FLARES Pants that fit tightly around the upper legs but flare out widely from the knee down; see also *Bell-bottoms, Loon pants*.
LATE 1960s ▷: SEE PP.366–367, 372–373, 382–383

FLAT CAP A soft, round cap of cloth or leather, with a low, flat crown and a small, stiff brim at the front.
16TH CENTURY ▷: SEE PP.227, 282

FLOUNCE A deep *ruffle* of gathered or *pleated* fabric used as decorative trimming for women's garments.
18TH CENTURY ▷: SEE PP.133, 143, 146–147

FLY FRONT A fold of cloth on a pair of pants covering a row of buttons or a zipper.
19TH CENTURY ▷: SEE P.217

FOLK COSTUME Style of dress traditionally worn by the inhabitants of a certain region, such as the *Dirndl* and *Lederhosen* in Germany.

FONTANGE A headdress for women first appearing in the French court, comprising a tower of *lace* or *linen* frills supported by a *commode*.
LATE 17TH–EARLY 18TH CENTURY: SEE P.139

FOUR-IN-HAND A simple and commonly used way to tie a necktie, forming a narrow and slightly asymmetrical knot.
1890 ▷: SEE PP.211, 263, 288

FRENCH CUFF Also called a double *cuff*, a long cuff that is folded back on itself and fastened with cuff links.
1850s ▷: SEE P.440

FRENCH HEEL A medium-high heel for women's shoes, in which the back curves inward and then flares out slightly just at the base; also called *pompadour heel* and Louis heel.
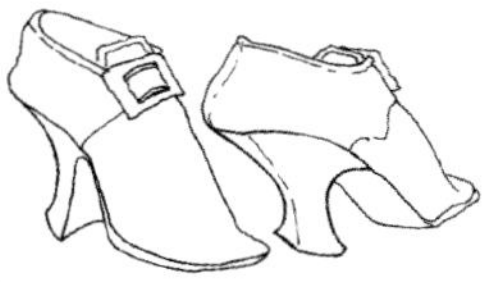
18TH CENTURY ▷

FRENCH HOOD A small, round hood with a stiff frame, worn far back over the crown of the head, with the ends extending forward over the ears.
1520s–1590

FRENCH KNICKERS A variety of (usually loose-fitting) women's underpants, extending from the waist to the upper thighs like a pair of shorts, typically made of *lace* or *satin*; see also *Teddy*, *Lingerie*.
1930s ▷

FRENCH POCKET An early form of flap pocket, comprising a horizontal slit with a flap to protect the opening; used on men's clothing.
17TH CENTURY: SEE P.453

FRENCH RUFF Also called the cartwheel *ruff*, a large, deep ruff forming a horseshoe shape or full circle around the neck.

1580s–c. 1610

FRENCH SEAM A seam in which the raw edges are enclosed within the body of the seam; especially suitable for sheer fabrics.

FRET A *coif* or skull cap made of gold fretwork or of fabric.

FROCK Old term for an informal gown or a child's dress.
MEDIEVAL ▷

FROCK COAT A man's coat reaching to the knee, buttoned down to waist level, and with full skirts.
18TH–EARLY 20TH CENTURY: SEE PP.184–185

FROGGING A coat closure comprising decorative braid and a spindle-shaped "frog button" that passes through a loop in the braid.
17TH CENTURY ▷: SEE PP.113, 205, 436

FRONTLET A decorative band worn across a woman's forehead, under a veil or other head covering.
MEDIEVAL–EARLY 17TH CENTURY

FULL-BOTTOMED WIG A large wig of closely curled hair, shoulder length or longer, with a center part.
1660–EARLY 18TH CENTURY: SEE PP.131, 137

FUN FUR A furlike material made from synthetic fiber, often dyed a bright color, or a garment made from such material.
1960s ▷

FURBELOW A *flounce,* or a wavy line of fabric, usually on a woman's garment and often made of the same material as the main garment.
18TH CENTURY

FUSTANELLA White *pleated* skirt traditionally worn as part of military dress in Albania and Greece; made from thick *linen*, often dipped in animal fat for waterproofing.
c. 13TH CENTURY ▷: SEE P.453

G

GABARDINE A *worsted* or *cotton/worsted twill* with diagonal *ribbing*, invented by Thomas Burberry; used to make weatherproof raincoats and the Burberry *trench coat*.
1879 ▷

GABRIELLE DRESS Dress with a skirt front, a *bodice* cut from one panel of fabric, and *box pleats* at the back; also known as fourreau.
1860s

GABRIELLE SLEEVE A sleeve used on women's dresses, full from shoulder to elbow and tapering to a deep *cuff*; also a sleeve with a series of *puffs* from shoulder to wrist.
19TH CENTURY

GALLIGASKINS Wide, loose *breeches*.
1570s–END OF 17TH CENTURY

GARÇONNE LOOK A style named for the French equivalent of the "flapper," with short hairstyles and an often androgynous shape to the clothes.
1920s: SEE PP.252–253

GARTER A band, often decorative, used to hold up the top of a stocking.

MEDIEVAL ▷: SEE PP.101, 104

GATHERING To make a fabric edge shorter and more full by sewing a line of *running stitch* and bunching the material closely along the thread.
MEDIEVAL ▷

GAUCHO PANTS Wide, calf-length pants first worn by the gauchos of South America but made popular by film star Rudolph Valentino.
1920s ▷

GAUNTLET An armored covering for the hand; also a sturdy glove with a flared *cuff* extending over the wrist.
15TH CENTURY ▷

GAUZE A thin, fine fabric made from *silk* or a similarly sheer material, used for veils and dress trimmings; see also *Cotton gauze*, *Organdie*.
13TH CENTURY ▷

GEORGETTE A light, sheer fabric of *silk* or synthetic fiber, with a *crêpe* texture, used in dresses and blouses.
1914 ▷

GHILLIES Soft, open-topped leather shoes secured by laces across the foot and around the ankle, worn with traditional Scottish dress.

GIBSON GIRL SKIRT A straight-sided, flat-fronted skirt with *gathers* at the back to give fullness.
1890: SEE P.457

GIBUS HAT A *top hat* with a collapsible crown; see also *Opera hat*.
19TH CENTURY ▷

GIGOT SLEEVE A sleeve that is very full from the shoulder to the elbow and fitted from elbow to wrist; also called a leg-of-mutton sleeve.
19TH CENTURY: SEE PP.179, 206–207, 209, 458

GINGHAM *Checked* or striped plain *weave* fabric, usually *cotton*, in which the pattern is made by stripes of *warp* and *weft* threads.
19TH CENTURY ▷

GIORNEA *Tabard*-style overdress with open front and sides, worn in Renaissance Italy by wealthy women as a way of displaying expensive fabric; especially popular in Florence.
LATE 14TH—MID-15TH CENTURY: SEE P.81

GIPON A close-fitting, padded *jacket* worn by men over the shirt; the forerunner of the *doublet.*
14TH CENTURY

GIRDLE (a) A belt or cord fastened around the waist or hips to secure the clothing; (b) An elastic *corset.*
ANTIQUITY ▷: SEE PP.25, 87, 107

GODETS Triangular panels sewn into the seams of a skirt to create a fluted, flared shape at the bottom.
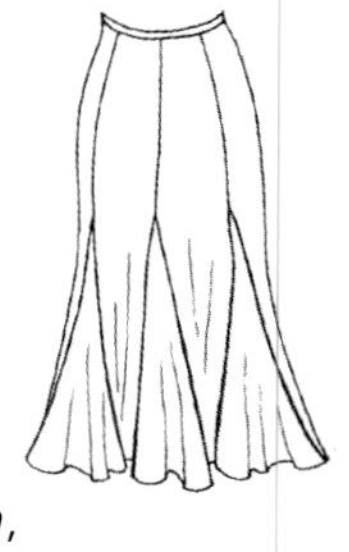
19TH CENTURY ▷

GOFFERING Creation of frills on *cotton*, *linen*, or delicate garments, by pressing the edges with heated tongs (goffering irons).
16TH CENTURY ▷

GO-GO BOOTS Knee-high boots for women, with a low or flat heel and often a chunky toe, inspired by Space Age style, usually made in shiny white or brightly colored material such as patent leather or vinyl.
1960s ▷: SEE PP.352, 361

GOLLAR Short, fitted cape that just covers the shoulders, upper chest, and upper back; closure at the front; worn in Renaissance Germany with low-cut gowns; often fur-lined.
EARLY–MID 16TH CENTURY: SEE P.86

GORES Tapered panels used to make a skirt fit closely around the hips but flare out at the bottom.
14TH CENTURY ▷

GOSSAMER A very light, fine, filmy fabric, often used for veils.
19TH CENTURY ▷

GOWN Originally a term for a long, loose outer garment for both sexes, but later a long, usually formal, dress for women, such as a *ball gown*.

GRAIN The lie of threads in a fabric, which affects the way a garment will hang; see also *Warp, Weft, Bias*.

GRASS SKIRT Traditional form of dress, usually made from leaves; worn in Polynesian cultures, as well as by coastal tribes of Papua New Guinea and Maori in New Zealand.
SEE P.463

GREATCOAT A heavy overcoat for men, worn especially by those in the armed forces.
18TH CENTURY ▷: SEE P.184

GRECIAN BEND A fashionable forward-tilted posture in women, often emphasized by a *bustle* and skirts that were puffed up at the back.
19TH CENTURY

GROSGRAIN A heavy *silk* fabric or ribbon with *ribs* across the surface.
19TH CENTURY ▷

GRUNGE An anti-materialistic, anti-fashion style originally from Seattle, which featured recycled clothing or outdoor wear and a messy appearance.
LATE 1980s ▷: SEE P.408

G-STRING Skimpy underpants, with a narrow elastic back that exposes the buttocks, worn to give a smooth line under clothes; see also *Thong*.
20TH CENTURY ▷

GUERNSEY A close-*knit wool sweater* first worn by fishermen in the Channel Islands, now a classic garment for both men and women.
16TH CENTURY ▷

GUSSET A piece of fabric, usually triangular or diamond in shape, which can be inserted into a garment seam to give extra width or improve the fit.

GYPSY STYLE An interpretation of Romani gypsy dress worn by women, with layered skirts, hoop earrings, and scarves tied around the head or hips.
20TH CENTURY

HABERDASHERY (a) British dressmaking term for small items required for sewing, such as thread, buttons, and zippers; see also *Notions*; (b) in the US a term for a men's clothier.
MEDIEVAL ▷: SEE P.214

HABIT (a) A woman's dress or skirt, worn for riding horses; (b) the traditional attire of monks or nuns; see also *Vestments*.
MEDIEVAL ▷: SEE P.214

HABOTAI SILK A light, inexpensive *silk* from Japan, also called China *silk*.
EARLY 19TH CENTURY

HACKING JACKET A *single-breasted tweed jacket* with slanted pockets and a back *vent*, first worn in the UK for riding horses, now a classic style.
SEE P.448

HAFERLSCHUH Sturdy, traditional Bavarian shoe with textured sole for traction on alpine terrain; low-cut under the ankle, with side lacing on the *vamp*.
EARLY 19TH CENTURY ▷: SEE PP.304, 446

HAIK A long wrap of translucent *linen* worn by high-status women in Ancient Egypt; today, a *wool* cloak worn by both men and women in Morocco.
1500 BCE ONWARD: SEE P.456

HALF BOOTS Ankle boots with the top reaching the base of the calf.
LATE 18TH–EARLY 20TH CENTURY: SEE P.225

HALF-WINDSOR KNOT A way of tying a necktie in which the wider end of the tie is looped around the narrower end and through the neck loop once (rather than twice, as in the *Windsor knot*), producing a neat, asymmetrical triangular knot.
20TH CENTURY ▷

HALTER NECK A soft, sleeveless *bodice* that is held up by straps tied behind the neck.
20TH CENTURY ▷: SEE PP.309, 382

GRAIN

The diagram above illustrates the elements that make up the grain of a woven fabric: the *warp* threads form the lengthwise grain, while the *weft* threads form the crosswise grain. The edges of the *weft* threads are looped back into the fabric to create the *selvage*. The *bias* runs at 45 degrees to the crosswise and lengthwise grains.

Basque dancer, southern France
The *beret* worn by this dancer is a style traditionally worn by Basque shepherds. Popularized in the 19th century, it has become synonymous with French culture.

Woman in Andalusian dress, Spain
Commonly associated with flamenco dancing, this style of dress originated within the gypsy community and is now a symbol of Andalusia the world over.

Tyrolean hat

Dirndl

Woman from Zillertal, Austria
Originally worn by peasant women, *Dirndls* were adopted by the upper classes in the 19th century and are now worn for festivals and other special occasions.

Tyrolean hat

Loden

Lederhosen

Haferlschuh

Man in Tyrolean dress, Austria
Like their Bavarian neighbors, Tyroleans wear *Lederhosen*, but the most distinctive features of their dress are the green *loden* jacket and the feathered *Tyrolean hat*.

HAND A term for the feel of a fabric when touched or rubbed between the fingers.

HAND RUFF A small *ruff* attached to the wrist.
1560s–1630s

HANGING SLEEVES Long, tubular sleeves with a slit at elbow level through which the forearm fits, with the rest of the sleeve hanging down.
c.1400–MID-16TH CENTURY: SEE PP.81, 85

HAORI A short, loose Japanese coat with an open front, traditionally worn over a *kimono*.

HAREM PANTS Loose, baggy pants for women, gathered at the ankles and worn under a *tunic*; inspired by Eastern dress and the costumes of the *Ballets Russes*.
c.1909 ▷: SEE P.367

HARRIS TWEED A handwoven *tweed* cloth made in the Western Isles of Scotland, now widely used, mainly for suits.
1846 ▷

HAUTE COUTURE The highest form of fashion, particularly from the great fashion houses of Paris; in France the term is protected and regulated by the Chambre Syndicale de la Haute Couture and can only be used by fashion houses who follow strict guidelines; see also *Couture*.
19TH CENTURY ▷: SEE PP.326–327

HENDIRA Arabic word for a blanketlike shawl traditionally made and worn by Berber women; often striped black, cream, and indigo; called tamizart or taderdouat in Berber.
ANTIQUITY ▷: SEE P.456

HERRINGBONE A *twill weave* in which the diagonal twill forms a zigzag pattern.
19TH CENTURY ▷: SEE PP.310–311

HIJAB Head scarf worn by Muslim women to cover the hair and neck; from the Arabic word for veil; a symbol of Islamic religious belief.
1ST CENTURY CE ▷: SEE PP.456, 458

HIMATION A rectangular *wool* cloak, worn over a *chiton*, draped over the left shoulder.
ANCIENT GREECE: SEE PP.24–25

HIPPIE STYLE A style mixing handmade or recycled clothes, *bell-bottoms*, *ethnic dress*, *tie-dye*, and psychedelic colors.
1960s ▷: SEE PP.374–377

HIPSTERS Pants cut to sit low on the hips; also referred to as "low-rise" in the US.
LATE 1960s ▷

H-LINE A slim, lean shape created by Christian Dior for dresses, with a small bust and slim hips.
1954 ▷: SEE P.319

HOBBLE SKIRT A long, slim skirt that was very narrow at the ankles, and sometimes included a decorative band around the knees.
1909–1915

HOLLAND A fine *linen* imported to Britain from Holland; later the term was used for any fine linen.
15TH–18TH CENTURY

HOMBURG A men's hat of stiff *felt* with a dent running along the center of the crown, a *grosgrain* ribbon band, and a slightly up-curved brim; see also *Trilby*.
1870s ▷: SEE PP.288–289, 303, 342–343

HOMESPUN A coarse *wool* cloth, often made at home or locally; also refers to *tweeds* made in Ireland or the Western Isles of Scotland.
16TH CENTURY ▷

HOOP PETTICOAT An under-*petticoat* that incorporated hoops of cane, wire, or *whalebone*.
EARLY 18TH–EARLY 19TH CENTURY: SEE P.141

HOPSACK A *wool* or *cotton* fabric woven with every two *weft* threads crossing two *warp* threads, making a pattern of tiny squares.
1860s ▷

HOSE Leg coverings for men, or an older word for stockings for men and women; used for any garment covering male legs and lower torso, separate until the Renaissance, then joined; see also *Trunk hose*.
MEDIEVAL ▷: SEE PP.84–85, 90–91

HOUNDSTOOTH A *twill weave* in which two colors of *yarn* are used to create a broken *checked* pattern or a pattern of abstract, four-pointed shapes.
1930s ▷

HOUPPELANDE A sumptuous outer garment for men or women, thigh length to full length, which is fitted at the shoulders and then flares into folds, and has very wide sleeves.
1380s–MID-15TH CENTURY: SEE PP.66, 72–75

HUIPIL Loose *tunic* in a rectangular shape, worn by women in southern Mexico and highland Guatemala; based on garments worn by the Maya people, huipils are colorful and elaborately decorated.
PREHISPANIC TIMES ▷: SEE P.438

IKAT An Indonesian term for a technique in which *yarn* is *tie-dyed* before weaving, producing a blurred design when woven.

INDIGO A deep violet-blue dye originally obtained from the indigo plant (*Indigofera* species), but now made synthetically, mainly to dye blue *jeans*.
ANTIQUITY ▷: SEE PP.38–39

INTARSIA A term for a *knit* fabric in which several colors are used, with separate *yarns* for each colored area, to create an "inlaid" look.

INTERFACING A stiffening material that is placed between the lining and the outer fabric of a garment piece to strengthen it and give structure.

INVERNESS COAT A full, knee-length overcoat for men, with a cape over the shoulders; different versions are made for day and evening wear.
1859 ▷

INVERTED PLEAT A *box pleat* that is reversed, causing the fullness of the fabric to go inward; commonly used in straight skirts to allow movement when walking.
SEE P.451

ITALIAN CLOAK A short, hooded cloak for men.
16TH–17TH CENTURY

ITALIAN HEEL On women's shoes, a small heel that tapers sharply toward the base and then flares out slightly, similar to the modern *kitten heel*.
1770s ▷

IVY LEAGUE Term describing the conservative styles worn by affluent students of the prestigious American "Ivy League" colleges and universities; similar to *Preppy style*.
1930s ▷

J

JABOT A *lacy* or frilled *ruffle* extending from the neck down the front of a blouse, shirt, or dress.
19TH CENTURY ▷:
SEE PP.154, 208–209

JACKET A short coat for informal or outdoor wear; see also *Hacking jacket*, *Norfolk jacket*.
18TH CENTURY ▷

JACQUARD FABRIC A fabric, such as a *damask* or a *brocade*, in which a design is woven into the cloth on an automated loom following a pattern punched in holes on a card.
18TH CENTURY ▷

JEANS Sturdy pants made of *denim*, which were first worn by miners in the US, then made widely popular by cowboys in American movies; now worn universally by men and women.
19TH CENTURY ▷: SEE PP.339, 345, 373

JACKETS

BLAZER   DINNER JACKET   DONKEY JACKET   DOUBLE-BREASTED

HACKING JACKET   MANDARIN JACKET   NEHRU JACKET   NORFOLK JACKET

PEA JACKET   SAFARI JACKET   SINGLE-BREASTED   SMOKING JACKET

JEBBA Traditional outer robe of Tunisia; rectangular in shape, with deep V-neck, usually edged with *embroidery*.
ANTIQUITY ▷: SEE P.454

JEGGINGS Tight, stretchy leggings styled to look like *denim jeans* (hence the name, a combination of "jeans" and "leggings"), and often made of *denim*-like fabric.
EARLY 21ST CENTURY

JERKIN A close-fitting *jacket* for men, worn over the *doublet*, and usually sleeveless, but with "wings" over the armholes.
1450–1630: SEE PP.88, 101, 110

JERSEY (a) A fine, stretchy *knit* fabric; (b) a knit garment covering the torso and arms; (c) a team shirt worn in sports.

JOCKEY BOOTS Calf-length leather boots like those worn by jockeys, often with a band of lighter-colored leather at the top.
1680s ▷

JODHPUR BOOTS Ankle boots for riding, made of sturdy leather and often with elastic sides; these gave rise to *Chelsea boots*.
19TH CENTURY ▷

JODHPURS Pants of Indian origin worn for riding horses; pre-1960s, usually made from *cotton twill* with voluminous thighs for ease of movement; now made of stretch *cotton*, with fabric or leather patches on the inner knees.
LATE 19TH CENTURY ▷: SEE PP.236, 280

JULIET CAP A *lace* or mesh cap worn by brides, named for the cap worn by the heroine in William Shakespeare's *Romeo and Juliet*.
LATE 19TH CENTURY ▷

JUMPER (a) A *tunic* with a square *yoke* and skirt with *box pleats*, derived from girls' school uniform; (b) UK term for *sweater*.
EARLY 20TH CENTURY ▷

JUSTAUCORPS A man's knee-length coat, close-fitting on the body but with flared skirts, and with large turned-back *cuffs*.
MID-17TH–EARLY 18TH CENTURY: SEE PP.130–131

K

KABOTEC *Blouse* with short *puffed sleeves* and a narrow collar; once worn by the highland Silesian women of Poland as everyday dress, but now as folk costume.
18TH CENTURY ▷: SEE P.450

KAFTAN Traditionally this was a long robe worn in the Middle East and central Asia; from the 1950s it denoted a long, loose tunic with a slit neckline and decoration around the neck and *cuffs*.
ANTIQUITY ▷: SEE PP.112–113

KALASIRIS A long, slim-fitting *linen* dress, covering the shoulders or with shoulder straps, worn by women.
2700 BCE ▷: SEE PP.16–17

KERSEY A coarse *wool* cloth widely used for making clothing in medieval times.
MEDIEVAL–19TH CENTURY

KICK PLEAT An *inverted pleat* (with the folds pointing inward) in the lower back seam of a tightly fitted skirt, to allow ease in walking.
SEE PP.275, 331, 396

KID LEATHER Fine leather made from the skin of young goats or lambs, used for gloves and shoes.
17TH CENTURY ▷

KILT A knee-length *plaid* skirt, *pleated* with a flat front and traditionally worn by Scotsmen; now also a style worn by women.
LATE 18TH CENTURY ▷: SEE PP.390, 442

KIMONO A Japanese garment for women or men made from *cotton* or *silk*, full-length and with very wide sleeves, worn crossed over at the front and fastened with an *obi*.
10TH CENTURY ▷: SEE PP.213, 459

KIMONO SLEEVE Wide sleeve like the sleeve on a *kimono*, cut as part of the *bodice*, with a deep *armscye*.
LATE 19TH CENTURY ▷: SEE PP.48–49, 458

KIRTLE In medieval times, a long supportive garment for women, worn over a *smock* but under a *gown*.
10TH CENTURY–c.1650: SEE PP.62–63, 75

KITTEN HEEL On women's shoes, a low heel that tapers sharply inward at the back, with a very narrow base.
1959 ▷

KNICKERBOCKERS Loose-fitting *breeches*, gathered just below the knee, mainly worn by men for golf and country pursuits.
1860 ▷: SEE PP.217, 226–227, 283

KNIFE PLEATS A series of *pleats* facing in one direction around a garment, as on a *kilt*.
SEE PP.230, 452

KNITTING A method of making fabric by interconnecting loops of *yarn* to form a weblike material.

KURTA PAJAMA An outfit, usually of *cotton* or *silk*, worn by Indian men; it comprises a kurta (a loose, knee-length shirt with slits up the sides) and pajama (lightweight pants).
SEE P.462

L

LACE (a) A delicate ornamental fabric with a weblike pattern; (b) a cord used to tie garments or shoes, often with *aglets* at each end.
MEDIEVAL ▷: SEE PP.98–99, 120–122

LAMCHU *Indigo*-dyed or black collarless *jacket*, with colorful *embroidery* around the neckline, front edges, and sleeve hems; worn by the Dao hill tribe of southeast Asia.
SEE P.460

LAMÉ A fabric woven with threads of gold- or silver-colored metal.
1920s ▷: SEE PP.274–275, 291

LAPELS Continuation of the turned-back collar on the front of a coat or *jacket*.
19TH CENTURY ▷: SEE PP.153, 263, 301

LAPPETS Pieces of fabric that hang from an indoor headdress, at the sides or the back.
18TH–19TH CENTURY: SEE PP.86, 132, 191

LATCHET Leather strip used to close shoes, from the Old French word "lacet," to lace; a latchet shoe has a single lacing; often with open sides.
13TH CENTURY ▷: SEE PP.104, 142

LAWN A fine, semitransparent cloth of *linen* or *cotton*.
14TH CENTURY ▷

LEDERHOSEN Traditional leather shorts with suspenders, worn by men in the high-altitude Alpine areas of Germany and Austria; see also *Bundhosen* and *Dirndl*.
SEE P.446

LEGHORN HAT A women's hat with a wide, soft brim, made from Italian Leghorn wheat straw.
EARLY 18TH CENTURY ▷

LEG-OF-MUTTON SLEEVE See *Gigot sleeve*.

LEI Garland of fresh flowers worn as decoration in Hawaii and originating in Polynesia; also made from other materials such as bone, shell, and feathers.
c.6TH CENTURY ▷: SEE P.463

LEOTARD A stretchy, close-fitting body covering worn by dancers and gymnasts, but also adopted for fashion; see also *Beatnik style*, *Body stocking*.
1880s ▷: SEE PP.217, 388

LE SMOKING A *dinner jacket* or *tuxedo* suit for women, first created by Yves Saint Laurent; see also *Androgynous style*.
LATE 1960s ▷: SEE PP.372–373, 381

LEVI'S® 501 *Jeans* created by the Levi Strauss Co. in 1873 and popularized by US cowboys; in the 1960s they became an icon of rebellious youth; very fashionable in the 1980s, they are widely worn as casual wear.
1873 ▷: SEE P.373

LIBERTY PRINTS Hand printed designs on Indian *silk*, created by Liberty of London, with floral or *paisley* patterns; now often used on *cotton*; see also *Aesthetic dress*.
1875 ▷: SEE P.237

LINEN A strong, fine fiber made from the stems of the flax plant (*Linum usitatissimum*); one of the oldest woven fabrics in the world.

LINGERIE French for *linen*, used to refer to women's underwear, often made from light, *silky* materials and trimmed with frills or *lace*.
c.1830s ▷: SEE PP.228, 252, 277, 316, 432–433

LINING A thin layer of fabric added to the inside of a garment to cover raw edges and improve comfort.

LIST The *selvage* of a fabric; "list slippers" were slippers made from strips of selvage.
18TH–19TH CENTURY

LIVERY Distinctive colors, insignia, or symbols attached to clothes, denoting a person of rank and his or her soldiers or followers; used to identify servants of an aristocratic household.
14TH CENTURY ▷: SEE PP.84, 117

LOAFERS Slip-on leather shoes like *moccasins*, often with decorative leather strips or tassels on the *vamp*.
1930s ▷: SEE P.419

LODEN A thick, *napped wool* fabric made in Austria and Germany, used for coats and *jackets* and typically dyed forest green; also a classic coat made from this fabric, with a long *pleat* at the back.
19TH CENTURY ▷: SEE PP.227, 446

LONG POCKET A vertical pocket on a coat or overcoat. Called a slash pocket in the US.
18TH–19TH CENTURY: SEE P.453

LONG STOCKING The stocking part of *trunk-hose*, joined to the upper part halfway up the thigh.
16TH–EARLY 17TH CENTURY

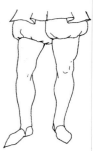

LOON (OR ELEPHANT-LEG) PANTS Flared pants similar to *bell-bottoms* but with a much wider flare from the knees down.
LATE 1960s–EARLY 1970s

LOUIS HEEL See *French heel*.

LOUNGE SUIT The most common form of suit for men, comprising a *jacket* and pants (and sometimes a *vest*), and used for day or business wear.
c.1860 ▷: SEE PP.224, 288

LUREX® A brand name for a type of synthetic fiber *yarn* coated with aluminum, or a metallic fabric made with this yarn.
1940s ▷

LYCRA® A brand name for a synthetic fiber with high elasticity, added to fabrics for use in garments such as underwear and swimwear; see also *Spandex*.
1958 ▷: SEE PP.382, 388

M

MACKINTOSH Rubberized *cotton* invented by Charles Mackintosh and used to make coats; now describes any waterproof coat.
1836 ▷: SEE P.356

MADE-TO-MEASURE A term for a garment made from a base pattern but adapted for an individual wearer; see also *Bespoke, Couture, Haute couture, Ready-to-wear*.

MADRAS Patterned *cotton* or *silk* fabric originally from Madras (now Chennai) in India; sometimes treated to give a lustrous surface.

MAGENTA The second *aniline dye* to be invented, after *mauve*; a pinkish crimson color; see also *Mauve*, *Solferino*.
1860 ▷

MAGYAR BLOUSE A style based on the traditional dress of a Hungarian ethnic group; long or short sleeves are cut as part of the bodice.
1890s–1910

MANDARIN COLLAR A short, unfolded *stand-up collar*, open at the front, for shirts or *jackets*.
20TH CENTURY ▷: SEE P.439

MANDARIN JACKET A Chinese men's *jacket* of plain fabric or *brocade*, with a *mandarin collar*, three-quarter length sleeves, and *frogging*, now also popular in the West.
20TH CENTURY ▷: SEE P.447

MANNEQUIN A life-size dummy for displaying clothes; also a word formerly used for a human *model*, particularly in French fashion houses.
MID-18TH CENTURY ▷

MANTILLA A large, lightweight veil or scarf, often of black *lace*, covering the head and shoulders, and typically worn by Catholic women in Spain and Latin American countries.
18TH CENTURY ▷

MANTLE A full-length garment similar to a cloak, but without a hood.
12TH CENTURY ▷: SEE PP.46–49, 74–75

MANTUA A women's gown, originally with an unboned *bodice* and an overskirt drawn back to show the *petticoat*, later becoming more structured, worn over wide *panniers*; see also *Robe à l'anglaise*.
MID-17TH–MID-18TH CENTURY: SEE PP.138–143

MAO SUIT A suit comprising a mandarin *jacket* and loose-fitting pants, made in somber colors, and formerly worn by Chinese people.
MID-20TH CENTURY

MARABOU Down from the Marabou stork (*Leptoptilos crumeniferus*), used for trimming women's garments and making feather *boas*.

MARY JANES Flat-heeled, round-toed shoes with a strap and buckle, first made for young girls but now adapted for adults.
EARLY 20TH CENTURY ▷: SEE P.356

MAUVE The color of mauveine, an *aniline dye*; on fabrics, it could make a range from bright purple to the typical faded lilac shade.
1850s ▷

MAXI SKIRT A full-length skirt, in contrast to the *miniskirt*.
SEE PP.359, 380

M-CUT COLLAR First seen on men's coats of the Regency period, a collar in which notches are cut at the ends just above the *lapels*.
c.1800–1870

MEDICI COLLAR An *embroidered* or *lace* collar on women's garments, standing up behind the head but tapering away toward the throat.
18TH–EARLY 20TH CENTURY

MEDLEY A cloth in which different colors are used for the *warp* and the *weft*, or mixed in the *yarn*.
MEDIEVAL ▷

MERINO Fine cloth made from the *wool* of the Merino sheep, used in suits and sportswear.
19TH CENTURY ▷

MICROMINI A very short *miniskirt*, reaching to the top of the thighs.
1960s ▷: SEE PP.356–357, 361

MIDI SKIRT A calf-length skirt, in contrast to the mini- and maxi skirt.
1960s ▷: SEE PP.359

MILLINER A maker and seller of high-quality or high-fashion hats; also sold *notions* in the 18th century.
LATE 18TH CENTURY ▷

MINISKIRT A term for a thigh-length skirt or dress, made popular by British designer Mary Quant.
MID-1960s ▷: SEE PP.352–353, 356–357

MINK Dense, glossy fur from the mink, a relative of the weasel.

MITER Stiffened cap of two parts that form a peak at the top; first worn by the pope, cardinals, and bishops of the Church in Rome; in white *silk* or *linen*.
c.10TH CENTURY ▷

MOCCASINS Soft leather shoes based on Native Americans' shoes, in which the lower part is wrapped around the foot and sewn to a flat top part; see also *Loafers*.
20TH CENTURY ▷:
SEE P.437

MOD STYLE A British youth style, featuring a clean, sharp appearance, and items such as *parkas* and *winklepickers* for men and *shift dresses* for women.
LATE 1950s–MID-1960s

MODEL A person employed to wear clothes for display at fashion shows or in photo shoots.
MID-20TH CENTURY ▷: SEE PP.355, 415

MOHAIR Fabric made from the hair of the *Angora* goat, now used for coats and *lounge suits*, or in a fluffier form for *sweaters*.
17TH CENTURY ▷

MOIRÉ FINISH A wavy pattern seen on watered fabrics, made by heating or wetting the fabric and running it through heavy, ribbed rollers.

MOLESKIN A tightly woven *cotton* fabric with a short, soft *pile*, often used for men's pants.
19TH CENTURY ▷

MOON BOOTS Thick-soled boots with a padded synthetic upper, first made as après-ski wear, and inspired by the boots worn by astronauts.
1970s ▷

Woman in Carnival costume, Venice
The costumes at Venice Carnival are based on a stock of traditional masks. The most common is the volto mask, a simple white mask that covers the whole face.

Woman in traditional Slovenian dress
In Slovenia unmarried women wear the triangular zavijacka head scarf, while married women wear an elaborately embroidered headdress called an avba.

Woman from Upper Silesia, Poland
Folk costumes in Poland, which are based on 18th- and 19th-century fashions, are intricately *embroidered,* and worn with silver jewelry, beads, and ribbons.

Kabotec
Wierzchen
Zapaska

Ukrainian girl in traditional dress
This girl wears a richly *embroidered* costume, or vyshyvanka, and a floral wreath called a vinok. The wreath is worn by unmarried women.

Vinok
Vyshyvanka
Plahta

MORNING COAT A men's *tailcoat* derived from the *Newmarket coat,* now worn for formal occasions.
1870s ▷: SEE PP.210, 224–225

MOROCCO LEATHER A leather first made in Moorish areas from finest kid hide and traditionally dyed red.
17TH CENTURY ▷

MOTLEY A term for a garment or fabric made with a mixture of colors.
14TH–17TH CENTURY

MUFF A tubular padded covering of fur or fabric, into which both hands are inserted for warmth.
c.1550 ▷: SEE PP.124–125, 192, 231

MULES Backless slip-on shoes with a closed toe, low- or high-heeled, now mainly worn by women.
16TH CENTURY ▷

MUSLIN A finely woven, medium to light *cotton* cloth; in the US, another name for a *toile;* known as *Calico* in the UK.
16TH CENTURY ▷

N

NANKEEN A sturdy *cotton* fabric with a natural yellow or buff color, originally made in China.
18TH CENTURY

NAP A term for raised fibers on a cloth surface, as in *flannel, suede,* or *velvet;* see also *Pile.*

NAPA LEATHER A fine, supple leather used for gloves and *jackets.*
c.1895 ▷

NATIONAL STANDARD DRESS A simple, standardized, calf-length dress for women, devised by the British government during World War I but never widely accepted.
1918

NEGLIGEE A light or sheer dressing gown for women.
19TH CENTURY ▷: SEE P.252

NECKLINES

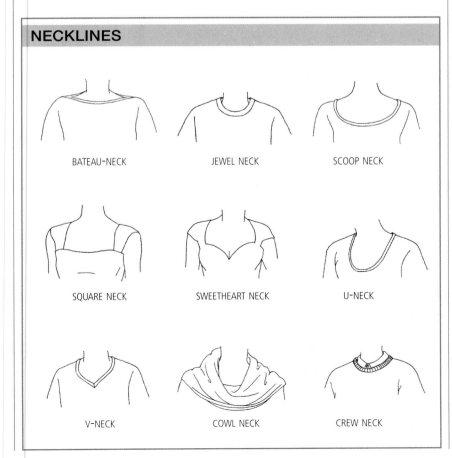

BATEAU-NECK   JEWEL NECK   SCOOP NECK

SQUARE NECK   SWEETHEART NECK   U-NECK

V-NECK   COWL NECK   CREW NECK

NEHRU JACKET A simple, hip-length *jacket* with a high, round collar, modeled on the jackets worn by Indian leader Jawaharlal Nehru; worn by The Beatles.
1960s ▷: SEE P.448

NEOCLASSICAL DRESS A style of women's dress that arose in reaction to the previous ornate formal styles, featuring simple, slim-fitting dresses inspired by Ancient Greek clothing.
LATE 18TH–EARLY 19TH CENTURY: SEE PP.168–169

NETWORK A form of *lace* in which a pattern is worked on to a ground of fine mesh.
16TH–17TH CENTURY

NEW LOOK The term used for the styles presented by Christian Dior in his first collections in 1947, featuring full, billowing skirts and small waists.
1947: SEE PP.316–319

NEWMARKET COAT A *tailcoat* originally designed for riding, either *single-breasted* or *double-breasted,* with the front sloping away from above waist level.
1830s–c.1900

NEW ROMANTIC STYLE A youth style that was a reaction to *punk style,* with frilled shirts, garments inspired by 18th-century dress, and makeup for both sexes.
LATE 1970s–MID-1980s: SEE P.405

NEWSBOY CAP Wide cap with a deep brim and peak, like the caps traditionally worn by tradesmen; in the 1960s, worn by men and women.
1960s ▷: SEE PP.382, 428

NORFOLK JACKET A man's *jacket* for country pursuits, often made of *Harris tweed* or *homespun,* with a belt, *bellows pockets,* and inverted *box pleats* at the front and back.
1880 ▷: SEE PP.217, 448

NOTCH A triangular mark on a garment pattern showing where the edge of one piece matches up with the edge of another.

NOTIONS US dressmaking term for items needed to complete a garment, such as zippers, buttons, and thread; see also *Haberdashery*.

NYLON A trade name for a range of synthetic fibers used to make a wide variety of garments, notably stockings and tights.
1935 ▷

NYLON TAFFETA A stiff, paperlike form of *nylon*, notably used to make the layers of *petticoats* under 1950s skirts; known as Paper Nylon in UK.
1950s ▷

O

OBI A long sash worn around the waist, over a *kimono*, as part of traditional Japanese dress; women wear a wide obi, which can be tied in a variety of decorative knots.
SEE P.459

OBLONG HOOPS *Whalebone* or willow structures that evolved from *panniers*, forming a wide, flat shape to support the *robe à la française*.
1740s–1760s

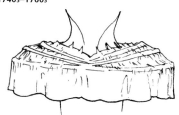

OFF-THE-PEG A UK term for a garment of a standard shape and size that is not customized for the wearer; see *Ready-to-wear*.

OPEN GOWN A style of women's dress in which the overskirt is open at the front to reveal a decorative underskirt or *petticoat*; see also *Mantua*.
18TH CENTURY ▷: SEE PP.87, 142–143

OPERA HAT A man's formal hat that could be compressed and easily carried under the arm; one form, the *gibus hat*, is still used today.
19TH CENTURY ▷

ORGANDIE A fine *cotton* or *nylon gauze* with a crisp finish.
19TH CENTURY ▷

ORGANZA A light, crisp, sheer fabric of *silk*, *polyester*, or *rayon*.
EARLY 19TH CENTURY ▷

ORIENTALISM The adoption of Middle Eastern and Far Eastern dress styles, or interpretations of these styles, in European or American fashion.
17TH CENTURY ▷: SEE PP.188–191, 212–213, 244–245, 267

ORPHREY A form of *embroidery* using gold thread.
13TH CENTURY ▷

OXFORD BAGS Very wide, baggy pants for men, often associated with students at Oxford University, UK; revived for both sexes in the 1970s.
1920s AND 1970s

OXFORD SHIRTING A plain *weave cotton* with narrow, colored stripes.
19TH CENTURY

P

PADDOCK COAT A knee-length, *single-breasted* or *double-breasted* overcoat for men, with two inverted *box pleats* at the rear.
1892 ▷

PAGODA SLEEVES Elbow-length, bell-shaped sleeves on dresses, with *engageantes* worn under them.
1849–1860s: SEE PP.196–197

PAISLEY PATTERN A distinctive teardrop-shaped motif adapted from Indian buteh patterns, named for the Scottish town that wove imitation Kashmiri shawls.
19TH CENTURY ▷: SEE PP.366, 377

PALAZZO PANTS Loose, wide-legged pants for women, often in a light, soft fabric.
1960s ▷: SEE P.451

PALETOT (a) A three-quarter-length *pleated* cloak with a stiff cape, for women, or a close-fitting, knee-length outdoor coat; (b) a short *greatcoat*, worn by men.
19TH CENTURY ▷: SEE P.216

PALLA A rectangular wrap draped around the body, worn by women.
ANCIENT ROME

PANAMA HAT A man's summer hat woven from fibers of the Central American toquilla palm, and flexible enough to be rolled up for carrying.
1830s ▷

PANES A decoration on sleeves or men's *trunk-hose*, made by slashing the fabric so that the *lining* or undergarments showed through.
1500–c.1660: SEE PP.88–93

PANNE VELVET Soft *velvet* with the *pile* pressed flat in one direction to give a highly lustrous surface.
LATE 18TH CENTURY ▷

PANNIERS Also known as side hoops, these were pads or frames attached to the hips to hold the skirt out at the sides; they evolved into large *oblong hoops*.
EARLY 18TH CENTURY: SEE PP.146, 149

PANTOFLES Slip-on overshoes for outdoor wear, or slippers for indoors.
LATE 15TH–MID-17TH CENTURY: SEE P.84

PANTSUIT A suit of *jacket* and pants designed for women but with masculine tailoring; see also *Androgynous style*, *Le smoking*.
20TH CENTURY ▷: SEE PP.359, 396–397

PAREO A traditional Tahitian wrap for women, originally made from bark cloth and tied around the waist; modern pareos are made of *cotton* and are popular as beachwear.

PARKA A coat worn by the Arctic peoples of North America; today a warm, protective, waterproof garment often made of synthetic material, with a fur-lined hood; see also *Anorak*, *Mod style*.
1960s ▷: SEE P.346

PLEATS

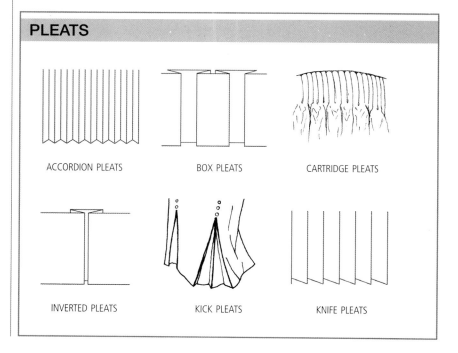

ACCORDION PLEATS BOX PLEATS CARTRIDGE PLEATS

INVERTED PLEATS KICK PLEATS KNIFE PLEATS

PARTLET *Yoke* piece with collar worn in Northern Europe over a low-cut gown to cover the *décolletage*; tied under the arms or pinned to clothes.
16TH–17TH CENTURY: SEE PP.86–87, 106

PARTI-COLORED A term for a garment made with the left and right sides in different-colored fabrics; also called mi-parti.
14TH–15TH CENTURY: SEE PP.62–63

PARURE A set of matching jewelry, such as earrings, necklace, and bracelet.
LATE 18TH CENTURY ▷: SEE P.175

PASHMINA (a) A fine, lightweight *cashmere* fabric made from pashm (a Persian word for the softest belly hair on goats), or a blend of pashm and *silk*, and usually woven in South Asia; (b) a shawl made from pashmina or from synthetic fiber with a similar texture.

PASSEMENTERIE Ornamental braids and other trimmings made with *silk*, gold or silver threads, and tassels.
16TH–19TH CENTURY: SEE PP.90–91

PATCH POCKET A pocket formed from a piece of fabric sewn on to the surface of a garment.
19TH CENTURY ▷: SEE PP.226, 335, 380, 453

PATCHWORK Cloth made from small pieces of fabric sewn together, often with a mixture of colors and patterns; popular in *hippie style*.
SEE P.381

PATENT LEATHER Leather coated with lacquer to give a high-gloss finish; used for men's formal shoes and women's shoes and handbags.
18TH CENTURY ▷: SEE P.367

PATTENS Wood-soled overshoes, sometimes with an iron ring underneath, for outdoor wear.
14TH–MID-19TH CENTURY: SEE P.85

PEACOAT A heavy, *double-breasted wool jacket* formerly worn by sailors in the US and European navies, and now a classic style for men; see also *Reefer*.
1830s ▷: SEE P.447

PEASCOD BELLY *Doublet* with extra padding at the waist to give the effect of a protruding stomach, or peapod ("peascod"); Dutch style.
LATE 16TH CENTURY: SEE PP.100, 105

PEIGNOIR A long, sheer outer garment for women, worn around the house like a dressing gown.
LATE 18TH CENTURY ▷

PELISSE A three-quarter-length fitted coat for women, often with a shoulder cape and fur, *silk*, or *satin* trim; also a women's cloak or *mantle*.
18TH–19TH CENTURY: SEE PP.171, 175–177

PENCIL SKIRT A narrow, close-fitting, knee-length skirt, often with a slit at the back for ease of movement.
1940s ▷: SEE PP.332, 396–397, 457

PEPLOS A woman's garment made from a rectangle or tube of fabric folded around the body, with an overhang above the waist, and held in place by brooches and a belt.
c.500–300 BCE: SEE P.25

PEPLUM In women's garments, a short, gathered overskirt sewn into the waistband of a *jacket*, skirt, or shirt, forming a *flounce* over the hips.
1940s ▷: SEE PP.203, 273, 397

PETER PAN COLLAR A soft, turned-down collar with rounded ends, usually seen on women's and children's clothing.
c.1909 ▷: SEE P.439

PETERSHAM CLOTH A heavy *wool* cloth, often dyed navy blue and formerly used for *peacoats*.
MID-19TH CENTURY ▷

PETERSHAM RIBBON Heavyweight ribbon with thick *ribbing*, used as a trim for hats and garments. *See* also *grograin*.
c.1840 ▷

PETTICOAT For men, a warm garment worn under a *doublet*; for women, an underskirt, sometimes reinforced with a frame to hold the skirt (see *Hoop petticoat*), and later an undergarment.
MEDIEVAL ▷: SEE PP.144–145, 344

PHRYGIAN CAP A soft, cone-shaped hat with the tip bending forward; worn by men in medieval times, and adopted by the "sans-culottes" in the French Revolution.
9TH–12TH CENTURY: 1790

PICKADIL Originally a tabbed or scalloped border on a *doublet*; later a support for a *ruff* or starched collar.
16TH CENTURY: SEE PP.118–119

PICOT A series of loops of twisted thread, forming an ornamental edging to lace, ribbon, or braid.
17TH CENTURY ▷

PICTURE HAT A wide-brimmed, brightly colored summer hat for women, often trimmed with ribbons and artificial flowers.
1890s ▷: SEE PP.428–429

PIKED SHOES Shoes with long, narrow points at the toes; see also *Poulaine*.
14TH–15TH CENTURY

PILE A form of *nap* made by adding an extra *yarn* to a fabric to give a raised surface; fabrics with a pile include *velvet*, *corduroy*, and *bouclé*.

PILLBOX HAT A woman's hat with straight sides, a flat crown, and no brim, made famous by US First Lady Jacqueline Kennedy.
1950s ▷: SEE PP.428–429

PILOT CLOTH A heavy, *twilled* cloth with a *nap*, used for men's overcoats; traditionally dyed blue and used by the navy.
19TH CENTURY ▷

PINAFORE DRESS A practical dress with a bib front or sleeveless *bodice*, worn over a *blouse* or thin *sweater*; often worn by young girls.
20TH CENTURY ▷

POCKETS

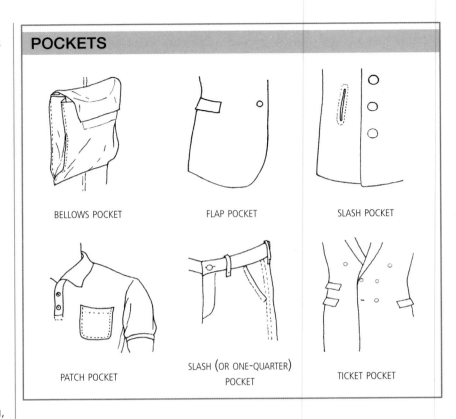

BELLOWS POCKET

FLAP POCKET

SLASH POCKET

PATCH POCKET

SLASH (OR ONE-QUARTER) POCKET

TICKET POCKET

PINKING (a) Also called pouncing, making a pattern of tiny holes or slits in a fabric; (b) trimming an unhemmed fabric edge by cutting it into a zigzag line with pinking shears.

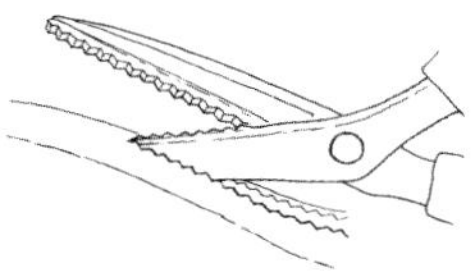

PINSONS Light indoor shoes, often adorned with fur.
14TH–LATE 16TH CENTURY ▷

PIN TUCKS Tiny *pleats* that are sewn along their edges to secure them.
SEE P.392

PIPING A strip of fabric-covered cord inserted into a seam as decorative edging or to accentuate the shapes of a garment.
SEE PP.181, 332, 388

PIQUÉ A *cotton* fabric with a raised, woven design, often a diamond or honeycomb pattern.
19TH CENTURY ▷

PLACKET A short opening at the top of a woman's skirt or pants, so that the garment can be pulled on easily.
16TH CENTURY ▷

PLAID A *wool twill* cloth, usually woven with a *tartan* or *checked* pattern, traditionally worn as part of Scottish Highlanders' dress; *see* also *Arisaid, Kilt.*
SEE P.408

PLASTRON Stiff panel in the center of a surcoat or panel worn underneath a *gown bodice*; popular in the French court of the 14th century.
14TH–15TH CENTURY: SEE PP.64, 81

PLATFORM SHOES Shoes with a high heel and a very thick, built-up sole, especially popular in the glam rock and disco styles of the 1970s.
1940s ▷: SEE PP.372, 376, 426–427

PLEAT A fold that is created by doubling fabric back on itself and securing one or both edges; may be pressed or unpressed, and may be used singly or as a series of parallel folds.

PLUS FOURS *Knickerbockers* with a puffed overhang ("plus four inches") at the knees; notably worn by golfers and popularized by British king Edward VIII.
1920s ▷: SEE PP.284–285

POKE BONNET A *bonnet* with a fabric-lined front brim that projects over the face; tied on with ribbons.
19TH CENTURY: SEE PP.192–193

POINTS Laces used to tie garments to one another: for example, attaching *trunk-hose* to *doublets*, or sleeves to *doublets* or *bodices*.
MEDIEVAL

POLLERA Full, gathered skirt, often *ruffled* or *tiered*; worn in several Latin American countries, including Panama and Bolivia; derived from 17th-century court dress.
MID-19TH CENTURY ▷: SEE P.441

POLO COAT A knee-length *camel hair* overcoat for men, often *double-breasted*, with *patch pockets*.
LATE 19TH CENTURY ▷

POLONAISE A style of women's dress with an overskirt that is hitched up with looped tapes or drawstrings, revealing the underskirt.
1770s–1870s: SEE PP.144–149

POLONY HEEL A high, *stacked heel* thought to have been made from pieces of leather.
17TH CENTURY

POLYESTER A synthetic fiber used to make crease-resistant, quick-drying, easy-care fabrics.
1940s ▷

POMPADOUR HEEL See *French heel.*

POM-POM A small ball of fabric, feathers, or tufts used as decoration for clothing, hats, or shoes.
MID-18TH CENTURY ▷: SEE P.204

PONCHO A *wool* cape first worn by South American gauchos and Andean peoples, made from a diamond or rectangle of fabric with a central hole for the head; popular in 1970s Western fashion.

POPLIN A strong fabric with fine crosswise *ribs*, originally with a *silk warp* and *wool* or *worsted weft*, but now made from a variety of fibers; watered poplin is called tabbinet.
LATE 17TH CENTURY ▷

PORKPIE HAT A man's hat with a narrow, turned-up brim and a low, flat crown with an indentation around the edge.
1860s ▷

POULAINE A medieval shoe worn by men and women, with a very long, pointed toe.
13TH–15TH CENTURY: SEE P.65

POURPOINT A buttoned or laced, fitted, and waisted man's *jacket* worn in medieval Europe; *hose* could be tied to it; also called a *doublet* or *gipon.*
MEDIEVAL: SEE P.64

POWER DRESSING Business wear for women that combined masculine elements, such as padded shoulders, with feminine elements, such as short skirts, high heels, and bowed neckline blouses.
1980s: SEE PP.396–399

PREPPY STYLE A classic style associated with wealthy American students, consisting of *chinos*, *blazers*, and *loafers* for men, and *Fair Isle sweaters* and *pleated* skirts for women.
MID-20TH CENTURY ▷

PRÊT-À-PORTER The French term for *ready-to-wear.*

PRINCE OF WALES CHECK A *wool* fabric with a *twill weave* and a pattern of small and large *checks*; popularized by Edward VIII when Prince of Wales.
1930s ▷: SEE PP.286, 381

PRINCESS-SEAMED DRESS A dress made with the *bodice* and skirt panels cut as one piece and *gores* in the skirt; the bodice is lightly fitted, and the skirt flares out; it has no waist seam but has darts at the waist to give shape.
1840s ▷: SEE P.326

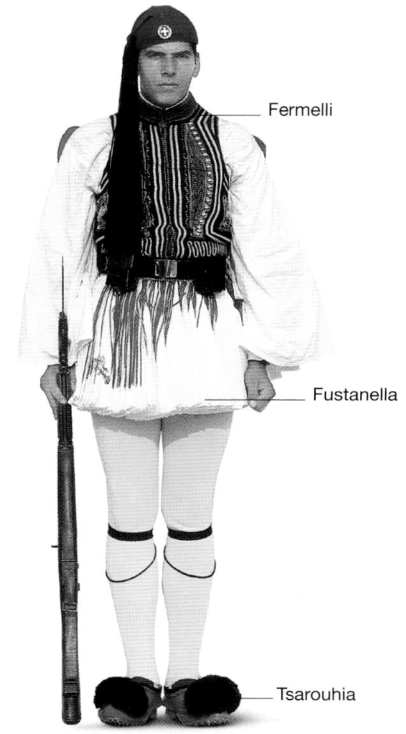
Fermelli
Fustanella
Tsarouhia

Presidential Guard, Athens, Greece
Traditional tsarouhia shoes have been part of Greek military dress since the Ottoman Occupation in 1821. The red color symbolizes the blood of fallen soldiers.

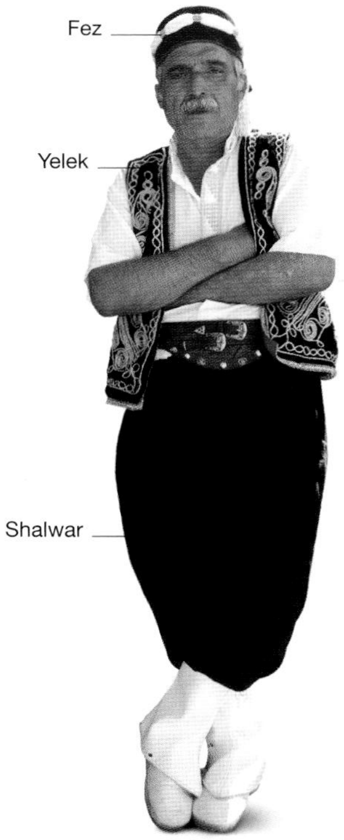
Fez
Yelek
Shalwar

Turkish man in traditional dress
The Moroccan *fez* spread throughout the Ottoman Empire when it was adopted as military dress in the 19th century. Today it is popular among tourists.

Sami man in traditional dress, Finland
This Sami man wears a wool hat and a *tunic* called a luhkka. The pattern on these garments indicates his origin or clan. His coat is made of reindeer hide.

Beaska

Luhkka

Howli

Jebba

Tunisian man in traditional dress
Though many Tunisians wear European clothes for daily wear, the traditional *jebba* is still worn by the older generation and for ceremonial events.

PSYCHEDELIC A term for bright colors and wild, swirling patterns, inspired by psychedelic rock and culture; clothing with these patterns was a feature of *hippie style*; see also *Patchwork, Tie-dye*.
LATE 1960s–EARLY 1970s: SEE PP.374–375

PUFFS A decorative effect created by pulling pieces of fabric from an underlying garment through *slashes* or *panes* in an overgarment.
1500–1650s: SEE PP.86, 90–91

PUFFED SLEEVES Very short sleeves that are *gathered* at the *armscye* so they puff out over the shoulders, and *gathered* in at the lower edge.
EARLY 19TH CENTURY ▷: SEE PP.90–91, 120–121, 174

PULLED-THREAD WORK A style of *embroidery* in which threads in a fabric are pulled together tightly to leave a pattern of small gaps; see also *Drawn-thread work*.

PUMPS Women's shoes with a low *vamp* and a medium-high heel; known in the UK as *Court shoes*.
20TH CENTURY ▷: SEE PP.273, 396, 426–427.

PUNK STYLE A youth fashion style designed specifically to challenge social norms and existing fashions, with features such as spiked hair, ripped clothes with safety pins, slim-fitting pants, and *Dr. (Doc) Martens* boots.
1970s–1980s: SEE PP.390, 404

PUPPYTOOTH A small *houndstooth checked* pattern.
1950s ▷

PURFLE A decorative trim or edging for a garment.
15TH–18TH CENTURY

PVC Polyvinyl chloride, a coating used on fabrics to give a high-gloss, waterproof finish.
20TH CENTURY ▷: SEE PP.360–361

Q

QUAIL-PIPE BOOTS Men's high-topped boots of soft leather that sagged into folds down the legs.
LATE 14TH–EARLY 17TH CENTURY

QUEUE (a) The tail of hair hanging from the back of some styles of wig; (b) a hairstyle typically worn by Manchurian or Native American men, consisting of a shaved head at the front, with a long, gathered ponytail at the back.
LATE 17TH CENTURY ▷: SEE P.152

QUILTING A technique used to combine two layers of fabric with padding between, by using lines of stitching, often making a pattern.
SEE P.377

R

RAGLAN SLEEVE A sleeve that runs from the underarm to the neckline, covering the entire shoulder.
1850s ▷: SEE PP.337, 399, 448

RANELAGH MOB A headdress of *gauze* or *lace*, folded diagonally and worn with the ends crossed under the chin and tied behind.
1760s

RA-RA SKIRT A short, frilled skirt. Briefly popular in the 1980s.
1960s ▷: SEE P.457

RASTA STYLE Originating in Jamaica, a style featuring dreadlocks in the hair, large *wool* caps, and the Rastafari colors of red, gold, and green; made world famous by the singer Bob Marley.
1930s ▷: SEE P.404

RATIONAL DRESS An early attempt to devise a practical dress style for women, including *bloomers* (divided skirts) for cycling and sports; despite its virtues, only a minority of women adopted the style.
1881–1900: SEE PP.236–237

RAYON An "artificial *silk*" made from cellulose (fibrous material from plants) and used to make stockings and other garments.
1910 ▷

READY-TO-WEAR Clothing sold in standard sizes and shapes that can be worn *off-the-peg*, in contrast to *made-to-measure* or *bespoke* items.
SEE PP.308–309, 334–335

REBATO A wired or starched collar, often of *lace*, that stood up around the neck of a woman's dress; also the wire support for a collar or *ruff*.
c.1580–1635

REDINGOTE Originally a traveling coat for men or women; later a long, close-fitting overcoat or dress worn by women, primarily for riding horses.
c.1790–EARLY 20TH CENTURY: SEE P.179

REEFER JACKET A hip-length, *double-breasted jacket* with a low collar and short *lapels*, two lines of buttons, and short side vents, formerly worn in the British Royal Navy, but now a classic coat for men; see also *Peacoat*.
1860 ▷: SEE P.289

REP A cloth with distinct horizontal *ribs*, such as *poplin*.
19TH CENTURY ▷

RETRO A term for a fashion inspired by the style of a few decades earlier.
LATE 20TH CENTURY

REVERS Originally a facing or edging on a garment; later a turned-back edge showing the reverse side, in particular a *lapel*.
14TH CENTURY ▷

RHINESTONE An imitation diamond made of glass or paste, often used in *costume jewelry* and *diamanté*.
LATE 19TH CENTURY ▷

RIBBING In *knitting*, a pattern in which vertical stripes are created by alternating plain and purl stitches; often used for socks and *sweaters*.

ROBE (a) For men, a formal garment in medieval times, and later a dressing gown; (b) for women, a garment with an overdress that was open in front to show an underskirt.
MEDIEVAL–19TH CENTURY

ROBE À L'ANGLAISE A *robe* with a fitted *bodice* and an overskirt that was open at the front; the skirt was supported by *panniers*, and the box pleats were stitched down to the small of the back; see also *Mantua*.
18TH CENTURY: SEE PP.138–143

ROBE À LA FRANÇAISE An elaborate, sumptuous dress worn in royal courts, comprising a tight-fitting *bodice* and *ruffled* sleeves, *box pleats* running down the back, and a wide skirt supported by *oblong hoops*.
1715–1775: SEE PP.144–147

ROBE DE STYLE A style of women's dress with a loosely fitted *bodice*, slightly dropped waist, and full skirt with *panniers*, associated with French designer Jeanne Lanvin.
1920s: SEE PP.246–247

ROCKER STYLE A youth style based on biker outfits, featuring leather *jackets*, often embellished with studs and badges, and scruffy *jeans*; a contrast to *mod style*.
1950s ▷: SEE PP.344–345

ROLL COLLAR A collar on a *jacket* or vest that folds over with no sharp crease, and has no notch between it and the *lapel*.
1840 ▷: SEE P.368

ROLLED HEM A very narrow hem made by folding a fabric edge two or three times and then sewing through the folded cloth; used on delicate items such as underwear and scarves.

ROMANTIC DRESS A style that arose in contrast to *Neoclassical dress*, with a more curved shape for women, greater use of *lace* and frills, and inspiration from medieval and Renaissance styles; see also *Medici collar*.
EARLY 19TH CENTURY: SEE PP.190–191

ROULEAUX Narrow strips of fabric, often cut on the *bias*, first used as trimming on dress hems, now used for features such as *spaghetti straps* on dresses and underwear.
19TH CENTURY ▷

ROULEAU LOOP Fabric loop that goes over a round, ball-shaped button, serving as a closure.
SEE P.436

ROUND DRESS/GOWN A term for a dress with a skirt that was closed at the front rather than open, showing the underskirt.
LATE 18TH–MID-19TH CENTURY

ROUND-EARED CAP A soft, *linen* cap, with a border of *ruffles* or *pleats*, that curved around the face to the level of the ears and was tied on with strings.
1730s–1760s

RUBEKA Length of *cotton* cloth, usually red and often *plaid*, worn by the Maasai in East Africa; wrapped around the body like a cloak; also called shúkà.
SEE P.458

RUBENS HAT A woman's hat with a high crown and a wide brim turned up on one side; named for Flemish painter Peter Paul Rubens.
1870s–1880s

RUCHING A sewing technique in which strips of fabric are *gathered* and then attached to a garment as decoration.

RUFF A detachable *pleated* collar in *linen* and/or *lace starched* into shape and sometimes supported underneath; see also *Pickadil*.
1560s–1640s: SEE PP.98, 118–121

RUFFLES Frills or *flounces*, often used on collars, *cuffs*, and shirt fronts.
MID-16TH CENTURY ▷: SEE PP.132–133, 140–141

RUNNING STITCH The most simple in-and-out stitch, often done in a straight line.

RUSSIAN HAT A soft fur or *astrakhan* hat with a medium-high crown and no brim; also called a Cossack hat or a Zhivago hat (after the hats worn by characters in the film *Dr. Zhivago*).

S

SABOT SLEEVE A sleeve with one or two *puffs* above the elbow.
9TH CENTURY: SEE PP.140–141

SACK Originally a loose, informal gown for women; later a dress with a more fitted body, a skirt open at the front to show the underskirt, and long *box pleats* running down the back; see also *Robe à la française*.
17TH–18TH CENTURY

SACK BACK A term for a dress with full-length *box pleats* running from the shoulders down the back; see also *Robe à la française*.

SACK DRESS A loose-fitting knee-length dress, hanging straight from the shoulder, created by Spanish designer Cristóbal Balenciaga.
1960 ▷: SEE P.329

SAFARI JACKET A sturdy *cotton jacket* worn by Europeans in tropical countries, with a belt, *bellows pockets*, and *epaulets*.
19TH CENTURY ▷: SEE P.448

SAMPOT Uncut rectangular cloth wrapped around the hips, *sarong*-style; worn by ethnic Khmer men and women in Cambodia.
c.1ST CENTURY CE▷: SEE P.460

SANDAL Shoe comprising a sole fastened to the foot by straps, used around the world since earliest history, especially in hot climates; today sandals can be flat or heeled.
ANTIQUITY ▷

SARI A long length of patterned *silk*, *cotton*, or light synthetic fabric worn by Indian women, *pleated* around the waist, with the end draped over one shoulder, and a *choli* underneath.
SEE PP.299, 462

SARONG A traditional Indonesian garment comprising a length of patterned fabric worn around the waist and legs by both women and men; now also popular outside Asia for casual and beachwear.

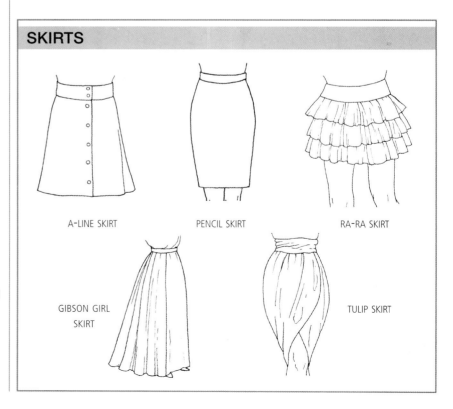

SKIRTS

A-LINE SKIRT PENCIL SKIRT RA-RA SKIRT

GIBSON GIRL SKIRT TULIP SKIRT

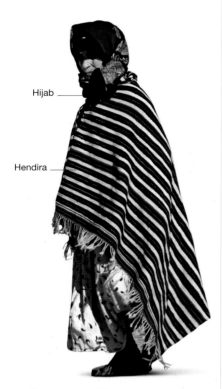

Berber woman, Morocco
Hijab
Hendira
Hendira are traditionally worn by the Berbers as cloaks but are now popular with people in Morocco as rugs or blankets. They are sold widely by carpet dealers.

Cowrie shell headdress

Haik

Tuareg dancer, Morocco
The nomadic Tuareg of North Africa are known as the "blue people" for their indigo clothing, as worn by this woman performing a guedra blessing dance.

SASH A wide band or scarf of ribbon or other soft fabric, worn around the waist or over the shoulder.
16TH CENTURY ▷

SATEEN *Cotton* fabric woven with a lustrous surface in *weft*-faced *satin weave*.

SATIN A fabric with a satin *weave*, in which *warp* threads are floated across several *weft* threads at a time (or vice versa); satin has a lustrous surface and a dull underside.
SEE P.463

SATIN STITCH In *embroidery*, a series of stitches side by side across a shape, producing a smooth surface.

S-BEND CORSET A *corset* with a wide *busk* that pushed the bust forward and the hips and bottom backward in an S shape.
c. 1900–1910 : SEE PP.228, 432–433

SCHENTI A knee-length *linen* wrap like a *kilt*, worn by men in Ancient Egypt.
c. 2686–2181 BCE : SEE PP.16–17

SCOOP NECK A low, round neckline on a woman's blouse or dress.
1950s ▷ : SEE PP.237, 338, 451

SEERSUCKER A lightweight, plain or striped *cotton* or synthetic fabric, with a puckered surface created by *warp* threads of varying tension.
18TH CENTURY ▷

SELVAGE The self-finished edge of a length of woven *fabric*, created by the *weft* threads being looped back into the fabric length; prevents the fabric from fraying or unraveling.
SEE PP.75, 446

SEQUINS Small, shiny disks of metal or plastic sewn on to garments for decoration; see also *Spangles*.
1880s ▷ : SEE PP.293, 361

SERAPE Long, woven striped blanket, worn over the shoulders; originally used by horsemen in northeast Mexico; became a national symbol after independence from Spain.
18TH CENTURY ▷

SERGE A sturdy *worsted* fabric with a *twill weave* and diagonal *ribbing*, made in different weights and types.
MEDIEVAL ▷

SHALWAR KAMEEZ A traditional form of dress for Indian women, comprising the shalwar (loosely fitted pants) and kameez, a knee-length shift or *tunic* with slits up the sides; often worn with a *dupatta*.

SHANTUNG A heavy, lustrous *silk* or synthetic fabric, with *slubs* in the fibers giving a slightly uneven texture.
1870s ▷

SHAWL COLLAR A broad, softly turned-down collar on a man's coat or *vest*, tapering to the front with no notch between it and the *lapel*; superseded by the *roll collar*.
1820s ▷ : SEE P.439

SHEATH DRESS A close-fitting dress for women, knee-length or mid-calf length, with *darts* at the bust and waist to follow the figure.
1920s ▷ : SEE P.323

SLEEVES

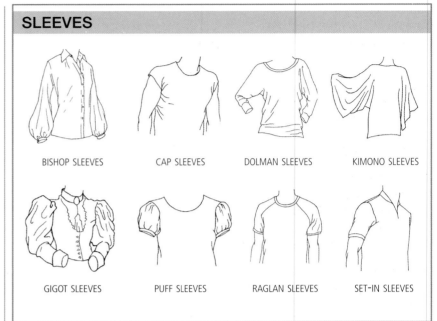

BISHOP SLEEVES   CAP SLEEVES   DOLMAN SLEEVES   KIMONO SLEEVES

GIGOT SLEEVES   PUFF SLEEVES   RAGLAN SLEEVES   SET-IN SLEEVES

SHEEPSKIN Treated sheep hides used with the fleece on the inside and the skin on the outside; used for *car coats*, and popular as part of the *hippie style*; sheepskin with a fleece of uniform depth is called shearling.
20TH CENTURY ▷

SHIFT Until the 19th century, a general term for a woman's undershirt with long sleeves, equivalent to a man's shirt; made of *linen*; the poor used *wool*.
MEDIEVAL ▷ : SEE PP.75, 80, 87

SHIFT DRESS A short, sleeveless dress with a straight or slightly flared shape that skims the figure.
1960s ▷ : SEE P.355

SHIRRING A technique in which parallel rows of tiny *gathers* are sewn into a garment, often using shirring elastic, to allow stretching of the area; see also *Smocking*.

SHIRTWAIST DRESS A classic dress style in which the *bodice* resembles a man's shirt, with a folded-down collar and *revers*.
1930s ▷ : SEE PP.228, 317

SHOT SILK A *silk* fabric woven with different-colored *warp* and *weft* threads to give an iridescent sheen.
MID-19TH CENTURY ▷

SHRUG A cropped, short-sleeved garment like a *bolero*, but *knit*.
EARLY 21ST CENTURY

SILK Fine, very long, lustrous fibers from the cocoons of various silk moth species, notably the domestic silk moth (*Bombyx mori*).

SILK HAT See *Top hat*.

SINGLE-BREASTED Men's coat or *jacket* that closes at the center front with a single row of buttons; see also *Double-breasted*.
LATE 18TH CENTURY ▷: SEE PP.303, 447

SKINHEAD STYLE A style originating among young working-class British people, featuring close-cropped hair, suspenders, *jeans*, and *Dr. (Doc) Martens* boots.
LATE 1960s ▷

SKI PANTS Narrow-fitting pants with elastic straps under the insteps, worn for skiing and as leisure wear.
20TH CENTURY: SEE P.346

SKORT Wide-legged shorts with a piece of fabric in front to give the appearance of a skirt.
20TH CENTURY ▷

SLACKS Casual pants.
1920s ▷

SLASHES Decorative slits cut into the surface of a garment so fabric from an underlying garment can show or be pulled through; see also *Puffs*.
1480s–1650s: SEE P.99

SLASH POCKET A pocket in a man's coat, with a slit opening and no covering flap.
19TH CENTURY: SEE P.453

SLEEVE HAND The open end of a sleeve, where the hand emerges.

SLEEVE HEAD The top of a sleeve, where it is attached to the *armscye*.

SLING BACKS Women's high-heeled shoes with either open or closed toes and with a strap around the heel to hold them on.
1930s ▷

SLIP A women's light *petticoat*, worn under dresses or skirts.
20TH CENTURY ▷

SLIPPERS Lightweight, low-heeled shoes that can easily be slipped on and off, often used for indoor wear.
16TH CENTURY ▷

SLIP SHOES Low-heeled *mules*.
16TH–MID-18TH CENTURY

SLIT POCKET A vertically cut pocket in a man's coat.
19TH CENTURY

SLOPPY JOE An oversized, loose-fitting *sweater*.
1950s ▷

SLOPS Very wide, loose knee *breeches* often worn by sailors.
LATE 16TH–18TH CENTURY

SLUBS Thickened, irregular areas in *silk* fiber, often seen as an attractive feature in silk fabrics.

SMOCK A loose-fitting *linen* or *cotton* overgarment worn by laborers, often with a *yoke* and *smocking* patterns on the front; adopted as informal dress by women.
16TH CENTURY ▷: SEE P.383

SMOCKING A decorative technique in which fabric is evenly gathered (see *Shirring*) and a pattern stitched on top of the *gathers*.
1880 ▷: SEE PP.205, 228, 241

SMOKING JACKET A short, *single-breasted* or *double-breasted jacket* for men, often in *velvet* or *silk* and lined with bright material, worn informally around the home.
1850s ▷

SNOOD (a) A fine mesh net worn by women to hold long hair or keep a hairstyle in place; (b) a tubular scarf pulled over the head.
19TH CENTURY ▷: SEE P.197

SOLFERINO An *aniline dye* used to produce a fuchsia color.
1860 ▷

SOMBRERO The Spanish term for a hat, typically referring in English to a traditional Mexican hat with a wide, upturned brim and a slightly pointed crown.
SEE PP.121, 438

SPAGHETTI STRAPS Very thin, light straps, often seen on women's sundresses, evening dresses, and undergarments.
20TH CENTURY ▷

SPANDEX A trade name for a light, elastic fiber used in underwear and swimwear; see also *Lycra®*.
1958 ▷

SPANGLES Small disks or lozenges of shiny metal with pierced centers, sewn on to garments for decoration; see also *Sequins*.
LATE 15TH–LATE 19TH CENTURY

SPANISH CLOAK Originally a short, hooded cloak for men; later a man's short evening cloak lined with bright-colored *silk*.
16TH–EARLY 20TH CENTURY

SPANISH FARTHINGALE The earliest form of *farthingale*, a garment that originated in Spain; made with a series of hoops that widened toward the feet, giving a funnel-shaped skirt.
c.1520s–1620s: SEE PP.432–433

SPATS Cloth or leather coverings for the uppers of men's shoes, worn by the military and as formal wear.
19TH–EARLY 20TH CENTURY: SEE PP.263, 442

SPECTATOR SHOES Men's shoes, usually *brogues*, made from two colors of leather, such as tan and white. Also corespondent shoes.
1934 ▷: SEE PP.298, 303, 333, 340

uPhaphe
umQhele
isiHlangu

Zulu warrior, South Africa
The rank of a Zulu warrior is indicated by the wearing of particular animal hides and feathers. The leopard-skin umQhele headdress is worn by those of high status.

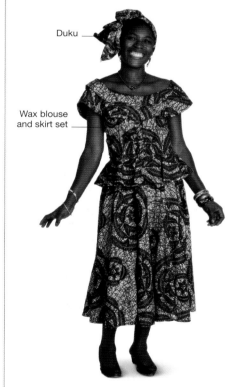

Duku
Wax blouse and skirt set

Ghanaian woman in typical dress
Said to have been introduced to West Africa by European traders in the 19th century, wax, or *batik*, is a textile used widely in West African traditional dress.

Maasai man, Tanzania
The Maasai live in Kenya and Tanzania and are well known for their distinctive dress of brightly colored, usually red, fabrics that are draped around the body.

Rubeka

Namuka

Jordanian woman in traditional dress
This woman wears a typical Muslim *hijab* and a *thawb*. Dress in Jordan is distinctive for its elaborate use of *embroidery*, with each village having its own designs.

Hijab

Thawb

SPENCER (a) A short, double-breasted men's *jacket*, often worn for country pursuits; (b) a short, close-fitting, high-waisted jacket worn by women in the Regency era, over an *Empire-line dress*; (c) a *wool* or wool mix vest or thermal garment worn by women.
18TH CENTURY ▷: SEE PP.171, 174, 187

SPUN SILK *Yarn* made from waste *silk* fiber, used to make *fabrics*, *embroidery silk*, and ribbons.
LATE 19TH CENTURY ▷

STACKED HEEL A heel made by stacking thin layers of wood, leather, or other material, or a heel designed to look as if it has been made in this way.
17TH CENTURY ▷

STAND COLLAR An upright collar.
19TH CENTURY ▷: SEE PP.155, 399, 439

STAND-FALL COLLAR A collar that is folded over, with the inner upright part called the "stand" and the downturned part called the "cape."
19TH CENTURY ▷: SEE P.439

STARCH A substance used to smooth and stiffen fabrics; most types are extracts from plants.
14TH CENTURY ▷: SEE P.124

STAYS The precursor of the *corset*: a tight undergarment for women, stiffened with *whalebone*, worn to give a fashionable shape; see also *Busk*.
17TH–18TH CENTURY: SEE P.139

STILETTO HEELS High, narrow heels, often reinforced with steel, seen on women's shoes.
1954 ▷: SEE PP.426–427

STIRRUP PANTS Close-fitting, stretchy pants for women, with the fabric forming a loop under the foot; see also *Ski pants*.

STOLA A full-length, sleeveless dress placed over the *tunica* and under the *palla*, and secured by brooches and a belt; worn by married Roman women.
c. 100 BCE–300 CE: SEE PP.34–37

STOLE A wide shawl or wrap of fur or luxury fabric, worn around the shoulders by women.
19TH CENTURY ▷: SEE PP.170, 236

STOMACHER A stiff, triangular panel, often heavily *embroidered*, worn over the chest and stomach, at the front of an open *bodice*.
15TH–18TH CENTURY: SEE PP.138–139, 145, 432–433

STONEWASHING A technique in which a fabric such as *denim* is artificially aged or distressed.
20TH CENTURY

STRAIGHT PANTS Pants for both men and women, in which the legs are the same width from hip to ankle.
19TH CENTURY ▷

STREET STYLE A term for styles created by young people for themselves and later taken up by fashion designers, for example, *beatnik*, *punk*, or *mod style*.
1960s ▷: SEE PP.404–405

STYLE WIDTH A tailoring term for the horizontal measurement from the center back seam of a coat to the armhole.

SUEDE Tanned leather with the flesh side treated to give a *nap*, and used with the napped side outward; often used for shoes and *jackets*.
19TH CENTURY ▷

SUGARLOAF HAT A hat with a high, conical crown and a broad brim, worn by both men and women.
1640s: SEE PP.73, 123, 159

SUIT An outfit comprising a *jacket* with pants or a skirt of the same material, worn as business or formal wear; some men's suits also have a *waistcoat*; see also *Lounge suit*.
19TH CENTURY ▷

SUIT OF APPAREL A man's outfit based on *doublet* and *hose*.
16TH–17TH CENTURY: SEE PP.90–91

SUMPTUARY LEGISLATION Laws governing garments and fabrics to be worn by (or forbidden for) specific levels of society, such as the law that only royalty could wear *ermine*.
MEDIEVAL–17TH CENTURY

SUPPORTASSE A decorated wire framework worn at the back of the neck to support a *ruff* or a *band*; see also *Pickadil, Rebato, Underpropper*.
c. 1550–1650: SEE P.99

SWALLOWTAIL A man's *tailcoat* in which the front part reaches to the waist and the back has knee-length *tails*; still worn for highly formal ("white tie") events.
19TH CENTURY ▷: SEE PP.262–263

SWEATER A loose-fitting *knit* garment pulled on over the head; usually informal or leisure wear.
c. 1890 ▷

SWEETHEART NECKLINE On women's dresses, a wide neckline forming a curved V at the front, with the point at the center of the bust.
20TH CENTURY: SEE PP.326, 451

SWING COAT A loose topcoat for women that flares from the shoulders.
20TH CENTURY ▷

T

TABARD (a) A short overgarment like a *tunic*, originally worn by peasants, or a more elaborate garment worn by a knight over armor, and bearing the knight's coat of arms; (b) a *jerkin* worn by a royal officer of arms, and emblazoned with the arms of the sovereign; (c) a loose, short-sleeved or open-sided top for women, especially one used as a beach robe; (d) an open-sided protective garment worn by uniformed workers.
ANTIQUITY ▷: SEE PP.39, 168

TABBY A thick, glossy *taffeta* with a watered surface (see *Watered fabrics*) giving a striped appearance.
17TH–EARLY 20TH CENTURY

PANTS

BELL-BOTTOMS   BOOT-CUT PANTS   CAPRI PANTS

CIGARETTE PANTS   DRAINPIPE PANTS   PALAZZO PANTS

TABI Traditional Japanese ankle socks, with thick soles and a division between the big toe and the other toes so they can be worn with shoes that have a strap between the toes.
SEE P.459

TABLET WEAVING Weaving technique for making bands, often patterned, using a hole-punched tablet made from bone, bark, wood, metal, or other material.
c.3RD–15TH CENTURY

TACKING See *Basting*.

TAFFETA A crisp, glossy fabric made of *silk* or synthetic fiber, with a shimmering luster; often used in *ball gowns* and *wedding dresses*; see also *Nylon taffeta*, *Tabby*.
14TH CENTURY ▷

TAIL (a) The *train* of a *wedding dress* or woman's formal *gown*; (b) the long rear skirt of a man's *dress coat*; see *Tailcoat*, *Swallowtail*, *Morning coat*; (c) as "tails," the term for a *dress suit* with tailcoat.
MEDIEVAL ▷: SEE PP.155, 185, 214

TAILCOAT A formal coat for men in which the front is cut short and the back has two long skirt pieces called *tails*; see also *Morning coat*, *Swallowtail*.
MID-19TH CENTURY ▷: SEE PP.262–263

TAILOR-MADE A term for garments made by a tailor to fit a specific person; in particular, garments for men or masculine-style clothing for women; see also *Bespoke*, *Couture*, *Haute couture*, *Made-to-measure*.
LATE 19TH CENTURY ▷

TAM O'SHANTER A round *wool* cap with a *pom-pom* in the center, worn traditionally by Scottish men, but now more often worn by women.
1880s ▷

TANGO STYLE A style inspired by the tango dancers of Argentina; in Europe, it gave rise to women's fashions such as the *tulip skirt*, and to shorter underwear that allowed freedom of movement.
c.1913 ▷

TARTAN A traditional Scottish *wool* cloth with a *twill weave*, in which stripes of different colors are interwoven to form a specific pattern of squares and bands called a sett; see also *Kilt*.
SEE PP.197, 273, 442

TATTERSALL VEST A fancy vest for men, with a *checked* pattern, usually worn for country pursuits.
1895 ▷

TATTING
A decorative technique in which thread is worked with a needle or shuttle to form a pattern of loops.

T-STRAP SHOES Women's flat or heeled shoes with a central strip joining the *vamp* to an ankle strap.
1930s ▷: SEE PP.273, 357, 426–427

TEDDY An item of *lingerie* that combines a *bodice* with a pair of panties; called *cami-knickers* in the UK.
1970s ▷

TEDDY-BOY STYLE A style that developed among young men in the UK, based on Edwardian fashions, and featuring knee-length *jackets*, close-fitting *drainpipe pants*, and very thin string ties.
1950s ▷: SEE PP.340–341

TENT DRESS A dress that is fitted at the shoulders and flares out to the hem; attributed to Spanish designer Cristóbal Balenciaga.
1951 ▷

Loowuuz
Deel

Mongolian man in traditional dress
Mongolian dress is ideal for the harsh cold of the steppes. The most common materials are leather (especially sheepskin), fur, and wool felt from sheep or camels.

Kimono
Obi
Tabi

Geisha, Japan
Japanese Geisha, female entertainers, regularly wear traditional Japanese dress, including a *kimono* and an *obi*. The hair is worn up with ornaments.

Dao girl, Northern Vietnam
The Dao are an ethnic minority living in China, Vietnam, and Thailand. They produce fine textiles of *embroidered batik* silk, frequently in geometric patterns.

Lamchu

Hang pen

Khmer Apsara dancer, Cambodia
The Khmer *sampot* dates back thousands of years and is made of silk using a unique, uneven twill technique. *Ikat* is a traditional method to create the patterns.

Av pak

Sampot

TEXTILE A term for any type of woven cloth or any synthetic fabric or thread.

THAWB Ankle-length *robe* constructed like a collarless shirt and worn by men and women in Arab countries to keep covered and cool.
ANTIQUITY ▷: SEE P.458

THONG Skimpy underpants, with a narrow back that exposes the buttocks, worn to give a smooth line under clothes; see also *G-string*.
c.1975 ▷

THREE-PIECE SUIT A term for a *lounge suit* comprising a *jacket*, pants, and *vest*.
20TH CENTURY

TICKET POCKET A small pocket just above the right front pocket on a man's *jacket* or coat, originally designed to hold train tickets.
LATE 1850s ▷: SEE P.453

TIE-DYE A traditional technique in Africa and Asia, in which fabric is tied at several points and then dyed; the ties keep the dye from reaching the cloth, thus forming a pattern against the colored areas; see also *Batik, Hippie style*.

TIERS Overlapping layered *ruffles* or *flounces* on a garment.
1850s ▷: SEE PP.205, 207

TIPPET A narrow wrap, often of fur, worn around a woman's shoulders, with the ends hanging down in front.
16TH CENTURY ▷: SEE PP.56, 64

TOGA A garment worn by male Roman citizens, comprising a semicircular piece of *wool* cloth draped round the body.
c.100 BCE–300 CE: SEE PP.34–35

TOGGLE A short, often cylindrical, bar pushed through a loop to fasten a garment such as a *duffle coat*.
20TH CENTURY ▷

TOILE In dressmaking, a term for a prototype of a new garment design, in an inexpensive fabric such as *muslin*, used to create the pattern for the actual garment.
LATE 19TH CENTURY ▷

TOP BOOTS An alternative, later name for *jockey boots*.
1680s ▷: SEE P.217

TOPCOAT A man's outdoor coat worn over a suit; usually knee length, and made of lightweight fabric.
18TH CENTURY ▷: SEE P.184

TOP HAT A man's hat with a tall, flat-topped crown, a narrow brim turned up at the sides, and a covering of black *silk* plush; worn for formal occasions (see also *Gibus hat*).
19TH CENTURY ▷: SEE PP.210–211, 262–263

TOQUE A close-fitting, brimless hat; particularly fashionable for women in the 1920s.
20TH CENTURY ▷: SEE P.175

TOURNURE The French word for a *bustle*, used by the English in polite society (as the word "bustle" was thought to be vulgar).
1880s

TRAIN An elongation of the back of a dress or cloak so that the fabric trails on the ground; still seen in costumes for ceremonial occasions, and as a feature on w*edding dresses*.
MEDIEVAL ▷: SEE PP.200–206

TRAPEZE LINE A term for full-skirted, knee-length dresses that flared out from fitted shoulders, with *petticoats* underneath to produce a rigid triangular outline.
1958: SEE P.381

TRENCH COAT A knee-length or long coat made from waterproof *cotton* or *wool*, with a belt and sometimes caped shoulders; first used by the military in World War I, it became popular after featuring in films such as *Casablanca*; see also *Gabardine*.
20TH CENTURY ▷: SEE PP.238, 280, 291

TREWS *Tartan hose* worn by Scottish men; later referred to tight-fitting pants, usually worn by horse-riders and soldiers; from the Scottish Gaelic triubhas.
c.16TH CENTURY

TRICORN HAT A hat with a low crown and the brim turned up at the back and sides to form a triangle; worn by both men and women.
1690–LATE 18TH CENTURY: SEE PP.136–137, 151, 157

TRICOT A fine, *knit, ribbed* fabric of *wool* or synthetic fiber, made on a special tricot machine; often used for women's undergarments.
19TH CENTURY ▷

TRILBY A man's soft *felt* hat, usually black, with a dent along the crown, and a narrow, flexible brim; named after the novel and play of the same name; see also *Homburg*.
1895 ▷: SEE P.283

TRUNK-HOSE Puffed-out *breeches* forming the top part of men's *hose*, extending from the waist to the tops of the thighs, to join the stockings.
c.1550–1610: SEE PP.90–91, 101

T-SHIRT A short-sleeved, round-necked *cotton* shirt, originally worn as an undershirt by US servicemen in World War II but has since become globally popular as leisure wear for both men and women.
MID-20TH CENTURY ▷: SEE P.345

TUBE TOP A cropped, sleeveless, and shoulderless top for women that wraps like a tube around the torso, and usually fits tightly around the bust so that it stays in place.
1970s ▷

TUCK A stitched fold of fabric used to shape a garment or for decoration.

TUCKER A piece of white fabric, such as *lace* or *lawn*, added to the neckline of a *bodice* on a low-cut dress; known as a "modesty piece."
18TH–19TH CENTURY

TULIP SKIRT A *wraparound* skirt with cross-over panels at the front that curve down from the waist, forming an inverted V at the front hem; a feature of *tango style*.
20TH CENTURY ▷: SEE P.457

TULLE A delicate net fabric made from *silk* or synthetic fibers, often starched to add structure, and used for bridal veils and stiff *petticoats*.
18TH CENTURY ▷

TUNIC A loose garment of varying lengths, either sleeved or sleeveless, worn over a shirt and pants or leggings, and usually made of *wool* or *linen*; worn from Ancient Greek and Roman to medieval times.

TUNICA A basic, T-shaped garment for both sexes in Ancient Rome, knee length for men and full length with long sleeves for women (see also *Dalmatic*).
c.100 BCE–300 CE: SEE PP.34–37

TUNIC DRESS A short dress worn over a *hobble skirt* in the early 20th century, or a short, loose dress worn over pants from the 1960s.
20TH CENTURY ▷

TURBAN (a) A headdress made by wrapping a long piece of cloth around the head, used by men in Middle-Eastern, Asian, and Islamic areas; (b) a woman's hat made to look like a turban.
LATE 18TH CENTURY ▷: SEE PP.112–113, 190–191, 171

TURTLENECK A *sweater* with a close-fitting, turned-down collar; known as a polo-neck in the UK.
EARLY 20TH CENTURY ▷: SEE PP.280, 352, 419

TUSSORE SILK A *silk* made from the cocoons of wild silkworms, and beige or light brown in its undyed state; also known as Tussah silk.
17TH CENTURY ▷

TUXEDO See *Dinner jacket*.

TWEED A rough *wool* cloth originating in Scotland, in a plain or *twill weave*, sometimes with a *checked* or *herringbone* pattern.
1825 ▷: SEE PP.217, 284–285

TWILL A type of *weave* with a pattern of diagonal *ribs*, formed when *weft* thread crosses over one or more *warp* threads and under two or more in a stepped fashion; also a fabric woven in this way.
SEE P.463

TWINSET A matching set of a light, sleeveless *sweater* and *cardigan* in the same fabric, usually *knit wool*, worn by women.
1920s ▷

TYRIAN PURPLE Natural deep purple dye obtained from the Murex mollusk; prized by ancient Phoenicians, Greeks, and Romans for its resistance to fading; expensive status symbol.
ANTIQUITY: SEE PP.38–39

TYROLEAN COSTUME Fashion inspired by traditional Austrian dress, such as *embroidered blouses* and Tyrolean hats.
1930s ▷: SEE PP.273, 299

TYROLEAN HAT A *felt* hat similar to a *fedora*, with a tapering crown, a brim turned up at the sides, and a feather cockade on one side; often moss green in color.
1860s ▷: SEE P.446

U

UGG BOOTS Traditional Australian soft *sheepskin* boots, originally worn by sheep-farm workers and as utility slippers; later popularized by surfers in the US to become a global fashion.
EARLY 20TH CENTURY ▷

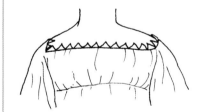

ULSTER A long, double-breasted overcoat for men, made of Donegal *tweed*, with a half or full belt.
1869 ▷

UNDERPROPPER Wired frame designed to support an Elizabethan *ruff*; tied to the inside of the *bodice*; also called a *supportasse*.
16TH CENTURY: SEE P.99

UNISEX CLOTHING Garments that can equally well be worn by men or women, such as *jeans* and *T-shirts*.
1960s ▷: SEE P.359

UTILITY CLOTHING A plan brought in by the British government during the period of austerity caused by World War II, in which a limited range of clothes was produced in styles that economized on the use of fabric and *notions*.
1941–1951: SEE PP.304–305

V

VAMP The front part of the upper on a shoe, covering the toes.

VANDYKING A decorative border of fabric or *lace*, with a series of V-shaped points, used as trimming on a garment; named after 17th-century styles painted by Paul van Dyk.
1750s ▷: SEE PP.174, 179

VARIEGATED Term describing fabric that has streaks, marks, or patches of various colors.

VELOUR A smooth plush fabric made of *cotton*, *wool*, or synthetic fiber, like *velvet* but with a shorter *pile*.
19TH CENTURY ▷

VELVET A *silk* or synthetic fabric with a short, dense *pile*, formed by weaving an extra set of looped *warp* threads into the fabric and then cutting them level, to give a soft, lustrous surface.
MEDIEVAL ▷

Cheongsam

Chinese woman wearing a *cheongsam*
The *cheongsam* (or qipao) is a style that originated in Shanghai in the 1920s. It was based on an old, loose-fitting style that was modified under European influence.

Jeogori

Chima

Korean woman in traditional dress
Women's hanbok, or traditional dress, in Korea consists of a long-sleeved blouse, or jeogori, and a long, full skirt, called a chima, worn with an underskirt.

Choli

Sari

Woman in Indian dress
Despite the variety in women's traditional dress in India, the *sari* is the most widespread garment. Each region's *sari* has its own draping style and material.

Kurta

Dhoti

Jutti

Man from West Bengal, India
The *kurta* and *dhoti* combination is a traditional men's dress worn in many parts of India, mostly for festivals. The style of draping the *dhoti* varies across regions.

VELVETEEN A fabric made to imitate *velvet*, with a *silk pile* on a *cotton* ground, or made entirely of cotton.
LATE 18TH CENTURY ▷

VENETIANS *Breeches* that were usually widest at the hips and sometimes padded with *bombast*, and narrowed toward the knees.
c.1570–1620: SEE P.105

VENT A vertical slit partway up the side or back seam of a coat or *jacket* to give ease of movement.
15TH CENTURY ▷

VEST Another name for *waistcoat*.
19TH CENTURY ▷

VESTMENTS *Robe* or *gown* worn to signify rank; worn by clerics of the Christian Church and others conducting services; based on everyday clothing of the 1st century CE.
MEDIEVAL ▷: SEE PP.56–57

VINTAGE CLOTHING Garments and accessories from previous eras, obtained for wearing or display, or collected as memorabilia.
LATE 20TH CENTURY ▷: SEE PP.408–409

VISCOSE Another name for *rayon*.
20TH CENTURY ▷

VOILE A sheer, lightweight fabric with a crisp surface finish, mainly made of *cotton* but also made of *silk* or synthetic fibers.
1885 ▷

VOLANT A small frill or *flounce* with wavy edges, used as trimming.
19TH CENTURY ▷

W

WAISTBAND The band encircling the waist at the top of lower-body garments such as pants and skirts.

WAISTCOAT Formerly a waist-length undercoat worn with a *doublet* or coat; today a vest; sleeveless garment worn with a coat or *jacket* on formal occasions, or as a decorative feature.
16TH CENTURY ▷: SEE PP.151, 155, 210

WAIST SEAM The seam running around the center of a formal coat or dress, joining the body to the skirts.

WARP The long threads running vertically on a loom, parallel to the *selvage*, creating the lengthwise grain of woven fabric; see also *Weft*.

WATERED FABRICS A term for fabrics that have a rippled pattern like a watermark on the surface, made by applying heat, moisture, and pressure; see *Tabby*, *Moiré finish*.

WATTEAU PLEATS A revival of the 18th-century *sack back* style, named for the dresses seen in paintings by 18th-century French artist Jean-Antoine Watteau.
c.1850–EARLY 20TH CENTURY: SEE P.117

WEAVE A term for the way in which the *warp* and *weft* are interwoven in a cloth; the basic types are plain (one *weft* thread crossing over one *warp* and under the next), *twill*, and *satin*.

WEDDING DRESS The bride's dress, typically white (made popular by the wedding of Queen Victoria in Britain in 1840); styles have usually been the "best dress" for the era, or, more recently, evening or Victorian-style dresses, or unusual styles and colors (such as pink).
19TH CENTURY ▷: SEE PP.189, 200, 320–321

WEDDING SUIT The groom's formal suit; an outfit of *morning coat* with striped pants, *vest*, and pale top hat became popular around 1920; a tuxedo is now more common formal wedding wear.
19TH CENTURY ▷

WEDDING VEIL The bridal veil, made popular after the British Queen Victoria wore a long *lace* veil for her wedding in 1840; 20th-century veils were often made of *tulle*, and various styles were adopted, but many reached to the waist or below.
19TH CENTURY ▷: SEE P.200

WEDGE-SOLED SHOES High-heeled shoes popularized by Italian designer Salvatore Ferragamo, in which the sole forms one triangular piece, often made of cork, wood, or plastic.
1930s ▷: SEE PP.305, 376

WEFT The horizontal threads that are interlaced with the *warp* as a cloth is being woven, and which create the crosswise *grain* in a fabric.

WELT (a) In shoe making, a strip of leather or other material sewn around the border between the upper and insole, to which the sole is attached; (b) a strengthened or raised border on a garment.

WHALEBONE Flexible cartilaginous material (baleen) from the upper jaw of a whale, used for *boning* in stays, *corsets*, and *bodices*.
MEDIEVAL–20TH CENTURY

WHEEL FARTHINGALE A wheel-shaped *farthingale* that fit around the waist, often tilted up at the back, and extended the skirts of a dress to form a cylinder shape.
1580–1620s

WHITE WORK A term for any kind of *embroidery* using white or undyed thread on a background of the same color, such as *broderie anglaise*.

WIG A headdress made of human or artificial hair, worn to conceal baldness or for decoration; wigs became a particular feature of dress in the 17th and 18th centuries, such as the *full-bottomed wig* worn by English King Charles II.
ANTIQUITY ▷: SEE PP.136–137, 150–153

WIMPLE A veil worn by medieval women, covering the head, neck and sides of the face; later adopted by nurses and nuns.
13TH CENTURY ▷: SEE P.158

WINDSOR KNOT A way of tying a necktie in which the wider end of the tie is wrapped around the

WEAVES

PLAIN WEAVE   SATIN WEAVE   TWILL WEAVE

narrower end and passed through the neck loop twice, producing a wide, symmetrical, triangular knot.
20TH CENTURY ▷: **SEE P.286**

WING COLLAR A *stand collar* on which the two points are bent outward; still worn by men on formal occasions.
19TH CENTURY ▷: **SEE PP.225, 289, 439**

WINKLEPICKERS A style of shoe or boot with very long, pointed toes, worn by both men and women, for example as part of the *mod style*.
1950s ▷

WOGGLE A loop or ring of wood, leather, or cord, through which the ends of a neckerchief are threaded; most typically worn by Boy Scouts and Girl Guides.
1930s ▷

WOOL Fiber collected from the fleece of sheep and similar domesticated animals, which has been used for thousands of years to make a variety of fabrics, and usually *knit*, woven, or matted to make *felt*.

WORSTED A *yarn* made from long strands of *wool* or other fibers that are combed (see *Combing*) and tightly twisted to make a smooth, woven fabric; or smooth fabric made from these yarns.
MEDIEVAL ▷

WRAPAROUND Any garment that is wrapped around the body and tied on, such as a *sarong*; also a classic dress by American designer

Diane von Furstenberg, the "wrap dress," wrapped around the body and tied with a belt of the same fabric.
1950s ▷: **SEE PP.323, 345**

X, Y

YARMULKE A Yiddish word for the skull-cap (called a kippah in Hebrew) worn by male Orthodox Jews at all times, and by other male Jews during prayer and on religious occasions.
TRADITIONAL

YARN Natural or synthetic fibers spun and twisted to make a thread for weaving or *knitting*.

Y-LINE A fashion created by French designer Christian Dior, which featured dramatic necklines and shoulder details that drew attention to the upper body; see also *A-line*.
1955: **SEE P.319**

YOUTHQUAKE A term coined by *Vogue* magazine editor Diana Vreeland to describe the impact of youth culture on 1960s fashion, and particularly linked to style icons such as teenage model Twiggy and young designers Mary Quant and Betsey Johnson; see *Mod style*, *Miniskirt*, *Shift dress*.
1960s: **SEE PP.361, 354–357**

YOKE A fitted piece from which lower parts of a garment hang, encircling the neck and shoulders on a shirt or coat, or encircling the waist on some types of skirt.

YUKATA An informal type of *kimono*, usually made of *cotton* and worn in summer, or worn as a covering at public baths.

Z

ZAZOU STYLE The French version of the *zoot suit*, but worn with narrow rather than baggy pants.
1940s ▷: **SEE P.302**

ZOOT SUIT A suit *comprising* high-waisted, wide-legged pants tapered at the ankle, and a long *jacket* with wide shoulders and lapels; introduced by Mexican-Americans and popular with African-Americans and rebellious youth.
1930s–1950s: **SEE P.341**

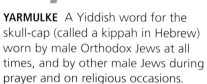

ZOUAVE JACKET A woman's *jacket* of *velvet* or *silk* with an open front that curved diagonally from the neck; named for the Algerian Zouave troops of the French army.
LATE 19TH CENTURY

Hula dancer, Hawaii, US
This dancer wears the traditional Hawaiian *lei* and *grass skirt*. The giving and wearing of *lei* can have many meanings, often symbolizing respect, affection, or rank.

Lei

Grass skirt

Maori warrior, New Zealand
The main elements of Maori men's dress are the piupiu flax skirt and ta moko traditional tattooing. Each tattoo represents the wearer's ancestry or tribe.

Ta moko

Piupiu

INDEX

Entries or page numbers in **bold** type refer to chapter headings, features, or boxes.

ACKNOWLEDGMENTS

The publisher would like to thank the following for their kind permission to reproduce their photographs:

(Key: a-above; b-below/bottom; c-center; f-far; l-left; r-right; t-top)

2-3 Corbis: Condé Nast Archive. **4 Fotolia:** Yuri Arcurs (l). **Getty Images:** DEA / G. Nimatallah / Votive relief with Artemis before god, Kephisos or Cephisus, river god, and three nymphs (r). **5 akg-images:** Sultane, (Jeanne Antoinette Poisson, Madame de Pompadour) by Charles André van Loo, Musée des Arts Décoratifs, Paris (r). **Corbis:** Gianni Dagli Orti / Detail of Bayeux Tapestry - Fortification Construction Underway at Hastings, Musée de la Tapisserie Bayeux (l). **Getty Images:** The Bridgeman Art Library / Ball at the Court of King Henri III of France or Ball of the Duke of Alencon, French School, Louvre Paris (c). **6 Corbis:** Condé Nast Archive (c); The Art Archive / Empress Eugenie of France with ladies of her court by Franz Xaver Winterhalter, Château de Compiègne (l). **Rex / Shutterstock:** MGM (r). **7 Corbis:** Condé Nast Archive (l). **Getty Images:** Niklas Halle'n / AFP (tr). **Rex by Shutterstock:** Paul Massey (r). **TopFoto.co.uk:** Colin Jones (c). **8-9 Corbis:** WWD / Condé Nast. **10 Getty Images:** The Bridgeman Art Library, London / Empress Theodora with her court of two ministers and seven women, detail San Vitale, Ravenna, Italy. **12-41 Getty Images:** Datacraft (t). **12-13 Fotolia:** Yuri Arcurs. **12 Alamy Stock Photo:** The Art Archive (cra). **Corbis:** Nathan Benn (cr); Frans Lemmens (bc). **13 Alamy Stock Photo:** The Art Archive / Men worshiping bare-breasted goddess, Minoan fresco, Heraklion Museum, Crete (c). **Dorling Kindersley:** The Trustees of the British Museum (cra, br). **Getty Images:** DEA / C. Moessner / Detail from Etruscan black-figure amphora depicting the Judgment of Paris, ; Staatliche Antikensammlung, Munich, Germany (crb); DEA / G. Dagli Orti / Detail antechamber fresco, Queen Nefertari playing Senet, Tomb of Nefertari, Egypt (bl). **14 akg-images:** Erich Lessing / Scythian rider, detail; carpet found Pasyryk, Kurgan 5 tomb, Ostaltai Mountain. State Hermitage, St Petersburg (bc). **Dorling Kindersley:** Bronze horned helmet, Iron Age / The Trustees of the British Museum (bl). **Getty Images:** DEA / M. Carrieri / Bronze statuette of tribe chief wearing a cloak, with a sword and a stick, from Mount Arcosu, Uta, Museo Archeologico Nazionale, Sardinia (r). **15 Alamy Stock Photo:** Ancient Art & Architecture Collection Ltd / Scythian Persian archer and trumpet by Psiax, detail (tc). **Bridgeman Images:** Boltin Picture Library / Dancer of goddess Demeter, Scythian, made of gold (tl). **Corbis:** Bettmann / A detail of the Stele of Ur-Nammu showing King Ur-Nammu making an offering to the moon god Nannar. (bl); Keren Su / Terra-cotta warrior with color still remaining, Emperor Qin Shihuangdi's Tomb, Xian, Shaanxi, China (bc). **Getty Images:** DEA / A. Dagli Orti (tr); The Bridgeman Art Library, London / Gold lunula, found Ross C. Westmeath Eire, National Museum of Ireland, Dublin (br). **16 Bridgeman Images:** Harvard University, Museum of Fine Arts Expedition / Beadnet dress, from Tomb G 2342 D (now G 5520 D) Giza, Old Kingdom (faience), Museum of Fine Arts Boston, Mass. (bl). **Corbis:** Sandro Vannini / Small standing statuette of a priest found in Saqqara in 1872, Egypt (br). **Getty Images:** DEA / A. Jemolo / Wood sculpture of female offering bearer from Thebes, Egypt (t); DEA / G. Dagli Orti / Detail antechamber fresco, Queen Nefertari playing Senet, Tomb of Nefertari, Egypt (bc). **17 Corbis:** Gianni Dagli Orti / detail fresco, Scribe Offering Flowers to the God of the West, Egypt (bl). **Dorling Kindersley:** Ancient Egyptian bracelet depicting the god Horus as a child, made for Prince Nemareth, British Museum. / The Trustees of the British Museum (cr, crb); An ancient Egyptian golden ringed "collar of honor" / The Trustees of the British Museum (cr, crb). **Getty Images:** DEA / S. Vannini / Tutankhamun and wife Ankhesenamon protected by solar disk on throne, from Treasure of Tutankhamun, Egypt (tl); DEA / A. Dagli Orti / Detail of the Book of the Dead of Heruben, Egypt (bc); DEA / G. Dagli Orti / Mural of prince and wife at Tomb of Senneferi detail, Shaykh 'Abd al-Qurnah, Ancient Thebes, Egypt (cra). **18 Getty Images:** AFP / Bust of Queen Nefertiti of Egypt is on display at Neues Museum, Berlin 2011 (cl); The Bridgeman Art Library, London / Female torso, probably Queen Nefertiti, Louvre, Paris (c). **19 Corbis:** Relief of a royal couple in the Armana style, Agyptisches Museum und Papyrussammlung. **20 Corbis:** Scott Smith / Faience figurine of the "Snake Goddess", found Knossos, Heraklion Archeological Museum, Crete (tr); Jean-Pierre Lescourret / Fresco from Thira at the National Archaeological Museum, Athens, detail (bc); Gianni Dagli Orti / Sarcophagus of Hagia Triada: Libation and Ritual Offerings to the Deceased, detail (br). **Getty Images:** Danita Delimont / Minoan ear pendant, Greece (bl). **21 Alamy Stock Photo:** The Art Archive / Men worshiping bare-breasted goddess, Minoan fresco, Heraklion Museum, Crete (tl). **Corbis:** Scott Smith / Faience figurine of the "Snake Goddess", found Knossos, Heraklion Archeological Museum, Crete (tr); Gianni Dagli Orti (bl); National Geographic Society / Maynard Owen Williams / Fresco of a Minoan Priest King at Knossos (br). **22-23 Corbis:** Wolfgang Kaehler / Minoan fresco of The Blue Ladies, found Palace of Knossos. **23 Fotolia:** Yuri Arcurs (r). **24 Corbis:** Ruggero Vanni / The Charioteer of Delphi by Pythagoras of Samos (br). **Getty Images:** DEA / G. Dagli Orti / Red-figure pottery, skyphos by Hieron the potter, detail with the capture of Briseis ; Red-figure pottery, skyphos by Hieron the potter, detail with the capture of Briseis (bl). **25 Corbis:** Araldo de Luca / Greek Statue of Woman from Tanagra (bl). **Getty Images:** DEA / G. Dagli Orti / Attic amphora black-figure pottery, detail from Vulci, Italy (tl, br); De Agostini / Red-figure pottery, Epinetron by Eretria Painter depicting woman at her toilet, detail (cr); Leemage / Universal Images Group / The Charioteer of Delphi by Pythagoras of Samos, detail, National Archaeological Museum, Athens, (bc); DEA / G. Dagli Orti / Statue of a lady, Kore, Acropolis Museum, Athens (tl, br). **26 Fotolia:** Yuri Arcurs (l). **26-27 Getty Images:** DEA / G. Nimatallah / Votive relief with Artemis before god, Kephisos or Cephisus, river god, and three nymphs. **28 Brendan Donovan:** Terracotta soldier, Heraklion Museum of Archaeology, Crete (r). **Getty Images:** DEA / G. Nimatallah / Feathered fabric headdress, from Peru, Chimu culture, Museo Preistorico Etnografico Pigorini, Rome (bl); DEA / M. Carrieri / Small bronze votive statue representing a warrior (or perhaps Mars) National Archaeological Museum, Florence (bc). **29 Alamy Stock Photo:** David Levenson / Gundestrup Cauldron in the Danish National Museum, Copenhagen, detail (tc); The Art Gallery Collection / Helmet fragment from Sutton Hoo Treasure, British Museum (bc); UK Alan King / Scottish stone warrior, gravestone West Highlands of Scotland (br). **Corbis:** Alfredo Dagli Orti / The Art Archive / Side View of West Pediment Sculpture from Temple of Aphaia (tl). **Dorling Kindersley:** Ancient Greek bronze muscled cuirass / The Trustees of the British Museum (cra). **Getty Images:** DEA Picture Library / Etruscan-Corinthian alabastron depicting a warrior figure, painted by the Pescia romana Painter, British Museum London (bl). **30 Corbis:** Asian Art & Archaeology Inc. / Western Han Dynasty Oil Lamp with Kneeling Servant Girl (bl); Lebrecht Music & Arts / Xuanzang returning from his pilgrimage to India to recover Buddhist texts (bc); Masked Caucasoid mummy from Tarim Basin, Xinjiang, Uygur utonomous Region, Bureau of Cultural Heritage, China (br). **Getty Images:** The Bridgeman Art Library / detail from transporting ceramics (painted silk), Topkapi Palace Museum, Istanbul (tr). **31 Alamy Stock Photo:** TAO Images Limited (c). **Corbis:** Asian Art & Archaeology Inc. (tr); Tibor Bognar (bl, br); Tibor Bognar / Sassanian bas-reliefs, Taq-é Bostan, Kermanshah, Iran, detail (bl, br). **Getty Images:** The Bridgeman Art Library / detail from transporting ceramics (painted silk), Topkapi Palace Museum, Istanbul (tl). **32 Corbis:** Charles & Josette Lenars / A mural painting on the wall of an Etruscan tomb in Tarquinia, Rome, detail (tc); Charles Lenars / Detail of a Woman from Tomb of the Jugglers Fresco Cycle, Tarquinia, Rome (bc). **Getty Images:** DEA / G. Nimatallah (clb); DEA / G. Dagli Orti (bl). **33 Corbis:** Reuters / A detail from an Etruscan vase is shown at the Etruscan Museum in Rome 2005 (bl); Alfredo Dagli Orti / The Art Archive / Detail of Tomb of the Augurs at Tarquinii, Italy (bc); Gianni Dagli Orti / Statuette of the Etruscan Goddess Turan (r). **Getty Images:** DEA / G. Nimatallah / Detail showing crowned Dionysus and Ariadne, red-figure pottery, Krater, from Civita Castellana, ancient Falerii, Rome province, Italy (tc). **34 Alamy Stock Photo:** The Art Archive / Detail of a marble statue of a woman of imperial period from Aptera, Archaeological Museum Istanbul (cla). **Corbis:** Bettmann / Portrait of Aulus Gabinius from Herculaneum (bl); Steven Vidler / Eurasia Press / Detail of fresco painting in House of the Vettii, Pompeii (br). **35 Alamy Stock Photo:** Peter Barritt / Hunting mosaic Villa Romana del Casale, Piazza Armerina Sicily (bl). **Corbis:** Peter Barritt / Detail from fresco depicting Artemis sending a deer to spare the sacrifice of Iphigenia, found in the House of Tragic Poet, Pompeii. National Archaeological Museum, Naples. (bc, br); Peter Barritt / Detail from fresco depicting Argos watching over the Nymph Io, House of Meleager from Pompeii, National Archaeological Museum, Naples. (bc, br). **Getty Images:** Altrendo (tl); DEA / A. Dagli Orti / Fresco portraying Jason and Pelias, Pompeii (tr). **36 Corbis:** Melvyn Longhurst (bc); Alinari Archives / Byzantine Diptych Panel Depicting the Empress Ariadne (r). **Getty Images:** The Bridgeman Art Library, London / Empress Theodora with her court of two ministers and seven women, detail San Vitale, Ravenna, Italy (bl). **37 Alamy Stock Photo:** Adam Eastland Italy / Detail from the mosaic depicting holy virgins bearing offerings to the Virgin, Basilica di Sant Apollinare Nuovo, Ravenna, Italy (bl). **Corbis:** Melvyn Longhurst / Detail from the mosaic of Saint Paul, depicting his flight from Damascus, Cappella Palatina, Palazzo dei Normanni, Palermo, Sicily (tc). **Getty Images:** The Bridgeman Art Library / Detail from the mosaic depicting Emperor Justinian I and his retinue of officials, guards and clergy, San Vitale, Ravenna, Italy (br). **Photo SCALA, Florence:** Ministero Beni e Att. Culturali / Detail from the mosaic of The Samaritan Woman at the Well, Church of Sant' Apollinare Nuovo, Ravenna, Italy (tl). **38 Corbis:** Reuters / Painted reproduction of the statue of Paris the archer, at the National Archaeological Museum in Athens (bl); Sandro Vannini / Detail of Mummy Mask of a Woman Wearing a Flower Garland excavated at Meir, Egypt (br). **Getty Images:** DEA / C. Moessner / Detail from Etruscan black-figure amphora depicting the Judgment of Paris, ; Staatliche Antikensammlung, Munich, Germany (tr). **39 Alamy Stock Photo:** www.BibleLandPictures.com / Detail of a wall painting depicting Semite women from Beni Hasan, Egypt (bc). **Corbis:** Mimmo Jodice / Detail from Fresco in the House of Marcus Lucretius Fronto, Pompeii (tl); Gianni Dagli Orti (tc); Frederic Soltan / Detail from the fresco representing the initiation into the cult of Dionysus at the Villa of the Mysteries in Pompeii (br). **Getty Images:** The Bridgeman Art Library / detail from transporting ceramics (painted silk), Topkapi Palace Museum, Istanbul (bl). **40 Bridgeman Images:** British Library / Detail from Cott Tib B V f.5 Peasants tending sheep (ca). **41 Getty Images:** Leemage / Universal Images Group / Detail from marble bas-relief of Ludovisi throne, depicting the birth of Aphrodite, Museo Nazionale Romano, Rome. (br). **42-43 Corbis:** Brooklyn Museum. **44-45 Fotolia:** Yuri Arcurs. **44 Bridgeman Images:** Seat Alinari / From mosaic depicting Christ Crowning King Roger II of Sicily, La Martorana, Palermo, Sicily (br). **Corbis:** Stapleton Collection (c); Bettmann (bc). **Getty Images:** De Agostini (cra). **45 Alamy Stock Photo:** The Art Gallery Collection / Detail of The Depiction of Christ in the Temple, Hans Holbein the Elder (cr). **Bridgeman Images:** British Library / From Roman du Roy Meliadus de Leonnoys, Ms Add 12228 f.202v, Merlin tutoring Arthur (c). **Courtesy of the Portable Antiquities Scheme:** (cla). **46 Alamy Stock Photo:** World History Archive / Detail from painting showing the peoples of the world adoring Otto III, from the Gospels of Otto III. (br). **Corbis:** Brooklyn Museum (bl). **Getty Images:** The Bridgeman Art Library / Detail from Ms Cim.4453 f.42r Holy Roman Emperor Otto III Enthroned, Bayerische Staatsbibliothek, Munich, Germany (bc). **47 Alamy Stock Photo:** The Art Archive / Detail from manuscript Codex Legum Longobardorum depicting Frankish King and Emperor Ludovic (tr); Photos 12 / Detail from The Sacramentary of Metz: a Frankish prince between two ecclesiastics, Snark Archives, France (c). **Bridgeman Images:** Archivo de la Corona de Aragon, Barcelona, Spain / Detail from Lord and vassal, from "Liber Feodorum Major" (bl). **Corbis:** Heritage Images / Wooden carving from Hylestad stave church, Norway, showing scene from the story of Sigurd: Regin the Smith reforges the broken sword, Universitetets Oldsaksamling, Oslo. (tl). **48 Bridgeman Images:** Landes Bibliothek, Filda / Detail from manuscript Aa 21 fol.2v Dedication of the book to Christ, from the Gospel of Countess Judith (tc); British Library / Detail from manuscript Cott Tib C VI f.30v David playing his harp, from the Tiberius Psalter, Winchester (tr, br); British Library / Detail from manuscript Add 33241 f.1v-2 from Encomium of Queen Emma or Gesta Cnutonis, Author offering his book to Queen Emma (tr, br). **Corbis:** Alfredo Dagli Orti / The Art Archive / Detail from De Rerum Naturis: Man Buying a Goose (bl, fbl); Alfredo Dagli Orti / The Art Archive / Detail from De Rerum Naturis: Woman Drawing Water From a Well (bl, fbl). **Getty Images:** Hulton Archive / Detail from an illustration of King Canute and his Queen Aelfgifu, taken from the register of Hyde Abbey. (bc). **49 Alamy Stock Photo:** The Art Archive / Detail from Bayeux Tapestry, depicting English soldier defending a hill at Battle of Hastings, Musée de la Tapisserie Bayeux (bl). **Bridgeman Images:** Bibliotheque Nationale, Paris, France / Detail from Ms Lat 1118 Illustration of a dancer, from the Tropary of St. Martial (tl); Giraudon / Detail from Ms 250 fol.43v St. Radegund on a throne, from the "Life of St. Radegund," Bibliotheque Municipale, Poitiers (r); Private Collection, Photo © Bonhams, London, UK / Collection of Anglo-Saxon and Celtic jewelry including gilt bronze mounts, saucer and cruciform brooches and a Merovingian pendant (br). **50-51 Corbis:** Gianni Dagli Orti / Detail of Bayeux Tapestry - Fortification Construction Underway at Hastings, Musée de la Tapisserie Bayeux . **51 Fotolia:** Yuri Arcurs. **52 Bridgeman Images:** Museum of Fine Arts, Boston, Massachusetts, USA (bl); Glasgow University Library, Scotland / Detail from MS Hunter 229 f.4v Virgo, from the Hunterian Psalter (br). **Corbis:** The Gallery Collection / Detail from Moralia in Job by Pope Gregory the Great, historiated initial R depicting a knight fighting a dragon (r). **53 Bridgeman Images:** Vannes Cathedral, France / Detail from a wedding chest depicting a musician and a dancer (tc); British Library / From "Passionale," f.218v detail of an inhabited initial "T" depicting a man playing a rebec (tr); Bibliotheque Nationale, Paris, France / From Moralia in Job by Pope Gregory the Great, depicting Satan armed with a torch killing two shepherds and their flock and a shepherd announcing the news to Job (br); Glasgow University Library, Scotland / From Hunterian Psalter, Ms Hunter 229 f.8r, depicting Expulsion from Paradise (bc). **Getty Images:** The Bridgeman Art Library / Detail from Liber Feudorum: marriage scene, Archivo de la Corona de Aragon, Barcelona, Spain (tl, bl); The Bridgeman Art Library / From panel door, Church of San Zeno Maggiore, Verona, Italy depicting An Exorcism (tl, bl). **54 Bridgeman Images:** De Agostini Picture Library / From fresco Royal cortege, Isabella of Angoulême and Eleanor of Aquitaine, Chapel of St. Radegund, Chinon, France. **55 akg-images:** (cr). **Bridgeman Images:** Giraudon / From window at Basilique Saint-Denis, France, depicting Moses saved from the water (c, br); Vannes Cathedral, France / Detail from a wedding chest depicting a musician and a dancer (bl); Giraudon / From St. Clotilda and Clovis I, from the Church Notre-Dame of Corbeil, Musée des Monuments Francais, Paris (c, br). **56 Bridgeman Images:** British Library / From Luttrell Psalter Add 42130 f.163v Sheep in pen being milked; women walking away bearing vessels (tr); Giraudon / From Liber notabilium Philippi Septimi, francorum regis, a libris Galieni extractus, by Guy of Pavia Ms 334/569 fig.18, Doctor Taking the Pulse of a Patient, Musée Conde, Chantilly (bc). **Corbis:** Alfredo Dagli Orti / The Art Archive / From Apse Mosaic of San Clemente, Rome (tc); Heritage Images / From manuscript depicting Dyers immersing bolt of cloth in vat of dye placed over a fire, British Museum, London (bl). **Getty Images:** The Bridgeman Art Library / From Historia Naturalis, depicting Pliny the Elder, detail of frontispiece to Book I, Biblioteca Marciana, Venice (br). **57 Alamy Stock Photo:** The Art Archive / From Moralia in Job by Saint Gregory, Saint GREGORY offering his book to Bishop Leander, folio 5R, Bibliothèque Municipale, Dijon (br). **Bridgeman Images:** Alinari / From fresco in Palazzo Pubblico, Siena, Effects of Good Government in the Countryside (c); Seat Alinari / From fresco in San Giacomo, Castelaz, Termeno, St. James Entering a House during a Meal, from the Story of St. James (bl). **Corbis:** Gianni Dagli Orti / From Breviaire d'Amour, French Breviary Illumination of the Month of March (tl); David Lees (tr). **58 Bridgeman Images:** Archives Charmet / From Ms Grec 2144 Apocauchus, Bibliothèque nationale de France, Paris (bl); Index / Miniature in a book of music from the Cantigas of Alfonso X the Wise,

4-0633321/1 A Moor and a Christian playing the ɘ, Monasterio de El Escorial, El Escorial (r). **59** **g-images:** Erich Lessing / Coronation robe of ger II, detail showing lion's head, Treasure amber, Palermo (br). **Bridgeman Images:** Index rom Book of Games, Chess, Dice and Boards, onso X, The Wise, King of Leon and Castile aying a game of chess. Biblioteca Monasterio del corial (tl); Krakjeva Crkva, Studenica Monastery, rbia / From fresco in the King's Church, depicting e presentation of the Virgin in the Temple (tc); at Alinari / From mosaic depicting Christ owning King Roger II of Sicily, La Martorana, lermo, Sicily (tr); Giraudon / From The Book of alila and Dimna from The Fables of Bidpay, l.101 A Woman Beseeching the Sultan, Egyptian ational Library, Cairo (bl); The Israel Museum, rusalem, Israel / From Birds' Head Haggadah (bc). **0 Bridgeman Images:** Vatican Library, Rome / om De Arte Venandi cum Avibus, Pal Lat 1071 ederick II, Two horsemen with falcons (b). **60-61** **etty Images:** Leemage / Universal Images Group / iniature from the Decretals, compiled by Giovanni Andrea under the direction of Pope Gregory IX, ibliothèque Municipale, Laon, France (tc). **61 akg-nages:** Album / Oronoz / Pellote de Infanta don ernando de la Cerda, Burgos (tr). **Bridgeman nages:** De Agostini Picture Library / From a iniature from Tristan, by Gottfried von Strassburg, ing Mark exiles Tristan and Isolde and King Mark nds Tristan and Isolde sleeping in a cave, ayerische Staatsbibliothek, Munich (bl); Pierpont Morgan Library, New York (br). **Corbis:** Gianni Dagli Orti / From Book of Games by Alfonso X, the King of Spain, detail depicting two ladies playing chess bc). **64 Bridgeman Images:** British Library / From uttrell Psalter, Add 42130 fol.76v, A King and Lady eated in a garden playing a board game resembling backgammon (tc, tr, br); British Library / From Golden Haggadah, Barcelona, Add 27210 f.15r, Preparations for the Passover (tc, tr, br); Giraudon / From Le Roman de la Rose, le testament, by Jean de Meung, Ms 482/665 f.1, The Lover Sleeping, Dressing, Sewing his Sleeve and Standing at the House of Love's Pleasure, Musée Condé, Chantilly (bl); British Library / From Dream of the Orchard Keeper, Roy 19 C IV f.298. Charles V enthroned in the garden with crown and scepter (tc, tr, br). **Getty Images:** The Bridgeman Art Library / Detail of two falconers, from the Stag Room, Palais des Papes, Avignon (bc). **65 Bridgeman Images:** Giraudon / From Ms Fr 1584 f.D The author receiving Love who brings to him Sweet Thoughts, Pleasure and Hope, Bibliothèque nationale de France, Paris (tl); British Library / From Roman du Roy Meliadus de Leonnoys, Ms Add 12228 f.202v, Merlin tutoring Arthur (bl, r); British Library / From St. Alban's Chronicle, Cotton Nero D VII fol.7 Queen Matilda holding a charter (bl, r). **Getty Images:** The Bridgeman Art Library / Medieval leather shoes, Museum of London (br). **66-67 Corbis:** Heritage Images / April from Les Tres Riches Heures du Duc de Berry, Musée Condé, Chantilly. **66 Fotolia:** Yuri Arcurs (l). **68 Alamy Stock Photo:** The Art Archive / From Bayeux Tapestry, Norman archer at the Battle of Hastings, Musée de la Tapisserie Bayeux (bc, tr); The Art Archive / From Manesse Codex, Walther von Klingen and Ulrich von Liechstenstein, noble German knights, jousting in a tournament, University Library Heidelberg (bc, tr). **Bridgeman Images:** British Library / From Cotton Nero D VI fol.31 Edward III granting the Black Prince the principality of Aquitaine (br). **69 Bridgeman Images:** British Library / From Westminster Psalter, Roy 2 A XXII f.220 Kneeling crusader with his horse behind him (tc). **Corbis:** Heritage Images / Manuscript illustration of a joust between Jean Chalons, an Englishman, and Loys de Beul of France at Tours, Royal Armouries Museum, Leeds (br). **Getty Images:** The Bridgeman Art Library / From The Temple Pyx, Burrell Collection, Glasgow (tl, tr); The Bridgeman Art Library / From tomb plaque of Geoffrey Plantagenet from the Cathedral of St. Julien, Musée de Tessé, Le Mans (tl, tr); SuperStock / From Capodilista Codex, Knight with Green and White Shields on Red Horse, Biblioteca Civica, Padua (bc). **72 Bridgeman Images:** Alinari / From fresco The Fountain of Life, detail of people arriving and bathing in the fountain, Castello della Manta, Saluzzo (tr); Paul Freeman (bl); Archives Charmet / From Tacuinum Sanitatis, Nouv Acq Lat 1673 fol.18 Harvesting Lemons, Bibliothèque nationale de France, Paris (c); Flammarion / From Roman de la Rose, Ms Fr 12595 fol.27v Bel Accueil Smelling a Rose, Bibliothèque nationale de France, Paris (br). **73 Bridgeman Images:** Osterreichische Nationalbibliothek, Vienna / From Tacuinum Sanitatis, Nova 2644 fol.96v Fencing (tl); Museo Episcopal de Vic, Osona, Spain / Love Scene, detail of paneling from the Penafiel Castle, Valladolid , workshop of Claustro de Silo (tc); National Gallery London / Arnolfini Portrait by Jan van Eyck (bc); Bibliotheque Nationale, Paris, France / From Roman de la Rose, Ms Fr 12595 fol.17 The God of Love Returns the Golden Key (br). **Corbis:** Gianni Dagli Orti / Renaissance manuscript illumination of textile merchants from a Book of Statutes of the Tailors' Guild (tr). **74 Bridgeman Images:** Index / From The Virgin Mary with her classmates showing needlework samplers to their teacher, detail from the Altarpiece of the Virgin and St. George, San Francesco, Vilafranca Penedes, Spain (tc); National Gallery London / Arnolfini Portrait by Jan van Eyck (bl); British Library / From Harl 4431 fol.183 Nine Muses Bathing, from the Collected Works of Christine de Pisan (bc); His Grace The Duke of Norfolk, Arundel Castle / Effigy of Beatrice Fitzalan, wife of the 5th Earl of Arundel, Fitzalan Chapel (tr). **Getty Images:** Leemage / Universal Images Group / From Roman du Chevalier Tristan, by the Master of Charles of Maine Isolde with her Ladies in Waiting, Musée Condé, Chantilly (br). **75 Bridgeman Images:** Alinari / From fresco, The Nine Worthies and the Nine Worthy Women, Castello della Manta, Saluzzo, Italy (tr); Giraudon / From April, Très Riches Heures du Duc de Berry Ms 65/1284 f.4v Courtly figures in the castle grounds, Musée Condé, Chantilly (br). **Corbis:** The Gallery Collection / From The Descent from the Cross by Rogier van der Weyden, Museo del Prado, Madrid (tl). **SuperStock:** Fine Art Images / The Magdalen Reading, detail by Rogier van der Weyden, National Gallery, London (c). **76-77 Photograph by John Chase:** Olive Matthews Collection, Chertsey Museum. **78 Alamy Stock Photo:** Zuma Wire Service (cb). **Bridgeman Images:** The Royal Collection © 2011 Her Majesty Queen Elizabeth II / Portrait of a man in red, Flemish School (cra). **Getty Images:** The Bridgeman Art Library / Man holding an Apple by Raphael, Galleria degli Uffizi Florence (cla); De Agostini / Lady with brocade dress, from The Book of the Tailor, plate 94 (bc). **79 Alamy Stock Photo:** The Art Archive / Cultivation of cochineal insects on prickly pear, Codex Kingsborough, illustrated manuscript, Mexico (cla, ca); Superstock / Laughing Cavalier by Frans Hals, Wallace Collection, London (br); The Art Archive / Pope Pius V at prayer, artist unknown, Santa Corona church Vicenza (cla, ca). **Getty Images:** DEA / A. Dagli Orti / Portrait of Gentlewoman by Unknown Venetian artist (cl). **V&A Images / Victoria and Albert Museum, London:** (bl). **80 Alamy Stock Photo:** V&A Images / Engraving The Ill Assorted Couple by Albrecht Dürer, Victoria & Albert Museum, London (tr). **Bridgeman Images:** Musée Condé, Chantilly / From Devotionary of Queen Juana the Mad Ms 604/1339 f.30v Queen Isabella of Castile (br). **Corbis:** The Gallery Collection / From Portrait of a Lady by workshop of Rogier van der Weyden, National Gallery London (c). **Getty Images:** The Bridgeman Art Library / Portrait of a Lady in Red, Anon, National Gallery, London (cl, bc); The Bridgeman Art Library / From Roman du Saint Graal Ms 527 fol.1r Court Ball, Bibliothèque Municipale, Dijon, France (cl, bc). **81 Alamy Stock Photo:** The Print Collector (tl). **Corbis:** Alinari Archives / Detail of Birth of the Virgin by Domenico Ghirlandaio, Santa Maria Novella, Florence, Italy (tc); Alfredo Dagli Orti / The Art Archive / From couple talking in their bedroom, folio 17R of 1475 French manuscript book of miniatures, Musée Condé, Chantilly (tr); Francis G. Mayer / Courtly Life, or "La Vie Seigneuriale", Musée National du Moyen Age et des Thermes de Cluny, Paris (bl); Historical Picture Archive / Manuscript Illumination Depicting Author Dedicating French Translation of Book to Unknown Woman by Giovanni Boccaccio (br). **82-83 Bridgeman Images:** Giraudon / The Miracle of the Relic of the True Cross on the Rialto Bridge, by Vittore Carpaccio, Galleria dell' Accademia, Venice. **83 Fotolia:** Yuri Arcurs. **84 Bridgeman Images:** British Library / From the Coronation of Richard II to 1387 Vol III by Jean de Batard Wavrin Roy 14 E IV f.244v Duke of Lancaster dines with the King of Portugal (bl). **Corbis:** Francis G. Mayer / From the miracle of Saint Quentin:a thief steals the horse from a priest's stable, ; MR R 825 Louvre, Departement des Objets d'Art, Paris (c, tr); Francis G. Mayer / Courtly Life, or "La Vie Seigneuriale", The Departure for the Hunt Musée National du Moyen Age et des Thermes de Cluny, Paris (c, tr); Stapleton Collection / Woodcut print showing medieval medical practitioners with an injured patient, detail (br). **85 Bridgeman Images:** Giraudon / From Hainaut Chronicles Ms 9242 Philip the Good, Duke of Burgundy, presented with the translation of the Chronicles by Jean Vauquelin, Bibliothèque Royale de Belgique, Brussels (tl); Galleria dell' Accademia, Florence / Frontal from the Adimari Cassone depicting a wedding scene in front of the Baptistry, detail of four men, Giovanni di Ser Giovanni Scheggia (tc); British Library / From Guild Book of the Barber Surgeons of York Eg 2572 f.51v The Four Humors (bl); Hospital Tavera, Toledo, Spain / Portrait of Juan II of Portugal (bc). **Corbis:** Gianni Dagli Orti / Types of Liberality From a French Renaissance Manuscript (br). **Getty Images:** The Bridgeman Art Library / Lorenzo de' Medici, the Magnificent as one of the Three Kings, detail from the Journey of the Magi cycle in the chapel Benozzo di Lese di Sandro Gozzoli, Palazzo Medici-Riccardi, Florence (tr). **86 Bridgeman Images:** Hamburger Kunsthalle, Hamburg, Germany, / Portrait of Mette (Mathildis) von Munchhausen, by Ludger Tom Ring the Younger (t); Musée Condé, Chantilly / From La Coche ou le Debat d'Amour Ms 522/1878 fol.11 Marguerite de Valois presenting her book to Anne de Pisseleu Duchesse d'Etampes (bc). **Corbis:** The Gallery Collection / Jane Seymour by Hans Holbein the Younger, Kunsthistorisches Museum, Vienna (br). **Getty Images:** The Bridgeman Art Library / Portrait of Catherine Parr, Hans the Younger Holbein (bl). **87 Bridgeman Images:** National Gallery London / Portrait of a Lady by Giovanni Battista Moroni (tc); Scuola del Santo, Padua, Italy / The Miracle of the Speech of the Newborn Child by Titian (tr); Prado, Madrid / Portrait of the Empress Isabella of Portugal by Titian (br). **Corbis:** Bass Museum of Art / Flemish Tapestry Tournament (tl). **Getty Images:** The Bridgeman Art Library / Philip II and Mary I by Hans Eworth or Ewoutsz, Trustees of the Bedford Estate, Woburn Abbey (bl); Hulton Archive / From Emperor Maximilian II, his wife Maria of Spain and children Anna, Rudolf and Ernst by Giuseppe Arcimboldo, Portraitgalerie Schloss Ambras, Innsbruck, Austria (bc). **88 Corbis:** Historical Picture Archive / Singers, engraving by Marcantonio Raimondi (bl). **Getty Images:** The Bridgeman Art Library / The Ambassadors by Hans Holbein the Younger, National Gallery London (r). **89 Bridgeman Images:** Staatliche Kunstsammlungen Dresden / Henry, Duke of Saxony by Lucas Cranach the Elder, Gemaeldegalerie Alte Meister, Dresden, Germany (tl); The Royal Collection © 2011 Her Majesty Queen Elizabeth II / Portrait of a man in red, Flemish School (tr). **Corbis:** Alfredo Dagli Orti / The Art Archive / Portrait of King Henry II, French School, Musée Condé Chantilly (bc); Austrian Archives / Archduke Karl II of Austria, Kunsthistorisches Museum (br). **Getty Images:** The Bridgeman Art Library / Archduke Ferdinand of Tirol, son of the Holy Roman Emperor Ferdinand I by Jakob Seisenegger, Kunsthistorisches Museum, Vienna (tc). **90 © Abegg-Stiftung, CH-3132 Riggisberg:** Rüstkammer, Staatliche Kunstsammlungen Dresden, inv. no. i.1, photo: Christoph von Viràg (bl, cb, bc, r). **91 © Abegg-Stiftung, CH-3132 Riggisberg:** Rüstkammer, Staatliche Kunstsammlungen Dresden, inv. no. i.1, photo: Christoph von Viràg (l, crb, tr, cra, cr, br). **92 akg-images:** From Charles V, Holy Roman Empire process through Bologna after the coronation of the Emperor by Hans Burgkmair (tr). **Getty Images:** Hulton Archive (br). **93 Alamy Stock Photo:** Interfoto (tl). **Corbis:** Summerfield Press / Alessandro de' Medici by Giorgio Vasari, Uffizi Gallery, Firenze (tc); Heritage Images / Robert Radcliffe, Earl of Sussex by Marcus Gheeraerts the Younger, Royal Armouries (br). **Getty Images:** The Bridgeman Art Library / Philip II (1527-98) of Spain by Sir Anthonis van Dashorst Mor, Prado, Madrid, (bl). **94 Corbis:** Alinari Archives / Laura da Pola by Lorenzo Lotto, Pinacoteca di Brera, Milan (bl). **Getty Images:** DEA / G. Nimatallah / Anna of Austria, Queen consort of Spain and Portugal (r). **95 Bridgeman Images:** Chatsworth House, Derbyshire, UK / Portrait of an unknown lady by Alonso Sanchez Coello (bl). **Corbis:** The Gallery Collection / Princess Elizabeth, Daughter of James I Attributed to Marcus Gheeraerts the Younger (br). **Getty Images:** Leemage / Universal Images Group / Ann of Denmark, the wife of the Prince elector August of Saxony by Lucas Cranach the Young, Vienne Kunsthistorisches Museum Austria (tc). **96 Bridgeman Images:** Walker Art Gallery, National Museums Liverpool / Queen Elizabeth I - The Pelican Portrait by Nicholas Hilliard . **97 Corbis:** The Art Archive / Queen Elizabeth I of England, copy of "Rainbow" portrait attributed to M. Gheeraerts or Isaac Oliver at Hatfield House, Musée du Château de Versailles (cr); The Gallery Collection / Queen Elizabeth I in Coronation Robes, National Portrait Gallery London (bc); Hoberman Collection / English Gold Pound Coin with Portrait of Queen Elizabeth I (br). **Rex by Shutterstock:** SIPA (c). **98 Corbis:** The Gallery Collection / Self-Portrait with Wife, Isabella Brandt by Peter Paul Rubens, Alte Pinakothek, Munich (bl, bc); The Gallery Collection / Anne of Denmark attributed to Marcus Gheeraerts the Younger, Woburn Abbey (bl, bc). **99 akg-images:** Album / Oronoz / Isabel de Valois by Anthonis Mor, Private Collection Madrid (tr). **Bridgeman Images:** Prado, Madrid / Infanta Isabella Clara Eugenia, daughter of King Philip II of Spain by Anguissola, Sofonisba (tl); Fitzwiliam Museum, University of Cambridge / Elizabeth Vernon, Countess of Southampton, English School (tc); Cowdray Park, Sussex, UK / Frances Howard, Countess of Hertford by Marcus Gheeraerts the Younger (bl); National Trust Photographic Library / Mrs. Penobscot in the manner of Daniel Mytens, The Vyne Hampshire UK (bc); Giraudon / Portrait presumed to be Henrietta Maria of France, French School, Château de Versailles France (br). **100 Corbis:** Arte & Immagini slr / Philip II of Spain by Titian and Workshop, Palazzo Pitti, Florence (tr). **Getty Images:** The Bridgeman Art Library / Don Carlos son of King Philip II of Spain by Alonso Sanches Coello, Kunsthistorisches Museum, Vienna, (c, br); The Bridgeman Art Library / From fresco Invitation to the Dance, by Giovanni Antonio Fasolo, Villa Caldogno-Nordera, Caldogna, Italy (c, br). **101 Corbis:** Burstein Collection / Charles IX of France by Francois Clouet, Musée Condé Chantilly France (bl). **Getty Images:** Leemage / Universal Images Group / Prince elector, August I of Saxony, called the pious by Lucas Cranach the Young, Vienne Kunsthistorisches Museum Austria (tc); The Bridgeman Art Library / Gian Gerolamo Grumelli by Giovanni Battista Moroni, collection of Count Antonio Moroni Bergamo Italy (r). **102-103 Getty Images:** The Bridgeman Art Library / Ball at the Court of King Henri III of France or Ball of the Duke of Alencon, French School, Louvre Paris. **103 Fotolia:** Yuri Arcurs. **104 Corbis:** Fine Art Photographic Library / The Sutherland Portrait of James VI of Scotland by John de Critz the Elder (tr); The Gallery Collection / Edward Sackville, 4th Earl of Dorset by William Larkin, Ranger's House, Blackheath, UK (c). **105 Bridgeman Images:** Private Collection / Edward Somerset, 4th Earl of Worcester from Queen Elizabeth I being carried in Procession (Eliza Triumphans) by Robert Peake (bl). **Corbis:** The Gallery Collection / Portrait of a Man (The Tailor) by Giovanni Battista Moroni, National Gallery London (br). **Getty Images:** Hulton Archive / King Henri III of France by Francois Quesnel, Portraitgalerie Schloss Ambras Innsbruck Austria (tl); The Bridgeman Art Library / A Young Man Leaning Against a Tree Among Roses by Nicholas Hilliard, Victoria & Albert Museum London (tr). **World Digital Library (WDL):** Tailor's pattern from Juan de Alcega, Libro de geometria, practica y traça, (Book on Geometry, Practice and Patterns) c1580. Publ Guillermo Drouy, Madrid http://www.wdl.org/en/item/7333/ (bc). **106 Bridgeman Images:** Galleria Degli Uffizi, Florence / Giuseppe da Porto and his Son Adriano by Veronese (Paolo Caliari) (tr); Private Collection / Photo © Philip Mould Ltd, London / Elizabeth I, "The Hampden Portrait" Anglo-Flemish School (c). **Getty Images:** The Bridgeman Art Library / From the tapestry The Lady and the Unicorn: "Smell," Musée National du Moyen Age et des Thermes de Cluny, Paris (bl, br); The Bridgeman Art Library / Portrait of a Young Girl by Adriaen van der Linde, Private Collection (bl, br). **107 Bayerische Staatsbibliothek:** Kostümbuch – Kopie nach dem Trachtenbuch des Christoph Weiditz - BSB Cod.icon. 342 (tc). **Bridgeman Images:** Staatliche Kunstsammlungen Dresden / Duchess Katharina of Mecklenburg by Lucas Cranach the Elder, Gemaeldegalerie Alte Meister, Dresden (tr); Walters Art Museum, Baltimore, USA / Portrait of Countess Livia da Porto Thiene and her Daughter, Portia by Veronese (l). **Getty Images:** The Bridgeman Art Library / Detail from a portrait of Anne Boleyn English School, Loseley Park, Guildford, Surrey, UK (br). **108 Bridgeman Images:** Walters Art Museum, Baltimore, USA / Kippell's costume book by Niclauss Kippell MS W.477 fol.16 (bc). **Corbis:** The Mariners' Museum / Hand-Colored Engraving by Theodor de Bry After Pictish Woman Warrier by John White (tr). **Getty Images:** The Bridgeman Art Library / Leo X, Cardinal Luigi de Rossi and Giulio de Medici by Raphael, Galleria degli Uffizi, Florence (bl); SuperStock / From Saint Catherine and Saint Marguerite, Flemish School, Louvre Paris (br). **109 Alamy Stock Photo:** The National Trust Photo Library / Queen Elizabeth I by studio of Nicholas Hilliard, Hardwick Hall The Devonshire Collection (tc); The Art Gallery Collection / An Unknown Lady in Fancy Dress also known as The Persian Lady by Marcus Gheeraerts the Younger, Hampton Court Palace, UK (tr). **Bridgeman Images:** Kunsthistorisches Museum, Vienna / From Jane Seymour by Hans Holbein the Younger (br);

Victoria & Albert Museum, London / Richard Sackville, 3rd Earl of Dorset by Isaac Oliver (l). **110 Corbis:** The Gallery Collection / From The Path of Life from The Haywain by Hieronymous Bosch, Museo del Prado (br). **Getty Images:** The Bridgeman Art Library / From Rustic Wedding, detail of people dancing by Pieter the Younger Brueghel, Museum voor Schone Kunsten, Ghent (tr, bl); The Bridgeman Art Library / Leather jerkin, Museum of London UK (tr, bl). **111 Alamy Stock Photo:** The Art Archive / French peasant carrying cheeses and poultry engraving from Habitus praecipuorum popularum, Biblioteca Nacional Madrid (tl). **Bridgeman Images:** Giraudon / Detail from Envy, a part of the Table of the Seven Deadly Sins and the Four Last Things by Hieronymus Bosch, Prado Madrid (tc); Ashmolean Museum / Young English Woman by Hans Holbein the Younger (r). **Getty Images:** DEA / G. Dagli Orti / Spanish peasant woman from Habitus praecipuorum popularum by Jost Amman (bl). **112 Alamy Stock Photo:** The Art Archive / Robe belonging to Ottoman Sultan Beyazid II, Topkapi Museum Istanbul (br). **Corbis:** Burstein Collection / A Turkish Artist Attributed to Gentile Bellini (bl). **Getty Images:** Leemage / Universal Images Group / Selim II 11th Sultan of the Ottoman Empire by Nigari Reis Haydar a.k.a Nakkep, Topkapi Sarayi Museum Library Istanbul (tc). **113 Bridgeman Images:** Private Collection / Hand-colored engraving from Omnium Poene Gentium Imagines by Abraham de Bruyn published in Cologne (br); Museumslandschaft Hessen Kassel / Nicolas de Respaigne by Peter Paul Rubens, Gemaeldegalerie Alte Meister, Kassel, Germany (l). **116-117 Fotolia:** Yuri Arcurs. **116 Getty Images:** Universal Images Group (ca); Hulton Archive (cr). **117 Alamy Stock Photo:** Old Paper Studios (cl). **Corbis:** Stapleton Collection / Madame de Pompadour by Francois Boucher (bl). **Getty Images:** The Bridgeman Art Library (c); Universal Images Group (cr). **V&A Images / Victoria and Albert Museum, London:** (cla, br). **118 Getty Images:** The Bridgeman Art Library / From Willem Van Heythuyzen by Frans Hals, Alte Pinakothek, Munich, Germany (tr). **119 Bridgeman Images:** Everard Studley Miller Bequest / From Sir John Ashburnham by Daniel Mytens, National Gallery of Victoria Melbourne (tl); National Trust Photographic Library / From Sir Alexander Carew by John Hammond, Antony House Cornwall UK (c). **Corbis:** Heritage Images / From Charles I of Great Britain and Ireland by Daniel Mytens the Elder, National Portrait Gallery London (bl). **120 Bridgeman Images:** © Bonhams, London, UK / From Portrait of a Lady by Gerrit van Donck (bl). **Getty Images:** SuperStock / From Presumed portrait of Marchesa Geromina (Spinola-Doria of Genoa) by Sir Anthony van Dyck (r). **121 Bridgeman Images:** © Devonshire Collection, Chatsworth Reproduced by permission of Chatsworth Settlement Trustees / From Christian Bruce Countess of Devonshire and her children by Daniel Mytens (tc); From Saint Margaret of Antioch by Francisco de Zurbaran, National Gallery, London, UK (bl, bc); From Portrait of a woman, by Sir Anthony van Dyck, The Royal Collection © 2011 Her Majesty Queen Elizabeth II (bl, bc); Private Collection, Wassenaar, Netherlands / From Dancing Party by Pieter Codde (tr). **Getty Images:** The Bridgeman Art Library (crb). **V&A Images / Victoria and Albert Museum, London:** Life-size dummy board depicting woman holding a mirror, East Sutton Park Kent UK (tl). **122 Alamy Stock Photo:** V&A Images (l). **Bridgeman Images:** National Trust Photographic Library / A cavalier by Edward Bower, Dunster Castle Somerset UK (c). **123 Getty Images:** DEA / A. Dagli Orti (tr); The Bridgeman Art Library / King Charles I of England out Hunting by Sir Anthony van Dyck, Louvre Paris (c). **124 Alamy Stock Photo:** The Art Archive / From Marguerite of Lorraine, Duchess of Orleans by Anthony Van Dyck, Galleria degli Uffizi Florence (tc). **125 Alamy Stock Photo:** Peter Horree / From Anne Kirke by Anthony van Dyck, Flemish Belgian Belgium (c). **Corbis:** Geoffrey Clements / From Anne, Countess of Clanbrassil by Anthony van Dyck (bl). **126 akg-images:** Memphis Brooks Museum of Art / Henrietta Maria of France Queen Consort of England by Anthony van Dyck (cl); From Henrietta Maria of England - Portrait with lute and dog by Cornelius Johnson and Gerard Houckgeest, Sotheby's 8 March 1989, Lot 24 (br). **Corbis:** Alinari Archives / Henrietta of France, Queen of England by Anthony van Dyck (c); The Gallery Collection / From Queen Henrietta Maria and Her Dwarf, Sir Jeffrey Hudson by Anthony van Dyck (bl). **127 Bridgeman Images:** Wallace Collection, London / Queen Henrietta Maria by Sir Anthony van Dyck. **128 Alamy Stock Photo:** Mary Evans Picture Library / From An English man and two women of the mid-17th century by Malcolm, from an old source, in his Anecdotes of the Manners and Customs of London, page 404 (tr). **Bridgeman Images:** Johnny Van Haeften Ltd., London / From A Conversation in the Street by Jacobus Vrel or Frel Private Collection (bl); From The Virtuous Woman by Nicolaes Maes, © Wallace Collection, London, UK (bc). **Getty Images:** DEA / G. Nimatallah / From Painted image of family in Delft by Pieter de Hooch, Vienna, Austria (br). **129 Bridgeman Images:** The Stapleton Collection / Habit of an Oliverian, English School, Private Collection (tl); From Prince Octavio Piccolomini, 1st Duke of Amalfi as a delegate of the Nuremberg peace congress by Anselmus van Hulle, Deutsches Historisches Museum, Berlin, Germany (r). **Getty Images:** Universal Images Group / From The Courtyard of a house in Delft by Pieter de Hooch (bl). **131 Getty Images:** The Bridgeman Art Library / Portrait of King Charles II by Sir Peter Lely, © Royal Hospital Chelsea, London, UK (tr). **132 Bridgeman Images:** Founders Society Purchase / From A Lady at Her Toilet by Gerard Terborch, Detroit Institute of Arts, USA (tc). **Getty Images:** The Bridgeman Art Library / From Portrait of Marie-Therese of Austria by Charles Beaubrun, Chateau de Versailles, France (tr). **133 Bridgeman Images:** From Anne Hyde, Duchess of York by Sir Peter Lely, Scottish National Portrait Gallery, Edinburgh, Scotland (tl). **134-135 Bridgeman Images:** Tichborne House, Hampshire UK / The Tichborne Dole by Gillis van Tilborgh. **135 Fotolia:** Yuri Arcurs. **136 Alamy Stock Photo:** Timewatch Images / The Old Cloak and Hat Seller, engraving by Marcellus Laroon or Lauron from the "Cryes and Habits of the City of London" (bl). **137 Corbis:** The Art Archive / © Alfredo Dagli Orti / From Charles VI of Habsburg, Holy Roman Empire, Charles III of Austria by Martin Mytens the Younger, Galleria degli Uffizi Florence (bl). **Getty Images:** Leemage / From Portrait of Marin Marais playing a 7 string viola by Andre Bouys, Opera Museum of Paris, France (tr); The Bridgeman Art Library / From The Duke of Marlborough in Garter Robes by, Sir Godfrey Kneller, Blenheim Palace, Oxfordshire, UK (br). **V&A Images / Victoria and Albert Museum, London:** (c). **138 Bridgeman Images:** From Louise de Kerouaille by Sir Godfrey Kneller (r). **Photo SCALA, Florence:** White Images / Marie Adelaide de Savoie, Duchesse de Bourgogne Dauphine of France, Musée du Château de Versailles (bc). **139 Bridgeman Images:** Philip Mould Ltd, London / Thought to be Elizabeth, Duchess of Beaufort by Michael Dahl, Private Collection (bl). **140-141 Museum of London**. **141 Museum of London:** (tl, cl, tc, cra, cr, crb, br). **142 Bridgeman Images:** From Portrait of Miss Elizabeth Hemyng by Arthur Devis, © Geffrye Museum, London, UK (c). **143 Alamy Stock Photo:** V&A Images (tl, bl). **V&A Images / Victoria and Albert Museum, London:** (tc, br, tr); Purchased with the assistance of the Elspeth Evans Bequest (bc). **146 Alamy Stock Photo:** The Art Archive / From Woman with clasped hands by Leclerc and Dupin, Bibliothèque des Arts Décoratifs Paris (bc, tr); The Art Archive / From Woman reading letter, wearing dress à la polonaise (Polish style) of painted fabric by Leclerc and Dupin, Bibliothèque des Arts Décoratifs Paris (bc, tr). **Corbis:** The Print Collector / Miss Calash by George Paston, illustration from "Social Caricature in the Eighteenth Century" (bl); Historical Picture Archive / From Costume Print of Lady's Ball Gown by Desrais and Le Clerc (br). **Getty Images:** De Agostin / From Fashionable clothes by Leclerc and Dupin, Paris, France (tc). **147 Corbis:** Historical Picture Archive / From Lady's Simple Promenade Gown by Palas (l, br, tr); Historical Picture Archive / From Lady's Ball Gown by Le Clerc (l, br, tr); Historical Picture Archive / From A lady's golden gown with a tight bodice and hooped skirt edged with pink gathered frill by Le Clerc (l, br, tr). **Getty Images:** The Bridgeman Art Library / From A Young Woman in a Peignoir with her Hairdresser, plate 31 from "Galerie des Modes et Costumes Francais" by Dupin (tc). **148 Corbis:** The Gallery Collection / Marie Antoinette by Elisabeth Vigee-Lebrun, Château de Versailles. **149 Alamy Stock Photo:** The Art Gallery Collection / Marie Antoinette and her Four Children by Elisabeth Louise Vigee-Lebrun, Château de Versailles (br). **Corbis:** The Gallery Collection / Archduchess Marie Antoinette Habsburg-Lotharingen by Martin Mytens the Younger, Schloss Schonbrunn, Vienna (cr). **Getty Images:** Hulton Archive / Queen Marie Antoinette of France in a fashion plate (c). **Mary Evans Picture Library:** Interfoto / Sammlung Rauch / Queen Marie Antoinette of France in hunting dress by Joseph Krazinger, Schoenbrunn Castle (bl). **150 Bridgeman Images:** Mark Fiennes / From Viscount Tyrconnel with his family by Philippe Mercier, Private Collection (tr); From Andrew Drummond by Johann Zoffany, Private Collection (bl); Giraudon / From Portrait of Charles John Crowle of Crowle Park by Pompeo Girolamo Batoni, Louvre, Paris, France (br). **Corbis:** Historical Picture Archive / From Nobleman's Dress by Le Clerc (c). **151 Bridgeman Images:** © Christie's Images / From Portrait of William Perry with the Colosseum beyond by David Antonio, Private Collection (tl); Giraudon / From Louis-Antoine-Auguste Comte de Chabot and Duc de Rohan by Carmontelle, Musee Conde, Chantilly, France (bl); Archives Charmet / The Salon of Philippe Egalite Duc d'Orleans by Carmontelle/ Private Collection (tc); From Thomas Graham, Baron Lynedoch by David Allan, Yale Center for British Art, Paul Mellon Collection, USA (bc). **152 Alamy Stock Photo:** The Print Collector / Portrait by Unknown Illustration from Social Caricature in the Eighteenth Century With over two hundred illustrations by George Paston pseudonym of Emily Morse Symonds London (r). **Bridgeman Images:** From "And catch the living Manners as they rise," published by Hannah Humphrey by James Gillray, © Courtesy of the Warden and Scholars of New College, Oxford (tc). **Getty Images:** DEA / De Agostini / From The Triumph of Ridicule from an engraving by Almanacby Basset (bl). **153 Bridgeman Images:** The Stapleton Collection / "L'Agiateur du Palais Royal," engraved by Baquoi, plate no.282 from "Galeries des Modes et Costumes Francais" 99:clothing; traditional dress; traditional costume; fashion; illustration; c18th; fashionable; clothes; male; striped waistcoat; dandy; hat; scalloped coat;, Watteau by Francois Louis Joseph/ Private Collection (c); Street Walkers, etched by B. Smith, pub. by S.W. Fores, English School/ © City of Westminster Archive Centre, London, UK (br). **Peter Kennedy:** Turf macaroni etching by Matthew Darly (tl). **Rex / Shutterstock:** Welladay! is this my son Tom?, satirical cartoon of a conservative father shocked by his son's new wig (bl). **Photo SCALA, Florence:** Heritage Images / The St. James's Macaroni by James Bretherton, Guildhall Library & Art Gallery (tr). **156 Alamy Stock Photo:** The Art Gallery Collection / From Mrs Richard Brinsley Sheridan by Thomas Gainsborough (br). **Bridgeman Images:** © The Huntington Library, Art Collections & Botanical Gardens / From Rose Milles by George Romney, Huntington Library and Art Gallery, San Marino, CA, USA (c). **Corbis:** Christie's Images / From Edwin from Dr. Beattie's by Joseph Wright of Derby (tr). **Getty Images:** Peter Barritt / From George Drummond by Thomas Gainsborough, Ashmolean Museum of Art, University of Oxford, Oxfordshire, England (bl). **157 Alamy Stock Photo:** Lebrecht Music and Arts Photo Library / From Mr and Mrs William Hallett ("The Morning Walk") by Thomas Gainsborough (bl). **Bridgeman Images:** From Watkin E. Wynne by William Parry, National Museum Wales (tl). **Corbis:** Historical Picture Archive / From Gentleman in Walking Dress by Le Clerc and Loysard (tr); From Goethe in the Roman Campagna by Johann H.W. Tischbein, Stadel Museum, Frankfurt, Germany (br). **V&A Images / Victoria and Albert Museum, London:** (tc). **158 Corbis:** Gustavo Tomsich / From The Charlatan by Pietro Longhi (bl). **Getty Images:** Hulton Archive / From The Masque (tr). **Rex / Shutterstock:** Dagli Orti / From Meeting at a ball, Bibliothèque des Arts Décoratifs Paris (br). **159 Bridgeman Images:** From The Fair Nun Unmasked by Henry Robert Morland, Leeds Museums and Art Galleries (Temple Newsam House) UK (br). **Getty Images:** Hulton Archive / From The Masque (l, tc); Hulton Archive / From The Masque (l, tc); The Bridgeman Art Library / From The Costume Ball (tr). **Rex / Shutterstock:** Bal de l'opera, or Opera Ball by Jean Francois Bosio (bc). **160-161 akg-images:** Sultane, (Jeanne Antoinette Poisson, Madame de Pompadour) by Charles André van Loo, Musée des Arts Décoratifs, Paris. **160 Fotolia:** Yuri Arcurs. **162 Alamy Stock Photo:** The Art Archive / From Racket player, from The Venetians by Grevenbroeck, Museo Correr Venice (bl). **Corbis:** Bettmann / From Full-Length Portrait of William St. Clair by George Chalmers (r). **163 Alamy Stock Photo:** The Art Gallery Collection / From Mr and Mrs Andrews by Thomas Gainsborough (tl); The Art Archive / From Resting while out hunting, from the Esterhazy Palace in Budapest, Hungary, Artist unknown, National Gallery Budapest (bl, tc); The Art Archive / From Resting while out hunting, from the Esterhazy Palace in Budapest, Hungary, Artist unknown, National Gallery Budapest (bl, tc). **Bridgeman Images:** From The Boy with a Bat by Walter Hawkesworth Fawkes, Breamore House, Hampshire, UK (bc, tr); From Cricket Match Played by the Countess of Derby and Other Ladies, Marylebone Cricket Club, London, UK (bc, tr). **Getty Images:** The Bridgeman Art Library / From John Ward of Squerrie by Arthur Devis (br). **166 Bridgeman Images:** Private Collection / George "Beau" Brummell by Robert Dighton (c). **Getty Images:** Popperfoto (cra); Hulton Archive (bl); Time & Life Pictures (br). **166-167 Fotolia:** Yuri Arcurs. **167 Alamy Stock Photo:** Archivart / Playbill poster Sarah Bernhardt in Gismonda Théâtre de la renaissance by Alphonse Mucha (Alfons Maria) (cr **Corbis:** Sean Sexton Collection (c). **Getty Image** Science & Society Picture Library (cr). **172-173 Get Images:** The Bridgeman Art Library / The Cloakroom, Clifton Assembly Rooms by Rolinda Sharples, Bristol City Museum and Art Gallery. **173 Fotolia:** Yuri Arcurs. **175 Dorling Kindersley:** Judith Miller / Sylvie Spectrum (cr). **182 Alamy Stock Photo:** Mary Evans Picture Library / George Bryan "Beau" Brummell, illustration from Jesse's Li (br). **Bridgeman Images:** Private Collection / George "Beau" Brummell by Robert Dighton (c). **Corbis:** Bettmann / George Brummel after a miniature by John Cook (cl). **183 Alamy Stock Photo:** Mary Evans Picture Library / Beau Brummell A young man asks "Who's your fat friend?" engraving after J. Godwin "The Wits and Beaux of Society". **194-195 Corbis:** The Art Archive / Empress Eugenie of France with ladies of her court by Franz Xaver Winterhalter, Château de Compiègne. **195 Fotolia:** Yuri Arcurs. **196 Getty Images:** Roger Viollet (cl). **Photo SCALA, Florence:** Brooklyn Museum Costume Collection a The Metropolitan Museum of Art, Gift of the Brooklyn Museum, 2009; Gift of Dr. and Mrs. Edward N. Goldstein, 1983 (2009.300.1000a, b) / Art Resource (br). **197 V&A Images / Victoria and Albert Museum, London:** (br). **198 Corbis:** The Gallery Collection / Elizabeth of Bavaria Empress of Austria by Franz Xavier Winterhalter, Bundesmobiliensammlung, Vienna. **199 Bridgeman Images:** Archives Charmet / Visiting card of Charles Frederick Worth in fancy dress, Bibliothèque Nationale de France, Paris (cr); Museum of Fine Arts, Boston, Massachusetts, USA (bc). **Getty Images:** DEA Picture Library (c). **TopFoto.co.uk:** Roger-Viollet (br). **200 V&A Images / Victoria and Albert Museum, London:** Given by Messrs Harrods Ltd (bl). **201 Photo SCALA, Florence:** Brooklyn Museum Costume Collection at The Metropolitan Museum of Art, Gift of the Brooklyn Museum, 2009; Gift of Ethel M. Dixon in memory of her mother, Annie Denton Merritt, 1953 (2009.300.777a–c) / Art Resource (tc). **205 Alamy Stock Photo:** Interfoto (tr). **208-209 Bridgeman Images:** Cincinnati Art Museum, Ohio, USA. **208 Bridgeman Images:** Cincinnati Art Museum, Ohio, USA (tc, tr). **209 Bridgeman Images:** Cincinnati Art Museum, Ohio, USA (tl, ca, tc, tr). **211 Alamy Stock Photo:** Mary Evans Picture Library / German gentleman (c); Thislife pictures (br). **Photo SCALA, Florence:** The Metropolitan Museum of Art / Art Resource / Purchase, The German Fur Federation Gift, 1981 (1981.12.4a–c) (tr). **212-213 Corbis:** The Print Collector. **213 Fotolia:** Yuri Arcurs. **214 Corbis:** Stapleton Collection (bl); Hulton-Deutsch Collection / From Empress Elizabeth of Austria and Bavaria (bc). **Photo SCALA, Florence:** Brooklyn Museum Costume Collection at The Metropolitan Museum of Art, Gift of the Brooklyn Museum, 2009; Dick S. Ramsay Fund, 1956 (2009.300.1900a–c) / Art Resource (tr). **215 Getty Images:** Stock Montage / From Coming Back From A Morning In The Bois by Francois Courboin (tl). **Photo SCALA, Florence:** Brooklyn Museum Costume Collection at The Metropolitan Museum of Art, Gift of the Brooklyn Museum, 2009; Mr and Mrs. Morton Sultzer, 1979 (2009.300.532a–d) / Art Resource (c, tr). **V&A Images / Victoria and Albert Museum, London:** (br). **216 Getty Images:** SSPL (bl); Hulton Archive (bc); Sean Sexton (br). **217 Bridgeman Images:** National Trust Photographic Library / John Hammond / Portrait of George William Henry Venables, 7th Lord Vernon (tc). **Getty Images:** Alinari Archives (tr); Hulton Archive (bc); London Stereoscopic Company (br). **218 Bridgeman Images:** Illustration from "Journal of Luxury and Fashion," French School/ Private Collection (tr, br); A Lady in her Costume Worn at the Eglington Tournament by Edward Henry Corbould/ Private Collection / © Mallett Gallery, London, UK (tr, br). **Getty Images:** Hulton Royals Collection / Lafayette (bl). **219 Bridgeman Images:** Archives Charmet / Fancy dress costume for Mephistopheles, from "L'Art du Travestissement" by Leon Salut, French School/ Bibliotheque des Arts Decoratifs, Paris, France (bl, c); Archives Charmet / Fancy dress costume for a female devil, from "L'Art du Travestissement" by Leon Salut, French School/ Bibliotheque des Arts Decoratifs, Paris, France (bl, c). **222-223 Fotolia:** Yuri Arcurs. **222 Corbis:**

Underwood & Underwood (ca). **Photo SCALA, Florence:** The Metropolitan Museum of Art / Art Resource (br). **223 Corbis:** Bettmann (cb, br). **Getty Images:** Science & Society Picture Library (ca). **224 Alamy Stock Photo:** Mary Evans Picture Library (c). **Corbis:** The Francis Frith Collection (bl). **Getty Images:** Hulton Archive (tr, br). **225 Alamy Stock Photo:** Mary Evans Picture Library (tl, bc, tc); Vintage Images (bl). **Getty Images:** Hulton Archive (r). **226 Alamy Stock Photo:** Mary Evans Picture Library (r). **Corbis:** Hulton-Deutsch Collection (bc). **Getty Images:** (bl). **227 Alamy Stock Photo:** Lordprice Collection (br). **Corbis:** Bettmann (tl); Austrian Archives (tc); Underwood & Underwood (bl). **Getty Images:** Hulton Archive (tr); Roger Viollet (bc). **228 Corbis:** Kirn Vintage Stock (bc). **230 Corbis:** Hulton-Deutsch Collection (c); Bettmann (bl). **Getty Images:** Hulton Archive (tr). **231 Corbis:** Hulton-Deutsch Collection (tl); Bettmann (bl, bc). **232 Getty Images:** Hulton Archive (bl). **Photo SCALA, Florence:** Brooklyn Museum Costume Collection at The Metropolitan Museum of Art, Gift of the Brooklyn Museum, 2009; Gift of the estate of Mrs. Arthur F. Schermerhorn, 1957 (2009.300.1250a, b) / Art Resource (br, tr, c). **233 Getty Images:** Hulton Archive (br). **Photo SCALA, Florence:** Brooklyn Museum Costume Collection at The Metropolitan Museum of Art, Gift of the Brooklyn Museum, 2009; Gift of Rodman A. Heeren, 1959 (2009.300.3196) / Art Resource (tc). **V&A Images / Victoria and Albert Museum, London:** Given by the House of Worth (tl). **234-235 Corbis:** Bettmann. **234 Fotolia:** Yuri Arcurs. **236 akg-images:** (bl). **Getty Images:** (c); Hulton Archive (br). **Mary Evans Picture Library:** Epic (tr). **237 Getty Images:** Hulton Archive (l, tr). **Mary Evans Picture Library:** (tc). **Photo SCALA, Florence:** Brooklyn Museum Costume Collection at The Metropolitan Museum of Art, Gift of the Brooklyn Museum, 2009; Gift of Jane Mead von Salis Funtanella, 1984 (2009.300.551) / Art Resource (bc). **238 Bridgeman Images:** Gift of Mrs. Francis John Rumpf, 1972 / Woman's WW1 American Red Cross Motor Services Uniform: Coat, Breeches, Coat Belt, Belt and Cap with Pin, 1917 (wool & leather), American School, (20th century) / Philadelphia Museum of Art, Pennsylvania, PA, USA (tr). **Getty Images:** Hulton Archive / F. J. Mortimer (br). **239 Getty Images:** Hulton Archive / Topical Press Agency (tl); Hulton Archive (bl); Archive Photos / Buyenlarge / Cover of The Gentlewoman, a patriotic magazine, showing "Miss 1918," a woman in uniform against an American flag background, 1918. Published by WJ Thompson & Company (br). **Photo SCALA, Florence:** The Metropolitan Museum of Art / Art Resource / Purchase, Irene Lewisohn Bequest, 1951 (C.I.51.97.26a–c) (tr); The Metropolitan Museum of Art / Art Resource / Gift of Jane Darlington Irwin, 1981 (1981.523.4a–d) (c). **240 Corbis:** (c). **241 Corbis:** Amanaimages (tc); PoodlesRock (bc). **Photo SCALA, Florence:** Brooklyn Museum Costume Collection at The Metropolitan Museum of Art, Gift of the Brooklyn Museum, 2009; Gift of Mrs. Dail Wolkowitz, 1982 (2009.300.540a–c) / Art Resource (bl). **V&A Images / Victoria and Albert Museum, London:** (tl). **242 Bridgeman Images:** Archives Charmet. **243 Corbis:** (cr). **Photo SCALA, Florence:** Metropolitan Museum of Art Brooklyn Museum Costume (c); The Metropolitan Museum of Art / Art Resource / Purchase, Friends of The Costume Institute Gifts, 2005 (2005.199) (bl); White Images (br). **244 Corbis:** (bl). **V&A Images / Victoria and Albert Museum, London:** Given by Lord and Lady Cowdray (tr). **245 Bridgeman Images:** Bibliothèque des Arts Décoratifs, Paris / Archives Charmet (tl). **Photograph by John Chase:** Olive Matthews Collection, Chertsey Museum (tr). **Corbis:** Philadelphia Museum of Art (bl). **Photo SCALA, Florence:** The Metropolitan Museum of Art / Art Resource (c); Brooklyn Museum Costume Collection at The Metropolitan Museum of Art, Gift of the Brooklyn Museum, 2009; Gift of Mary Cheney Platt, 1966 (2009.300.23a, b) / Art Resource (br). **246 Getty Images:** Hulton Archive (bl). **Photo SCALA, Florence:** The Metropolitan Museum of Art / Art Resource (bc); Brooklyn Museum Costume Collection at The Metropolitan Museum of Art, Gift of the Brooklyn Museum, 2009; Gift of Mrs. V. D. Crisp, 1963 (2009.300.3248) / Art Resource (br). **247 Photo SCALA, Florence:** Brooklyn Museum Costume Collection at The Metropolitan Museum of Art, Gift of the Brooklyn Museum, 2009; Gift of Mrs. Norman W. Wassman, 1956 (2009.300.2802) / Art Resource (tc, tr); The Metropolitan Museum of Art / Art Resource / Gift of Mrs. George Henry O'Neil, 1968 (C.I.68.48a–e) (bc); The Metropolitan Museum of Art / Art Resource (bl). **248 Getty Images.** **249 Alamy Stock Photo:** Pictorial Press Ltd (cr). **Corbis:** DPA (c). **Photo SCALA, Florence:** The Metropolitan Museum of Art / Art Resource / Purchase, Friends of The Costume Institute Gifts, 2005 (2005.114a, b) (bl); The Metropolitan Museum of Art / Art Resource / Gift of Mrs. John Chambers Hughes, 1958 (C.I.58.34.18a–c) (bc). **250 Alamy Stock Photo:** Amoret Tanner (c). **Corbis:** Bettmann (tr); Condé Nast Archive (bl). **Photo SCALA, Florence:** The Metropolitan Museum of Art / Art Resource / Purchase, The New York Historical Society, by exchange, 1984 (1984.28a–c) (br). **251 Alamy Stock Photo:** Mary Evans Picture Library (tc); Lordprice Collection (br). **Corbis:** Bettmann (tl). **Getty Images:** Hulton Archive (bl, tr). **252 Corbis:** Minnesota Historical Society (tr); Hulton-Deutsch Collection (br). **V&A Images / Victoria and Albert Museum, London:** (bc). **253 Corbis:** Hulton-Deutsch Collection (tl); National Geographic Society / Clifton R. Adams (br). **Photo SCALA, Florence:** Brooklyn Museum Costume Collection at The Metropolitan Museum of Art, Gift of the Brooklyn Museum, 2009; Gift of Mrs. Egbert J. Sormani, 1966 (2009.300.400a–c) / Art Resource (bl, tr). **254-255 Corbis:** Condé Nast Archive. **255 Fotolia:** Yuri Arcurs. **256 Photo SCALA, Florence:** Brooklyn Museum Costume Collection at The Metropolitan Museum of Art, Gift of the Brooklyn Museum, 2009; Gift of Mrs. Howard C. Brokaw, 1960 (2009.300.1276) / Art Resource (bl). **257 V&A Images / Victoria and Albert Museum, London:** Given by Lord and Lady Cowdray (tc). **260 Alamy Stock Photo:** Trinity Mirror / Mirrorpix (c). **Corbis:** Bettmann (br, tr, r). **261 Corbis:** National Geographic Society / Clifton R. Adams (bc). **Getty Images:** Hulton Archive (tc, tr). **262 Corbis:** (bl). **Photo SCALA, Florence:** Brooklyn Museum Costume Collection at The Metropolitan Museum of Art, Gift of the Brooklyn Museum, 2009; Gift of Albert Moss, 1967 (2009.300.906a–f) / Art Resource (bc). **V&A Images / Victoria and Albert Museum, London:** (r). **263 Corbis:** Bettmann (tl, bc); John Springer Collection (tr). **Getty Images:** Hulton Archive (tc); Science & Society Picture Library (bl, br). **264 Corbis:** Bettmann (bl); Underwood & Underwood (bc). **265 Corbis:** The Francis Frith Collection (tl); Hulton-Deutsch Collection (tc); Bettmann (bc). **Getty Images:** Hulton Archive (bl). **266 Corbis:** John Springer Collection (c). **Photo SCALA, Florence:** Modello di Tuta (model of overalls) Michehelles Ernesto Thayaht, Michehelles Collection (bl); The Metropolitan Museum of Art / Art Resource (bc). **267 akg-images:** Les Arts Décoratifs, Paris / Jean Tholance (tc). **Getty Images:** Hulton Archive (tr). **Photo SCALA, Florence:** Brooklyn Museum Costume Collection at The Metropolitan Museum of Art, Gift of the Brooklyn Museum, 2009; Gift of Arturo and Paul Peralta-Ramos, 1955 (2009.300.2423a, b) / Art Resource (tl); (bl). **270 Alamy Stock Photo:** Pictorial Press Ltd (bc). **Corbis:** Bettmann (bl). **Getty Images:** Hulton Archive (br). **270-271 Fotolia:** Yuri Arcurs. **271 Alamy Stock Photo:** MPVHistory (ca). **Getty Images:** (cl); AFP (bl); Hulton Archive (bc). **Photo SCALA, Florence:** Brooklyn Museum Costume Collection at The Metropolitan Museum of Art, Gift of the Brooklyn Museum, 2009; Gift of Arturo and Paul Peralta-Ramos, 1954 (2009.300.2785a, b) (br). **273 Bridgeman Images:** The Stapleton Collection (cb). **274 Photo SCALA, Florence:** Brooklyn Museum Costume Collection at The Metropolitan Museum of Art / gift of Mrs. Frederick H. Prince, Jr / Art Resource (bl); The Metropolitan Museum of Art / Art Resource / Gift of Madame Madeleine Vionnet, 1952 (C.I.52.18.4) (bc); Brooklyn Museum Costume Collection at The Metropolitan Museum of Art,Gift of the estate of Mary / Art Resource (r). **275 Corbis:** Bettmann (br). **Photo SCALA, Florence:** Brooklyn Museum Costume Collection at The Metropolitan Museum of Art, Gift of Mrs. Hollis K. Thayer / Art Resource (tl); The Metropolitan Museum of Art / Art Resource (bl, bc, tr). **276 Getty Images:** George Marks (tr); Roger Viollet (bl). **Photo SCALA, Florence:** Brooklyn Museum Costume Collection at The Metropolitan Museum of Art, Gift of the Brooklyn Museum, 2009; Gift of Bettina Ballard, 1952 (2009.300.1174) / Art Resource (c, br). **277 Corbis:** Hulton-Deutsch Collection (tc). **Photo SCALA, Florence:** The Metropolitan Museum of Art / Art Resource / Brenner Couture Inc. Fund, 1978 (1978.278.4) (tr); The Metropolitan Museum of Art / Art Resource / Gift of Mrs. Harrison Williams, 1948 (C.I.48.15.3a, b) (bl); Brooklyn Museum Costume Collection at The Metropolitan Museum of Art, Gift of the Brooklyn Museum, 2009; Gift of Madame Eta Hentz, 1946 (2009.300.119) / Art Resource (bc). **V&A Images / Victoria and Albert Museum, London:** (tl). **278-279 Corbis:** Condé Nast Archive. **278 Fotolia:** Yuri Arcurs. **279 Getty Images:** Hulton Archive (ca). **280 Bridgeman Images:** Private Collection (c). **Corbis:** Bettmann (tr). **Getty Images:** Hulton Archive (br). **281 Getty Images:** Hulton Archive (bc); Science & Society Picture Library (l); Gamma-Keystone (br). **V&A Images / Victoria and Albert Museum, London:** Given by Margaret, Duchess of Argyll and worn by her while she was Mrs. Charles Sweeny (tc). **282 Corbis:** Hulton-Deutsch Collection (c); Bettmann (br). **Getty Images:** Science & Society Picture Library (tr); Hulton Archive (bl). **283 Alamy Stock Photo:** Amoret Tanner (br). **Corbis:** Hulton-Deutsch Collection (bl); Bettmann (bc). **Getty Images:** Science & Society Picture Library (tl, tc, tr). **286 Bridgeman Images:** Royal and Ancient Golf Club of St. Andrew's, Scotland / Edward, Prince of Wales by Sir William Orpen (c). **Corbis:** Hulton-Deutsch Collection (cl, bl); Condé Nast Archive (br). **287 Corbis:** Bettmann. **288 Corbis:** Hulton-Deutsch Collection (bc). **Getty Images:** Hulton Archive (bl); Roger Viollet (br). **TopFoto.co.uk:** (tr). **289 Corbis:** Hulton-Deutsch Collection (bl); Bettmann (r). **Getty Images:** Hulton Archive (tl); (tc). **290 akg-images:** Ullstein bild (tc); (bl). **Getty Images:** Gamma-Keystone (c); Hulton Archive (br). **291 akg-images:** (tl, tr). **Getty Images:** Hulton Archive (bl, br). **292 Alamy Stock Photo:** Trinity Mirror / Mirrorpix (tr). **Photo SCALA, Florence:** The Metropolitan Museum of Art / Art Resource / Gift of Mrs. John Chambers Hughes, 1958 (C.I.58.34.19a, b) (bl); The Metropolitan Museum of Art / Art Resource / Gift of Mrs. Harrison Williams, 1948 (C.I.48.15.1a–c) (bc); Brooklyn Museum Costume Collection at The Metropolitan Museum of Art, Gift of the Brooklyn Museum, 2009; Gift of Mrs. Anthony Wilson, 1963 (2009.300.2522a, b) / Art Resource (br). **293 Corbis:** Bettmann (tr). **Getty Images:** Time & Life Pictures (bl). **Photo SCALA, Florence:** The Metropolitan Museum of Art / Art Resource / Gift of Paulette Winston Zerner, 1964 (C.I.64.21.1) (tl); Brooklyn Museum Costume Collection at The Metropolitan Museum of Art, Gift of the Brooklyn Museum, 2009; Gift of Millicent Huttleston Rogers, 1949 (2009.300.2754) / Art Resource (br). **V&A Images / Victoria and Albert Museum, London:** (c). **294 Corbis:** Philadelphia Museum of Art (tr). **Dorling Kindersley:** Judith Miller (bl, fbl). **Photo SCALA, Florence:** Brooklyn Museum Costume Collection at The Metropolitan Museum of Art, Gift of the Brooklyn Museum, 2009; Gift of the estate of Elinor S. Gimbel, 1984 (2009.300.1008a–c) / Art Resource (br). **V&A Images / Victoria and Albert Museum, London:** (c). **295 akg-images:** Les Arts Décoratifs, Paris / Jean Tholance (tl). **Photo SCALA, Florence:** The Metropolitan Museum of Art / Art Resource / Gift of Mrs. Lawrence W. Snell, 1973 (1973.199.1) (c); Brooklyn Museum Costume Collection at The Metropolitan Museum of Art, Gift of the Brooklyn Museum, 2009; Gift of Mrs. V. D. Crisp, 1963 (2009.300.324) / Art Resource (br); The Metropolitan Museum of Art / Art Resource (bl). **V&A Images / Victoria and Albert Museum, London:** (tr). **296 Corbis:** Bettmann. **297 Bridgeman Images:** Philadelphia Museum of Art, Pennsylvania, PA, USA / Gift of Mme Elsa Schiaparelli, 1969 (br). **Corbis:** Hulton-Deutsch Collection (cr); Philadelphia Museum of Art (bc). **V&A Images / Victoria and Albert Museum, London:** Given by Miss Ruth Ford (c). **298 Getty Images:** Eggit (tc). **299 Corbis:** J. Baylor Roberts / National Geographic Society (bc). **Getty Images:** Planet News Archive / SSPL (br); J. A. Hampton (l). **302 Getty Images:** Hulton Archive (bl); Popperfoto (bc). **303 Getty Images:** Hulton Archive (tc); Gamma-Keystone (bl); Michael Ochs Archives (tr). **304 Getty Images:** Popperfoto (br). **305 Getty Images:** Hulton Archive (tl); (tr). **V&A Images / Victoria and Albert Museum, London:** Given by the Board of Trade, through Sir Thomas Barlow, Director-General of Civilian Clothing (c). **306-307 Rex / Shutterstock:** MGM. **306 Fotolia:** Yuri Arcurs. **308 Corbis:** Bettmann (tr). **Getty Images:** (bl). **Photo SCALA, Florence:** The Metropolitan Museum of Art / Art Resource / Gift of Janet Chatfield-Taylor, 1962 (C.I.62.4.4a, b) (bc); The Metropolitan Museum of Art / Art Resource / Gift of Claire McCardell, 1949 (C.I.49.37.15a, b) (br). **309 Corbis:** Bettmann (tr). **Photo SCALA, Florence:** Brooklyn Museum Costume Collection at The Metropolitan Museum of Art, Gift of the Brooklyn Museum, 2009; Gift of Helen Cookman, 1957 (2009.300.240a–c) / Art Resource (tl, bl); The Metropolitan Museum of Art / Art Resource / Gift of Claire McCardell, 1949 (C.I.49.37.30a–d) (c). **310 Corbis:** Genevieve Naylor (tr); Hulton-Deutsch Collection (br). **Getty Images:** Hulton Archive (bc). **Mary Evans Picture Library:** National Magazine Company (bl). **311 Corbis:** Bettmann (bc, br). **Getty Images:** Hulton Archive (tc, tr). **Photo SCALA, Florence:** The Metropolitan Museum of Art / Art Resource (l). **314-315 Fotolia:** Yuri Arcurs. **314 Corbis:** Bettmann (c, bl); Sunset Boulavard (bc). **315 Corbis:** Bettmann (cra); Sunset Boulavard (c). **Getty Images:** Bob Thomas (bl); Redferns (br). **316 Getty Images:** Pat English (br). **TopFoto.co.uk:** Topham Picturepoint (tr). **317 Getty Images:** Keystone (tr). **Photo SCALA, Florence:** Brooklyn Museum Costume Collection at The Metropolitan Museum of Art, Gift of the Brooklyn Museum, 2009; Gift of Claire Ramsay Roman, 1986 (2009.300.1370) / Art Resource (tl). **V&A Images / Victoria and Albert Museum, London:** (br). **318 Getty Images:** Gamma-Keystone. **319 Corbis:** Condé Nast Archive (cra); Bettmann (c); Reuters (br). **V&A Images / Victoria and Albert Museum, London:** Given by the Baroness Alain de Rothschild (bc). **320 Photograph by John Chase:** Olive Matthews Collection, Chertsey Museum (r, bl, cb). **321 Photograph by John Chase:** Olive Matthews Collection, Chertsey Museum (cra, cr, crb, l, tr, br). **322 TopFoto.co.uk:** Roger-Viollet (c). **V&A Images / Victoria and Albert Museum, London:** (bl, tr). **323 TopFoto.co.uk:** Roger-Viollet (tc). **V&A Images / Victoria and Albert Museum, London:** (tl, bl, br). **324-325 Corbis:** Condé Nast Archive. **325 Fotolia:** Yuri Arcurs. **326 Mary Evans Picture Library:** National Magazine Company (tr). **TopFoto.co.uk:** Roger-Viollet (c). **V&A Images / Victoria and Albert Museum, London:** (bl). **327 Dorling Kindersley:** Judith Miller / William Wain at Antiquarius (crb); Judith Miller / Cristobal (br). **Photo SCALA, Florence:** Brooklyn Museum Costume Collection at The Metropolitan Museum of Art, Gift of the Brooklyn Museum, 2009; Gift of Josephine Abercrombie, 1953 (2009.300.784) / Art Resource (tc). **V&A Images / Victoria and Albert Museum, London:** (bl, tr). **328-329 Mary Evans Picture Library:** National Magazine Company. **329 Alamy Stock Photo:** Allstar Picture Library (br). **Corbis:** Ramon Manent courtesy of Museum of Textil y de la indumentaria, Barcelona (c). **Getty Images:** Roger Viollet (cr). **Mary Evans Picture Library:** National Magazine Company (bl). **330 Bridgeman Images:** (tr). **Photo SCALA, Florence:** Brooklyn Museum Costume Collection at The Metropolitan Museum of Art, Gift of the Brooklyn Museum, 2009; Gift of the estate of Sophy Tepperman, 1978 (2009.300.528a, b) / Art Resource (br). **V&A Images / Victoria and Albert Museum, London:** (c). **331 Bridgeman Images:** Gift of Marilyn M. Maxwell (c). **Corbis:** Bettmann (bl, tr). **V&A Images / Victoria and Albert Museum, London:** (br, tl). **332 Alamy Stock Photo:** Interfoto / fashion, Defaka (department store) fashion catalogue, Germany, 1957, title page, illustration showing Petra Schuermann, Miss World of 1956, advertising, men's fashion, ladies' fashion, tippet, tippets, wool, jacket, coat, hat, handbag, purse, 1950s, 50s, historic, historical, skirt, elegant, elegance, Schurmann, Schuermann (bc). **Corbis:** Blue Lantern Studio / Two Women with Prize Winning Cat (bl). **333 Getty Images:** Art Rickerby (br). **Photo SCALA, Florence:** Brooklyn Museum Costume Collection at The Metropolitan Museum of Art, Gift of the Brooklyn Museum, 2009; Gift of Mr. and Mrs. Robert Zicklin, 1985 (2009.300.555) / Art Resource (c). **334 Dorling Kindersley:** Judith Miller / Wallis and Wallis (ca, bl); Judith Miller / Richard Gibbon (cl). **336 The Advertising Archives:** (bl). **Alamy Stock Photo:** Trinity Mirror / Mirrorpix (br). **337 Alamy Stock Photo:** Trinity Mirror / Mirrorpix (bc). **Corbis:** Bettmann (br). **Dorling Kindersley:** Judith Miller / Cloud Cuckoo Land (cra, crb); Judith Miller / Sparkle Moore at The Girl Can't Help It (cr). **Getty Images:** Cheryl Maeder (tr); Archivio Cameraphoto Epoche (bl). **338 Corbis:** Bettmann (bc). **Getty Images:** Hulton Archive / Brian Challis (tc); Retrofile / George Marks (fbl); Hulton Archive / Keystone (bl). **V&A Images / Victoria and Albert Museum, London:** (br). **339 Getty Images:** Paramount Pictures (l). **340 Corbis:** Bettmann (l). **Rex by Shutterstock:** Daily Mail (tr). **TopFoto.co.uk:** Ken Russell (br). **341 TopFoto.co.uk:** Ken Russell (bl). **V&A Images / Victoria and Albert Museum, London:** (tl, c, tr). **342-343 Corbis:** John Springer Collection. **343 Fotolia:** Yuri Arcurs. **344 Alamy Stock Photo:** Interfoto (bc). **Getty Images:** Popperfoto (r). **345 The Advertising Archives:** (br). **Corbis:** William Gottlieb (tr). **Getty Images:** Keystone Features (tl); Michael Ochs Archives (bl); Don Cravens (bc). **346 Corbis:** H. Armstrong Roberts / ClassicStock (bc); Camerique / ClassicStock (r). **Getty Images:** Hulton Archive (bl). **347 Alamy Stock Photo:** Keystone Pictures USA (bl). **Corbis:** Bettmann (tc); Universal / TempSport (tr). **Getty Images:** Orlando (br). **348 Dorling Kindersley:** Judith Miller / Wallis and Wallis. **350**

Alamy Stock Photo: Zuma Press Inc (c); B Christopher (cr). **Corbis:** Condé Nast Archive (br). **Getty Images:** Hulton Archive (bc). **351 Alamy Stock Photo:** Richard Levine (crb). **Corbis:** Rune Hellestad (c); (bl); Neal Preston (br); Douglas Kirkland (cr). **Getty Images:** Hulton Archive (tl, clb); Henry Diltz / Corbis Premium Historical (cla) **352 Dorling Kindersley:** Judith Miller / Freeman's (br). **V&A Images / Victoria and Albert Museum, London:** (bc). **352-383 Dorling Kindersley:** Judith Miller (t). **353 Corbis:** Condé Nast Archive (l). **Dorling Kindersley:** Judith Miller / Steinberg and Tolkien (tc); Judith Miller / Roxanne Stuart (crb); Judith Miller / Wallis and Wallis (bc, br). **354 Alamy Stock Photo:** Interfoto (cl); Pictorial Press Ltd (bl). **Getty Images:** Popperfoto (c); (bc). **355 Getty Images:** Popperfoto. **356 Bridgeman Images:** Museum Purchase (tr). **Corbis:** Bettmann (bl); Condé Nast Archive (bc, br). **V&A Images / Victoria and Albert Museum, London:** (tc). **357 Corbis:** Condé Nast Archive (r). **TopFoto.co.uk:** Roger-Viollet (bl). **V&A Images / Victoria and Albert Museum, London:** (tl). **358-359 Mirrorpix:** Julian Brown. **359 Fotolia:** Yuri Arcurs. **360 Corbis:** Hulton-Deutsch Collection (tr). **Getty Images:** Terry O'Neill (c). **V&A Images / Victoria and Albert Museum, London:** (bl). **361 Corbis:** Condé Nast Archive (cr); CinemaPhoto (bc). **Dorling Kindersley:** Judith Miller / Linda Bee (tr); Judith Miller / Mary Ann's Collectible (cra); Judith Miller (ftr). **362 Photo SCALA, Florence:** The Metropolitan Museum of Art / Art Resource / Gift of Mrs. Claus von Bülow, 1971 (1971.79.4) (r). **V&A Images / Victoria and Albert Museum, London:** (bl, bc). **362-363 Bridgeman Images:** Gift of Judy Robinson. **363 Dorling Kindersley:** Judith Miller / Sara Covelli (bc); Judith Miller (br). **Photo SCALA, Florence:** The Metropolitan Museum of Art / Art Resource / Gift of Baron Philippe de Rothschild, 1983 (1983.619.1a, b) (tc). **V&A Images / Victoria and Albert Museum, London:** (tl, tr). **364 Dorling Kindersley:** Judith Miller (br). **Getty Images:** Hulton Archive (cla). **Mary Evans Picture Library:** National Magazine Company (bc). **Rex by Shutterstock:** David Graves (c). **365 TopFoto.co.uk.** **366 Alamy Stock Photo:** Pictorial Press Ltd (tr). **Getty Images:** Terrence Spencer (bl). **V&A Images / Victoria and Albert Museum, London:** (bc, br). **367 Rex by Shutterstock:** (br). **V&A Images / Victoria and Albert Museum, London:** (tc, l). **368 Bridgeman Images:** (bl). **Rex by Shutterstock:** Pierluigi Praturlon (r). **369 Getty Images:** Evening Standard (tl); Terrence Spencer (br); Frederic Lewis (tr). **V&A Images / Victoria and Albert Museum, London:** (tc, bl). **370 Corbis:** John Springer Collection. **371 Alamy Stock Photo:** Interfoto (bl). **Corbis:** Bettmann (cra); Sygma (c). **Rex by Shutterstock:** Evening Standard / Alex Lentati (br). **372 V&A Images / Victoria and Albert Museum, London:** (tr). **373 The Advertising Archives:** (cra). **Getty Images:** AFP (tl). **V&A Images / Victoria and Albert Museum, London:** (c). **374-375 TopFoto.co.uk:** Colin Jones. **374 Fotolia:** Yuri Arcurs. **376 V&A Images / Victoria and Albert Museum, London:** (tr, bc, br). **378-379 Photograph by John Chase:** Olive Matthews Collection, Chertsey Museum. **378 Photograph by John Chase:** Olive Matthews Collection, Chertsey Museum (tc, ca, cl, cr). **379 Photograph by John Chase:** Olive Matthews Collection, Chertsey Museum (cl, c, cr, fcl, fcr). **380 Getty Images:** Hulton Archive / Frank Barralt (bc). **V&A Images / Victoria and Albert Museum, London:** (r). **381 Alamy Stock Photo:** Trinity Mirror / Mirrorpix (bl, bc). **Corbis:** Condé Nast Archive (tr). **Getty Images:** Hulton Archive / Roy Jones (tl); Hulton Archive (br). **382 Corbis:** Condé Nast Archive (tr); Bettmann (bc). **Dorling Kindersley:** Judith Miller (fbl, fclb). **V&A Images / Victoria and Albert Museum, London:** (bl). **383 Alamy Stock Photo:** Trinity Mirror / Mirrorpix (bl). **Corbis:** Steve Schapiro (bc, r). **V&A Images / Victoria and Albert Museum, London:** (tc, tl). **384 Dorling Kindersley:** Dominic Winter / Fieldings Auctioneers. **386 Alamy Stock Photo:** AF archive (bc); Trinty Mirror / Mirrorpix (tl). **Andy Lane:** (br). **Corbis:** Quadrillion (cra); Jan Butchofsky (c); Rune Hellestad (cr). **387 Alamy Stock Photo:** Photo 12 (bl); Jennifer Wright (bc); WENN Rights Ltd (crb).**catwalking.com:** (c). **Corbis:** Neal Preston (l). **Getty Images:** Hulton Archive (tc);Danny Lawson / AFP (cra). **388 Alamy Stock Photo:** xMarshall (clb). **Getty Images:** Archive Photos (tr); WireImage (br). **389 Rex by Shutterstock:** EPA-EFE / Yoan Valat (br); Sipa (tl); Imaginechina (bc). **The Kobal Collection:** Paramount (tr). **V&A Images / Victoria and Albert Museum, London:** (bl). **390 Alamy Stock Photo:** Trinity Mirror / Mirrorpix (tl). **Corbis:** Condé Nast Archive (cl); WWD / Condé Nast (br). **Dorling Kindersley:** Dominic Winter / Fieldings Auctioneers (bc). **Getty Images:** WireImage (c). **391 Corbis:** DPA. **392 Alamy Stock Photo:** Trinity Mirror / Mirrorpix (tl). **Corbis:** Pierre Vauthey / Sygma (tr); Jean-François Rault / Kipa (bc); Julio Donoso / Sygma (br). **V&A Images / Victoria and Albert Museum, London:** (tc, l). **393 Alamy Stock Photo:** Trinity Mirror / Mirrorpix (tr). **Corbis:** Pierre Vauthey / Sygma (bc). **Getty Images:** Princess Diana Archive (crb, cr); Tim Graham (br). **V&A Images / Victoria and Albert Museum, London:** (tc). **394 Corbis:** Reuters. **395 Alamy Stock Photo:** Trinity Mirror / Mirrorpix (tr). **Corbis:** Reuters (c); Kipa / Eric Fougere (cr). **Getty Images:** AFP (br). **Press Association Images:** (bl). **396 Alamy Stock Photo:** Trinity Mirror / Mirrorpix (tl). **Corbis:** Vittoriano Rastelli (bc); Petre Buzoianu (br). **Getty Images:** Andrea Blanch (bl). **397 Alamy Stock Photo:** Trinity Mirror / Mirrorpix (tr). **Corbis:** Condé Nast Archive (tl); Bettmann (tc); Stephen Lock / I-Images / ZUMA Press (r). **Getty Images:** Stan Honda (bl); AFP / Yoshikazu Tsuno (bc). **398 Alamy Stock Photo:** Trinity Mirror / Mirrorpix (tl). **Photograph by John Chase:** Olive Matthews Collection, Chertsey Museum (r, l). **399 Alamy Stock Photo:** Trinity Mirror / Mirrorpix (tr). **Photograph by John Chase:** Olive Matthews Collection, Chertsey Museum (cra, cr, c, br, fbr, l). **400 Alamy Stock Photo:** Trinity Mirror / Mirrorpix (tl). **Bridgeman Images:** Gift of Hess's Department Store, Allentown, 1974 / Cape, Pants, and Clogs, 1973 (cotton plain weave), Yamamoto, Kansai (b.1944) / Philadelphia Museum of Art, Pennsylvania, PA, USA (tr). **Corbis:** William Coupon (clb). **Getty Images:** Daniel Simon (bc). **V&A Images / Victoria and Albert Museum, London:** (br). **401 Alamy Stock Photo:** Trinity Mirror / Mirrorpix (ftr). **Getty Images:** Gamma-Rapho (tc); Francois Guillot (bc); Bettmann (cra); Guy Marineau / Conde Nast Collection (bl). **Rex by Shutterstock:** SIPA / Pixelformula (br).**V&A Images / Victoria and Albert Museum, London:** (tl). **402 Corbis:** WWD / Condé Nast. **403 Alamy Stock Photo:** Trinity Mirror / Mirrorpix (tr). **Corbis:** WWD / Condé Nast (c). **Getty Images:** Gamma-Rapho (bc). **Rex by Shutterstock:** SIPA (cr); Evening Standard (br). **404 Getty Images**: Lynn Goldsmith / Corbis Premium Historical (bc); Dave Hogan (br); Michael Ochs Archives / Stringer (clb); Julian Yewdall / Hulton Archive (tr). **405 Alamy Stock Photo:** Vibrant Pictures (r); PYMCA (bl); Pictorial Press Ltd (tr). **Getty Images:** Slaven Vlasic / Stringer / Getty Images Entertainment (bc); ullstein bild Dtl. (tc). **406 Corbis:** Condé Nast Archive (bl); Reuters (r). **Getty Images:** Pierre Verdy (br). **Rex by Shutterstock:** Penske Media / Robert Mitra (tc). **407 Corbis:** Condé Nast Archive (tc). **Getty Images:** Pascal Le Segretain / Getty Images Entertainment (bl); Victor VIRGILE / Gamma-Rapho (bc); Estrop / Getty Images Entertainment (r). **Photo SCALA, Florence:** The Metropolitan Museum of Art / Art Resource (tl). **408 Corbis:** Mauro Carraro / Sygma (tr). **Getty Images:** Michael Cole / Getty Images Entertainment (clb); Eddy LEMAISTRE / Corbis Sport (c). **Rex by Shutterstock:** David Heerde (br). **409 Getty Images:** Dave M. Benett / Getty Images Entertainment (tr); MJ Kim / Getty Images Entertainment (tl); Venturelli / Getty Images Entertainment (bl); Pascal Le Segretain / Getty Images Entertainment (br). **Rex by Shutterstock:** WWD / Giovanni Giannoni (bc). **410 Alamy Stock Photo:** Storms Media Group (br); USA / Tsuni (tr). **Corbis:** Leonard Ortiz / ZUMA Press (bl). **Getty Images:** Steve Granitz / WireImage (bc); Steve. Granitz / INACTIVE / WireImage (tc). **411 Alamy Stock Photo:** dpa picture alliance (r). **Getty Images:** Stefania D'Alessandro / Getty Images Entertainment (bl); Steve Granitz / WireImage (tc) ; SGranitz (tl). **412 Corbis:** Reuters. **413 Alamy Stock Photo:** Trinity Mirror / Mirrorpix (tr). **Corbis:** WWD / Condé Nast (c, bl, br); Condé Nast Archive (cr). **414-415 Alamy Stock Photo:** Trinity Mirror / Mirrorpix (tr). **Getty Images:** NIKLAS HALLE'N / AFP. **416 Alamy Stock Photo:** Chris Yates (br). **Corbis:** Andrew Gombert / epa (tr). **Getty Images:** Darren Gerrish / WireImage (clb). **Rex by Shutterstock:** Sipa / Pixelformula (bc). **417 Alamy Stock Photo:** Trinity Mirror / Mirrorpix (tr); Marco Mega (br) **Getty Images:** Pascal Le Segretain / Getty Images Entertainment (c); Arun Nevader / Stringer / Getty Images Entertainment (tr). **Rex by Shutterstock:** David Fisher (tl); Richard Isaac (bl); SIPA / Pixelformula (br) **418 Alamy Stock Photo:** Trinity Mirror / Mirrorpix (tl); AlamyCelebrity (tr). **Corbis:** WWD / Condé Nast (c, br). **Getty Images:** Samir Hussein (bl).**419 Alamy Stock Photo:** Marco Mega (tr); Trinity Mirror / Mirrorpix (ftr). **Corbis:** WWD / Condé Nast (tl, tc). **Getty Images:** Ben A. Pruchnie / Getty Images Entertainment (bc); Tim Whitby / BFC / Getty Images Entertainment (br); Victor VIRGILE / Gamma-Rapho (bl). **420-421 Getty Images:** Estrop / Getty Images Entertainment **423 Getty Images:** Joe McNally (br); FilmMagic (fbr). **424 Corbis:** Sandro Vannini / Small standing statuette of a priest found in Saqqara in 1872, Egypt (tc); Historical Picture Archive / From Nobleman's Dress by Le Clerc (cl). **Getty Images:** (bl); Hulton Archive (bc, fbr). **V&A Images / Victoria and Albert Museum, London:** (br). **425 Getty Images:** The Bridgeman Art Library / Detail of two falconers, from the Stag Room, Palais des Papes, Avignon (tl); Hulton Archive (cl, fbl); DEA Picture Library (c); Science & Society Picture Library (cr); NBC (bl); (bc); FilmMagic (br); WireImage (fbr). **426 V&A Images / Victoria and Albert Museum, London:** (tr). **427 Dorling Kindersley:** Dominic Winter / Fieldings Auctioneers (bc). **V&A Images / Victoria and Albert Museum, London:** (tl). **428 V&A Images / Victoria and Albert Museum, London:** (ca, bl, bc). **429 Getty Images:** FilmMagic (bc); AFP (br). **V&A Images / Victoria and Albert Museum, London:** (tl, bl, cr). **430 Alamy Stock Photo:** Peter Horree (bc). **431 Dorling Kindersley:** Judith Miller (cra); Judith Miller / Wallis and Wallis (cl). **Getty Images:** MCT (bl); (br). **432 Photograph by John Chase:** Olive Matthews Collection, Chertsey Museum (ca). **V&A Images / Victoria and Albert Museum, London:** (bl, bc). **433 Bridgeman Images:** Hamburger Kunsthalle, Hamburg, Germany, / Portrait of Mette (Mathildis) von Munchhausen, by Ludger Tom Ring the Younger (ca). **Photograph by John Chase:** Olive Matthews Collection, Chertsey Museum (cl, cra, tl). **V&A Images / Victoria and Albert Museum, London:** (crb, bc). **434 Getty Images:** Hola Images (t). **437 Corbis:** Marilyn Angel Wynn / Nativestock Pictures (t); Biserka Livaja (b). **445 Fotolia:** Franck Boston (b). **449 Alamy Stock Photo:** imagebroker (t). **450 Getty Images:** Jupiter Images (b). **454 Getty Images:** Alison Wright (t). **457 Corbis:** Stapleton Collection / Zulu Hunting Dance Near the Engooi Mountains by George French Angas, from The Kafirs Illustrated by George French Angas (1849) (t). **459 Dorling Kindersley:** Bethany Dawn (br). **461 Getty Images:** Imagemore Co., Ltd. (t); Runstudio (b). **462 Getty Images:** Uniquely India (b). **463 Getty Images:** Photodisc (t); (b)

Front Endpapers: Getty Images: Altrendo 0

All other images © Dorling Kindersley. For further information see: www.dkimages.com

The publisher would also like to thank the following companies, organizations, museums and individuals for their generosity in allowing Dorling Kindersley access to their exhibits and private collections for photography:

Museum of London
150 London Wall, London, EC2Y 5HN, UK
www.museumoflondon.org.uk
Features: *Embroidered Mantua; Streamlined Court Suit; Dance Dress; Plus Fours Suit*

The Blandford Fashion Museum
Lime Tree House, The Plocks, Blandford Forum, Dorset, DT11 7AA, UK
www.theblandfordfashionmuseum.co.uk
Assistance on photoshoots: Isobel Gilpin, Ann Bell, June Boutelle, Jean Longley, Stella Walker, Diana Foster-Williams, and Maureen Strong
Features: *Sack Back Dress; Regency Pelisse; Bustle Skirt; Women's Legion* (see picture credits for full listing)

The Shoe Museum
C & J Clark Ltd, High Street, Street, BA16 0EQ, UK
Features: *Women's Shoes* (see picture credits for full listing)

The Olive Matthews Collection
Chertsey Museum, 33 Windsor Street, Chertsey, Surrey KT16 8AT; www.chertseymuseum.org.uk
Features: *Wedding Dress; Jean Muir Classic; Power Suit*

Central Saint Martins College of Art and Design
Museum and Study Collection,
Granary Building, 1 Granary Square, King's Cross, London, N1C 4AA, UK; www.csm.arts.ac.uk

Banbury Museum
Spiceball Park Road, Banbury, OX16 2PG, UK
www.banburymuseum.org

Museum Resource Centre
Cotswold Dene, Standlake, Witney, OXON, OX29 7QG, UK

Felicity J Warnes
The Old Bookshop, 36 Gordon Road, Enfield, North London, EN2 0PZ, UK
www.fjwarnes.u-net.com
Over 20,000 books on costume, jewelry, lace, textiles, fashion, beads, embroidery, and needlework

Angels the Costumiers & Angels Fancy Dress
1 Garrick Road, London, NW9 6AA, UK
www.angels.uk.com

Sarah Thursfield
The Medieval Tailor
www.sarahthursfield.com
Features: *Short Tunic and Peplos Style; Cote-hardie; Doublet and hose*
Sarah Thursfield started to sew over 50 years ago and took City and Guilds Fashion in the early 1980s, since when she has been supplying clothing to reenactors and museums. She researched and wrote *The Medieval Tailor's Assistant* (Ruth Bean 2001) and continues to investigate and reconstruct the methods of early tailors and seamstresses and to teach these to others.

The publisher would like to thank the following people from Smithsonian Enterprises:
Carol LeBlanc, Vice President;
Brigid Ferraro, Director of Licensing;
Ellen Nanney, Licensing Manager;
Kealy Wilson, Product Development Coordinator

Susan Brown, Associate Curator, Cooper-Hewitt, National Design Museum, Smithsonian

Dorling Kindersley would like to thank the following people for their help in the preparation of this book:

UK
Additional editing: Paula Regan, Sam Atkinson, Laura Wheadon, and Wendy Horobin.
Additional design: Maxine Pedliham (*Timelines/ Reference features)*, Helen Spencer, and Jacqui Swan.
Design assistance: Johnny Pau, Laura Roberts, and Natalie Godwin.
Production editor: Rebekah Parsons-King.
Proofreading: Caroline Hunt and Joanna Chisholm.
Index: Helen Peters.

Delhi
Editorial assistance: Gaurav Joshi, Vibha Malhotra, Suparna Sengupta, Antara Moitra, and Monica Saigal. Design assistance: Jomin Johny, Priyanka Singh, and Shreya Sadhan